Mazda 323
Service and Repair Manual

Louis LeDoux

Models covered

(3455-288-10AG2)

Mazda 323 3-door hatchback and 4-door saloon models with
1324 cc, 1489 cc, 1598 cc and 1840 cc engines

Does not cover 5-door hatchback/fastback or estate models
Does not cover 1.3 litre carburettor or V6 engines

© J H Haynes & Co. Ltd. 2003

A book in the **Haynes Service and Repair Manual Series**

ISBN **978 0 85733 659 0**

British Library Cataloguing in Publication Data
A catalogue record for this book is available from the British Library.

J H Haynes & Co. Ltd.
Haynes North America, Inc

www.haynes.com

Contents

LIVING WITH YOUR MAZDA 323

Roadside Repairs

Weekly Checks

Lubricants, fluids and tyre pressures

MAINTENANCE

Routine Maintenance and Servicing

Contents

The transversely mounted inline four-cylinder engines used in these models are equipped with electronic fuel injection.

The engine drives the front wheels through a manual or automatic transmission via independent driveshafts.

Independent suspension, featuring coil spring/strut damper units, is used on the front wheels, while independent suspension using shock absorbers and coil springs or coil spring/strut dampers is used at the rear. The rack and pinion steering unit is mounted behind the engine with power assistance available as an option.

The brakes are disc at the front and drums or disc at the rear, with servo assistance as standard. An Anti-lock Brake System (ABS) became available on later models.

Your Mazda 323 manual

The aim of this manual is to help you get the best from your vehicle. It can do so in several ways. It can help you decide what work must be done (even should you choose to get it done by a garage), provide information on routine maintenance and servicing and give a logical course of action and diagnosis when random faults occur. However, it is hoped that you will use the manual by tackling the work yourself. On simpler jobs it may even be quicker than booking the vehicle into a garage and going there twice to leave and collect it. Perhaps most important, a lot of money can be saved by avoiding the costs the garage must charge to cover its labour and overheads.

The manual has drawings and descriptions to show the function of the various components so that their layout can be understood. Then the tasks are described and photographed in a step-by-step sequence so that even a novice can do the work.

References to the 'left' or 'right' of the vehicle are in the sense of a person in the driver's seat facing forwards.

Acknowledgements

We are grateful for the help and cooperation of the Mazda Motor Corporation for their assistance with technical information and certain illustrations. The technical writer who contributed to this project is Jay Storer.

Thanks are due to Draper Tools Limited, who provided some of the workshop tools. Special thanks are due to all those people at Sparkford who helped in the production of this manual.

We take great pride in the accuracy of information given in this manual, but vehicle manufacturers make alterations and design changes during the production run of a particular vehicle of which they do not inform us. No liability can be accepted by the authors or publishers for loss, damage or injury caused by any errors in, or omissions from the information given.

Mazda 323 3-door Hatchback

Mazda 323 4-door Saloon

Working on your car can be dangerous. This page shows just some of the potential risks and hazards, with the aim of creating a safety-conscious attitude.

General hazards

Scalding

• Don't remove the radiator or expansion tank cap while the engine is hot.
• Engine oil, automatic transmission fluid or power steering fluid may also be dangerously hot if the engine has recently been running.

Burning

• Beware of burns from the exhaust system and from any part of the engine. Brake discs and drums can also be extremely hot immediately after use.

Crushing

• When working under or near a raised vehicle, always supplement the jack with axle stands, or use drive-on ramps. *Never venture under a car which is only supported by a jack.*
• Take care if loosening or tightening high-torque nuts when the vehicle is on stands. Initial loosening and final tightening should be done with the wheels on the ground.

Fire

• Fuel is highly flammable; fuel vapour is explosive.
• Don't let fuel spill onto a hot engine.
• Do not smoke or allow naked lights (including pilot lights) anywhere near a vehicle being worked on. Also beware of creating sparks (electrically or by use of tools).
• Fuel vapour is heavier than air, so don't work on the fuel system with the vehicle over an inspection pit.
• Another cause of fire is an electrical overload or short-circuit. Take care when repairing or modifying the vehicle wiring.
• Keep a fire extinguisher handy, of a type suitable for use on fuel and electrical fires.

Electric shock

• Ignition HT voltage can be dangerous, especially to people with heart problems or a pacemaker. Don't work on or near the ignition system with the engine running or the ignition switched on.

• Mains voltage is also dangerous. Make sure that any mains-operated equipment is correctly earthed. Mains power points should be protected by a residual current device (RCD) circuit breaker.

Fume or gas intoxication

• Exhaust fumes are poisonous; they often contain carbon monoxide, which is rapidly fatal if inhaled. Never run the engine in a confined space such as a garage with the doors shut.
• Fuel vapour is also poisonous, as are the vapours from some cleaning solvents and paint thinners.

Poisonous or irritant substances

• Avoid skin contact with battery acid and with any fuel, fluid or lubricant, especially antifreeze, brake hydraulic fluid and Diesel fuel. Don't syphon them by mouth. If such a substance is swallowed or gets into the eyes, seek medical advice.
• Prolonged contact with used engine oil can cause skin cancer. Wear gloves or use a barrier cream if necessary. Change out of oil-soaked clothes and do not keep oily rags in your pocket.
• Air conditioning refrigerant forms a poisonous gas if exposed to a naked flame (including a cigarette). It can also cause skin burns on contact.

Asbestos

• Asbestos dust can cause cancer if inhaled or swallowed. Asbestos may be found in gaskets and in brake and clutch linings. When dealing with such components it is safest to assume that they contain asbestos.

Special hazards

Hydrofluoric acid

• This extremely corrosive acid is formed when certain types of synthetic rubber, found in some O-rings, oil seals, fuel hoses etc, are exposed to temperatures above 400°C. The rubber changes into a charred or sticky substance containing the acid. *Once formed, the acid remains dangerous for years. If it gets onto the skin, it may be necessary to amputate the limb concerned.*
• When dealing with a vehicle which has suffered a fire, or with components salvaged from such a vehicle, wear protective gloves and discard them after use.

The battery

• Batteries contain sulphuric acid, which attacks clothing, eyes and skin. Take care when topping-up or carrying the battery.
• The hydrogen gas given off by the battery is highly explosive. Never cause a spark or allow a naked light nearby. Be careful when connecting and disconnecting battery chargers or jump leads.

Air bags

• Air bags can cause injury if they go off accidentally. Take care when removing the steering wheel and/or facia. Special storage instructions may apply.

Diesel injection equipment

• Diesel injection pumps supply fuel at very high pressure. Take care when working on the fuel injectors and fuel pipes.

⚠ *Warning: Never expose the hands, face or any other part of the body to injector spray; the fuel can penetrate the skin with potentially fatal results.*

Remember...

DO

• Do use eye protection when using power tools, and when working under the vehicle.

• Do wear gloves or use barrier cream to protect your hands when necessary.

• Do get someone to check periodically that all is well when working alone on the vehicle.

• Do keep loose clothing and long hair well out of the way of moving mechanical parts.

• Do remove rings, wristwatch etc, before working on the vehicle – especially the electrical system.

• Do ensure that any lifting or jacking equipment has a safe working load rating adequate for the job.

DON'T

• Don't attempt to lift a heavy component which may be beyond your capability – get assistance.

• Don't rush to finish a job, or take unverified short cuts.

• Don't use ill-fitting tools which may slip and cause injury.

• Don't leave tools or parts lying around where someone can trip over them. Mop up oil and fuel spills at once.

• Don't allow children or pets to play in or near a vehicle being worked on.

Jump starting

When jump-starting a car using a booster battery, observe the following precautions:

✔ Before connecting the booster battery, make sure that the ignition is switched off.

✔ Ensure that all electrical equipment (lights, heater, wipers, etc) is switched off.

✔ Take note of any special precautions printed on the battery case.

✔ Make sure that the booster battery is the same voltage as the discharged one in the vehicle.

✔ If the battery is being jump-started from the battery in another vehicle, the two vehicles MUST NOT TOUCH each other.

✔ Make sure that the transmission is in neutral (or PARK, in the case of automatic transmission).

 Jump starting will get you out of trouble, but you must correct whatever made the battery go flat in the first place. There are three possibilities:

1 The battery has been drained by repeated attempts to start, or by leaving the lights on.

2 The charging system is not working properly (alternator drivebelt slack or broken, alternator wiring fault or alternator itself faulty).

3 The battery itself is at fault (electrolyte low, or battery worn out).

1 Connect one end of the red jump lead to the positive (+) terminal of the flat battery

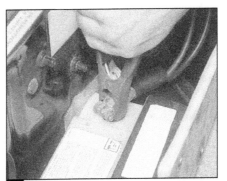

2 Connect the other end of the red lead to the positive (+) terminal of the booster battery.

3 Connect one end of the black jump lead to the negative (-) terminal of the booster battery

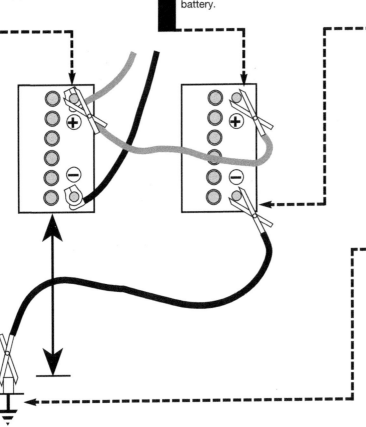

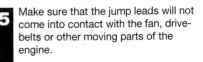

4 Connect the other end of the black jump lead to a bolt or bracket on the engine block, well away from the battery, on the vehicle to be started.

5 Make sure that the jump leads will not come into contact with the fan, drive-belts or other moving parts of the engine.

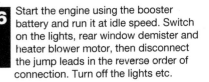

6 Start the engine using the booster battery and run it at idle speed. Switch on the lights, rear window demister and heater blower motor, then disconnect the jump leads in the reverse order of connection. Turn off the lights etc.

Jacking and wheel changing

Warning: The jack supplied with the vehicle should only be used for changing a tyre or placing axle stands under the frame. Never work under the vehicle or start the engine while this jack is being used as the only means of support.

The vehicle should be on level earth. Place the shift lever in Park, if you have an automatic, or Reverse if you have a manual transmission. Chock the wheel diagonally opposite the wheel being changed. Set the handbrake.

Remove the spare tyre and jack from stowage. Remove the wheel cover and trim ring (if so equipped) with the tapered end of the wheel nut spanner by inserting and twisting the handle and then levering against the back of the wheel cover. Loosen the wheel nuts about 1/4-to-1/2 turn each.

Place the scissors-type jack under the side of the vehicle and adjust the jack height until it fits in the notch in the flange nearest the wheel to be changed. There is a front and rear jacking point on each side of the vehicle **(see illustration)**.

Turn the jack handle clockwise until the tyre clears the ground. Remove the wheel nuts and pull the wheel off. Replace it with the spare.

Refit the wheel nuts with the beveled edges facing in. Tighten them snugly. Don't attempt to tighten them completely until the vehicle is lowered or it could slip off the jack. Turn the jack handle anti-clockwise to lower the vehicle. Remove the jack and tighten the wheel nuts in a diagonal pattern.

Refit the cover (and trim ring, if used) and be sure it's snapped into place all the way around.

Stow the tyre, jack and spanner. Unchock the wheel.

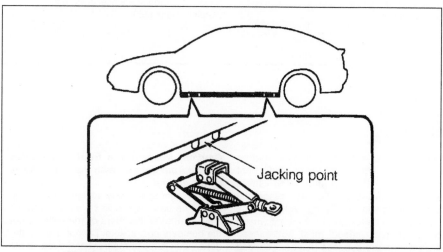

The jack fits under the vehicle, indicated by notches in the sills

Identifying leaks

Puddles on the garage floor or drive, or obvious wetness under the bonnet or underneath the car, suggest a leak that needs investigating. It can sometimes be difficult to decide where the leak is coming from, especially if the engine bay is very dirty already. Leaking oil or fluid can also be blown rearwards by the passage of air under the car, giving a false impression of where the problem lies.

⚠ *Warning: Most automotive oils and fluids are poisonous. Wash them off skin, and change out of contaminated clothing, without delay.*

 The smell of a fluid leaking from the car may provide a clue to what's leaking. Some fluids are distinctively coloured. It may help to clean the car and to park it over some clean paper as an aid to locating the source of the leak.
Remember that some leaks may only occur while the engine is running.

Sump oil

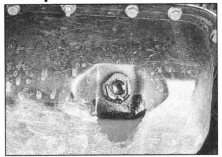

Engine oil may leak from the drain plug...

Oil from filter

...or from the base of the oil filter.

Gearbox oil

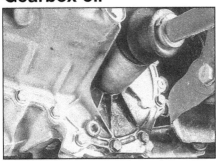

Gearbox oil can leak from the seals at the inboard ends of the driveshafts.

Antifreeze

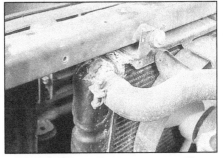

Leaking antifreeze often leaves a crystalline deposit like this.

Brake fluid

A leak occurring at a wheel is almost certainly brake fluid.

Power steering fluid

Power steering fluid may leak from the pipe connectors on the steering rack.

Towing

As a general rule, the vehicle should be towed from the front with the front (drive) wheels off the ground. If the vehicle must be towed from the rear, place the front wheels on a towing dolly. If the vehicle has to be towed with the front wheels on the ground, speed must not exceed 35 mph, and the distance must not exceed 50 miles.

Caution: Never tow a front wheel drive vehicle from the rear with the front wheels on the ground.

Equipment specifically designed for towing should be used. It should be attached to the main structural members of the vehicle, not the bumpers or brackets. Do not use the tie-down hook loops at the front or the rear of the vehicle for towing. These hooks loops are designed for securing the vehicle during transport, if used for towing, damage to the front or rear bumper may occur.

The ignition key must be in the ACC position, since the steering lock mechanism isn't strong enough to hold the front wheels straight while towing. Place the gear lever in neutral and release the handbrake.

Introduction

There are some very simple checks which need only take a few minutes to carry out, but which could save you a lot on inconvenience and expense.

☐ These *Weekly Checks* require no great skill or special tools, and the small amount of time they take to perform could well prove to be very well spent, for example;

☐ Keeping an eye on tyre condition and pressures will not only help to stop them wearing out prematurely, but could also save your life.

☐ If your car develops a brake fluid leak, the first time you might know about it is when your brakes don't work properly. Checking the level regularly will give advance warning of this kind of problem.

☐ If the oil or coolant levels run low, the cost of repairing any engine damage will be far greater than fixing the leak.

Underbonnet check points

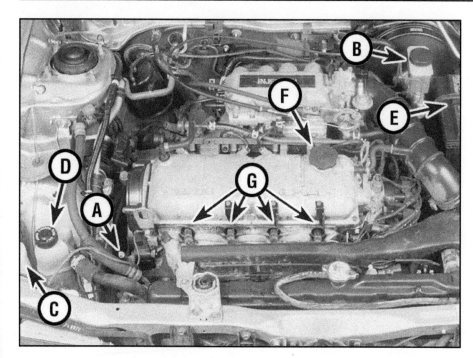

1.6 litre SOHC engine

A *Engine oil level dipstick*
B *Brake/clutch fluid reservoir*
C *Windscreen washer fluid reservoir*
D *Power steering fluid reservoir*
E *Battery*
F *Engine oil filler cap*
G *Spark plug caps*

Note: *Project vehicle is left-hand drive; component locations may vary*

Engine oil level

 HAYNES HiNT *If the oil level is checked immediately after driving the vehicle, some of the oil will remain in the upper engine components, resulting in an inaccurate reading on the dipstick!*

Before you start

✔ Make sure that your car is on level ground.
✔ Check the oil level before the car is driven, or at least 5 minutes after the engine has been switched off.

The correct oil

It is important to use a suitable oil (see *Lubricants and fluids*).

Vehicle care

● If you have to add oil frequently, you should check whether you have any oil leaks. Place some clean paper under the car overnight, and check for stains in the morning. If there are no leaks, the engine may be burning oil (see *Fault Finding*). A continually dropping oil level indicates oil leakage through damaged seals, from loose connections, or past worn rings or valve guides.

● If the oil looks milky in colour or has water droplets in it, a cylinder head gasket may be blown. The engine should be checked immediately.

● Each time you check the oil level, slide your thumb and index finger up the dipstick before wiping off the oil. If you see small dirt or metal particles clinging to the dipstick, the oil should be changed.

● Do not allow the level to drop below the L mark or oil starvation may cause engine damage. Conversely, overfilling the engine (adding oil above the F mark) may cause oil fouled spark plugs, oil leaks or oil seal failures.

1 The engine oil level is checked with a dipstick located on the right side of the engine compartment at the front of the engine. The dipstick extends through a metal tube from which it protrudes down into the engine sump.

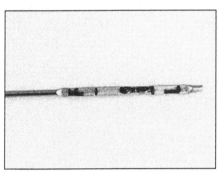

3 Observe the oil at the end of the dipstick. At its highest point, the level should be between the L (Low) and F (Full) marks.

2 Using a clean rag or paper towel remove all oil from the dipstick. Insert the clean dipstick into the tube as far as it will go, then withdraw it again.

4 Remove the threaded cap from the valve cover to add oil. Use a funnel to prevent spills. After adding the oil, refit the filler cap hand tight. Check the oil level again after it has had sufficient time to drain from the upper block and cylinder head.

Windscreen/window washer fluid

Before you start

✔ Fluid for the windscreen washer system is stored in a plastic reservoir which is located in the right front corner of the engine compartment. Fluid for the rear hatchback window washer system is stored in a plastic reservoir located in the right rear corner of the boot space.

 Warning: On no account use engine coolant antifreeze in the screen washer system - this may damage the paintwork.

Car care

● Screenwash additives not only keep the windscreen clean during bad weather, they also prevent the washer system freezing in cold weather - which is when you are likely to need it most. Don't top-up using plain water, as the screenwash will become diluted, and will freeze in cold weather.

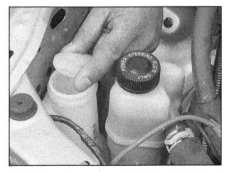

1 If topping-up is necessary, remove the cap, and fill the reservoir with a mixture of screenwash additive and water.

Brake/clutch fluid level

Before you start
✔ Make sure that the car is on level ground.

Safety first
● If a leak is suspected, the car should not be driven until the braking system has been checked. Never take any risks where brakes are concerned.
● While the reservoir cap is removed, inspect the fluid for contamination. If deposits, dirt particles or water droplets are present, the system should be drained and refilled (see Chapter 8 for clutch fluid renewal and Chapter 9 for brake fluid renewal).
● The fluid in the reservoir will drop slightly as the brake pads wear down during normal operation. If the fluid requires repeated replenishing to keep it at the proper level, this is an indication of leakage which should be corrected immediately. Check all brake and clutch lines and connections.
● If, upon checking the fluid level, you discover the reservoir empty or nearly empty, the brake and clutch system must be inspected immediately (see Chapters 8 and 9).

✔ Cleanliness is of great importance when dealing with the braking system, so take care to clean around the reservoir cap before topping-up. Use only clean brake fluid.

✔ A common reservoir is used for the brake and clutch hydraulic systems. The reservoir is mounted in front of the brake servo unit in the engine compartment.

⚠ *Warning: Brake fluid can harm your eyes and damage painted surfaces, so use extreme caution when handling and pouring it. Do not use fluid which has been standing open for some time, as it absorbs moisture from the air, which can cause a dangerous loss of braking effectiveness.*

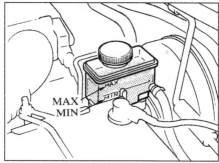

 To check the fluid level of the brake/clutch reservoir, simply look at the MAX (Maximum) and MIN (Minimum) marks on the reservoir. The level should be at or near the MAX fill line on the reservoir.

2 If the level is low, wipe the top of the reservoir cap with a clean rag to prevent contamination of the brake and clutch systems before lifting the cap. Add only the specified brake fluid to the brake/clutch reservoir (refer to *Lubricants and fluids*). Mixing different types of brake fluid can damage the system. Fill the reservoir to the MAX level.

3 After filling the reservoir to the proper level, make sure the cap is properly seated to prevent fluid leakage and/or system pressure loss.

Coolant level

⚠ *Warning: Never remove the radiator cap or the coolant recovery reservoir cap when the engine is running or has just been switched off, because the cooling system is hot. Escaping steam and scalding liquid could cause serious injury.*
Warning: On no account use engine coolant antifreeze in the screen washer system - this may damage the paintwork.

Before you start
✔ The coolant level should be checked before the vehicle has been driven when the engine is cool.

 The coolant level must be between the F (Full) and L (Low) marks on the dipstick attached to the reservoir cap.

Vehicle care
● With a sealed-type cooling system, adding coolant should not be necessary on a regular basis. If the coolant level drops within a short time after replenishment, there may be a leak

2 Use only ethylene-glycol type coolant and soft (demineralized) water. Do not use supplemental inhibitor additives. If only a small amount of coolant is required to bring the system up to the proper level, water can be used. However, repeated additions of water will dilute the recommended antifreeze and water solution. In order to maintain the proper ratio of antifreeze and water, it is advisable to top up the coolant level with the correct mixture.

in the system. Inspect the radiator, hoses, engine coolant filler cap, drain plugs, air bleeder plugs and water pump. If no leak is evident, have the radiator cap pressure tested by your dealer.
● It is important that antifreeze is used in the cooling system all year round, not just during the winter months. Don't top-up with water alone, as the antifreeze will become diluted.
● When checking the coolant level, always note its condition. It should be relatively clear. If it is brown or rust coloured, the system should be drained, flushed and refilled. Even if the coolant appears to be normal, the corrosion inhibitors wear out with use, so it must be renewed at the specified intervals.
● Do not allow antifreeze to come in contact with your skin or painted surfaces of the vehicle. Flush contacted areas immediately with plenty of water.

Tyre condition and pressure

It is very important that tyres are in good condition, and at the correct pressure - having a tyre failure at any speed is highly dangerous. Tyre wear is influenced by driving style - harsh braking and acceleration, or fast cornering, will all produce more rapid tyre wear. As a general rule, the front tyres wear out faster than the rears. Interchanging the tyres from front to rear ("rotating" the tyres) may result in more even wear. However, if this is completely effective, you may have the expense of replacing all four tyres at once! Remove any nails or stones embedded in the tread before they penetrate the tyre to cause deflation. If removal of a nail does reveal that the tyre has been punctured, refit the nail so that its point of penetration is marked. Then immediately change the wheel, and have the tyre repaired by a tyre dealer.

Regularly check the tyres for damage in the form of cuts or bulges, especially in the sidewalls. Periodically remove the wheels, and clean any dirt or mud from the inside and outside surfaces. Examine the wheel rims for signs of rusting, corrosion or other damage. Light alloy wheels are easily damaged by "kerbing" whilst parking; steel wheels may also become dented or buckled. A new wheel is very often the only way to overcome severe damage.

New tyres should be balanced when they are fitted, but it may become necessary to re-balance them as they wear, or if the balance weights fitted to the wheel rim should fall off. Unbalanced tyres will wear more quickly, as will the steering and suspension components. Wheel imbalance is normally signified by vibration, particularly at a certain speed (typically around 50 mph). If this vibration is felt only through the steering, then it is likely that just the front wheels need balancing. If, however, the vibration is felt through the whole car, the rear wheels could be out of balance. Wheel balancing should be carried out by a tyre dealer or garage.

1 *Tread Depth - visual check*

The original tyres have tread wear safety bands (B), which will appear when the tread depth reaches approximately 1.6 mm. The band positions are indicated by a triangular mark on the tyre sidewall (A).

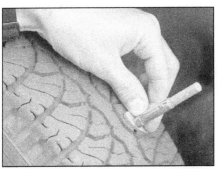

2 *Tread Depth - manual check*

Alternatively, tread wear can be monitored with a simple, inexpensive device known as a tread depth indicator gauge.

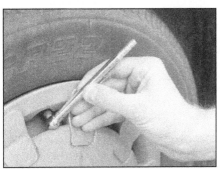

3 *Tyre Pressure Check*

Check the tyre pressures regularly with the tyres cold. Do not adjust the tyre pressures immediately after the vehicle has been used, or an inaccurate setting will result.

Tyre tread wear patterns

Shoulder Wear

Underinflation (wear on both sides)
Under-inflation will cause overheating of the tyre, because the tyre will flex too much, and the tread will not sit correctly on the road surface. This will cause a loss of grip and excessive wear, not to mention the danger of sudden tyre failure due to heat build-up.
Check and adjust pressures
Incorrect wheel camber (wear on one side)
Repair or renew suspension parts
Hard cornering
Reduce speed!

Centre Wear

Overinflation
Over-inflation will cause rapid wear of the centre part of the tyre tread, coupled with reduced grip, harsher ride, and the danger of shock damage occurring in the tyre casing.
Check and adjust pressures

If you sometimes have to inflate your car's tyres to the higher pressures specified for maximum load or sustained high speed, don't forget to reduce the pressures to normal afterwards.

Uneven Wear

Front tyres may wear unevenly as a result of wheel misalignment. Most tyre dealers and garages can check and adjust the wheel alignment (or "tracking") for a modest charge.
Incorrect camber or castor
Repair or renew suspension parts
Malfunctioning suspension
Repair or renew suspension parts
Unbalanced wheel
Balance tyres
Incorrect toe setting
Adjust front wheel alignment
Note: *The feathered edge of the tread which typifies toe wear is best checked by feel.*

Lubricants and fluids

Engine . . . . Multigrade engine oil, viscosity SAE 10W-30 to 20W-50, to API SG or better

Cooling system . . . . Water and ethylene glycol based antifreeze

Automatic transmission fluid . . . . Dexron II automatic transmission fluid

Manual transmission oil . . . . Gear oil, viscosity SAE 75W-90, to API GL-4 or GL-5

Brake/clutch fluid . . . . Hydraulic fluid to SAE J1703 or FMVS116 DOT 3

Power steering fluid . . . . Dexron II automatic transmission fluid

Choosing your engine oil

Engines need oil, not only to lubricate moving parts and minimise wear, but also to maximise power output and to improve fuel economy.

HOW ENGINE OIL WORKS

• *Beating friction*

Without oil, the moving surfaces inside your engine will rub together, heat up and melt, quickly causing the engine to seize. Engine oil creates a film which separates these moving parts, preventing wear and heat build-up.

• *Cooling hot-spots*

Temperatures inside the engine can exceed 1000° C. The engine oil circulates and acts as a coolant, transferring heat from the hot-spots to the sump.

• *Cleaning the engine internally*

Good quality engine oils clean the inside of your engine, collecting and dispersing combustion deposits and controlling them until they are trapped by the oil filter or flushed out at oil change.

OIL CARE - FOLLOW THE CODE

To handle and dispose of used engine oil safely, always:

• *Avoid skin contact with used engine oil. Repeated or prolonged contact can be harmful.*
• *Dispose of used oil and empty packs in a responsible manner in an authorised disposal site. Call 0800 663366 to find the one nearest to you. Never tip oil down drains or onto the ground.*

Tyre pressures

Note: *Recommended tyre pressures are marked on a label attached to the driver's door edge or frame. Pressures apply to original-equipment tyres, and may vary if any other make or type of tyre is fitted; check with the tyre manufacturer or supplier for correct pressures if necessary.*

Typical pressures for up to 3 people	Front	Rear
1.3 litre models		
Up to 1994	1.9 bar (28 psi)	1.8 bar (26 psi)
1995 and later	2.2 bar (32 psi)	2.2 bar (32 psi)
1.5 litre models	2.1 bar (30 psi)	2.1 bar (30 psi)
1.6 litre models	1.9 bar (28 psi)	1.8 bar (26 psi)
1.8 litre models		
Up to 1994	2.1 bar (30 psi)	1.9 bar (28 psi)
1995 and later		
185/65x14 tyres	2.1 bar (30 psi)	2.1 bar (30 psi)
195/55x15 tyres	2.2 bar (32 psi)	2.1 bar (30 psi)

Advanced driving

Many people see the words 'advanced driving' and believe that it won't interest them or that it is a style of driving beyond their own abilities. Nothing could be further from the truth. Advanced driving is straightforward safe, sensible driving - the sort of driving we should all do every time we get behind the wheel.

An average of 10 people are killed every day on UK roads and 870 more are injured, some seriously. Lives are ruined daily, usually because somebody did something stupid. Something like 95% of all accidents are due to human error, mostly driver failure. Sometimes we make genuine mistakes - everyone does. Sometimes we have lapses of concentration. Sometimes we deliberately take risks.

For many people, the process of 'learning to drive' doesn't go much further than learning how to pass the driving test because of a common belief that good drivers are made by 'experience'.

Learning to drive by 'experience' teaches three driving skills:

☐ Quick reactions. (Whoops, that was close!)
☐ Good handling skills. (Horn, swerve, brake, horn).
☐ Reliance on vehicle technology. (Great stuff this ABS, stop in no distance even in the wet...)

Drivers whose skills are 'experience based' generally have a lot of near misses and the odd accident. The results can be seen every day in our courts and our hospital casualty departments.

Advanced drivers have learnt to control the risks by controlling the position and speed of their vehicle. They avoid accidents and near misses, even if the drivers around them make mistakes.

The key skills of advanced driving are **concentration,** effective all-round **observation, anticipation** and **planning.** When **good vehicle handling** is added to these skills, all driving situations can be approached and negotiated in a safe, methodical way, leaving nothing to chance.

Concentration means applying your mind to safe driving, completely excluding anything that's not relevant. Driving is usually the most dangerous activity that most of us undertake in our daily routines. It deserves our full attention.

Observation means not just looking, but seeing and seeking out the information found in the driving environment.

Anticipation means asking yourself what is happening, what you can reasonably expect to happen and what could happen unexpectedly. (One of the commonest words used in compiling accident reports is 'suddenly'.)

Planning is the link between seeing something and taking the appropriate action. For many drivers, planning is the missing link.

If you want to become a safer and more skilful driver and you want to enjoy your driving more, contact the Institute of Advanced Motorists at www.iam.org.uk, phone 0208 996 9600, or write to IAM House, 510 Chiswick High Road, London W4 5RG for an information pack.

Chapter 1 Part A
Routine maintenance and servicing – models up to 1994

Contents

Degrees of difficulty

| **Easy,** suitable for novice with little experience | | **Fairly easy,** suitable for beginner with some experience | | **Fairly difficult,** suitable for competent DIY mechanic |  | **Difficult,** suitable for experienced DIY mechanic | | **Very difficult,** suitable for expert DIY or professional | |

Specifications

Capacities*
Engine oil (including filter)
1.3 litre engine	3.2 litres
1.5 litre engine	3.5 litres
1.6 litre engine	3.2 litres
1.8 litre engine	3.8 litres

Engine coolant
1.3 litre engine	5.0 litres
1.5 litre engine	
Manual transmission	5.0 litres
Automatic transmission	6.0 litres
1.6 litre engine	
Manual transmission	5.0 litres
Automatic transmission	6.0 litres
1.8 litre engine	3.8 litres
1991 to 1994	5.0 litres
1995 and later	6.0 litres

Transmission lubricant
Manual
1.3, 1.5, 1.6 litre	2.7 litres
1.8 litre engine	
1991 to 1994	3.4 litres
1995 and later	2.7 litres

Automatic
1.5 litre engine	4.9 litres
1.6 litre engine	5.8 litres
1.8 litre engine	4.9 litres

*All capacities approximate. Add as necessary to bring up to appropriate level.

Recommended lubricants and fluids

Refer to *Weekly checks*

Ignition system

Spark plugs	Type	Electrode gap
All engines	Bosch FR 7 D+X	1.1 mm

Spark plug lead resistance .... 16 k-ohms per metre at 20° C (68° F)
Engine firing order 1-3-4-2

Valve clearance

1.3 litre engine (engine hot) .... 0.30 mm (inlet and exhaust)
1.5 litre engine (engine cold) .... 0.25 to 0.31 mm (inlet and exhaust)
1.6 & 1.8 litre engine .... Hydraulic adjustment

Cooling system

Thermostat opening temperature
  1.3 & 1.5 litre engine .... 87 to 90° C
  1.6 litre engine
    All except Estate models .... 87 to 90° C
    Estate models .... 82 to 85° C
  1.8 litre engine
    1991 to 1994 .... 87 to 90° C
    1994 and later .... 84 to 89° C

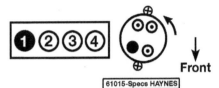

Cylinder location and distributor rotation

Accessory drivebelt deflection

Used belt
  Alternator and water pump (crankshaft-to-alternator pulleys) ...... 6.0 to 7.5 mm
  Power steering .... 9.0 to 10.0 mm
  Air conditioning compressor .... 9.0 to 10.0 mm
  Power steering pump and air conditioning
    compressor (crankshaft-to-power steering pump pulleys) .... 9.0 to 10.0 mm
New belt
  Alternator and water pump (crankshaft-to-alternator pulleys) ...... 5.5 to 7.0 mm
  Power steering pump .... 8.0 to 9.0 mm
  Air conditioning compressor .... 8.0 to 9.0 mm
  Power steering pump and air conditioning
    compressor (crankshaft-to-power steering pump pulleys) .... 8.0 to 9.0 mm

Clutch pedal

Height (including carpet) .... 210.0 to 217.0 mm
Freeplay .... 5.8 to 16.0 mm
Disengagement height (minimum - including carpet) .... 70.5 mm

Brakes

Front disc brake pad lining thickness (minimum) .... 1.0 mm
Rear disc brake pad lining thickness (minimum) .... 1.0 mm
Drum brake shoe lining thickness (minimum) .... 1.0 mm
Handbrake adjustment .... 5 to 7 clicks

Suspension and steering

Steering wheel freeplay limit .... 0 to 30.0 mm
Balljoint allowable movement .... 0 mm

Torque specifications

	lbf ft	Nm
Engine oil drain plug	22 to 30	30 to 41
Spark plugs	11 to 16	15 to 22
Automatic transmission		
Drain plug	29 to 39	39 to 53
Sump bolts	6 to 8	8 to 11
Oil strainer/filter bolts	6 to 8	8 to 11
Manual transmission		
Speedometer driven gear retaining bolt	6 to 9	8 to 12
Level and fill plug	29 to 43	39 to 58
Drain plug	29 to 43	39 to 58
Wheel nuts	65 to 87	89 to 118

The maintenance intervals in this manual are provided with the assumption that you, not the dealer, will be doing the work. These are the minimum maintenance intervals recommended by the factory for vehicles that are driven daily. If you wish to keep your vehicle in peak condition at all times, you may wish to perform some of these procedures even more often. Because frequent maintenance enhances the efficiency, performance and resale value of your car, we encourage you to do so. If you drive in dusty areas, tow a trailer, idle or drive at low speeds for extended periods, or drive for short distances (less than four miles) in below freezing temperatures, shorter intervals are also recommended.

When your vehicle is new, it should be serviced by a dealer to protect the factory warranty. In many cases, the initial maintenance check is done at no cost to the owner.

Every 6000 miles or 6 months, whichever comes first

Note: *Frequent oil and filter changes are good for the engine. We recommend changing the oil at the mileage specified here, or at least twice a year if the mileage covered is less.*

☐ Change the engine oil and oil filter (Section 3)
☐ Check the power steering fluid level (Section 4)
☐ Check the clutch pedal for proper height and freeplay (Section 5)
☐ Check and adjust if necessary the engine drivebelts (Section 6)
☐ Check the ignition timing (Chapter 5)

Every 12 000 miles or 12 months, whichever comes first

☐ Inspect and renew if necessary the windscreen wiper blades (Section 7)
☐ Check and service the battery (Section 8)
☐ Inspect and renew if necessary all underbonnet hoses (Section 9)
☐ Inspect the braking system (Section 10)*
☐ Inspect the steering and suspension components (Section 11)*
☐ Check and adjust the valve clearances - 1.3 litre engines (Section 12)
☐ Check the air conditioning system operation (Chapter 3)
☐ Lubricate the hinges and catches (Chapter 11)
☐ Check for bodywork corrosion
☐ Tighten the fasteners on the body and chassis
☐ Check the cooling system (Section 13)
☐ Inspect the fuel system (Section 14)
☐ Inspect the spark plugs (Section 15)
☐ Inspect the fuel evaporative emissions control system (Section 16)
☐ Check the seat belts (Chapter 11)
☐ Check the EGR system (Chapter 6)
☐ Check the headlight alignment (Chapter 10)

Every 24 000 miles or 24 months, whichever comes first

☐ Check the manual transmission lubricant level (Section 17)
☐ Check the automatic transmission fluid level (Section 18)
☐ Check the driveshaft gaiters (Section 19)
☐ Renew the spark plugs (Section 15)
☐ Inspect and renew if necessary the spark plug leads, distributor cap and rotor (Section 20)
☐ Service the cooling system (drain, flush and refill) (Section 21)
☐ Inspect the exhaust system (Section 22)
☐ Check and renew if necessary the PCV valve (Section 23)
☐ Renew the brake fluid (Section 24)
☐ Renew the air filter (Section 25)
☐ Renew the fuel filter (Section 26)

Every 48 000 miles or 48 months, whichever comes first

☐ Change the automatic transmission fluid (Section 27)**
☐ Change the manual transmission lubricant (Section 28)**

Every 60 000 miles

☐ Renew the timing belt (Chapter 2A)
☐ Check and adjust the valve clearances - 1.5 litre engines (Section 12)

This item is affected by 'severe' operating conditions as described below. If your vehicle is operated under 'severe' conditions, perform all maintenance indicated with an asterisk at 6000 mile/6 month intervals. Severe conditions are indicated if you mainly operate your vehicle under one or more of the following conditions:
  Operating in dusty areas
  Towing a trailer
  Idling for extended periods and/or low speed operation
  Operating when outside temperatures remain below freezing and when most trips are less than four miles

**If operated under one or more of the following conditions, change the manual or automatic transmission fluid and differential lubricant at 36 000 miles/36 month intervals:*
  In heavy city traffic where the outside temperature regularly reaches 32° C (90° F) or higher
  In hilly or mountainous terrain
  Frequent trailer pulling

Typical engine compartment components

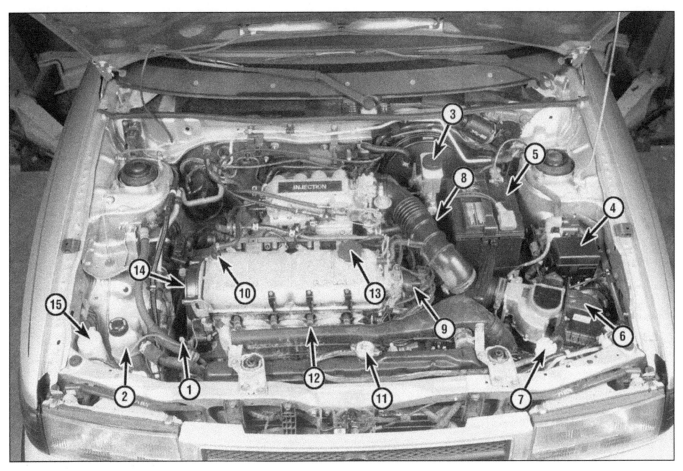

1	Engine oil dipstick	6	Air cleaner assembly	11	Radiator cap
2	Power steering fluid reservoir	7	Coolant reservoir	12	Spark plug
3	Brake/clutch fluid reservoir	8	Automatic transmission dipstick	13	Oil filler cap
4	Main fuse/relay block	9	Distributor	14	Drivebelts
5	Battery	10	PCV valve	15	Windscreen washer fluid reservoir

Note: The vehicle shown is left-hand drive, component locations may vary

Typical front underside components

1 Driveshaft boot
2 Automatic transmission drain plug
3 Exhaust system catalytic converter
4 Engine oil drain plug
5 Front suspension strut unit
6 Radiator drain fitting
7 Front disc brake caliper

Typical rear underside components

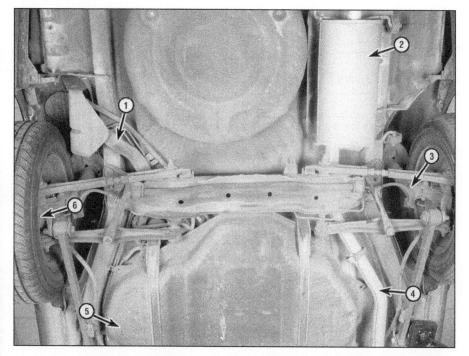

1 Fuel tank filler pipe
2 Silencer
3 Suspension strut
4 Exhaust pipe
5 Fuel tank
6 Rear brake assembly

1 Introduction

This Chapter is designed to help the home mechanic maintain the Mazda 323 for peak performance, economy, safety and long life.

Included is a master maintenance schedule, followed by sections dealing specifically with each item on the schedule. Visual checks, adjustments, component renewal and other helpful items are included.

Servicing your 323 in accordance with the mileage/time maintenance schedule and the following Sections will provide it with a planned maintenance program that should result in a long and reliable service life. This is a comprehensive plan, so maintaining some items but not others at the specified service intervals will not produce the same results.

As you service your 323, you will discover that many of the procedures can - and should - be grouped together because of the nature of the particular procedure you're performing or because of the close proximity of two otherwise unrelated components to one another.

For example, if the vehicle is raised for any reason, you should inspect the exhaust, suspension, steering and fuel systems while you're under the vehicle.

Finally, let's suppose you have to borrow or rent a torque wrench. Even if you only need to tighten the spark plugs, you might as well check the torque of as many critical fasteners as time allows.

The first step of this maintenance program is to prepare yourself before the actual work begins. Read through all Sections pertinent to the procedures you're planning to do, then make a list of and gather together all the parts and tools you will need to do the job. If it looks as if you might run into problems during a particular segment of some procedure, seek advice from your local parts specialist or service department.

2 General information

If, from the time the vehicle is new, the routine maintenance schedule is followed closely and frequent checks are made of fluid levels and high wear items, as suggested throughout this manual, the engine will be kept in relatively good running condition and the need for additional work will be minimised.

More likely than not, however, there will be times when the engine is running poorly due to lack of regular maintenance. This is even more likely if a used vehicle, which has not received regular and frequent maintenance checks, is purchased. In such cases, extra work will be needed outside of the regular routine maintenance intervals.

The first step in any procedure to help correct a poor running engine would be a cylinder compression check. A check of the engine compression (Chapter 2, Part B) will give valuable information regarding the overall performance of many internal components and should be used as a basis for servicing and repair procedures. If, for instance, a compression check indicates serious internal engine wear, a conventional service will not help the running condition of the engine and would be a waste of time and money.

The following series of operations are those most often needed to bring a generally poor running engine back into a proper state of tune.

Primary operations

Clean, inspect and test the battery
Check all engine related fluids
Check and adjust the drivebelts
Renew the spark plugs
Inspect the distributor cap and rotor
Inspect the spark plug and coil leads
Check all underbonnet hoses
Check the cooling system
Check the air filter

Secondary operations

Check the ignition system
Check the charging system
Check the fuel system
Renew the air filter
Renew the distributor cap and rotor
Renew the spark plug leads

Every 6000 miles or 6 months, whichever comes first

3 Engine oil and oil filter change

> **HAYNES HiNT** *Frequent oil changes are the best preventive maintenance the home mechanic can give the engine, because ageing oil becomes diluted and contaminated, which leads to premature engine wear.*

1 Make sure that you have all the necessary tools before you begin this procedure **(see illustration)**.
2 You should also have plenty of rags or newspapers handy for mopping up any spills.
3 Access to the underside of the vehicle is greatly improved if the vehicle can be lifted on a hoist, driven onto ramps or supported by axle stands.

3.1 These tools are required when changing the engine oil and filter

1 **Drain pan** - *It should be fairly shallow in depth, but wide in order to prevent spills*
2 **Rubber gloves** - *When removing the drain plug and filter, it is inevitable that you will get oil on your hands (the gloves will prevent burns)*
3 **Breaker bar** - *Sometimes the oil drain plug is pretty tight and a long breaker bar is needed to loosen it*
4 **Socket** – *To be used with the breaker bar or a ratchet (must be the correct size to fit the drain plug)*
5 **Filter spanner** - *This is a metal band-type spanner, which requires clearance around the filter to be effective*
6 **Filter spanner** - *This type fits on the bottom of the filter and can be turned with a ratchet or beaker bar (different size spanners are available for different types of filters)*

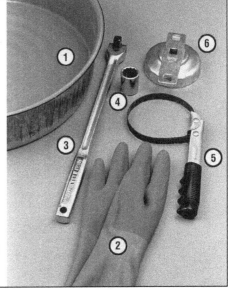

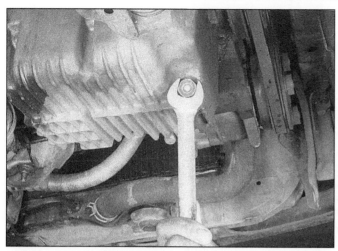

3.7 Use a proper size spanner or socket to remove the oil drain plug and avoid rounding it off

3.12   You'll need a special spanner for oil filter removal - DO NOT use it to tighten the new filter

 Warning: Do not work under a vehicle which is supported only by a bumper, hydraulic or scissors-type jack.

4 If this is your first oil change familiarise yourself with the location of the oil drain plug. The engine and exhaust components will be warm during the actual work, so try to anticipate any potential problems before the engine and accessories are hot.

5 Park the vehicle on a level spot. Start the engine and allow it to reach its normal operating temperature (the needle on the temperature gauge should be at least above the bottom mark). Warm oil and sludge will flow out more easily. Turn off the engine when it's warmed up. Remove the filler cap in the valve cover.

6 Raise the vehicle and support it on axle stands.

 Warning: To avoid personal injury, never get beneath the vehicle when it is supported only by a jack. The jack provided with your vehicle is designed solely for raising the vehicle to remove and renew

3.14 Lubricate the oil filter gasket with clean engine oil before refitting the filter on the engine

the wheels. *Always use axle stands to support the vehicle when it becomes necessary to place your body underneath the vehicle.*

7 Being careful not to touch the hot exhaust components, place the drain pan under the drain plug in the bottom of the pan and remove the plug **(see illustration)**. You may want to wear gloves while unscrewing the plug the final few turns if the engine is really hot.

8 Allow the old oil to drain into the pan. It may be necessary to move the pan farther under the engine as the oil flow slows to a trickle. Inspect the old oil for the presence of metal shavings and chips.

9 After all the oil has drained, wipe off the drain plug with a clean rag. Even minute metal particles clinging to the plug would immediately contaminate the new oil.

10 Clean the area around the drain plug opening, refit the plug and tighten to 30 to 41 Nm (22 to 30 lbf ft)

11 Move the drain pan into position under the oil filter.

12 Loosen the oil filter **(see illustration)** by turning it anti-clockwise with the filter spanner. Any standard filter spanner should work. Once the filter is loose, use your hands to unscrew it from the block. Just as the filter is detached from the block, immediately tilt the open end up to prevent the oil inside the filter from spilling out.

 Warning: The engine exhaust components may still be hot, so be careful.

13 With a clean rag, wipe off the mounting surface on the block. Also make sure that the none of the old gasket remains stuck to the mounting surface. It can be removed with a scraper if necessary.

14 Compare the old filter with the new one to make sure they are the same type. Smear some engine oil on the rubber gasket of the

new filter and screw it into place **(see illustration)**. Because overtightening the filter will damage the gasket, do not use a filter spanner to tighten the filter. Tighten it by hand until the gasket contacts the seating surface. Then seat the filter by giving it an additional 3/4-turn.

15 Remove all tools, rags, etc. from under the vehicle, being careful not to spill the oil in the drain pan, then lower the vehicle.

16 Add new oil to the engine through the oil filler cap in the valve cover. Use a spout or funnel to prevent oil from spilling onto the top of the engine. Pour 3 litres of fresh oil (3.5 litres in the 1.8 litre engine) into the engine. Wait a few minutes to allow the oil to drain into the pan, then check the level on the oil dipstick (see *Weekly checks* if necessary). If the oil level is at or near the F mark, refit the filler cap hand tight, start the engine and allow the new oil to circulate.

17 Allow the engine to run for about a minute. While the engine is running, look under the vehicle and check for leaks at the sump drain plug and around the oil filter. If either is leaking, stop the engine and tighten the plug or filter slightly.

18 Wait a few minutes to allow the oil to trickle down into the pan, then recheck the level on the dipstick and, if necessary, add enough oil to bring the level to the F mark.

19 During the first few trips after an oil change, make it a point to check frequently for leaks and proper oil level.

20 The old oil drained from the engine cannot be reused in its present state and should be discarded. Check with your local refuse disposal company, disposal facility or environmental agency to see if they will accept the oil for recycling. Don't pour used oil into drains or onto the earth. After the oil has cooled, it can be drained into a suitable container for transport to one of these disposal sites.

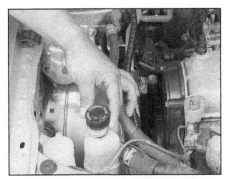

4.2 The power steering fluid reservoir is located in the right front corner of the engine compartment

4 Power steering fluid level check

1 Unlike manual steering, the power steering system relies on fluid which may, over a period of time, require replenishing.

2 The fluid reservoir for the power steering pump is located in the right front corner of the engine compartment, next to the windscreen washer fluid reservoir **(see illustration)**.

3 For the check, the front wheels should be pointed straight ahead and the engine should be off.

4 To check the fluid level, simply look at the F (Full) and L (Low) lines on the reservoir **(see illustration)**. The fluid level should be between the F and L lines.

5 If additional fluid is required, pour the specified type (see *Lubricants and fluids* in *Weekly checks*) directly into the reservoir, using a funnel to prevent spills. Fill the reservoir to the F line.

6 If the reservoir requires frequent fluid additions, all power steering hoses, hose

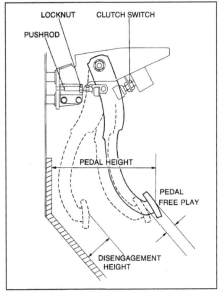

5.1 Clutch pedal adjustment details

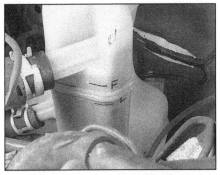

4.4 The fluid level is checked by looking at the lines on the reservoir and can be checked hot or cold

connections, the power steering pump and the rack and pinion assembly should be carefully checked for leaks.

5 Clutch pedal height and freeplay check and adjustment

1 To check the clutch pedal height, measure the horizontal distance from the centre of the clutch pedal surface to the carpet or pad on the bulkhead **(see illustration)**. The height should be within the limits listed in this Chapter's Specifications. If it isn't, it must be adjusted.

2 To adjust the clutch pedal height, disconnect the clutch switch electrical connector.

3 Loosen the switch locknut **(see illustration 5.1)**.

4 Turn the clutch switch until the pedal height is correct.

5 Tighten the locknut and recheck the pedal height to verify it is correct. **Note:** *Whenever the pedal height is adjusted it will most likely be necessary to adjust the freeplay, because increasing or decreasing pedal height will cause a similar change in pedal freeplay.*

6 Check the clutch pedal freeplay by lightly pushing the clutch pedal down and, with a small steel ruler, measure the distance that it moves freely before the clutch resistance is felt **(see illustration 5.1)**. The freeplay should be within the limits listed in this Chapter's Specifications. If it isn't, it must be adjusted.

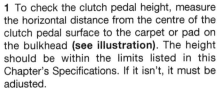

6.1 Drivebelts (arrowed) stretch and deteriorate as they age and must be carefully inspected

7 To adjust the clutch pedal freeplay, loosen the locknut on the pedal end of the clutch pushrod **(see illustration 5.1)**.

8 Turn the pushrod until pedal freeplay is correct.

9 Tighten the locknut and recheck the pedal freeplay to verify it is correct.

10 Complete this procedure by checking the disengagement height (from the upper surface of the pedal to the floor carpet). The disengagement height should be equal to or more than the minimum listed in this Chapter's Specifications.

6 Drivebelt check, adjustment and renewal

Check

1 The alternator/water pump and power steering pump/air conditioning compressor drivebelts, are located at the front of the engine **(see illustration)**. Because of their composition and the high stresses to which they are subjected, drivebelts stretch and deteriorate as they get older. They must therefore be periodically inspected. The good condition and proper adjustment of the alternator/water pump drivebelt is especially critical because it effects the operation of the engine.

2 Vehicles equipped with power steering and air conditioning have a second drivebelt dedicated to these accessories. This

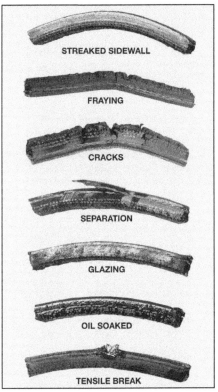

STREAKED SIDEWALL

FRAYING

CRACKS

SEPARATION

GLAZING

OIL SOAKED

TENSILE BREAK

6.3a Here are some of the more common problems associated with drivebelts

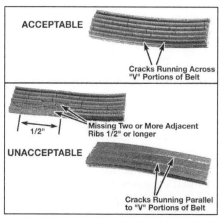

6.3b Small cracks in a V-ribbed belt are acceptable - other damage is cause for renewal

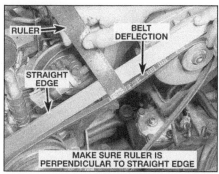

6.4 Measuring drivebelt deflection with a straightedge and ruler

6.5 Loosen the mounting and adjusting bolts (arrows) and move the alternator to tension the drivebelt

accessory drivebelt is mounted outboard of the alternator/water pump drivebelt on the crankshaft pulley.

3 With the engine off, open the bonnet and locate the drivebelts. With an electric torch, visually check the belts. Look for cracking, fraying, separation, tears and glazing, which gives the belt a shiny appearance **(see illustrations)**. Both sides of the belt should be inspected, which means you will have to twist the belt to check the underside. Use your fingers to feel the belt where you can't see it. If any of the above conditions are evident, renew the belt (go to paragraph 8).

4 To check the tension of each belt in accordance with factory specifications, apply moderate pressure (10 kg/22 pounds) midway between the specified pulleys. Measure the deflection **(see illustration)** and compare your measurement to the specified drivebelt deflection for either a used or new belt. **Note:** *A 'used' belt is defined as any belt which has been operated more than five minutes on the engine; a 'new' belt is one that has been used for less than five minutes.*

Adjustment

5 If the alternator/water pump belt must be adjusted, loosen the alternator mounting bolt located under the alternator. Loosen the

adjusting bolt on the top of the alternator and lever the alternator away from the engine to tension the belt **(see illustration)**. Tighten the mounting and adjusting bolt. Measure the belt deflection in accordance with the above method. Repeat this procedure until the drivebelt is properly adjusted.

6 Adjust the power steering pump belt by loosening the bolt and the locknut that secure the pump to the engine and the adjusting locknut under the pump. Adjust the belt tension by turning the adjusting bolt **(see illustration)**. Tighten the adjusting locknut and the pump bolt and nut. Measure the belt deflection in accordance with the above method. Repeat this procedure until the drivebelt is properly adjusted.

7 Vehicles that do not have power steering but are equipped with air conditioning have an idler pulley installed above the compressor. Loosen the idler pulley locknut and turn the adjusting bolt to tension the drivebelt. Tighten the locknut. Measure the belt deflection in accordance with the above method. Repeat this procedure until the drivebelt is properly adjusted.

Renewal

8 To renew a belt, follow the above tensioning procedures but loosen the drivebelt enough to slip the belt off the crankshaft pulley and remove it. If you are replacing the alternator/water pump belt, you will have to remove the power steering and/or

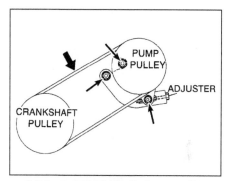

6.6 Loosen the bolts that secure the pump, turn the adjusting bolt to tension the drivebelt

air conditioning belt first because of the way they are arranged on the crankshaft pulley. Because of this and because belts tend to wear out more or less together, it is a good idea to renew both belts at the same time. Mark each belt and its appropriate pulley groove so the renewal belts can be installed in their proper positions.

9 Take the old belts to the parts specialist in order to make a direct comparison for length, width and design.

10 After replacing the drivebelt, make sure that it fits properly. When refitting a multi-ribbed belt, make sure that it is centred - it must not overlap either edge of the pulley.

11 Adjust the drivebelt(s) in accordance with the procedure outlined above.

Every 12 000 miles or 12 months, whichever comes first

---

7 Windscreen wiper blade inspection and renewal

1 The windscreen wiper and blade assembly should be inspected periodically for damage, loose components and cracked or worn blade elements.

 Road film can build up on the wiper blades and affect their efficiency, so they should be washed regularly with a mild detergent solution.

2 The action of the wiping mechanism can loosen bolts, nuts and fasteners, so they

should be checked and tightened, as necessary, at the same time the wiper blades are checked.

3 If the wiper blade elements are cracked, worn or warped, or no longer clean adequately, they should be replaced with new ones.

4 Remove the wiper blade assembly from the arm by pushing on the release lever, then

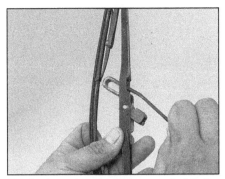

7.4 Push on the release lever and slide the wiper assembly out of the hook in the end of the wiper arm

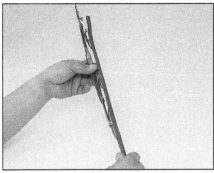

7.5 After detaching the end of the element, slide it out of the end of the frame

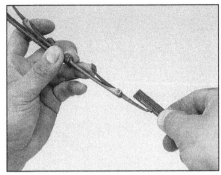

7.6 Insert the end of the element with the protrusions in first

8.1 Tools and materials required for battery maintenance

1 **Face shield/safety goggles** - *When removing corrosion with a brush, the acidic particles can easily fly up into your eyes*

2 **Baking soda** - *A solution of baking soda and water can be used to neutralise corrosion*

3 **Petroleum jelly** - *A layer of this on the battery posts will help prevent corrosion*

4 **Battery post/cable cleaner** - *This wire brush cleaning tool will remove all traces of corrosion from the battery posts and cable clamps*

5 **Treated felt washers** - *Placing one of these on each post, directly under the cable clamps, will help prevent corrosion*

6 **Puller** - *Sometimes the cable clamps are very difficult to pull off the posts, even after the nut/bolt has been completely loosened. This tool pulls the clamp straight up and off the post without damage*

7 **Battery post/cable cleaner** - *Here is another cleaning tool which is a slightly different version of number 4 above, but it does the same thing*

8 **Rubber gloves** - *Another safety item to consider when servicing the battery; remember that's acid inside the battery*

sliding the assembly down and out of the hook in the end of the arm **(see illustration)**.
5 Detach the blade insert element and pull it out of the right end of the wiper frame **(see illustration)**.
6 Insert the new element end with the small protrusions into the right side of the wiper frame **(see illustration)**. Slide the element fully into place, then seat the protrusions in the end of the frames to secure it.

8 Battery check, maintenance and charging

![Warning] **Warning: Certain precautions must be followed when checking and servicing the battery. Hydrogen gas, which is highly flammable, is always present in the battery cells, so keep lighted tobacco and all other open flames and sparks away from the battery. The electrolyte inside the battery is actually dilute sulphuric acid, which will cause injury if splashed on your skin or in your eyes. It will also ruin clothes and painted surfaces. When removing the battery cables, always detach the negative cable first and connect it last!**

1 A routine preventive maintenance program for the battery in your vehicle is the only way to ensure quick and reliable starts. But before performing any battery maintenance, make sure that you have the proper equipment necessary to work safely around the battery **(see illustration)**.

2 There are also several precautions that should be taken whenever battery maintenance is performed. Before servicing the battery, always turn the engine and all accessories off and disconnect the cable from the negative terminal of the battery.

3 The battery produces hydrogen gas, which is both flammable and explosive. Never create a spark, smoke or light a match around the battery. Always charge the battery in a ventilated area.

4 Electrolyte contains poisonous and corrosive sulphuric acid. Do not allow it to get in your eyes, on your skin on your clothes. Never ingest it. Wear protective safety glasses when working near the battery. Keep children away from the battery.

5 Note the external condition of the battery. If the positive terminal and cable clamp on your vehicle's battery is equipped with a rubber protector, make sure that it's not torn or damaged. It should completely cover the terminal. Look for any corroded or loose connections, cracks in the case or cover or loose hold-down clamps. Also check the entire length of each cable for cracks and frayed conductors.

6 If corrosion, which looks like white, fluffy deposits **(see illustration)** is evident, particularly around the terminals, the battery should be removed for cleaning. Loosen the cable clamp bolts with a spanner, being careful to remove the earth cable first, and slide them off the terminals **(see illustration)**.

8.6a Battery terminal corrosion usually appears as light, fluffy powder

8.6b Removing a cable from the battery post with a spanner

8.7a When cleaning the cable clamps, all corrosion must be removed

8.7b When cleaning the battery posts, a clean, shiny surface should be the result

8.8 Make sure the battery clamp nut and bolt (arrowed) are tight

Then disconnect the hold-down clamp bolt and nut, remove the clamp and lift the battery from the engine compartment.

7 Clean the cable clamps thoroughly with a battery brush or a terminal cleaner and a solution of warm water and baking soda **(see illustration)**. Wash the terminals and the top of the battery case with the same solution but make sure that the solution doesn't get into the battery. When cleaning the cables, terminals and battery top, wear safety goggles and rubber gloves to prevent any solution from coming in contact with your eyes or hands. Wear old clothes too - even diluted, sulphuric acid splashed onto clothes will burn holes in them. If the terminals have been extensively corroded, clean them up with a terminal cleaner **(see illustration)**. Thoroughly wash all cleaned areas with plain water.

8 Make sure that the battery tray is in good condition and the hold-down nut and bolt are tight **(see illustration)**. If the battery is removed from the tray, make sure no loose nuts or bolts remain in the bottom of the tray when the battery is reinstalled. When refitting the hold-down clamp bolt or nut, do not overtighten it.

9 Information on removing and refitting the battery can be found in Chapter 5. Information on jump starting can be found at the front of this manual. For more detailed battery checking procedures, refer to the *Haynes Automotive Electrical and Electronic Systems Manual.*

Cleaning

10 Corrosion on the hold-down components, battery case and surrounding areas can be removed with a solution of water and baking soda. Thoroughly rinse all cleaned areas with plain water.

11 Any metal parts of the vehicle damaged by corrosion should be covered with a zinc-based primer, then painted.

Charging

 Warning: When batteries are being charged, hydrogen gas, which is very explosive and flammable, is produced. Do not

smoke or allow open flames near a charging or a recently charged battery. Wear eye protection when near the battery during charging. Also, make sure the charger is unplugged before connecting or disconnecting the battery from the charger.

12 Slow-rate charging is the best way to restore a battery that's discharged to the point where it will not start the engine. It's also a good way to maintain the battery charge in a vehicle that's only driven a few miles between starts. Maintaining the battery charge is particularly important in the winter when the battery must work harder to start the engine and electrical accessories that drain the battery are in greater use.

13 It's best to use a one or two-amp battery charger (sometimes called a 'trickle' charger). They are the safest and put the least strain on

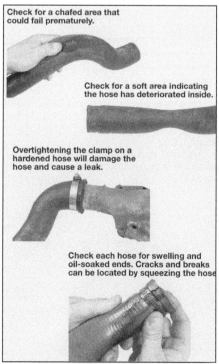

Check for a chafed area that could fail prematurely.

Check for a soft area indicating the hose has deteriorated inside.

Overtightening the clamp on a hardened hose will damage the hose and cause a leak.

Check each hose for swelling and oil-soaked ends. Cracks and breaks can be located by squeezing the hose

9.2 Inspect hoses carefully

the battery. They are also the least expensive. For a faster charge, you can use a higher amperage charger, but don't use one rated more than 1/10th the amp hour rating of the battery. Rapid boost charges that claim to restore the power of the battery in one to two hours are hardest on the battery and can damage batteries not in good condition. This type of charging should only be used in emergency situations.

14 The average time necessary to charge a battery should be listed in the instructions that come with the charger. As a general rule, a trickle charger will charge a battery in 12 to 16 hours.

9 Underbonnet hose check and renewal

Caution: Renewal of air conditioning hoses must be left to a dealer service department or air conditioning workshop that has the equipment to depressurise the system safely. Never remove air conditioning components or hoses until the system has been depressurised.

General

1 High temperatures in the engine compartment can cause the deterioration of the rubber and plastic hoses used for engine, accessory and emission systems operation. Periodic inspection should be made for cracks, loose clamps, material hardening and leaks.

2 Information specific to the cooling system hoses can be found in Section 13 **(see illustration).**

3 Some, but not all, hoses are secured to the fittings with clamps. Where clamps are used, check to be sure they haven't lost their tension, allowing the hose to leak. If clamps aren't used, make sure the hose has not expanded and/or hardened where it slips over the fitting, allowing it to leak.

Vacuum hoses

4 It's quite common for vacuum hoses, especially those in the emissions system, to be colour-coded or identified by coloured stripes moulded into them. Various systems require hoses with different wall thickness, collapse resistance and temperature resistance. When replacing hoses, be sure the new ones are made of the same material.

5 Often the only effective way to check a hose is to remove it completely from the vehicle. If more than one hose is removed, be sure to label the hoses and fittings to ensure correct refitting.

6 When checking vacuum hoses, be sure to include any plastic T-fittings in the check. Inspect the fittings for cracks and the hose where it fits over the fitting for distortion, which could cause leakage.

7 A small piece of vacuum hose can be used as a stethoscope to detect vacuum leaks. Hold one end of the hose to your ear and probe around vacuum hoses and fittings, listening for the 'hissing' sound characteristic of a vacuum leak.

 Warning: When probing with the vacuum hose stethoscope, be very careful not to come into contact with moving engine components such as the drivebelts, cooling fan, etc.

Fuel hose

 Warning: There are certain precautions which must be taken when inspecting or servicing fuel system components. Work in a well ventilated area and do not allow open flames (cigarettes, appliance pilot lights, etc.) or bare light bulbs near the work area. Mop up any spills immediately and do not store fuel soaked rags where they could ignite.

8 Check all rubber fuel lines for deterioration and chafing. Check especially for cracks in areas where the hose bends and just before fittings, such as where a hose attaches to the fuel filter.

9 High quality fuel line, specifically designed for fuel injection systems, must be used for fuel line renewal.

 Warning: Never use anything other than the proper fuel line for fuel line renewal.

10 Spring-type clamps are commonly used on fuel lines. These clamps often lose their tension over a period of time, and can be 'sprung' during removal. Renew all spring-type clamps with screw clamps whenever a hose is replaced.

Metal lines

11 Sections of metal line are often used for fuel line between the fuel pump and fuel injection unit. Check carefully to be sure the line has not been bent or crimped and that cracks have not started in the line.

12 If a section of metal fuel line must be replaced, only seamless steel tubing should be used, since copper and aluminium tubing

don't have the strength necessary to withstand normal engine vibration.

13 Check the metal brake lines where they enter the master cylinder and brake proportioning unit (if used) for cracks in the lines or loose fittings. Any sign of brake fluid leakage calls for an immediate thorough inspection of the brake system.

10 Braking system check

Note: For detailed photographs of the braking system, refer to Chapter 9.

HAYNES HINT *In addition to the specified intervals, the brakes should be inspected every time the wheels are removed.*

1 Any of the following symptoms could indicate a potential braking system defect: The vehicle pulls to one side when the brake pedal is depressed; the brakes make squealing or dragging noises when applied; brake travel is excessive; the pedal pulsates; brake fluid leaks, usually onto the inside of the tyre or wheel.

2 The disc brake pads have built-in wear indicators which should make a high-pitched squealing or scraping noise when they are worn to the renewal point. When you hear this noise, renew the pads immediately or expensive damage to the discs can result.

3 Loosen the wheel nuts.

4 Raise the vehicle and place it securely on axle stands.

5 Remove the wheels (see *Jacking and wheel changing* at the front of this book, or your owner's manual, if necessary).

Disc brakes

6 There are two pads - an outer and an inner - in each caliper. The pads are visible by looking at the top of the caliper **(see illustration)**.

7 Check the pad thickness by measuring the pad lining. If the lining material is less than the thickness listed in this Chapter's

10.6 Measure the thickness of remaining pad material for both inner and outer pads

Specifications, renew the pads. **Note:** *Keep in mind that the lining material is riveted or bonded to a metal backing plate and the metal portion is not included in this measurement.*

8 If it is difficult to determine the exact thickness of the remaining pad material by the above method, or if you are at all concerned about the condition of the pads, remove them from the calipers for further inspection (see Chapter 9).

9 Once the pads are removed from the calipers, clean them with brake cleaner and re-measure them with a small steel pocket ruler or a vernier caliper.

10 Measure the disc thickness with a micrometer to make sure that it still has service life remaining. If any disc is thinner than the specified minimum thickness, renew it (see Chapter 9). Even if the disc has service life remaining, check its condition. Look for scoring, gouging and burned spots. If these conditions exist, remove the disc and have it resurfaced (see Chapter 9).

11 Before refitting the wheels, check all brake lines and hoses for damage, wear, deformation, cracks, corrosion, leakage, bends and twists, particularly in the vicinity of the rubber hoses at the calipers. Check the clamps for tightness and the connections for leakage. Make sure that all hoses and lines are clear of sharp edges, moving parts and the exhaust system. If any of the above conditions are noted, repair, reroute or renew the lines and/or fittings as necessary (see Chapter 9).

Rear drum brakes

12 To check the brake shoe lining thickness without removing the brake drums, remove the rubber plug from the backing plate and use an electric torch to inspect the linings. For a more thorough brake inspection, follow the procedure below.

13 Refer to Chapter 9 and remove the rear brake drums.

 Warning: Brake dust produced by lining wear and deposited on brake components contains asbestos, which is hazardous to your health. DO NOT blow it out with compressed air and DO NOT inhale it! DO NOT use petrol or solvents to remove the dust. Brake system cleaner should be used to flush the dust into a drain pan. After the brake components are wiped clean with a damp rag, dispose of the contaminated rag(s) and solvent in a covered and labelled container. Try to use non-asbestos renewal parts whenever possible.

14 Note the thickness of the lining material on the rear brake shoes **(see illustration)** and look for signs of contamination by brake fluid and grease.

15 If the lining material is within 1.5 mm (0.06 in) of the recessed rivets or metal shoes, renew the brake shoes with new ones. The shoes should also be replaced if they are cracked, glazed (shiny lining surfaces) or

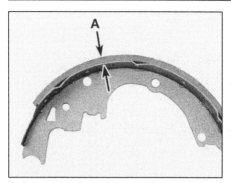

10.14 If the lining is bonded to the shoe, measure the thickness from the outer surface to the shoe

10.17 Peel back the wheel cylinder boot and check for leaking fluid

contaminated with brake fluid or grease. See Chapter 9 for the renewal procedure.

16 Check the shoe return and hold-down springs and the adjusting mechanism to make sure they're installed correctly and in good condition. Deteriorated or distorted springs, if not replaced, could allow the linings to drag and wear prematurely.

17 Check the wheel cylinders for leakage by carefully peeling back the rubber boots **(see illustration)**. If brake fluid is noted behind the boots, the wheel cylinders must be replaced (see Chapter 9).

18 Check the drums for cracks, score marks, deep scratches and hard spots, which will appear as small discoloured areas. If imperfections cannot be removed with emery cloth, the drums must be resurfaced by an automotive machine workshop (see Chapter 9 for more detailed information).

19 Refer to Chapter 9 and refit the brake drums.

20 Refit the wheels and wheel nuts.

21 Remove the axle stands and lower the vehicle.

22 Tighten the wheel nuts to the torque listed in this Chapter's Specifications.

Brake servo check

23 Sit in the driver's seat and perform the following sequence of tests.

24 With the engine stopped, depress the brake pedal several times - the distance of travel should not change.

25 With the brake fully depressed, start the engine - the pedal should move down a little when the engine starts.

26 Depress the brake, stop the engine and hold the pedal in for about 30 seconds - the pedal should neither sink nor rise.

27 Restart the engine, run it for about a minute and turn it off. Then firmly depress the brake several times - the pedal travel should decrease with each application.

28 If your brakes do not operate as described above, the brake servo is either in need of repair or has failed. Refer to Chapter 9 for the removal procedure.

Handbrake

29 Slowly pull up on the handbrake and count the number of clicks you hear until the handle is

up as far as it will go. The adjustment is correct if you hear the specified number of clicks. If you hear more or fewer clicks, it's time to adjust the handbrake (refer to Chapter 9).

30 An alternative method of checking the handbrake is to park the vehicle on a steep hill with the handbrake set and the transmission in Neutral. If the handbrake cannot prevent the vehicle from rolling, it is in need of adjustment (see Chapter 9).

11 Steering and suspension check

Note: *For detailed illustrations of the steering and suspension components, refer to Chapter 10.*

With the wheels on the ground

1 With the vehicle stopped and the front wheels pointed straight ahead, rock the steering wheel gently back and forth. If freeplay is excessive, a front wheel bearing, main shaft yoke, intermediate shaft yoke, lower arm balljoint or steering system joint is worn, or the steering gear is out of adjustment or broken. Refer to Chapter 10 for the appropriate repair procedure.

2 Other symptoms, such as excessive vehicle body movement over rough roads and binding as the steering wheel is turned, may indicate faulty steering and/or suspension components.

3 Check the shock absorbers by pushing down and releasing the vehicle several times at each corner. If the vehicle does not come back to a level position within one or two bounces, the shock absorbers/struts are worn and must be replaced. When bouncing the vehicle up and down, listen for squeaks and noises from the suspension components. Additional information on suspension components can be found in Chapter 10.

Under the vehicle

Front

4 Raise the vehicle with a trolley jack and support it securely on axle stands. See *Jacking and wheel changing* at the front of this manual for the proper jacking points.

5 Check the tyres for irregular wear patterns and proper inflation. See *Weekly checks* for information regarding tyre wear and Chapter 10 for the wheel bearing renewal procedures.

6 Inspect the universal joint between the steering shaft and the steering gear housing. Check the steering gear housing for grease leakage. Make sure that the dust seals and boots are not damaged and that the boot clamps are not loose. Check the steering linkage for looseness or damage. Check the tie-rod ends for excessive play. Look for loose bolts, broken or disconnected parts and deteriorated rubber bushings on all suspension and steering components. While an assistant turns the steering wheel from side to side, check the steering components for free movement, chafing and binding. If the steering components do not seem to be reacting with the movement of the steering wheel, try to determine where the slack is located.

7 Check the balljoints for wear by placing an 180 mm (7 in) thick wooden block under each tyre. Lower the jack until there is about half the load on the coil spring. Make sure that the front wheels are in a straight-ahead position and chock the rear wheels. Move each lower arm up and down **(see illustration)** to ensure that its balljoint has no play. If any balljoint does have play, renew it. See Chapter 10 for the front balljoint renewal procedure.

8 Inspect the balljoint boots for damage and leaking grease **(see illustration)**. Renew the

11.7 Move the lower arm up and down to make sure there is no play in the balljoint

11.8 Push on the balljoint boot to check for damage

12.6 Measure valve clearance with a feeler gauge between the valve stem and the adjusting screw

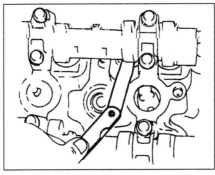

12.11a Measure valve clearance with a feeler gauge between the camshaft lobe and valve tappet shim

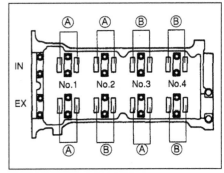

12.11b Valve clearance measurement positions

balljoints with new ones if they are damaged (see Chapter 10).

Rear

9 Raise the vehicle with a trolley jack and support it securely on axle stands. See *Jacking and wheel changing* at the front of this manual for the proper jacking points.
10 Check the tyres for irregular wear patterns and proper inflation. See *Weekly checks* for information regarding tyre wear and Chapter 10 for the wheel bearing renewal procedures.
11 Look for loose bolts, broken or disconnected parts and deteriorated rubber bushings on all suspension and steering components.

12 Valve clearance check

1 1.3 litre engines have valves which are adjusted by a screw with a locknut; 1.5 litre engines have valves which are adjusted by a shim which sits on top of a tappet bucket, and do not need to be checked or adjusted very frequently. All others engines are equipped with hydraulic clearance adjusters which automatically maintain the correct valve clearance and adjustment is not required.

1.3 litre engines

2 Warm the engine up to normal operating temperature then switch the engine off.
3 Remove the cylinder head cover as described in Chapter 2.
4 Turn the crankshaft clockwise so that the No. 1 piston is at TDC of the compression stroke.
5 With the engine in this position the following four valves can be adjusted:
   No 1 cylinder inlet
   No 1 cylinder exhaust
   No 2 cylinder inlet
   No 3 cylinder exhaust
6 Check the valve clearances are as stated in the Specifications by inserting a feeler gauge of the correct thickness between the valve stem and the rocker adjusting screw **(see**

illustration)**. If adjustment is necessary, slacken the adjusting screw locknut and turn the screw as necessary until the feeler blade is a light sliding fit. Once the correct clearance is obtained, hold the adjusting screw and securely tighten the locknut. Recheck the valve clearance and adjust if necessary.
7 Once all four clearances are as specified, turn the crankshaft one complete turn so that the engine is once again at TDC, but this time with No 4 cylinder on compression. With the engine in this position the remaining four valves can be adjusted:
   No 3 cylinder inlet
   No 2 cylinder exhaust
   No 4 cylinder inlet
   No 4 cylinder exhaust
8 Once all valve clearances are correct refit the cylinder head cover as described in Chapter 2.

1.5 litre engines

Check

9 Remove the valve/camshaft cover (see Chapter 2)
10 With the engine in a cold condition, measure the valve clearance as follows.
11 Turn the crankshaft clockwise so that the No. 1 piston is at TDC of the compression stroke. Measure the valve clearance at the 'A' positions **(see illustrations)**.
12 Compare the measured clearance to that listed in this Chapter's Specifications. If the clearance exceeds specifications the adjustment shim will have to be replaced.
13 Turn the crankshaft 360° clockwise so that the No. 4 piston is at TDC on the compression stroke. Measure the valve clearance at the 'B' positions.
14 Again, if the clearance exceeds specifications the adjustment shim will have to be replaced.

Adjustment

15 Valve adjustment requires numerous special fixtures and tools and for this reason it is strongly recommended that you take the vehicle to your dealer to ensure that this critical job is performed correctly.

13 Cooling system check

1 Many major engine failures can be attributed to a faulty cooling system. If the vehicle is equipped with an automatic transmission, the cooling system also cools the transmission fluid and thus plays an important role in prolonging transmission life.
2 The cooling system should be checked with the engine cold. Do this before the vehicle is driven for the day or after the engine has been shut off for at least three hours.
3 Remove the radiator cap by turning it to the left until it reaches a stop. If you hear a hissing sound (indicating there is still pressure in the system), wait until it stops. Now press down on the cap with the palm of your hand and continue turning to the left until the cap can be removed. Thoroughly clean the cap, inside and out, with clean water. Also clean the filler neck on the radiator. All traces of corrosion should be removed. The coolant inside the radiator should be relatively transparent. If it's rust-coloured, the system should be drained and refilled (see Section 21). If the coolant level isn't up to the top, add additional antifreeze/coolant mixture (see *Weekly checks*).
4 Carefully check the large upper and lower radiator hoses along with the smaller diameter heater hoses which run from the engine to the bulkhead. Inspect each hose along its entire length, replacing any hose which is cracked, swollen or shows signs of deterioration. Cracks may become more apparent if the hose is squeezed **(see illustration 9.2)**. Regardless of condition, it's a good idea to renew hoses with new ones every two years.
5 Make sure that all hose connections are tight. A leak in the cooling system will usually show up as white or rust-coloured deposits on the areas adjoining the leak. If wire-type clamps are used at the ends of the hoses, it may be a good idea to renew them with more secure screw-type clamps.
6 Use compressed air or a soft brush to

remove bugs, leaves, etc. from the front of the radiator or air conditioning condenser. Be careful not to damage the delicate cooling fins or cut yourself on them.

14 Fuel system check

⚠️ **Warning: Certain precautions should be observed when inspecting or servicing the fuel system components. Work in a well ventilated area and do not allow open flames (cigarettes, appliance pilot lights, etc.) near the work area. Mop up spills immediately and do not store fuel soaked rags where they could ignite. It is a good idea to keep a dry chemical (Class B) fire extinguisher near the work area any time the fuel system is being serviced.**

1 If you smell petrol while driving or after the vehicle has been sitting in the sun, inspect the fuel system immediately.

2 Remove the filler cap and inspect if for damage and corrosion. The gasket should have an unbroken sealing imprint. If the gasket is damaged or corroded, remove it and refit a new one **(see illustration)**.

3 Inspect the fuel feed and return lines for cracks. Make sure that the threaded flare-nut type connectors which secure the metal fuel lines to the fuel injection system are tight.

4 Since some components of the fuel system - the fuel tank and part of the fuel feed and

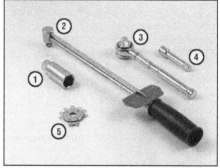

15.1 Tools required for changing spark plugs

1 *Spark plug socket - This will have special padding inside to protect the spark plug porcelain insulator*
2 *Torque wrench - Although not mandatory, use of this tool is the best way to ensure that the plugs are tightened properly*
3 *Ratchet - Standard hand tool to fit the plug socket*
4 *Extension - Depending on model and accessories, you may need special extensions and universal joints to reach one or more of the plugs*
5 *Spark plug gap gauge - This gauge for checking the gap comes in a variety of styles. Make sure the gap for your engine is included*

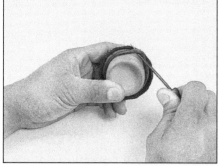

14.2 Use a small screwdriver to carefully lever out the old gasket - take care not to damage the cap

return lines, for example - are underneath the vehicle, they can be inspected more easily with the vehicle raised on a hoist. If that's not possible, raise the vehicle and support it securely on axle stands.

5 With the vehicle raised and safely supported, inspect the tank and filler neck for punctures, cracks and other damage. The hose connecting the filler neck to the tank is particularly critical. Sometimes this hose will leak because of loose clamps or deteriorated rubber **(see illustration)**. These are problems a home mechanic can usually rectify.

⚠️ **Warning: Do not, under any circumstances, try to repair a fuel tank (except rubber components). A welding torch or any open flame can easily cause fuel vapours inside the tank to explode.**

6 Carefully check all rubber hoses and metal lines leading away from the fuel tank. Check for loose connections, deteriorated hoses, crimped lines and other damage. Carefully inspect the lines from the tank to the fuel injection system. Repair or renew damaged sections as necessary (see Chapter 4).

15 Spark plug check and renewal

1 Spark plug renewal requires a spark plug socket which fits onto a ratchet spanner. This

15.4a Spark plug manufacturers recommend using a wire-type gauge when checking the gap

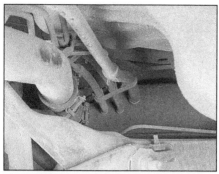

14.5 Inspect the filler/tank connecting hose for cracks and make sure the clamps are tight

socket is lined with a rubber grommet to protect the porcelain insulator of the spark plug and to hold the plug while you insert it into the spark plug hole. You will also need a wire-type feeler gauge to check and adjust the spark plug gap and a torque wrench to tighten the new plugs to the specified torque **(see illustration)**.

2 If you are replacing the plugs, purchase the new plugs, adjust them to the proper gap and then renew each plug one at a time. **Note:** *When buying new spark plugs, it's essential that you obtain the correct plugs for your specific vehicle.*

3 Inspect each of the new plugs for defects. If there are any signs of cracks in the porcelain insulator of a plug, don't use it.

4 Check the electrode gaps of the new plugs. Check the gap by inserting the wire gauge of the proper thickness between the electrodes at the tip of the plug **(see illustration)**. The gap between the electrodes should be identical to that listed in this Chapter's Specifications. If the gap is incorrect, use the notched adjuster on the feeler gauge body to bend the curved side electrode slightly **(see illustration)**.

5 If the side electrode is not exactly over the centre electrode, use the notched adjuster to align them.

Caution: If the gap of a new plug must be adjusted, bend only the base of the earth electrode – do not touch the tip.

15.4b To change the gap, bend the side electrode only

15.8 Use a spark plug socket with a long extension to unscrew the spark plug

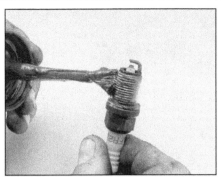

15.10 Apply a thin coat of anti-seize compound to the spark plug threads

16.2 Check the evaporative emissions control canister and the hoses for cracks and damage (arrowed)

HAYNES HiNT

It's often difficult to insert spark plugs into their holes without cross-threading them. To avoid this possibility, fit a short piece of rubber hose over the end of the spark plug. The flexible hose acts as a universal joint to help align the plug with the plug hole. Should the plug begin to cross-thread, the hose will slip on the spark plug, preventing thread damage.

Removal

6 To prevent the possibility of mixing up spark plug leads, work on one spark plug at a time. Remove the lead and boot from one spark plug. Grasp the boot - not the cable - give it a half twisting motion and pull straight up.

7 If compressed air is available, blow any dirt or foreign material away from the spark plug area before proceeding (a common bicycle pump will also work).

8 Remove the spark plug **(see illustration)**.

9 Whether you are replacing the plugs at this time or intend to reuse the old plugs, compare each old spark plug with the chart on the inside back cover of this manual to determine the overall running condition of the engine.

Refitting

10 Prior to refitting, it's a good idea to coat the spark plug threads with anti-seize compound **(see illustration)**. Tighten the plug to the torque listed in this Chapter's Specifications.

11 Attach the plug lead to the new spark plug, again using a twisting motion on the

boot until it is firmly seated on the end of the spark plug.

12 Follow the above procedure for the remaining spark plugs, replacing them one at a time to prevent mixing up the spark plug leads.

16 Evaporative emissions control system check

1 The function of the evaporative emissions control system is to draw fuel vapours from the petrol tank and fuel system, store them in a charcoal canister and then burn them during normal engine operation.

2 The most common symptom of a fault in the evaporative emissions system is a strong fuel odour in the engine compartment. If a fuel odour is detected, inspect the charcoal canister, located at the front of the engine compartment. Check the canister and all hoses for damage and deterioration **(see illustration)**.

3 The evaporative emissions control system is explained in more detail in Chapter 6.

Every 24 000 miles or 2 years, whichever comes first

17 Manual transmission lubricant level check

1 The oil level is checked by removing the speedometer cable and driven gear from the transmission in the engine compartment. The speedometer cable and driven gear are located at the left rear of the engine compartment on the top of the transmission.

2 Park the vehicle on level ground and set the handbrake firmly. Turn the engine off.

3 Disconnect the speedometer cable by turning the knurled nut securing it to the driven gear assembly.

4 Remove the hex head bolt securing the driven gear assembly to the transmission and slowly pull the driven gear assembly from the transmission.

5 Wipe the driven gear clean and reinsert the assembly in the transmission.

6 Pull it out again. The oil level should be between L (Low) and F (Full) **(see illustrations)**.

7 If the oil level is low, add oil until it is at the proper level.

⚠ *Warning: Do not overfill.*

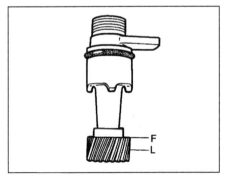

17.6a Transmission oil level should be between the F and L points

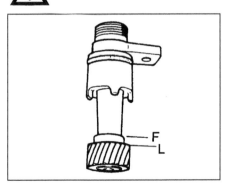

17.6b Transmission oil level should be between the F and L points

18.4 The automatic transmission dipstick is located in a tube near the battery

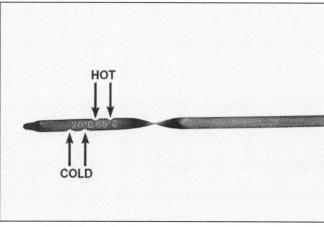

18.6 Pull the dipstick out and note the fluid level.

8 Inspect the O-ring seal on the driven gear. Renew it if it appears damaged, flattened or age hardened. Refit the driven gear in the transmission and tighten the retaining bolt to the torque listed in this Chapter's Specifications. Then refit the speedometer cable.

9 Drive the vehicle a short distance, then check carefully for leaks.

18 Automatic transmission fluid level check

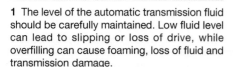

1 The level of the automatic transmission fluid should be carefully maintained. Low fluid level can lead to slipping or loss of drive, while overfilling can cause foaming, loss of fluid and transmission damage.

2 The transmission fluid level should only be checked when the transmission is hot (at its normal operating temperature). If the vehicle has just been driven over 10 miles, and the fluid temperature is about 65° C, the transmission is hot.

Caution: If the vehicle has just been driven for a long time at high speed or in city traffic in hot weather, or if it has been pulling a trailer, an accurate fluid level reading cannot be obtained. Allow the fluid to cool down for about 30 minutes.

3 If the vehicle has not just been driven, park the vehicle on level earth, set the handbrake and start the engine. While the engine is idling, depress the brake pedal and move the selector lever through all the gear ranges, beginning and ending in Park.

4 With the engine still idling, remove the dipstick from its tube **(see illustration)**.

5 Wipe the fluid from the dipstick with a clean rag and reinsert it back into the filler tube until the cap seats.

6 Pull the dipstick out again and note the fluid level **(see illustration)**. If the transmission is cold, the level should be in the 20° C (COLD) range on the dipstick. If it is hot, the fluid level

should be in the 65° C (HOT) range. Use the cold scale as a rough reference only; if the level is low on the COLD scale, recheck the level when the transmission is at normal operating temperature. If the level is at the low side of the HOT range, add the specified automatic transmission fluid through the dipstick tube with a funnel.

7 Add just enough of the recommended fluid to fill the transmission to the proper level. It takes about one pint to raise the level from the low notch to the full notch on the dipstick when the fluid is hot, so add the fluid a little at a time and keep checking the level until it is correct. Do not use the transmission if the level is above the full notch; drain some fluid out (see Section 27).

8 The condition of the fluid should also be checked along with the level. If the fluid at the end of the dipstick is black or a dark reddish brown colour, or if it emits a burned smell, the fluid should be changed (see Section 27). If you are in doubt about the condition of the fluid, purchase some new fluid and compare the two for colour and smell.

19 Driveshaft boot check

1 The driveshaft boots are very important because they prevent dirt, water and foreign material from entering and damaging the constant velocity (CV) joints. Oil and grease can cause the boot material to deteriorate prematurely, so it's a good idea to wash the boots with soap and water. Because it constantly pivots back and forth following the steering action of the front hub, the outer CV boot wears out and should be inspected regularly.

2 Inspect the boots for tears and cracks as well as loose clamps **(see illustration)**. If there is any evidence of cracks or leaking lubricant, they must be renewed as described in Chapter 8.

20 Spark plug lead, distributor cap and rotor check and renewal

1 The spark plug leads should be checked whenever new spark plugs are installed.

2 Begin this procedure by making a visual check of the spark plug leads while the engine is running. In a darkened garage (make sure there is ventilation) start the engine and observe each plug lead. Be careful not to come into contact with any moving engine parts. If there is a break in the wire, you will see arcing or a small spark at the damaged area. If arcing is noticed, make a note to obtain new wires, then allow the engine to cool and check the distributor cap and rotor.

3 The spark plug leads should be inspected one at a time to prevent mixing up the order, which is essential for proper engine operation. Each original plug lead should be numbered to help identify its location. If the number is illegible, a piece of tape can be marked with the correct number and wrapped around the plug lead.

4 Disconnect the plug lead from the spark plug. A removal tool can be used for this purpose or you can grasp the rubber boot,

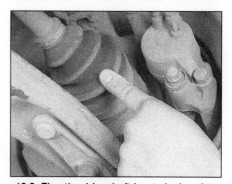

19.2 Flex the driveshaft boots by hand to check for cracks and/or leaking grease

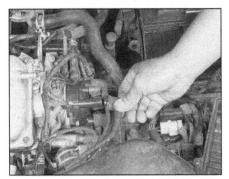

20.8 Pull only on the boot when removing ignition wires from the distributor

20.11a Remove the two screws and detach the distributor cap

20.11b Inspect the distributor cap for carbon tracks, charred or eroded terminals and other damage

twist the boot half a turn and pull the boot free. Do not pull on the wire itself.

5 Check inside the boot for corrosion, which will look like a white crusty powder.

6 Push the wire and boot back onto the end of the spark plug. It should fit tightly onto the end of the plug. If it doesn't, remove the wire and use pliers to carefully crimp the metal connector inside the wire boot until the fit is snug.

7 Using a clean rag, wipe the entire length of the wire to remove built-up dirt and grease. Once the wire is clean, check for burns, cracks and other damage. Do not bend the wire sharply, because the conductor might break.

8 Disconnect the wire from the distributor cap. Again, pull only on the boot **(see illustration)**. Check for corrosion and a tight fit. Renew the wire in the distributor cap.

9 Inspect the remaining spark plug leads, making sure that each one is securely fastened at the distributor and spark plug when the check is complete.

10 If new spark plug leads are required, purchase a set for your specific engine model. Pre-cut wire sets with the boots already installed are available. Remove and renew the wires one at a time to avoid mix-ups in the firing order.

11 Detach the distributor cap by removing the two retaining screws **(see illustration)**.

Look inside it for cracks, carbon tracks and worn, burned or loose contacts **(see illustration)**.

12 Pull the rotor off the distributor shaft and examine it for cracks and carbon tracks **(see illustration)**. Renew the cap and rotor if any damage or defects are noted.

13 It is common practice to refit a new cap and rotor whenever new spark plug leads are installed, but if you wish to continue using the old cap, check the resistance between the spark plug leads and the cap first **(see illustration)**. If the indicated resistance is more than the maximum value listed in this Chapter's Specifications, renew the cap and/or leads.

14 When refitting a new cap, remove the wires from the old cap one at a time and attach them to the new cap in the exact same location – do not simultaneously remove all the wires from the old cap or firing order mix-ups may occur.

21 Cooling system servicing (draining, flushing and refilling)

⚠️ **Warning: Do not allow engine coolant (antifreeze) to come in contact with your skin or painted surfaces of the vehicle. Rinse off spills immediately with plenty of water. Antifreeze is highly toxic if ingested.**

Never leave antifreeze laying around in an open container or in puddles on the floor; children and pets are attracted by it's sweet smell and may drink it. Check with local authorities about disposing of used antifreeze.

1 Periodically, the cooling system should be drained, flushed and refilled to replenish the antifreeze mixture and prevent formation of rust and corrosion, which can impair the performance of the cooling system and cause engine damage. When the cooling system is serviced, all hoses and the radiator cap should be checked and replaced if necessary.

Draining

2 Apply the handbrake and chock the wheels. If the vehicle has just been driven, wait several hours to allow the engine to cool down before beginning this procedure.

3 Once the engine is completely cool, remove the radiator cap.

4 Move a large container under the radiator drain to catch the coolant. On most models you will have to remove a cover for access to the radiator drain fitting located at the bottom of the radiator. Attach a suitable hose to the drain fitting to direct the coolant into the container (some models are already equipped with a hose), then open the drain fitting (a pair of pliers may be required to turn it) **(see illustration)**.

20.12 Check the rotor for damage, wear and corrosion (if in doubt about its condition, buy a new one)

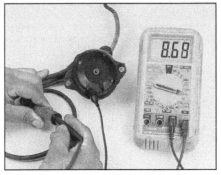

20.13 Measure the resistance value of the distributor cap and the spark plug leads

21.4 The radiator drain fitting located at the bottom of the radiator

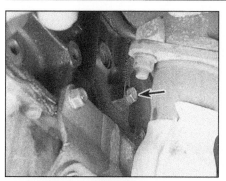

21.5 Fully drain the coolant by removing the drain plug (arrowed) on the side of the engine block

5 After the coolant stops flowing out of the radiator, move the container under the engine block drain plug **(see illustration)**. Loosen the plug and allow the coolant in the block to drain.

6 While the coolant is draining, check the condition of the radiator hoses, heater hoses and clamps (refer to Section 9 if necessary).

7 Renew any damaged clamps or hoses (see Chapter 3).

Flushing

8 Once the system is completely drained, flush the radiator with fresh water from a garden hose until water runs clear at the drain. The flushing action of the water will remove sediments from the radiator but will not remove rust and scale from the engine and cooling tube surfaces.

9 These deposits can be removed by the chemical action of a cleaner. Follow the procedure outlined in the manufacturer's instructions. If the radiator is severely corroded, damaged or leaking, it should be removed (see Chapter 3) and taken to a radiator repair specialist.

10 Remove the overflow hose from the coolant reservoir. Drain the reservoir and flush it with clean water, then reconnect the hose.

Refilling

11 Close and tighten the radiator drain. Refit and tighten the block drain plug.

12 Place the heater temperature control in the maximum heat position.

13 Slowly add new coolant (a 50/50 mixture of water and antifreeze) to the radiator until it's full. Add coolant to the reservoir up to the lower mark.

14 Leave the radiator cap off and run the engine in a well-ventilated area until the thermostat opens (coolant will begin flowing through the radiator and the upper radiator hose will become hot).

15 Turn the engine off and let it cool. Add more coolant mixture to bring the level back up to the lip on the radiator filler neck.

16 Squeeze the upper radiator hose to expel air, then add more coolant mixture if necessary. Renew the radiator cap.

17 Start the engine, allow it to reach normal operating temperature and check for leaks.

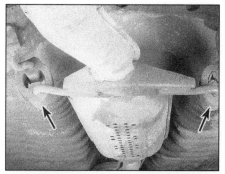

22.4 Be sure to check each exhaust system component rubber hanger (arrowed) for damage

22 Exhaust system check

1 With the engine cold (at least three hours after the vehicle has been driven), check the complete exhaust system from its starting point at the engine to the end of the tailpipe. This should be done on a hoist where unrestricted access is available.

2 Check the pipes and connections for evidence of leaks, severe corrosion or damage. Make sure that all brackets and hangers are in good condition and tight.

3 At the same time, inspect the underside of the body for holes, corrosion, open seams, etc. which may allow exhaust gases to enter the passenger compartment. Seal all body openings with silicone or body putty.

4 Rattles and other noises can often be traced to the exhaust system, especially the mounts and hangers. Try to move the pipes, silencer and catalytic converter. If the components can come in contact with the body or suspension parts, secure the exhaust system with new mounts **(see illustration)**.

5 Check the running condition of the engine by inspecting inside the end of the tailpipe. The exhaust deposits here are an indication of engine state-of-tune. If the pipe is black and sooty or coated with white deposits, the engine is in need of a full service, including a thorough fuel system inspection.

23.2 Grasp the hose securely and pull the PCV valve out of the cover

23 Positive Crankcase Ventilation (PCV) valve and hose check and renewal

1 The PCV valve and hose is located in the valve cover.

2 Pull the PCV valve from the cover **(see illustration)**.

3 With the engine idling at normal operating temperature, place your finger over the end of the valve. If there's no vacuum at the valve, check for a plugged hose or valve. Renew any plugged or deteriorated hoses.

4 Turn off the engine. Remove the PCV valve from the hose. Connect a clean piece of hose and blow through the valve from the valve cover (cylinder head) end. If air will not pass through the valve in this direction, renew it with a new one **(see illustration)**.

5 When purchasing a renewal PCV valve, make sure it's for your particular vehicle and engine size. Compare the old valve with the new one to make sure they're the same.

24 Brake fluid renewal

Brake fluid renewal is similar to bleeding the brake hydraulic system (see Chapter 9, Section 12), except that the aim is to replace all the old fluid rather than removing air from the system.

> **HAYNES HiNT**
> *Old brake fluid is generally much darker in colour than new fluid, making it easier to see when old fluid has been expelled from the system.*

25 Air filter renewal

1 The air filter is located inside a housing in the left front corner of the engine compartment.

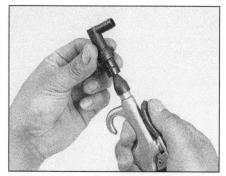

23.4 To check the PVC valve, blow air through it

25.2a Remove the air intake duct and the cover bolts

25.2b Remove the cover and lift the element out

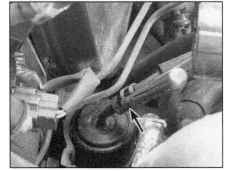

26.4 Disconnect the fuel hoses and remove the filter and bracket

2 To remove the air filter, loosen the intake air duct band and remove the duct/hose **(see illustration)**. Remove the five bolts attaching the air cleaner cover the box, then lift the cover up and remove the air filter element **(see illustration)**.

3 Inspect the outer surface of the filter element. If it is dirty, renew it. If it is only moderately dusty, it can be reused by blowing it clean from the back to the front surface with compressed air. Because it is a pleated paper type filter, it cannot be washed or oiled. If it cannot be cleaned satisfactorily with compressed air, discard and renew it. While the cover is off, be careful not to drop anything down into the housing.

Caution: Never drive the vehicle with the air cleaner removed. Excessive

engine wear could result and backfiring could even cause a fire under the bonnet.

4 Wipe out the inside of the air cleaner housing with a damp cloth.

5 Place the new filter into the air cleaner housing, making sure it seats properly.

6 Refitting of the cover is the reverse of removal.

26 Fuel filter renewal

1 Disconnect the battery negative cable.

2 The canister filter is mounted in a bracket

on the bulkhead near the brake master cylinder.

3 Remove any components that would interfere with access to the top of the filter.

4 Disconnect the fuel hoses from the fuel filter **(see illustration)**.

5 Remove the bracket bolt(s) from the bulkhead and remove the old filter and the filter support bracket assembly.

6 Note that the inlet and outlet pipes are clearly labelled on their respective ends. Make sure the new filter is installed so that it's facing the proper direction as noted above. When correctly installed, the filter should be installed so that the outlet pipe faces up and the inlet pipe faces down.

7 Refitting is the reverse of the removal procedure.

Every 48 000 miles or 4 years, whichever comes first

27 Automatic transmission fluid and filter change

1 Before beginning work, purchase the specified transmission fluid (see *Lubricants and fluids* in *Weekly checks*).

2 Other tools necessary for this job include axle stands to support the vehicle in a raised position, spanners, drain pan capable of holding at least 7 litres, newspapers and clean rags.

3 The fluid should be drained immediately after the vehicle has been driven. Hot fluid is more effective than cold fluid at removing built up sediment.

 Warning: Fluid temperature can exceed 180° C in a hot transmission. Wear protective gloves.

4 After the vehicle has been driven to warm up the fluid, raise it and support it securely on axle stands.

5 Position a drain pan under the transmission drain plug and remove the plug **(see illustration)**.

6 Allow the oil to completely drain, then refit

the plug and tighten it to the torque listed in this Chapter's Specifications.

7 Move the drain pan under the transmission pan and remove the rear and side pan mounting bolts.

8 Loosen the front pan bolts approximately four turns.

9 Carefully lever the transmission pan loose allowing the fluid to drain. Once the fluid has drained, remove the remaining bolts and lower the pan.

27.5 Remove the transmission drain plug

10 Remove the remaining bolts, pan and gasket. Carefully clean the gasket surface of the transmission to remove all traces of the old gasket and sealant.

11 Remove the oil strainer/filter retaining bolts and lower the filter from the transmission **(see illustration)**. Be careful when lowering the filter as it contains residual fluid.

12 Place the new filter in position, and refit the bolts. Tighten the bolts to the torque listed in this Chapter's Specifications.

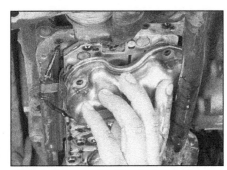

27.11 Remove the filter bolts and lower the filter (be careful, there will be some residual fluid)

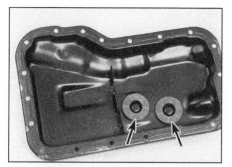

27.13 Wash the pan in clean solvent and remove metal filings from the magnet (arrowed)

13 Carefully clean the gasket surfaces of the fluid pan, removing all traces of old gasket material. Wash the pan in clean solvent and dry it with compressed air. Be sure to clean the metal filings from the magnet **(see illustration)**.

14 Refit a new gasket, place the fluid pan in position and refit the bolts in their original positions. Tighten the bolts to the torque listed in this Chapter's Specifications.

15 Lower the vehicle.

16 With the engine off, add new fluid to the transmission through the dipstick. Use a funnel to prevent spills. It is best to add a little fluid at a time, continually checking the level

with the dipstick (see Section 18). Allow the fluid time to drain into the pan.

17 Start the engine and shift the selector into all positions from P through L, then shift into P and apply the handbrake.

18 With the engine idling, check the fluid level. Add fluid up to the COLD level on the dipstick.

19 Warm the engine and transmission with a short run and recheck the level.

28 Manual transmission lubricant change

1 Before beginning work, purchase the specified lubricant (see *Lubricants and fluids* in *Weekly checks*) and a new drain plug washer/seal.

2 Other tools necessary for this job include axle stands to support the vehicle in a raised position, spanners, drain pan capable of holding at least 5 litres, newspapers and clean rags.

3 The oil should be drained immediately after the vehicle has been driven. Hot oil is more effective than cold oil at removing built up sediment.

 Warning: Oil temperature can exceed 180° C in a hot transmission. Wear protective gloves.

4 After the vehicle has been driven to warm up the oil, disconnect the speedometer cable and remove the speedometer driven gear assembly on early models; later models have an oil level and filler plug (See Section 15) which should be removed.

5 Raise the vehicle and support it securely on axle stands. Make sure it is safely supported and as level as possible.

6 Move the necessary equipment under the vehicle, being careful not to touch any of the hot exhaust components.

7 Place the drain pan under the transmission drain plug and loosen the drain plug.

8 Carefully unscrew the drain plug and washer with your fingers. Be careful not to burn yourself on the oil.

9 Allow the oil to drain completely. Clean the drain plug then refit it with a new washer. Tighten the drain plug to the torque listed in this Chapter's Specifications.

10 Lower the vehicle.

11 Add new oil to the transmission. Use a funnel to prevent spills. It is best to add a little oil at a time, continually checking the level (see Section 15).

12 Refit the oil level and filler plug, or the speedometer driven gear assembly and reconnect the speedometer cable, where applicable.

Notes

Chapter 1 Part B
Routine maintenance and servicing - models from 1995

Contents

Degrees of difficulty

Easy, suitable for novice with little experience	Fairly easy, suitable for beginner with some experience	Fairly difficult, suitable for competent DIY mechanic	Difficult, suitable for experienced DIY mechanic	Very difficult, suitable for expert DIY or professional

Specifications

Refer to specifications listed in Chapter 1A

Component locations

Refer to Chapter 1A

The maintenance intervals in this manual are provided with the assumption that you, not the dealer, will be doing the work. These are the minimum maintenance intervals recommended by the factory for vehicles that are driven daily. If you wish to keep your vehicle in peak condition at all times, you may wish to perform some of these procedures even more often. Because frequent maintenance enhances the efficiency, performance and resale value of your car, we encourage you to do so. If you drive in dusty areas, tow a trailer, idle or drive at low speeds for extended periods, or drive for short distances (less than four miles) in below freezing temperatures, shorter intervals are also recommended.

When your vehicle is new, it should be serviced by a dealer to protect the factory warranty. In many cases, the initial maintenance check is done at no cost to the owner.

Every 4500 miles or 6 months, whichever comes first

Note: *Frequent oil and filter changes are good for the engine. We recommend changing the oil at the mileage specified here, or at least twice a year if the mileage covered is less.*

☐ Change the engine oil and oil filter (Section 3)

Every 9000 miles or 12 months, whichever comes first

☐ Check the power steering fluid level (Section 4)
☐ Inspect and renew if necessary the windscreen wiper blades (Section 5)
☐ Check the clutch pedal for proper height and freeplay (Section 6)
☐ Check and service the battery (Section 7)
☐ Check and adjust if necessary the engine drivebelts (Section 8)
☐ Inspect and renew if necessary all underbonnet hoses (Section 9)
☐ Inspect the braking system (Section 10)*
☐ Inspect the steering and suspension components (Section 11)*
☐ Check and adjust the valve clearances - 1.3 litre engines (Section 12)
☐ Check the air conditioning system operation (Chapter 3)
☐ Lubricate the hinges and catches (Chapter 11)
☐ Check for bodywork corrosion
☐ Tighten the fasteners on the body and chassis

This item is affected by 'severe' operating conditions as described below. If your vehicle is operated under 'severe' conditions, perform all maintenance indicated with an asterisk at 4500 mile/6 month intervals. Severe conditions are indicated if you mainly operate your vehicle under one or more of the following conditions:
    Operating in dusty areas
    Towing a trailer
    Idling for extended periods and/or low speed operation
    Operating when outside temperatures remain below freezing and when most trips are less than four miles

**If operated under one or more of the following conditions, change the manual or automatic transmission fluid and differential lubricant at 27 000 miles/36 month intervals:*
    In heavy city traffic where the outside temperature regularly reaches 32° C (90° F) or higher
    In hilly or mountainous terrain
    Frequent trailer pulling

Every 18 000 miles or 24 months, whichever comes first

☐ Check the automatic transmission fluid level (Section 13)
☐ Check the cooling system (Section 14)
☐ Check the manual transmission lubricant level (Section 15)
☐ Check the driveshaft boot (Section 16)
☐ Inspect the fuel system (Section 17)
☐ Renew the spark plugs (Section 18)
☐ Inspect and renew if necessary the spark plug leads, distributor cap and rotor (Section 19)
☐ Service the cooling system (drain, flush and refill) (Section 20)
☐ Inspect the fuel evaporative emissions control system (Section 21)
☐ Inspect the exhaust system (Section 22)
☐ Check and renew if necessary the PCV valve (Section 23)
☐ Check the ignition timing (Chapter 5)
☐ Check the seat belts (Chapter 11)
☐ Check the EGR system (Chapter 6)
☐ Check the headlight alignment (Chapter 12)
☐ Renew the brake fluid (Section 24)

Every 27 000 miles or 36 months, whichever comes first

☐ Renew the air filter (Section 25)

Every 36 000 miles or 48 months, whichever comes first

☐ Renew the fuel filter (Section 26)
☐ Change the automatic transmission fluid (Section 27)**
☐ Change the manual transmission lubricant (Section 28)**

Every 60 000 miles

☐ Renew the timing belt (Chapter 2A)
☐ Check and adjust the valve clearances - 1.5 litre engines (Section 12)

1 Introduction

This Chapter is designed to help the home mechanic maintain the Mazda 323 for peak performance, economy, safety and long life.

Included is a master maintenance schedule, followed by sections dealing specifically with each item on the schedule. Visual checks, adjustments, component renewal and other helpful items are included.

Servicing your 323 in accordance with the mileage/time maintenance schedule and the following Sections will provide it with a planned maintenance program that should result in a long and reliable service life. This is a comprehensive plan, so maintaining some items but not others at the specified service intervals will not produce the same results.

As you service your 323, you will discover that many of the procedures can - and should - be grouped together because of the nature of the particular procedure you're performing or because of the close proximity of two otherwise unrelated components to one another.

For example, if the vehicle is raised for any reason, you should inspect the exhaust, suspension, steering and fuel systems while you're under the vehicle.

Finally, let's suppose you have to borrow or rent a torque wrench. Even if you only need to tighten the spark plugs, you might as well check the torque of as many critical fasteners as time allows.

The first step of this maintenance program is to prepare yourself before the actual work begins. Read through all Sections pertinent to the procedures you're planning to do, then make a list of and gather together all the parts and tools you will need to do the job. If it looks as if you might run into problems during a particular segment of some procedure, seek advice from your local parts specialist or service department.

2 General information

If, from the time the vehicle is new, the routine maintenance schedule is followed closely and frequent checks are made of fluid levels and high wear items, as suggested throughout this manual, the engine will be kept in relatively good running condition and the need for additional work will be minimised.

More likely than not, however, there will be times when the engine is running poorly due to lack of regular maintenance. This is even more likely if a used vehicle, which has not received regular and frequent maintenance checks, is purchased. In such cases, extra work will be needed outside of the regular routine maintenance intervals.

The first step in any procedure to help correct a poor running engine would be a cylinder compression check. A check of the engine compression (Chapter 2, Part B) will give valuable information regarding the overall performance of many internal components and should be used as a basis for servicing and repair procedures. If, for instance, a compression check indicates serious internal engine wear, a conventional service will not help the running condition of the engine and would be a waste of time and money.

The following series of operations are those most often needed to bring a generally poor running engine back into a proper state of tune.

Primary operations

Clean, inspect and test the battery
Check all engine related fluids
Check and adjust the drivebelts
Renew the spark plugs
Inspect the distributor cap and rotor
Inspect the spark plug and coil leads
Check all underbonnet hoses
Check the cooling system
Check the air filter

Secondary operations

Check the ignition system
Check the charging system
Check the fuel system
Renew the air filter
Renew the distributor cap and rotor
Renew the spark plug leads

Every 4500 miles or 6 months

3 Engine oil and oil filter change

HAYNES HiNT *Frequent oil changes are the best preventive maintenance the home mechanic can give the engine, because ageing oil becomes diluted and contaminated, which leads to premature engine wear.*

1 Make sure that you have all the necessary tools before you begin this procedure (**see illustration**).
2 You should also have plenty of rags or newspapers handy for mopping up any spills.
3 Oil and filter renewal for later models is very similar to the procedure given in Section 3, Chapter 1A.

3.1 These tools are required when changing the engine oil and filter

1 **Drain pan** - It should be fairly shallow in depth, but wide in order to prevent spills
2 **Rubber gloves** - When removing the drain plug and filter, it is inevitable that you will get oil on your hands (the gloves will prevent burns)
3 **Breaker bar** - Sometimes the oil drain plug is pretty tight and a long breaker bar is needed to loosen it
4 **Socket** – To be used with the breaker bar or a ratchet (must be the correct size to fit the drain plug)
5 **Filter spanner** - This is a metal band-type spanner, which requires clearance around the filter to be effective
6 **Filter spanner** - This type fits on the bottom of the filter and can be turned with a ratchet or beaker bar (different size spanners are available for different types of filters)

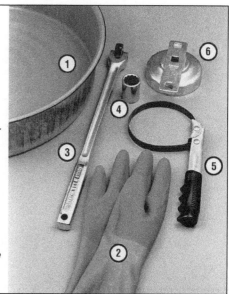

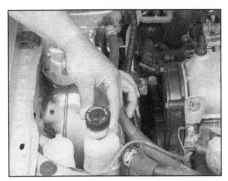

4.2 The power steering fluid reservoir is located in the right front corner of the engine compartment

4.4 The fluid level is checked by looking at the lines on the reservoir and can be checked hot or cold

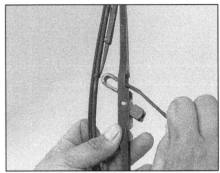

5.4 Push on the release lever and slide the wiper assembly out of the hook in the end of the wiper arm

Every 9,000 miles or 12 months

4 Power steering fluid level check

1 Unlike manual steering, the power steering system relies on fluid which may, over a period of time, require replenishing.
2 The fluid reservoir for the power steering pump is located in the right front corner of the engine compartment, next to the windscreen washer fluid reservoir (see illustration).
3 For the check, the front wheels should be pointed straight ahead and the engine should be off.
4 To check the fluid level, simply look at the F (Full) and L (Low) lines on the reservoir (see illustration). The fluid level should be between the F and L lines.
5 If additional fluid is required, pour the specified type (see *Lubricants and fluids* in *Weekly checks*) directly into the reservoir, using a funnel to prevent spills. Fill the reservoir to the F line.
6 If the reservoir requires frequent fluid additions, all power steering hoses, hose connections, the power steering pump and the rack and pinion assembly should be carefully checked for leaks.

5 Windscreen wiper blade inspection and renewal

1 The windscreen wiper and blade assembly should be inspected periodically for damage, loose components and cracked or worn blade elements.

 HAYNES HiNT *Road film can build up on the wiper blades and affect their efficiency, so they should be washed regularly with a mild detergent solution.*

2 The action of the wiping mechanism can loosen bolts, nuts and fasteners, so they should be checked and tightened, as necessary, at the same time the wiper blades are checked.
3 If the wiper blade elements are cracked, worn or warped, or no longer clean adequately, they should be replaced with new ones.
4 Remove the wiper blade assembly from the arm by pushing on the release lever, then sliding the assembly down and out of the hook in the end of the arm (see illustration).

5 Detach the blade insert element and pull it out of the right end of the wiper frame (see illustration).
6 Insert the new element end with the small protrusions into the right side of the wiper frame (see illustration). Slide the element fully into place, then seat the protrusions in the end of the frames to secure it.

6 Clutch pedal height and freeplay check and adjustment

1 To check the clutch pedal height, measure the horizontal distance from the centre of the clutch pedal surface to the carpet or pad on the bulkhead (see illustration). The height should be within the limits listed in this Chapter's Specifications. If it isn't, it must be adjusted.

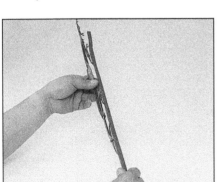

5.5 After detaching the end of the element, slide it out of the end of the frame

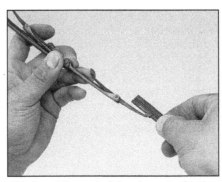

5.6 Insert the end of the element with the protrusions in first

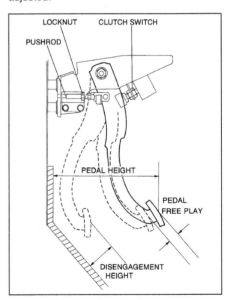

6.1 Clutch pedal adjustment details

2 To adjust the clutch pedal height, disconnect the clutch switch electrical connector.

3 Loosen the switch locknut **(see illustration 6.1)**.

4 Turn the clutch switch until the pedal height is correct.

5 Tighten the locknut and recheck the pedal height to verify it is correct. **Note**: *Whenever the pedal height is adjusted it will most likely be necessary to adjust the freeplay, because increasing or decreasing pedal height will cause a similar change in pedal freeplay.*

6 Check the clutch pedal freeplay by lightly pushing the clutch pedal down and, with a small steel ruler, measure the distance that it moves freely before the clutch resistance is felt **(see illustration 6.1)**. The freeplay should be within the limits listed in this Chapter's Specifications. If it isn't, it must be adjusted.

7 To adjust the clutch pedal freeplay, loosen the locknut on the pedal end of the clutch pushrod **(see illustration 6.1)**.

8 Turn the pushrod until pedal freeplay is correct.

9 Tighten the locknut and recheck the pedal freeplay to verify it is correct.

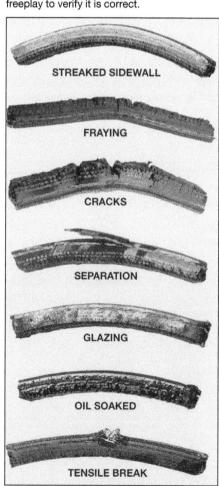

8.3a Here are some of the more common problems associated with drivebelts

10 Complete this procedure by checking the disengagement height (from the upper surface of the pedal to the floor carpet). The disengagement height should be equal to or more than the minimum listed in this Chapter's Specifications.

7 Battery check, maintenance and charging

> ⚠️ **Warning: Certain precautions must be followed when checking and servicing the battery. Hydrogen gas, which is highly flammable, is always present in the battery cells, so keep lighted tobacco and all other open flames and sparks away from the battery. The electrolyte inside the battery is actually dilute sulphuric acid, which will cause injury if splashed on your skin or in your eyes. It will also ruin clothes and painted surfaces. When removing the battery cables, always detach the negative cable first and connect it last!**

1 A routine preventive maintenance program for the battery in your vehicle is the only way to ensure quick and reliable starts. Refer to Section 8, Chapter 1A for more details.

8 Drivebelt check, adjustment and renewal

Check

1 The alternator/water pump and power steering pump/air conditioning compressor drivebelts, are located at the front of the engine **(see illustration)**. Because of their composition and the high stresses to which they are subjected, drivebelts stretch and deteriorate as they get older. They must therefore be periodically inspected. The good condition and proper adjustment of the alternator/water pump drivebelt is especially

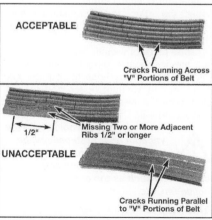

8.3b Small cracks in a V-ribbed belt are acceptable - other damage is cause for renewal

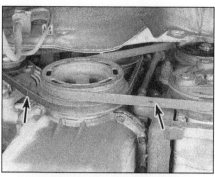

8.1 Drivebelts (arrowed) stretch and deteriorate as they age and must be carefully inspected

critical because it effects the operation of the engine.

2 Vehicles equipped with power steering and air conditioning have a second drivebelt dedicated to these accessories. This accessory drivebelt is mounted outboard of the alternator/water pump drivebelt on the crankshaft pulley.

3 With the engine off, open the bonnet and locate the drivebelts. With an electric torch, visually check the belts. Look for cracking, fraying, separation, tears and glazing, which gives the belt a shiny appearance **(see illustrations)**. Both sides of the belt should be inspected, which means you will have to twist the belt to check the underside. Use your fingers to feel the belt where you can't see it. If any of the above conditions are evident, renew the belt (go to paragraph 8).

4 To check the tension of each belt in accordance with factory specifications, apply moderate pressure (10 kg/22 pounds) midway between the specified pulleys. Measure the deflection **(see illustration)** and compare your measurement to the specified drivebelt deflection for either a used or new belt. **Note**: *A 'used' belt is defined as any belt which has been operated more than five minutes on the engine; a 'new' belt is one that has been used for less than five minutes.*

Adjustment

5 If the alternator/water pump belt must be adjusted, loosen the alternator mounting bolt

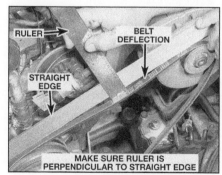

8.4 Measuring drivebelt deflection with a straightedge and ruler

located under the alternator. Loosen the adjusting bolt on the top of the alternator and lever the alternator away from the engine to tension the belt **(see illustration)**. Tighten the mounting and adjusting bolt. Measure the belt deflection in accordance with the above method. Repeat this procedure until the drivebelt is properly adjusted.

6 Adjust the power steering pump belt by loosening the bolt and the locknut that secure the pump to the engine and the adjusting locknut under the pump. Adjust the belt tension by turning the adjusting bolt **(see illustration)**. Tighten the adjusting locknut and the pump bolt and nut. Measure the belt deflection in accordance with the above method. Repeat this procedure until the drivebelt is properly adjusted.

7 Vehicles that do not have power steering but are equipped with air conditioning have an idler pulley installed above the compressor. Loosen the idler pulley locknut and turn the adjusting bolt to tension the drivebelt. Tighten the locknut. Measure the belt deflection in accordance with the above method. Repeat this procedure until the drivebelt is properly adjusted.

Renewal

8 To renew a belt, follow the above tensioning procedures but loosen the drivebelt enough to slip the belt off the crankshaft pulley and remove it. If you are replacing the alternator/water pump belt, you will have to remove the power steering and/or air conditioning belt first because of the way they are arranged on the crankshaft pulley. Because of this and because belts tend to wear out more or less together, it is a good idea to renew both belts at the same time. Mark each belt and its appropriate pulley groove so the renewal belts can be installed in their proper positions.

9 Take the old belts to the parts specialist in order to make a direct comparison for length, width and design.

10 After replacing the drivebelt, make sure that it fits properly. When refitting a multi-ribbed belt, make sure that it is centred - it must not overlap either edge of the pulley.

11 Adjust the drivebelt(s) in accordance with the procedure outlined above.

9   Underbonnet hose check and renewal

Caution: Renewal of air conditioning hoses must be left to a dealer service department or air conditioning workshop that has the equipment to depressurise the system safely. Never remove air conditioning components or hoses until the system has been depressurised.

General

1 High temperatures in the engine compartment can cause the deterioration of

8.5 Loosen the mounting and adjusting bolts (arrows) and move the alternator to tension the drivebelt

the rubber and plastic hoses used for engine, accessory and emission systems operation. Periodic inspection should be made for cracks, loose clamps, material hardening and leaks.

2 Information specific to the cooling system hoses can be found in Section 14 **(see illustration)**.

3 Some, but not all, hoses are secured to the fittings with clamps. Where clamps are used, check to be sure they haven't lost their tension, allowing the hose to leak. If clamps aren't used, make sure the hose has not expanded and/or hardened where it slips over the fitting, allowing it to leak.

Vacuum hoses

4 It's quite common for vacuum hoses, especially those in the emissions system, to be colour-coded or identified by coloured stripes moulded into them. Various systems require hoses with different wall thickness, collapse resistance and temperature resistance. When replacing hoses, be sure the new ones are made of the same material.

5 Often the only effective way to check a hose is to remove it completely from the vehicle. If more than one hose is removed, be sure to label the hoses and fittings to ensure correct refitting.

6 When checking vacuum hoses, be sure to include any plastic T-fittings in the check. Inspect the fittings for cracks and the hose where it fits over the fitting for distortion, which could cause leakage.

7 A small piece of vacuum hose can be used as a stethoscope to detect vacuum leaks. Hold one end of the hose to your ear and probe around vacuum hoses and fittings, listening for the 'hissing' sound characteristic of a vacuum leak.

   Warning: When probing with the vacuum hose stethoscope, be very careful not to come into contact with moving engine components such as the drivebelts, cooling fan, etc.

Fuel hose

   Warning: There are certain precautions which must be taken when inspecting or

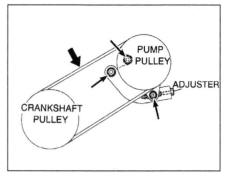
8.6 Loosen the bolts that secure the pump, turn the adjusting bolt to tension the drivebelt

servicing fuel system components. Work in a well ventilated area and do not allow open flames (cigarettes, appliance pilot lights, etc.) or bare light bulbs near the work area. Mop up any spills immediately and do not store fuel soaked rags where they could ignite.

8 Check all rubber fuel lines for deterioration and chafing. Check especially for cracks in areas where the hose bends and just before fittings, such as where a hose attaches to the fuel filter.

9 High quality fuel line, specifically designed for fuel injection systems, must be used for fuel line renewal.

   Warning: Never use anything other than the proper fuel line for fuel line renewal.

10 Spring-type clamps are commonly used on fuel lines. These clamps often lose their

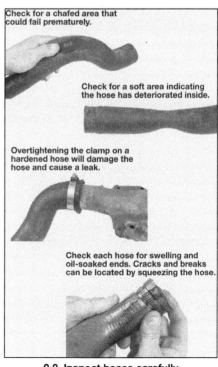
9.2 Inspect hoses carefully

tension over a period of time, and can be 'sprung' during removal. Renew all spring-type clamps with screw clamps whenever a hose is replaced.

Metal lines

11 Sections of metal line are often used for fuel line between the fuel pump and fuel injection unit. Check carefully to be sure the line has not been bent or crimped and that cracks have not started in the line.

12 If a section of metal fuel line must be replaced, only seamless steel tubing should be used, since copper and aluminium tubing don't have the strength necessary to withstand normal engine vibration.

13 Check the metal brake lines where they enter the master cylinder and brake proportioning unit (if used) for cracks in the lines or loose fittings. Any sign of brake fluid leakage calls for an immediate thorough inspection of the brake system.

10 Braking system check

Refer to Section 10, Chapter 1A for braking system check procedures.

11 Steering and suspension check

Note: *For detailed illustrations of the steering and suspension components, refer to Chapter 10.*

With the wheels on the ground

1 With the vehicle stopped and the front wheels pointed straight ahead, rock the steering wheel gently back and forth. If freeplay is excessive, a front wheel bearing, main shaft yoke, intermediate shaft yoke, lower arm balljoint or steering system joint is worn, or the steering gear is out of adjustment or broken. Refer to Chapter 10 for the appropriate repair procedure.

2 Other symptoms, such as excessive vehicle body movement over rough roads and binding as the steering wheel is turned, may indicate faulty steering and/or suspension components.

3 Check the shock absorbers by pushing down and releasing the vehicle several times at each corner. If the vehicle does not come back to a level position within one or two bounces, the shock absorbers/struts are worn and must be replaced. When bouncing the vehicle up and down, listen for squeaks and noises from the suspension components. Additional information on suspension components can be found in Chapter 10.

Under the vehicle
Front

4 Raise the vehicle with a trolley jack and support it securely on axle stands. See *Jacking and wheel changing* at the front of this manual for the proper jacking points.

5 Check the tyres for irregular wear patterns and proper inflation. See *Weekly checks* for information regarding tyre wear and Chapter 10 for the wheel bearing renewal procedures.

6 Inspect the universal joint between the steering shaft and the steering gear housing. Check the steering gear housing for grease leakage. Make sure that the dust seals and boots are not damaged and that the boot clamps are not loose. Check the steering linkage for looseness or damage. Check the tie-rod ends for excessive play. Look for loose bolts, broken or disconnected parts and deteriorated rubber bushings on all suspension and steering components. While an assistant turns the steering wheel from side to side, check the steering components for free movement, chafing and binding. If the steering components do not seem to be reacting with the movement of the steering wheel, try to determine where the slack is located.

7 Check the balljoints for wear by placing an 180 mm (7 in) thick wooden block under each tyre. Lower the jack until there is about half the load on the coil spring. Make sure that the front wheels are in a straight-ahead position and chock the rear wheels. Move each lower arm up and down **(see illustration)** to ensure that its balljoint has no play. If any balljoint does have play, renew it. See Chapter 10 for the front balljoint renewal procedure.

8 Inspect the balljoint boots for damage and leaking grease **(see illustration)**. Renew the balljoints with new ones if they are damaged (see Chapter 10).

Rear

9 Raise the vehicle with a trolley jack and support it securely on axle stands. See *Jacking and wheel changing* at the front of this manual for the proper jacking points.

10 Check the tyres for irregular wear patterns and proper inflation. See *Weekly checks* for information regarding tyre wear and Chapter 10 for the wheel bearing renewal procedures.

11 Look for loose bolts, broken or disconnected parts and deteriorated rubber bushings on all suspension and steering components.

12 Valve clearance check

1 1.3 litre engines have valves which are adjusted by a screw with a locknut; 1.5 litre engines have valves which are adjusted by a shim which sits on top of a tappet bucket, and do not need to be checked or adjusted very frequently. All others engines are equipped with hydraulic clearance adjusters which automatically maintain the correct valve clearance and adjustment is not required.

1.3 litre engines

2 Warm the engine up to normal operating temperature then switch the engine off.

3 Remove the cylinder head cover as described in Chapter 2.

4 Turn the crankshaft clockwise so that the No. 1 piston is at TDC of the compression stroke.

5 With the engine in this position the following four valves can be adjusted:

No 1 cylinder inlet
No 1 cylinder exhaust
No 2 cylinder inlet
No 3 cylinder exhaust

6 Check the valve clearances are as stated in the Specifications by inserting a feeler gauge of the correct thickness between the valve stem and the rocker adjusting screw **(see illustration)**. If adjustment is necessary,

11.7 Move the lower arm up and down to make sure there is no play in the balljoint

11.8 Push on the balljoint boot to check for damage

12.6 Measure valve clearance with a feeler gauge between the valve stem and the adjusting screw

slacken the adjusting screw locknut and turn the screw as necessary until the feeler blade is a light sliding fit. Once the correct clearance is obtained, hold the adjusting screw and securely tighten the locknut. Recheck the valve clearance and adjust if necessary.

7 Once all four clearances are as specified, turn the crankshaft one complete turn so that the engine is once again at TDC, but this time with No 4 cylinder on compression. With the engine in this position the remaining four valves can be adjusted:

No 3 cylinder inlet
No 2 cylinder exhaust
No 4 cylinder inlet
No 4 cylinder exhaust

8 Once all valve clearances are correct refit the cylinder head cover as described in Chapter 2.

1.5 litre engines

Check

9 Remove the valve/camshaft cover (see Chapter 2)

10 With the engine in a cold condition, measure the valve clearance as follows.

11 Turn the crankshaft clockwise so that the No. 1 piston is at TDC of the compression

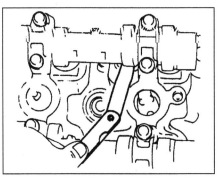

12.11a Measure valve clearance with a feeler gauge between the camshaft lobe and valve tappet shim

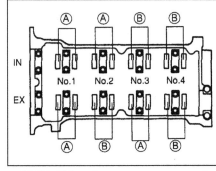

12.11b Valve clearance measurement positions

stroke. Measure the valve clearance at the 'A' positions **(see illustrations)**.

12 Compare the measured clearance to that listed in this Chapter's Specifications. If the clearance exceeds specifications the adjustment shim will have to be replaced.

13 Turn the crankshaft 360° clockwise so that the No. 4 piston is at TDC of the compression stroke. Measure the valve clearance at the 'B' positions.

14 Again, if the clearance exceeds specifications the adjustment shim will have to be replaced.

Adjustment

15 Valve adjustment requires numerous special fixtures and tools and for this reason it is strongly recommended that you take the vehicle to your dealer to ensure that this critical job is performed correctly.

Every 18 000 miles or 24 months

13 Automatic transmission fluid level check

1 The level of the automatic transmission fluid should be carefully maintained. Low fluid level can lead to slipping or loss of drive, while overfilling can cause foaming, loss of fluid and transmission damage.

2 The transmission fluid level should only be checked when the transmission is hot (at its normal operating temperature). If the vehicle has just been driven over 10 miles, and the fluid temperature is about 65° C, the transmission is hot.

Caution: If the vehicle has just been driven for a long time at high speed or in city traffic in hot weather, or if it has been

pulling a trailer, an accurate fluid level reading cannot be obtained. Allow the fluid to cool down for about 30 minutes.

3 If the vehicle has not just been driven, park the vehicle on level earth, set the handbrake and start the engine. While the engine is idling, depress the brake pedal and move the selector lever through all the gear ranges, beginning and ending in Park.

4 With the engine still idling, remove the dipstick from its tube **(see illustration)**.

5 Wipe the fluid from the dipstick with a clean rag and reinsert it back into the filler tube until the cap seats.

6 Pull the dipstick out again and note the fluid level **(see illustration)**. If the transmission is cold, the level should be in the 20° C (COLD) range on the dipstick. If it is hot, the fluid level should be in the 65° C (HOT) range. Use the

cold scale as a rough reference only; if the level is low on the COLD scale, recheck the level when the transmission is at normal operating temperature. If the level is at the low side of the HOT range, add the specified automatic transmission fluid through the dipstick tube with a funnel.

7 Add just enough of the recommended fluid to fill the transmission to the proper level. It takes about one pint to raise the level from the low notch to the full notch on the dipstick when the fluid is hot, so add the fluid a little at a time and keep checking the level until it is correct. Do not use the transmission if the level is above the full notch; drain some fluid out (see Section 27).

8 The condition of the fluid should also be checked along with the level. If the fluid at the end of the dipstick is black or a dark reddish brown colour, or if it emits a burned smell, the fluid should be changed (see Section 27). If you are in doubt about the condition of the fluid, purchase some new fluid and compare the two for colour and smell.

14 Cooling system check

1 Many major engine failures can be attributed to a faulty cooling system. If the vehicle is equipped with an automatic transmission, the cooling system also cools the transmission fluid and thus plays an important role in prolonging transmission life.

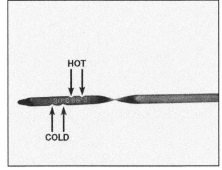

13.4 The automatic transmission dipstick is located in a tube near the battery

13.6 Pull the dipstick out and note the fluid level.

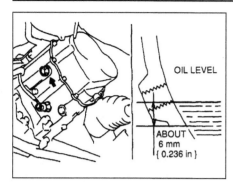

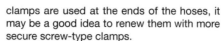

15.2 Oil level and filler plug

2 The cooling system should be checked with the engine cold. Do this before the vehicle is driven for the day or after the engine has been shut off for at least three hours.

3 Remove the radiator cap by turning it to the left until it reaches a stop. If you hear a hissing sound (indicating there is still pressure in the system), wait until it stops. Now press down on the cap with the palm of your hand and continue turning to the left until the cap can be removed. Thoroughly clean the cap, inside and out, with clean water. Also clean the filler neck on the radiator. All traces of corrosion should be removed. The coolant inside the radiator should be relatively transparent. If it's rust-coloured, the system should be drained and refilled (see Section 20). If the coolant level isn't up to the top, add additional antifreeze/coolant mixture (see *Weekly checks*).

4 Carefully check the large upper and lower radiator hoses along with the smaller diameter heater hoses which run from the engine to the bulkhead. Inspect each hose along its entire length, replacing any hose which is cracked, swollen or shows signs of deterioration. Cracks may become more apparent if the hose is squeezed **(see illustration 9.2)**. Regardless of condition, it's a good idea to renew hoses with new ones every two years.

5 Make sure that all hose connections are tight. A leak in the cooling system will usually show up as white or rust-coloured deposits on the areas adjoining the leak. If wire-type clamps are used at the ends of the hoses, it may be a good idea to renew them with more secure screw-type clamps.

6 Use compressed air or a soft brush to remove bugs, leaves, etc. from the front of the radiator or air conditioning condenser. Be careful not to damage the delicate cooling fins or cut yourself on them.

15 Manual transmission lubricant level check

1 Park the vehicle on level ground and set the handbrake firmly. Turn the engine off.

2 The oil level is checked by removing the oil level and filler plug **(see illustration)**.

3 If the oil level is low, add oil until it is at the proper level.

 Warning: Do not overfill.

4 Refit the oil level and filler plug. Tighten the plug to the torque listed in this Chapter's Specifications.

5 Drive the vehicle a short distance, then check carefully for leaks.

16 Driveshaft boot check

1 The driveshaft boots are very important because they prevent dirt, water and foreign material from entering and damaging the constant velocity (CV) joints. Oil and grease can cause the boot material to deteriorate prematurely, so it's a good idea to wash the boots with soap and water. Because it constantly pivots back and forth following the steering action of the front hub, the outer CV boot wears out and should be inspected regularly.

2 Inspect the boots for tears and cracks as well as loose clamps **(see illustration)**. If there is any evidence of cracks or leaking lubricant, they must be renewed as described in Chapter 8.

17 Fuel system check

 Warning: Certain precautions should be observed when inspecting or servicing the fuel system components. Work in a well ventilated area and do not allow open flames (cigarettes, appliance pilot lights, etc.) near the work area. Mop up spills immediately and do not store fuel soaked rags where they could ignite. It is a good idea to keep a dry chemical (Class B) fire extinguisher near the work area any time the fuel system is being serviced.

1 If you smell petrol while driving or after the vehicle has been sitting in the sun, inspect the fuel system immediately.

2 Remove the filler cap and inspect if for damage and corrosion. The gasket should have an unbroken sealing imprint. If the gasket is damaged or corroded, remove it and refit a new one **(see illustration)**.

3 Inspect the fuel feed and return lines for cracks. Make sure that the threaded flare-nut type connectors which secure the metal fuel lines to the fuel injection system are tight.

4 Since some components of the fuel system - the fuel tank and part of the fuel feed and return lines, for example - are underneath the vehicle, they can be inspected more easily with the vehicle raised on a hoist. If that's not possible, raise the vehicle and support it securely on axle stands.

5 With the vehicle raised and safely supported, inspect the tank and filler neck for punctures, cracks and other damage. The hose connecting the filler neck to the tank is particularly critical. Sometimes this hose will leak because of loose clamps or deteriorated rubber **(see illustration)**. These are problems a home mechanic can usually rectify.

Warning: Do not, under any circumstances, try to repair a fuel tank (except rubber components). A welding torch or any open flame can easily cause fuel vapours inside the tank to explode.

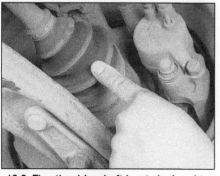

16.2 Flex the driveshaft boots by hand to check for cracks and/or leaking grease

17.2 Use a small screwdriver to carefully lever out the old gasket - take care not to damage the cap

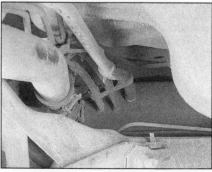

17.5 Inspect the filler/tank connecting hose for cracks and make sure the clamps are tight

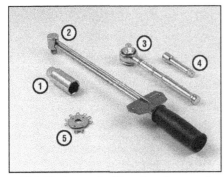

18.1 Tools required for changing spark plugs

1 **Spark plug socket** - This will have special padding inside to protect the spark plug porcelain insulator
2 **Torque wrench** - Although not mandatory, use of this tool is the best way to ensure that the plugs are tightened properly
3 **Ratchet** - Standard hand tool to fit the plug socket
4 **Extension** - Depending on model and accessories, you may need special extensions and universal joints to reach one or more of the plugs
5 **Spark plug gap gauge** - This gauge for checking the gap comes in a variety of styles. Make sure the gap for your engine is included

18.4a Spark plug manufacturers recommend using a wire-type gauge when checking the gap

18.4b To change the gap, bend the side electrode only

18.8 Use a spark plug socket with a long extension to unscrew the spark plug

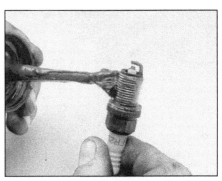

18.10 Apply a thin coat of anti-seize compound to the spark plug threads

6 Carefully check all rubber hoses and metal lines leading away from the fuel tank. Check for loose connections, deteriorated hoses, crimped lines and other damage. Carefully inspect the lines from the tank to the fuel injection system. Repair or renew damaged sections as necessary (see Chapter 4).

18 Spark plug check and renewal

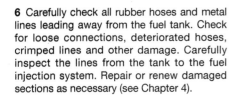

1 Spark plug renewal requires a spark plug socket which fits onto a ratchet spanner. This socket is lined with a rubber grommet to protect the porcelain insulator of the spark plug and to hold the plug while you insert it into the spark plug hole. You will also need a wire-type feeler gauge to check and adjust the spark plug gap and a torque wrench to tighten the new plugs to the specified torque **(see illustration)**.
2 If you are replacing the plugs, purchase the new plugs, adjust them to the proper gap and then renew each plug one at a time. **Note:** *When buying new spark plugs, it's essential that you obtain the correct plugs for your specific vehicle.*
3 Inspect each of the new plugs for defects. If there are any signs of cracks in the porcelain insulator of a plug, don't use it.
4 Check the electrode gaps of the new plugs. Check the gap by inserting the wire gauge of the proper thickness between the electrodes

at the tip of the plug **(see illustration)**. The gap between the electrodes should be identical to that listed in this Chapter's Specifications. If the gap is incorrect, use the notched adjuster on the feeler gauge body to bend the curved side electrode slightly **(see illustration)**.
5 If the side electrode is not exactly over the centre electrode, use the notched adjuster to align them.

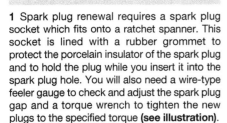

HAYNES HINT

It's often difficult to insert spark plugs into their holes without cross-threading them. To avoid this possibility, fit a short piece of rubber hose over the end of the spark plug. The flexible hose acts as a universal joint to help align the plug with the plug hole. Should the plug begin to cross-thread, the hose will slip on the spark plug, preventing thread damage.

Caution: If the gap of a new plug must be adjusted, bend only the base of the earth electrode – do not touch the tip.

Removal

6 To prevent the possibility of mixing up spark plug leads, work on one spark plug at a time. Remove the lead and boot from one spark plug. Grasp the boot - not the cable - give it a half twisting motion and pull straight up.
7 If compressed air is available, blow any dirt or foreign material away from the spark plug area before proceeding (a common bicycle pump will also work).
8 Remove the spark plug **(see illustration)**.
9 Whether you are replacing the plugs at this time or intend to reuse the old plugs, compare each old spark plug with the chart on the inside back cover of this manual to determine the overall running condition of the engine.

Refitting

10 Prior to refitting, it's a good idea to coat the spark plug threads with anti-seize compound **(see illustration)**. Tighten the plug to the torque listed in this Chapter's Specifications.
11 Attach the plug lead to the new spark plug, again using a twisting motion on the boot until it is firmly seated on the end of the spark plug.
12 Follow the above procedure for the remaining spark plugs, replacing them one at a time to prevent mixing up the spark plug leads.

19.8 Pull only on the boot when removing ignition wires from the distributor

19.11a Remove the two screws and detach the distributor cap

19.11b Inspect the distributor cap for carbon tracks, charred or eroded terminals and other damage

19 Spark plug lead, distributor cap and rotor check and renewal

1 The spark plug leads should be checked whenever new spark plugs are installed.

2 Begin this procedure by making a visual check of the spark plug leads while the engine is running. In a darkened garage (make sure there is ventilation) start the engine and observe each plug lead. Be careful not to come into contact with any moving engine parts. If there is a break in the wire, you will see arcing or a small spark at the damaged area. If arcing is noticed, make a note to obtain new wires, then allow the engine to cool and check the distributor cap and rotor.

3 The spark plug leads should be inspected one at a time to prevent mixing up the order, which is essential for proper engine operation. Each original plug lead should be numbered to help identify its location. If the number is illegible, a piece of tape can be marked with the correct number and wrapped around the plug lead.

4 Disconnect the plug lead from the spark plug. A removal tool can be used for this purpose or you can grasp the rubber boot, twist the boot half a turn and pull the boot free. Do not pull on the wire itself.

5 Check inside the boot for corrosion, which will look like a white crusty powder.

6 Push the wire and boot back onto the end of the spark plug. It should fit tightly onto the end of the plug. If it doesn't, remove the wire and use pliers to carefully crimp the metal connector inside the wire boot until the fit is snug.

7 Using a clean rag, wipe the entire length of the wire to remove built-up dirt and grease. Once the wire is clean, check for burns, cracks and other damage. Do not bend the wire sharply, because the conductor might break.

8 Disconnect the wire from the distributor cap. Again, pull only on the boot **(see illustration)**. Check for corrosion and a tight fit. Renew the wire in the distributor cap.

9 Inspect the remaining spark plug leads, making sure that each one is securely fastened at the distributor and spark plug when the check is complete.

10 If new spark plug leads are required, purchase a set for your specific engine model. Pre-cut wire sets with the boots already installed are available. Remove and renew the wires one at a time to avoid mix-ups in the firing order.

11 Detach the distributor cap by removing the two retaining screws **(see illustration)**. Look inside it for cracks, carbon tracks and worn, burned or loose contacts **(see illustration)**.

12 Pull the rotor off the distributor shaft and

examine it for cracks and carbon tracks **(see illustration)**. Renew the cap and rotor if any damage or defects are noted.

13 It is common practice to refit a new cap and rotor whenever new spark plug leads are installed, but if you wish to continue using the old cap, check the resistance between the spark plug leads and the cap first **(see illustration)**. If the indicated resistance is more than the maximum value listed in this Chapter's Specifications, renew the cap and/or leads.

14 When refitting a new cap, remove the wires from the old cap one at a time and attach them to the new cap in the exact same location – do not simultaneously remove all the wires from the old cap or firing order mix-ups may occur.

20 Cooling system servicing (draining, flushing and refilling)

 Warning: Do not allow engine coolant (antifreeze) to come in contact with your skin or painted surfaces of the vehicle. Rinse off spills immediately with plenty of water. Antifreeze is highly toxic if ingested. Never leave antifreeze laying around in an open container or in puddles on the floor; children and pets are attracted by it's sweet smell and may drink it. Check with local authorities about disposing of used antifreeze.

1 Periodically, the cooling system should be drained, flushed and refilled to replenish the antifreeze mixture and prevent formation of rust and corrosion, which can impair the performance of the cooling system and cause engine damage. When the cooling system is serviced, all hoses and the radiator cap should be checked and replaced if necessary.

Draining

2 Apply the handbrake and chock the wheels. If the vehicle has just been driven, wait several hours to allow the engine to cool down before beginning this procedure.

19.12 Check the rotor for damage, wear and corrosion (if in doubt about its condition, buy a new one)

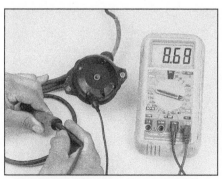

19.13 Measure the resistance value of the distributor cap and the spark plug leads

20.4 The radiator drain fitting located at the bottom of the radiator

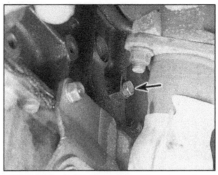

20.5 Fully drain the coolant by removing the drain plug (arrowed) on the side of the engine block

3 Once the engine is completely cool, remove the radiator cap.

4 Move a large container under the radiator drain to catch the coolant. On most models you will have to remove a cover for access to the radiator drain fitting located at the bottom of the radiator. Attach a suitable hose to the drain fitting to direct the coolant into the container (some models are already equipped with a hose), then open the drain fitting (a pair of pliers may be required to turn it) **(see illustration)**.

5 After the coolant stops flowing out of the radiator, move the container under the engine block drain plug **(see illustration)**. Loosen the plug and allow the coolant in the block to drain.

6 While the coolant is draining, check the condition of the radiator hoses, heater hoses and clamps (refer to Section 9 if necessary).

7 Renew any damaged clamps or hoses (see Chapter 3).

Flushing

8 Once the system is completely drained, flush the radiator with fresh water from a garden hose until water runs clear at the drain. The flushing action of the water will remove sediments from the radiator but will not remove rust and scale from the engine and cooling tube surfaces.

9 These deposits can be removed by the chemical action of a cleaner. Follow the procedure outlined in the manufacturer's instructions. If the radiator is severely corroded, damaged or leaking, it should be removed (see Chapter 3) and taken to a radiator repair specialist.

10 Remove the overflow hose from the coolant reservoir. Drain the reservoir and flush it with clean water, then reconnect the hose.

Refilling

11 Close and tighten the radiator drain. Refit and tighten the block drain plug.

12 Place the heater temperature control in the maximum heat position.

13 Slowly add new coolant (a 50/50 mixture of water and antifreeze) to the radiator until it's full. Add coolant to the reservoir up to the lower mark.

14 Leave the radiator cap off and run the engine in a well-ventilated area until the thermostat opens (coolant will begin flowing through the radiator and the upper radiator hose will become hot).

15 Turn the engine off and let it cool. Add more coolant mixture to bring the level back up to the lip on the radiator filler neck.

16 Squeeze the upper radiator hose to expel air, then add more coolant mixture if necessary. Renew the radiator cap.

17 Start the engine, allow it to reach normal operating temperature and check for leaks.

21 Evaporative emissions control system check

1 The function of the evaporative emissions control system is to draw fuel vapours from the petrol tank and fuel system, store them in a charcoal canister and then burn them during normal engine operation.

2 The most common symptom of a fault in the evaporative emissions system is a strong fuel odour in the engine compartment. If a fuel odour is detected, inspect the charcoal canister, located at the front of the engine compartment. Check the canister and all hoses for damage and deterioration **(see illustration)**.

3 The evaporative emissions control system is explained in more detail in Chapter 6.

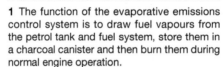

21.2 Check the evaporative emissions control canister and the hoses for cracks and damage (arrowed)

22 Exhaust system check

1 With the engine cold (at least three hours after the vehicle has been driven), check the complete exhaust system from its starting point at the engine to the end of the tailpipe. This should be done on a hoist where unrestricted access is available.

2 Check the pipes and connections for evidence of leaks, severe corrosion or damage. Make sure that all brackets and hangers are in good condition and tight.

3 At the same time, inspect the underside of the body for holes, corrosion, open seams, etc. which may allow exhaust gases to enter the passenger compartment. Seal all body openings with silicone or body putty.

4 Rattles and other noises can often be traced to the exhaust system, especially the mounts and hangers. Try to move the pipes, silencer and catalytic converter. If the components can come in contact with the body or suspension parts, secure the exhaust system with new mounts **(see illustration)**.

5 Check the running condition of the engine by inspecting inside the end of the tailpipe. The exhaust deposits here are an indication of engine state-of-tune. If the pipe is black and sooty or coated with white deposits, the engine is in need of a full service, including a thorough fuel system inspection.

23 Positive Crankcase Ventilation (PCV) valve and hose check and renewal

1 The PCV valve and hose is located in the valve cover.

2 Pull the PCV valve from the cover **(see illustration overleaf)**.

3 With the engine idling at normal operating temperature, place your finger over the end of the valve. If there's no vacuum at the valve, check for a plugged hose or valve. Renew any plugged or deteriorated hoses.

4 Turn off the engine. Remove the PCV valve from the hose. Connect a clean piece of hose

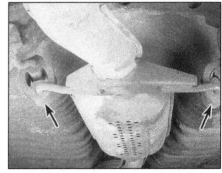

22.4 Be sure to check each exhaust system component rubber hanger (arrowed) for damage

23.2 Grasp the hose securely and pull the PCV valve out of the cover

23.4 To check the PVC valve, blow air through it

and blow through the valve from the valve cover (cylinder head) end. If air will not pass through the valve in this direction, renew it with a new one **(see illustration)**.

5 When purchasing a renewal PCV valve, make sure it's for your particular vehicle and engine size. Compare the old valve with the new one to make sure they're the same.

24 Brake fluid renewal

Brake fluid renewal is similar to bleeding the brake hydraulic system (see Chapter 9, Section 12), except that the aim is to replace all the old fluid rather than removing air from the system.

> **HAYNES HiNT** *Old brake fluid is generally much darker in colour than new fluid, making it easier to see when old fluid has been expelled from the system.*

Every 27 000 miles or 36 months

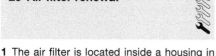

25 Air filter renewal

1 The air filter is located inside a housing in the left front corner of the engine compartment.
2 To remove the air filter, loosen the intake air duct band and remove the duct/hose **(see illustration)**. Remove the five bolts attaching the air cleaner cover the box, then lift the

cover up and remove the air filter element **(see illustration)**.
3 Inspect the outer surface of the filter element. If it is dirty, renew it. If it is only moderately dusty, it can be reused by blowing it clean from the back to the front surface with compressed air. Because it is a pleated paper type filter, it cannot be washed or oiled. If it cannot be cleaned satisfactorily with compressed air, discard and renew it. While the cover is off, be careful not to drop anything down into the housing.

Caution: Never drive the vehicle with the air cleaner removed. Excessive engine wear could result and backfiring could even cause a fire under the bonnet.

4 Wipe out the inside of the air cleaner housing with a damp cloth.
5 Place the new filter into the air cleaner housing, making sure it seats properly.
6 Refitting of the cover is the reverse of removal.

Every 36 000 miles or 48 months

26 Fuel filter renewal

1 Disconnect the battery negative cable.
2 The canister filter is mounted in a bracket on the bulkhead near the brake master cylinder.

3 Remove any components that would interfere with access to the top of the filter.
4 Disconnect the fuel hoses from the fuel filter **(see illustration)**.
5 Remove the bracket bolt(s) from the bulkhead and remove the old filter and the filter support bracket assembly.
6 Note that the inlet and outlet pipes are

clearly labelled on their respective ends. Make sure the new filter is installed so that it's facing the proper direction as noted above. When correctly installed, the filter should be installed so that the outlet pipe faces up and the inlet pipe faces down.
7 Refitting is the reverse of the removal procedure.

25.2a Remove the air intake duct and the cover bolts

25.2b Remove the cover and lift the element out

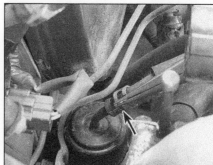

26.4 Disconnect the fuel hoses and remove the filter and bracket

27 Automatic transmission fluid and filter change

1 Before beginning work, purchase the specified transmission fluid (see *Lubricants and fluids* in *Weekly checks*).

2 Other tools necessary for this job include axle stands to support the vehicle in a raised position, spanners, drain pan capable of holding at least 7 litres, newspapers and clean rags.

3 The fluid should be drained immediately after the vehicle has been driven. Hot fluid is more effective than cold fluid at removing built up sediment.

 Warning: Fluid temperature can exceed 180° C in a hot transmission. Wear protective gloves.

4 After the vehicle has been driven to warm up the fluid, raise it and support it securely on axle stands.

5 Position a drain pan under the transmission drain plug and remove the plug **(see illustration)**.

6 Allow the oil to completely drain, then refit the plug and tighten it to the torque listed in this Chapter's Specifications.

7 Move the drain pan under the transmission pan and remove the rear and side pan mounting bolts.

8 Loosen the front pan bolts approximately four turns.

9 Carefully lever the transmission pan loose allowing the fluid to drain. Once the fluid has drained, remove the remaining bolts and lower the pan.

10 Remove the remaining bolts, pan and gasket. Carefully clean the gasket surface of the transmission to remove all traces of the old gasket and sealant.

11 Remove the oil strainer/filter retaining bolts and lower the filter from the transmission **(see illustration)**. Be careful when lowering the filter as it contains residual fluid.

12 Place the new filter in position, and refit the bolts. Tighten the bolts to the torque listed in this Chapter's Specifications.

13 Carefully clean the gasket surfaces of the fluid pan, removing all traces of old gasket material. Wash the pan in clean solvent and dry it with compressed air. Be sure to clean the metal filings from the magnet **(see illustration)**.

14 Refit a new gasket, place the fluid pan in position and refit the bolts in their original positions. Tighten the bolts to the torque listed in this Chapter's Specifications.

15 Lower the vehicle.

16 With the engine off, add new fluid to the transmission through the dipstick. Use a funnel to prevent spills. It is best to add a little fluid at a time, continually checking the level with the dipstick (see Section 13). Allow the fluid time to drain into the pan.

17 Start the engine and shift the selector into all positions from P through L, then shift into P and apply the handbrake.

18 With the engine idling, check the fluid level. Add fluid up to the COLD level on the dipstick.

19 Warm the engine and transmission with a short run and recheck the level.

28 Manual transmission lubricant change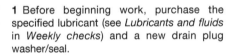

1 Before beginning work, purchase the specified lubricant (see *Lubricants and fluids* in *Weekly checks*) and a new drain plug washer/seal.

2 Other tools necessary for this job include axle stands to support the vehicle in a raised position, spanners, drain pan capable of holding at least 5 litres, newspapers and clean rags.

3 The oil should be drained immediately after the vehicle has been driven. Hot oil is more effective than cold oil at removing built up sediment.

 Warning: Oil temperature can exceed 180° C in a hot transmission. Wear protective gloves.

4 After the vehicle has been driven to warm up the oil, disconnect the speedometer cable and remove the speedometer driven gear assembly on early models; later models have an oil level and filler plug (See Section 15) which should be removed.

5 Raise the vehicle and support it securely on axle stands. Make sure it is safely supported and as level as possible.

6 Move the necessary equipment under the vehicle, being careful not to touch any of the hot exhaust components.

7 Place the drain pan under the transmission drain plug and loosen the drain plug.

8 Carefully unscrew the drain plug and washer with your fingers. Be careful not to burn yourself on the oil.

9 Allow the oil to drain completely. Clean the drain plug then refit it with a new washer. Tighten the drain plug to the torque listed in this Chapter's Specifications.

10 Lower the vehicle.

11 Add new oil to the transmission. Use a funnel to prevent spills. It is best to add a little oil at a time, continually checking the level (see Section 15).

12 Refit the oil level and filler plug, or the speedometer driven gear assembly and reconnect the speedometer cable, where applicable.

27.5 Remove the transmission drain plug

27.11 Remove the filter bolts and lower the filter (be careful, there will be some residual fluid)

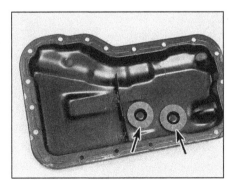

27.13 Wash the pan in clean solvent and remove metal filings from the magnet (arrowed)

Chapter 2 Part A
Engines

Contents

Degrees of difficulty

Easy, suitable for novice with little experience	**Fairly easy,** suitable for beginner with some experience	**Fairly difficult,** suitable for competent DIY mechanic	**Difficult,** suitable for experienced DIY mechanic	**Very difficult,** suitable for expert DIY or professional

Specifications

Timing belt

Tensioner spring free length
1.3 litre and 1.6 litre	64.0 mm
1.5 litre	71.0 mm
1.8 litre	
1991 to 1994	58.8 mm
1995 and later	59.2 mm

Timing belt deflection
1.3 litre and 1.6 litre	11.0 to 13.0 mm
1.5 litre	7.0 to 9.0 mm
1.8 litre	9.0 to 11.5 mm

Valves

Valve spring free length
1.3 litre	38.0 mm minimum
1.5 litre	39.5 mm minimum
1.6 litre	
Inlet	39.0 mm minimum
Exhaust	38.0 mm minimum
1.8 litre	39.5 mm minimum
Valve stem-to-guide-clearance	0.20 mm maximum

Rocker arm and shaft (SOHC engines)

1.3 litre
Rocker shaft diameter	18.959 mm minimum
Oil clearance	0.10 mm maximum
Rocker arm inside diameter	19.000 mm maximum

1.6 litre 8-valve
Rocker shaft diameter	17.959 mm minimum
Oil clearance	0.10 mm maximum
Rocker arm inside diameter	18.000 mm maximum

1.6 litre 16-valve
Rocker shaft diameter	18.959 mm minimum
Oil clearance	0.10 mm maximum
Rocker arm inside diameter	19.000 mm maximum

Camshaft

1.3 litre

Lobe height
Inlet	35.787 mm minimum
Exhaust	35.626 mm minimum

Journal diameter
Front and rear journals (journals 1 and 5)	43.440 mm minimum
Journals 2 and 4	43.425 mm minimum
Centre journal (journal 3)	43.410 mm minimum
Out-of-round limit	0.05 mm maximum
Journal oil clearance	0.15 mm maximum
Endplay	0.15 mm maximum

1.5 litre
Lobe height - inlet and exhaust	40.70 mm minimum
Journal diameter	25.91 mm minimum
Out-of-round limit	0.05 mm maximum
Journal oil clearance	0.08 mm maximum
Endplay	0.20 mm maximum

1.6 litre 8-valve
Lobe height - inlet and exhaust	35.251 mm minimum

Journal diameter
Front and rear journals (journals 1 and 5)	43.440 mm minimum
Centre journals (journals 2, 3 and 4)	43.410 mm minimum
Out-of-round limit	0.05 mm maximum
Journal oil clearance	0.15 mm maximum
Endplay	0.20 mm maximum

1.6 litre 16-valve

Lobe height
Inlet	35.629 mm minimum
Exhaust	35.459 mm minimum

Journal diameter
Front and rear journals (journals 1 and 5)	43.440 mm minimum
Journals 2 and 4	43.425 mm minimum
Centre journal (journal 3)	43.410 mm minimum
Out-of-round limit	0.05 mm maximum
Journal oil clearance	0.15 mm maximum
Endplay	0.15 mm maximum

1.8 litre

Lobe height
Inlet	43.894 mm minimum
Exhaust	44.400 mm minimum
Journal diameter	25.940 mm minimum
Out-of-round limit	0.05 mm maximum
Journal oil clearance	0.015 mm maximum
Camshaft runout	0.03 mm maximum
Endplay	0.20 mm maximum

Oil pump

Driven rotor-to-pump housing clearance	0.20 mm maximum
Outer rotor-to-body clearance	0.22 mm maximum
Rotor set-to-oil pump housing (side clearance)	0.14 mm maximum
Oil pump relief valve spring free length	45.5 mm minimum

Valve clearance

Refer to Chapter 1 *Routine maintenance and servicing*

Torque specifications

	lbf ft	Nm
Camshaft bearing cap bolts (1.5 litre and 1.8 litre)	8 to 10	11 to 14
Camshaft idler pulley bolts		
1.3 litre and 1.6 litre	14 to 19	19 to 26
1.5 litre and 1.8 litre	27 to 38	37 to 52
Camshaft seal plate bolts (1.5 litre and 1.8 litre)	6 to 8	8 to 11
Camshaft sprocket bolt	36 to 45	49 to 61
Camshaft thrust plate bolt (1.6 litre 8-valve)	6 to 8	8 to 11
Crankshaft pulley bolts	9 to 13	12 to 18
Crankshaft sprocket bolt	116 to 123	157 to 167
Cylinder head bolts		
1.3 litre, 1.6 litre and 1.8 litre	56 to 60	76 to 81
1.5 litre		
Stage 1	13 to 16	18 to 22
Stage 2 . . . . Tighten an additional 85 to 95°		
End plate bolts	6 to 8	8 to 11
Engine mount bolts/nuts		
No. 1 engine mount bracket bolts to engine	50 to 68	68 to 92
No. 1 engine rubber mount through-bolt	48 to 65	65 to 88
No. 1 engine mount to crossmember nut	50 to 65	68 to 88
No. 2 engine mount bracket bolts to engine	28 to 38	38 to 52
No. 2 engine mount bracket to crossmember	28 to 38	38 to 52
No. 3 engine mount bracket to engine	55 to 77	75 to 104
No. 3 engine mount bracket small bolts	14 to 16	19 to 22
No. 3 engine mount bracket nuts	69 to 83	94 to 113
No. 3 engine mount brackets large bolt	50 to 68	68 to 92
No. 4 left (driver's side) engine/transmission		
bracket-to-transmission nuts	50 to 68	68 to 92
No. 4 left (driver's side) engine/transmission		
bracket-to-frame bolts	32 to 44	43 to 60
Exhaust manifold bolts/nuts		
1.3 litre and 1.6 litre	12 to 17	16 to 23
1.5 litre and 1.8 litre	28 to 34	38 to 46
Exhaust manifold heat shield bolts/nuts	6 to 8	8 to 11
Exhaust pipe bracket bolts	27 to 38	37 to 52
Flywheel cover bolts		
1.3 litre and 1.6 litre	27 to 38	37 to 52
1.5 litre and 1.8 litre	48 to 65	65 to 88
Flywheel/driveplate bolts	71 to 76	96 to 103
Front cover bolts	14 to 19	19 to 16
Inlet manifold bolts	14 to 19	19 to 16
Main Bearing Support Plate (MBSP) bolts	12 to 15	16 to 20
Oil pump bolts	14 to 19	19 to 16
Oil pump cover	4 to 7	6 to 9
Oil pump strainer	6 to 8	8 to 11
Rear cover screws	6 to 8	8 to 11
Rocker arm shaft bolts (1.3 litre and 1.6 litre)	16 to 21	22 to 28
Sump bolts	6 to 8	8 to 11
Sump stiffener bolts (models with separate sump)	27 to 38	37 to 52
Tensioner pulley bolt		
1.3 litre and 1.6 litre	14 to 19	19 to 16
1.5 litre and 1.8 litre	28 to 38	38 to 52
Timing belt cover bolts	6 to 8	8 to 11
Timing belt idler pulley bolts		
1.3 litre and 1.6 litre	14 to 19	19 to 16
1.5 litre and 1.8 litre	28 to 38	38 to 52
Valve cover bolts		
1.3 litre and 1.6 litre	4 to 6	5 to 7
1.5 litre	5 to 8	7 to 11
1.8 litre		
Two bolts at end of valve cover	6 to 8	8 to 11
Screws on top of valve cover	4 to 6	5 to 7
Water pump pulley	6 to 8	8 to 11

1 General information

This Part of Chapter 2 is devoted to in-vehicle repair procedures for all engines. All information concerning engine removal and refitting, and engine block and cylinder head overhaul can be found in Part B of this Chapter.

The following repair procedures are based on the assumption that the engine is installed in the vehicle. If the engine has been removed from the vehicle and mounted on a stand, many of the paragraphs outlined in this Part of Chapter 2 will not apply.

The Specifications included in this Part of Chapter 2 apply only to the procedures contained in this Part. Part B of Chapter 2 contains the Specifications necessary for cylinder head and engine block rebuilding. *Caution: If the stereo in your vehicle is equipped with an anti-theft system, make sure you have the correct code before disconnecting the battery in any of the following procedures.*

2 Repair operations possible with the engine in the vehicle

Many major repair operations can be accomplished without removing the engine from the vehicle.

Clean the engine compartment and the exterior of the engine with some type of degreaser before any work is done. It will make the job easier and help keep dirt out of the internal areas of the engine.

Depending on the components involved, it may be helpful to remove the bonnet to improve access to the engine as repairs are performed (refer to Chapter 11 if necessary). Cover the wings to prevent damage to the paint. Special pads are available, but a substitute such as a thick bedspread or blanket will also work.

If vacuum, exhaust, oil or coolant leaks develop, indicating a need for gasket or seal renewal, the repairs can generally be made with the engine in the vehicle. The inlet and exhaust manifold gaskets, sump gasket, crankshaft oil seals and cylinder head gasket are all accessible with the engine in place.

Exterior engine components, such as the inlet and exhaust manifolds, the sump, the oil pump, the water pump, the starter motor, the alternator, the distributor and the fuel system components can be removed for repair with the engine in place.

Since the cylinder head can be removed without removing the engine, camshaft and valve component servicing can also be accomplished with the engine in the vehicle. Renewal of the timing belt and sprockets is also possible with the engine in the vehicle.

In extreme cases caused by a lack of necessary equipment, repair or renewal of piston rings, pistons, connecting rods and rod bearings is possible with the engine in the vehicle. However, this practice is not recommended because of the engine cleaning and other preparation work, such as driveshaft, steering, anti-roll bar, engine mount members that may require partial dismantling or removal for access to the engine.

3 Top Dead Centre (TDC) - locating

Note: *The following procedure is based on the assumption that the distributor is correctly installed. If you are trying to locate TDC to refit the distributor correctly, piston position must be determined by feeling for compression at the number one spark plug hole, then aligning the ignition timing marks as described in paragraph 8.*

1 Top Dead Centre (TDC) is the highest point in the cylinder that each piston reaches travelling up-and-down as the crankshaft turns. Each piston reaches TDC on the compression stroke and again on the exhaust stroke, but TDC generally refers to piston position on the compression stroke.

2 Positioning the piston(s) at TDC is an essential part of many procedures such as camshaft and timing belt/sprocket removal and distributor removal.

3 Before beginning this procedure, be sure to place the transmission in Neutral and apply the handbrake or block the rear wheels. Also, disable the ignition system by detaching the primary (low voltage) wires from the coil (see Chapter 5). Remove the spark plugs (see Chapter 1).

4 In order to bring any piston to TDC, the crankshaft must be turned using one of the methods outlined below. When looking at the front of the engine, normal crankshaft rotation is clockwise.

a) *The preferred method is to turn the crankshaft with a socket and ratchet attached to the bolt threaded into the front of the crankshaft.*

b) *If an assistant is available to turn the ignition switch to the Start position in short bursts, you can get the piston close to TDC. Make sure your assistant is out of the vehicle, away from the ignition switch, then use a socket and ratchet as described in Paragraph a) to complete the procedure.*

5 Note the position of the terminal for the number one spark plug lead on the distributor cap. If the terminal is not marked, follow the plug lead from the number one cylinder spark plug to the cap.

6 Use a felt-tip pen or chalk to make a mark on the distributor body and the cap - directly at the terminal.

7 Detach the cap from the distributor and set it aside (see Chapter 1 if necessary).

3.8 To bring No 1 piston to TDC, align the timing notch on the edge of the pulley with the T-degree mark

8 Turn the crankshaft (see paragraph 4 above) until the notch in the crankshaft sprocket is aligned with the T on the timing plate (located at the front of the engine) **(see illustration)**.

9 Look at the distributor rotor - it should be pointing directly at the mark you made on the distributor body.

10 If the rotor is 180° off, the number one piston is at TDC on the exhaust stroke.

11 To get the piston to TDC on the compression stroke, turn the crankshaft one complete turn (360°) clockwise. The rotor should now be pointing at the mark on the distributor. When the rotor is pointing at the number one spark plug lead terminal in the distributor cap and the ignition timing marks are aligned, the number one piston is at TDC on the compression stroke. **Note:** *If it is impossible to align the ignition timing marks when the rotor is pointing at the mark on the distributor body, the timing belt may have jumped the teeth on the sprockets or may have been installed incorrectly.*

12 After the number one piston has been positioned at TDC on the compression stroke, TDC for any of the remaining pistons can be located by turning the crankshaft and following the firing order. Mark the remaining spark plug lead terminal locations on the distributor body just like you did for the number one terminal, then number the marks to correspond with the cylinder numbers. As you turn the crankshaft, the rotor will also turn. When it's pointing directly at one of the marks on the distributor, the piston for that particular cylinder is at TDC on the compression stroke.

4 Valve cover - removal and refitting

Removal

1 Disconnect the negative cable from the battery.

2 Detach the PCV (Positive Crankcase Ventilation) valve and breather hoses from the valve cover.

4.4 Remove the timing belt cover bolts (SOHC engine shown)

4.5 Remove the valve cover bolts (SOHC engine shown)

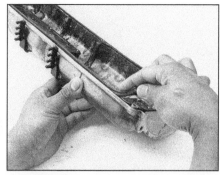

4.12 Press the valve cover gasket into the groove by hand (SOHC engine shown)

1.3 litre and 1.6 litre models

3 Disconnect the spark plug leads from the clips.

4 Remove the two upper bolts from the timing belt cover **(see illustration)**. Loosen, but do not remove the lower timing belt cover bolts.

5 Remove the valve cover bolts **(see illustration)**.

6 Lift the valve cover from the cylinder head. If it sticks, knock it loose with a rubber mallet or a hammer and a block of wood. Don't lever between the sealing surfaces.

7 Visually check the valve cover gasket for damage and to ensure that has not hardened and is still flexible. Save it for reuse if satisfactory.

1.5 litre and 1.8 litre models

8 Label the spark plug cables, then remove them from the spark plugs.

9 Remove the distributor, leaving the spark plug cables connected to the distributor.

10 Remove the bolts attaching the upper timing belt cover, then remove the cover.

11 Remove the bolts holding the valve cover in place, disconnect any tubing or other connected components and move them out of the way, and remove the valve cover. If the cover sticks, knock it loose with a rubber mallet or a hammer and a block of wood. Do not lever between the sealing surfaces.

Refitting

1.3 litre and 1.6 litre models

12 If a new valve cover gasket is being installed, clean the groove of the valve cover. Apply silicone sealant in the groove of the valve cover and press the new gasket into the groove **(see illustration)**.

13 If the valve cover gasket is being reused, remove the gasket, make sure the groove is clean and the gasket is clean. Apply silicone sealant in the groove of the valve cover, and refit the gasket.

14 Position the valve cover in place and insert the bolts by hand, starting the threads several turns before using a spanner.

15 Tighten the valve cover bolts/screws in several steps to the torque listed in this Chapter's Specifications.

16 Refitting of the remaining parts is the reverse of removal.

17 Run the engine and check for oil leaks.

1.5 litre and 1.8 litre models

18 The mating surfaces of the housing or cylinder head and cover must be clean when the cover is installed. Carefully use a gasket scraper to remove all traces of sealant and old gasket material - be careful to not gouge the gasket surfaces when cleaning. Then clean the mating surfaces with a rag with gasket cleaner or solvent. If there is residue or oil on the mating surfaces when the cover is installed, oil leaks may develop.

19 If a new valve cover gasket is being installed, apply silicone sealant in the groove of the valve cover and press the new gasket into the groove **(see illustration 4.12)**.

20 If the valve cover gasket is being reused, remove the gasket, make sure the groove is clean and the gasket is clean. Apply silicone sealant in the groove of the valve cover, and refit the gasket.

21 Apply a light coating of silicone sealant to the areas shown **(see illustrations)**.

22 Position the valve cover in place and insert the bolts by hand, starting the threads several turns before using a spanner.

23 Tighten the bolts in two or three steps (except the 1.5 litre engine) to the torque listed in this Chapter's Specifications. For the 1.5 litre engine, tighten in five or six steps in the sequence shown **(see illustration)** to the torque listed in this Chapter's Specifications.

24 Refitting of the remaining parts is the reverse of removal.

25 Run the engine and check for oil leaks.

5 Inlet manifold - removal and refitting

Removal

1 Disconnect the negative cable from the battery.

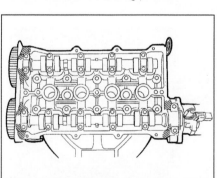

4.21a Apply sealant to the shaded areas on the cylinder head before refitting the cover (1.8 litre DOHC)

4.21b Apply silicone sealant to the areas shown before refitting the valve cover (1.5 litre DOHC)

DISTRIBUTOR CAP

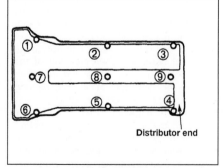

Distributor end

4.23 Valve cover tightening sequence (1.5 litre DOHC)

5.4 Remove the resonance chamber above the radiator, as applicable

5.9 Remove the fuel regulator vacuum solenoid

2 Drain the cooling system (see Chapter 1).

3 Remove the air inlet hose assembly from the inlet manifold assembly (see Chapter 4).

4 Remove the resonance chamber, as applicable **(see illustration)**.

5 Disconnect the accelerator cable and the throttle cable from the inlet assembly (see Chapter 4).

6 Label and detach all wire harness, control cables and hoses connected to the inlet manifold.

7 Remove the air inlet plenum and throttle body (see Chapter 4).

8 Remove the fuel rail (see Chapter 4).

9 Remove the electrical connector and vacuum lines to the fuel regulator vacuum solenoid, and remove the fuel regulator vacuum solenoid **(see illustration)**.

10 Raise the vehicle and support it securely on axle stands. Under the inlet manifold, remove the inlet manifold bracket, as applicable **(see illustration)**.

11 Remove the inlet manifold mounting bolts, while supporting the inlet manifold from above the engine.

12 Lower the vehicle if necessary.

13 Remove the inlet manifold.

Refitting

14 Carefully use a gasket scraper to remove all traces of old gasket material and any sealant from the manifold and cylinder head, then clean the mating surfaces with gasket cleaner or solvent - be careful to not gouge the gasket surfaces when cleaning. If the gasket was leaking, have the manifold checked for warpage at an engineering workshop and resurfaced if necessary.

15 Refit a new gasket, then position the manifold on the head and refit the nuts/bolts.

16 Tighten the nuts/bolts in three or four equal steps to the torque listed in this Chapter's Specifications. Work from the centre out towards the ends, while alternating upper to lower bolts/nuts to avoid warping the manifold.

17 Refit the remaining parts in the reverse order of removal.

18 Before starting the engine, check the throttle linkage for smooth operation.

19 Check coolant level. Run the engine and check for coolant and vacuum leaks.

20 Road test the vehicle and check for proper operation of all accessories, including the cruise control system (if equipped).

6 Exhaust manifold - removal and refitting

> ⚠ *Warning: The engine must be completely cool before beginning this procedure.*

Removal

1 Disconnect the negative cable from the battery.

2 Unplug the oxygen sensor electrical connector from the exhaust manifold. If you are refitting a new manifold, remove the sensor (see Chapter 6).

3 Remove the heat shield bolts and remove the heat shield from the manifold **(see illustration)**.

4 Apply penetrating oil to the exhaust manifold mounting bolts/nuts and to the exhaust pipe nuts.

5 Raise the vehicle and support it securely on axle stands (see "*Jacking and wheel changing*").

6 Disconnect the exhaust pipe from the exhaust manifold. Lower the vehicle.

7 Remove the manifold bolts/nuts and detach the manifold from the cylinder head. **Note:** *If any bolts/nuts are difficult to remove, apply penetrating oil to the bolts/nuts and let them soak for at least 15 minutes. If any bolts or studs break during removal, you may be able to use self-locking pliers after the manifold is removed to unscrew the broken bolt/stud. If unable to remove the broken bolt/stud, see your parts specialist for stud removal tools. Renew any damaged parts with factory parts, or parts specifically designed for exhaust system application.*

Refitting

8 Use a scraper to remove all traces of old gasket material and carbon deposits from the manifold and cylinder head mating surfaces. If the gasket was leaking, have the manifold checked for warpage at an automotive engineering workshop and resurfaced if necessary.

5.10 Remove the inlet manifold support bracket

6.3 Remove the exhaust manifold heat shield

7.3 Remove the undercover splash shield for access to engine

7.9 Remove the bolt from the crankshaft sprocket using a large socket and ratchet or breaker bar

Caution: When scraping, be very careful not to gouge or scratch the delicate aluminium cylinder head manifold mounting surface.

9 Position a new exhaust manifold gasket over the studs on the cylinder head.

10 Refit the manifold and thread the mounting bolts/nuts into place.

11 Working from the centre out, tighten the bolts/nuts to the torque listed in this Chapter's Specifications in several equal steps.

12 Refit the remaining parts in the reverse order of removal. If refitting the oxygen sensor, use a special anti-seize thread lubricant available at your dealer.

13 Run the engine and check for exhaust leaks.

7 Timing belt and sprockets - removal and refitting

Removal

1 Disconnect the negative cable from the battery

2 Chock the rear wheels and set the handbrake.

1.3 litre and 1.6 litre models

3 Remove the under cover splash shield (**see illustration**).

4 Remove the power steering and air conditioner drivebelt, if applicable (see Chapter 1).

5 Remove the alternator drivebelt (see Chapter 1). Remove the spark plugs from all cylinders.

6 Remove the water pump pulley bolts and remove the water pump pulley.

7 Remove the four crankshaft pulley bolts.

8 Remove the crankshaft pulley.

9 Remove the crankshaft sprocket centre bolt (**see illustration**). **Note:** *If necessary to prevent the crankshaft from turning, remove the flywheel/driveplate access cover and carefully wedge a screwdriver between the ring gear teeth and the engine block. Do not damage the gear teeth when holding the flywheel/driveplate.*

10 Remove the timing belt guide (**see illustration**). If necessary, carefully lever the guide off using two large screwdrivers or a puller.

11 Remove the timing belt upper cover and lower cover.

7.10 Slide the timing belt guide from the crankshaft

12 Temporarily refit the crankshaft sprocket bolt, rotate the engine to align the crankshaft and camshaft sprocket marks (**see illustrations**). The crankshaft sprocket pulley Woodruff key should be facing upwards (top).

13 Remove the crankshaft sprocket bolt.

14 If reusing the timing belt, paint matching marks on the sprockets and belt and an arrow indicating direction of travel on the belt.

15 Loosen the timing belt tensioner (**see illustration**), and temporarily tighten the tensioner with the spring fully extended. Remove the timing belt.

7.12a Timing belt camshaft sprocket alignment mark (SOHC engines)

7.12b Timing belt crankshaft sprocket alignment mark (SOHC engines)

7.15 Loosen the timing belt tensioner pulley bolt and rotate the pulley away from the belt

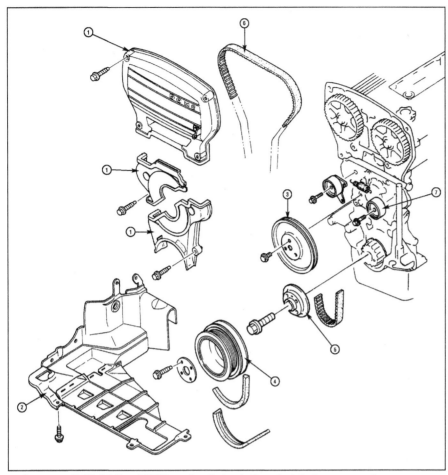

7.17 1.8 litre DOHC engine timing belt and related components

1 Timing belt covers
2 Engine under cover
   splash shield
3 Water pump pulley
4 Crankshaft pulley
5 Timing belt guide
6 Timing belt
7 Timing belt tensioner
   pulleys

16 If it is necessary to remove the camshaft sprocket(s) to renew the seal(s), remove the valve cover (see Section 4). Remove the camshaft sprocket bolt(s) and remove the sprocket(s) from the camshaft(s). Prevent the camshaft from turning by placing a spanner on the hex surface of the camshaft (see illustration 7.31). If it is necessary to remove the crankshaft sprocket, carefully lever it off.

1.5 litre and 1.8 litre models

17 Remove the engine under cover shield **(see Illustration)**.
18 Remove the power steering and/or air conditioning drivebelt (see Chapter 1).
19 Remove the alternator drivebelt (see Chapter 1).
20 Remove the water pump pulley bolts and remove the pulley.
21 Remove the spark plugs from all cylinders.
22 Remove the oil dipstick.
23 Remove the four crankshaft pulley plate bolts and remove the pulley.
24 Remove the timing belt upper cover, middle cover, and lower cover.

25 Remove the crankshaft sprocket centre bolt. **Note:** *If necessary to prevent the crankshaft from turning, remove the flywheel/driveplate access cover and carefully wedge a screwdriver between the ring gear teeth and the engine block. Do not damage the gear teeth when holding the flywheel/driveplate.*

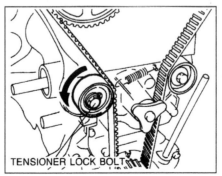

7.29 Loosen the timing belt tensioner pulley bolt and rotate the pulley away from the belt

26 Remove the timing belt guide **(see illustration 7.10)**.
27 Temporarily refit the crankshaft sprocket bolt, and rotate the engine to align the crankshaft and camshaft sprocket marks **(see illustrations 7.41b and 7.41c)**. The timing belt guide dowel pin should be facing upward (top). Remove the crankshaft sprocket bolt.
28 If reusing the timing belt, paint matching marks on the pulley and belt and an arrow indicating direction of travel on the belt.
29 Loosen the timing belt tensioner **(see illustration)**. Cover the tensioner with a rag to protect it while levering the tensioner outwards. Temporarily tighten the tensioner with the spring fully extended.
30 Remove the timing belt.
31 If it is necessary to remove the camshaft sprocket(s) to renew the seal(s), remove the valve cover (see Section 4). Remove the camshaft sprocket bolt(s) and remove the sprocket(s) from the camshaft(s). Prevent the camshaft from turning by placing a spanner on the hex surface on the shaft **(see illustration)**. If it is necessary to remove the crankshaft sprocket, carefully lever it off.

Inspection

Caution: Do not bend, twist or turn the timing belt inside out. Do not allow it to come in contact with oil, coolant or fuel. Do not use timing belt tension to keep the camshaft or crankshaft from turning when refitting the sprocket bolt(s). Do not turn the crankshaft or camshaft more than a few degrees (necessary for tooth alignment) while the timing belt is removed.

32 Remove the idler pulleys and check the bearings for smooth operation and excessive play. Inspect the spring for damage.
33 If the timing belt was broken during engine operation, the belt may have been fouled by debris or may have been damaged by a defective component in the area of the timing belt; check for belt material in the teeth of the sprockets. Any defective parts or debris in the sprockets must be cleaned out of all the sprockets before refitting the new belt or the belt will not mesh properly when installed.

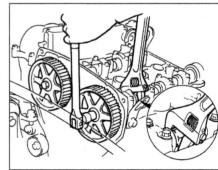

7.31 Hold the camshaft with a spanner on the hex while loosening the sprocket bolt

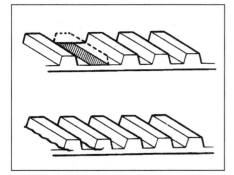

7.34 Check the timing belt for cracked and missing teeth

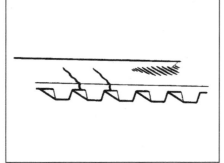

7.35 If the belt is cracked or worn, check the pulleys for nicks and burrs

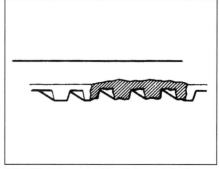

7.36 Wear on one side of the belt indicates pulley misalignment problems

34 If the belt teeth are cracked or pulled off **(see illustration)**, the distributor, water pump, oil pump or camshaft(s) may have seized.

35 If there is noticeable wear or cracks in the belt **(see illustration)**, check to see if there are nicks or burrs on the sprockets.

36 If there is wear or damage on only one side of the belt **(see illustration)**, check the belt guide and the alignment of all sprockets. Also check the oil seals at the front of the engine and renew them if they are leaking.

37 Renew the timing belt with a new one if obvious wear or damage is noted or if it is the least bit questionable. Correct any problems which contributed to belt failure prior to belt refitting. **Note:** *We recommend replacing the belt whenever it is removed, since belt failure can lead to expensive engine damage.*

Refitting

38 Remove all dirt and oil from the timing belt area at the front of the engine.

39 If they were removed, refit the idler pulleys and tensioner. The idler pulley should be pulled back against spring tension with the spring fully extended and the idler pulley bolt temporarily tightened.

40 If they were removed, refit the camshaft(s) and crankshaft sprocket(s). Make sure the sprocket Woodruff key is installed with the tapered side toward the oil pump body. Tighten the sprocket bolt(s) to the torque

listed in this Chapter's Specifications, referring to paragraphs 16 or 31 above.

41 Recheck the camshaft sprocket and crankshaft sprocket timing marks to be sure they are properly aligned **(see illustrations)**. The crankshaft sprocket is aligned with the mark upwards. On 1.3 litre and 1.6 litre engines, the camshaft sprocket has two marks, one at the 12 o'clock and one at the 3 o'clock position, when looking at the sprocket, which must be in alignment with the marks on the cylinder head. On the 1.5 litre engine, the 'Z' mark on the larger diameter camshaft sprocket should be upward. On the 1.8 litre engine the 'I' and 'E' markings are upward in alignment with the two notches in the seal plate. **Note:** *If necessary, rotate the camshaft sprocket(s) slightly to achieve proper alignment.*

42 Slip the timing belt over the crankshaft sprocket and camshaft sprocket(s), and position the belt with no looseness on the side opposite the tensioner pulley. If the original belt is being reinstalled, align the marks made during removal with the marks on the sprockets, and be sure to refit the timing belt so that it will rotate in the same direction as removed (the direction of rotation was marked during removal).

1.3 litre and 1.6 litre models

43 Refit the timing belt guide and crankshaft sprocket bolt.

44 Rotate the crankshaft two turns clockwise, align the crankshaft sprocket timing marks.

Caution: If you feel resistance while rotating the engine by hand, do not continue. The valves may be contacting the pistons due to incorrect valve timing. Recheck the camshaft and crankshaft sprockets to be sure they are correctly aligned with their marks.

45 Verify the camshaft sprocket marks are properly aligned with the marks on the cylinder head **(see illustration 7.41a)**.

46 Loosen the tensioner (idler) pulley bolt to apply tension to the timing belt. **Note:** *The tensioner pulley spring applies the proper tension to the belt.*

47 Tighten the tensioner pulley bolt.

48 Again, rotate the crankshaft two turns clockwise, align the crankshaft sprocket timing marks and verify the camshaft sprocket marks are aligned with the marks on the cylinder head **(see illustration 7.41a)**.

49 Check the timing belt tension by applying moderate force by hand (about 20 pounds force) midway between the crankshaft sprocket and camshaft sprocket (*not the tensioner pulley side*) and measure the belt deflection. Deflection should be approximately 13 mm (0.5 in), but not less than 11 mm (0.44 in).

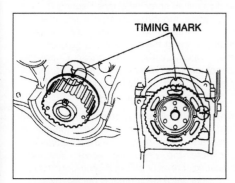

TIMING MARK

7.41a SOHC engines camshaft and crankshaft sprocket timing marks

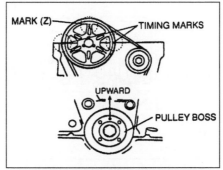

MARK (Z) — TIMING MARKS

UPWARD

PULLEY BOSS

7.41b 1.5 litre DOHC camshaft and crankshaft sprocket timing marks

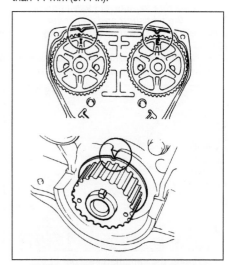

7.41c 1.8 litre DOHC camshaft and crankshaft sprocket timing marks

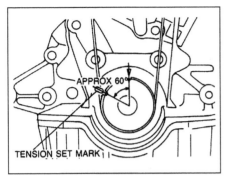

7.54 Align the crankshaft sprocket timing mark with the Tension Set Mark

50 If belt deflection is *not* correct, loosen the tensioner pulley bolt, set the tensioner pulley with the spring fully extended and temporarily tighten the tensioner pulley bolt. Repeat paragraphs 44 to 48. If the proper tension is still not obtained, renew the tensioner spring with a new spring and reset belt tension as described above.

51 Tighten the crankshaft sprocket bolt to the torque listed in this Chapter's Specifications.

52 Refit the remaining parts in the reverse order of removal. Run the engine and check for proper operation.

Caution: DO NOT start the engine until you are absolutely certain that the timing belt is installed correctly. Serious and costly engine damage could occur if the belt is improperly installed.

1.5 litre and 1.8 litre models

53 Refit the timing belt guide and crankshaft sprocket bolt.

54 Rotate the crankshaft 1-5/6 turns clockwise and align the crankshaft sprocket timing mark with the tension set mark on the engine block **(see illustration)**.

Caution: If you feel resistance while rotating the engine by hand, do not continue. The valves may be contacting the pistons due to incorrect valve timing. Recheck the camshaft and crankshaft sprockets to be sure they are correctly aligned with their marks.

55 Loosen the tensioner pulley bolt and allow the tensioner spring to apply tension to the

8.5 Lever the camshaft seal out of the bore - DO NOT nick or scratch the camshaft or seal bore

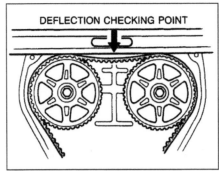

7.58 Check the timing belt deflection (1.8 litre DOHC)

timing belt. **Note:** *The tensioner pulley spring applies the proper tension to the belt.*

56 Tighten the tensioner pulley bolt.

57 Turn the crankshaft 2-1/6 turns clockwise and verify that the crankshaft sprocket timing mark and the camshaft sprocket timing marks are correctly aligned **(see illustrations 7.41b and 7.41c)**. If the timing marks do not align, remove the timing belt and repeat the refitting procedure.

58 Check the timing belt deflection at a point midway between the camshaft sprockets (or camshaft sprocket and idler pulley on the 1.5 litre engine) by applying moderate force by hand (about 9 kg/20 pounds force) **(see illustration)**. 1.5 litre engine belt deflection should be 7.1 to 8.7 mm (0.28 to 0.34 in). 1.8 litre engine belt deflection should be 9.5 to 11.1 mm (0.38 to 0.44 in).

59 If belt deflection is not correct, repeat the refitting procedure. If the proper tension is still not obtained, renew the tensioner spring with a new spring and reset belt tension as described above.

60 Tighten the crankshaft sprocket bolt to the torque listed in this Chapter's Specifications.

61 Refit the remaining parts in the reverse order of removal. Run the engine and check for proper operation.

Caution: DO NOT start the engine until you are absolutely certain that the timing belt is installed correctly. Serious and costly engine damage could occur if the belt is improperly installed.

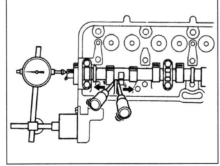

9.4 Lever the camshaft back-and-forth to check the endplay (thrust clearance)

8 Camshaft oil seal(s) - renewal

Removal

1 Disconnect the cable from the negative battery terminal.

2 Chock the rear wheels and set the handbrake.

3 Position cylinder number one to TDC on the compression stroke (see Section 3).

4 Remove the camshaft sprocket bolt(s) and sprocket(s) (see Section 7). On 1.8 litre models, remove the timing belt sprocket rear shield.

5 Carefully lever the camshaft seal out of the bore using a thin screwdriver **(see illustration)**. Or drill a small hole in the seal midway between the camshaft and cylinder head; thread a small screw into the camshaft oil seal one or two threads and use the screw to pull the seal from the bore.

Caution: DO NOT nick or scratch the camshaft or seal bore.

Refitting

6 Apply some clean engine oil to the lip of the new camshaft oil seal. Push the seal in slightly by hand.

7 Hold a short length of pipe or tube sized to fit the camshaft oil seal bore against the seal, and lightly tap the seal in, flush to the edge of the camshaft cap or to the depth of the original seal.

8 Refit the remaining parts in the reverse order of removal.

9 Run the engine and check for proper operation.

9 Rocker arms, clearance adjusters and camshaft(s) - removal, inspection and refitting

Removal

1 Remove the valve cover (see Section 4).

2 Remove the distributor (see Chapter 5).

3 Remove the timing belt covers, timing belt, and camshaft sprocket(s) (see Section 7).

4 Measure the thrust clearance (endplay) of the camshaft(s) with a dial indicator **(see illustration)**. If the clearance is greater than the value listed in this Chapter's Specifications, renew the camshaft thrust plate, camshaft, and/or the cylinder head.

1.3 litre and 1.6 litre models

Note: *The 1.6 litre engines use a rocker shaft and rocker arm with hydraulic clearance adjusters. The hydraulic clearance adjusters eliminate the need for valve clearance adjusting screws or shims. After initial refitting, no further valve adjustment is necessary.*

5 Number or mark the components before removal to be sure that the parts will be

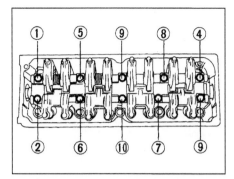

9.6 Loosen the camshaft bearing cap bolts, in several steps, in the sequence shown (SOHC engine)

9.9 Pull the camshaft straight out of the cylinder head

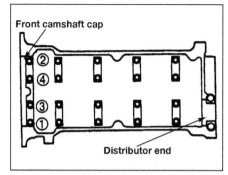

9.11a Loosen the two front camshaft caps in two or three steps in sequence (1.5 litre DOHC)

reinstalled in the same location when reassembled.

6 Loosen the rocker arm bolts in the sequence shown **(see illustration)** in two or three steps. **Note:** *Unscrew the bolts fully from the cylinder head but do not remove the bolts from the rocker shafts.*

7 Remove the rocker arm and rocker shaft assembly. Mark or otherwise store the rocker arms and springs for later refitting in the same locations from which they were removed.

8 In order to remove the camshaft without removing the cylinder head from the engine, remove the air cleaner assembly and reposition the underbonnet fusebox.

9 Pull the camshaft straight out of the cylinder head **(see illustration)**. Remove the camshaft oil seal.

1.5 litre and 1.8 litre models

Note: *The 1.8 litre engine uses two overhead camshafts to directly-actuate hydraulic valve adjusters, which control the valves. After initial refitting, no further valve adjustments are necessary. The hydraulic adjusters eliminate the need for an adjusting shim. The 1.5 litre engine uses shim-on-bucket type tappets, which require adjustment by measuring a clearance and refitting new shims of proper thickness. The need to properly mark or store parts for later refitting in the same locations*

*from which they were removed is very important **(see illustration 9.14)**.*

10 Remove the camshaft sprocket bolts (see Section 7) and remove the sprockets. Remove the timing belt sprocket rear shield.

11 Loosen the camshaft bearing cap bolts in two or three steps in the sequence shown **(see illustrations)**. Remove the camshaft bearing caps, marking or packaging them to record their locations for correct refitting later. To further ensure correct refitting later, take note of the factory camshaft cap stamped numbers and direction arrows.

12 Make note how far into the bearing cap the old oil seal is located and use this as a guide for the refitting depth later.

13 Mark the camshafts to ensure proper refitting later. Remove the camshafts. Remove the oil seals from the camshafts.

14 Using a magnet or tweezers, as applicable, lift out each hydraulic valve adjuster or shim/bucket tappet and set them in numbered boxes, plastic bags or other containers so they can be reinstalled in the same position during reassembly **(see illustration)**. **Note:** *Do not scratch the components when removing them.*

Inspection

15 Examine all parts, looking for signs of pitting, scoring or scuffing.

1.3 litre and 1.6 litre models

16 Examine the rocker arm bearing surfaces which contact the camshaft lobes for wear ridges and scoring. Renew any rocker arms on which these conditions are apparent.

17 If the rocker gear has been dismantled, examine the rocker arm and shaft bearing surfaces for wear ridges and scoring. If the necessary measuring equipment is available, measure the internal diameter of the rocker arm and the outside diameter of the rocker shaft at the point where the rocker pivots and calculate the clearance **(see illustrations)**. If the clearance exceeds the figure given in the Specifications at the start of this Chapter or there are obvious signs of wear, the rocker arm and/or shaft must be renewed.

18 On 1.6 litre and 1.8 litre engines, check the operation of the hydraulic valve adjusters by pushing down on the plunger at the end of each rocker arm. If the plunger moves when pressure is applied, the assembly is faulty and must be renewed. Remove any faulty hydraulic valve adjuster assemblies from their respective rocker arms using a pair of pliers.

19 Measure the camshaft journals and camshaft lobes. Measure each camshaft bore inside diameter and subtract the camshaft journal outside diameter measurement to determine the camshaft journal oil clearance

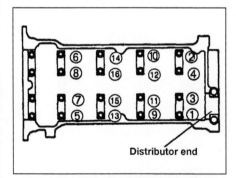

9.11b Loosen the remaining camshaft caps in two or three steps in sequence (1.5 litre DOHC)

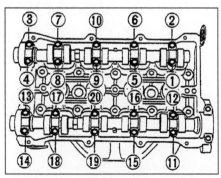

9.11c Loosen the camshaft caps in two or three steps in sequence (1.8 litre DOHC)

9.14 Mark up a cardboard box to store the components to relocate for refitting

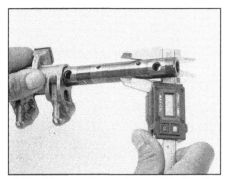

9.17a Measure the rocker arm shaft outer diameter

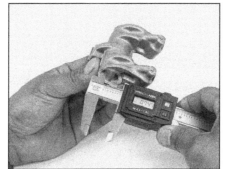

9.17b Measure the rocker arm inside diameter

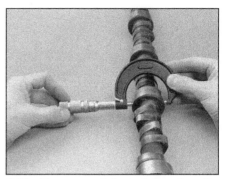

9.19a Measure each journal diameter with a micrometer

(see illustrations). Compare your measurements to the values listed in this Chapter's Specifications.

1.5 litre and 1.8 litre models

20 Check the oil clearance for each camshaft journal as follows:

a) *Clean the bearing caps and the camshaft journals with cleaning solvent and dry thoroughly.*

b) *Carefully lay the camshaft(s) in place in the head. Do not refit the tappets/valve adjusters and do not use any lubrication.*

c) *Lay a strip of Plastigauge on each journal* **(see illustration).**

d) *Refit the camshaft bearing caps in the proper locations as removed with the arrows pointing as removed.*

e) *Tighten the bolts IN SEQUENCE* **(see illustrations 9.40a and 9.40b)** *to the torque listed in this Chapter's Specifications in two or three steps.* **Note:** *Do not turn the camshaft while the Plastigauge is in place.*

f) *Remove the camshaft bearing cap bolts IN SEQUENCE* **(see illustrations 9.11a, 9.11b, and 9.11c)** *and detach the caps.*

g) *Compare the width of the crushed Plastigauge (at its widest point) to the scale on the Plastigauge envelope* **(see illustration).**

h) *If the clearance is greater than specified, renew the camshaft and/or cylinder head.*

i) *Scrape off the Plastigauge with your fingernail or the edge of a credit card - do not scratch or nick the journals or bearing caps.*

21 On 1.5 litre models, inspect each bucket shim surface for scuffing and scoring marks or other surface defects. If defective, renew the shim. Inspect each tappet for scuffing and scoring marks **(see illustration).** On 1.8 litre models, press the hydraulic adjuster plunger in by hand, checking for movement. If the plunger moves, renew the hydraulic adjuster.

22 Measure the outside diameter of each tappet or valve adjuster and measure the bore diameter **(see illustration).** Renew any component that is worn excessively.

23 Visually examine the camshaft lobes and bearing journals for scoring marks, pitting and evidence of overheating (blue, discoloured areas). Look for flaking away of the hardened surface of each lobe.

24 Using a micrometer, measure the diameter of each camshaft journal **(see illustration 9.19a).** If the diameter of any one journal is less than specified, renew the camshaft.

25 Using a micrometer, measure the height of each lobe **(see illustration 9.19b).** If the height for any one lobe is less than the specified minimum, renew the camshaft.

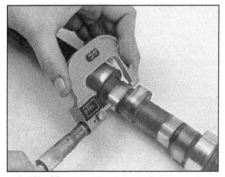

9.19b Measure the lobe heights on the camshaft(s)

9.20a Lay a strip of Plastigauge on each camshaft journal

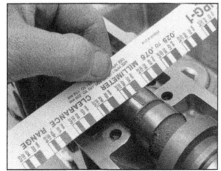

9.20b Compare the width of the crushed Plastigauge with the scale to determine the oil clearance

9.21 Wipe off the oil and inspect each tappet for wear and scuffing

1 Tappet wall   2 Shim

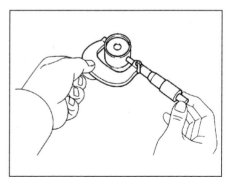

9.22 Use a micrometer to measure tappet diameter

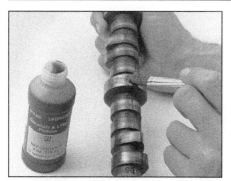

9.29 Coat the lobes and journals with lubricant

9.30 Position the camshaft against the thrust plate

9.31a Apply oil to the hydraulic valve adjuster O-ring (arrowed). . .

26 Renew any parts that are worn beyond specifications.

Refitting

1.3 litre and 1.6 litre models

27 Apply clean engine oil to the new camshaft oil seal and the cylinder head camshaft bore.
28 Hold a short length of pipe or tube sized to fit the camshaft oil seal bore against the seal, and lightly tap the seal in, flush to the edge of the cylinder head.
29 Apply camshaft assembly lubricant to the camshaft lobes and bearing journals **(see illustration)**.
30 Refit the camshaft in the cylinder head and into position with the thrust plate **(see illustration)**.
31 If the hydraulic clearance adjusters were removed from the rocker arms, or are being replaced, fill the rocker arm cavity with clean engine oil, coat the clearance adjusters with clean engine oil, and refit them into the rocker arm **(see illustrations)**.
32 Assemble and refit the rocker arm assembly as it was removed. Make sure that the rocker shaft oil holes face downward. **Note:** *There are two types of rocker arms used on the 1.6 litre model; one type is used on cylinders no. 1 and 2, while the other type is used on cylinders No. 3 and 4 - be careful to*

9.31b . . . and press the valve adjuster into the rocker arm

refit them exactly as removed, and if replacing any rocker arms, be sure to obtain the correct parts **(see illustrations)**.
33 Tighten the rocker arm bolts to the torque listed in this Chapter's Specifications in several steps and in the recommended sequence **(see illustration)**. **Note:** *Take great care to ensure that the rocker shaft springs do not become trapped between the shaft and cylinder head or retaining plates whilst tightening the bolts.*
34 Refit the camshaft sprocket (see Section 7) and tighten the bolt to the torque listed in this Chapter's Specifications.
35 Refit the timing belt (see Section 7).

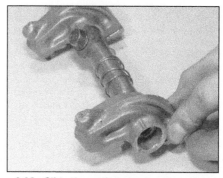

9.32a Slide the springs and rocker arms onto the shaft . . .

36 The remainder of refitting is the reverse of the removal procedure. On 1.3 litre engines, check the valve clearances as described in Chapter 1.

1.5 litre and 1.8 litre models

37 Apply engine assembly lubricant or clean engine oil to the hydraulic valve assemblies, or tappets, and refit into the bores in their original locations. Check that the components travel smoothly in their bores.
38 Apply camshaft assembly lubricant or clean engine oil to the camshaft lobes and bearing journals. Refit the camshafts. On the 1.5 litre engine, also install the camshaft chain

9.32b . . . and refit the retaining bolts and plates

9.32c Align the rocker shaft and cylinder head oilways (arrowed)

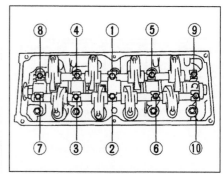

9.33 Rocker arm bolt tightening sequence - SOHC models

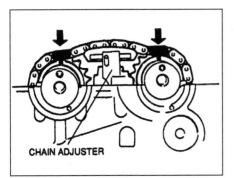

9.38 Install the 1.5L DOHC camshaft drive chain adjuster and chain, with alignment marks as shown

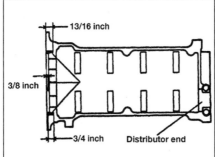

9.39a Apply silicone sealant to the shaded surfaces (1.5 litre DOHC)

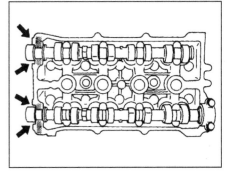

9.39b Apply silicone sealant to the shaded surfaces (1.8 litre DOHC)

adjuster between the camshafts and align the marks on the camshaft gears and the timing chain **(see illustration)**. Make sure the exhaust camshaft is reinstalled on the exhaust manifold side of the engine, and the inlet camshaft is reinstalled on the inlet manifold side of the engine. **Note:** *Make sure the correct camshaft is installed on the side that drives the distributor. The camshaft that drives the distributor has a groove or slot for distributor engagement.*

39 Apply silicone sealant to the shaded areas of the bearing caps surfaces as shown **(see illustrations)**.

40 Refit the camshaft bearing caps in the proper order as marked when removed, in the stamped numerical order with the arrows pointing as removed. Then tighten the cap bolts in two or three steps IN SEQUENCE **(see illustrations)** to the torque listed in this Chapter's Specifications.

41 Apply clean engine oil to the lips of the new camshaft oil seals and refit the oil seals (see Section 8).

42 Refit the camshaft sprockets on their correct camshafts (see Section 8).

43 Refit the timing belt (see Section 7).

44 Before refitting the distributor, refit a new distributor O-ring. Apply grease to the O-ring and apply grease or engine assembly lubricant to the distributor drive lugs.

45 Refit the distributor and loosely tighten the distributor timing adjustment bolt(s). Connect the distributor electrical connector.

46 Refit the remaining parts in the reverse order of removal. On 1.5 litre engines, check the valve clearances as described in Chapter 1.

47 Run the engine and adjust the timing (see Chapter 5). Check the engine for proper operation.

10 Valve springs, retainers and seals - renewal

Note: *Broken valve springs and defective valve stem seals can be replaced without removing the cylinder head. Two special tools and a compressed air source are normally required to perform this operation, so read through this Section carefully and rent or buy the tools before beginning the job. If compressed air isn't available, a length of nylon rope can be used to keep the valves from falling into the cylinder during this procedure.*

1 On SOHC models, remove the rocker arms and shafts (Section 9), there is no need to remove the camshaft or timing belt. On DOHC models refer to Section 9 and remove the camshaft(s). Remove the valve clearance adjusting components from the defective valves. Keep them in order so they may be reinstalled in their original location.

2 Remove the spark plug from the cylinder which has the defective component. If all of

the valve stem seals are being replaced, all of the spark plugs should be removed.

3 Turn the crankshaft until the piston in the affected cylinder is at Top Dead Centre (TDC) on the compression stroke (refer to Section 3 for instructions). If you are replacing all of the valve stem seals, begin with cylinder number one and work on the valves for one cylinder at a time. Move from cylinder-to-cylinder following the firing order sequence.

4 Thread an adapter into the spark plug hole **(see illustration)** and connect an air hose from a compressed air source. Most car accessory outlets can supply the air hose adapter. **Note:** *Many cylinder compression gauges utilise a screw-in fitting that may work with your air hose quick-disconnect fitting.*

5 Apply compressed air to the cylinder.

⚠️ *Warning: The piston may be forced down by compressed air, causing the crankshaft to turn suddenly. If the spanner used when positioning the number one piston at TDC is still attached to the bolt in the crankshaft pulley end, damage or injury could occur if the crankshaft moves.*

6 The valves for that cylinder should now be held in place by the air pressure.

7 If you do not have access to compressed air, an alternative method can be used. Position the piston at a point approximately 45° before TDC on the compression stroke, then feed a long piece of *nylon* rope through the spark plug hole until it fills the combustion

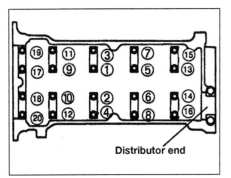

9.40a Camshaft bearing cap bolt tightening sequence - 1.5 litre DOHC engine

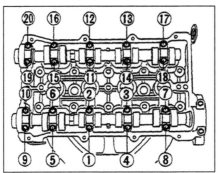

9.40b Camshaft bearing cap bolt tightening sequence - 1.8 litre DOHC engine

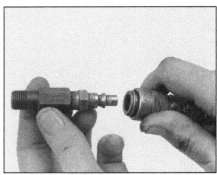

10.4 Air hose adapter that threads into the spark plug hole

10.9 Remove the collets from the valve stem with a magnet or small needle-nose pliers

10.10 Remove the valve guide oil seal with an oil seal removal tool or a pair of pliers

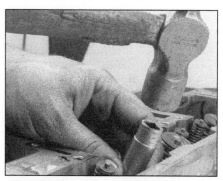

10.15 Gently tap the seal into place with a hammer and a deep socket

chamber. Be sure to leave the end of the rope hanging out of the engine so it can be removed easily.

8 Use a large ratchet and socket to rotate the crankshaft in the normal direction of rotation (clockwise, when viewed from the front) until slight resistance is felt.

9 Stuff clean workshop rags into any cylinder head holes above and below the valves to prevent parts and tools from falling into the engine, then use a suitable valve spring compressor to compress the spring. Remove the collets with small needle-nose pliers or a magnet **(see illustration)**. **Note:** *Different types of tools are available for compressing the valve springs with the head in place. One type grips the lower spring coils and presses on the retainer as the knob is turned, while the other type uses a bolt or stud and nut for leverage. Both types work well, although the lever type is usually less expensive.*

10 Remove the spring retainer and valve spring (mark the top end of the valve spring for later refitting). On DOHC engines, measure the depth to the upper side of the valve stem oil seal, then remove the oil seal **(see illustration)**. **Note:** *If using air pressure to hold the valve(s) and this fails to hold the valve in the closed position during this operation, the valve face and/or seat is probably damaged. If so, the cylinder head will have to be removed, the alternative procedure for holding the valves described above may be used, or the cylinder head will require removal for additional repair operations.*

11 Wrap a rubber band or tape around the top of the valve stem so the valve won't fall into the combustion chamber, then release the air pressure. **Note:** *If a rope was used instead of air pressure, turn the crankshaft slightly in the direction opposite normal rotation.*

12 Inspect the valve spring for cracks or damage and check free length is as listed in this Chapter's Specifications. Inspect the valve stem for damaged or rough face or an unevenly worn stem tip. Rotate the valve in its guide and check the end of the valve stem for eccentric movement, which would indicate that the valve is bent.

13 Move the valve up-and-down in the guide and make sure there is no binding. If the valve stem binds, either the valve is bent or the guide

is damaged. Rock the valve stem side-to-side; clearance should not exceed the valve stem-to-valve guide clearance in this Chapter's Specifications. If the valve stem is defective, the cylinder head will have to be removed for repair of valves and/or valve guides.

14 Reapply air pressure to the cylinder to retain the valve in the closed position, then remove the tape or rubber band from the valve stem. If a nylon rope was used instead of air pressure, rotate the crankshaft in the normal direction of rotation until slight resistance is felt.

15 Lubricate the valve stem with engine oil or engine assembly lubricant and refit a new oil seal using an oil seal installer tool or deep socket **(see illustration)**, measuring the installed depth as necessary. On DOHC engines, refit the oil seal to the depth measured before seal removal (paragraph 10 above). On 1.8 litre engines, the oil seal should be to a depth such that the upper side of the oil seal is 20.0 mm (0.787 in) above the bottom of the oil seal bore.

16 Refit the spring in position over the valve. Renew any springs not meeting the inspection above. Be sure the spring is installed as marked during removal (top of the spring is up) and also note that the end of the spring with a closer pitch is toward the cylinder head.

17 Refit the valve spring retainer. Compress the valve spring and carefully position the keepers in the groove.

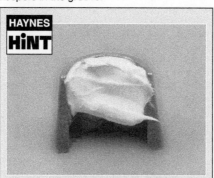

HAYNES HiNT

Apply a small dab of grease to each collet before refitting - it'll hold them in place on the valve stem as the spring is released

18 Remove the pressure from the spring tool and make sure the collets are seated.

19 Disconnect the compressed air hose and remove the adapter from the spark plug hole. If a nylon rope was used in place of air pressure, pull it out of the cylinder.

20 Refer to Section 9 and refit the camshaft(s), or rocker arms, as applicable.

21 Refit the rest of the parts in the reverse order of the removal procedure.

22 Start and run the engine, then check for oil leaks and unusual sounds coming from the valve cover area

11 Cylinder head - removal and refitting

Caution: The engine must be completely cool before beginning this procedure.

Removal

1 Disconnect the negative cable from the battery.

2 Remove the spark plugs.

3 Drain the coolant from the engine block and radiator (see Chapter 1).

4 Remove the air inlet tube assembly from the inlet plenum (see Chapter 4).

5 Remove the resonance tube above the radiator, as applicable.

6 Remove the throttle cable (on automatic transmission models) and accelerator cable.

7 Remove the brake vacuum hose, fuel hose, radiator hoses, the purge control vacuum hose (from inlet plenum-to-bulkhead area), cruise control vacuum hose (as applicable), and the heater hoses. Mark the hoses for later refitting.

8 Remove all electrical connectors/wiring harness connections to the cylinder head. Mark the connectors for later refitting.

9 Remove water bypass tubing bolts/nuts (where applicable, the bypass tubing is mounted on engine head).

10 Remove the water pump pulley and drive belt.

11 Remove the air inlet plenum and the fuel rail (see Chapter 4).

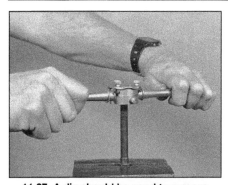

11.27 A die should be used to remove sealant and corrosion from the head bolt threads prior to refitting

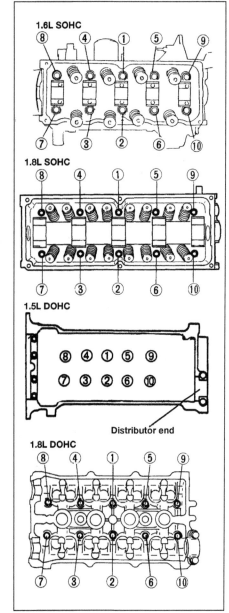

11.33 Cylinder head bolt TIGHTENING sequence

12 Remove the inlet manifold (see Section 5).

13 Detach the exhaust pipe from the exhaust manifold. Remove the exhaust manifold (see Section 6).

14 Remove the valve cover (see Section 4).

15 Remove the timing belt covers and the timing belt (see Section 7).

16 Remove the power steering pump and alternator drive belt(s) (see Chapter 5).

17 Remove the alternator/generator brackets.

18 Remove the distributor (see Chapter 5).

19 Unbolt the power steering pump, as applicable, and lay it to the side without disconnecting the hoses (see Chapter 10).

20 Check the cylinder head. Label and detach any remaining components that would interfere with cylinder head removal.

21 Using a breaker bar and the appropriate Allen-head driver or socket, loosen the cylinder head bolts in 1/4-turn increments, loosening in the reverse of the tightening sequence **(see illustration 11.33)** until they can be removed by hand.

22 Lift the cylinder head off the engine block. If it is stuck, very carefully lever up at the transmission end, away from the head gasket surface. **Note:** *The cylinder head is positioned on dowels, so will not rotate.*

23 Remove all external components from the head to allow for thorough cleaning and inspection. See Chapter 2, Part B, for cylinder head servicing procedures.

Refitting

24 The mating surfaces of the cylinder head and block must be perfectly clean when the head is installed.

25 Use a gasket scraper to remove all traces of carbon and old gasket material, then clean the mating surfaces with lacquer thinner or acetone. If any oil residue is on the mating surfaces when the head is installed, the gasket may not seal correctly and leaks could develop. When working on the block, stuff the cylinders with clean workshop rags to prevent the entry of debris. Use a vacuum cleaner to remove material that falls into the cylinders. *Caution: Be careful not to gouge the soft aluminium of the cylinder head.*

26 Check the block and head mating surfaces for nicks, deep scratches and other damage. If damage is slight, it can be removed with a file; if it's excessive, machining may be the only alternative.

27 Use a thread die of the correct thread size to clean up the head bolt threads **(see illustration)**. **Note:** *Cleaning up the threads using a thread die should not cut any metal from the threads. If you observe any metal cuttings while cleaning the threads, stop and renew the bolt with a new one from an automotive parts store or dealer. Make sure the renewal bolt is a OEM (Original Equipment Manufacturer) renewal cylinder head bolt specifically designed for this engine, and is the correct length and thread type. Discard the defective bolt. Use a tap of the correct thread size to clean the threads in the head bolt*

holes, then clean the holes with compressed air - make sure that no residue such as dirt, corrosion, and sealant remains in the holes and the threads are not damaged as this will affect torque readings, which affects the quality of the head refitting job.

 Warning: Wear eye protection when using compressed air!

28 Refit the components that were removed from the head.

29 Position the new gasket over the dowel pins in the block.

30 Carefully set the head on the block without disturbing the gasket.

31 Before refitting the head bolts, apply a small amount of clean engine oil to the threads.

32 Refit the bolts and tighten them finger tight.

33 Tighten the bolts following the recommended sequence in several steps to the torque listed in this Chapter's Specifications **(see illustration)**.

34 The remaining refitting steps are the reverse of removal.

35 Refill the cooling system, refit a new oil filter and add oil to the engine (see Chapter 1).

36 Run the engine and check for leaks. Set the ignition timing (see Chapter 5) and road test the vehicle.

37 Frequently recheck coolant level for the first few hundred miles to be sure that no leakage exists.

12 Sump - removal and refitting

Removal

1 Disconnect the negative cable from the battery.

2 Set the handbrake and block the rear wheels. Raise the front of the vehicle and support it securely on axle stands.

3 Remove the under cover splash shield(s) from under the engine **(see illustration 7.3)**.

4 Drain the engine oil and remove the oil filter (see Chapter 1).

5 Disconnect the exhaust pipe from the exhaust manifold **(see illustrations)**.

12.5a Remove the exhaust pipe flange connection . . .

12.5b . . . and remove the pipe from the exhaust manifold - remove the catalytic converter if necessary

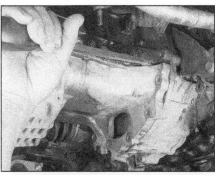

12.7a Carefully lever the sump away from the Main Bearing Support Plate (MBSP)

12.7b Remove the oil pickup tube/screen assembly

6 Remove the sump as follows. **Note:** *Sump bolts may be of varying sizes. Mark, tag, or store each sump bolt/nut with the location removed from the sump for correct refitting later.*
Caution: Do not insert the screwdriver or levering tool between the Main Bearing Support Plate (MBSP) and the engine block. Be very careful not to scratch, bend, or otherwise damage the mating surfaces of the sump, MBSP, and block or oil leaks could develop.
7 On 1.6 litre models, the sump may be one piece, or it may be a two-piece design with an Sump Stiffener at the transmission end of the engine which attaches to the sump. Also, this engine has a MBSP between the sump and the engine, attached at the main journals and the sump bolts. If the vehicle you are working on has a two-piece sump, first remove the sump stiffener bolts around the bottom of the transmission and at the engine block, then remove the sump stiffener. Remove the remaining sump bolts and then remove the sump. If the sump is stuck, carefully lever it loose by inserting a screwdriver or small lever at the engine block ears located at the transmission end of the engine **(see illustration)**. Do not lever along the sump lip and the MBSP. With the sump removed, detach the oil strainer from the MBSP **(see illustration)**. Then remove the MBSP bolts **(see illustration)**, and very carefully lever the MBSP against the main bearing journal or at the corners of the MBSP **(see illustration)**.
Caution: Do not lever on the rod bearing caps.
8 On 1.8 litre models, remove the sump bolts and then remove the sump. If the sump is stuck, lever it loose very carefully by inserting a screwdriver or putty knife at the engine block ears at the flywheel end of the engine block. Then, remove the MBSP attaching bolts and remove the MBSP, levering as necessary against the main bearing journal or at the corners of the MBSP.
Caution: Do not insert the screwdriver or levering tool at any other area.
9 On 1.3 litre and 1.5 litre models, remove the sump bolts and then remove the sump. If the sump is stuck, lever it loose carefully by

12.7c Remove the MBSP bolts

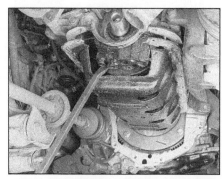

12.7d Carefully lever the MBSP from the engine block

inserting a screwdriver or putty knife at the corners of the sump.

Refitting

10 Use a scraper to remove all traces of old gasket material and sealant from the block, MBSP, and sump. Clean the mating surfaces with gasket cleaner or equivalent solvent, available at automotive parts stores.
Caution: Be very careful not to scratch, bend, or otherwise damage the mating surfaces of the pan and block or oil leaks could develop.
11 Make sure the threaded bolt holes in the block are clean. Visually check the condition of the oil strainer.
12 Check the sump flange for cracks or distortion, particularly at the bolting flange.

13 On all except the 1.3 litre and 1.5 litre models, apply silicone sealant to the shaded areas of the engine block **(see illustration)**. **Note:** *The next step must be completed so that the MBSP can be installed within 5 minutes after the sealant in this step was applied.*
14 On all except the 1.3 litre and 1.5 litre models, apply a continuous bead of silicone sealant to the bolting flange (lip) of the MBSP inside the bolt holes **(see illustration)**. Refit the MBSP bolts and tighten them to the torque listed in this Chapter's Specification. **Note:** *The MBSP must be installed within 5 minutes of application of the sealant applied in paragraph 13 above.*
15 On 1.3 litre and 1.5 litre models, apply a continuous bead of silicone sealant to the

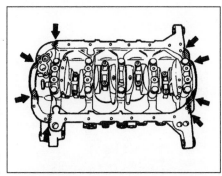

12.13 Apply silicone sealant to the engine block at the shaded areas shown

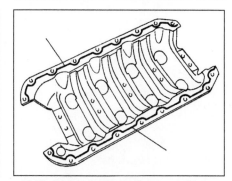

12.14 Apply a bead of silicone sealant to the Main Bearing Support Plate or sump inside the bolt holes

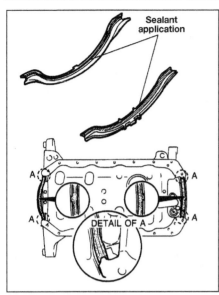

12.16 Location of projections on gasket/seal refitting for the oil pump body and the rear cover

bolting flange (lip) of the sump inside the bolt holes. Refit the sump bolts and tighten them to the torque listed in this Chapter's Specification. **Note:** *The sump must be installed within 5 minutes of application of the sealant.*

16 On all except the 1.3 litre and 1.5 litre models, apply silicone sealant to new gaskets for the oil pump body and rear cover. Refit the new gaskets on the oil pump body and rear cover on the engine block, with the projections on the gaskets in the notches **(see illustration)**.

17 On all except the 1.3 litre and 1.5 litre model, apply a continuous bead of silicone sealant to the sump bolting flange (lip) inside the bolt holes.

18 On all except the 1.3 litre and 1.5 litre models, carefully position the sump on the engine block and refit the bolts/nuts. Working from the centre out, tighten them to the torque listed in this Chapter's Specifications in three or four steps.

19 The remainder of refitting is the reverse of

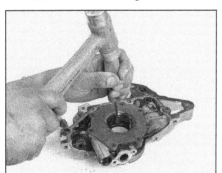

14.2 Remove the front oil seal using screwdriver or punch

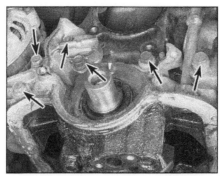

13.6 Remove the bolts (arrowed) and separate the front cover from the engine block

removal. Be sure to add oil and fit a new oil filter.

20 Let the silicone sealant set for approximately 12 hours before running the engine.

21 After sufficient time for the silicone sealant to set, run the engine and check for oil leaks.

13 Front cover - removal and refitting

Removal

1 Disconnect the negative battery cable.
2 Remove the under cover splash shield.
3 Securely support the front of the vehicle on axle stands, and remove the front driver's side wheel for access to the front cover. Remove the alternator (see Chapter 5). Remove the air conditioning compressor (without disconnecting the hoses) and secure it aside (see Chapter 3).
4 Remove the crankshaft pulley, water pump pulley, timing belt covers, timing belt, and timing belt guide (see Section 7), remove the sump (Section 13).
5 Remove the crankshaft sprocket using a puller or two screwdrivers placed behind the gear to apply even pressure on the gear to slide it off the crankshaft.
6 Remove the front cover bolts/nuts from the engine block **(see illustration)** and separate the front cover from the engine block. You

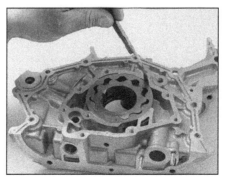

14.5a Measure the clearance between the oil pump driven rotor and the pump housing . . .

may have to lever carefully between the front main bearing cap and the pump housing with a screwdriver.

Refitting

7 Use a scraper to remove all traces of gasket and sealant from the cover and engine block, then clean the mating surfaces with solvent.
8 Refit new gasket with a thin coat of silicone sealant on the front cover gasket surface. Refit the front cover to the engine block. **Note:** *Be sure the sealant doesn't plug or cover any oil passages.*
9 Refit the bolts/nuts, tightening them to the torque listed in this Chapter's Specifications.
10 The remainder of refitting is the reverse of the removal procedure.

14 Oil pump - removal, inspection and refitting

Note: *If you are replacing the front oil seal only and not removing, inspecting, repairing or replacing the oil pump, the front oil seal can be replaced without oil pump removal as described in Section 15.*

Removal

1 Remove the front cover, which is also the housing for the oil pump assembly (see Section 13).
2 Place the front cover/oil pump on a workbench. Note how far the oil seal is seated in the bore. Using a seal removal tool or a screwdriver taped or wrapped with a rag to protect the pump bore, remove the oil seal from the housing **(see illustration)**.
Caution: Do not scratch the housing bore.
3 Remove the screws that hold the oil pump cover (slotted plate) to the front cover/oil pump housing. Inspect the oil pump cover for distortion or damage.
4 Remove the oil pressure relief valve. Note or mark the direction of the components as installed, then remove the oil pump inner and outer rotors from the housing.

Inspection

5 Refit the oil pump inner and outer rotors

14.5b . . . then measure the clearance between the drive and driven rotor . . .

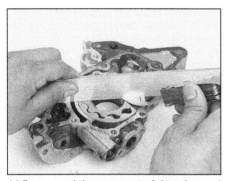

14.5c ... and then use a straight-edge and measure the endplay between the rotors and the housing

into the oil pump housing **(see illustrations)** and measure the clearance of:

a) *The driven rotor-to-pump housing.*
b) *The drive rotor-to-oil pump driven rotor.*
c) *The rotor set-to-oil pump housing endplay clearance.*

Compare your measurements to the clearance listed in this Chapter's Specifications.

6 Check the length of the oil pressure relief spring when removed from the oil pump. Compare the length measured with the free length listed in this Chapter's Specifications. Renew the spring if necessary.

7 Be sure the surfaces of the pump housing are clean and dry before reassembly.

8 Lightly coat the outer edge of a new oil seal with engine assembly lubricant or clean engine oil. Using a socket with an outside diameter slightly smaller than the outside diameter of the seal, carefully drive the new seal into place with a hammer. Make sure it's installed squarely and driven in to the same depth as the original. If a socket is not available, a short section of large diameter pipe will also work. Apply engine assembly lubricant to the seal lip surface that contacts the crankshaft.

9 Lubricate the oil pressure relief valve piston with clean engine oil and refit the valve components into the pump case.

10 Lubricate the rotor set with clean engine oil. Refit the rotors.

11 Pack the pump cavities with petroleum

jelly (this will prime the pump and ensure good suction when the engine is started).

12 Refit the cover and tighten the screws to the torque listed in this Chapter's Specifications.

13 It is a good idea to inspect the screen at the end of the oil pick-up tube (see Section 12) for any debris that might plug it. Either clean the tube and screen completely or renew it with a new one at this time.

Refitting

14 Refit the front cover (see Section 13).

15 Refit the remaining parts in the reverse order of removal.

16 Add oil (see Chapter 1), start the engine and check for oil pressure and leaks.

15 Crankshaft front oil seal - renewal

1 Disconnect the negative battery cable.

2 Remove the under cover splash shield.

3 Securely support the front of the vehicle on axle stands, and remove the front driver's side wheel for access to the front cover.

4 Remove the crankshaft pulley, timing belt covers, timing belt, and timing belt guide (see Section 7).

5 Remove the crankshaft sprocket using a puller or two screwdrivers placed behind the gear to apply even pressure on the gear to slide it off the crankshaft.

6 Cut the front oil seal lip with a razor knife.

7 Note how far the seal is seated in the bore and the direction the oil seal lip faces (the oil seal should be flush with the face of the oil pump body. Remove the front oil seal with a screwdriver taped or wrapped with a rag to protect the crankshaft surface and engine block **(see illustration)**.

8 Clean the bore in the engine block and clean the crankshaft surface. Coat the outside of the new front oil seal with engine oil. Apply engine assembly lubricant or clean engine oil to the seal lip.

9 Press the oil seal in slightly by hand, with the oil seal lip facing the same direction as

removed. Using a seal driver or a socket with an outside diameter slightly smaller than the outside diameter of the front oil seal, carefully tap the new seal into place with a hammer **(see illustration)** until the oil seal is flush with the face of the oil pump body. Make sure the oil seal is installed squarely.

10 Refit the crankshaft timing belt sprocket and timing belt (see Section 7).

11 The remainder of the refitting is the reverse of the removal procedure.

12 Run the engine and check for oil leaks at the front oil seal.

16 Flywheel/driveplate - removal and refitting

Removal

1 Raise the vehicle and support it securely on axle stands, then refer to Chapter 7 and remove the transmission.

2 If you're working on a model with a manual transmission, remove the clutch cover and clutch disc (see Chapter 8). Now is a good time to check/renew the clutch components and pilot bearing.

3 Use a centre-punch or paint to make alignment marks on the flywheel/driveplate and crankshaft to ensure correct refitting alignment later **(see illustration)**. **Note:** *The flywheel can be marked prior to transmission removal if desired through the access hole at the sump/transmission housing area (1.5 litre engine access method may vary from other models).*

4 Remove the bolts that secure the flywheel/driveplate to the crankshaft. If the crankshaft turns, wedge a screwdriver in the ring gear teeth to jam the flywheel.

5 Remove the flywheel/driveplate from the crankshaft. On the automatic transmission models, also remove the driveplate backing plate and adapter, taking note of which sides of the driveplate the adapter plates are mounted for correct refitting later. Since the flywheel is fairly heavy, be sure to support it while removing the last bolt.

6 Clean the flywheel to remove grease and

15.7 Remove the oil seal with a screwdriver

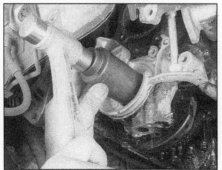

15.9 Using a large socket or suitable pipe or tubing to fit the seal

16.3 Mark the flywheel/driveplate and the crankshaft

17.4 The quick way to renew the rear main oil seal is to simply lever the old one out . . .

oil. Inspect the surface for cracks, rivet grooves, burned areas and score marks. Light scoring can be removed with emery cloth. Check for cracked and broken ring gear teeth. Lay the flywheel on a flat surface and use a straight-edge to check for warpage. If necessary, take the flywheel to an automotive machine workshop to have it resurfaced.

7 Clean and inspect the mating surfaces of the flywheel/driveplate and the crankshaft. If the crankshaft rear seal is leaking, renew it before refitting the flywheel/driveplate (see Section 17).

Refitting

8 Remove any thread sealant from the crankshaft flywheel bolt holes and bolts. *Caution: If all the thread sealant cannot be removed from a bolt, renew that bolt. Do not apply sealant when refitting a new bolt.*

9 For manual transmission models, position the flywheel at the crankshaft. For automatic transmission models, position the adapter, driveplate, and backing plate at the crankshaft. Be sure to align the marks made during removal. Before refitting the bolts, apply thread sealant to the threads of any bolts except new bolts used.

10 Wedge a screwdriver in the ring gear teeth to keep the flywheel/driveplate from turning as you tighten the bolts to the torque listed in this Chapter's Specifications. Follow a criss-cross pattern and work up to the final torque in three or four steps.

11 The remainder of refitting is the reverse of the removal procedure.

---

17 Rear main oil seal - renewal

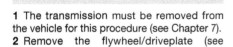

1 The transmission must be removed from the vehicle for this procedure (see Chapter 7).

2 Remove the flywheel/driveplate (see Section 16).

3 Cut the rear main oil seal lip with a razor knife.

4 Lever out the old seal with a screwdriver taped or wrapped in a rag, or use a seal removal tool to lever the seal out **(see illustration)**.

17.5 . . . then lubricate the crankshaft and the lip of the new seal with oil and tap the seal into place

5 Apply engine oil to the crankshaft seal journal and to the lip of the new seal. Carefully push the new seal part way into place by hand. Carefully tap into place using a flat punch, large socket, or a suitable short pipe or tubing of the correct diameter until the oil seal is flush with the edge of the rear cover **(see illustration)**.

6 Refit the flywheel/driveplate (see Section 16).

7 The remaining steps are the reverse of removal.

---

18 Engine mounts - check and renewal

1 Engine mounts seldom require attention, but broken or deteriorated mounts should be replaced immediately or the added strain placed on the driveline components may cause damage or wear.

 Warning: Do not remove any engine mounts or components of engine mounts if the engine is not properly supported as described. DO NOT place any part of your body directly under the engine when performing engine mount work and when the engine is supported only by a jack.

Check

2 During the check, the engine must be raised slightly to remove the weight from the mounts.

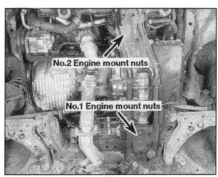

18.8a Transmission/engine mounts are attached to this crossmember which is removable

3 Raise the vehicle and support it securely on axle stands, then position a jack with a block of wood under the engine sump or use an engine support fixture from above. Carefully raise the engine just enough to take the weight off the mounts.

 Warning: DO NOT place any part of your body under the engine when it's supported only by a jack. Support the engine just enough to take the weight off the engine mounts but without lifting the weight of the car from the axle stands

4 Check the mounts to see if the rubber is cracked, hardened or separated from the metal portion. Occasionally, the rubber will split down the centre.

5 Check for relative movement between the mounts and the engine or frame, using a large screwdriver or other lever to attempt to move the mounts. If movement is noted, lower the engine and tighten the mount fasteners.

6 Rubber preservative liquid, available from any automotive parts store, should be applied to the engine mounts (and other chassis rubber components) to help protect from deterioration.

Renewal

7 Disconnect the negative battery cable from the battery, then raise the vehicle and support it securely on axle stands (if not already done). Support the engine as described in paragraph 3.

8 Renew the transmission/engine mounts No. 1 and 2 as follows:

a) *Detach the engine mount nuts located on the bottom of the engine mount crossmember (see illustration).*

b) *Remove the engine mount through bolts/nuts to detach from the rubber mount from the mount bracket.*

c) *Remove the crossmember mounting bolts and remove the crossmember for access.*

 Warning: Do not remove the crossmember if the engine is not supported as described above.

d) *Refit the transmission/engine mounts by attaching the mount brackets to the transmission (see illustration), refitting*

18.8b Refit the transmission/engine mounts by attaching the mount brackets to the transmission

18.9 Engine mount on the right, below the timing belt cover, is removed by detaching the through-bolt

1 *Engine mount No. 3 through-bolt*
2 *Engine mount Dynamic damper*

3 *Engine mount bracket nuts*

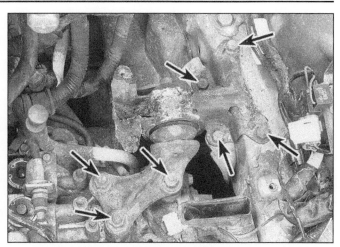

18.10 Transmission/engine mount at the right side of the engine

the mount through-bolts, washers and nuts, and then refitting the crossmember.
e) *Tighten all bolts/nuts to the torque listed in this Chapter's Specifications.*

9 Renew the engine mount No. 3 (located on the right side, near the engine timing belt cover) as follows **(see illustration)**:
a) *Remove the through-bolt nut and washer and withdraw the through-bolt from the frame bracket.*
b) *Detach the dynamic damper block on the top of the engine mount (if fitted) by removing the bolt and.*
c) *Remove the engine mount bracket nuts and remove the engine mount.*
d) *Refit the right side engine mount by*

refitting the mount bracket onto the vehicle frame, inserting the through-bolt to connect the engine bracket, and using a new washer, refit the washer and nut.
e) *Refit the dynamic damper and its bolt and nut (if fitted).*
f) *Tighten all bolts and nuts to the torque listed in this Chapter's Specifications.*

10 Renew engine mount No. 4 (located at the left side of the engine compartment at the battery tray area, attaching the transmission/engine to the vehicle body) as follows **(see illustration)**:
a) *Remove the battery and battery tray.*
b) *Remove the engine mount bracket bolts/nuts at the engine bracket.*

c) *Remove the engine mount bolts/nuts at the vehicle body bracket.*
d) *Remove the engine mount.*
e) *Refit the left side engine mount by refitting the mount bracket onto the vehicle frame, fit new washers (if applicable) and fit the nut(s). Tighten the left side engine mount bracket-to-vehicle body bolts to the torque listed in this Chapter's Specifications in several steps and in the following sequence: Tighten one of the bolts closest to the rubber mount first, then using a criss-cross pattern, tighten the remaining bolts and nuts.*

Notes

Chapter 2 Part B
General engine overhaul procedures

Contents

Degrees of difficulty

| **Easy,** suitable for novice with little experience | | **Fairly easy,** suitable for beginner with some experience | | **Fairly difficult,** suitable for competent DIY mechanic | | **Difficult,** suitable for experienced DIY mechanic | | **Very difficult,** suitable for expert DIY or professional | 🔧 |

Specifications

General

Displacement

1.3 litre	1324 cm³
1.5 litre	1489 cm³
1.6 litre	1598 cm³
1.8 litre	1840 cm³

Cylinder compression pressure @ 300 rpm

1.3 litre
Standard	14.5 bar (210 psi)
Minimum	10.9 bar (158 psi)
Maximum difference between cylinders	1.9 bar (28 psi)

1.5 litre
Standard	13.4 bar (195 psi)
Minimum	10.1 bar (146 psi)
Maximum difference between cylinders	1.9 bar (28 psi)

1.6 litre
Standard	13.2 bar (192 psi)
Minimum	9.3 bar (135 psi)
Maximum difference between cylinders	1.9 bar (28 psi)

1.8 litre
Standard	12.8 bar (185 psi)
Minimum	9.6 bar (139 psi)
Maximum difference between cylinders	1.9 bar (28 psi)

Oil pressure @ idle (warm)

1.3 litre and 1.5 litre	1.0 to 2.0 bar (15 to 28 psi)
1.6 litre and 1.8 litre	2.0 to 2.9 bar (28 to 43 psi)

Cylinder head

Warpage limits
    1.3 litre, 1.5 litre and 1.6 litre . . . . 0.15 mm
    1.8 litre . . . . 0.10 mm
    Manifold surfaces (all engines) . . . . 0.15 mm

Valves and related components

Valve margin thickness (minimum)
1.3 litre
    Inlet . . . . 1.0 mm
    Exhaust . . . . 1.0 mm
1.5 litre
    Inlet . . . . 1.1 mm
    Exhaust . . . . 1.2 mm
1.6 litre
    Inlet . . . . 0.9 mm
    Exhaust . . . . 1.0 mm
1.8 litre
    Inlet . . . . 0.850 mm
    Exhaust . . . . 0.925 mm

Valve stem diameter
1.3 litre, 1.6 litre and 1.8 litre
    Inlet . . . . 5.970 to 5.985 mm
    Exhaust . . . . 5.965 to 5.980 mm
1.5 litre
    Inlet . . . . 5.471 to 5.484 mm
    Exhaust . . . . 5.466 to 5.479 mm

Valve stem-to-guide clearance
Inlet . . . . 0.025 to 0.060 mm
Exhaust . . . . 0.030 to 0.065 mm
Maximum . . . . 0.20 mm

Valve spring
Out-of-square limit
    1.3 litre . . . . 1.50 mm
    1.5 litre . . . . N/A
    1.6 litre
        Inlet . . . . 1.61 mm
        Exhaust . . . . 1.50 mm
    1.8 litre . . . . 1.62 mm
Free length
    1.3 litre . . . . 38.0 mm minimum
    1.5 litre . . . . 39.5 mm minimum
    1.6 litre
        Inlet . . . . 39.0 mm minimum
        Exhaust . . . . 38.0 mm minimum
    1.8 litre . . . . 39.5 mm minimum

Engine block

Warpage limit . . . . 0.15 mm
Cylinder bore diameter
    1.3 litre . . . . 71.006 to 71.013 mm
        Oversize 1 . . . . 71.256 to 71.263 mm
        Oversize 2 . . . . 71.506 to 71.513 mm
        Oversize 3 . . . . 71.756 to 71.763 mm
        Oversize 4 . . . . 72.006 to 72.013 mm
    1.5 litre . . . . 75.281 to 75.300 mm
        Oversize 1 . . . . 75.552 to 75.568 mm
        Oversize 2 . . . . 75.801 to 75.816 mm
    1.6 litre . . . . 78.006 to 78.013 mm
        Oversize 1 . . . . 78.256 to 78.263 mm
        Oversize 2 . . . . 78.506 to 78.513 mm
    1.8 litre . . . . 83.006 to 83.013 mm
        Oversize 1 . . . . 83.256 to 83.263 mm
        Oversize 2 . . . . 83.506 to 83.513 mm

Crankshaft and connecting rods

Small-end bearing diameter
1.3 litre	19.943 to 19.961 mm
1.5 litre	20.003 to 20.014 mm
1.6 litre	19.943 to 19.961 mm
1.8 litre	20.003 to 20.014 mm

Big-end bearing journal
Diameter
1.3 litre and 1.5 litre	39.940 to 39.956 mm
1.6 litre and 1.8 litre	44.940 to 44.956 mm
Out-of-round	0.05 mm

Oil clearance
Standard	0.028 to 0.068 mm
Service limit	0.10 mm
Undersize bearing inserts	**Undersize**

Journal diameter

1.3 litre and 1.5 litre
39.690 to 39.706 mm	0.25 mm
39.440 to 39.456 mm	0.50 mm
39.190 to 39.206 mm	0.75 mm

1.6 litre and 1.8 litre
44.690 to 44.706 mm	0.25 mm
44.440 to 44.456 mm	0.50 mm
44.190 to 44.206 mm	0.75 mm

Main bearing journal
Diameter	49.938 to 49.956 mm
Out-of-round	0.05 mm
Runout limit	0.04 mm

Oil clearance
Standard	0.018 to 0.036 mm
Service limit	0.10 mm
Undersize bearing inserts	**Undersize**

Journal diameter
49.704 to 49.708 mm	0.25 mm
49.454 to 49.458 mm	0.50 mm
49.204 to 49.208 mm	0.75 mm (not 1.6 litre)

Connecting rod side clearance
Standard	0.110 to 0.262 mm
Service limit	0.30 mm

Crankshaft endplay
Standard	0.080 to 0.282 mm
Service limit	0.30 mm
Thrust washer thickness	2.500 to 2.925 mm
Taper and out-of-round limits	0.019 mm

Pistons and rings

Piston diameter
1.3 litre	70.954 to 70.974 mm
Oversize 1	71.211 to 71.217 mm
Oversize 2	71.461 to 71.467 mm
Oversize 3	71.711 to 71.717 mm
Oversize 4	71.961 to 71.967 mm
1.5 litre	75.265 to 75.281 mm
Oversize 1	75.514 to 75.531 mm
Oversize 2	75.763 to 75.781 mm
1.6 litre	77.954 to 77.974 mm
Oversize 1	78.211 to 78.217 mm
Oversize 2	78.461 to 78.467 mm
1.8 litre	82.954 to 82.974 mm
Oversize 1	83.211 to 83.217 mm
Oversize 2	83.461 to 83.467 mm

Piston-to-bore clearance
Standard	0.039 to 0.052 mm
Service limit	0.15 mm

Pistons and rings (continued)

Piston ring end gap
Top compression ring	0.15 to 0.30 mm
Middle compression ring	0.15 to 0.30 mm
Oil ring	0.20 to 0.70 mm
Service limit	1.0 mm

Piston ring groove clearance
1.3 litre
Top compression ring	0.030 to 0.65 mm
Middle compression ring	0.030 to 0.070 mm
Service limit	0.15 mm

1.5 litre
Top compression ring	0.036 to 0.64 mm
Middle compression ring	0.030 to 0.64 mm
Service limit	0.15 mm

1.6 litre
Top compression ring	0.030 to 0.070 mm
Middle compression ring	0.030 to 0.070 mm
Service limit	0.15 mm

1.8 litre
Top compression ring	0.030 to 0.65 mm
Middle compression ring	0.030 to 0.070 mm
Service limit	0.15 mm

Torque specifications*

	lbf ft	Nm
Connecting rod cap nuts/bolts		
1.3 litre and 1.5 litre	22 to 25	30 to 34
1.6 litre	35 to 38	47 to 52
1.8 litre	37 to 40	50 to 54
Main bearing cap bolts	40 to 43	54 to 58
Oil jets	9 to 13	12 to 18

*Note: Refer to Part A for additional torque specifications.

1 General information

Included in this portion of Chapter 2 are the general overhaul procedures for the cylinder head(s) and internal engine components.

The information ranges from advice concerning preparation for an overhaul and the purchase of renewal parts to detailed, step-by-step procedures covering removal and refitting of internal engine components and the inspection of parts.

The following Sections have been written based on the assumption that the engine has been removed from the vehicle. For information concerning in-vehicle engine repair, as well as removal and refitting of the external components necessary for the overhaul, see Chapter 2A and Section 8 of this Chapter.

The Specifications included in this Part are only those necessary for the inspection and overhaul procedures which follow. Refer to Chapter 2, Part A for additional Specifications.

2 Engine overhaul - general information

It's not always easy to determine when, or if, an engine should be completely overhauled, as a number of factors must be considered.

High mileage is not necessarily an indication that an overhaul is needed, while low mileage doesn't preclude the need for an overhaul. Frequency of servicing is probably the most important consideration. An engine that's had regular and frequent oil and filter changes, as well as other required maintenance, will most likely give many thousands of miles of reliable service. Conversely, a neglected engine may require an overhaul very early in its life.

Excessive oil consumption is an indication that piston rings, valve seals and/or valve guides are in need of attention. Make sure that oil leaks aren't responsible before deciding that the rings and/or guides are faulty. Perform a cylinder compression check to determine the extent of the work required (see Section 4). Also check the vacuum readings under various conditions (see Section 3).

Check the oil pressure with a gauge installed in place of the oil pressure sender unit (see illustrations) and compare it to this Chapter's Specifications. If it's extremely low, the bearings and/or oil pump are probably worn out.

Loss of power, rough running, knocking or metallic engine noises, excessive valve train noise and high fuel consumption may also point to the need for an overhaul, especially if they're all present at the same time. If a complete service doesn't remedy the

2.4a Oil pressure can be checked by removing the sender unit and fitting a pressure gauge in its place

2.4b The oil pressure sender unit (arrowed) is located near the oil filter

situation, major mechanical work is the only solution.

An engine overhaul involves restoring the internal parts to the specifications of a new engine. During an overhaul, the piston rings are replaced and the cylinder walls are reconditioned (re-bored and/or honed). If a re-bore is done by an automotive machine workshop, new oversize pistons will also be installed. The main bearings, big-end bearings and camshaft bearings are generally replaced with new ones and, if necessary, the crankshaft may be reground to restore the journals. Generally, the valves are serviced as well, since they're usually in less-than-perfect condition at this point. While the engine is being overhauled, other components, such as the distributor, starter and alternator, can be rebuilt as well. The end result should be a like new engine that will give many trouble free miles. **Note:** *Critical cooling system components such as the hoses, drivebelts, thermostat and water pump should be replaced with new parts when an engine is overhauled. The radiator should be checked carefully to ensure that it isn't clogged or leaking (see Chapter 3). If you purchase a rebuilt engine or short block, some rebuilders will not warranty their engines unless the radiator has been professionally flushed. Also, we don't recommend overhauling the oil pump - always refit a new one when an engine is rebuilt.*

Before beginning the engine overhaul, read through the entire procedure to familiarise yourself with the scope and requirements of the job. Overhauling an engine isn't difficult, but it is time-consuming. Plan on the vehicle being tied up for a minimum of two weeks, especially if parts must be taken to an automotive machine workshop for repair or reconditioning. Check on availability of parts and make sure that any necessary special tools and equipment are obtained in advance. Most work can be done with typical hand tools, although a number of precision measuring tools are required for inspecting parts to determine if they must be replaced. Often an automotive machine workshop will handle the inspection of parts and offer advice concerning reconditioning and

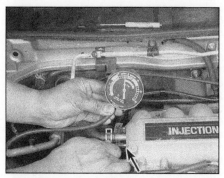

3.4 The vacuum gauge is easily attached to this unused port (arrowed) on the inlet manifold

renewal. **Note:** *Always wait until the engine has been completely dismantled and all components, especially the engine block, have been inspected before deciding what service and repair operations must be performed by an automotive machine workshop.* Since the block's condition will be the major factor to consider when determining whether to overhaul the original engine or buy a rebuilt one, never purchase parts or have machine work done on other components until the block has been thoroughly inspected. As a general rule, time is the primary cost of an overhaul, so it doesn't pay to refit worn or substandard parts.

As a final note, to ensure maximum life and minimum trouble from a rebuilt engine, everything must be assembled with care in a spotlessly-clean environment.

3 Vacuum gauge diagnostic checks

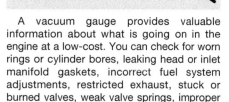

A vacuum gauge provides valuable information about what is going on in the engine at a low-cost. You can check for worn rings or cylinder bores, leaking head or inlet manifold gaskets, incorrect fuel system adjustments, restricted exhaust, stuck or burned valves, weak valve springs, improper ignition or valve timing and ignition problems.

Unfortunately, vacuum gauge readings are easy to misinterpret, so they should be used in conjunction with other tests to confirm the diagnosis.

Both the absolute readings and the rate of needle movement are important for accurate interpretation. Most gauges measure vacuum in inches of mercury (in-Hg). As vacuum increases (or atmospheric pressure decreases), the reading will increase. Also, for every 1000 foot increase in elevation above sea level, the gauge readings will decrease about one inch of mercury.

Connect the vacuum gauge directly to inlet manifold vacuum, not to ported (above the throttle plate) vacuum **(see illustration)**. Be sure no hoses are left disconnected during the test or false readings will result.

Before you begin the test, allow the engine to warm up completely. Chock the wheels and set the handbrake. With the transmission in neutral (or Park, on automatics), start the engine and allow it to run at normal idle speed.

⚠ **Warning: Carefully inspect the fan blades for cracks or damage before starting the engine. Keep your hands and the vacuum tester clear of the fan and do not stand in front of the vehicle or in line with the fan when the engine is running.**

Read the vacuum gauge; an average, healthy engine should normally produce between 17 and 22 inches of vacuum with a fairly steady needle.

Refer to the following vacuum gauge readings and what they indicate about the engines condition:

1 A low steady reading usually indicates a leaking gasket between the inlet manifold and carburettor or throttle body, a leaky vacuum hose, late ignition timing or incorrect camshaft timing. Check ignition timing with a timing light and eliminate all other possible causes, utilising the tests provided in this Chapter before you remove the timing belt cover to check the timing marks.

2 If the reading is three to eight inches below normal and it fluctuates at that low reading, suspect an inlet manifold gasket leak at an inlet port or a faulty injector.

3 If the needle has regular drops of about two to four inches at a steady rate the valves are probably leaking. Perform a compression or leak-down test to confirm this.

4 An irregular drop or down-flick of the needle can be caused by a sticking valve or an ignition misfire. Perform a compression or leak-down test and check the spark plugs.

5 A rapid vibration of about four in-Hg vibration at idle combined with exhaust smoke indicates worn valve guides. Perform a leak-down test to confirm this. If the rapid vibration occurs with an increase in engine speed, check for a leaking inlet manifold gasket or head gasket, weak valve springs, burned valves or ignition misfire.

6 A slight fluctuation, say one inch up and down, may mean ignition problems. Check all the usual servicing items and, if necessary, run the engine on an ignition analyser.

7 If there is a large fluctuation, perform a compression or leak-down test to look for a weak or dead cylinder or a blown head gasket.

8 If the needle moves slowly through a wide range, check for a clogged PCV system, incorrect idle fuel mixture, throttle body or inlet manifold gasket leaks.

9 Check for a slow return after revving the engine by quickly snapping the throttle open until the engine reaches about 2500 rpm and let it shut. Normally the reading should drop to near zero, rise above normal idle reading (about 5 in-Hg over) and then return to the previous idle reading. If the vacuum returns slowly and doesn't peak when the throttle is snapped shut, the rings may be worn. If there is a long delay, look for a restricted exhaust system (often the silencer or catalytic converter). An easy way to check this is to temporarily disconnect the exhaust ahead of the suspected part and redo the test.

4 Compression check

1 A compression check will tell you what mechanical condition the upper end (pistons, rings, valves, head gasket) of your engine is in. Specifically, it can tell you if the compression is down due to leakage caused by worn piston rings, defective valves and seats or a blown head gasket. **Note:** *The engine must be at normal operating temperature and the battery must be fully charged for this check.*

2 Begin by cleaning the area around the spark plugs before you remove them (compressed air should be used, if available, otherwise a small brush or even a bicycle tyre pump will work). The idea is to prevent dirt from getting into the cylinders as the compression check is being done.

3 Remove all of the spark plugs from the engine (see Chapter 1).

4 Chock the throttle wide open.

5 Detach the coil wire from the centre of the distributor cap and earth it on the engine block. Use a jumper wire with alligator clips on each end to ensure a good earth. It is also a good idea to pull the EFI fuse from the fuse panel to disable the fuel pump during the compression test.

6 Fit the compression gauge in the spark plug hole **(see illustration)**. A compression gauge with a threaded fitting for the spark plug hole is preferred over the type that requires hand pressure to maintain the seal - be sure to block open the throttle valve as far as possible during the compression check!

7 Crank the engine over at least seven compression strokes and watch the gauge. The compression should build up quickly in a healthy engine. Low compression on the first stroke, followed by gradually increasing pressure on successive strokes, indicates worn piston rings. A low compression reading on the first stroke, which doesn't build up during successive strokes, indicates leaking valves or a blown head gasket (a cracked head could also be the cause). Deposits on the undersides of the valve heads can also cause low compression. Record the highest gauge reading obtained.

8 Repeat the procedure for the remaining cylinders and compare the results to this Chapter's Specifications.

9 Add some engine oil (about three squirts from a plunger-type oil can) to each cylinder, through the spark plug hole, and repeat the test.

10 If the compression increases after the oil is added, the piston rings are definitely worn.

4.6 A compression gauge with a threaded fitting for the spark plug hole

If the compression doesn't increase significantly, the leakage is occurring at the valves or head gasket. Leakage past the valves may be caused by burned valve seats and/or faces or warped, cracked or bent valves.

11 If two adjacent cylinders have equally low compression, there's a strong possibility that the head gasket between them is blown. The appearance of coolant in the combustion chambers or the crankcase would verify this condition.

12 If one cylinder is 20-percent lower than the others, and the engine has a slightly rough idle, a worn exhaust lobe on the camshaft could be the cause.

13 If the compression is unusually high, the combustion chambers are probably coated with carbon deposits. If that's the case, the cylinder head should be removed and decarbonised.

14 If compression is way down or varies greatly between cylinders, it would be a good idea to have a leak-down test performed by an automotive repair workshop. This test will pinpoint exactly where the leakage is occurring and how severe it is.

5 Engine removal - methods and precautions

If you've decided that an engine must be removed for overhaul or major repair work, several preliminary steps should be taken.

Locating a suitable place to work is extremely important. Adequate work space, along with storage space for the vehicle, will be needed. If a workshop or garage isn't available, at the very least a flat, level, clean work surface made of concrete or asphalt is required.

Cleaning the engine compartment and engine before beginning the removal procedure will help keep tools clean and organised.

An engine hoist or A-frame will also be necessary. Make sure the equipment is rated in excess of the combined weight of the engine and transmission. Safety is of primary importance, considering the potential hazards involved in lifting the engine out of the vehicle.

If the engine is being removed by a novice, a helper should be available. Advice and aid from someone more experienced would also be helpful. There are many instances when one person cannot simultaneously perform all of the operations required when lifting the engine out of the vehicle.

Plan the operation ahead of time. Arrange for or obtain all of the tools and equipment you'll need prior to beginning the job. Some of the equipment necessary to perform engine removal and refitting safely and with relative ease are (in addition to an engine hoist) a heavy duty trolley jack, complete sets of

spanners and sockets as described in the rear of this manual, wooden blocks and plenty of rags and cleaning solvent for mopping up spilled oil, coolant and petrol. If the hoist must be rented, make sure that you arrange for it in advance and perform all of the operations possible without it beforehand. This will save you money and time.

Plan for the vehicle to be out of use for quite a while. A machine workshop will be required to perform some of the work which the do-it-yourselfer can't accomplish without special equipment. These shops often have a busy schedule, so it would be a good idea to consult them before removing the engine in order to accurately estimate the amount of time required to rebuild or repair components that may need work.

Always be extremely careful when removing and refitting the engine. Serious injury can result from careless actions. Plan ahead, take your time and a job of this nature, although major, can be accomplished successfully.

6 Engine - removal and refitting

Note: *Read through the entire Section before beginning this procedure. The factory recommends removing the engine and transmission from the top as a unit, then separating the engine from the transmission on the workshop floor.*

Note: *The following sequence for engine removal and renewal can be utilised for all engines covered in this manual. The paragraphs may be varied to accommodate combinations of accessories.*

Removal

 Warning: Some models are equipped with airbags. The airbag is armed and can inflate anytime the battery is connected. To prevent accidental deployment (and possible injury), turn the ignition key to LOCK and disconnect the negative battery cable whenever working near airbag components. After the battery is disconnected, wait at least two minutes before beginning work (the system has a back-up capacitor that must fully discharge). See Chapter 12 for more information.

1 Relieve the fuel system pressure (see Chapter 4).

2 Disconnect the negative cable from the battery.

Caution: If the stereo in your vehicle is equipped with an anti-theft system, make sure you have the correct activation code before disconnecting the battery.

3 Place protective covers on the wings and cowl and remove the bonnet (see Chapter 11).

4 Raise the vehicle and support it securely on axle stands.

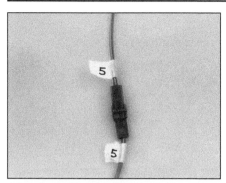

6.7 Label both ends of each wire and hose before disconnecting it

6.24 Attach the engine hoist

6.25 Lower the engine outside of the vehicle, and attach the engine to a suitable workstand

5 Drain the cooling system, engine oil, transmission oil and remove the drivebelts (see Chapter 1).

6 Remove front wheels.

7 Clearly label, then disconnect all vacuum lines, coolant and emissions hoses, wiring harness connectors, earth straps and fuel lines. Masking tape and/or a touch-up paint applicator work well for marking items **(see illustration)**. Take instant photos or sketch the locations of components and brackets.

8 Remove the air cleaner housing assembly and the resonance chamber (see Chapter 4).

9 Remove the engine undercover to provide access to the bottom of the engine (see Chapter 2A).

10 Remove the battery bracket, the battery cover, the battery, the battery carrier and the battery duct.

11 Disconnect the accelerator cable.

12 Remove the windscreen washer tank and coolant reservoir tank.

13 Disconnect the heater hoses.

14 Remove the cooling fan(s), the radiator hoses and the radiator (see Chapter 3)

15 Release the residual fuel pressure in the tank by removing the fuel cap, then detach the fuel lines connecting the engine to the chassis (see Chapter 4). Plug or cap all open fittings.

16 On power steering-equipped vehicles, unbolt the power steering pump. If clearance allows, tie the pump aside without disconnecting the hoses. If necessary, remove the pump (see Chapter 10).

17 On air-conditioned models, unbolt the compressor and set it aside. **Do not** disconnect the refrigerant hoses. **Note:** *Wire the compressor out of the way with a coat hanger, don't let the compressor hang on the hoses.*

18 Disconnect the throttle linkage, transmission Throttle Valve (TV) linkage, speedometer cable, and speed control cable, if equipped, from the engine (see Chapter 4).

19 Disconnect the clutch release cylinder, the shift control rod and cable and the extension bar (see Chapter 8).

20 Disconnect the front exhaust pipe, the anti-roll bar, the tie-rod end and the driveshaft (see Chapter 10).

21 Attach a lifting sling to the engine. Position a hoist and connect the sling to it. Take up the slack until there is slight tension on the hoist.

22 Recheck to be sure nothing except the mounts are still connecting the engine/transmission to the vehicle. Disconnect and label anything still remaining.

23 Support the transmission with a trolley jack. Place a block of wood on the jack head to prevent damage to the transmission. Remove the dynamic damper, the mount brackets, and the engine support bracket.

 Warning: Do not place any part of your body under the engine/transmission when it's supported only by a hoist or other lifting device.

24 Slowly lift the engine and transmission out of the vehicle **(see illustration)**. It may be necessary to lever the mounts away from the frame brackets.

25 Move the engine away from the vehicle and carefully lower the hoist until the engine can be set on the floor; or remove the transmission and flywheel/driveplate and mount the engine on an engine stand **(see illustration)**. **Note:** *On automatic transmission-equipped models, mark the front and rear spacer plates and keep them with the driveplate.*

26 On automatic transmission-equipped models, remove the torque converter-to-driveplate fasteners (see Chapter 7B) and push the converter back slightly into the bellhousing.

27 Remove the engine-to-transmission bolts and separate the engine from the transmission. The torque converter should remain in the automatic transmission.

Refitting

28 Check the engine/transmission mounts. If they're worn or damaged, renew them.

29 On manual transmission-equipped models, inspect the clutch components (see Chapter 8) and on automatic models inspect the converter seal and bushing.

30 On automatic transmission-equipped models, apply a dab of grease to the nose of the converter. Make sure the converter is completely seated on the transmission input

shaft and the front pump splines. To do this, push in on the converter and turn it, feeling for a 'clunk' - it may even 'clunk' more than once. If you feel nothing, the converter is already completely seated.

31 Carefully guide the transmission into place, following the procedure outlined in Chapter 7.

Caution: Do not use the bolts to force the engine and transmission into alignment. It may crack or damage major components.

32 Refit the engine-to-transmission bolts and tighten them to the torque listed in the Chapter 7 Specifications.

33 Attach the hoist to the engine and carefully lower the engine/transmission assembly into the engine compartment.

34 Refit the mount bolts and tighten them securely.

35 Refit the remaining components and fasteners in the reverse order of removal.

36 Add coolant, oil, power steering and transmission fluids as needed (see Chapter 1).

37 Run the engine and check for proper operation and leaks. Shut off the engine and recheck the fluid levels.

7 Engine rebuilding alternatives

The do-it-yourselfer is faced with a number of options when performing an engine overhaul. The decision to renew the engine block, piston/connecting rod assemblies and crankshaft depends on a number of factors, with the number one consideration being the condition of the block. Other considerations are cost, access to machine workshop facilities, parts availability, time required to complete the project and the extent of prior mechanical experience on the part of the do-it-yourselfer.

Some of the rebuilding alternatives include:

Individual parts - If the inspection procedures reveal that the engine block and most engine components are in reusable condition, purchasing individual parts may be the most economical alternative. The block, crankshaft and piston/connecting rod assemblies should all be inspected carefully. Even if the block shows little wear, the cylinder bores should be surface honed.

Short block - A short block consists of an engine block with a crankshaft and piston/connecting rod assemblies already installed. All new bearings are incorporated and all clearances will be correct. The existing camshafts, valve train components, cylinder head and external parts can be bolted to the short block with little or no machine workshop work necessary.

Long block - A long block consists of a short block plus an oil pump, sump, cylinder head, valve cover, camshaft and valve train components, timing sprockets and chain or gears and timing cover. All components are installed with new bearings, seals and gaskets incorporated throughout. The refitting of manifolds and external parts is all that's necessary.

Give careful thought to which alternative is best for you and discuss the situation with local automotive engineering shops, auto parts dealers and experienced rebuilders before ordering or purchasing renewal parts.

8 Engine overhaul - dismantling sequence

1 It's much easier to dismantle and work on the engine if it's mounted on a portable engine stand. A stand can often be rented quite cheaply from an equipment rental yard. Before the engine is mounted on a stand, the flywheel/driveplate and rear oil seal retainer should be removed from the engine.

2 If a stand isn't available, it's possible to dismantle the engine with it blocked up on the floor. Be extra careful not to tip or drop the engine when working without a stand.

3 If you're going to obtain a rebuilt engine, all external components must come off first, to be transferred to the renewal engine, just as they will if you're doing a complete engine overhaul yourself. These include:

Alternator and brackets
Emissions control components
Distributor, spark plug leads and spark plugs
Thermostat and housing cover
Water pump
EFI components
Inlet/exhaust manifolds
Oil filter
Engine mounts
Clutch and flywheel/driveplate
Engine rear plate

Note: *When removing the external components from the engine, pay close attention to details that may be helpful or important during refitting. Note the installed position of gaskets, seals, spacers, pins, brackets, washers, bolts and other small items.*

4 If you're obtaining an exchange short block, which consists of the engine block, crankshaft, pistons and connecting rods all assembled, then the cylinder head, sump and oil pump will have to be removed from your engine so that your short block can be returned to the rebuilder. See *Engine rebuilding alternatives* for additional information regarding the different possibilities to be considered.

5 If you're planning a complete overhaul, the engine must be dismantled and the internal components removed **(see illustration)**. The engine cylinder head is first removed in Chapter 2 Part A, then the following engine block components are dismantled:

Sump
Main bearing support plate (if fitted)
Front cover (oil pump assembly)
Rear cover
Piston/connecting rod assemblies
Crankshaft rear oil seal retainer
Crankshaft and main bearings

6 Before beginning the dismantling and overhaul procedures, make sure the following items are available. Also, refer to Section 21 for a list of tools and materials needed for engine reassembly.

8.5 Four-cylinder engine lower end components - exploded view

1 Crankshaft timing belt sprocket
2 Front cover (oil pump assembly)
3 Rear cover end plate
4 Rear cover
5 Sump
6 Oil pump pickup tube & screen
7 Main Bearing Support Plate (MBSP)
8 Connecting rod cap
9 Lower connecting rod bearing
10 Main bearing cap
11 Lower main bearing
12 Crankshaft
13 Upper main bearing
14 Thrust bearings
15 Oil jet assembly (one per cylinder)
16 Upper connecting rod bearing
17 Piston ring set
18 Piston pin clips
19 Piston gudgeon pin
20 Piston
21 Connecting rod
22 Cylinder block

Common hand tools
Small cardboard boxes or plastic bags for
storing parts
Gasket scraper
Ridge reamer
Micrometer
Telescoping gauges
Dial indicator set
Valve spring compressor
Cylinder surfacing hone
Piston ring groove-cleaning tool
Electric drill
Tap and die set
Wire brushes
Oil gallery brushes
Cleaning solvent

9 Cylinder head - dismantling

Note: *New and rebuilt cylinder heads are commonly available for most engines at dealerships and car accessory outlets. Due to the fact that some specialised tools are necessary for the dismantling and inspection procedures, and renewal parts may not be readily available, it may be more practical and economical for the home mechanic to purchase a renewal head rather than taking the time to dismantle, inspect and recondition the original.*

1 Cylinder head dismantling involves removal of the inlet and exhaust valves and related components. It's assumed that the valve adjusting mechanisms and camshafts have already been removed (see Part A as needed).
2 Before the valves are removed, arrange to label and store them, along with their related components, so they can be kept separate and reinstalled in the same valve guides they are removed from **(see illustration)**.
3 Compress the springs on the first valve with a spring compressor and remove the collets **(see illustrations)**. Carefully release the valve spring compressor and remove the retainer, the spring and the spring seat (if used). **Note:** *If your spring compressor does not have an end (such as the one shown) with cut-outs on*

the side, an adapter is available to use with a standard spring compressor.
Caution: Be very careful not to nick or otherwise damage the cylinder head when compressing the valve springs.
4 Pull the valve out of the head, then remove the oil seal from the guide. If the valve binds in the guide (won't pull through), push it back into the head and deburr the area around the collet groove with a fine file or whetstone.
5 Repeat the procedure for the remaining valves. Remember to keep all the parts for each valve together so they can be reinstalled in the same locations.
6 Once the valves and related components have been removed and stored in an organised manner, the head should be thoroughly cleaned and inspected. If a complete engine overhaul is being done, finish the engine dismantling procedures before beginning the cylinder head cleaning and inspection process.

10 Cylinder head - cleaning and inspection

1 Thorough cleaning of the cylinder head(s) and related valve train components, followed by a detailed inspection, will enable you to decide how much valve service work must be done during the engine overhaul. **Note:** *If the engine was severely overheated, the cylinder head is probably warped (see paragraph 12).*

Cleaning

2 Scrape all traces of old gasket material and sealing compound off the head gasket, inlet manifold and exhaust manifold sealing surfaces. Be very careful not to gouge the cylinder head. Special gasket-removal solvents that soften gaskets and make removal much easier are available at car accessory outlets.
3 Remove all built up scale from the coolant passages.
4 Run a stiff wire brush through the various holes to remove deposits that may have formed in them. If there are heavy rust

deposits in the water passages, the bare head should be professionally cleaned at a suitable workshop.
5 Run an appropriate-size tap into each of the threaded holes to remove corrosion and thread sealant that may be present. If compressed air is available, use it to clear the holes of debris produced by this operation.

 Warning: Wear eye protection when using compressed air!

6 Clean the exhaust and inlet manifold stud threads with a wire brush.
7 Clean the cylinder head with solvent and dry it thoroughly. Compressed air will speed the drying process and ensure that all holes and recessed areas are clean. **Note:** *Decarbonising chemicals are available and may prove very useful when cleaning cylinder heads and valve train components. They are very caustic and should be used with caution. Be sure to follow the instructions on the container.*
8 Clean the valve adjusters with solvent and dry them thoroughly. Compressed air will speed the drying process and can be used to clean out the oil passages. Don't mix them up during the cleaning process; keep them in a box with numbered compartments.
9 Clean all the valve springs, spring seats, collets and retainers with solvent and dry them thoroughly. Work on the components from one valve at a time to avoid mixing up the parts.
10 Scrape off any heavy deposits that may have formed on the valves, then use a motorised wire brush to remove deposits from the valve heads and stems. Again, make sure the valves don't get mixed up.

Inspection

Note: *Be sure to perform all of the following inspection procedures before concluding that engineering workshop work is required. Make a list of the items that need attention. The inspection procedures for the valve adjusters and camshafts, can be found in Part A.*

Cylinder head

11 Inspect the head very carefully for cracks, evidence of coolant leakage and other

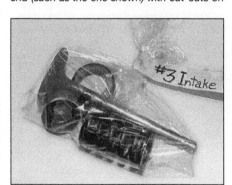

9.2 A small plastic bag, with an appropriate label, can be used to store the valve train components

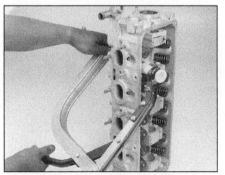

9.3a Compress the spring to expose the collets

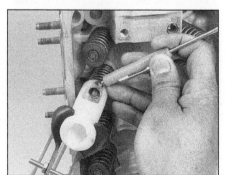

9.3b Remove the collets with a small magnetic screwdriver or needle-nose pliers

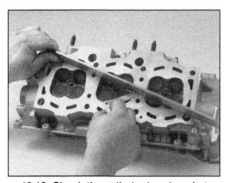

10.12 Check the cylinder head gasket surfaces for warpage (typical head shown)

10.14 A dial indicator can be used to determine the valve stem-to-guide clearance

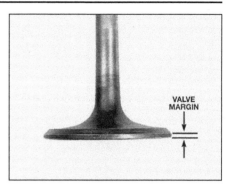

10.16 The margin width on each valve must be as specified

damage. If cracks are found, check with an automotive machine workshop concerning repair. If repair isn't possible, a new cylinder head should be obtained.

12 Using a straight-edge and feeler gauge, check the head gasket mating surface for warpage **(see illustration)**. If the warpage exceeds the limit found in this Chapter's Specifications, it can be resurfaced at an automotive machine workshop.

13 Examine the valve seats in each of the combustion chambers. If they're pitted, cracked or burned, the head will require valve service that's beyond the scope of the home mechanic.

14 Check the valve stem-to-guide clearance with a small hole gauge and micrometer, or a dial indicator. Check the valve stem movement with a dial indicator attached securely to the head **(see illustration)**. The valve must be in the guide and approximately 1.6 mm (0.063 in) off the seat. Move the entire valve stem between the guide walls; 'rocking the valve will give a false reading. The total valve stem movement indicated by the gauge needle must be noted, then divided by two to obtain the actual clearance value. If it exceeds the stem-to-guide clearance limit found in this Chapter's Specifications, the valve guides should be replaced. After this is done, if there's still some doubt regarding the condition of the valve guides they should be checked by an automotive engineering workshop (the cost should be minimal). **Note:** *Most home mechanics will not have a*

precision small bore gauge, but your local engineering workshop can measure the guides for you.

Valves

15 Carefully inspect each valve face for uneven wear, deformation, cracks, pits and burned areas. Check the valve stem for scuffing and galling and the neck for cracks. Rotate the valve and check for any obvious indication that it's bent. Look for pits and excessive wear on the end of the stem. The presence of any of these conditions indicates the need for valve service by an automotive engineering workshop.

16 Measure the margin width on each valve **(see illustration)**. Any valve with a margin narrower than that listed in this Chapter's Specifications will have to be replaced with a new one.

Valve components

17 Check each valve spring for wear (on the ends) and pits. Measure the free length and compare it to this Chapter's Specifications **(see illustration)**. Any springs that are shorter than specified have sagged and should not be re-used. The tension of all springs should be pressure checked with a special fixture before deciding that they're suitable for use in a rebuilt engine (take the springs to an automotive engineering workshop for this check).

18 Stand each spring on a flat surface and check it for squareness **(see illustration)**. If any of the springs are distorted or sagged, renew all of them with new parts.

19 Check the spring retainers and collets for obvious wear and cracks. Any questionable parts should be replaced with new ones, as extensive damage will occur if they fail during engine operation.

20 Any damaged or excessively worn parts must be replaced with new ones.

21 If the inspection process indicates that the valve components are in generally poor condition and worn beyond the limits specified, which is usually the case in an engine that's being overhauled, contact a suitable workshop, as some prefer you to reassemble the valves in the cylinder head for valve servicing.

11 Valves - servicing

1 Because of the complex nature of the job and the special tools and equipment needed, servicing of the valves, the valve seats and the valve guides, should be done by a professional.

2 The home mechanic can remove and dismantle the head, do the initial cleaning and inspection, then reassemble and deliver them to a dealer service department or an automotive machine workshop for the actual service work. Doing the inspection will enable you to see what condition the head and valve train components are in and will ensure that you know what work and new parts are required when dealing with an automotive engineering workshop.

3 The dealer service department, or automotive engineering workshop, will remove the valves and springs, recondition or renew the valves and valve seats, recondition the valve guides, check and renew the valve springs, spring retainers and collets (as necessary), renew the valve seals with new ones, reassemble the valve components and make sure the installed spring height is correct. The cylinder head gasket surface will also be resurfaced if it's warped.

4 After the work has been performed by a professional, the head will be in like new condition. When the head is returned, be sure

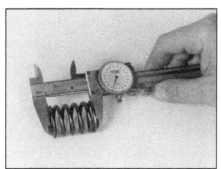

10.17 Measure the free length of each valve spring with a dial or vernier caliper

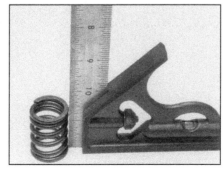

10.18 Check each valve spring for squareness

12.3 Gently tap the valve seals into place with a deep socket and hammer

to clean them again before refitting on the engine to remove any metal particles and abrasive grit that may still be present from the valve service or head resurfacing operations. Use compressed air, if available, to blow out all the oil holes and passages.

12 Cylinder head - reassembly

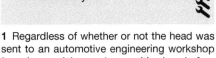

1 Regardless of whether or not the head was sent to an automotive engineering workshop for valve servicing, make sure it's clean before beginning reassembly. Note that there are several small core plugs in the head. These should be replaced whenever the engine is overhauled or the cylinder head is reconditioned (see Section 15 for the renewal procedure).
2 If the head was sent out for valve servicing, the valves and related components will already be in place. Begin the reassembly procedure with paragraph 8.
3 Refit new seals on each of the valve guides. **Note:** *Inlet and exhaust valves require different seals - DO NOT mix them up!* Gently tap each inlet valve seal into place until it's seated on the guide **(see illustration)**.
Caution: Don't hammer on the valve seals once they're seated or you may damage them. Don't twist or cock the seals during refitting or they won't seat properly on the valve stems.

13.3 Check the connecting rod side clearance with a feeler gauge

13.1 A ridge reamer is required to remove the ridge from the top of each cylinder

4 Beginning at one end of the head, lubricate and refit the first valve. Apply moly-base grease or clean engine oil to the valve stem.
5 Drop the spring seat or shim(s) over the valve guide and set the valve spring and retainer in place.
6 Compress the springs with a valve spring compressor and carefully refit the collets in the upper groove, then slowly release the compressor and make sure the collets seat properly.

Apply a small dab of grease to each collet to hold it in place if necessary.

7 Repeat the procedure for the remaining valves. Be sure to return the components to their original locations - don't mix them up!
8 Tap the end of the valve stem lightly two or three times with a plastic hammer to verify that the collets are all fully seated.

13.4 The connecting rods and caps should be marked to indicate which cylinder they're installed in

13 Pistons/connecting rods - removal

Note: *Prior to removing the piston/connecting rod assemblies, remove the cylinder head, the sump and the oil pump pick-up tube by referring to the appropriate Sections in Chapter 2A.*
1 Use your fingernail to feel if a ridge has formed at the upper limit of ring travel (about 6 mm/0.25 in down from the top of each cylinder). If carbon deposits or cylinder wear have produced ridges, they must be completely removed with a special tool **(see illustration)**. Follow the manufacturer's instructions provided with the tool. Failure to remove the ridges before attempting to remove the piston/connecting rod assemblies may result in piston damage.
2 After the cylinder ridges have been removed, turn the engine upside-down so the crankshaft is facing up.
3 Before the connecting rods are removed, check the side clearance with feeler gauges. Slide them between the first connecting rod and the crankshaft throw until the play is removed **(see illustration)**. The side clearance is equal to the thickness of the feeler gauge(s). If the side clearance exceeds the specified service limit, new connecting rods will be required. If new rods (or a new crankshaft) are installed, the side clearance may fall under the standard minimum (if it does, the rods will have to be machined to restore it - consult an automotive engineering workshop for advice if necessary). Repeat the procedure for the remaining connecting rods.
4 Check the connecting rods and caps for identification marks. If they aren't plainly marked, use a small centre punch to make the appropriate number of indentations on each rod and cap (1, 2, 3, etc., depending on the cylinder they're associated with) **(see illustration)**.
5 Loosen each of the connecting rod cap nuts 1/2-turn at a time until they can be removed by hand. Remove the number one connecting rod cap and bearing insert. Don't drop the bearing insert out of the cap.
6 Slip a short length of plastic or rubber hose over each connecting rod cap bolt to protect the crankshaft journal and cylinder wall as the piston is removed **(see illustration)**.

13.6 Prevent damage to the crankshaft journals and cylinder walls with sections of hose

7 Remove the bearing insert and push the connecting rod/piston assembly out through the top of the engine. Use a wooden hammer handle to push on the upper bearing surface in the connecting rod. If resistance is felt, double-check to make sure that all of the ridge was removed from the cylinder.

8 Repeat the procedure for the remaining cylinders. **Note:** *Turn the crankshaft as needed to put the rod to be removed close to parallel with the cylinder bore, i.e. don't try to drive it out while at a large angle to the bore.*

9 After removal, reassemble the connecting rod caps and bearing inserts in their respective connecting rods and refit the cap nuts/bolts finger tight. Leaving the old bearing inserts in place until reassembly will help prevent the connecting rod bearing surfaces from being accidentally nicked or gouged.

10 Don't separate the pistons from the connecting rods (see Section 18 for additional information).

14 Crankshaft - removal

Note: *The crankshaft can be removed only after the engine has been removed from the vehicle. It's assumed that the flywheel or driveplate, crankshaft sprocket, timing belt, sump, oil pick-up tube, oil pump and piston/connecting rod assemblies have already been removed. The rear main oil seal and retainer must be removed from the block before proceeding with crankshaft removal.*

1 Before the crankshaft is removed, check the endplay. Mount a dial indicator with the stem in line with the crankshaft and touching end of the crank **(see illustration)**.

2 Push the crankshaft all the way to the rear and zero the dial indicator. Next, lever the crankshaft to the front as far as possible and check the reading on the dial indicator. The distance that it moves is the endplay. If it's

14.1 Checking crankshaft endplay with a dial indicator

greater than specified, check the crankshaft thrust surfaces for wear. If no wear is evident, new thrust washers should correct the endplay.

3 If a dial indicator is not available, feeler gauges can be used. Gently lever or push the crankshaft all the way to the front of the engine. Slip feeler gauges between the crankshaft and the front face of the number 4 (thrust) main bearing to determine the clearance **(see illustration)**. **Note**: *Not all engines have the thrust washers at number 4 main bearing. If they are in a different location, measure the endplay there. If it's greater than specified, check the crankshaft thrust surfaces for wear. If no wear is evident, new thrust washers should correct the endplay. Make a note of the thrust washer location.*

4 Check the main bearing caps to see if they're marked to indicate their locations. They should be numbered consecutively from the front of the engine to the rear. If they aren't, mark them with number stamping dies or a centre punch. Main bearing caps generally have a cast-in arrow, which points to the front of the engine. Loosen the main bearing cap bolts 1/4-turn at a time each, in the reverse order of the recommended tightening sequence **(see illustration 23.12)**, until they can be removed by hand.

5 Gently tap the caps with a soft-face

14.3 Checking crankshaft endplay with a feeler gauge

hammer, then separate them from the engine block. Try not to drop the bearing inserts if they come out with the caps.

6 Carefully lift the crankshaft out of the engine. It may be a good idea to have an assistant available, since the crankshaft is quite heavy. With the bearing inserts in place in the engine block and main bearing caps or cap assembly, return the caps to their respective locations on the engine block and tighten the bolts finger tight.

15 Engine block - cleaning

Caution: The core plugs may be difficult or impossible to retrieve if they're driven completely into the block coolant passages.

1 Using the blunt end of a punch, tap on the outer edge of the core plug to turn the plug sideways in the bore. Then, using pliers, pull the core plug from the engine block **(see illustrations)**.

2 Using a gasket scraper, remove all traces of gasket material from the engine block. Be very careful not to nick or gouge the gasket sealing surfaces.

3 Remove the main bearing caps or cap

15.1a A hammer and a large punch can be used to knock the core plugs sideways in their bores

15.1b Pull the core plugs from the block with pliers

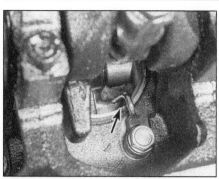

15.6 After the block is returned, clean all oil holes, oil galleries and oil jets (arrowed)

15.8 All bolt holes in the block should be cleaned and restored with a tap

15.10 A large socket on an extension can be used to drive the new core plugs into the bores

assembly and separate the bearing inserts from the caps and the engine block. Tag the bearings, indicating which cylinder they were removed from and whether they were in the cap or the block, then set them aside.

4 Remove all of the threaded oil gallery plugs from the block. The plugs are usually very tight - they may have to be drilled out and the holes retapped. Use new plugs when the engine is reassembled.

5 If the engine is extremely dirty, it should be taken to an automotive engineering workshop to be steam cleaned.

6 After the block is returned, clean all oil holes, oil galleries, and oil jets, where fitted **(see illustration)** one more time. Brushes specifically designed for this purpose are available at most car accessory outlets. Flush the passages with warm water until the water runs clear, dry the block thoroughly and wipe all machined surfaces with a light, rust preventive oil. If you have access to compressed air, use it to speed the drying process and to blow out all the oil holes and galleries.

⚠️ *Warning: Wear eye protection when using compressed air!*

7 If the block is not extremely dirty or sludged up, you can do an adequate cleaning job with hot soapy water and a stiff brush. Take plenty of time and do a thorough job. Regardless of the cleaning method used, be sure to clean all oil holes and galleries very thoroughly, dry the

block completely and coat all machined surfaces with light oil.

8 The oil jet and the threaded holes in the block must be clean to ensure accurate torque readings during reassembly. Run the proper size tap into each of the holes to remove rust, corrosion, thread sealant or sludge and restore damaged threads **(see illustration)**. If possible, use compressed air to clear the holes of debris produced by this operation. Now is a good time to clean the threads on the head bolts and the main bearing cap bolts as well.

9 Refit the main bearing caps and tighten the bolts finger tight.

10 After coating the sealing surfaces of the new core plugs with suitable non-hardening sealant, refit them in the engine block **(see illustration)**. Make sure they are driven in straight and seated properly or leakage could result. Special tools are available for this purpose, but a large socket, with an outside diameter that will just slip into the core plug, a 1/2-inch drive extension and a hammer will work just as well.

11 Apply non-hardening sealant to the new oil gallery plugs and thread them into the holes in the block. Make sure they are tightened securely.

12 If the engine isn't going to be reassembled right away, cover it with a large plastic bag to keep it clean.

16 Engine block - inspection

1 Before the block is inspected, it should be cleaned as described in Section 15.

2 Visually check the block for cracks, rust and corrosion. Look for stripped threads in the threaded holes. It's also a good idea to have the block checked for hidden cracks by an automotive engineering workshop that has the special equipment to do this type of work, especially if the vehicle had a history of overheating or using coolant. If defects are found, have the block repaired, if possible, or replaced.

3 Check the cylinder bores for scuffing and scoring.

4 Check the cylinders for taper and out-of-round conditions as follows **(see illustrations)**:

5 Measure the diameter of each cylinder at the top (just under the ridge area), centre and bottom of the cylinder bore, parallel to the crankshaft axis.

6 Next, measure each cylinder's diameter at the same three locations perpendicular to the crankshaft axis.

7 The taper of each cylinder is the difference between the bore diameter at the top of the cylinder and the diameter at the bottom. The out-of-round specification of the cylinder bore is the difference between the parallel and

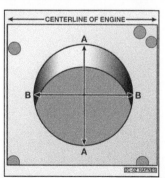

16.4a Measure cylinder diameter at a right angle to the centreline (A), and parallel to the centreline (B)

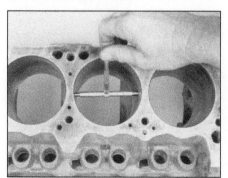

16.4b Measure cylinder diameter. Repeat until you're sure that the measurement is accurate (typical engine shown)

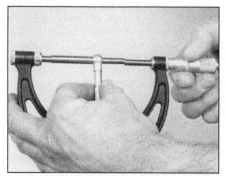

16.4c The gauge is then measured with a micrometer to determine the bore size

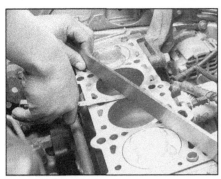

16.9 Check the block deck for distortion with a precision straight-edge and feeler gauges

17.3a A 'bottle brush' hone will produce better results if you have never done cylinder honing before

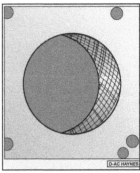

17.3b The cylinder hone should leave a smooth, crosshatch pattern

perpendicular readings. Compare your results to this Chapter's Specifications.

8 If the cylinder walls are badly scuffed or scored, or if they're out-of-round or tapered beyond the limits given in this Chapter's Specifications, have the engine block rebored and honed at an automotive engineering workshop. If a rebore is done, oversize pistons and rings will be required.

9 Using a precision straight-edge and feeler gauge, check the block deck (the surface that mates with the cylinder head) for distortion **(see illustration)**. If it's distorted beyond the specified limit, it can be resurfaced by an automotive engineering workshop.

10 If the cylinders are in reasonably good condition and not worn to the outside of the limits, and if the piston-to-cylinder clearances can be maintained properly, then they don't have to be rebored. Honing is all that's necessary (Section 17).

17 Cylinder honing

1 Prior to engine reassembly, the cylinder bores must be honed so the new piston rings will seat correctly and provide the best possible combustion chamber seal. **Note:** *If you don't have the tools or don't want to tackle the honing operation, most automotive engineering shops will do it for a reasonable fee.*

2 Before honing the cylinders, refit the main bearing caps or cap assembly (without bearing inserts) and tighten the bolts to the specified torque.

3 Two types of cylinder hones are commonly available - the flex hone or 'bottle brush' type and the more traditional surfacing hone with spring-loaded stones. Both will do the job, but for the less-experienced mechanic the 'bottle brush' hone will probably be easier to use. You'll also need some paraffin or honing oil, rags and an electric drill motor. The drill motor should be operated at a steady, slow speed. Proceed as follows:

a) *Mount the hone in the drill motor, compress the stones and slip it into the first cylinder* **(see illustration).**

 *Warning: **Be sure to wear safety goggles or a face shield!***

b) *Lubricate the cylinder with plenty of honing oil, turn on the drill and move the hone up-and-down in the cylinder at a pace that will produce a fine crosshatch pattern on the cylinder walls. Ideally, the crosshatch lines should intersect at approximately a 60-degree angle* **(see illustration).** *Be sure to use plenty of lubricant and don't take off any more material than is absolutely necessary to produce the desired finish.* **Note:** *Piston ring manufacturers may specify a smaller crosshatch angle than the traditional 60° - read and follow any instructions included with the new rings.*

c) *Don't withdraw the hone from the cylinder while it's running. Instead, turn off the drill and continue moving the hone up-and-down in the cylinder until it comes to a complete stop, then compress the stones and withdraw the hone. If you're using a 'bottle brush' type hone, stop the drill motor, then turn the chuck in the normal direction of rotation while withdrawing the hone from the cylinder.*

d) *Wipe the oil out of the cylinder and repeat the procedure for the remaining cylinders.*

4 After the honing job is complete, chamfer the top edges of the cylinder bores with a small file so the rings won't catch when the pistons are installed. Be very careful not to nick the cylinder walls with the end of the file.

5 The entire engine block must be washed again very thoroughly with warm, soapy water to remove all traces of the abrasive grit produced during the honing operation. **Note:** *The bores can be considered clean when a lint-free white cloth - dampened with clean engine oil - used to wipe them out doesn't pick up any more honing residue, which will show up as grey areas on the cloth. Be sure to run a brush through all oil holes and galleries and flush them with running water.*

6 After rinsing, dry the block and apply a coat of light rust preventive oil to all machined surfaces. Wrap the block in a plastic bag to keep it clean and set it aside until reassembly.

18 Pistons/connecting rods - inspection

1 Before the inspection process can be carried out, the piston/connecting rod assemblies must be cleaned and the original piston rings removed from the pistons. **Note:** *Always use new piston rings when the engine is reassembled.*

2 Using a piston ring refitting tool, carefully remove the rings from the pistons. Be careful not to nick or gouge the pistons in the process.

3 Scrape all traces of carbon from the top of the piston. A hand-held wire brush or a piece of fine emery cloth can be used once the majority of the deposits have been scraped away. **Do not**, under any circumstances, use a wire brush mounted in a drill motor to remove deposits from the pistons. The piston material is soft and may be eroded away by the wire brush.

4 Use a piston ring groove-cleaning tool to remove carbon deposits from the ring grooves. If a tool isn't available, a piece broken off the old ring will do the job. Be very careful to remove only the carbon deposits - don't remove any metal and do not nick or scratch the sides of the ring grooves **(see illustrations)**.

5 Once the deposits have been removed,

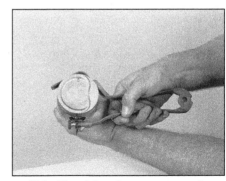

18.4a The piston ring grooves can be cleaned with a special tool, as shown here . . .

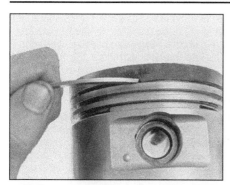

18.4b ... or a section of a broken ring

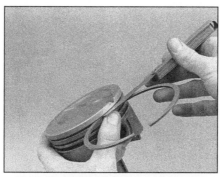

18.10 Check the ring groove clearance with a feeler gauge at several points around the groove

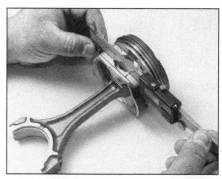

18.11 Measure the piston diameter at a 90-degree angle to the piston pin

clean the piston/rod assemblies with solvent and dry them with compressed air (if available). Make sure the oil return holes in the ring grooves and the oil hole in the lower end of each rod are clear.

6 Normal piston wear appears as even vertical wear on the piston thrust surfaces and slight looseness of the top ring in its groove. If the pistons and cylinder walls aren't damaged or worn excessively, and if the engine block is not rebored, new pistons won't be necessary. New piston rings, however, should always be used when an engine is rebuilt.

7 Carefully inspect each piston for cracks around the skirt, at the gudgeon pin bosses and at the ring lands.

8 Look for scoring and scuffing on the thrust faces of the skirt, holes in the piston crown and burned areas at the edge of the crown. If the skirt is scored or scuffed, the engine may have been suffering from overheating and/or abnormal combustion, which caused excessively high operating temperatures. The cooling and lubrication systems should be checked thoroughly. A hole in the piston crown is an indication that abnormal combustion (pre-ignition) was occurring. Burned areas at the edge of the piston crown are usually evidence of spark knock (detonation). If any of the above problems exist, the causes must be corrected or the damage will occur again. The causes may include inlet air leaks, incorrect air/fuel mixture, incorrect ignition timing and EGR system malfunctions.

9 Corrosion of the piston, in the form of small pits, indicates that coolant is leaking into the combustion chamber and/or the crankcase. Again, the cause must be corrected or the problem may persist in the rebuilt engine.

10 Measure the piston ring groove clearance by laying a new piston ring in each ring groove and slipping a feeler gauge in beside it **(see illustration)**. Check the clearance at three or four locations around each groove. Be sure to use the correct ring for each groove - they are different. If the clearance is greater than that listed in this Chapter's Specifications, new pistons will have to be used.

11 Check the piston-to-bore clearance by measuring the bore (see Section 16) and the piston diameter. Make sure the pistons and bores are correctly matched. Measure the piston across the skirt, at a 90-degree angle to the gudgeon pin **(see illustration)**. Subtract the piston diameter from the bore diameter to obtain the clearance. If it's greater than specified, the block will have to be rebored and new pistons and rings installed.

12 Check the piston-to-rod clearance by twisting the piston and rod in opposite directions. Any noticeable play indicates excessive wear, which must be corrected.

13 If the pistons must be removed from the connecting rods for any reason, the rods should be taken to an automotive engineering workshop, and also to be checked for bend and twist, since automotive engineering shops have special equipment for this purpose.

14 Check the connecting rods for cracks and other damage. Temporarily remove the rod caps, lift out the old bearing inserts, wipe the rod and cap bearing surfaces clean and inspect them for nicks, gouges and scratches. After checking the rods, renew the old bearings, slip the caps into place and tighten the nuts finger tight.

19 Crankshaft - inspection

1 Clean the crankshaft with solvent and dry it with compressed air (if available).

2 Check the main and connecting rod bearing journals for uneven wear, scoring, pits and cracks.

3 Remove all burrs from the crankshaft oil holes with a stone, file or scraper.

4 Clean the oil holes with a stiff brush and flush them with solvent.

5 Check the rest of the crankshaft for cracks and other damage. It should be magnafluxed to reveal hidden cracks - an automotive machine workshop will handle the procedure.

6 Using a micrometer, measure the diameter of the main and big-end journals and compare the results to this Chapter's Specifications **(see illustration)**. By measuring the diameter at a number of points around each journal's circumference, you'll be able to determine whether or not the journal is out-of-round. Take the measurement at each end of the journal, near the crank throws, to determine if the journal is tapered. Crankshaft runout should be checked also, but large V-blocks and a dial indicator are needed to do it correctly. If you don't have the equipment, have a engineering workshop check the runout.

7 If the crankshaft journals are damaged, tapered, out-of-round or worn beyond the limits given in the Specifications, have the crankshaft reground by an automotive engineering workshop. Be sure to use the correct size bearing inserts if the crankshaft is reconditioned.

8 Check the oil seal journals at each end of the crankshaft for wear and damage. If the seal has worn a groove in the journal, or if it's nicked or scratched, the new seal may leak when the engine is reassembled. In some cases, an automotive engineering workshop may be able to repair the journal by pressing on a thin sleeve. If repair isn't feasible, a new or different crankshaft should be installed.

9 Refer to Section 20 and examine the main and big-end bearing inserts.

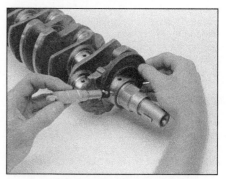

19.6 Measure the diameter of each crankshaft journal to detect taper and out-of-round conditions

20 Main and big-end bearings - inspection and selection

Inspection

1 Even though the main and big-end bearing inserts should be replaced with new ones during the engine overhaul, the old bearings should be retained for close examination, as they may reveal valuable information about the condition of the engine (see illustration).

2 Bearing failure occurs because of lack of lubrication, the presence of dirt or other foreign particles, overloading the engine and corrosion. Regardless of the cause of bearing failure, it must be corrected before the engine is reassembled to prevent it from happening again.

3 When examining the bearings, remove them from the engine block, the main bearing caps, the connecting rods and the rod caps and lay them out on a clean surface in the same general position as their location in the engine. This will enable you to match any bearing problems with the corresponding crankshaft journal.

4 Dirt and other foreign particles get into the engine in a variety of ways. It may be left in the engine during assembly, or it may pass through filters or the PCV system. It may get into the oil, and from there into the bearings. Metal chips from machining operations and normal engine wear are often present. Abrasives are sometimes left in engine components after reconditioning, especially when parts are not thoroughly cleaned using the proper cleaning methods. Whatever the source, these foreign objects often end up embedded in the soft bearing material and are easily recognised. Large particles will not embed in the bearing and will score or gouge the bearing and journal. The best prevention for this cause of bearing failure is to clean all parts thoroughly and keep everything spotlessly clean during engine assembly. Frequent and regular engine oil and filter changes are also recommended.

5 Lack of lubrication (or lubrication breakdown) has a number of interrelated causes. Excessive heat (which thins the oil), overloading (which squeezes the oil from the bearing face) and oil leakage or throw off (from excessive bearing clearances, worn oil pump or high engine speeds) all contribute to lubrication breakdown. Blocked oil passages, which usually are the result of misaligned oil holes in a bearing shell, will also oil starve a bearing and destroy it. When lack of lubrication is the cause of bearing failure, the bearing material is wiped or extruded from steel backing of the bearing. Temperatures may increase to the point where the steel backing turns blue from overheating.

6 Driving habits can have a definite effect on bearing life. Low speed operation in too high a

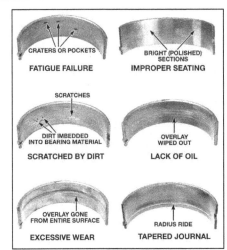

20.1 When inspecting the main and connecting rod bearings, look for these problems

gear puts very high loads on bearings, which tends to squeeze out the oil film. These loads cause the bearings to flex, which produces fine cracks in the bearing face (fatigue failure). Eventually the bearing material will loosen in pieces and tear away from the steel backing. Short trip driving leads to corrosion of bearings because insufficient engine heat is produced to drive off the condensed water and corrosive gases. These products collect in the engine oil, forming acid and sludge. As the oil is carried to the engine bearings, the acid attacks and corrodes the bearing material.

7 Incorrect bearing fitting during engine assembly will lead to bearing failure as well. Tight-fitting bearings leave insufficient bearing oil clearance and will result in oil starvation. Dirt or foreign particles trapped behind a bearing insert result in high spots on the bearing which lead to failure.

Selection

8 If the original bearings are worn or damaged, or if the oil clearances are incorrect (see Section 23 or 25), the following procedures should be used to select the correct new bearings for engine reassembly. However, if the crankshaft has been reground, new undersize bearings must be installed - the following procedure should not be used if undersize bearings are required! The automotive engineering workshop that reconditions the crankshaft will provide or help you select the correct size bearings. Regardless of how the bearing sizes are determined, use the oil clearance, measured with Plastigauge, as a guide to ensure the bearings are the right size.

Main bearings

9 If you need to use a standard size main bearing, fit one that is the same size as the original bearing listed in the specifications in

the front of this Chapter. If the journal diameter is less than the standard minimum, have a qualified engine engineering workshop grind the journals to match the undersize bearings. There are three different sizes of undersized main bearings.

Big-end bearings

10 If you need to use a standard size rod bearing, fit one that is the same size as the original bearing listed in the specifications in the from of this Chapter. If the journal diameter is less than the standard minimum, have a qualified engine engineering workshop grind the journals to match the undersize bearings. There are three different sizes of undersized rod bearings.

All bearings

11 Remember, the oil clearance is the final judge when selecting new bearing sizes. If you have any questions or are unsure which bearings to use, get help from a dealer parts or service department.

21 Engine overhaul - reassembly sequence

1 Before beginning engine reassembly, make sure you have all the necessary new parts, gaskets and seals as well as the following items on hand:

Common hand tools
A 1/2-inch drive torque wrench
Piston ring refitting tool
Piston ring compressor
Short lengths of rubber or plastic hose to fit over connecting rod bolts
Plastigauge
Feeler gauges
A fine-tooth file
New engine oil
Engine assembly lube or moly-base grease
Camshaft refitting lube
Gasket sealant
Thread locking compound

2 In order to save time and avoid problems, engine reassembly must be done in the following general order:

Piston rings (Part B)
Crankshaft and main bearings (Part B)
Piston/connecting rod assemblies (Part B)
Rear main (crankshaft) oil seal (Part B)
Cylinder head and DOHC valve adjusters components (Part A)
Camshaft(s) (Part A)
SOHC rocker gear (Part A)
Oil pump (Part A)
Timing belt and sprockets (Part A)
Timing belt covers (Part A)
Oil pick-up (Part A)
Sump (Part A)
Inlet and exhaust manifolds (Part A)
Valve cover (Part A)
Flywheel/driveplate (Part A)

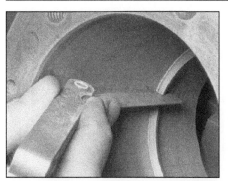

22.4 With the ring square in the cylinder, measure the end gap with a feeler gauge

22.9a Refit the spacer/expander in the oil control ring groove

22.9b DO NOT use a piston ring refitting tool when refitting the oil ring side rails

22 Piston rings - refitting

1 Before refitting the new piston rings, the ring end gaps must be checked. It's assumed that the piston ring groove clearance has been checked and verified correct (see Section 18).

2 Lay out the piston/connecting rod assemblies and the new ring sets so the ring sets will be matched with the same piston and cylinder during the end gap measurement and engine assembly.

3 Insert the top (number one) ring into the first cylinder and square it up with the cylinder walls by pushing it in with the top of the piston. The ring should be near the bottom of the cylinder, at the lower limit of ring travel.

4 To measure the end gap, slip feeler gauges between the ends of the ring until a gauge equal to the gap width is found **(see illustration)**. The feeler gauge should slide between the ring ends with a slight amount of drag. Compare the measurement to that found in this Chapter's Specifications. If the gap is larger or smaller than specified, double-check to make sure you have the correct rings before proceeding.

5 If the gap is too small, renew the rings - DO NOT file the ends to increase the clearance.

6 Excess end gap is not critical unless it's greater than the service limit listed in this Chapter's Specifications. Again, double-check to make sure you have the correct rings for your engine.

7 Repeat the procedure for each ring that will be installed in the first cylinder and for each ring in the remaining cylinders. Remember to keep rings, pistons and cylinders matched up.

8 Once the ring end gaps have been checked/corrected, the rings can be installed on the pistons.

9 The oil control ring (lowest one on the piston) is usually installed first. It's composed of three separate components. Slip the spacer/expander into the groove **(see illustration)**. If an anti-rotation tang is used, make sure it's inserted into the drilled hole in

the ring groove. Next, refit the lower side rail. Don't use a piston ring refitting tool on the oil ring side rails, as they may be damaged. Instead, place one end of the side rail into the groove between the spacer/expander and the ring land, hold it firmly in place and slide a finger around the piston while pushing the rail into the groove **(see illustration)**. Next, refit the upper side rail in the same manner.

10 After the three oil ring components have been installed, check to make sure that both the upper and lower side rails can be turned smoothly in the ring groove.

11 The number two (middle) ring is installed next. It's usually stamped with a mark which must face up, toward the top of the piston. **Note:** *Always follow the instructions printed on the ring package or box - different manufacturers may require different approaches. Do not mix up the top and middle rings, as they have different cross-sections.*

12 Use a piston ring refitting tool and make sure the ring's identification mark is facing the top of the piston, then slip the ring into the middle groove on the piston **(see illustration)**. Don't expand the ring any more than necessary to slide it over the piston.

13 Refit the number one (top) ring in the same manner. Make sure the mark is facing up. Be careful not to confuse the number one and number two rings.

14 Repeat the procedure for the remaining pistons and rings.

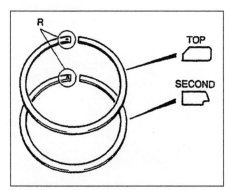

22.12 Refit the compression rings with a ring expander - the mark must face up

23 Crankshaft - refitting and main bearing oil clearance check

1 Crankshaft refitting is the first major step in engine reassembly. It's assumed at this point that the engine block and crankshaft have been cleaned, inspected and repaired or reconditioned.

2 Position the engine with the bottom facing up.

3 Remove the main bearing cap bolts and lift out the caps. Lay the caps out in the proper order.

4 If they're still in place, remove the old bearing inserts from the block and the main bearing caps. Wipe the main bearing surfaces of the block and caps with a clean, lint free cloth. They must be kept spotlessly clean!

Main bearing oil clearance check

5 Clean the backs of the new main bearing inserts and lay the bearing half with the oil groove in each main bearing in the block. Lay the other bearing half from each bearing set in the corresponding main bearing cap. Make sure the tab on each bearing insert fits into the recess in the block or cap. Also, the oil holes in the block must line up with the oil holes in the bearing insert.

Caution: Do not hammer the bearings into place and don't nick or gouge the bearing faces. No lubrication should be used at this time.

6 The thrust bearings (washers) must be installed in the number four bearing in the block. **Note:** *Not all engines have the thrust washers at number 4 main bearing, as noted in Section 14; install them where they came from.*

7 Clean the faces of the bearings in the block and the crankshaft main bearing journals with a clean, lint free cloth. Check or clean the oil holes in the crankshaft, as any dirt here can go only one way - straight through the new bearings.

8 Once you're certain the crankshaft is clean, carefully lay it in position in the main bearings.

23.10 Lay the Plastigauge strips on the main bearing journals, parallel to the crankshaft centreline

23.12 Main bearing cap bolt tightening sequence

23.14 Compare the width of the crushed Plastigauge to the scale on the envelope

9 Before the crankshaft can be permanently installed, the main bearing oil clearance must be checked.

10 Trim several pieces of the appropriate size Plastigauge (they must be slightly shorter than the width of the main bearings) and place one piece on each crankshaft main bearing journal, parallel with the journal axis **(see illustration)**.

11 Clean the faces of the bearings in the caps and refit the caps in their respective positions (don't mix them up) with the arrows pointing toward the front of the engine. Don't disturb the Plastigauge. Apply a light coat of oil to the bolt threads and the under-sides of the bolt heads, then refit them.

12 Following the recommended sequence **(see illustration)**, tighten the main bearing cap bolts, in three steps, to the torque listed in this Chapter's Specifications. Do not rotate the crankshaft at any time during this operation!

13 Remove the bolts and carefully lift off the main bearing caps. Keep them in order. Don't disturb the Plastigauge or rotate the crankshaft. If any of the main bearing caps are difficult to remove, tap them gently from side-to-side with a soft-face hammer to loosen them.

14 Compare the width of the crushed Plastigauge on each journal to the scale printed on the Plastigauge envelope to obtain the main bearing oil clearance **(see illustration)**. Check the Specifications to make sure it's correct.

15 If the clearance is not as specified, the bearing inserts may be the wrong size (which means different ones will be required - see Section 20). Before deciding that different inserts are needed, make sure that no dirt or oil was between the bearing inserts and the caps or block when the clearance was measured. If the Plastigauge is noticeably wider at one end than the other, the journal may be tapered (see Section 19).

16 Carefully scrape all traces of the Plastigauge material off the main bearing journals and/or the bearing faces. Don't nick or scratch the bearing faces.

Final crankshaft refitting

17 Carefully lift the crankshaft out of the engine. Clean the bearing faces in the block, then apply a thin, uniform layer of clean moly-base grease or engine assembly lube to each of the bearing surfaces. Coat the thrust washers as well. **Note:** *Be sure to refit the thrust washers.*

18 Lubricate the crankshaft surfaces that contact the oil seals with multi-purpose grease, engine assembly lube or clean engine oil.

19 Make sure the crankshaft journals are clean, then lay the crankshaft back in place in the block. Clean the faces of the bearings in the caps, then apply lubricant to them. Refit the caps in their respective positions with the arrows pointing toward the front of the engine.

20 Apply a light coat of oil to the bolt threads and the undersides of the bolt heads, then refit them. Tighten all main bearing cap bolts

to the torque listed in this Chapter's Specifications, following the recommended sequence **(see illustration 23.12)**.

21 Rotate the crankshaft a number of times by hand to check for any obvious binding.

22 Check the crankshaft endplay with a feeler gauge or a dial indicator as described in Section 14.

23 Refit a new rear main oil seal, then bolt the retainer to the block (see Section 24).

24 Rear main oil seal - fitting

1 The crankshaft must be installed first and the main bearing caps bolted in place, then the new seal should be installed in the retainer and the retainer bolted to the block.

2 Check the seal contact surface on the crankshaft very carefully for scratches and nicks that could damage the new seal lip and cause oil leaks. If the crankshaft is damaged, the only alternative is a new or different crankshaft.

3 The old seal can be removed from the retainer by driving it out with a hammer and punch **(see illustration)**. Be sure to note how far it's recessed into the bore before removing it; the new seal will have to be recessed an equal amount. Be very careful not to scratch or otherwise damage the bore in the retainer or oil leaks could develop.

4 Make sure the retainer is clean, then apply a thin coat of engine oil to the outer edge of the new seal. The seal must be pressed squarely into the bore, so hammering it into place isn't recommended. If you don't have access to a press, sandwich the housing and seal between two smooth pieces of wood and press the seal into place with the jaws of a large vice. The pieces of wood must be thick enough to distribute the force evenly around the entire circumference of the seal. Work slowly and make sure the seal enters the bore squarely.

5 As a last resort, the seal can be tapped into the retainer with a hammer using a block of wood to distribute the force evenly and make sure the seal is driven in squarely **(see illustration)**.

24.3 Drive out the old seal with a punch or screwdriver and hammer

24.5 Drive the new seal into the retainer with a wood block or a section of pipe

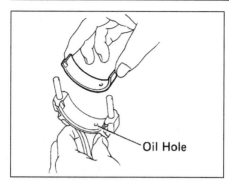

25.3 Align the oil hole in the bearing with the oil hole in the rod

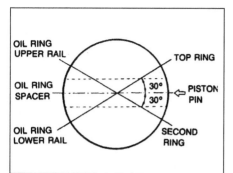

25.5 Ring end gap positions

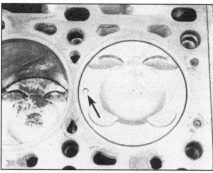

25.9 Check to assure the mark on the piston (arrowed) is towards the front of the engine

6 The seal lips must be lubricated with clean engine oil or multi-purpose grease before the seal/retainer is slipped over the crankshaft and bolted to the block, using a new gasket.

7 Tighten the bolts a little at a time to the torque listed in the Chapter 2A Specifications.

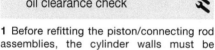

25 Pistons/connecting rods - refitting and big-end bearing oil clearance check

1 Before refitting the piston/connecting rod assemblies, the cylinder walls must be perfectly clean, the top edge of each cylinder must be chamfered, and the crankshaft must be in place.

2 Remove the cap from the end of the number one connecting rod (refer to the marks made during removal). Remove the original bearing inserts and wipe the bearing surfaces of the connecting rod and cap with a clean, lint-free cloth. They must be kept spotlessly clean.

Big-end rod bearing oil clearance check

3 Clean the back of the new upper bearing insert, then lay it in place in the connecting rod. Make sure the tab on the bearing fits into the recess in the rod so the oil holes line up **(see illustration)**. Don't hammer the bearing insert into place and be very careful not to nick or gouge the bearing face. Don't lubricate the bearing at this time.

4 Clean the back of the other bearing insert and fit it in the rod cap. Again, make sure the tab on the bearing fits into the recess in the cap, and don't apply any lubricant. It's critically important that the mating surfaces of the bearing and connecting rod are perfectly clean and oil free when they're assembled.

5 Position the piston ring gaps at staggered intervals around the piston **(see illustration)**.

6 Slip a section of plastic or rubber hose over each connecting rod cap bolt.

7 Lubricate the piston and rings with clean engine oil and attach a piston ring compressor to the piston. Leave the skirt protruding about 1/4-inch to guide the piston into the cylinder. The rings must be compressed until they're flush with the piston.

8 Rotate the crankshaft until the number one connecting rod journal is at BDC (bottom dead centre) and apply a coat of engine oil to the cylinder wall.

9 With the dimple on top of the piston **(see illustration)** facing the front of the engine, gently insert the piston/connecting rod assembly into the number one cylinder bore

and rest the bottom edge of the ring compressor on the engine block.

10 Tap the top edge of the ring compressor to make sure it's contacting the block around its entire circumference.

11 Gently tap on the top of the piston with the end of a wooden hammer handle **(see illustration)** while guiding the end of the connecting rod into place on the crankshaft journal. The piston rings may try to pop out of the ring compressor just before entering the cylinder bore, so keep some downward pressure on the ring compressor. Work slowly, and if any resistance is felt as the piston enters the cylinder, stop immediately. Find out what's stopping it before proceeding. *Caution: Do not, for any reason, force the piston into the cylinder - you might break a ring and/or the piston.*

12 Once the piston/connecting rod assembly is installed, the connecting rod bearing oil clearance must be checked before the rod cap is permanently bolted in place.

13 Cut a piece of the appropriate size Plastigauge slightly shorter than the width of the connecting rod bearing and lay it in place on the number one connecting rod journal, parallel with the journal axis **(see illustration)**.

14 Clean the connecting rod cap bearing face, remove the protective hoses from the

25.11 The piston can be driven (gently) into the cylinder bore with the end of a hammer handle (typical engine shown)

25.13 Lay the Plastigauge strips (arrowed) on each rod bearing journal, parallel to the crankshaft centreline

connecting rod bolts and refit the rod cap. Make sure the mating mark on the cap is on the same side as the mark on the connecting rod. Check the cap to make sure the front mark is facing the timing belt end of the engine.

15 Apply a light coat of oil to the undersides of the nuts, then refit and tighten them to the torque listed in this Chapter's Specifications, working up to it in three steps. Use a thin-wall socket to avoid erroneous torque readings that can result if the socket is wedged between the rod cap and nut. If the socket tends to wedge itself between the nut and the cap, lift it up slightly until it no longer contacts the cap. Do not rotate the crankshaft at any time during this operation.

16 Remove the nuts and detach the rod cap, being very careful not to disturb the Plastigauge.

17 Compare the width of the crushed Plastigauge to the scale printed on the Plastigauge envelope to obtain the oil clearance **(see illustration)**. Compare it to this Chapter's Specifications to make sure the clearance is correct.

18 If the clearance is not as specified, the bearing inserts may be the wrong size (which means different ones will be required). Before deciding that different inserts are needed, make sure that no dirt or oil was between the bearing inserts and the connecting rod or cap when the clearance was measured. Also, recheck the journal diameter. If the

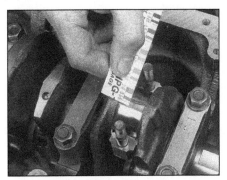

25.17 Measure the width of the crushed Plastigauge to determine the rod bearing oil clearance

Plastigauge was wider at one end than the other, the journal may be tapered (refer to Section 19).

Final connecting rod refitting

19 Carefully scrape all traces of the Plastigauge material off the rod journal and/or bearing face. Be very careful not to scratch the bearing, use your fingernail or the edge of a credit card to remove the Plastigauge.

20 Make sure the bearing faces are perfectly clean, then apply a uniform layer of clean moly-base grease or engine assembly lube to both of them. You'll have to push the piston higher into the cylinder to expose the face of the bearing insert in the connecting rod, be sure to slip the protective hoses over the rod bolts first.

21 Slide the connecting rod back into place on the journal, remove the protective hoses from the rod cap bolts, refit the rod cap and tighten the nuts to the torque listed in this Chapter's Specifications. Again, work up to the torque in three steps.

22 Repeat the entire procedure for the remaining pistons/connecting rods.

23 The important points to remember are:
a) *Keep the bearing inserts and the insides of the connecting rods and caps perfectly clean when assembling them.*
b) *Make sure you have the correct piston/rod assembly for each cylinder.*
c) *The dimple on the piston must face the front of the engine.*
d) *Lubricate the cylinder walls with clean oil.*
e) *Lubricate the bearing faces when refitting the rod caps after the oil clearance has been checked.*

24 After all the piston/connecting rod assemblies have been properly installed, rotate the crankshaft a number of times by hand to check for any obvious binding.

25 As a final step, the connecting rod side clearance must be checked. Refer to Section 13 for this procedure.

26 Compare the measured clearance to this Chapter's Specifications to make sure it's correct. If it was correct before dismantling and the original crankshaft and rods were reinstalled, it should still be right. If new rods or a new crankshaft were installed, the clearance may be inadequate. If so, the rods

will have to be removed and taken to an automotive engineering workshop for resizing.

26 Initial start-up and running-in after overhaul

⚠️ *Warning: Have a fire extinguisher handy when starting the engine for the first time.*

1 Once the engine has been installed in the vehicle, double-check the engine oil and coolant levels.

2 With the spark plugs out of the engine and the ignition system and fuel pump disabled (see Section 4), crank the engine until oil pressure registers on the gauge or the light goes out.

3 Refit the spark plugs, connect the plug leads and restore the ignition system and fuel pump functions (see Section 4).

4 Start the engine. It may take a few moments for the fuel system to build up pressure, but the engine should start without a great deal of effort.

5 After the engine starts, it should be allowed to warm up to normal operating temperature. While the engine is warming up, make a thorough check for fuel, oil and coolant leaks.

6 Turn the engine off and recheck the engine oil and coolant levels.

7 Drive the vehicle to an area with minimum traffic, accelerate from 30 to 50 mph, then allow the vehicle to slow to 30 mph with the throttle closed. Repeat the procedure 10 or 12 times. This will load the piston rings and cause them to seat properly against the cylinder walls. Check again for oil and coolant leaks.

8 Drive the vehicle gently for the first 500 miles (no sustained high speeds) and keep a constant check on the oil level. It is not unusual for an engine to use oil during the break-in period.

9 At approximately 500 to 600 miles, change the oil and filter.

10 For the next few hundred miles, drive the vehicle normally. Do not pamper it or abuse it.

11 After 2000 miles, change the oil and filter again and consider the engine run in.

Chapter 3
Cooling, heating and air conditioning systems

Contents

Degrees of difficulty

Easy, suitable for novice with little experience		**Fairly easy,** suitable for beginner with some experience		**Fairly difficult,** suitable for competent DIY mechanic		**Difficult,** suitable for experienced DIY mechanic		**Very difficult,** suitable for expert DIY or professional	

Specifications

General
Radiator cap pressure rating . . . . 0.74 to 1.03 bar (10.7 to 14.9 psi)
Thermostat rating . . . . 87 to 90° C (188 to 193° F)

Torque specifications

	lbf ft	Nm
Radiator drain plug (1995 and later)	0.5 to 0.8	0.7 to 1.1
Thermostat housing bolts	14 to 19	19 to 26
Water pump-to-block bolts	14 to 19	19 to 26

---

1   General information

Engine cooling system

All vehicles covered by this manual employ a pressurised engine cooling system with thermostatically-controlled coolant circulation. An impeller type water pump mounted on the front of the block pumps coolant through the engine. The coolant flows around each cylinder and toward the rear of the engine. Cast-in coolant passages direct coolant around the inlet and exhaust ports, near the spark plug areas and in proximity to the exhaust valve guides.

A wax-pellet type thermostat is located in the thermostat housing at the transmission end of the engine. During war- up, the closed thermostat prevents coolant from circulating through the radiator. When the engine reaches normal operating temperature, the thermostat opens and allows hot coolant to travel through the radiator, where it is cooled before returning to the engine.

The cooling system is sealed by a pressure-type radiator cap. This raises the boiling point of the coolant, and the higher boiling point of the coolant increases the cooling efficiency of the radiator. If the system pressure exceeds the cap pressure-relief value, the excess pressure in the system forces the spring-loaded valve inside the cap off its seat and allows the coolant to escape through the

overflow tube into a coolant reservoir. When the system cools, the excess coolant is automatically drawn from the reservoir back into the radiator.

The coolant reservoir does double duty as both the point at which fresh coolant is added to the cooling system to maintain the proper fluid level and as a holding tank for overheated coolant.

This type of cooling system is known as a closed design because coolant that escapes past the pressure cap is saved and reused.

Heating system

The heating system consists of a blower fan and heater core located within the heater box under the right end of the dashboard, the inlet and outlet hoses connecting the heater core to the engine cooling system and the heater/air conditioning control head on the dashboard. Engine coolant is circulated through the heater core. When the heater mode is activated, a flap door opens to expose the heater box to the passenger compartment. A fan switch on the controls activates the blower motor, which forces air through the core, heating the air.

Air conditioning system

The air conditioning system consists of a condenser mounted in front of the radiator, an evaporator mounted adjacent to the heater core, a compressor mounted on the engine, a filter-drier which contains a high pressure relief valve and the plumbing connecting all of the above.

A blower fan forces the warmer air of the passenger compartment through the evaporator core (similar to a radiator in reverse), transferring the heat from the air to the refrigerant. The liquid refrigerant boils off into low pressure vapour, taking the heat with it when it leaves the evaporator. The compressor keeps refrigerant circulating through the system, pumping the warmed coolant through the condenser where it is cooled and then circulated back to the evaporator.

2 Antifreeze - general information

⚠️ **Warning: Do not allow antifreeze to come in contact with your skin or painted surfaces of the vehicle. Rinse off spills immediately with plenty of water. Antifreeze is highly toxic if ingested. Never leave antifreeze lying around in an open container or in puddles on the floor; children and pets are attracted by it's sweet smell and may drink it. Check with local authorities about disposing of used antifreeze. Never dump used antifreeze on the ground or into drains.**

1 The cooling system should be filled with a water/ethylene-glycol based antifreeze solution, which will prevent freezing down to at least −29° C (−20° F), or lower if local climate requires it. It also provides protection against corrosion and increases the coolant boiling point.

2 The cooling system should be drained, flushed and refilled every 18 000 miles or every two years (see Chapter 1). The use of antifreeze solutions for periods of longer than two years is likely to cause damage and encourage the formation of rust and scale in the system. If your tap water is 'hard,' i.e. contains a lot of dissolved minerals, use distilled water with the antifreeze.

3 Before adding antifreeze to the system, check all hose connections, because antifreeze tends to search out and leak through very minute openings. Engines do not normally consume coolant. Therefore, if the level goes down, find the cause and correct it.

4 The exact mixture of antifreeze-to-water you should use depends on the relative weather conditions. The mixture should contain at least 50 percent antifreeze, but should never contain more than 70 percent antifreeze. Consult the mixture ratio chart on the antifreeze container before adding coolant. Hydrometers are available at most car accessory outlets to test the ratio of antifreeze to water **(see illustration)** or antifreeze test strips are available instead of the hydrometer gauge. Use antifreeze which meets the vehicle manufacturer's specifications.

3 Thermostat - check and renewal

⚠️ **Warning: Do not attempt to remove the radiator cap, coolant or thermostat until the engine has cooled completely.**

Check

1 Before assuming the thermostat is responsible for a cooling system problem, check the coolant level (*Weekly checks*), drivebelt tension (Chapter 1) and temperature gauge (or light) operation.

2 If the engine takes a long time to warm up (as indicated by the temperature gauge), the thermostat is probably stuck open. Replace the thermostat with a new one.

3 If the engine runs hot, use your hand to check the temperature of the lower radiator hose. If the hose is not hot, but the engine is, the thermostat is probably stuck in the closed position, preventing the coolant inside the engine from travelling through the radiator. Renew the thermostat.

Caution: Do not drive the vehicle without a thermostat. The computer may stay in open loop and emissions and fuel economy will suffer.

4 If the lower radiator hose is hot, it means that the coolant is flowing and the thermostat is open. Consult the Fault finding Section at the rear of this manual for further diagnosis.

Renewal

5 Disconnect the negative cable from the battery.

6 Drain the coolant from the radiator (see Chapter 1).

7 Disconnect the thermoswitch electrical connector from the thermostat cover located at the left end of the cylinder head **(see illustration)**.

8 Detach the thermostat cover from the engine. **Note:** *The radiator hose can be left attached to the thermostat cover, unless the thermostat cover itself is to be replaced.*

9 Be prepared for some coolant to spill as the gasket seal is broken.

10 Remove the thermostat, noting the direction in which it was installed in the block.

11 Remove the gasket and thoroughly clean the sealing surfaces.

12 Refit the thermostat with the spring end towards the engine **(see illustration)**, and with the small bypass hole in the thermostat at the high point (top).

13 Fit a new gasket, aligning the gasket with the bolt holes in the block. On 1995 and later models, refit the gasket with the print side facing the cylinder head.

14 Refitting is the reverse of removal. Tighten the thermostat cover fasteners to the torque listed in this Chapter's Specifications.

15 Refill the cooling system, run the engine and check for leaks and proper operation.

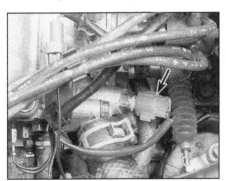

2.4 An inexpensive hydrometer can be used to test the condition of your coolant

3.7 Disconnect the electrical connector from the thermoswitch located in the thermostat housing

3.12 The thermostat is installed with the spring end into the cylinder head and the bypass hole up

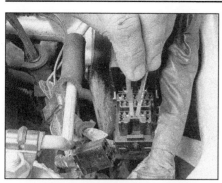

4.1 Check the radiator fan operation

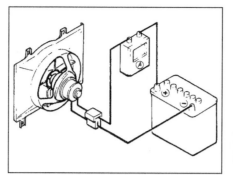

4.2 Disconnect the fan electrical connector and connect fused jumper wires directly to the battery

4.5a Disconnect the electrical connector . . .

4 Engine cooling fan and circuit - check and renewal

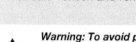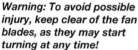

> ⚠ **Warning: To avoid possible injury, keep clear of the fan blades, as they may start turning at any time!**

Check

1 Refit a jumper wire across the fan test (TFA) terminal and the earth (GND) terminal of the diagnosis connector, located on the engine compartment bulkhead **(see illustration)**. With the ignition key ON, the fan should now operate. If the fan does not operate, check the fan system components including the fan relay, fan thermoswitch, and fan motor itself.

2 To test an inoperative fan motor (one that doesn't come on when the engine gets hot or when the air conditioner is on), first check the fuses and/or fusible links (see Chapter 12). Then disconnect the electrical connector at the fan motor and use fused jumper wires to connect the fan directly to the battery **(see illustration)**. If the fan still does not work, renew the fan motor. Some 1.8 litre models with an automatic transmission are equipped with a two-speed fan. Fans with a four-prong connector are two-speed. Be sure to check both fan speeds of two-speed fans by connecting both positive (+) connectors and negative (–) connectors to the test battery using fused jumper wires.

> ⚠ **Warning: Do not allow the test clips to contact each other or any metallic part of the vehicle.**

3 If the fan motor tested OK in the previous test but is still inoperative, then the fault lies in the fuse, relays, thermoswitch or wiring. The relays and thermoswitch can be tested as described below. **Note:** *On 1995 and later models, the cooling fan relay is controlled by the PCM with information supplied by the engine coolant temperature sensor. See Chapter 6 for testing the coolant temperature sensor. If the fan motor, relay and related circuits all test good and the cooling fan fails to operate normally, the fault may lie with the PCM. Have the PCM diagnosed by a dealer or other qualified repair facility.*

4 On all 1990 to 1994 models, the fan thermoswitch can be tested for continuity with an ohmmeter. Disconnect the wiring connector **(see illustration 3.7)** and attach one lead of the ohmmeter to the electrical connector prong on the thermoswitch, and the other lead to the body of the thermoswitch. When the engine is cold (below 91° C/194° F) there should be NO continuity. When the engine is hot (above 98° C/207° F), there should be continuity.

Renew the thermoswitch if necessary (see Section 9).

5 On 1990 to 1994 models with a two-speed fan, the second fan thermoswitch actuates relays No. 2 and No. 3. Test the thermoswitch for continuity with an ohmmeter by disconnecting the fan thermoswitch wiring connector and attaching the ohmmeter leads to the two terminals in the thermoswitch connector **(see illustrations)**. When the engine is cold (below 97° C/205° F) there should be NO continuity. When the engine is hot (above 106° C/221° F), there should be continuity.

6 Renew the thermoswitch if necessary (see Section 9).

Relay check

7 On all models, locate No. 1 fan relay in the main relay box **(see illustration)**. On models with a two-speed cooling fan, locate the No. 2 fan relay and the No. 3 fan relay located forward of the main relay box (No. 2 fan relay is closest to the inner wing, while the No. 3 fan relay is mounted inboard of the No. 2 fan relay) **(see illustration)**.

8 Remove the cooling fan relays, beginning with the No. 1 fan relay. Using an ohmmeter, test for continuity. On 1994 and earlier models, two types of relays are used by the manufacturer, and the terminals are numbered differently. Be sure to test the relay as shown **(see**

4.5b . . . and check for continuity

4.7a Cooling fan relay No. 1 is located in the main fuse block (1990 through 1994 model shown)

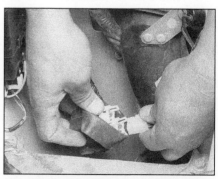

4.7b Cooling fan relays No. 2 and No. 3 are located on a separate bracket in front of the main relay box

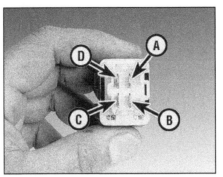

4.8a No. 1 cooling fan relay (Type 1) terminal guide for continuity test (1990 to 1994 shown)

4.8b No. 2 fan relay (Type 2) and No. 3 fan relay (Type 2) terminal guide for continuity test

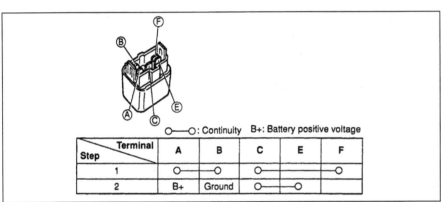

Step \ Terminal	A	B	C	E	F
1	O——O		O——		——O
2	B+	Ground	O——	——O	

O——O : Continuity   B+: Battery positive voltage

4.8c 1995 and later fan relay terminal guide and continuity table

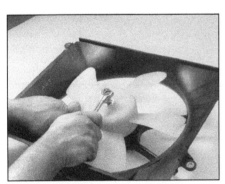

4.16 Hold the cooling fan blades and remove the fan retaining nut

4.17 Remove the screws retaining the motor to the shroud

5.8 Remove the automatic transmission cooler lines

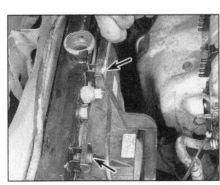

5.9a Remove the radiator fan assembly bolts . . .

illustrations). With no voltage applied, there should be NO continuity between terminals A and C. There should be continuity between terminals B and D. With battery voltage applied across terminals B and D, there should be continuity between terminals A and C. On 1995 and later models, remove the fan relay and test the relay as shown **(see illustration)**.

9 If the fan relays, thermoswitch and fan motors all test okay, take the vehicle to a dealer service department or other qualified repair facility for further diagnosis, due to the complexity and variety of the circuits involved.

Fan renewal

10 Disconnect the negative battery cable.

11 Drain the cooling system (see Chapter 1) below the level of the upper radiator hose.

12 On 1990 to 1994 models, remove the resonance chamber.

13 Disconnect the wiring connector at the fan motor.

14 Loosen the radiator upper hose clamps and remove the upper hose.

15 Unbolt the fan shroud and lift the fan shroud from the engine compartment. On 1995 and later models, move the coolant fan assembly to the side after removing the bolts and remove the radiator (see Section 5). Remove the fan assembly.

16 While holding the fan blades, remove the fan retaining nut **(see illustration)**. Remove the fan from the fan motor.

17 Remove the fan motor from the fan shroud **(see illustration)**.

18 Refitting is the reverse of removal. When refitting the fan shroud and the resonance chamber, tighten the mounting bolts securely.

5 Radiator and coolant reservoir - removal and refitting

⚠ Warning: Do not start this procedure until the engine is completely cool.

Radiator

1 Disconnect the negative battery cable.

2 Drain the engine coolant into a container (see Chapter 1).

3 On 1990 to 1994 models, remove the resonance chamber.

4 Disconnect the wiring connector at the fan motor.

5 On 1990 to 1994 models with a two-speed fan, disconnect the wiring connector at the fan thermoswitch.

6 Disconnect the coolant reservoir hose from the radiator filler neck. Then remove the coolant reservoir.

7 Loosen the radiator hose clamps and remove both the upper and lower hoses.

8 If equipped with an automatic transmission, disconnect the oil cooler hose from the radiator **(see illustration)**. Place a drip pan to catch the transmission fluid and cap the fittings.

9 Remove the fan retaining bolts and lift out the fan assembly **(see illustrations)**. On 1995

5.9b . . . and lift out the radiator fan assembly

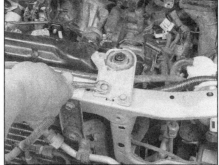

5.10a Remove the two radiator upper mounting assemblies and . . .

5.10b . . . remove the radiator carefully

and later models, move the fan assembly to the side while the radiator is removed. **Note:** *The bottom of the radiator is retained, without bolts, by the radiator support frame.*

10 Detach and lift out the radiator **(see illustrations)**. Be aware of dripping fluids and the sharp fins.

11 On 1995 and later models, the cooling fan and fan shroud can now be removed, if necessary (see Section 4).

12 With the radiator removed, it can be inspected for leaks, damage and internal blockage. If in need of repairs, have a professional radiator workshop or dealer service department perform the work as special techniques are required.

13 Insects and dirt can be cleaned from the radiator with compressed air and a soft brush. Don't bend the cooling fins as this is done.

Warning: Wear eye protection when using compressed air.

14 Refitting is the reverse of the removal procedure. Be sure the bottom of the radiator is located properly. When refitting the radiator fan shroud and the resonance chamber, tighten the mounting bolts securely.

15 After refitting, fill the cooling system with the proper mixture of antifreeze and water. Refer to Chapter 1 if necessary.

16 Start the engine and check for leaks. Allow the engine to reach normal operating temperature, indicated by both radiator hoses becoming hot. Recheck the coolant level and add more if required.

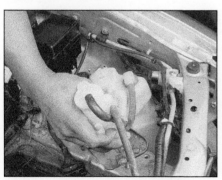

5.18 Remove the reservoir bottle

17 On automatic transmission equipped models, check and add automatic transmission fluid as needed.

Coolant reservoir

18 Unbolt the coolant reservoir and lift it out of engine compartment **(see illustration)**.

19 Pour the coolant into a container. Wash out and inspect the reservoir for cracks and chafing. Renew it if damaged.

20 Refitting is the reverse of removal.

---

6 Water pump - check

1 A failure in the water pump can cause serious engine damage due to overheating. If the pump is defective, it should be replaced with a new or rebuilt unit.

2 Remove the timing belt cover(s) (see Chapter 2A).

3 Water pumps are equipped with weep or vent holes. If a failure occurs in the pump seal, coolant will leak from the hole. In most cases you'll need an electric light to find the hole on the water pump from underneath to check for leaks. On 1.8 litre engines any water coming from this hole is vented to the outside of the timing belt cover on the back side of the engine in order to not damage the timing belt.

4 Check the water pump shaft bearing for wear by grasping the pump hub and gently

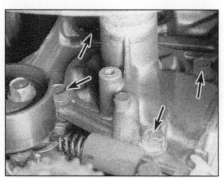

7.7 After removing the front covers and timing belt, remove the water pump mounting bolts (arrowed)

rocking the hub and shaft from side to side. If any looseness is apparent, excessive water pump shaft/bearing wear is possible.

5 If the water pump shaft bearings fail there may be a howling sound at the drivebelt end of the engine while it's running. Don't mistake drivebelt slippage, which causes a squealing sound, for water pump bearing failure. If a squealing sound is heard, check belt condition and belt tension.

---

7 Water pump - removal and refitting

⚠ *Warning: Wait until the engine is completely cool before beginning this procedure. Do not allow antifreeze to come in contact with your skin or painted surfaces of the vehicle. Rinse off spills immediately with plenty of water. Antifreeze is highly toxic if ingested. Never leave antifreeze lying around in an open container or in puddles on the floor; children and pets are attracted by its sweet smell and may drink it. Check with local authorities about disposing of used antifreeze.*

Removal

1 Disconnect the negative battery cable from the battery.

2 Drain the cooling system (see Chapter 1). If the coolant is relatively new or in good condition, save it and reuse it.

3 Remove the water pump drivebelt, pulley, timing belt cover(s) and timing belt (see Chapter 2A).

4 Remove the water inlet pipe and gasket from the water pump.

5 On 1990 to 1994 models, remove the water bypass pipe and O-ring, located on the water inlet pipe.

6 On 1990 to 1994 1.8 litre models, remove the oil level gauge (dipstick) tube clamp located at the engine block.

7 Remove the water pump mounting bolts **(see illustration)** and detach the water pump from the engine. If the water pump is stuck, gently tap it with a soft-faced hammer to break the seal.

Refitting

8 Clean the bolt threads and the threaded holes in the engine to remove corrosion and sealant.

9 Remove all traces of old gasket material from the sealing surfaces.

10 Compare the new water pump to the old one to make sure they are identical.

11 Apply a thin film of silicone sealant to the new gasket and refit it on the water pump.

12 Carefully mate the water pump to the engine.

13 Refit the water pump mounting bolts. Tighten them to the torque listed in this Chapter's Specifications. Don't over-tighten them or the pump may be damaged.

14 Refit all parts removed for access to the water pump.

15 Refill the cooling system (see Chapter 1) and check the timing belt tension (see Chapter 2A). Run the engine and check for leaks.

8 Coolant temperature gauge sending unit - check and renewal

Warning: Do not start this procedure until the engine is completely cool.

Check

1 If the coolant temperature gauge is inoperative, check the fuses first (see Chapter 12).

2 If the temperature gauge indicates excessive temperature after running awhile, see the *Fault Finding* Section in the rear of the manual.

3 If the temperature gauge indicates HOT as soon as the engine is started cold, disconnect the electrical connector at the coolant gauge sending unit, located in the engine compartment **(see illustration)**. If the gauge reading drops, renew the sending unit. If the reading remains high, the wire to the gauge may be shorted to earth or the gauge is faulty.

4 If the coolant temperature gauge fails to show any indication after the engine has been warmed up, (approximately 10 minutes) and

the fuses are good, turn off the engine. Disconnect the electrical connector at the sending unit and, using a jumper wire, connect the wire to a clean earth on the engine. Briefly turn on the ignition without starting the engine. If the gauge now indicates HOT, renew the sending unit.

5 Additionally, the sending unit may be checked for resistance using an ohmmeter; with the engine coolant hot, resistance should be 190 to 260 ohms.

6 If the gauge fails to respond, the circuit may be open or the temperature gauge may be faulty.

Renewal

7 Drain the coolant (see Chapter 1).

8 Disconnect the wiring connector from the sending unit.

9 Using a deep socket or a spanner, remove the sending unit.

10 Refit the new sending unit, and tighten it securely. Do not use thread sealer as it may electrically insulate the sending unit. Connect the electrical connector.

11 Refill the cooling system and check for coolant leakage and proper gauge operation.

9 Radiator cooling fan thermoswitch - renewal

Note: *1990 to 1994 models use either one of two cooling fan thermoswitches to control the operation of the cooling fan. On 1.8 litre engines with an automatic transmission, the second thermoswitch controls the high speed operation of the dual-speed fan. See Section 4 for information on checking the thermo-switches. On 1995 and later models, the cooling fan relay is controlled by the PCM with information supplied by the engine coolant temperature sensor, see Chapter 6 for information on the coolant temperature sensor.*

1 Drain the cooling system (see Chapter 1).

2 To renew the main radiator cooling fan thermoswitch, disconnect the electrical connector and unscrew the switch from the thermostat housing **(see illustration 3.7)**.

3 Refit the new switch with a new O-ring and tighten it securely. Connect the electrical connector and refill the cooling system.

4 To renew the secondary radiator cooling fan thermoswitch on models with a two-speed fan, remove the radiator resonance chamber. Disconnect the electrical connector and remove the radiator fan thermoswitch and gasket **(see illustration 4.5a)**. Refit the new radiator fan thermoswitch with a new gasket. Tighten the radiator thermoswitch securely. Connect the radiator thermoswitch electrical connector.

5 Refit the radiator resonance chamber. Tighten the fasteners securely.

6 Refill the cooling system.

10 Blower motor and circuit - check and component renewal

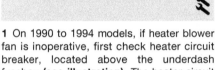

1 On 1990 to 1994 models, if heater blower fan is inoperative, first check heater circuit breaker, located above the underdash fusebox **(see illustration)**. The heater circuit breaker is a 30A fuse with a reset button feature. On 1995 and later models, check the 40A fuse located in the underdash fusebox (see Chapter 12).

2 If the reset button is OUT on 1990 to 1994 models, or if the fuse is blown on 1995 and later models, first check for a short circuit in the blower wiring by disconnecting the electrical connector at the blower. Check for any shorts (continuity) between the blower electrical connector **(see illustration)** and any convenient body earth. Renew or repair the harness if necessary.

3 On 1990 to 1994 models, depress the reset button to reset the heater circuit breaker.

4 Measure the voltage at the heater blower motor as follows:

a) *Remove the glovebox for access to the blower.*

b) *Turn the ignition switch on, and turn the blower switch to the Position 4 (high speed).*

c) *Using a voltmeter, test the blower motor terminal wires.*

8.3 Location of the temperature gauge sending unit (arrowed)

10.1 Check the circuit breaker reset button (arrowed), located above the fuse box

10.2 Check for shorts between the electrical connector and any convenient chassis earth

10.6a Remove the blower motor resistor assembly mounting screws . . .

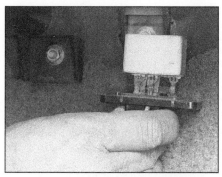

10.6b . . . and withdraw the resistor assembly to test continuity

12 Heater core - renewal

Warning: 1995 and later models are equipped with airbags. The airbag is armed and can inflate anytime the battery is connected. To prevent accidental deployment (and possible injury), turn the ignition key to LOCK and disconnect the negative battery cable whenever working near airbag components. After the battery is disconnected, wait at least two minutes before beginning work (the system has a back-up capacitor that must fully discharge). For more information see Chapter 12.

Warning: The air conditioning system is under high pressure. Do not loosen any hose fittings or remove any components until the system has been discharged. Air conditioning refrigerant should be properly discharged by a dealer service department or an automotive air conditioning repair facility.

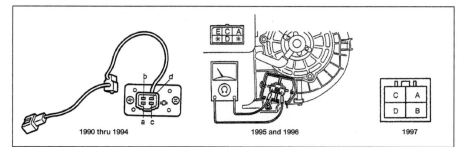

10.6c Blower resistor terminal guide

d) *The voltage should measure 12-volts. If 12-volts is present and the blower doesn't run, renew the blower (see Section 11).*

5 With the voltmeter still connected to the blower electrical connector, turn the blower switch down to Position 3, Position 2, and finally, Position 1, checking the voltage is less at each lower position of the blower switch. Renew the resistor assembly if necessary.

6 Further checks of the resistors can be made by removing the resistor assembly and checking terminal continuity as follows **(see illustrations)**:

a) *On 1990 to 1994 models, if no continuity is measured between resistor assembly terminals a and b, a and c, and a and d, renew the resistor assembly.*

b) *On 1995 and 1996 models, if no continuity is measured between resistor assembly terminals A and C, C and E, and C and D, renew the resistor assembly.*

c) *On 1997 models, if no continuity is measured between resistor assembly terminals A and C, B and C, and B and D, renew the resistor assembly.*

11 Blower motor - removal and refitting

1 Remove the trim panel underneath the glovebox.
2 Disconnect the electrical connector from the blower motor.
3 Remove the three screws retaining the blower motor to the housing.
4 Withdraw the blower motor straight down and out of the housing **(see illustration)**.
5 To remove the blower fan, remove the fastener from the shaft and withdraw the fan from the motor.
6 Refitting is the reverse of removal.

1 If equipped with air conditioning, have the refrigerant discharged and recovered by a qualified repair facility.
2 Disconnect the cable from the negative battery terminal.
3 Drain the engine coolant (see Chapter 1).
4 Remove the instrument panel (Refer to Chapter 11).

Models without air conditioning

5 Remove the seal plate on the right side of the heater unit by unlatching the seal plate latch **(see illustration)**.
6 Disconnect the heater hoses from the heater core by unlocking the hose connections at the bulkhead **(see illustration)**. Keep plenty of towels or rags on the carpeting to catch any coolant that may drip.
7 Remove the three nuts from the studs retaining the heater unit to the dash.
8 Remove the heater unit from the dash. The seal plate will come out with the heater unit as an assembly.

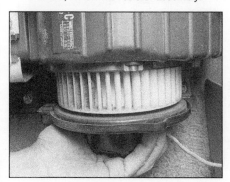

11.4 Remove the blower motor from the housing

12.5 Unlatch the heater unit seal plate

12.6 Disconnect the heater hose from the heater unit by unlocking the hose connector

12.9 Remove the heater core from of the heater unit

9 Remove the heater core from the heater unit **(see illustration)**.

10 Reassembly is the reverse of removal. When refitting the heater hoses on the heater core, make sure the hose connectors are securely locked.

Models with air conditioning

11 Remove the evaporator unit (see Section 18).

12 Disconnect the heater hoses from the heater core by unlocking the hose connections at the bulkhead. Keep plenty of towels or rags on the carpeting to catch any coolant that may drip inside.

13 Disconnect the heater electrical connectors.

14 Remove the three nuts from the studs retaining the heater unit to the dash.

15 Remove the heater unit from the dash.

16 Remove the heater core from the heater unit.

17 Reassembly is the reverse of removal. When refitting the heater hoses on the heater unit, check the hose connectors are securely locked.

---

13 Heater and air conditioning control assembly - removal, refitting, check and adjustment

 Warning: 1995 and later models are equipped with airbags. The airbag is armed and can inflate anytime the battery is connected. To prevent accidental deployment (and possible injury), turn the ignition key to LOCK and disconnect the negative battery cable whenever working near airbag components. After the battery is disconnected, wait at least two minutes before beginning work (the system has a back-up capacitor that must fully discharge). For more information see Chapter 12.

Note: Two types on control systems are used on the models covered by this manual; a manual 'wire type' control system and an electronic 'logic type' system. Logic controls can be distinguished from the wire type control by the type of control unit at the

dashboard. Logic controls have a series of push buttons for the heater and air conditioning operation, a fan switch, and a lever for air mix. Logic controls use only one air MIX wire plus electrical switches for the remaining heater and air conditioning functions. Electrically-driven actuators are used at the blower unit and the heater units instead of mechanical levers.

Removal and refitting

1 Disconnect the negative battery cable.

2 Remove the side panel below the dash on the passenger side (see Chapter 11).

3 Remove the underdash panel on the passenger side.

4 Remove the centre heater and radio control panel (see Chapter 11).

5 Remove the instrument cluster bezel (see Chapter 11).

6 Remove the glovebox (see Chapter 11).

7 Remove the glovebox cover inside the dash (see Chapter 11).

8 On models with manual wire type controls, disconnect the heater control wires behind the heater control (MODE wire, MIX wire, and REC-FRESH wire, as applicable). Remove the heater control assembly.

9 On models with electronic 'Logic' type controls, disconnect the heater air MIX wire, the control unit retaining screws, and as the control unit is pulled out, disconnect the two electrical connectors. Remove the heater/air conditioning control assembly.

10 Refitting is the reverse of the removal procedure. When refitting of the heater/air conditioning control assembly is complete, connect and adjust the heater control wires as follows.

Check and adjustment

11 On 1990 to 1994 models with wire-type controls:

a) To connect and adjust the REC-FRESH wire, set the REC-FRESH lever to the Fresh position, connect the REC-FRESH wire to the REC-FRESH door, set the door to FRESH position and clamp the wire in place. Check the lever moves its full stroke.

b) To connect and adjust the MIX wire, set the MIX lever to the COLD position, connect the MIX wire to the MIX door, set the door to the COLD position and clamp the wire in place. Check the lever moves its full stroke.

c) To connect and adjust the MODE wire, set the MODE lever to the DEFROST position, remove the MODE wire from Clip A **(see illustration)**. Align the set pin hole at B of the link with the matching hole of the heater unit and temporarily insert a 6.0 mm (0.24 in) diameter set pin. Use a suitable diameter drill bit as a set pin. Holding the MODE wire housing and with the wire straight , push the MODE wire into Clip A. Check the operation of the MODE lever. If the result is not correct, pull the MODE wire approximately 1.6 mm (0.16 in) toward the heater unit link. Remove the set pin that was installed for adjustment.

12 On 1995 and 1996 models with wire-type controls:

a) Adjust the airflow MODE wire by setting the MODE lever to DEFROSTER, connect the wire at the heater, set the MODE wire link to DEFROSTER and insert a screwdriver at the set hole near the bottom of the unit, clamp the MODE wire and verify that the MODE control lever on the dashboard moves full stroke.

b) Adjust the air MIX wire by setting the temperature control lever to MAX COLD, connect the wire at the heater, set the air mix link to MAX COLD and insert a screwdriver at the set hole. Clamp the air MIX wire and verify that the temperature control lever on the dashboard moves full stroke.

c) Adjust the air INTAKE wire by setting the REC/FRESH lever to FRESH, connecting the air INTAKE wire to the air intake link at the heater, set the air INTAKE link to FRESH and clamp the wire in place. Verify the REC/FRESH lever on the dashboard moves full stroke.

d) To check control unit switches, access the back of the control unit and backprobe the fan switch electrical

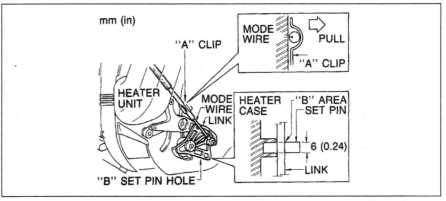

13.11 Remove the heater MODE wire from Clip A and complete the MODE wire adjustment

FAN SWITCH CONNECTOR

H	F	[X]	D	C	A
	G		E		B

A/C SWITCH CONNECTOR

F	E	D	*	B	A

HEATER CONTROL UNIT CONNECTOR

B	A

O——O : Continuity

Terminal / Switch position	Fan switch								A/C switch					Heater control unit	
	A	B	C	D	E	F	G	H	A	B	D	E	F	A	B
Constant	○		○		○				○	○		○	○	○	○
OFF															
1		○		○											
2		○				○		○							
3		○			○			○							
4		○					○	○							

13.12a Terminal guide and continuity table for 1995 and later models with wire type controls

connector, the A/C switch electrical connector, and the heater unit electrical connector, checking for continuity between connector terminals as shown **(see illustrations)**.

e) *Disconnect the fan switch electrical connector and check for continuity between fan switch terminals as shown in the illustration. Renew the fan switch if defective.*

13 On 1995 and later models with logic controls:

a) *Check and adjust the MIX wire as above.*

b) *To check the fan switch, disconnect the fan switch electrical connector and check for continuity as shown* **(see illustrations)**. *Renew fan switch if defective.*

c) *To check the REC switch, disconnect the REC switch electrical connector. Connect a 1 k-ohm reslstor between terminals C and F* **(see illustrations)** *of the switch, connect the vehicle battery to terminal F and battery earth to terminal J. Connect a voltmeter between terminals C and J. With the REC switch ON, voltage should be 1-volt or less. With the REC switch OFF, 12-volts should be present. Renew the control unit if defective.*

d) *To check the FRESH switch, disconnect the REC switch electrical connector. Connect a 1 k-ohm resistor between terminals A and F* **(see illustrations)** *of the switch, connect the vehicle battery to terminal F and battery earth to terminal J. Connect a voltmeter between terminals A and J. With the REC switch ON, voltage should be 1-volt or less. With the REC switch OFF, 12-volts should be present. Renew the control unit if defective.*

e) *To check the MODE switch, disconnect the REC switch electrical connector. Connect a 1 k-ohm resistor between terminals J and L* **(see illustrations)** *of the control unit, connect the vehicle*

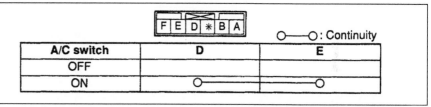

F	E	D	*	B	A

O——O : Continuity

A/C switch	D	E
OFF		
ON	○	○

13.12b Terminal guide and continuity table for wire type control fan switch

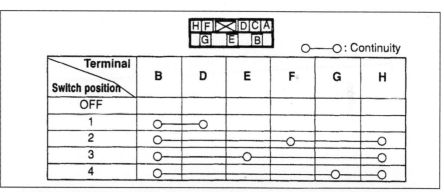

H	F	[X]	D	C	A
	G		E		B

O——O : Continuity

Terminal / Switch position	B	D	E	F	G	H
OFF						
1	○	○				
2	○			○		○
3	○		○			○
4	○				○	○

13.13a Fan switch terminal guide and continuity table for 1995 and later with logic control

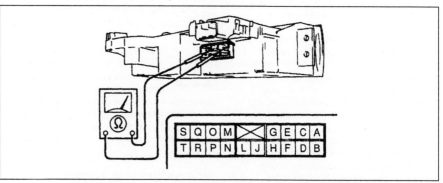

13.13b Heater unit connector terminal guide for 1995 and later with logic control

O——O : Continuity

Switch \ Terminal	J	T	S	Q	O	M
VENT	O	O				
BI–LEVEL	O		O			
HEAT	O			O		
HEAT/DEF	O				O	
DEFROSTER	O					O

13.13c MODE switch continuity table for 1995 and later with logic control

O——O : Continuity

A/C switch \ Terminal	B	D
OFF		
ON	O	O

13.13d A/C switch continuity table for 1995 and later with logic control

battery to terminal F and battery earth to terminal J, connect a jumper wire between terminals J and R, connect a voltmeter between terminals J and L; voltage should measure 12-volts. Renew the control unit if defective.

f) Connect a 1 k-ohm resistor between terminals J and N **(see illustrations)** of the control unit, connect the vehicle battery to terminal F and battery earth to terminal J, connect a jumper wire between terminals J and P, connect a voltmeter (DC voltage setting) between terminals J and N; voltage should measure 12-volts. Renew the control unit if defective.

g) Connect a 1 k-ohm resistor between terminals J and L **(see illustrations)** of the control unit, connect the vehicle battery to terminal F and battery earth to terminal J, connect a jumper wire between terminals J and P, connect a voltmeter between terminals J and L; voltage should measure 1-volt or less. Renew the control unit if defective.

h) Connect a 1 k-ohm resistor between terminals J and N **(see illustrations)** to the control unit, connect the vehicle battery to terminal F and battery earth to terminal J, connect a jumper wire between terminals J and R, connect a voltmeter between terminals J and N; voltage should measure 1-volt or less. Renew the control unit if defective.

i) Check the continuity of terminals listed **(see illustrations)** while pressing the mode switch to the positions shown. Renew the control unit if defective.

j) Check the continuity of the A/C switch terminals **(see illustrations)**, pressing the

A/C switch to ON and OFF positions. Renew the control unit if defective.

14 On 1997 models with wire-type controls:

a) Adjust the airflow MODE wire by setting the MODE lever to VENT, connect the wire at the heater, set the MODE wire link at the heater to VENT and insert a screwdriver at the set hole near the bottom of the unit. Clamp the MODE wire and verify that the MODE control lever on the dashboard moves full stroke.

b) Adjust the air MIX wire by setting the temperature control lever to MAX HOT, connect the wire at the heater, set the air mix link to MAX HOT and insert a screwdriver at the set hole. Clamp the air MIX wire and verify that the HOT-COLD control lever on the dashboard moves full stroke.

c) Adjust the air INTAKE wire the same as the 1995 to 1996 wire type controls above.

14 Air conditioning and heating system - check and maintenance

Warning: The air conditioning system is under high pressure. Do not loosen any hose fittings or remove any components until the system has been discharged. Air conditioning refrigerant should be properly discharged by a dealer service department or an automotive air conditioning repair facility.

Air conditioning system

1 The following maintenance checks should be performed on a regular basis to ensure that

the air conditioning system continues to operate at peak efficiency:

a) Inspect the condition of the compressor drivebelt. If it is worn or deteriorated, renew it (see Chapter 1).

b) Check the drivebelt tension and, if necessary, adjust it (see Chapter 1).

c) Inspect the system hoses. Look for cracks, bubbles, hardening and deterioration. Inspect the hoses and all fittings for oil bubbles or seepage. If there is any evidence of wear, damage or leakage, renew the hose(s).

d) Inspect the condenser fins for leaves, insects and any other foreign material that may have embedded itself in the fins. Use a soft brush or compressed air to remove debris from the condenser.

e) Make sure the system has the correct refrigerant charge.

2 It's a good idea to operate the system for about ten minutes at least once a month. This is particularly important during the winter months because long term non-use can cause hardening, and subsequent failure, of the seals.

3 Leaks in the air conditioning system are best spotted when the system is brought up to operating temperature and pressure, by running the engine with the air conditioning ON for five minutes. Turn the engine off and inspect the air conditioning hoses and connections. Traces of oil usually indicate refrigerant leaks.

4 Because of the complexity of the air conditioning system and the special equipment required to effectively work on it, accurate troubleshooting of the system should be left to a professional technician.

5 If the air conditioning system doesn't operate at all, check the fuse panel and the air conditioning relay, located in the fuse/relay box in the engine compartment. Refer to Sections 4, 9 and 11 for electrical checks of heating/air conditioning system components.

6 The most common cause of poor cooling is simply a low system refrigerant charge. If a noticeable drop in cool air output occurs, the following quick check will help you determine if the refrigerant level is low.

Checking the refrigerant charge

7 Warm the engine up to normal operating temperature.

8 With the engine at fast idle, place the air conditioning temperature selector at the coldest setting and put the blower at the highest setting. Open the doors (to make sure the air conditioning system doesn't cycle off as soon as it cools the passenger compartment).

9 With the compressor engaged, the clutch will make an audible click and the centre of the clutch will rotate. After the system reaches operating temperature, feel the two pipes

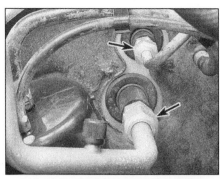

14.9 The evaporator outlet line (large tubing) should feel slightly cooler than the inlet line (small tubing)

14.10 Check the temperature of the output air in the centre register with a thermometer

14.11 The sight glass is located on top of the receiver/drier (1990 to 1994 shown)

connected to the evaporator at the bulkhead **(see illustration)**.

10 The pipe leading from the condenser outlet to the evaporator (small tubing) should be cold, and the evaporator outlet line (the larger tubing that leads back to the compressor) should be slightly colder (2 to 6° C/3 to 10° F). If the evaporator outlet is considerably warmer than the inlet, the system needs a charge. Insert a thermometer in the centre air distribution duct while operating the air conditioning system **(see illustration)** - the temperature of the output air should be 20 to 22° C (35 to 40° F) below the ambient air temperature (down to approximately 5° C/40° F). If the ambient (outside) air temperature is very high, say 44° C (110° F), the duct air temperature may be as high as 16° C (60° F), but generally the air conditioning is 20 to 22° C (35 to 40° F) cooler than the ambient air. If the air isn't as cold as it used to be, the system probably needs a charge. Further inspection or testing of the system is beyond the scope of the home mechanic and should be left to a professional.

11 Inspect the sight glass. If the refrigerant looks foamy when running, it's low **(see illustration)**. When ambient temperatures are very hot, bubbles may show in the sight glass even with the proper amount of refrigerant. With the proper amount of refrigerant, when the air conditioning is turned off, the sight glass should show refrigerant that foams, then clears.

Heating systems

12 If the air coming out of the heater vents isn't hot, the problem could stem from any of the following causes:

a) *The thermostat is stuck open, preventing the engine coolant from warming up quickly to carry heat to the heater core. Renew the thermostat (see Section 3).*

b) *A heater hose is blocked, preventing the flow of coolant through the heater core. Feel both heater hoses at the bulkhead. They should be hot. If one of them is cold, there is an obstruction in one of the hoses or in the heater core. Detach the hoses and back flush the heater core with a*

water hose. If the heater core is clear but circulation is impeded, remove the two hoses and flush them out with a water hose.

c) *If flushing fails to remove the blockage from the heater core, the core must be replaced (see Section 12).*

13 If the blower motor speed does not correspond to the setting selected on the blower switch, the problem could be a bad fuse, circuit, switch, blower motor resistor or motor (see Sections 10 and 11).

14 If there isn't any air coming out of the vents:

a) *Turn the ignition ON and activate the fan control. Place your ear at the heating/air conditioning register (vent) and listen. Most motors are audible. Can you hear the motor running?*

b) *If you can't (and have already verified that the blower switch and the blower motor resistor are good), the blower motor itself is probably bad (see Section 10).*

15 If the carpet under the heater core is damp, or if antifreeze vapour or steam is coming through the vents, the heater core is leaking. Remove it (see Section 12) and refit a new unit (most radiator specialists will not repair a leaking heater core).

16 Inspect the drain hose from the heater/air conditioning assembly located under the vehicle; make sure it is not clogged.

15.3 Remove the refrigerant line clamp bolt and disconnect the two refrigerant lines and cap them

15 Air conditioning receiver/drier - removal and refitting

> **Warning: The air conditioning system is under high pressure. Do not loosen any hose fittings or remove any components until the system has been discharged. Air conditioning refrigerant should be properly discharged by a dealer service department or an automotive air conditioning repair facility.**

1 Have the refrigerant discharged and recovered by a qualified repair facility.

2 On 1990 to 1994 models, refer to Chapter 11 and remove the radiator grille. On 1995 and later models, remove the driver's side undercar splash shield and wing mud guard.

3 On 1995 and later models, remove the receiver/drier pressure switch electrical connector. Then, for all models, remove the refrigerant line clamp bolt and disconnect the refrigerant lines from the receiver/drier **(see illustration)**. Cap the open fittings to prevent entry of moisture.

4 Remove the receiver/drier mounting bolts and remove the receiver/drier.

5 Refitting is the reverse of removal. Renew any O-rings with new ones specifically for the type of refrigerant in your system and lubricate them with refrigerant oil prior to refitting.

> **Warning: Do not apply compressor oil to the fitting nuts. Tighten the receiver/drier inlet and outlet fittings securely.**

6 Have the system evacuated, charged and leak tested by the workshop that discharged it.

16 Air conditioning compressor - removal and refitting

> **Warning: The air conditioning system is under high pressure. Do not loosen any hose fittings or remove any components until**

the system has been discharged. Air conditioning refrigerant should be properly discharged by a dealer service department or an automotive air conditioning repair facility.

1 Have the refrigerant discharged and recovered by a qualified repair facility.

2 Disconnect the negative cable from the battery.

3 Remove the undercover and splash shield on the passenger side from under the vehicle.

4 Remove the drivebelt from the compressor (see Chapter 1).

5 Disconnect the refrigerant lines and compressor electrical connector **(see illustration)**.

6 Unbolt the compressor and lift it from the vehicle **(see illustration)**.

7 If a new or rebuilt compressor is being installed, follow the directions supplied with the compressor regarding the proper level of refrigerant oil prior to refitting.

8 Refitting is the reverse of removal. Tighten the compressor mounting bolts securely. Renew any O-rings with new ones specifically for the type of refrigerant in your system and lubricate them with refrigerant oil prior to refitting.

 Warning: Do not apply compressor oil to the fitting nuts. Tighten the refrigerant line bolts securely.

9 Have the system evacuated, recharged and leak tested by the workshop that discharged it.

17 Air conditioning condenser - removal and refitting

 Warning: The air conditioning system is under high pressure. Do not loosen any hose fittings or remove any components until the system has been discharged. Air conditioning refrigerant should be properly discharged by a dealer service department or an automotive air conditioning repair facility.

1 Have the refrigerant discharged and recovered by a qualified repair facility.

2 Refer to Chapter 11 and remove the radiator grille.

3 On 1990 to 1994 models, remove the receiver/drier (see Section 15).

4 Remove the undercover shield from under the vehicle. Insert a fin protector such as a sheet of cardboard between the radiator and condenser.

5 On 1990 to 1994 models, remove the radiator (see Section 5).

6 Disconnect the condenser inlet and outlet fittings. Immediately cap the open fittings to keep moisture and contamination out of the system.

7 Remove the condenser.

8 Check the condenser for cracks, damage,

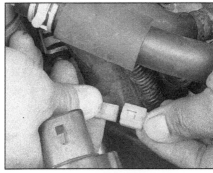

16.5 Disconnect the wiring harness connector at the compressor

refrigerant leakage, bent fins, and distorted or damaged condenser inlet and outlet. Repair or renew the condenser as necessary.

9 Refitting is the reverse of removal. Renew any O-rings with new ones specifically for the type of refrigerant in your system and lubricate them with refrigerant oil prior to refitting.

 Warning: Do not apply compressor oil to the fitting nuts. Tighten the condenser inlet and outlet fittings securely.

10 Have the system evacuated, recharged and leak tested by the workshop that discharged it.

18 Air conditioning evaporator and expansion valve - removal and refitting

 Warning: 1995 and later models are equipped with airbags. The airbag is armed and can inflate anytime the battery is connected. To prevent accidental deployment (and possible injury), turn the ignition key to LOCK and disconnect the negative battery cable whenever working near airbag components. After the battery is disconnected, wait at least two minutes before beginning work . For more information see Chapter 12.

18.2 Use a back-up spanner when disconnecting the air conditioning lines at the bulkhead

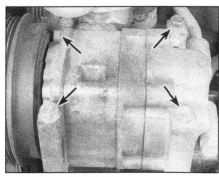

16.6 Remove the compressor mounting bolts (arrowed) and remove the compressor

 Warning: The air conditioning system is under high pressure. Do not loosen any hose fittings or remove any components until the system has been discharged. Air conditioning refrigerant should be properly discharged by a dealer service department or an automotive air conditioning repair facility.

1 Have the refrigerant discharged and recovered by a qualified repair facility.

2 Disconnect the air conditioning lines at the bulkhead; use a back-up spanner to prevent damage the fittings **(see illustration)**. Cap the open fittings after dismantling to prevent the entry of air or dirt.

3 Remove the glovebox (see Chapter 11). Remove the glovebox cover inside the dash.

4 Remove the side panel from the dash on the passenger side.

5 Remove the underdash panel on the passenger side.

6 On 1995 and later models, remove the cooling unit duct. Disconnect the air INTAKE wire from the blower unit link.

7 On 1990 to 1994 models, disconnect the evaporator cooling unit electrical connector.

8 Unlatch the seal plates on each side of the evaporator cooling unit **(see illustration)**.

9 Remove the evaporator cooling unit nuts from the mounting studs at the bulkhead.

10 Remove the evaporator cooling unit.

18.8 Unlatch the seal plates on each side of the evaporator cooling unit

11 Separate the lower and upper cooling unit housings **(see illustration)**.

12 Remove the evaporator.

13 Disconnect the expansion valve fittings and remove the expansion valve from the evaporator. Immediately cap the open fittings to keep moisture and contamination out of the system.

14 On 1990 to 1994 models, if necessary, remove the air conditioning thermoswitch from the upper cooling unit housing.

15 On 1995 and later models, if necessary, remove the air conditioning thermoswitch from the evaporator core and renew in the same location as removed.

16 Check the evaporator core and fittings for cracks or any other damage. Renew the evaporator if necessary.

17 Refit the expansion valve, replacing the gaskets on the expansion valve. Tighten the expansion valve inlet and outlet fittings securely.

18 Evaporator cooling unit refitting is the reverse of removal. Renew any O-rings with new ones specifically for the type of refrigerant in your system and lubricate them with refrigerant oil prior to refitting.

 Warning: Do not apply compressor oil to the fitting nuts. Tighten the evaporator cooling unit inlet and outlet fittings securely.

19 Have the system evacuated, charged and leak tested by the workshop that discharged it.

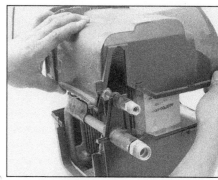

18.11 Separate the two halves of the cooling unit housing and remove the evaporator core

Notes

Chapter 4
Fuel and exhaust systems

Contents

Degrees of difficulty

| Easy, suitable for novice with little experience | | Fairly easy, suitable for beginner with some experience | | Fairly difficult, suitable for competent DIY mechanic | | Difficult, suitable for experienced DIY mechanic | | Very difficult, suitable for expert DIY or professional | |

Specifications

Fuel system

Fuel pressure

Fuel pump pressure (maximum)
1.3 litre models	5.0 to 6.4 bar (72 to 93 psi)
1.5 litre models	5.0 to 6.4 bar (72 to 93 psi)
1.6 litre models	4.4 to 5.9 bar (64 to 85 psi)
1.8 litre models	5.0 to 6.4 bar (72 to 93 psi)

Ignition ON, engine not running
1.3 litre models	2.7 to 3.1 bar (39 to 45 psi)
1.5 litre models	2.7 to 3.1 bar (39 to 45 psi)
1.6 litre models	2.5 to 3.2 bar (36 to 46 psi)
1.8 litre models	2.8 to 3.1 bar (40 to 45 psi)

Engine idling
1.3 litre models	2.0 to 2.3 bar (29 to 34 psi)
1.5 litre models	2.0 to 2.3 bar (29 to 34 psi)
1.6 litre models	2.1 to 2.6 bar (30 to 37 psi)
1.8 litre models	2.0 to 2.3 bar (29 to 34 psi)

Engine idling (vacuum hose from pressure regulator disconnected)
1.3 litre models	2.8 to 3.1 bar (40 to 45 psi)
1.5 litre models	2.8 to 3.1 bar (40 to 45 psi)
1.6 litre models	2.6 to 3.2 bar (38 to 46 psi)
1.8 litre models	2.8 to 3.1 bar (40 to 45 psi)

Fuel system hold pressure (minimum) . . . . 1.4 bar (21 psi)

Fuel system (continued)

Fuel injector resistance

1.3 litre models	13.8 ohms at 20° C (68° F)
1.5 litre models	13.8 ohms at 20° C (68° F)
1.6 litre models	12 to 16 ohms
1.8 litre models	13.8 ohms at 20° C (68° F)

Idle Air Control (IAC) valve resistance

1.3 litre models	7.7 to 9.3 ohms at 23° C (73° F)
1.5 litre models	7.7 to 9.3 ohms at 23° C (73° F)
1.6 litre models	N/A
1.8 litre models	10.7 to 12.3 ohms at 20° C (68° F)
Accelerator cable freeplay	1.0 to 3.0 mm (0.04 to 0.12 in)

Idle speed

1.3 litre models	800 to 900 rpm
1.5 litre models	
Manual transmission	650 to 750 rpm
Automatic transmission	700 to 800 rpm
1.6 litre models	
Estate models	800 to 900 rpm
All other models	700 to 800 rpm
1.8 litre models	700 to 800 rpm

Torque specification

	lbf ft	Nm
Air inlet plenum bolts/nuts	14 to 18	19 to 26
Fuel rail mounting bolts	14 to 19	19 to 26
Throttle body mounting bolts	14 to 19	19 to 26

1 General information

The fuel system consists of a fuel tank, an electric fuel pump (located in the fuel tank), an EFI/fuel pump relay, fuel injectors, a fuel pressure regulator, an air cleaner assembly and a throttle body unit. All models covered by this manual are equipped with the Multi Point Fuel Injection (MPFI) system.

Multi Point Fuel Injection (MPFI) system

Multi point fuel injection uses timed impulses to sequentially inject the fuel directly into the inlet port of each cylinder. The injectors are controlled by the Powertrain Control Module (PCM). The PCM monitors various engine parameters and delivers the exact amount of fuel, in the correct sequence, into the inlet ports. The 1.8 litre engine is also equipped with a Variable Inertia Charging System (VICS) which effectively varies the length of the inlet air path, yielding higher torque and a wider torque band. The throttle body serves only to control the amount of air passing into the system. Because each cylinder is equipped with an injector mounted immediately adjacent to the inlet valve, much better control of the fuel/air mixture ratio is possible.

Fuel pump and lines

Fuel is circulated from the fuel tank to the fuel injection system, and back to the fuel tank, through a pair of metal lines running along the underside of the vehicle. An electric fuel pump is attached to the fuel level sender unit inside the fuel tank. All excess fuel is routed back to the fuel tank through a separate return line.

The fuel pump will operate as long as the engine is cranking or running and the PCM is receiving ignition reference pulses from the electronic ignition system (see Chapter 5). If there are no reference pulses, the fuel pump will stop after 2 or 3 seconds.

Exhaust system

The exhaust system includes an exhaust manifold fitted with an exhaust oxygen sensor, a catalytic converter, an exhaust pipe, and a silencer.

The catalytic converter is an emission control device added to the exhaust system to reduce pollutants. A single-bed converter is used in combination with a three-way (reduction) catalyst. Refer to Chapter 6 for more information regarding the catalytic converter.

2 Fuel pressure relief

 Warning: Petrol is extremely flammable, so take extra precautions when you work on any part of the fuel system. **Don't smoke or allow open flames or bare light bulbs near the work area, and don't work in a garage where a natural gas-type appliance (such as a water heater or a clothes dryer) with a pilot light is present. Since petrol is carcinogenic, wear latex gloves when there's a possibility of being exposed to fuel, and, if you spill any fuel on your skin, rinse it off immediately with soap and water. Mop up any spills immediately and do not store fuel-soaked rags where they could ignite. The fuel system is under constant pressure, so, if any fuel lines are to be disconnected, the fuel pressure in the system must be relieved first. When you perform any kind of work on the fuel system, wear safety glasses and have a Class B type fire extinguisher on hand.**

1 Before servicing any fuel system component, you must relieve the fuel pressure to minimise the risk of fire or personnel injury.
2 Remove the fuel filler cap - this will relieve any pressure built up in the tank.
3 Remove the rear seat cushion (see Chapter 11).
4 On 1995 and later models remove the fuel pump access cover.
5 Disconnect the fuel pump electrical connector **(see illustration)**.

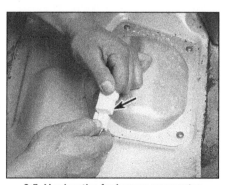

2.5 Unplug the fuel pump connector (arrowed)

6 Start the engine and wait for the engine to stall, then turn the ignition key to OFF.

7 The fuel system is now depressurised.

Note: *Place a rag around the fuel line before removing any hose clamp or fitting to prevent any residual fuel from spilling onto the engine.*

8 Connect the fuel pump electrical connector.

9 Refit the rear seat cushion (see Chapter 11).

3 Fuel pump/fuel pressure - check

Warning: Petrol is extremely flammable, so take extra precautions when you work on any part of the fuel system. See the Warning in Section 2.

Fuel pump operation check

1 Connect the diagnostic connector terminals F/P and GND with a jumper wire **(see illustration)**.

2 Remove the fuel filler cap.

3 Turn the ignition switch to ON (but do not start the engine).

4 The fuel pump is now activated. Listen for fuel pump noises from the fuel tank (under the rear seat).

5 Turn the ignition switch OFF.

6 Remove the jumper wire. Close the cap on the test connector.

7 If the fuel pump did not operate, measure the voltage between the fuel pump connector wire B/P and earth. You should read full battery voltage **(see illustration)**.

8 If not correct, check the EFI 30-amp fuse and the circuit opening/fuel pump relays (see paragraphs 32 to 38).

9 If the relay checks correctly, check for continuity between fuel pump connector terminals B/P and B (on the pump side) **(see illustration)**.

10 If there is no continuity, check the pump's earth circuit for continuity and repair it as necessary.

11 If there is still no continuity, renew the fuel pump (see Section 5).

12 Reconnect the cable to the battery.

3.1 Connect a jumper wire to the GND and F/P terminals of the diagnostic connector

Fuel pressure check

13 Relieve the fuel pressure (Section 2). Using a T-fitting, refit the fuel pressure gauge in the main fuel hose going from the top of the fuel filter to the engine **(see illustration)**.

14 Perform the pressure check procedure (see paragraphs 1 to 4) and compare your pressure readings with the pressures in this Chapter's Specifications.

a) If the pressure is high, check for a restricted fuel return line. If the line is clear, renew the pressure regulator.

b) If the pressure is low, pinch the fuel return line. If the pressure goes up, renew the fuel pressure regulator. If the pressure does not increase, check the fuel feed line, the fuel pump and the fuel filter.

15 Remove the jumper wire from the diagnostic connector.

16 Start the engine and with the engine idling:

a) Measure the fuel pressure and compare your reading to the fuel pressure listed in this Chapter's Specifications.

b) If the pressure is not as specified, check the vacuum sensing hose and fuel pressure regulator (see paragraphs 18 to 22).

17 Stop the engine and verify that the fuel pressure remains above the minimum system hold pressure listed in this Chapter's Specifications for five minutes after the engine is turned off. If the pressure bleeds down, the fuel pressure regulator, the fuel pump or a fuel injector may be leaking.

3.7 Check for battery voltage at the fuel pump electrical connector

Fuel pressure regulator check

18 Disconnect the pressure regulator vacuum hose and plug the supply hose or pipe. Connect a hand-held vacuum pump to the regulator. Start the engine and read the fuel pressure gauge without vacuum applied to the fuel pressure regulator. Apply vacuum to the regulator and check the fuel pressure again **(see illustration)**. The fuel pressure should decrease as vacuum increases.

19 Reconnect the vacuum hose to the regulator and check the fuel pressure at idle, comparing your reading with the value listed in this Chapter's Specifications. Disconnect the vacuum hose and watch the gauge - the pressure should increase as soon as the hose is disconnected. If the pressure at idle was too high (with the hose connected), connect a vacuum gauge and check for vacuum in the supply line. If there is no reading on the gauge, check the air inlet plenum and inlet manifold for a vacuum leak.

20 If the fuel pressure is LOW, pinch the fuel return line shut and watch the gauge. If the pressure doesn't rise, the fuel pump is defective or there is a restriction in the fuel feed line. If the pressure rises sharply, renew the fuel pressure regulator (see Section 13).

21 If the indicated fuel pressure is too high, relieve the fuel pressure (see Section 2), disconnect the fuel return line and blow through it to check for blockage. If there is no blockage, renew the fuel pressure regulator (see Section 13).

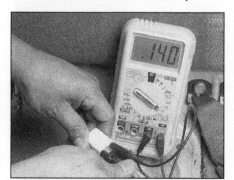

3.9 Check for continuity between B/P and B terminals of the fuel pump connector

3.13 Measure the fuel pump pressure at the fuel filter

3.18 Check the fuel pressure

22 If the fuel pressure does not fluctuate as described In Paragraph 19, and vacuum is present at the hose, renew the fuel pressure regulator (see Section 13).

23 Depressurise the fuel system (see Section 2). Carefully remove the fuel pressure gauge. Be sure to cover the fitting with a rag before loosening it.

24 Wipe up any spilled petrol.

25 Start the engine and check for leaks.

EFI main relay, circuit opening relay (early models) and fuel pump relay checks (late models)

Voltage checks

26 There are two relays involved in the fuel pump circuit. First, test for battery voltage to the EFI main relay and then the circuit opening relay (fuel pump relay on later models).

27 Remove the EFI main relay from the main fuse block **(see illustration)** in the engine compartment and with the ignition key ON (engine not running), check for battery voltage across the A and B terminals **(see illustration 3.32).**

28 If battery voltage is present, insert the relay back in the fuse block and check for battery voltage at the circuit opening/fuel pump relay. To access the relay you will have to remove the console and the passenger side wall (see Chapter 11).

29 Leave the circuit opening/fuel pump relay in place and check for battery voltage at the relay by probing the terminals where the wires enter the connector. The following conditions should exist.

a) *For 1990 to 1994 models, with the ignition switch ON there should be full battery voltage at the LIGHT GREEN and WHITE/RED STRIPE wire terminals* **(see illustration).**

b) *For 1995 and later models, with the ignition switch ON there should be full battery voltage at the two WHITE/RED STRIPE wire terminals.*

30 If battery voltage is present at the relay connectors, check the relays.

EFI main relay

31 Verify that the relay clicks when turning the ignition switch from OFF to ON and back

3.27 Remove the EFI main relay (arrowed)

to OFF, then remove the EFI main relay **(see illustration 3.27)** from the fuse block.

32 Using an ohmmeter check for continuity across A and B **(see illustration).** Check that there is no continuity across terminals C and D.

33 Apply battery voltage across terminals A and B. Using an ohmmeter, check across terminals C and D. Continuity should exist. If the test results are incorrect, renew the relay.

Circuit opening relay (1990 to 1992 models) and fuel pump relay (1993 and 1994 models)

34 Using an ohmmeter, check the resistance between the terminals **(see illustration):**

a) *Between STA and E1, there should be 21 to 43 ohms*

b) *Between B and Fc, there should be 109 to 226 ohms*

c) *Between B and Fp there should be infinite resistance*

35 Apply battery voltage across terminals STA and E1. Using an ohmmeter, check for continuity across terminals +B and Fp. Continuity should exist. If the test results are incorrect, renew the relay.

Fuel pump relay (1995 and later models)

36 Using an ohmmeter, check for continuity across terminals A and B **(see illustration);** there should be continuity. Check that there is no continuity across terminals C and D.

37 Apply battery voltage across terminals A and B. Using an ohmmeter, check for continuity across terminals C and D **(see illustration 3.36).** Continuity should exist. If the test results are incorrect, renew the relay.

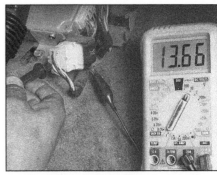

3.29 Using a voltmeter, probe the wire terminals for presence of battery voltage

4 Fuel lines and fittings - inspection and renewal

> *Warning: Petrol is extremely flammable, so take extra precautions when you work on any part of the fuel system. See the Warning in Section 2.*

Inspection

1 Once in a while, you will have to raise the vehicle to service or renew some component (an exhaust pipe support, for example). Whenever you work under the vehicle, always inspect fuel lines and all fittings and connections for damage or deterioration.

2 Check all hoses and pipes for cracks, kinks, deformation or obstructions.

3 Make sure all hoses and pipe clips attach their associated hoses or pipes securely to the underside of the vehicle.

4 Verify all hose clamps attaching rubber hoses to metal fuel lines or pipes are secure enough to assure a tight fit between the hoses and pipes.

Renewal

5 If you must renew any damaged sections, use original equipment renewal hoses or pipes constructed from exactly the same material as the section you are replacing. Do not fit substitutes constructed from inferior or inappropriate material or you could cause a fuel leak or a fire.

6 Always, before detaching or dismantling any part of the fuel line system, note the

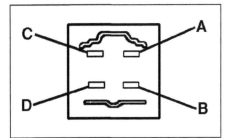

3.32 EFI main relay terminal identification (1990 to 1994 models)

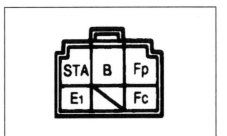

3.34 Circuit opening relay/fuel pump relay terminal identification

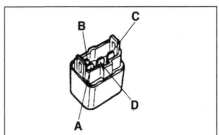

3.36 Fuel pump relay terminal identification (1995 and later models)

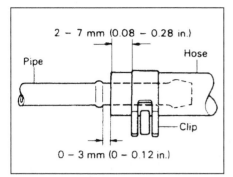

4.6 When attaching a section of rubber hose to a metal fuel line, be sure to overlap the hose

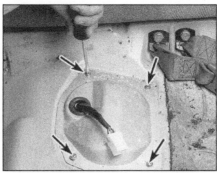

5.4 Remove the access cover screws (arrowed) and pull up the cover

5.5a Unplug the fuel pump electrical connector . . .

routing of all hoses and pipes and the orientation of all clamps and clips to assure that renewal sections are installed in exactly the same manner. When attaching hoses to metal lines, overlap them as shown **(see illustration)**.

7 Before detaching any part of the fuel system, be sure to relieve the fuel line and tank pressure (see Section 2).

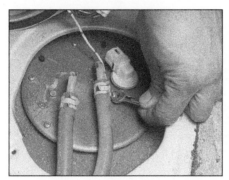

5.5b . . . then remove the terminal nut and wire on the top of the pump

5.6 Disconnect the fuel supply hose (right arrow) and fuel return hose (left arrow)

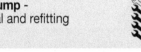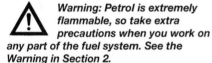

5 Fuel pump - removal and refitting

> ⚠ **Warning: Petrol is extremely flammable, so take extra precautions when you work on any part of the fuel system. See the Warning in Section 2.**

1 Remove the fuel tank cap. Depressurise the fuel system (see Section 2).
2 Disconnect the cable from the negative terminal of the battery.
3 Remove the rear seat cushion (see Chapter 11).
4 Remove the fuel pump access cover **(see illustration)**.
5 Unplug the electrical connector and disconnect the wire attached to the top of the fuel pump **(see illustrations)**.
6 Disconnect the fuel supply and return hoses from the pump **(see illustration)**.

7 Remove the fuel pump retaining screws **(see illustration)**.
8 Carefully lift the fuel pump assembly out of the fuel tank **(see illustration)**.
9 Disconnect the electrical connector and move the hose clamp clear of the pump fitting **(see illustration)**.
10 Remove the band securing the pump to the bracket.
11 Remove the bracket at the bottom of the pump with the rubber mount.
12 Remove the fuel pump.
13 Remove the sock filter from the bottom of the pump and inspect it for contamination. If it is dirty, renew it.
14 Refitting is the reverse of removal. Refit a new O-ring set (O-ring, cap and spacer) at the

hose connection and a new tank seal during refitting. **Note:** *After refitting the fuel pump to the bracket, pull the pump down so it is seated tightly against the pad on the bottom of the bracket, then position the hose clamps.*

6 Fuel level sender unit - check and renewal

> ⚠ **Warning: Petrol is extremely flammable, so take extra precautions when you work on any part of the fuel system. See the Warning in Section 2.**

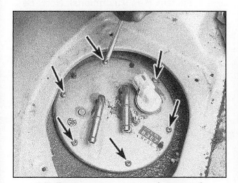

5.7 Remove the screws (arrowed) securing the pump in the fuel tank

5.8 Lift the fuel pump from the fuel tank at an angle so as not to damage the inlet screen or float arm

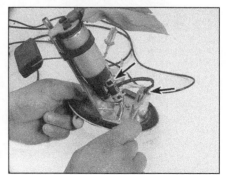

5.9 Disconnect the fuel pump electrical connector and the hose clamp (arrowed)

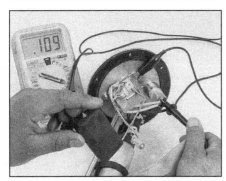

6.3a Resistance with the float arm down (tank empty) should be about 110 ohms

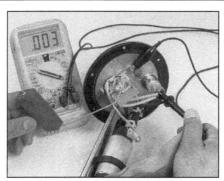

6.3b Resistance with the float arm up (tank full) should be 2 to 4 ohms

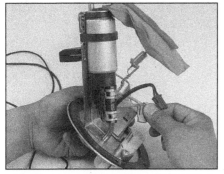

6.6 Disconnect the sender unit electrical connector

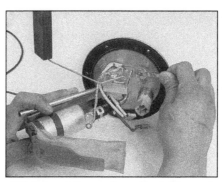

6.7 Remove the sender unit retaining nut

Check

1 The fuel level sender unit is part of the fuel pump assembly mounted in the fuel tank.
2 Remove the fuel pump assembly (see Section 5).
3 Using an ohmmeter, check the resistance of the sender unit with the float arm completely down (tank empty) and with the arm up (tank full) **(see illustrations)**. The resistance should change steadily from 110 ohms to approximately 2 to 4 ohms.
4 If the readings are incorrect, renew the sender unit.

Renewal

5 Remove the fuel pump assembly from the fuel tank (see Section 5).
6 Disconnect the electrical connection to the fuel level sender unit **(see illustration)**.
7 Remove the nut securing the sending unit bracket and separate the sending unit from the assembly **(see illustration)**.
8 Refitting is the reverse of removal.

7 Fuel tank - removal and refitting

> **Warning: Petrol is extremely flammable, so take extra precautions when you work on any part of the fuel system. See the Warning in Section 2.**

1 This procedure is much easier to perform if the fuel tank is empty. Some models may have a drain plug for this purpose. If for some reason the drain plug can't be removed, postpone the job until the tank is empty or siphon the fuel into an approved container using a siphoning kit (available at most car accessory outlets).

> **Warning: Do not start the siphoning action by mouth!**

2 Remove the fuel filler cap to relieve fuel tank pressure. Relieve the fuel system pressure (see Section 2).
3 Detach the cable from the negative terminal of the battery.
4 If the tank is full or nearly full, drain the fuel into an approved container.
5 Raise the vehicle and place it securely on axle stands.
6 Familiarise yourself with the layout of the fuel tank assembly before proceeding **(see illustration)**.
7 Remove the insulator from the front of the fuel tank. Refer to Section 5 and disconnect the fuel pump hoses and electrical connectors.
8 Support the fuel tank with a trolley jack. Place a sturdy plank between the jack head and the fuel tank to protect the tank.
9 Disconnect the fuel lines and the evaporative hoses at the tank **(see illustrations)**. **Note:** *Be*

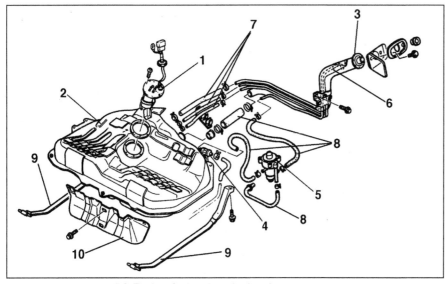

7.6 Typical fuel tank and related components

1 Fuel pump assembly	5 Check and cut valve	8 Fuel hoses
2 Fuel tank	6 Separator	9 Tank strap
3 Filler pipe	7 Evaporative hoses	10 Insulator
4 Check valve		

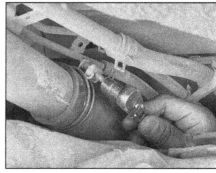

7.9a Loosen the clamp that retains the fuel filler hose

sure to plug the hoses to prevent leakage and contamination of the fuel system.

10 Remove the bolts from the fuel tank retaining straps **(see illustration)**.

11 Remove the tank from the vehicle.

12 Refitting is the reverse of removal.

8 Fuel tank cleaning and repair - general information

1 Any repairs to the fuel tank or filler neck should be carried out by a professional who has experience in this critical and potentially dangerous work. Even after cleaning and flushing of the fuel system, explosive fumes can remain and ignite during repair of the tank.

2 If the fuel tank is removed from the vehicle, it should not be placed in an area where sparks or open flames could ignite the fumes coming out of the tank. Be especially careful inside garages where a natural gas-type appliance is located, because the pilot light could cause an explosion.

9 Air cleaner assembly - removal and refitting

1 Familiarise yourself with the inlet air system components before proceeding **(see illustration)**.

2 Disconnect the mass airflow sensor electrical connector **(see illustration)**.

3 Locate the hose going from the air inlet to the valve cover and disconnect it from the valve cover **(see illustration)**.

4 Loosen the air inlet hose clamp at the throttle body and detach the air inlet hose **(see illustration)**.

5 Loosen the air inlet hose clamp at the resonance chamber and remove the hose **(see illustration overleaf)**.

6 Use a needle-nose pliers to release the clamp on the small hose at the resonance

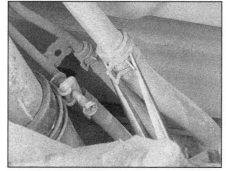

7.9b Loosen the clamp and detach the fuel evaporative hoses from the tank

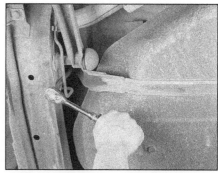

7.10 Remove the fuel tank strap bolts from the body

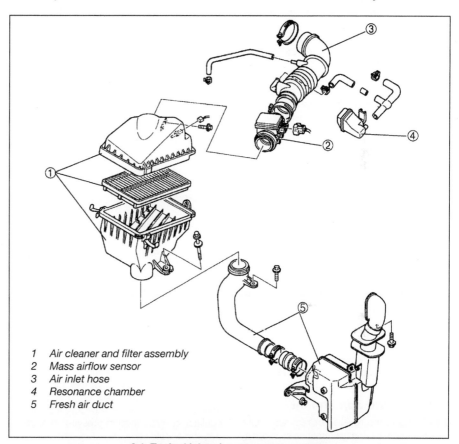

1 Air cleaner and filter assembly
2 Mass airflow sensor
3 Air inlet hose
4 Resonance chamber
5 Fresh air duct

9.1 Typical inlet air system components

9.2 Release the electrical connector lock tabs and unplug the connector

9.3 Remove the clamp and separate the hose from the valve cover

9.4 Loosen the clamp and pull the air inlet hose from the throttle body

9.5 Loosen the clamp and pull the air inlet hose from the resonance chamber

9.6 Disconnect the smaller air hose from the resonance chamber

9.7 Loosen the hose clamp at the air filter and remove the resonance chamber

chamber and disconnect the hose (see illustration).

7 Loosen the hose clamp at the air cleaner housing and remove the resonance chamber (see illustration).

8 Remove the attaching bolt(s) (see illustration) and remove the air cleaner assembly from the engine compartment.

9 Refitting is the reverse of removal.

10 Accelerator cable - removal, refitting and adjustment

Removal

1 Detach the cable from the negative terminal of the battery.

2 Loosen the locknut on the threaded portion of the throttle cable at the plenum chamber (see illustration).

3 Rotate the throttle lever and slip the throttle cable end out of the slot in the lever (see illustration).

4 Detach the throttle cable from the accelerator pedal and release the cable guide attached to the bulkhead.

5 From the engine compartment side of the bulkhead, pull the cable through the bulkhead.

Refitting and adjustment

6 Refitting is the reverse of removal. Make sure the cable casing grommet seats properly in the bulkhead.

7 To adjust the cable, fully depress the accelerator pedal and check that the throttle is fully opened.

8 Measure the play in the accelerator and compare your measurement to that listed in this Chapter's Specifications.

9 If the throttle is not fully opened and/or if the play is incorrect, loosen the locknuts, and adjust the cable.

10 Tighten the locknuts and recheck the adjustment. Make sure the throttle closes fully when the pedal is released.

11 Electronic Fuel Injection (EFI) system - general information

1 These models are equipped with an Electronic Fuel Injection (EFI) system. The EFI system is composed of three basic subsystems: fuel system, air induction system and electronic control system (see illustrations on opposite page).

Fuel system

2 An electric fuel pump located inside the fuel tank supplies fuel under constant pressure to the fuel rail, which distributes fuel evenly to all injectors. From the fuel rail, fuel is injected into the inlet ports, just above the inlet valves, by fuel injectors. The amount of fuel supplied by the injectors is precisely controlled by a Powertrain Control Module (PCM). A pressure regulator controls system pressure in relation to inlet manifold vacuum. A fuel filter between the fuel pump and the fuel rail filters fuel to protect the components of the system.

Air induction system

3 The air induction system consists of an air filter housing, the throttle body and the duct connecting the two. An Inlet Air Temperature (IAT) sensor monitors the temperature of the incoming air. This information helps the PCM determine the amount of fuel to be injected by the injectors. The throttle plate inside the throttle body is controlled by the driver. As the throttle plate opens, the speed of the incoming air increases, which lowers the temperature of the air. The IAT sends this information to the PCM and the PCM signals the injectors to increase the amount of fuel delivered to the inlet ports.

Electronic control system

4 The Computer Control System controls the EFI and other systems by means of an Powertrain Control Module (PCM), which employs a microcomputer. The PCM receives signals from a number of information sensors which monitor such variables as inlet air temperature, throttle angle, coolant temperature, engine rpm, vehicle speed and exhaust oxygen content. These signals help the PCM determine the injection duration necessary for the optimum air/fuel ratio. Some of these sensors and their corresponding PCM-controlled relays are not contained within EFI components, but are located throughout the engine compartment. For further information regarding the PCM and its relationship to the engine electrical and ignition system, see Chapter 6.

9.8 Remove the air cleaner housing mounting bolts

10.2 Loosen the locknuts on the accelerator cable

10.3 Rotate the throttle lever and remove the cable end from the slot

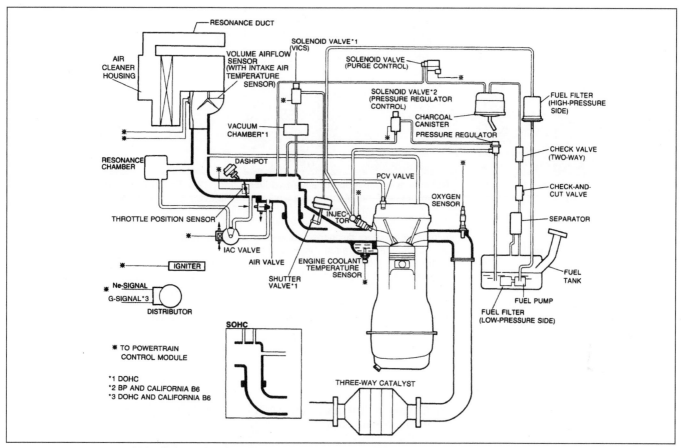

11.1a Schematic of the Electronic Fuel Injection (EFI) system for 1990 to 1994 models

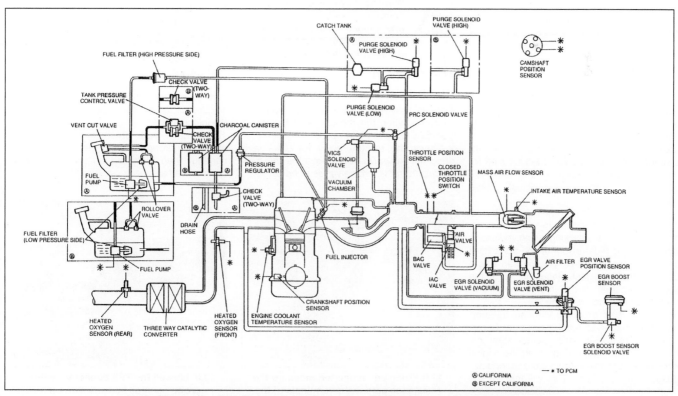

11.1b Schematic of the Electronic Fuel Injection (EFI) system for 1995 and later models

12.6 With the engine off, clean the throttle body

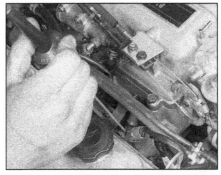

12.7 Use a stethoscope or a screwdriver to determine if the injectors are working properly

12.8 Fit the 'noid' light into the fuel injector connector and check that it blinks with the engine running

12 Electronic Fuel Injection (EFI) system - check

1 Check the earth wire connections for tightness. Check all wiring and electrical connectors that are related to the system. Loose electrical connectors and poor earths can cause many problems that resemble more serious malfunctions.
2 Check to see that the battery is fully charged, as the control unit and sensors depend on an accurate supply voltage in order to properly meter the fuel.
3 Check the air filter element - a dirty or partially blocked filter will severely impede performance and economy (see Chapter 1).
4 If a blown fuse is found, renew it and see if it blows again. If it does, search for an earthed wire in the harness related to the system.
5 Check the air inlet duct from the air cleaner housing to the inlet manifold for leaks, which will result in an excessively lean mixture. Also check the condition of the vacuum hoses connected to the inlet manifold.
6 Remove the air inlet duct from the throttle body and check for carbon and residue build-up. If it's dirty, clean it with aerosol carburettor cleaner (make sure the can says it's safe for use with oxygen sensors and catalytic converters) and a toothbrush (see illustration).
7 With the engine running, place a stethoscope against each injector, one at a time, and listen for a clicking sound, indicating operation (see illustration). If you don't have an automotive stethoscope you can use a long screwdriver; just place the tip of the screwdriver against the injector body and press your ear against the handle.
8 If there is a problem with an injector, purchase a special injector test light ('noid' light) and refit it into the injector electrical connector (see illustration). Start the engine and make sure that each injector connector flashes the noid light. This will test for the proper voltage signal to the injector.
9 With the engine OFF and the fuel injector

electrical connectors disconnected, measure the resistance of each injector (see illustration). Compare the measured resistance to the values listed in this Chapter's Specifications. Out of range injectors are probably faulty.
10 The remainder of the system checks should be left to a dealer service department or other qualified repair workshop, as there is a chance that the control unit may be damaged if not performed properly.

13 Electronic Fuel Injection (EFI) system - component check and renewal

⚠ **Warning: Petrol is extremely flammable, so take extra precautions when you work on any part of the fuel system. See the Warning in Section 2.**

Throttle body

Check

1 Verify that the throttle linkage operates smoothly when the throttle lever is moved from fully closed to fully open.
2 Check the throttle body for wear and deposits. Note: *Do not remove the thin seal coating from the throttle valves or bore.*

Renewal

⚠ **Warning: Wait until the engine is completely cool before beginning this procedure.**

3 Detach the cable from the negative terminal of the battery.
4 Loosen the hose clamps and remove the air inlet duct.
5 Detach the accelerator cable from the throttle lever (see Section 10).
6 If your vehicle is equipped with an automatic transmission, detach the throttle valve cable from the throttle linkage (see Chapter 7B), detach the cable bracket from the engine and set the cable and bracket aside.
7 Clearly label, then detach, all vacuum hoses from the throttle body.
8 Clearly label, then detach, all coolant hoses from the throttle body. Plug the coolant hoses to prevent coolant loss.
9 Disconnect the electrical connector from the throttle position sensor (TPS) (see illustration).
10 Remove the four throttle body mounting bolts (see illustration).
11 Detach the throttle body and gasket from the inlet manifold.
12 Using a soft brush and carburettor cleaner, thoroughly clean the throttle body casting, then blow out all passages with compressed air.

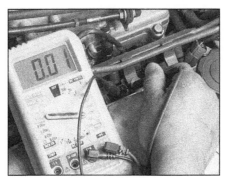

12.9 Using an ohmmeter, measure the resistance across the terminals of the injector

13.9 Loosen the TPS connector with a probe or small screwdriver, then disconnect the TPS connector

13.10 A typical throttle body is retained by four bolts/nuts (arrowed)

Caution: Do not clean the throttle position sensor with anything. Just wipe it off carefully with a clean, soft cloth.
13 Refitting of the throttle body is the reverse of removal.
14 Be sure to tighten the throttle body mounting bolts to the torque listed in this Chapter's Specifications.

Variable Inlet Control System (VICS) shutter valve actuator (1.8 litre engine only)

Check

15 Remove the vacuum hose from the actuator located on the opposite end of the plenum chamber from the throttle body.
16 Verify that the actuator rod can move in and out smoothly **(see illustration)**.
17 Start the engine and run it at idle.
18 Place a finger over the end of the vacuum hose and verify that there is vacuum **(see illustration)**.
19 Refit the vacuum hose and verify that the rod is pulled inward.

Throttle position sensor (TPS)

Check

20 Disconnect the electrical connector from the throttle position sensor (TPS).
21 Insert a feeler gauge of the specified thickness between the throttle stop screw and the stop lever **(see illustration)**.

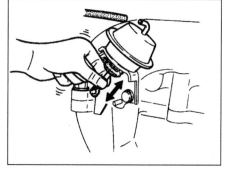

13.16 Actuator rod should move in and out smoothly

a) *On 1990 to 1994 models with an automatic transmission use a 0.6 mm (0.024 in) feeler gauge.*
b) *On 1990 to 1994 models with a manual transmission use a 1.0 mm (0.039 in) feeler gauge.*
c) *On all 1995 and later models use a 1.3 mm (0.050 in) feeler gauge.*

22 With the correct feeler gauge in position, use an ohmmeter to verify that there is no continuity between the specified terminal pairs **(see illustrations)**.
a) *The two lower terminals (E and IDL) on all 1990 to 1994 models, regardless of transmission type.*
b) *Terminals A and B on 1995 and later models.*

23 On 1990 to 1994 models with an automatic transmission, connect the ohmmeter probes to the 2nd terminal from the top and the lowest terminal. Then slowly rotate the throttle lever toward the wide-open position; there should be no continuity until the throttle reaches the wide-open position. In the closed throttle position there should be less than 1 k-ohm of resistance and at the wide-open position approximately 5 k-ohm resistance.
24 On 1990 to 1994 models with a manual transmission, connect the ohmmeter probes to the top two terminals. Then slowly rotate the throttle lever toward the wide-open position; there should be no continuity until the throttle reaches the wide-open position.

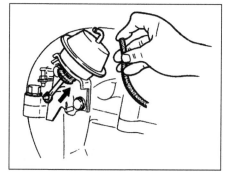

13.18 You should be able to feel the vacuum with your finger

13.21 Insert a feeler gauge between the throttle stop screw and stop lever (arrowed)

25 If the continuity and/or resistance is not as specified, adjust the TPS.

Adjustment

26 Disconnect the electrical connector from the throttle position sensor (TPS) and verify that the throttle valve is in the closed position.
27 Connect an ohmmeter between the throttle position sensor lower terminals **(see illustration 13.22a and 13.22b)**.
28 Loosen the two TPS attaching screws **(see illustration)**.
29 Insert a feeler gauge of the specified thickness between the throttle stop screw and the stop lever:
a) *On 1990 to 1994 models with an automatic transmission use a 0.25 mm (0.010 in) feeler gauge.*

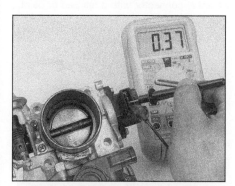

13.22a On 1990 to 1994 models there should be no continuity between the lower TPS terminals

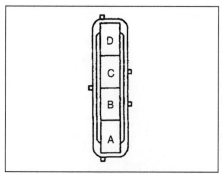

13.22b Typical TPS terminal configuration on 1995 and later models

13.28 Loosen the two screws (arrowed) holding the TPS in place

b) On 1990 to 1994 models with a manual transmission use a 0.4 mm (0.016 in) feeler gauge.

c) On 1995 and later models use a 0.15 mm (0.006 in) feeler gauge.

30 Rotate the throttle position sensor clockwise approximately 30°, then rotate it back (anti-clockwise) until there is continuity.

31 Renew the feeler gauge with a gauge of the specified thickness and verify that there is no continuity:

a) On 1990 to 1994 models with an automatic transmission use a 0.016 inch (0.4 mm) feeler gauge.

b) On 1990 to 1994 models with a manual transmission use a 0.027 inch (0.7 mm) feeler gauge.

c) On 1995 and later models use a 0.020 inch (0.50 mm) feeler gauge.

32 If there is continuity, repeat paragraphs 29 to 31.

33 Tighten the two attaching screws. **Note:** *Do not move the TPS from the set position when tightening the screws.*

34 If you cannot successfully adjust the TPS, renew it.

Renewal

35 If adjustment doesn't bring the sensor within specifications, disconnect it, remove the screws and renew it with a new one, then adjust it as described in paragraphs 26 to 33.

Fuel pressure regulator

Check

36 Refer to the fuel pump/fuel pressure check procedure (see Section 3).

Renewal

37 Relieve the fuel pressure (see Section 2) and detach the cable from the negative terminal of the battery.

38 Detach the vacuum sensing hose from the regulator.

39 Place a metal container or workshop towel under the fuel return hose.

40 Slide the clamp down the hose and remove the fuel return hose from the regulator.

41 Remove the pressure regulator mounting bolts **(see illustration)** and detach the pressure regulator from the fuel rail.

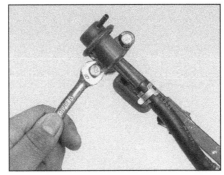

13.41 Remove the fuel pressure regulator from the fuel rail

42 Use a new O-ring and make sure that the pressure regulator is installed properly on the fuel rail **(see illustration)**.

43 The remainder of refitting is the reverse of removal.

Idle air control (IAC) valve

Note: *The minimum idle speed is pre-set at the factory and should not require adjustment under normal operating conditions; however if the throttle body has been replaced or you suspect the minimum idle speed has been tampered with (for example, if the idle speed screw was removed from the throttle body) have the vehicle checked by a dealer service department or a qualified automotive repair workshop.*

Check

44 Apply the handbrake, shift the transmission to Neutral (manual) or Park (automatic) and chock the drive wheels. Refit the lead of a tachometer to the IG (–) terminal on the diagnostic test connector. Start the engine and allow it to reach normal operating temperature. Check the idle speed and compare it to the idle speed listed in this Chapter's Specifications.

45 Check if a click sound is heard and the engine speed increases to approximately 1200 rpm when the IAC valve is disconnected at idle. If the engine speed does not increase, renew the IAC.

46 Disconnect the IAC valve electrical connector.

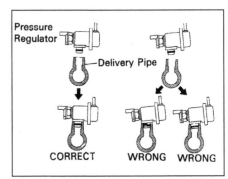

13.42 If the fuel pressure regulator is cocked during refitting, it will not seal properly

47 Measure the resistance between the two terminals **(see illustration)**. Compare your results to the IAC valve resistance in this Chapter's Specifications.

48 If the resistance is not as specified, renew the IAC valve.

49 Connect the IAC valve electrical connector.

Renewal

50 Remove the throttle body (see paragraphs 3 to 11).

51 Remove the mounting screws and detach the IAC valve and gasket **(see illustration)**.

52 Refitting of the IAC valve is the reverse of removal. Be sure to use a new gasket when refitting the IAC valve.

Fuel rail and fuel injectors

Check

53 Refer to the fuel injection system checking procedure (see Section 12).

Renewal

54 Relieve the fuel pressure (see Section 2).

55 Detach the cable from the negative terminal of the battery (see the **Warning** at the beginning of this Section).

56 Remove the PCV hose from the cylinder head and inlet manifold.

57 Remove the hose clamps/hoses from the air valve, then remove the air valve from the side of the air inlet plenum chamber **(see illustrations)**.

58 Carefully mark each injector and its electrical connector with a felt pen or paint,

13.47 Using an ohmmeter, check the resistance across the IAC valve terminals

13.51 Remove the screws that retain the IAC valve to the throttle body

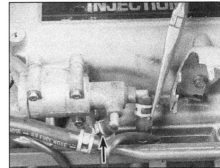

13.57a Release the hose clamps with pliers and slide the clamps down the hose

13.57b Remove the air valve mounting screws (arrowed)

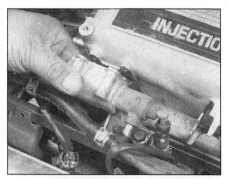

13.57c Remove the air valve

13.58a Release the fuel injection harness clips

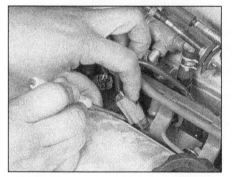

13.58b Disconnect the injector electrical connectors

13.61 Remove the bolts (arrowed) that retain the fuel rail to the inlet manifold

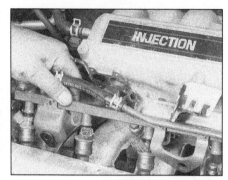

13.62a Lift the fuel rail assembly from the engine

then carefully release the two harness clips and remove the connectors **(see illustrations)** from each injector and set the wire harness aside. **Note:** *Use a small flat blade screwdriver to release the connectors lock lever while gently pulling the connector.*

59 Detach the vacuum sensing hose from the fuel pressure regulator.

60 Disconnect the fuel lines from the fuel pressure regulator and the fuel rail.

61 Remove the fuel rail mounting bolts **(see illustration)**.

62 Remove the fuel rail with the fuel injectors attached and if you intend to reuse the injectors number the injector and its position on the rail so you can refit them in the same position **(see illustrations)**.

63 Remove the fuel injectors from the fuel rail **(see illustration)** and set them aside in a

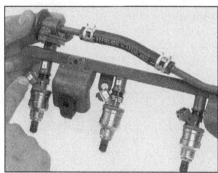

13.62b Number each injector and its rail position

clearly labelled storage container. **Note:** *The seals sometimes stick on the injectors when removed.*

13.63 Gently pull on the injectors to remove them from the rail

64 If you intend to re-use the same injectors, renew the grommets and O-rings **(see illustrations)**.

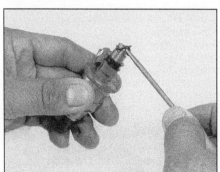

13.64a Remove the O-ring from the injector

13.64b Remove the grommet from the top of the injector

13.64c Remove the insulator from the bores in the inlet manifold

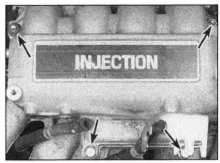

13.72 Remove the upper bolts/nuts (arrowed) that fasten the air inlet plenum to the inlet manifold

65 Refitting of the fuel injectors is the reverse of removal.
66 Tighten the fuel rail mounting bolts to the torque listed in this Chapter's Specifications.

Air inlet plenum chamber

Removal

 Warning: Wait until the engine is completely cool before beginning this procedure.

67 Detach the cable from the negative terminal of the battery.
68 Detach the accelerator cable (see Section 10) and the throttle cable (see Chapter 7) from the plenum chamber and throttle body assembly.
69 On the 1.8 litre engine, disconnect the vacuum hose from the VICS vacuum chamber to the plenum chamber and the vacuum hose attached to the VICS shutter valve on the plenum chamber.
70 Clearly label, then detach, any other vacuum lines connected to the air inlet plenum chamber.

13.73 Remove the bolt (arrowed) from the underside of the inlet manifold

71 Detach the throttle body assembly from the plenum chamber (see paragraphs 10 and 11).
72 Remove the air inlet plenum chamber upper retaining bolts and nuts **(see illustration)**. Note: *Models with the 1.6 litre engine have 1 bolt and 2 nut; and models with the 1.8 litre engine have 5 bolts and 2 nuts.*
73 Raise the vehicle and support it securely, then from under the vehicle, remove the bolts going from the inlet manifold into the air inlet plenum chamber **(see illustration)**. Note: *Models with the 1.6 litre engine have three bolts underneat; and models with the 1.8 litre engine have four bolts underneath.*
74 Lift the air inlet plenum chamber off the lower inlet manifold.

Refitting

75 Be sure to clean and inspect the mounting surface of the lower inlet manifold (see Chapter 2A) and the air inlet plenum chamber before positioning the new gasket onto the lower inlet mounting face. Refit the air inlet plenum chamber onto the inlet manifold.

Ensure the gasket remains in place. Refit the upper inlet manifold retaining bolts and tighten the bolts/nuts to the torque listed in this Chapter's Specifications. Refitting is otherwise the reverse of removal.

14 Exhaust system servicing - general information

 Warning: Inspection and repair of exhaust system components should be done only after the system components have cooled completely.

1 The exhaust system consists of the exhaust manifold, catalytic converter, the silencer, the tailpipe and all connecting pipes, brackets, supports and clamps. The exhaust system is attached to the body with mounting brackets and rubber hangers **(see illustration)**. If any of these parts are damaged or deteriorated, excessive noise and vibration will be transmitted to the body.
2 Conducting regular inspections of the exhaust system will keep it safe and quiet. Look for any damaged or bent parts, open seams, holes, loose connections, excessive corrosion or other defects which could allow exhaust fumes to enter the vehicle. Deteriorated exhaust system components should not be repaired - they should be replaced with new parts.
3 If the exhaust system components are extremely corroded or rusted together, they will probably have to be cut from the exhaust system. The convenient way to accomplish this is to simply cut off the old components with a hack-saw. If you do decide to tackle the job at home, be sure to wear eye protection to guard your eyes from metal chips and work gloves to protect your hands.
4 Here are some simple guidelines to apply when repairing the exhaust system:
a) *Work from the back to the front when removing exhaust system components.*
b) *Apply penetrating oil to the exhaust system component fasteners to make them easier to remove.*
c) *Use new gaskets, supports and clamps when refitting exhaust system components.*
d) *Apply anti-seize compound to the threads of all exhaust system fasteners during reassembly.*
Be sure to allow sufficient clearance between newly installed parts and all points on the underbody to avoid overheating the floor pan and possibly damaging the interior carpet and insulation. Pay particularly close attention to the catalytic converter and its heat shield.

 Warning: The catalytic converter operates at very high temperatures and takes a long time to cool. Wait until it's completely cool before attempting to remove the converter. Failure to do so could result in serious burns.

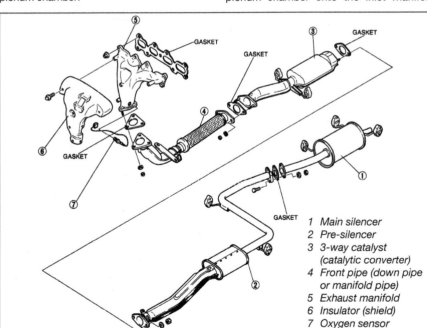

1 Main silencer
2 Pre-silencer
3 3-way catalyst (catalytic converter)
4 Front pipe (down pipe or manifold pipe)
5 Exhaust manifold
6 Insulator (shield)
7 Oxygen sensor

14.1 Exploded view of a typical exhaust system

Chapter 5
Engine electrical systems

Contents

Degrees of difficulty

Easy, suitable for novice with little experience		**Fairly easy,** suitable for beginner with some experience		**Fairly difficult,** suitable for competent DIY mechanic		**Difficult,** suitable for experienced DIY mechanic		**Very difficult,** suitable for expert DIY or professional	

Specifications

Ignition timing
1.3 litre engine .... 10 ± 1° BTDC at idle
1.5 litre engine .... 0 ± 1° at idle
1.6 litre engine .... 7 ± 1° BTDC at idle
1.8 litre engine .... 0 ± 1° at idle

Ignition coil resistance (cold)
Primary resistance
  1.3 litre and 1.5 litre engines .... 0.49 to 0.73 ohms at 20° C (68° F)
  1.6 litre engine
    All models except Estate .... 0.81 to 0.99 ohms at 20° C (68° F)
    Estate .... 1.04 to 1.27 ohms at 20° C (68° F)
  1.8 litre engine .... 0.49 to 0.73 ohms at 20° C (68° F)
Secondary resistance
  1.3 litre and 1.5 litre engines .... 20 to 31 k-ohms at 20° C (68° F)
  1.6 litre engine .... 10 to 16 k-ohms at 20° C (68° F)
  1.8 litre engine .... 20 to 31 k-ohms at 20° C (68° F)

Charging system

Charging voltage	14.1 to 14.7 volts
Standard amperage	
All lights and accessories turned off	Less than 12 amps
Headlights (main beam) and heater blower motor turned on	65 amps or more at 2500 to 3000 rpm
Alternator brush length	
Standard	
1.3 litre engine and 1.5 litre engine	20.0 mm
1.6 litre engine	21.5 mm
1.8 litre engine	16.5 mm
Minimum	
1.3 litre engine and 1.5 litre engine	5.0 mm
1.6 litre engine and 1.8 litre engine	8.0 mm

Torque specifications

	lbf ft	Nm
Alternator mounting bolts		
Adjusting bolt	12 to 16	16 to 22
Pivot bolt	24 to 33	33 to 45
Distributor mounting bolt	14 to 18	19 to 24
Starter mounting bolts	24 to 33	33 to 46

1 General information

The engine electrical systems include all ignition, charging and starting components. Because of their engine related functions, these components are discussed separately from chassis electrical devices such as the lights, the instruments, etc. (which are included in Chapter 12).

Always observe the following precautions when working on the electrical systems:

a) Be extremely careful when servicing engine electrical components. They are easily damaged if checked, connected or handled improperly.

b) Never leave the ignition switch on for long periods of time (10 minutes maximum) with the engine off.

c) Don't disconnect the battery cables while the engine is running.

d) Maintain correct polarity when connecting a battery cable from another vehicle during jump starting.

Always disconnect the negative cable first and hook it up last or the battery may be shorted by the tool being used to loosen the cable clamps.

3.1 Remove the battery

Caution: If the stereo in your vehicle is equipped with an anti-theft system, make sure you have the correct code before disconnecting the battery in any of the following procedures.

It's also a good idea to review the safety-related information regarding the engine electrical systems located in the *Safety First* section near the front of this manual before beginning any operation included in this Chapter.

2 Battery - emergency jump starting

Refer to the *Jump starting* procedure at the front of this manual.

3 Battery - removal and refitting

1 Beginning with the negative battery cable **(see illustration)**, disconnect both cables from the battery terminals.

2 Remove the battery hold-down clamp.

3 Lift out the battery. Be careful, it's heavy.

4 While the battery is out, inspect the carrier (tray) for corrosion.

5 If you are replacing the battery, make sure that you get one that is identical, with the same dimensions, amperage rating, cold cranking amperage rating, etc., as the original.

6 Refitting is the reverse of removal.

4 Battery cables - check and renewal

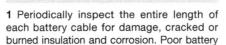

1 Periodically inspect the entire length of each battery cable for damage, cracked or burned insulation and corrosion. Poor battery cable connections can cause starting problems and decreased engine performance.

2 Check the cable-to-terminal connections at the ends of the cables for cracks, loose wire strands and corrosion. The presence of white, fluffy deposits under the insulation at the cable terminal connection is a sign that the cable is corroded and should be replaced. Check the terminals for distortion, missing mounting bolts and corrosion.

3 When removing the cables, always disconnect the negative cable first and hook it up last or the battery may be shorted by the tool used to loosen the cable clamps. Even if only the positive cable is being replaced, be sure to disconnect the negative cable from the battery first .

4 Disconnect the old cables from the battery, then trace each of them to their opposite ends and detach them from the starter solenoid and earth terminals. Note the routing of each cable to ensure correct refitting.

5 If you are replacing either or both of the old cables, take them with you when buying new cables. It is vitally important that you renew the cables with identical parts. Cables have characteristics that make them easy to identify: positive cables are usually red, larger in cross-section and have a larger diameter battery post clamp; earth cables are usually black, smaller in cross-section and have a slightly smaller diameter clamp for the negative post.

6 Clean the threads of the solenoid or earth connection with a wire brush to remove rust and corrosion. Apply a light coat of battery terminal corrosion inhibitor, or petroleum jelly, to the threads to prevent future corrosion.

7 Attach the cable to the solenoid or earth connection and tighten the mounting nut/bolt securely.

8 Before connecting a new cable to the battery, make sure that it reaches the battery post without having to be stretched.

9 Connect the positive cable first, followed by the negative cable.

5 Ignition system - general information and precautions

1 The electronic ignition system includes the ignition switch, the battery, the igniter (1994 and earlier models), the ignition coil, the primary (low voltage) and secondary (high voltage) coils, the distributor and the spark plugs. The ignition system is controlled by the Powertrain Control Module (PCM). Using data provided by information sensors which monitor various engine functions (such as rpm, intake air volume, engine temperature, etc.), the PCM ensures a perfectly timed spark under all conditions. **Note:** *In 1995 and later models the igniter and the coil have been integrated into the distributor body, now called the ignition control module and ignition coil.*
2 The electronic ignition systems are divided into two groups: External ignition coil distributor (1994 and earlier models) and the internal ignition coil distributor (1995 and later models) which also include the ICM **(see illustrations)**. When diagnosing the electronic ignition system, be sure to make all the necessary ignition system checks before replacing any components, as they are expensive and usually non-returnable.
3 When working on the ignition system, take the following precautions:
a) *Do not keep the ignition switch on for more than 10 seconds if the engine will not start.*
b) *Always connect a tachometer in accordance with the manufacturer's instructions. Some tachometers may be incompatible with this ignition system. Consult a dealer service department before buying a tachometer for use with this vehicle.*
c) *Never allow the ignition coil terminals to touch earth. Earthing the coil could result in damage to the igniter and/or the ignition coil.*
d) *Do not disconnect the battery when the engine is running.*
e) *On 1994 and earlier models, make sure the igniter is properly earthed.*

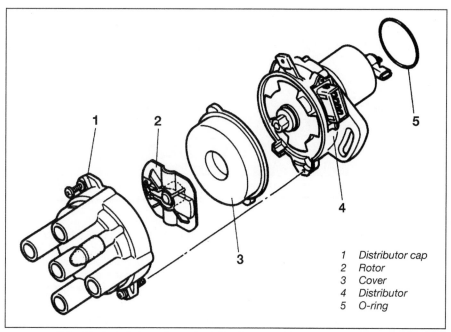

1	Distributor cap
2	Rotor
3	Cover
4	Distributor
5	O-ring

5.2a Exploded view of a typical distributor - 1994 and earlier models

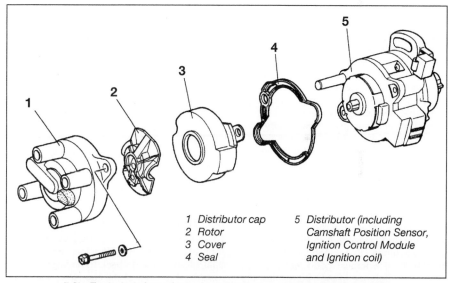

1	Distributor cap	5	Distributor (including
2	Rotor		Camshaft Position Sensor,
3	Cover		Ignition Control Module
4	Seal		and Ignition coil)

5.2b Exploded view of a typical distributor - 1995 and later models

6 Ignition system - check

⚠ **Warning: Because of the high voltage generated by the ignition system, extreme care should be taken whenever an operation is performed involving ignition components. This not only includes the igniter, coil, distributor and spark plug leads, but related components such as plug connectors, tachometer and other test equipment also.**

1 If the engine turns over but will not start, disconnect the spark plug lead from any spark plug and attach it to a calibrated tester available at most car accessory outlets **(see illustration)**. Connect the clip on the tester to a bolt or metal bracket on the engine. If you're unable to obtain a calibrated ignition tester, remove the lead from one of the spark plugs and, using an insulated tool, pull back the boot and hold the end of the lead about 6 mm (0.25 in) from a good earth.
2 Crank the engine and watch the end of the tester or spark plug lead to see if bright blue, well-defined sparks occur.
3 If sparks occur, sufficient voltage is reaching the plug to fire it (repeat the check at the remaining plug leads to verify that the

6.1 Using a calibrated ignition tester

6.5 Disconnect the high tension lead from the distributor and hold it with insulated pliers

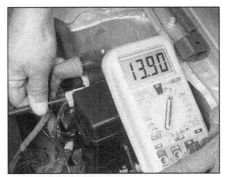

6.7 Check for battery voltage to the positive side (+) of the ignition coil

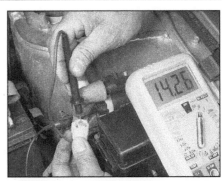

6.9 Disconnect the electrical connector and check for battery voltage to the igniter

distributor cap and rotor are OK). However, the plugs themselves may be fouled, so remove and check them as described in Chapter 1.

4 If no sparks or intermittent sparks occur, remove the distributor cap and check the cap and rotor as described in Chapter 1. If moisture is present, dry out the cap and rotor, then refit the cap and repeat the spark test.

1994 and earlier models

5 If there is still no spark, detach the coil secondary wire from the distributor cap and hook it up to the tester (re-attach the plug lead to the spark plug), then repeat the spark check. Again, if you don't have a tester, hold the end of the wire about 6 mm (0.25 in) from a good earth **(see illustration)**.

6 If sparks now occur, the distributor cap, rotor or plug lead(s) may be defective.

7 If no sparks occur, check the primary wire connections at the coil to make sure they're clean and tight. Check for voltage to the coil on the primary circuit from the ignition switch **(see illustration)**. Check the ignition coil (see Section 7). Make any necessary repairs, then repeat the check again.

8 If there's still no spark, the coil-to-cap lead may be faulty (check the resistance with an ohmmeter and compare it to the spark plug lead resistance Specifications found in Chapter 1). If a known good lead doesn't make any difference in the test results, the igniter may be defective .

9 Check for battery voltage to the igniter **(see illustration)** with the ignition key ON, engine not running. If voltage is available and there is still no spark, remove the igniter (see Section 8) and have it checked at a properly-equipped repair workshop.

1995 and later models

10 Check the ignition coil, ignition control module-related voltages (3 volts when idling at no load), wiring harness, and distributor connector.

11 If all of these are normal and no firing is observed, renew the distributor.

---

7 Ignition coil - check and renewal

Check

1 Perform the ignition system checks as described in Section 6.

2 Crank the engine and verify that a strong blue spark is visible at the coil wire or spark plug lead.

1994 and earlier models

3 If there is no spark, disconnect the connector from the ignition coil **(see illustration 6.7)** and check for voltage at the positive (+) terminal of the connector with the ignition switch in the ON position.

4 If there is no battery voltage, check the main fuse, ignition switch, and wiring harness.

5 Use an ohmmeter to measure the resistance of the primary coil winding **(see illustration)**. If not within specifications identified in this Chapter's Specifications, renew the coil.

6 Use an ohmmeter to measure the resistance of the secondary coil winding **(see illustration)**. If not within the specifications listed in this Chapter's Specifications, renew the coil.

1995 and later models

7 Perform the ignition system checks as described in Section 6.

8 Disconnect the 3-pin connector from the distributor.

9 Using an ohmmeter, measure the primary coil resistance between terminals A and B on the distributor **(see illustration)**. Measure the secondary coil resistance between terminal A and the distributor body.

10 Renew the distributor if the resistance is not within the values listed in this Chapter's specifications.

Renewal

Note: The coil is replaceable on 1994 and earlier models only. On 1995 and later models, renew the complete distributor assembly.

11 Detach the cable from the negative terminal of the battery.

12 Remove the heat shield from the coil.

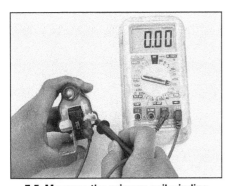

7.5 Measure the primary coil winding resistance

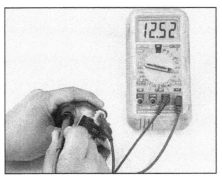

7.6 Measure the resistance of the secondary coil winding

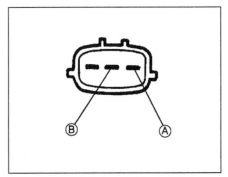

7.9 Distributor 3-pin connector terminal identification

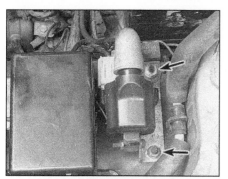

7.14 Remove the coil mounting bolts (arrowed)

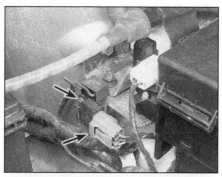

8.3 Remove the screws (arrowed) from the bracket assembly and remove the igniter/bracket assembly

9.5 Make a mark on the distributor (arrowed) . Also mark the distributor base and the engine (arrowed)

13 Label and disconnect the wires from the coil terminals.
14 Remove the coil mounting bolts **(see illustration)**.
15 Refitting is the reverse of removal.

8 Igniter (1994 and earlier models) - renewal

Note: *A special igniter checker is required to check the function of the igniter. Some automotive parts stores will perform the check for you.*
1 Detach the cable from the negative terminal of the battery.
2 Disconnect the electrical connector from the igniter.
3 Remove the screws from the bracket assembly and remove the igniter and bracket assembly from the engine compartment **(see illustration)**.
4 Refitting is the reverse of removal.

9 Distributor - removal and refitting

Removal

1 Detach the cable from the negative battery terminal.

2 Look for a raised '1' on the distributor cap. This marks the location for the number one cylinder spark plug lead terminal. If the cap does not have a mark for the number one terminal, locate the number one spark plug and trace the lead back to the terminal on the cap.
3 Remove the distributor cap (see Chapter 1) and turn the engine over until the rotor is pointing toward the number one spark plug terminal (see locating TDC procedure in Chapter 2A).
4 Disconnect and label the electrical connectors from the distributor.
5 Make a mark on the edge of the distributor base directly below the rotor tip and in line with it. Also, mark the distributor base and the engine block to ensure that the distributor is installed correctly **(see illustration)**.
6 If equipped with collar bolts, loosen but do not remove the two bolts in the distributor collar. This will give the distributor shaft clearance.
7 Remove the distributor hold-down bolt **(see illustration)**, then pull the distributor straight out to remove it.
Caution: DO NOT turn the crankshaft while the distributor is out of the engine, or the alignment marks will be useless.

Refitting

Note: *If the crankshaft has been moved while the distributor is out, locate Top Dead Centre*

(TDC) for the number one piston (see Chapter 2A) and position the distributor and the rotor accordingly.
8 Refit a new O-ring onto the distributor housing **(see illustration)**.
9 Align the cut-out portion of the coupling with the groove in the housing **(see illustration)**.
10 Insert the distributor into the engine in exactly the same relationship to the block that it was in when removed.
11 If the distributor does not seat completely, recheck the alignment marks between the distributor base and the block to verify that the distributor is in the same position it was in before removal. Also check the rotor to see if it's aligned with the mark you made on the edge of the distributor base.
12 Loosely refit the distributor hold-down bolt(s).
13 Refit the distributor cap and connect the electrical connectors.
14 Check the ignition timing (see Section 10) and tighten the distributor hold-down bolt securely.

10 Ignition timing - check and adjustment

1 Connect a tachometer according to the manufacturer's specifications.

9.7 Remove the distributor hold-down bolt (arrowed) and pull the distributor straight out

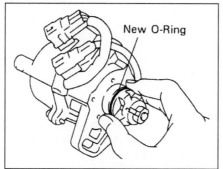

New O-Ring

9.8 Refit a new O-ring onto the distributor housing

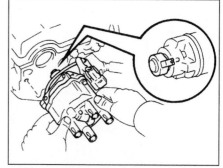

9.9 Align the cut-out portion of the coupling with the groove in the housing

10.2 Attach a jumper wire between terminals TEN and GND of the test connector

10.3 Tools needed to check and adjust the ignition timing

1   *Vacuum plugs - Vacuum hoses will, in most cases, have to be disconnected and plugged. Moulded plugs in various shapes and sizes are available for this*
2   *Inductive pick-up timing light - Flashes a bright, concentrated beam of light when the number one spark plug fires. Connect the leads according to the instructions supplied with the light*
3   *Distributor spanner - On some models, the hold-down bolt for the distributor is difficult to reach and turn with conventional spanners or sockets. A special spanner like this must be used*

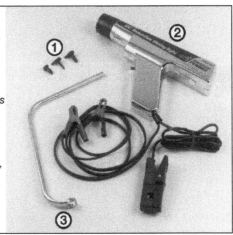

2 Locate the diagnostic connector and insert a jumper wire between terminals TEN and GND **(see illustration). Note:** *This is not necessary on the 1995 and later models.*
3 With the ignition switch off, connect a timing light according to the manufacturer's specifications **(see illustration)**. Most timing lights are powered by the battery. Also, an inductive style pick-up is installed onto the number one cylinder spark plug lead.
4 Locate the timing marks on the pointer index and the crankshaft pulley.
5 Start the engine and allow it to warm up to normal operating temperature (upper radiator hose hot). Verify that the engine idle is correct (750 rpm with an automatic transmission and 700 rpm with a manual transmission). Aim the timing light at the index pointer **(see illustration)**. The mark on the crankshaft pulley should line up with the timing indicator. If necessary, loosen the distributor hold-down bolt and slowly rotate the distributor until the timing marks align. Tighten the hold-down bolt and recheck the timing.
6 Remove the jumper wire from the diagnostic connector and confirm that the ignition timing advances to 12 to 22° BTDC.
7 Turn the engine off and remove the tachometer and the timing light.

10.5 Point the timing light at the timing marks with the engine at idle

11 Charging system - general information and precautions

The charging system includes the alternator, an internal voltage regulator, a charge indicator, the battery and the wiring between all the components **(see illustration)**. The charging system supplies electrical power for the ignition system, the lights, the radio, etc. The alternator is driven by a drivebelt at the front of the engine.

The purpose of the voltage regulator is to limit the alternator's voltage to a preset value. This prevents power surges, circuit overloads,

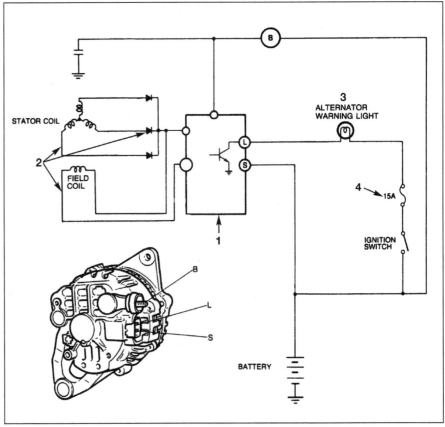

11.1 Typical charging system schematic diagram

B *Battery connection (high current large wire connection)*
L *Indicator connection*
S *Voltage sensing connection*

1 *Voltage regulator*
2 *Stator and field excitation windings, diode bridge*
3 *Alternator warning light on dashboard*
4 *Alternator fuse in fuse box*

etc., during peak voltage output.

The charging system doesn't ordinarily require periodic maintenance. However, the drivebelt, battery and wires and connections should be inspected at the intervals outlined in Chapter 1.

The dashboard warning light should come on when the ignition key is turned to Start, then should go off immediately. If it remains on, there is a malfunction in the charging system. Some vehicles are also equipped with a voltage gauge. If the voltage gauge indicates abnormally high or low voltage, check the charging system (see Section 12).

Be very careful when making electrical circuit connections to a vehicle equipped with an alternator and note the following:

a) When reconnecting wires to the alternator from the battery, be sure to note the polarity.
b) Before using arc welding equipment to repair any part of the vehicle, disconnect the wires from the alternator and the battery terminals.
c) Never start the engine with a battery charger connected.
d) Always disconnect both battery leads before using a battery charger.
e) The alternator is driven by an engine drivebelt which could cause serious injury if your hand, hair or clothes become entangled in it with the engine running.
f) Because the alternator is connected directly to the battery, it could arc or cause a fire if overloaded or shorted out.
g) Wrap a plastic bag over the alternator and secure it with rubber bands before steam cleaning the engine.

12 Charging system - check

1 If a malfunction occurs in the charging circuit, don't automatically assume that the alternator is causing the problem. First check the following items:

a) Check the drivebelt tension and its condition. Renew it if worn or deteriorated.
b) Make sure the alternator mounting and adjustment bolts are tight.
c) Inspect the alternator wiring harness and the electrical connectors at the alternator and voltage regulator. They must be in good condition and tight.
d) Check the large main fuse in the engine compartment. If it's burned, determine the cause, repair the circuit and renew the fuse (the vehicle won't start and/or the accessories won't work if the fuse blows).
e) Check all the fuses that are in series with the charging system circuit. The location of these fuses may vary from year and model but the designations are the same.
f) Start the engine and check the alternator for abnormal noises (a shrieking or squealing sound indicates faulty bushes).
g) Check the specific gravity of the battery electrolyte. If it's low, charge the battery (doesn't apply to maintenance free batteries).
h) Make sure that the battery is fully charged (one bad cell in a battery can cause overcharging by the alternator).
i) Disconnect the battery cables (negative first, then positive). Inspect the battery posts and the cable clamps for corrosion. Clean them thoroughly if necessary (see Chapter 1). Reconnect the positive cable, then the negative cable.

2 Using a voltmeter, check the battery voltage with the engine off. It should be approximately 12 volts.

3 Start the engine and check the battery voltage again. It should now be approximately 13.5 to 15.1 volts.

4 Turn on the headlights. The voltage should drop and then come back up, if the charging system is working properly.

5 If the voltage reading is greater than the specified charging voltage, renew the voltage regulator (see Section 14).

6 If the voltmeter reading is less than standard voltage, check the regulator and alternator as follows.

7 Remove the cover from the alternator. Start the engine and check the voltages at the alternator terminals are as specified (see illustration).

a) If the voltmeter readings are greater than standard voltage, renew the regulator.
b) If the voltmeter reading is less than standard voltage, check the alternator (or have it checked by a dealer service department if you do not have an ammeter).

8 If you have an ammeter, hook it up to the charging system as shown (see illustration). If you do not have an ammeter, you can also use an inductive-type current indicator. This device is inexpensive, readily available at car accessory outlets and accurate enough to perform simple amperage checks like the following test.

9 With the engine running at 2,000 rpm, check the reading on the ammeter with all accessories and lights off, then again with the high-beam headlights on and the heater blower switch turned to the HI position. Compare your readings to the standard amperage listed in this Chapter's Specifications.

10 If the ammeter reading is less than standard amperage, repair or renew the alternator.

13 Alternator - removal and refitting

Removal

1 Detach the cable from the negative terminal of the battery.

2 Remove the power steering pressure line brace, if equipped.

3 Remove the EGR solenoid valve bracket, if equipped.

4 Detach the electrical connector from the alternator (see illustration).

5 Loosen the alternator adjustment, pivot and

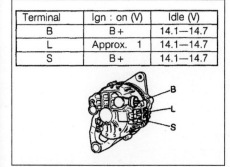

Terminal	Ign : on (V)	Idle (V)
B	B +	14.1—14.7
L	Approx. 1	14.1—14.7
S	B +	14.1—14.7

12.7 Check the voltages at the alternator terminals with the ignition On (engine not running) and at idle

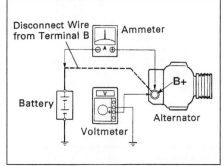

12.8 Hook up an ammeter as shown to check the alternator output

13.4 Detach the electrical connector from the alternator (arrowed)

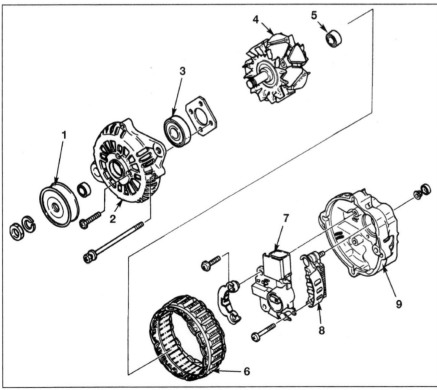

13.5 Alternator refitting details

1 *Terminal wire B*
2 *Alternator connector (terminals L and S)*
3 *Belt tensioner*
4 *Drive belt*
5 *Alternator adjusting arm/bracket*
6 *Alternator*

lock bolts **(see illustration)** and detach the drivebelt.

6 Remove the adjustment and lock bolts from the alternator adjustment bracket.

7 Separate the alternator and bracket from the engine.

8 If you are replacing the alternator, take the old alternator with you when purchasing a renewal unit. Make sure that the new/rebuilt unit is identical to the old alternator. Look at the terminals - they should be the same in number, size and locations as the terminals

on the old alternator. Finally, look at the identification markings - they will be stamped in the housing or printed on a tag or plaque affixed to the housing. Make sure that these numbers are the same on both alternators.

9 Many new/rebuilt alternators do not have a pulley installed, so you may have to switch the pulley from the old unit to the new/rebuilt one. When buying an alternator, find out the store policy regarding refitting of pulleys - some stores will perform this service free of charge.

Refitting

10 Refit in the reverse order of refitting
11 After the alternator is installed, adjust the drivebelt tension (see Chapter 1).
12 Check the charging voltage to verify proper operation of the alternator (see Section 12).

14 Alternator components - check and renewal

Dismantling

1 Remove the alternator (see Section 13) and place it on a clean workbench.

2 Remove the nut, lock-washer, pulley, and the four small bolts located behind the pulley **(see illustration)**.

3 Remove the four large bolts that hold the front cover to the rear housing and separate them **(see illustration 14.2)**.

4 Remove the stator, the two bolts holding the brush holder assembly and the nut on the back of the rear housing which retains the rectifier **(see illustration 14.2)**. If you are going to renew the brushes, proceed with the next paragraph.

5 Measure the exposed length of each brush **(see illustration)** and compare it to the minimum length listed in this Chapter's Specifications. If the length of either brush is less than the specified minimum, renew the brushes.

6 Make sure that each brush moves smoothly in the brush holder.

14.2 Exploded view of an alternator

1 *Pulley*
2 *Front cover*
3 *Bearing*
4 *Rotor*
5 *Bearing*
6 *Stator*
7 *Brush holder*
8 *Rectifier*
9 *Rear cover*

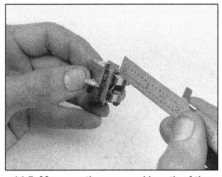

14.5 Measure the exposed length of the brushes

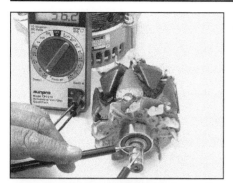

14.7a Continuity should exist between the rotor slip rings

14.7b Check the continuity between the rotor and the slip rings. There should be NO continuity

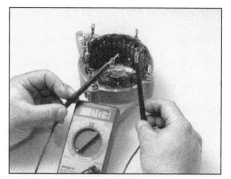

14.8 Check for continuity between the stator windings

Component checks

7 Check for an open circuit between the two slip rings **(see illustration)**. There should be 3.5 to 4.5 ohms resistance between the slip rings. Check for earths between each slip ring and the rotor **(see illustration)**. There should be no continuity (infinite resistance) between the rotor and either slip ring. If the rotor fails either test, or if the slip rings are excessively worn, the rotor is defective.

8 Check for open circuits between each end terminal of the stator windings **(see illustration)**. If either reading is open (infinite resistance), the stator is defective. Check for a earthed stator winding between each stator terminal and the frame. If there's continuity between any stator winding and the frame, the stator is defective.

9 Using an ohmmeter, check the rectifier as shown **(see illustration)**. Renew the rectifier if it fails any of the tests.

Reassembly

10 Refit the components in the reverse order of removal, noting the following.

11 Refit the brush holder by depressing each brush with a small screwdriver to clear the shaft **(see illustration)**.

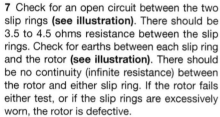

Negative	Positive	Continuity
E		Yes
B	P1, P2, P3	No
T		No
P1, P2, P3	E	No
	B	Yes
P1, P2, P3	T	Yes

14.9 Rectifier terminal guide and continuity chart

electrical energy to the starter motor, which does the actual work of cranking the engine.

5 The starter motor on a vehicle equipped with an automatic transmission can be operated only when the transmission selector lever is in Park or Neutral.

14.11 Depress each brush with a small screwdriver to clear the shaft

6 Always observe the following precautions when working on the starting system:

a) *Excessive cranking of the starter motor can overheat it and cause serious damage. Never operate the starter motor for more than 15 seconds at a time without pausing to allow it to cool for at least two minutes.*

15 Starting system - general information and precautions

1 The sole function of the starting system is to turn over the engine quickly enough to allow it to start.

2 The starting system consists of the battery, the starter motor, the starter solenoid and the electrical circuit connecting the components. The solenoid is mounted directly on the starter motor **(see illustration)**.

3 The solenoid/starter motor assembly is installed on the upper part of the engine, next to the transmission bellhousing.

4 When the ignition key is turned to the START position, the starter solenoid is actuated through the starter control circuit. The starter solenoid then connects the battery to the starter. The battery supplies the

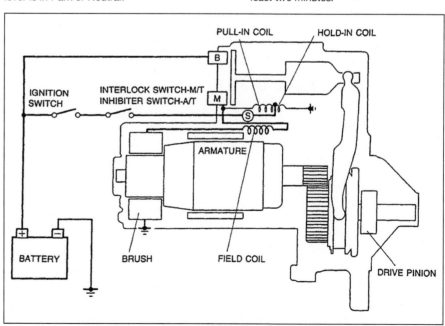

15.2 Wiring schematic of a typical starter/solenoid assembly

b) *The starter is connected directly to the battery and could arc or cause a fire if mishandled, overloaded or short circuited.*

c) *Always detach the cable from the negative terminal of the battery before working on the starting system.*

16 Starter motor - testing in vehicle

Note: *Before diagnosing starter problems, make sure the battery is fully charged.*

1 If the starter motor does not turn at all when the switch is operated, make sure that the shift lever is in Neutral or Park (automatic transmission).

2 Make sure that the battery is charged and that all cables, both at the battery and starter solenoid terminals, are clean and secure.

3 If the starter motor spins but the engine is not cranking, the overrunning clutch in the starter motor is slipping and the starter motor must be replaced.

4 If, when the switch is actuated, the starter motor does not operate at all but the solenoid clicks, then the problem lies with either the battery, the main solenoid contacts or the starter motor itself (or the engine is seized).

5 If the solenoid plunger cannot be heard when the switch is actuated, the battery is faulty, the circuit is open, or the starter solenoid itself is defective.

6 To check the solenoid, connect a jumper lead between the battery (+) and the ignition switch terminal (the small terminal) on the solenoid. If the starter motor now operates, the solenoid is OK and the problem is in the ignition switch, Neutral start switch or in the wiring.

7 If the starter motor still does not operate, remove the starter/solenoid assembly for dismantling, testing and repair.

8 If the starter motor cranks the engine at an abnormally slow speed, first make sure that the battery is charged and that all terminal connections are tight. If the engine is partially

seized, or has the wrong viscosity oil in it, it will crank slowly.

9 Run the engine until normal operating temperature is reached, then disconnect the coil wire from the distributor cap and earth it on the engine.

10 Connect a voltmeter positive lead to the battery positive post and connect the negative lead to the negative post.

11 Crank the engine and take the voltmeter readings as soon as a steady figure is indicated. Do not allow the starter motor to turn for more than 15 seconds at a time. A reading of nine volts or more, with the starter motor turning at normal cranking speed, is normal. If the reading is nine volts or more but the cranking speed is slow, the motor is faulty. If the reading is less than nine volts and the cranking speed is slow, the solenoid contacts are probably burned, the starter motor is faulty, the battery is discharged or there is a bad connection.

17 Starter motor - removal and refitting

Note: *The starter/solenoid assembly cannot be repaired using separate components. In*

17.7 Disconnect the solenoid electrical connector and remove the battery cable from the starter

the event of failure, exchange the starter/solenoid assembly for a new or rebuilt unit.

1 Detach the cable from the negative terminal of the battery.

2 On 1994 and earlier models, remove the battery from the engine compartment.

3 On 1995 and later models, remove the air cleaner assembly (see Chapter 4).

4 Raise the vehicle and support it securely on axle stands.

5 Disconnect the exhaust pipe from the exhaust manifold and remove the catalytic converter, if fitted (see Chapter 4).

6 Remove the inlet manifold bracket and the starter bracket from the starter.

7 Disconnect the electrical connector from the solenoid, remove the nut and disconnect the battery cable from the starter **(see illustration)**.

8 Remove starter mounting bolts and remove the starter **(see illustration)**.

9 Refitting is the reverse of removal.

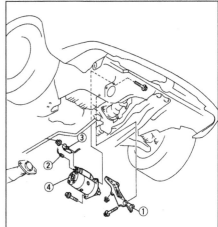

17.8 Starter motor refitting details

1 *Intake manifold support bracket*
2 *Terminal S connector*
3 *Terminal B connector*
4 *Starter*

Chapter 6
Emissions and engine control systems

Contents

Degrees of difficulty

Easy, suitable for novice with little experience	Fairly easy, suitable for beginner with some experience	Fairly difficult, suitable for competent DIY mechanic	Difficult, suitable for experienced DIY mechanic	Very difficult, suitable for expert DIY or professional

1 General Information

Note: *It should be noted that the illustrations of the various systems may not exactly match the system installed on your vehicle because of changes made by the manufacturer during production or from year-to-year.*

1 To minimise pollution of the atmosphere from incompletely burned and evaporating gases and to maintain good driveability and fuel economy, a number of emission control systems may be used on these vehicles **(see illustrations)**. They include the:

Positive Crankcase Ventilation (PCV) system
Evaporative Emission Control (EVAP) system
Exhaust Gas Recirculation (EGR) system (1995 and later)
Three-way catalytic converter (TWC) system
Powertrain Control Module (PCM)
Idle Speed Control (ISC) System

2 The Sections in this Chapter include general descriptions, checking procedures within the scope of the home mechanic and component renewal procedures (when

1.1a Typical emission and engine control components - items may vary with model year of vehicle

1 Idle Speed Control (ISC) valve
2 Solenoid valve (purge control)
3 Intake Air Temperature (IAT) sensor
4 Oxygen sensor (not visible this view)
5 Positive Crankcase Ventilation (PCV) valve
6 Coolant temperature sensor
7 Diagnostic connector
8 Throttle position sensor

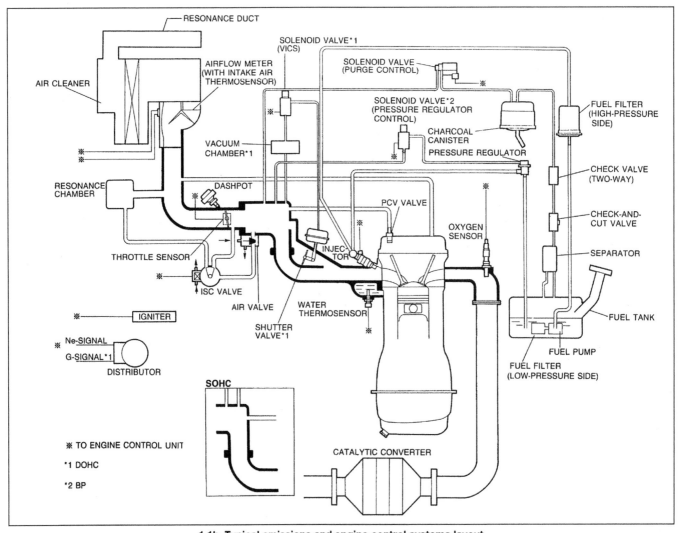

1.1b Typical emissions and engine control systems layout

possible) for each of the systems listed above.

3 Before assuming an emissions control system is malfunctioning, check the fuel and ignition systems carefully (see Chapters 4 and 5). The diagnosis of some emission control devices requires specialised tools, equipment and training. If checking and servicing become too difficult or if a procedure is beyond the scope of your skills, consult your dealer service department or other repair workshop.

4 This doesn't mean, however, that emission control systems are particularly difficult to maintain and repair. You can quickly and easily perform many checks and do most of the regular maintenance at home with common hand tools. **Note:** *The most frequent cause of emissions problems is simply a loose or broken electrical connector or vacuum hose, so always check the vacuum hoses and electrical connectors.*

5 Pay close attention to any special precautions outlined in this Chapter.

2 Engine control system - general information

General information

1 The fuel injection system is controlled by means of a microcomputer known as the Powertrain Control Module (PCM).

2 The PCM receives signals from various sensors which monitor changing engine operating conditions such as inlet air volume, inlet air temperature, coolant temperature, engine rpm, acceleration/deceleration, exhaust oxygen content, etc. These signals are utilised by the PCM to determine the correct fuel injection duration.

3 Here's a specific example of how one portion of this system operates: An oxygen sensor, located in the exhaust manifold, constantly monitors the oxygen content of the exhaust gas. If the percentage of oxygen in the exhaust gas is incorrect, an electrical

signal is sent to the PCM. The PCM takes this information, processes it and then sends a command to the fuel injection system telling it to change the air/fuel mixture. This happens in a fraction of a second and it goes on continuously when the engine is running. The end result is an air/fuel mixture ratio which is constantly maintained at a predetermined ratio, regardless of driving conditions.

4 In the event of a sensor malfunction, a backup circuit will take over to provide driveability until the problem is identified and fixed.

Precautions

5 Follow these steps:

a) *Always disconnect the power by disconnecting the battery terminals before unplugging any electrical connectors.*

b) *When reconnecting a battery, be particularly careful to avoid reversing the positive and negative battery cables.*

c) *Do not subject Electronic Fuel Injection components, emissions-related* components or the PCM to severe impact during removal or refitting.

d) Do not be careless during fault finding. Even slight terminal contact can invalidate a testing procedure and damage one of the numerous transistor circuits.

e) Never attempt to work on the PCM or open the PCM cover.

f) If you are inspecting Engine control system components during rainy weather, make sure that water does not enter any part. When washing the engine compartment, do not spray these parts or their electrical connectors with water.

3 On-Board Diagnostic (OBD) System and trouble codes

Note: *This procedure does not include the diagnostic codes or the code extracting procedure for 1995 or later models equipped with the OBD II system. These models require a special SCAN tool to read out the various levels of coded information. Have the 1995 or later models diagnosed by a dealer service department or other qualified repair workshop in the event of computer failure.*

1 The PCM (computer) has a built-in self-diagnosis system which detects malfunctions in the system sensors and alerts the driver by illuminating a CHECK ENGINE warning light in the instrument panel **(see illustration)**. The computer stores the failure code until the diagnostic system is cleared by disconnecting

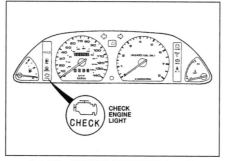

3.1 The CHECK ENGINE light will illuminate if a problem is detected with the engine control system

the negative battery cable then depressing the brake pedal for a period of five seconds or longer. The warning light goes out automatically when the malfunction is repaired.

2 The CHECK ENGINE warning light should come on when the ignition switch is placed in the ON position, this checks the bulb for proper operation. When the engine is started the warning light should go out. If the light remains on, the diagnostic system has detected a malfunction or abnormality in the system.

3 To determine which sensor or system component is malfunctioning, connect a jumper wire between the TEN and GND terminals at the DIAGNOSTIC test connector **(see illustration)** in the engine compartment. Make sure the battery voltage is greater than 11 volt, the transmission is in Neutral, the

3.3 Connect the TEN terminal and GND terminal of the Diagnostic Connector

accessories are off, the throttle valve is closed and the engine is at normal operating temperature, then turn the ignition switch to the ON position but do not start the engine.

4 The diagnostic code is the number of flashes indicated on the CHECK ENGINE light. If no codes are stored, the CHECK ENGINE light will come on for a few moments, then go out. If any malfunction has been detected, the light will blink the first digit(s) of the code at a long interval(s) and then blink the second digit of the code at short interval(s). For example, a code 34 (IAC valve) will first blink three long flashes and then pause and blink four quick flashes. **Note:** *If the code is simply a single digit number, the CHECK ENGINE light will flash in the quick mode.*

5 The accompanying tables indicate the diagnostic code, the system, diagnosis, and specific areas.

Diagnostic code chart

Note: *Not all codes apply to all vehicles.*

Code	Circuit or system	Corrective action
03	Camshaft position sensor	Check the wiring from the sensor to the PCM and from the ignition switch to the distributor for an open or short circuit, and the sensor for malfunction.
04	Camshaft position sensor	Check the wiring from the sensor to the PCM and from the ignition switch to the distributor for an open or short circuit, and the sensor for malfunction.
08	Airflow sensor	Check the wiring from the sensor to the PCM and from the sensor to the ignition switch for an open or short circuit, and the sensor for malfunction.
09	Coolant temperature sensor	Check the wiring from the sensor to the PCM for an open or short circuit, and the sensor for malfunction.
10	Inlet air temperature sensor	Check the wiring from the sensor to the PCM for an open or short circuit, and the sensor for malfunction.
12	Throttle position sensor	Check the wiring from the sensor to the PCM for an open or short circuit, and the sensor for malfunction.
14	Barometric pressure sensor	The barometric pressure sensor is integrated within the PCM. Check the PCM power and earth circuits. If no fault is found with the circuits, renew the PCM.
15	Oxygen sensor	Check the wiring from the sensor to the PCM for an open or short circuit, and the inlet air system, fuel system, ignition system and sensor for malfunction.
16	EGR valve position sensor	Check the wiring from the sensor to the PCM for an open or short circuit, and the sensor for malfunction.
17	Oxygen sensor	Check the wiring from the sensor to the PCM for an open or short circuit, and the inlet air system, fuel system, ignition system and sensor for malfunction.
25	Solenoid valve	Check the wiring from the valve to the PCM and from the valve to the fuel injection main relay for an open or short circuit, and the valve for malfunction.
26	Purge solenoid valve	Check the wiring from the valve to the PCM and from the valve to the ignition switch for an open or short circuit, and the valve for malfunction.
28	EGR solenoid valve	Check the wiring from the valve to the PCM and from the valve to the ignition switch for an open or short circuit, and the valve for malfunction.
29	EGR solenoid valve	Check the wiring from the valve to the PCM and from the valve to the ignition switch for an open or short circuit, and the valve for malfunction.
34	IAC valve	Check the wiring from the valve to the PCM and from the valve to the ignition switch for an open or short circuit, and the valve for malfunction.

Clearing the codes

6 After the self-diagnosis check, remove the jumper wire and close the cover on the DIAGNOSTIC electrical connector. Check the indicated system or component or take the vehicle to a dealer service department to have the malfunction repaired.

7 After repairs have been made, the diagnostic code must be canceled by detaching the cable from the negative terminal of the battery, then depressing the brake pedal for more than 5 seconds.

8 After cancellation, perform a road test and make sure the warning light does not come on. If the original trouble code is repeated, additional repairs are required.

4 Information sensors

Note: *Refer to Chapters 4 and 5 for additional information on the location and the diagnostic procedures for the sensors that are not directly covered in this Section.*

Coolant temperature sensor

General description

1 The coolant temperature sensor is a thermistor (a resistor which varies the value of

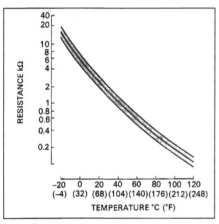

4.1 Compare the resistance values with the temperature specified on this graph

its voltage output in accordance with temperature changes). As the sensor temperature DECREASES, the resistance values will INCREASE. As the sensor temperature INCREASES, the resistance values will DECREASE **(see illustration)**. A failure in this sensor circuit should set a Code 09. This code indicates a failure in the coolant temperature sensor circuit, so in most cases the appropriate solution to the problem will be either repair of a connector or wire, or renewal of the sensor.

Check

2 To check the sensor, depress the locking tabs, disconnect the electrical connector **(see illustration)** and measure the resistance across the terminals of the engine-mounted sensor **(see illustration)**. With the engine completely cold 20° C (68° F) the resistance should be 2000 to 3000 ohms. Next, start the engine and warm it up until it reaches operating temperature 83° C (180° F) - the resistance should be 200 to 400 ohms. **Note:** *If necessary, remove the sensor and perform the tests in a pan of heated water to simulate the conditions. Compare the resistance values with the accompanying graph.*

3 If the resistance values of the coolant temperature sensor are correct, check the circuit for the proper signal voltage. Turn the ignition key ON (engine not running) and check for reference voltage **(see illustration)**. It should be approximately 5 volts.

Renewal

4 To remove the sensor, carefully unscrew the sensor.
Caution: Handle the coolant sensor with care. Damage to this sensor will affect the operation of the entire fuel injection system.
5 Before refitting the new sensor, wrap the threads with Teflon sealing tape to prevent leakage and thread corrosion.
6 Refitting is the reverse of removal.

Oxygen sensor

General description

7 These models are equipped with either a single oxygen sensor system or a dual-stage

oxygen sensor system. On dual-stage systems, the main oxygen sensor is mounted ahead of the front catalytic converter and monitors the exhaust gases exiting the engine. The sub oxygen sensor monitors the exhaust gases after they have passed through the front catalytic converter. Each oxygen sensor monitors the oxygen content of the exhaust gas stream. The oxygen content in the exhaust reacts with the oxygen sensor to produce a voltage output which varies from 0.1 volt (high oxygen, lean mixture) to 0.9 volts (low oxygen, rich mixture). The PCM constantly monitors this variable voltage output to determine the ratio of oxygen to fuel in the mixture. The PCM alters the air/fuel mixture ratio by controlling the pulse width (open time) of the fuel injectors. A mixture ratio of 14.7 parts air to 1 part fuel is the ideal mixture ratio for minimising exhaust emissions, thus allowing the catalytic converter to operate at maximum efficiency. It is this ratio of 14.7 to 1 which the PCM and the oxygen sensor attempt to maintain at all times.

8 The oxygen sensor produces no voltage when the oxygen sensor is below its normal operating temperature of about 318° C (600° F). During this initial period before warm-up, the PCM operates in open loop mode.

9 If the engine reaches normal operating temperature and/or has been running for two or more minutes, and if the main oxygen sensor is producing a steady signal voltage below 0.70 volts at 1500 or more rpm, the PCM will set a Code 15.

10 When there is a problem with the oxygen sensor or its circuit, the PCM operates in the open loop mode - that is, it controls fuel delivery in accordance with a programmed default value instead of feedback information from the oxygen sensor.

11 The proper operation of the oxygen sensor depends on four conditions:

a) *Electrical - The low voltages generated by the sensor depend upon good, clean connections which should be checked whenever a malfunction of the sensor is suspected or indicated.*

b) *Outside air supply - The sensor is designed to allow air circulation to the*

4.2a Location of the coolant temperature sensor (arrowed)

4.2b To check the temperature sensor, measure the resistance between the terminals

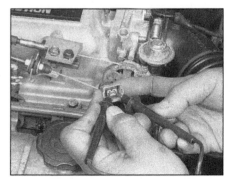

4.3 Use a voltmeter and probe the coolant temperature sensor connector for reference voltage

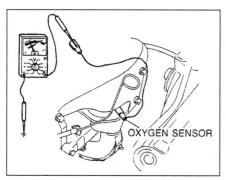

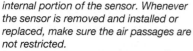

4.13 Insert a pin into the back of the oxygen sensor connector and check for an output signal

4.21 Slotted sockets are available for easing oxygen sensor removal

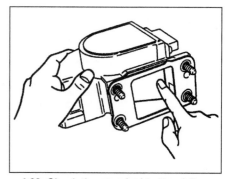

4.29 Check the vane inside the airflow sensor for smooth operation

internal portion of the sensor. Whenever the sensor is removed and installed or replaced, make sure the air passages are not restricted.

c) **Proper operating temperature** - *The PCM will not react to the sensor signal until the sensor reaches approximately 318° C (600° F). This factor must be taken into consideration when evaluating the performance of the sensor.*

d) **Unleaded fuel** - *The use of unleaded fuel is essential for proper operation of the sensor. Make sure the fuel you are using is of this type.*

12 In addition to observing the above conditions, special care must be taken whenever the sensor is serviced.

a) *The oxygen sensor has a permanently attached pigtail and electrical connector which should not be removed from the sensor. Damage to or removal of the pigtail or electrical connector can adversely affect operation of the sensor.*

b) *Grease, dirt and other contaminants should be kept away from the electrical connector and the louvered end of the sensor.*

c) *Do not use cleaning solvents of any kind on the oxygen sensor.*

d) *Do not drop or roughly handle the sensor.*

e) *The silicone boot must be installed in the correct position to prevent the boot from being melted and to allow the sensor to operate properly.*

Check

13 To check the oxygen sensor use a digital voltmeter to monitor the millivolt signal from the oxygen sensor during actual operating conditions. Locate the oxygen sensor electrical connector and backprobe the sensor wire on the harness side of the oxygen sensor connector **(see illustration)**. To properly backprobe the connector insert a long straight pin (a T-pin is preferred) alongside the wire until the pin contacts the metal wire terminal inside the connector. Connect the positive probe of a voltmeter onto the pin and the negative probe to earth. **Note:** *Refer to the wiring diagrams at the end of Chapter 12 to determine the correct*

terminals to probe when performing the oxygen sensor checks.

14 Warm up the engine and monitor the voltage signal of the main oxygen sensor as the engine warms up. Run the engine at 3000 rpm until the voltmeter indicates approximately 0.55 volt. Increase and decrease the engine speed suddenly several times. Verify that when the speed is increased the meter reads 0.5 to 1.0 volt, and when the speed is decreased it reads zero to 0.4 volt. If the oxygen sensor fails to operate as described, renew it.

15 On models equipped with a heated oxygen sensor, check the oxygen sensor heater as follows: Disconnect the oxygen sensor electrical connector and connect an ohmmeter between the positive and negative terminals on the oxygen sensor side of the connector. It should measure approximately 11.0 to 17.0 ohms. **Note:** *Not all models are equipped with a heated oxygen sensor. Models with heated oxygen sensors will be equipped with a four-wire electrical connector.*

16 Check for proper supply voltage to the oxygen sensor heater. With the ignition key ON (engine not running), check for battery voltage at the positive and negative terminals on the harness side of the connector.

17 To check the heated rear oxygen sensor on 1995 and later models, locate the electrical connector at the catalytic converter and check it in the same manner as the main oxygen sensor.

Renewal

Note: *Because it is installed in the exhaust manifold or pipe, which contracts when cool, the oxygen sensor may be very difficult to loosen when the engine is cold. Rather than risk damage to the sensor (assuming you are planning to reuse it in another manifold or pipe), start and run the engine for a minute or two, then shut it off. Be careful not to burn yourself during the following procedure.*

18 Disconnect the cable from the negative terminal of the battery.

19 Raise the vehicle and place it securely on axle stands.

20 Carefully disconnect the electrical connector from the sensor pigtail lead.

21 Remove the oxygen sensor from the exhaust system **(see illustration)**. **Note:** *Some oxygen sensors are threaded directly into the exhaust manifold while others are mounted in the exhaust manifold or pipe with two bolts.*

Caution: Excessive force may damage the threads.

22 Anti-seize compound must be used on the threads of the sensor to facilitate future removal. The threads of new sensors will already be coated with this compound, but if an old sensor is removed and reinstalled, recoat the threads.

23 Refit the sensor and tighten it securely.

24 Reconnect the electrical connector of the pigtail lead to the main engine wiring harness.

25 Lower the vehicle and reconnect the cable to the negative terminal of the battery.

Throttle Position Sensor (TPS)

General description

26 The Throttle Position Sensor (TPS) is located on the end of the throttle shaft on the throttle body (see Chapter 4). By monitoring the output voltage from the TPS, the PCM alters fuel delivery based on throttle valve angle (driver demand). A broken or loose TPS can cause intermittent bursts of fuel from the injector and an unstable idle because the PCM receives a signal that the throttle is moving. All the checks and renewal procedures are covered in Chapter 4.

Airflow sensor/inlet air temperature sensor (1994 and earlier models)

General description

Note: *On 1994 and earlier models, the inlet air temperature sensor is incorporated into the airflow sensor.*

27 The airflow sensor (located on top of the air cleaner housing) measures the volume or air entering the inlet system using a vane-type potentiometer device. As air enters the air by-pass passage, the measuring plate (vane) swings open and allows an electrical device (potentiometer) to vary its voltage signal according to the position of the measuring

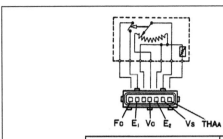

Terminal	Resistance (Ω)	
	Closed throttle position	Wide open throttle
E₂ ↔ Vs	20—600	20—1,000
E₂ ↔ Vc	200—400	
E₂ ↔ THAA (Intake air temperature sensor)	−20°C { −4°F}: 13.6—18.4 KΩ 20°C { 68°F}: 2.21—2.69 kΩ 60°C {140°F}: 493— 667Ω	
E₁ ↔ Fc	∞	0

4.30 Airflow sensor and intake air temperature sensor terminal guide and continuity chart

plate. This information is relayed to the computer and is used to determine the correct amount of fuel to inject into the combustion chamber for the volume of air (load) that is demanded.

28 The inlet air temperature sensor is located inside the airflow sensor. This sensor is a resistor which changes value according to the temperature of the air entering the engine. Low temperatures produce a high resistance value (for example, at 20° C/68° F the resistance is 2000 to 3000 ohms) while high temperatures produce low resistance values (at 81° C/176° F the resistance is 200 to 400 ohms (see illustration 4.43b). The PCM supplies approximately 5 volt (reference voltage) to the air temperature sensor. The IAT sensor alters the voltage according to the temperature of the incoming air. The signal voltage sent back to the PCM will be high when the air temperature is cold and low when the air temperature is warm. Any problems with the air temperature sensor will usually set a diagnostic code 10.

Check

29 Remove the airflow sensor and check the body for cracks or damage. with your finger, press the vane in and make sure it moves smoothly and does not bind (see illustration).
30 Using the accompanying terminal guide and chart (see illustration), measure the resistance of the airflow meter on the designated terminals with the vane in the closed throttle position, then in the open throttle position. Measure the resistance of the inlet air temperature sensor and compare it with the chart. If the values are not as specified, renew the sensor.

Renewal

31 Disconnect the electrical connector from the sensor.
32 Remove the inlet duct from the sensor and remove the sensor and air cleaner housing top cover from the vehicle.

33 Remove the screws retaining the sensor to the housing and remove the sensor.
34 Refitting is the reverse of removal.

Airflow sensor (1995 and later models)

General description

35 The airflow sensor is located in the air inlet duct. The sensor uses a hot wire sensing element to measure the amount of air entering the inlet system. The air passing over the hot wire causes it to cool. Consequently, this change in temperature can be converted into an analog voltage signal to the PCM which in turn, calculates the required fuel injector pulse width.

Check

36 Disconnect the electrical connector from the airflow sensor and check for battery voltage on the white/red wire terminal with the ignition key ON. Check for continuity to earth on the black wire terminal. Repair the circuits if necessary.
37 Reconnect the connector and, using a straight pin, backprobe the light green/blue wire terminal, on most models (refer to the wiring diagrams at the end of Chapter 12).

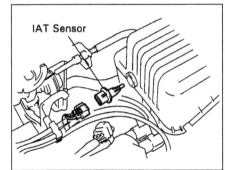

IAT Sensor

4.43a The IAT sensor is located at the intake air cleaner housing

38 With the ignition ON, there should be approximately 2.0 volt present. Start the engine and allow it to idle, the voltmeter should now read 1.0 to 2.5 volt. If the voltage is not as specified check the connectors and the circuit from the PCM to the airflow sensor. If the connectors and circuit are good, renew the airflow sensor.

Renewal

39 Disconnect the electrical connector from the sensor.
40 Loosen the hose clamp and remove the inlet duct from the sensor.
41 Remove the screws attaching the sensor to the air cleaner housing and remove the sensor.
42 Refitting is the reverse of removal.

Inlet Air Temperature (IAT) sensor (1995 and later models)

General description

43 The inlet air temperature (IAT) sensor is located inside the air cleaner housing. This sensor is a resistor which changes value according to the temperature of the air entering the engine. Low temperatures produce a high resistance value (for example, at 20° C/68° F the resistance is 2000 to 3000 ohms) while high temperatures produce low resistance values (at 81° C/176° F the resistance is 200 to 400 ohms (see illustrations). The PCM supplies approximately 5 volt (reference voltage) to the

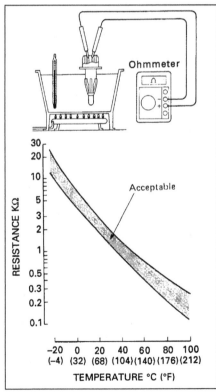

Ohmmeter

4.43b The air intake temperature (IAT) sensor resistance

5.3 The PCM is located behind the centre console

air temperature sensor. The IAT sensor alters the voltage according to the temperature of the incoming air. The signal voltage sent back to the PCM will be high when the air temperature is cold and low when the air temperature is warm. Any problems with the air temperature sensor will usually set a diagnostic code 10.

Check

44 To check the air temperature sensor, disconnect the two prong electrical connector. Turn the ignition key ON, but do not start the engine.
45 Measure the voltage (reference voltage) on the yellow/black wire terminal. The VOM should read approximately 5 volt.

46 If the reference voltage is not correct, have the PCM diagnosed by a dealer service department or other repair workshop.
47 Measure the resistance across the air temperature sensor terminals. The resistance should be HIGH when the air temperature is LOW. Next, start the engine and let it idle. Wait awhile and let the engine reach operating temperature. Turn the ignition OFF, disconnect the air temperature sensor and measure the resistance across the terminals. The resistance should be LOW when the air temperature is HIGH. If the sensor does not exhibit this change in resistance, renew the sensor.

Renewal

48 Disconnect the electrical connector from the sensor.
49 Detach the sensor from the air cleaner housing.
50 Refit the sensor and connect the electrical connector.

Crankshaft Position Sensor - 1995 and later models

General Description

51 The crankshaft position sensor is located in the timing belt cover near the crankshaft pulley . The crankshaft position sensor relays a signal to the PCM to indicate the exact position (angle) of the crankshaft.

Check

52 Using an ohmmeter, measure the resistance of the crankshaft position sensor . It should be between 500 and 600 ohms depending on the temperature; the warmer the temperature of the sensor, the higher the resistance value. If the resistance is not within the specified range, renew the sensor.
53 Using a feeler gauge measure the air gap between the crankshaft pulley and the crankshaft position sensor. The gap specification should be 0.020 to 0.059 inch (0.5 to 1.5 mm). If not as specified, renew the crankshaft pulley or the crankshaft position sensor.

Renewal

54 To renew the sensor, remove the engine undercover, disconnect the electrical connector and remove the bolts from the crankshaft position sensor.
55 Refitting is the reverse of removal.

5 Powertrain Control Module (PCM) - removal and refitting

1 Disconnect the negative cable from the battery .
2 Remove the front and rear centre console (see Chapter 11).
3 Carefully disconnect the electrical connectors from the PCM **(see illustration)**. Each connector has a locking tab which must be disengaged before the connector is unplugged.
4 Remove the nuts and bolts from the PCM brackets.
5 Lift the PCM from the vehicle.
6 Refitting is the reverse of removal.
7 Securely tighten the PCM retaining fasteners during refitting.

6 Evaporative Emission Control (EVAP) system

General description

1 This system is designed to trap and store fuel that evaporates from the fuel tank, throttle body and inlet manifold that would normally enter the atmosphere in the form of hydrocarbon (HC) emissions.
2 The Evaporative Emission Control (EVAP) system consists of a charcoal-filled canister, the lines connecting the canister to the fuel tank, a temperature controlled vacuum valve and a check valve **(see illustration)**.
3 Fuel vapours are transferred from the fuel tank and throttle body to a canister where they are stored when the engine isn't running. When the engine is running, the fuel vapours are purged from the canister by inlet airflow and consumed in the normal combustion process.

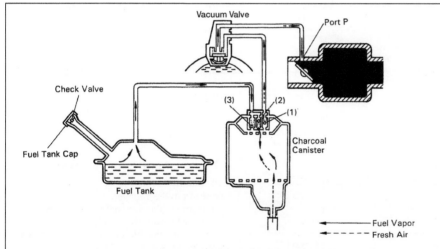

Engine Temp. Sensor	Temp. Controlled Vacuum Valve	Throttle Position	Canister Check Valve			Check Valve in Cap	Evaporated Fuel (HC)
			(1)	(2)	(3)		
Cold/Warm	CLOSED	—	—	—	—	—	HC from tank is absorbed into the canister.
Hot	OPEN	Below port P	CLOSED	—	—	—	HC from tank is absorbed into the canister.
		Above port P	OPEN	—	—	—	HC from canister is led into air intake chamber.
High pressure in tank	—	—	—	OPEN	CLOSED	CLOSED	HC from tank is absorbed into the canister.
High vacuum in tank	—	—	—	CLOSED	OPEN	OPEN	Air is led into the fuel tank.

6.2 Typical EVAP system and operation chart

6.10 Apply air pressure into the charcoal canister purge control valve inlet side

6.11 Apply air pressure to port A on the temperature controlled vacuum valve

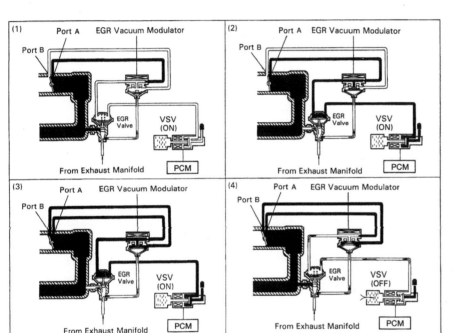

To reduce NOx emissions, part of the exhaust gases are recirculated through the EGR valve to the intake manifold to lower the maximum combustion temperature.

Engine Temp. Sensor	RPM	VSV	Throttle Position	Pressure in the EGR Valve Pressure Chamber		EGR Vacuum Modulator	EGR Valve	Exhaust Gas
COLD	ANY	**** OFF	—		—	—	CLOSED	Not recirculated
WARM/ HOT	LOW	*** ON	OFF		—	—	CLOSED	Not recirculated
			Below port A		—	—	CLOSED	Not recirculated
			Between port A and port B	(1) LOW	* Pressure constantly alternating between low and high	OPENS passage to atmosphere	CLOSED	Not recirculated
				(2) HIGH		CLOSES passage to atmosphere	OPEN	Recirculated
			Above port B	(3) HIGH	**	CLOSES passage to atmosphere	OPEN	Recirculated (increase)
	HIGH	(4) OFF	—		—	—	CLOSED	Not recirculated

Remarks: * Pressure increase ───► Modulator closes ───► EGR valve opens ───► Pressure drops
　　　　　　　　　　　　　EGR valve closes ◄─── Modulator opens ◄───

** When the throttle valve is positioned above port R, the EGR vacuum modulator will close the atmosphere passage and open the EGR valve to increase the exhaust gas, even if the exhaust pressure is insufficiently low.

*** VSV switched ON when product of engine speed multiplied by vacuum sensor valve exceeds a specified valve.

**** If terminals TE1 and E1 of data link connector 1 are connected, the VSV switches ON.

7.1 Typical EGR system and operation chart - 1995 and later

4 The charcoal canister is equipped with a check valve that incorporates three check balls. Depending upon the running conditions and the pressure in the fuel tank, the check balls open and close the passageways to the vacuum valve (consequently the throttle body) and fuel tank.

Check

5 Poor idle, stalling and poor driveability can be caused by an inoperative check valve, a damaged canister, split or cracked hoses or hoses connected to the wrong fittings. Check the fuel filler cap for a damaged or deformed gasket (see Chapter 1).

6 Evidence of fuel loss or fuel odour can be caused by liquid fuel leaking from fuel lines, a cracked or damaged canister, an inoperative check valve, disconnected, misrouted, kinked, deteriorated or damaged vapour or control hoses.

7 Inspect each hose attached to the canister for kinks, leaks and cracks along its entire length. Repair or renew as necessary.

8 Look for fuel leaking from the bottom of the canister. If fuel is leaking, renew the canister and check the hoses and hose routing.

9 Inspect the canister. If it's cracked or damaged, renew it.

10 Check for a clogged filter or a stuck check valve. Using low pressure compressed air, blow into the canister tank pipe (**see illustration**). Air should flow freely from the other pipes. If a problem is found, renew the canister.

11 Check the operation of the temperature controlled vacuum valve. With the engine completely cold, use a hand-held pump and direct air into port A (**see illustration**). Air should not pass through the valve. Now warm the engine to operating temperature (above 54° C/129° F) and observe that air passes through the valve. Renew the valve if the test results are incorrect.

Charcoal canister renewal

12 Clearly label, then detach the vacuum hoses from the canister.

13 Remove the mounting clamp bolts, lower the canister with the bracket, disconnect the hoses from the check valve and remove it from the vehicle.

14 Refitting is the reverse of removal.

7 Exhaust Gas Recirculation (EGR) system

General description

1 To reduce oxides of nitrogen emissions, some of the exhaust gases are recirculated through the EGR valve to the inlet manifold to lower combustion temperatures (**see illustration**).

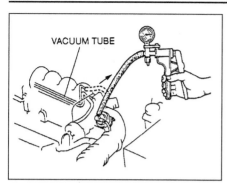

7.4 Vacuum should remain steady and the engine should run rough

7.7 EGR valve position sensor connector details

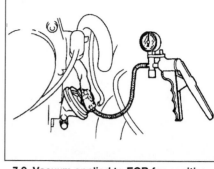

7.9 Vacuum applied to EGR for position sensor voltage check

2 The EGR system consists of the EGR valve, the EGR modulator, vacuum switching valve (VSV), the Powertrain Control Module (PCM) and the EGR gas temperature sensor.

Check

EGR valve

3 Start the engine and allow it to idle.
4 Detach the vacuum hose from the EGR valve and attach a hand-held vacuum pump in its place **(see illustration)**.
5 Apply vacuum to the EGR valve. Vacuum should remain steady and the engine should run poorly.
a) *If the vacuum does not remain steady and the engine does not run poorly, renew the EGR valve and recheck it.*
b) *If the vacuum remains steady but the engine does not run poorly, remove the EGR valve and check the valve and the inlet manifold for blockage. Clean or renew parts as necessary and recheck.*

EGR valve position sensor

6 Disconnect the EGR valve position sensor connector.
7 Measure the resistance between terminals A and B at the sensor connector with an ohmmeter **(see illustration)**. The meter reading should be 2.7 k-ohms. If not as specified, renew the EGR valve.
8 Connect the EGR valve position sensor connector.
9 Disconnect the vacuum hose from the EGR valve and refit a vacuum pump at the valve **(see illustration)**.
10 Turn ignition switch on and measure the voltage at terminal B of the connector **(see illustration 7.7)**.
11 Voltmeter should read approximately 0.8 volt with no vacuum applied and approximately 5.0 volt with 5.0 in-Hg applied.
12 If not as specified, inspect the harness and connector between the EGR valve and the PCM terminal.
13 If the harness and connector are OK, renew the EGR valve.

8 Positive Crankcase Ventilation (PCV) system

General information

1 The Positive Crankcase Ventilation (PCV) system reduces hydrocarbon emissions by scavenging crankcase vapours. It does this by circulating fresh air from the air cleaner through the crankcase, where it mixes with blow-by gases and is then rerouted through a PCV valve to the inlet manifold **(see illustration)**.
2 The main components of the PCV system are the PCV valve, a fresh air inlet and the vacuum hoses connecting these components to the engine.
3 To maintain idle quality, the PCV valve restricts the flow when the inlet manifold vacuum is high. If abnormal operating conditions (such as piston ring problems) arise, the system is designed to allow excessive amounts of blow-by gases to flow back through the crankcase vent tube into the air cleaner to be consumed by normal combustion.
4 This system directs the blow-by into the throttle body which, over time, can cause an oily residue build up in the area near the throttle plate. Consequently, it is a good idea to periodically clean this residue from the throttle body. Refer to Chapter 4 for this cleaning procedure.

Check

5 To check the valve, first pull it out of the grommet in the valve cover and shake the valve. It should rattle, indicating that it's not clogged with deposits. If the valve does not rattle, renew it with a new one.
6 Start the engine and allow it to idle, then place your finger over the valve opening. If vacuum is felt, the PCV valve is working properly. If no vacuum is felt, the PCV valve may be bad or the hose may be plugged. Also, check for vacuum leaks at the valve, filler cap and all the hoses.

Renewal

7 Pull straight up on the valve to remove it.

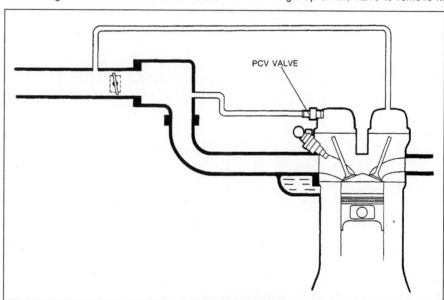

8.1 Typical PCV system

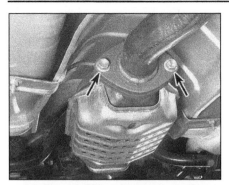

9.2 The catalytic converter mounting bolts (arrowed)

Check the rubber grommet for cracks and distortion. If it's damaged, renew it.

8 If the valve is clogged, the hose is also probably plugged. Remove the hose and clean it with solvent.

9 After cleaning the hose, inspect it for damage, wear and deterioration. Make sure it fits snugly on the fittings.

10 If necessary, refit a new PCV valve.

11 Refit the clean PCV hose. Make sure that the PCV valve and hose are secure.

9 Catalytic converter

General description

1 To reduce hydrocarbon, carbon monoxide and oxides of nitrogen emissions, all vehicles are equipped with a three-way catalyst system which oxidises and reduces these chemicals, converting them into nitrogen, carbon dioxide and water.

2 The catalytic converter is mounted in the exhaust system much like a silencer (see illustration).

Check

3 Periodically inspect the catalytic converter-to-exhaust pipe mating flanges and bolts. Make sure that there are no loose bolts and no leaks between the flanges.

4 Look for dents in or damage to the catalytic converter protector (see illustration). If any part of the protector is damaged or dented enough to touch the converter, repair or renew it.

5 Inspect the heat insulator for damage. Make sure that there is adequate clearance between the heat insulator and the catalytic converter (see illustration).

Renewal

6 To renew the catalytic converter, refer to Chapter 4.

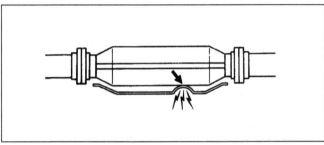

9.4 Periodically inspect the shield for dents and other damage

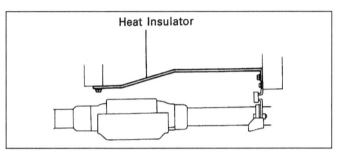

9.5 Periodically inspect the heat insulator

Chapter 7 Part A
Manual transmission

Contents

Degrees of difficulty

Easy, suitable for novice with little experience		**Fairly easy,** suitable for beginner with some experience		**Fairly difficult,** suitable for competent DIY mechanic		**Difficult,** suitable for experienced DIY mechanic		**Very difficult,** suitable for expert DIY or professional	

Specifications

Torque specifications	lbf ft	Nm
Engine mount-to-support subframe nuts	28 to 38	38 to 52
Gear lever control rod-to-transmission change rod bolt	12 to 16	16 to 22
Gear lever extension bar-to-transmission nut	28 to 34	38 to 46
No. 4 engine mount-to-transmission bolts	50 to 68	68 to 92
Reversing light switch	15 to 21	20 to 38
Support subframe-to-vehicle frame bolts	48 to 65	65 to 88
Transmission-to-engine bolts	48 to 65	65 to 88

1 General information

The vehicles covered by this manual are equipped with a 5-speed manual transmission or 4-speed automatic transmission. Information on the manual transmission is included in this Part of Chapter 7. Service procedures for the automatic transmission are contained in Chapter 7, Part B.

The manual transmission is a compact, two-piece, lightweight aluminum alloy housing containing both the transmission and differential assemblies. All transmissions are virtually identical except for different gear ratios. If attempting repairs, it is important to tell any parts supplier as much information as possible about the transmission fitted to get the correct spares.

Because of the complexity, unavailability of renewal parts and special tools necessary, internal repair procedures for the manual transmission are beyond the scope of this manual. For readers who wish to tackle a transmission rebuild, a brief *Manual transmission overhaul, general information* Section is provided. The bulk of information in this Chapter is devoted to removal and refitting procedures.

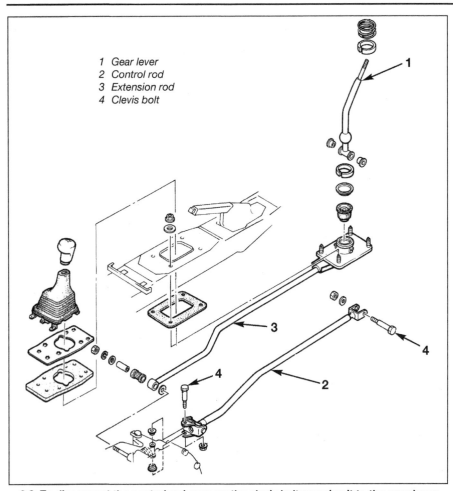

1 Gear lever
2 Control rod
3 Extension rod
4 Clevis bolt

2.3 To disconnect the control rod, remove the clevis bolt securing it to the gear lever

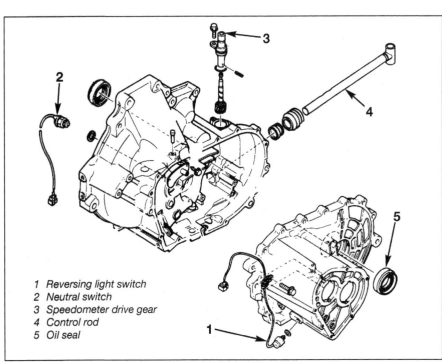

1 Reversing light switch
2 Neutral switch
3 Speedometer drive gear
4 Control rod
5 Oil seal

3.8 Transmission external components

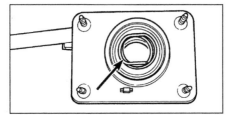

2.4 Remove the spring from the bracket with a needle nose pliers

2 Gear lever - removal and refitting

1 Remove the centre console (see Chapter 11) and the rubber boot.
2 Raise the vehicle and support it securely on axle stands.
3 From under the vehicle disconnect the control rod from the gear lever **(see illustration)** and remove the bushings from the lever foot.
4 Inside the vehicle remove the hooked part of the spring from the bracket groove **(see illustration)** then remove the spring and upper ball seat.
5 Remove the gear lever.
6 Refitting is the reverse of removal.

3 Reversing light switch - check and renewal

Check

1 The reversing light switch is located on the front side, near the bottom of the transmission case.
2 Turn the ignition key to the ON position and move the shift lever to the Reverse position. The switch should close the reversing light circuit and turn on the reversing lights.
3 If it doesn't, check the reversing light fuse (see Chapter 12).
4 If the fuse is okay, verify that there's voltage available on the battery side of the switch (with the ignition turned to ON).
5 If there's no voltage on the battery side of the switch, check the wire between the fuse and the switch; if there is voltage, put the shift lever in reverse and see if there's voltage on the earth side of the switch.
6 If there's no voltage on the earth side of the switch, renew the switch (see below); if there is voltage, note whether one or both reversing lights are out.
7 If only one bulb is out, renew it; if they're both out, the bulbs could be the problem, but it's more likely that the wire between the switch and the bulbs has an open circuit somewhere.

Renewal

8 Unplug the electrical connector in the harness to the reversing light switch **(see illustration)**.

9 Unscrew and remove the old switch.

10 To test the new switch before refitting, simply check continuity across the switch terminals: with the plunger depressed, there should be continuity; with the plunger free, there should be no continuity.

11 Screw in the new switch and tighten it to the torque listed in this Chapter's Specifications.

12 Connect the electrical connector.

13 Check the switch to ensure that the circuit is working properly.

4 Manual transmission - removal and refitting

Removal

1 Disconnect the cables from the battery.

 Warning: When removing the battery cables always detach the negative cable first and connect it up last.

2 Remove the battery and battery tray.

3 Remove the inlet air hose and resonance chamber (see Chapter 4).

4 Set the handbrake and move the gear shift lever into the Neutral position.

5 Loosen the front wheel nuts no more than 1/4 turn, then raise the vehicle and support it securely on axle stands. Remove the wheels.

6 Remove the starter (see Chapter 5).

7 Drain the transmission lubricant into a suitable container (see Chapter 1).

8 Separate the driveshaft(s) from the transmission and remove the intermediate shaft if so equipped (see Chapter 8). Support the end of the driveshaft with a wire or rope. **Note:** *It is not necessary to remove the driveshafts from the hub.*

9 Remove the anti-roll bar (see Chapter 10).

10 Remove the clutch release cylinder (see Chapter 8).

11 Unplug the reversing light switch pigtail at the connector **(see illustration 3.8)**.

12 Unplug the neutral switch pigtail at the connector **(see illustration 3.8)**.

13 Locate the electrical system earth cable on the clutch pipe bracket near the top of the transmission. Remove the cable lug bolt and detach the earth cable.

14 Detach any wire harness clamps from the engine and/or transmission and set the harnesses aside.

15 Disconnect the gear lever extension bar from the transmission and support the bar with a wire **(see illustration 2.3)**.

16 Disconnect the gear lever control rod from the transmission and support the rod with a wire **(see illustration 2.3)**.

17 Support the engine. This can be done from above by using an engine hoist, or by placing a jack (with a wood block as an insulator) under the engine sump. The engine must be securely supported at all times while the transmission is out of the vehicle.

18 Remove the engine support subframe **(see Chapter 7B, illustration 4.24)**.

19 Remove the front exhaust pipe assembly (see Chapter 4).

20 Remove the No. 1 engine mount located at the rear side of the transmission toward the bulkhead, and remove the No. 2 engine mount located on the front side of the transmission.

21 Remove the No. 4 engine mount located above the transmission near the battery/battery tray area.

22 Support the transmission with a jack (preferably a special jack made for this purpose). If you're using a trolley jack, be sure to place a wood block between the lifting pad and the transmission to protect the cast aluminium housing. Safety chains will help steady the transmission on the jack.

23 Remove the bolts attaching the transmission to the engine **(see illustration)**.

24 Make a final check that all wires and hoses have been disconnected from the transmission.

25 Lower the left end of the engine, then roll the transmission and jack toward the side of the vehicle. Once the input shaft is clear of the splines in the clutch hub, lower the transmission and remove it from under the vehicle. Try to keep the transmission as level as possible.

Caution: Do not depress the clutch pedal while the transmission is removed from the vehicle.

26 The clutch components can now be inspected (see Chapter 8). In most cases, new clutch components should be routinely installed whenever the transmission is removed.

Refitting

27 If removed, fit clutch components (see Chapter 8).

28 With the transmission secured to the jack as on removal, raise it into position and then carefully slide it forward, engaging the input shaft with the splines in the clutch hub. Do not use excessive force to fit the transmission - if the input shaft does not slide into place, readjust the angle of the transmission so it is level and/or turn the input shaft so the splines engage properly with the clutch.

29 Fit the transmission-to-engine bolts.

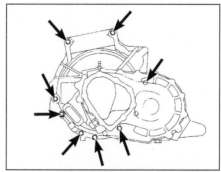

4.23 Remove the bolts (arrowed) that attach the transmission to the engine

Tighten the bolts to the torque listed in this Chapter's Specifications.

30 Remove the transmission support jack.

31 Fit the back, No. 4 engine mount (located above the transmission, near the battery tray area) on the transmission. Loosely tighten the bolts.

32 Fit the front, No. 2 engine mount on the transmission, and make sure the rear, No. 1 engine mount is attached to the transmission. Tighten the bolts securely.

33 Fit the front exhaust pipe (down pipe or manifold pipe) assembly (see Chapter 4).

34 Fit the engine mount crossmember bolts and nuts to the body attachment points and then fit and tighten the engine mount bolts/nuts. Tighten to the torque listed in this Chapter's Specifications.

35 Tighten the rear, No. 4 engine mount-to-transmission bolts to the torque listed in this Chapter's Specifications, following the torque sequence given in Chapter 2A.

36 Remove the engine support jack or hoist.

37 Fit the gear lever extension bar and control rod. Tighten the extension bar nut and control rod bolt to the torque listed in this Chapter's Specifications.

38 Attach any wire harness clamps removed from the engine and/or transmission.

39 Attach the electrical system earth to the clutch pipe bracket and tighten the bolt securely.

40 Reconnect the neutral switch and reversing light switch pigtails.

41 Fit the clutch release cylinder (see Chapter 8).

42 Fit the anti-roll bar (see Chapter 10).

43 Fit the driveshaft(s) in the transmission and the intermediate shaft if so equipped (see Chapter 8).

44 Fit the starter (see Chapter 5).

45 Fit the wheels. Lower the vehicle and tighten the wheel nuts to the torque listed in Chapter 1 Specifications.

46 Fill the transmission with lubricant (see Chapter 1).

47 Fit the inlet air hose and resonance chamber.

48 Fit the battery tray and battery.

49 Connect the battery cables.

 Warning: When connecting the battery cables always attach the positive cable first.

50 Road test the vehicle to check for proper transmission operation and check for leakage.

5 Manual transmission overhaul - general information

Note: *Although very similar, many different transmissions were used on these vehicles, so it is important to give any parts supplier as much information as possible about the transmission fitted to get the correct spares.*

Overhauling a manual transmission unit is a difficult and involved job for the DIY home mechanic. In addition to dismantling and reassembling many small parts, clearances must be precisely measured and, if necessary, changed by selecting shims and spacers. Internal transmission components are also often difficult to obtain, and in many instances, are extremely expensive. Because of this, if the transmission develops a fault or becomes noisy, the best course of action is to have the unit overhauled by a specialist repairer, or to obtain an exchange reconditioned unit.

Nevertheless, it is not impossible for the more experienced mechanic to overhaul the transmission, provided the special tools are available, and that the job is done in a deliberate step-by-step manner so that nothing is overlooked.

The tools necessary for an overhaul may include internal and external circlip pliers, bearing pullers, a slide hammer, a set of pin punches, a dial test indicator, and possibly a hydraulic press. In addition, a large, sturdy workbench and a vice will be required.

During dismantling of the transmission, make careful notes of how each component is fitted, to make reassembly easier and accurate.

Before dismantling the transmission, it will help if you have some idea which area is malfunctioning. Certain problems can be closely related to specific areas in the gearbox, which can make component examination and renewal easier.

Chapter 7 Part B
Automatic transmission

Contents

Degrees of difficulty

Easy, suitable for novice with little experience	Fairly easy, suitable for beginner with some experience	Fairly difficult, suitable for competent DIY mechanic	Difficult, suitable for experienced DIY mechanic	Very difficult, suitable for expert DIY or professional

Specifications

Oil Pressure (engine idling)
Throttle cable, specified pressure . . . . 62 to 81 psi
Throttle cable, adjustment pressure . . . . 71 psi

Torque specifications

	lbf ft	Nm
Control valve body bolts	6 to 8	8 to 11
Engine mount-to-support subframe nuts	28 to 38	38 to 52
Engine sump-to-transmission bolts	28 to 38	38 to 52
Support subframe-to-vehicle frame bolts	48 to 65	65 to 88
Torque converter-to-driveplate bolts	26 to 36	35 to 49
Transmission-to-engine bolts		
1990 to 1994 models	48 to 65	65 to 88
1995 and later models	41 to 59	56 to 80
Transverse subframe-to-vehicle frame bolts	69 to 97	94 to 132

1 General information

All vehicles covered in this manual are equipped with either a 5-speed manual transmission or a 4-speed automatic transmission. All information on the automatic transmission is included in this Part of Chapter 7. Information for the manual transmission can be found in Part A of this Chapter.

The 4-speed automatic transmission is electronically controlled with fourth gear being an overdrive gear. Gearchanges (shifts) are attained by the use of shift solenoids, which are controlled by the Powertrain Control Module. The transmissions utilise a lock-up torque converter.

Because of the complexity of the automatic transmissions and the specialised equipment necessary to perform most service operations, this Chapter contains only those procedures related to general fault diagnosis, routine maintenance, adjustment, and removal and refitting.

If the transmission requires major repair work, it should be left to a dealer service department or an automotive or transmission repair workshop. You can, however, remove and fit the transmission yourself and save the expense, even if the repair work is done by a transmission workshop. **Note**: *Accurate fault diagnosis often needs to be done with the transmission in the vehicle, so don't remove it until the fault has been identified.*

2 Diagnosis - general

Note: *Automatic transmission malfunctions may be caused by five general conditions: poor engine performance, improper adjustments, hydraulic malfunctions, mechanical malfunctions or malfunctions in the computer or its signal network. Diagnosis of these problems should always begin with a check of the easily repaired items: fluid level*

and condition (see Chapter 1), shift linkage adjustment and throttle linkage adjustment. Next, perform a road test to determine if the problem has been corrected or if more diagnosis is necessary. If the problem persists after the preliminary tests and corrections are completed, additional diagnosis should be done by a dealer service department or transmission repair workshop. Refer to the Fault finding section at the rear of this manual for information on symptoms of transmission problems.

Preliminary checks

1 Drive the vehicle to warm the transmission to normal operating temperature.
2 Check the fluid level as described in Chapter 1:
a) *If the fluid level is unusually low, add enough fluid to bring the level within the designated area of the dipstick, then check for external leaks (see below).*
b) *If the fluid level is abnormally high, drain off the excess, then check the drained fluid for contamination by coolant. The presence of engine coolant in the automatic transmission fluid indicates that a failure has occurred in the internal radiator walls that separate the coolant from the transmission fluid (see Chapter 3).*
c) *If the fluid is foaming, drain it and refill the transmission, then check for coolant in the fluid, or a high fluid level.*
3 Check the engine idle speed. **Note:** *If the engine is malfunctioning, do not proceed with the preliminary checks until it has been repaired and runs normally.*
4 Check the throttle valve cable for freedom of movement. Adjust it if necessary (see Section 4). **Note:** *The throttle cable may function properly when the engine is turned off and cold, but it may malfunction once the engine is hot. Check it cold and at normal engine operating temperature.*
5 Inspect the shift cable (see Section 5). Make sure that it's properly adjusted and that the cable operates smoothly.

Fluid leak diagnosis

6 Most fluid leaks are easy to locate visually. Repair usually consists of replacing a seal or gasket. If a leak is difficult to find, the following procedure may help.
7 Identify the fluid. Make sure its transmission fluid and not engine oil or brake fluid (automatic transmission fluid is a deep red colour).
8 Try to pinpoint the source of the leak. Drive the vehicle several miles, then park it over a large sheet of cardboard. After a minute or two, you should be able to locate the leak by determining the source of the fluid dripping onto the cardboard.
9 Make a careful visual inspection of the suspected component and the area immediately around it. Pay particular attention to gasket mating surfaces. A mirror is often

helpful for finding leaks in areas that are hard to see.
10 If the leak still cannot be found, clean the suspected area thoroughly with a degreaser or solvent, then dry it.
11 Drive the vehicle for several miles at normal operating temperature and varying speeds. After driving the vehicle, visually inspect the suspected component again.
12 Once the leak has been located, the cause must be determined before it can be properly repaired. If a gasket is replaced but the sealing flange is bent, the new gasket will not stop the leak. The bent flange must be straightened.
13 Before attempting to repair a leak, check to make sure that the following conditions are corrected or they may cause another leak. **Note:** *Some of the following conditions cannot be fixed without highly specialised tools and expertise. Such problems must be referred to a transmission workshop or a dealer service department.*

Gasket leaks

14 Check the pan periodically. Make sure the bolts are tight, no bolts are missing, the gasket is in good condition and the pan is flat (dents in the pan may indicate damage to the valve body inside).
15 If the pan gasket is leaking, the fluid level or the fluid pressure may be too high, the vent may be plugged, the pan bolts may be too tight, the pan sealing flange may be warped, the sealing surface of the transmission housing may be damaged, the gasket may be damaged or the transmission casting may be cracked or porous. If sealant instead of gasket material has been used to form a seal between the pan and the transmission housing, it may be the wrong sealant.

Seal leaks

16 If a transmission seal is leaking, the fluid level or pressure may be too high, the vent may be plugged, the seal bore may be damaged, the seal itself may be damaged or improperly installed, the surface of the shaft protruding through the seal may be damaged or a loose bearing may be causing excessive shaft movement.
17 Make sure the dipstick tube seal is in good condition and the tube is properly

seated. Periodically check the area around the speedometer gear or sensor for leakage. If transmission fluid is evident, check the O-ring for damage.

Case leaks

18 If the case itself appears to be leaking, the casting is porous and will have to be repaired or replaced.
19 Make sure the oil cooler hose fittings are tight and in good condition.

Fluid comes out vent pipe or fill tube

20 If this condition occurs, the transmission is overfilled, there is coolant in the fluid, the case is porous, the dipstick is incorrect, the vent is plugged or the drain-back holes are plugged.

3 Oil seal renewal

1 Oil leaks frequently occur due to wear of the driveshaft oil seals and/or the speedometer drive gear oil seal and O-rings. Renewal of these seals is relatively easy, since the repairs can usually be performed without removing the transmission from the vehicle.

Driveshaft oil seals

2 The driveshaft oil seals are located on the sides of the transmission, where the inner ends of the driveshafts are splined into the differential side gears. If you suspect that a driveshaft oil seal is leaking, raise the vehicle and support it securely on axle stands. If the seal is leaking, you'll see lubricant on the side of the transmission, below the seal.
3 Remove the driveshaft (see Chapter 8).
4 Using a screwdriver, carefully lever the oil seal out of the transmission bore **(see illustration)**.
5 If the oil seal cannot be removed with a screwdriver, a special oil seal removal tool (available at car accessory outlets) will be required.
6 Using a seal installer, a large section of pipe or a large deep socket as a drift, fit the new oil seal. Drive it into the bore squarely and make sure it's completely seated **(see illustration)**.

3.4 Carefully lever out the driveshaft oil seal with a seal removal tool or a large screwdriver

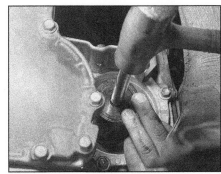

3.6 Use a seal installer, a large socket or a piece of pipe to fit the new seal

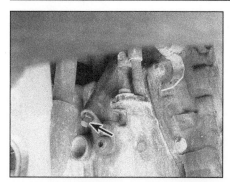

4.4 Remove the square head plug (arrowed) on the front side of the transmission

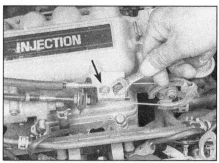

4.7 Loosen the cable mounting bolt on the left side first and then the bolt on the right side (arrowed)

4.10 Pull the throttle cable toward the right side (arrow direction) of the vehicle

A fully-seated seal should be flush with the surface of the transmission housing.

7 Lubricate the lip of the new seal with multi-purpose grease, then fit the driveshaft (see Chapter 8). Be careful not to damage the lip of the new seal.

4 Throttle cable - check, adjustment and renewal

Note: *The cable adjustment and renewal procedures require a 0 to 100 psi oil pressure gauge and suitable adapters to connect the gauge to the transmission test port. If you do not have a suitable pressure gauge have the cable adjusted and/or replaced by a dealer service department or other qualified automotive repair workshop.*

Check

1 Check the cable and housing for damage.
2 Actuate the accelerator through its full range of travel and ensure it operates smoothly.
3 Renew the throttle cable assembly if necessary.

Adjustment

4 Remove the square-head plug on the front of the transmission and fit a 0 to 100 psi oil pressure gauge in the test port **(see illustration)**.
5 With the shift lever in the Park (P) position, start the engine and let it warm up to normal operating temperature.

6 Check the idle speed adjustment (see Chapter 4) and ensure that it is adjusted correctly.
7 Loosen the bolts securing the throttle cable to the bracket on the front side of the throttle body assembly.
Caution: First loosen the bolt on the left side (closest to the throttle valve) (see illustration) and then the bolt on the right side.
8 Check and ensure that the throttle valve lever is in the closed throttle position.
9 Tighten the left cable bolt **(see illustration 4.7)** securely.
10 Pull the throttle cable toward the right side of the vehicle **(see illustration)** until the line pressure exceeds the specified pressure range listed in this Chapter's Specifications.
11 Push the throttle cable toward the left side of the vehicle until the line pressure decreases to the adjustment pressure listed in this Chapter's Specifications.
12 Tighten the right cable bolt securely.
Note: *If the line pressure will not decrease to the adjustment pressure, tighten the right bolt with the line pressure at the closest reading to the adjustment pressure.*
13 Stop the engine and ensure that the throttle cable moves smoothly.
14 Restart the engine and accelerate it slightly, then let it run at idle speed.
15 Verify that the line pressure is within the specified pressure range listed in this Chapter's Specifications.
16 If the line pressure is not correct repeat this adjustment procedure.

17 Turn off the engine, remove the pressure gauge and fit the square-head plug.

Renewal

18 Disconnect the negative cable from the battery.
19 Loosen and remove the bolts securing the throttle cable to the bracket on the front side of the throttle body assembly.
Caution: First loosen the bolt on the left side (closest to the throttle valve) (see illustration 4.7) and then the bolt on the right side.
20 Remove the throttle cable from the bracket and from the throttle lever on the throttle body **(see illustration)**.
21 Loosen the left front wheel nuts no more than 1/4 turn, then raise the vehicle and support it securely on axle stands. Remove the wheel and the splash shield.
22 Drain the transmission lubricant into a suitable container (see Chapter 1).
23 Support the engine. This can be done from above by using an engine hoist, or by placing a jack (with a wood block as an insulator) under the engine sump.
24 Remove the engine support subframe **(see illustration)** and on 1995 and later models with the 1.8 litre engine remove the transverse subframe.
25 Remove the transmission sump and gasket (see Chapter 1).
26 Disconnect the solenoid connectors **(see illustration)**.
27 Remove the control valve body mounting

4.20 Remove the cable from the throttle lever

4.24 Remove the engine mount nuts and the nuts/bolts securing the engine support subframe (arrowed)

4.26 Disconnect the four solenoid connectors (arrowed)

4.27 Remove the control valve body mounting bolts (there are nine of them - arrows point to three)

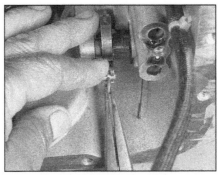

4.28 Remove the cable from the throttle cam in the transmission

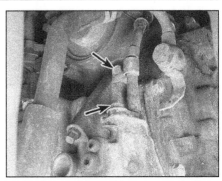

4.29 Remove the cable-to-transmission mounting bolts (arrowed)

bolts **(see illustration)** and lower the valve body from the transmission.

28 Remove the throttle cable from the throttle cam in the transmission **(see illustration)**.

29 Remove the mounting bolts and throttle cable from the transmission **(see illustration)**.

30 Fit a new throttle cable to the throttle cam in the transmission.

31 Connect the throttle cable to the throttle lever on the throttle body.

32 Attach the throttle cable to the transmission using new bolts and tighten the bolts securely.

33 Fit the control valve body tightening the bolts to the torque listed in this Chapter's Specifications.

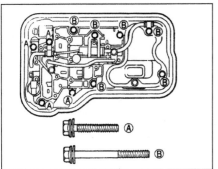

4.33 Fit the short bolts (A) and the long bolts (B) in the indicated locations

Caution: There are 2 bolt lengths; refitting the long bolts in the wrong position could cause severe damage (see illustration).

34 Reconnect the solenoid connectors.

35 Fit the transmission sump (see Chapter 1).

36 Fit the engine support subframe. Tighten the bolts to the torque listed in this Chapter's Specifications.

37 Remove the engine support jack or hoist.

38 Connect the battery cables.

> ⚠ *Warning: When connecting the battery cables always attach the positive cable first.*

39 Fill the transmission with the proper type and amount of fluid (see Chapter 1).

40 Adjust the throttle cable.

5.2a Remove the retaining clip and the shift cable (arrowed) from the shift lever on the transmission

5 Shift cable - removal, refitting and adjustment

Removal and refitting

1 Remove the battery and battery tray (see Chapter 5) and air cleaner assembly (see Chapter 4) to access the top of the transmission where the shift cable is attached.

2 Disconnect the shift cable end from the transmission **(see illustrations)**.

3 Remove the consoles and control box side covers (see Chapter 11).

4 Remove the indicator panel screws and lift up the indicator panel **(see illustration)**.

5 Unscrew the nut securing the shift cable to the shift lever **(see illustration)** and pull the cable end from the lever. **Note:** *With the consoles removed you will see two cables coming into the front of the shift mechanism. The shift cable is on the left and the shift-lock cable is on the right.*

6 Unscrew the bolts securing the cable to the vehicle **(see illustration)**.

7 Lift the cable clear of the shift lever assembly and carefully pull the cable through the grommet in the bulkhead.

8 Refitting is the reverse of removal.

9 When you're done, adjust the shift cable.

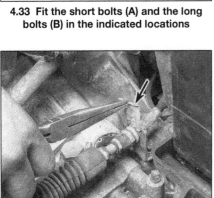

5.2b Remove the bracket clip (arrowed) and lift the shift cable off the bracket

5.4 Remove the four screws holding the shift indicator panel in place and lift the panel up

5.5 Remove the retaining nut and pull the cable end from the lever

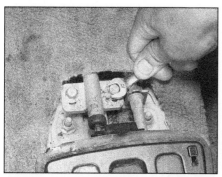

5.6 Remove the shift cable bolts and move the cable clear of the shifter mechanism

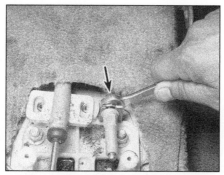

6.7 Loosen the nut on the front of the shift-lock cable bracket (arrowed) to remove the cable

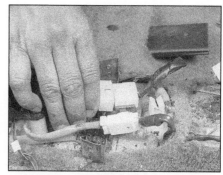

6.8 Unplug the shift assembly electrical connector

Adjustment

10 Move the shift lever to the Park (P) position.
11 Loosen the two cable mounting bolts in front of the shift assembly **(see illustration 5.6)**.
12 While holding the shift lever forward against the stop, tighten the shift cable mounting bolts securely.
13 Check the operation of the transmission in each shift lever position (try to start the engine in each gear - the starter should operate in the Park and Neutral positions only).

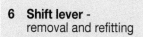

6 Shift lever - removal and refitting

Removal and refitting

1 Disconnect the negative cable from the battery.
2 Remove the consoles and control box side covers (see Chapter 11).
3 Remove the indicator panel screws and lift up the indicator panel **(see illustration 5.4)**.
4 Unscrew the nut securing the shift cable to the shift lever **(see illustration 5.5)** and pull the cable end from the lever. Note: *With the consoles removed you will see two cables coming into the front of the shift mechanism. The shift cable is on the left and the shift-lock cable is on the right.*
5 Unscrew the bolts securing the shift cable to the vehicle **(see illustration 5.6)**.
6 Lay the cable clear of the shift assembly.
7 Loosen the nut on the front, cable side of the shift-lock cable and move the cable clear of the shift assembly **(see illustration)**.
Caution: Be careful not to turn/loosen the nut on the rear, shift assembly side of the bracket.
8 Disconnect the electrical connectors **(see illustration)**.
9 Remove the four nuts that secure the shift assembly to the vehicle **(see illustrations)**.
10 Lift the shift assembly clear of the mounting studs to remove it from the vehicle.
11 Refitting is the reverse of removal.
12 Adjust the shift cable (see Section 5).

6.9a Remove the two mounting nuts at the back . . .

7 Inhibitor switch - check, adjustment and renewal

Adjustment

1 If the engine will start with the shift lever in any position other than Park or Neutral, adjust the neutral start switch.
2 Apply the handbrake and chock the rear wheels. Raise the front of the vehicle and place it securely on axle stands. Shift the transmission into Neutral.
3 Unplug the electrical connector from the switch and loosen the switch retaining bolts.
4 Touch the ohmmeter leads to the switch terminals inside the electrical connector and rotate the switch until there is continuity

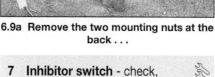

7.4a Touch the leads to terminals A and B

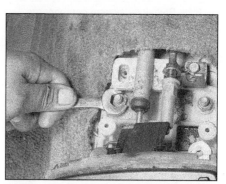

6.9b . . . then remove the two nuts at the front of the shift assembly

between the terminals, indicating that it's now in the Neutral position **(see illustrations)**. Tighten the bolts securely.

Renewal

5 Disconnect the negative cable from the battery.
6 Shift the transmission into Neutral.
7 Remove the nut and lift off the shift lever.
8 Unplug the electrical connector.
9 Remove the retaining bolts and lift the switch off the shift shaft.
10 To fit, line up the flats on the shift shaft with the flats in the switch and push the switch onto the shaft.
11 Position the switch on the transmission and loosely tighten the bolts.
12 Fit the shift lever and follow the adjustment procedure above.

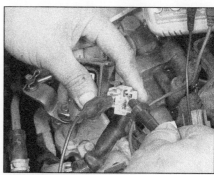

7.4b Check continuity with an ohmmeter

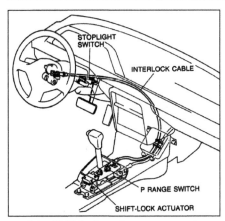

8.1a Shift-lock system components

13 Connect the negative battery cable and verify the engine will not start with the shift lever in any position other than Park or Neutral.

8 Shift-lock system -
description, check and component renewal

Description

1 The shift lock system (see illustrations) prevents the shift lever from being shifted out of the Park (P) position unless the ignition switch is ON and the brake pedal is applied.

Shift-lock

2 Turn the ignition switch ON (engine OFF).
3 Without the brake pedal depressed, verify that the shift lever cannot be shifted from Park (P) position.
4 Depress the brake pedal and verify that the selector lever can be shifted from the P position.
5 If the shift-lock does not function correctly, check the P position switch continuity and/or shift-lock actuator terminal voltage and continuity.

Emergency override button

6 Turn the ignition switch OFF.

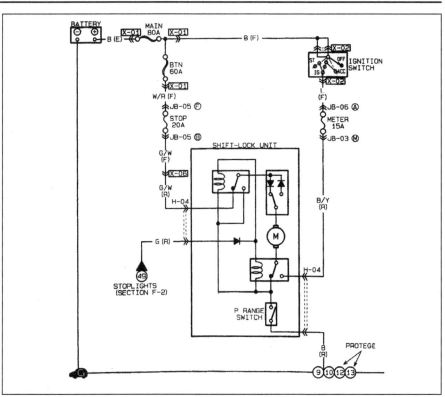

8.1b Shift-lock system electrical schematic

7 Verify that the selector lever is in P position.
8 Without the brake pedal depressed, verify that the selector lever cannot be shifted from P position.
9 On 1990 to 1994 models, slide back the emergency override button located on the shift indicator panel (see illustration).
10 On 1995 and later models, remove the cover on the shift indicator panel. Insert a screwdriver into the hole and push the emergency override button down (see illustration).
11 Verify that the selector lever can be shifted from P position. If not, renew the emergency override button.

Key interlock

12 Turn the ignition switch ON (engine OFF).

13 With the brake pedal depressed, shift the selector lever to R position.
14 Verify that the ignition key cannot be turned to the LOCK position.
15 If ignition switch can be turned to the LOCK position, the ignition switch may need to be replaced.

Park (P) position switch

16 Disconnect the negative cable from the battery.
17 Remove the front and rear console (see Chapter 11).
18 Remove the indicator panel screws and lift up the indicator panel (see illustration 5.4).
19 Disconnect the P-range switch connector (see illustration).

8.9 Slide back the emergency override button to verify that the selector lever can be shifted from P

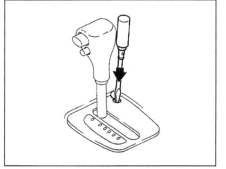

8.10 Remove the cover on the shift indicator panel and push down on the emergency override button

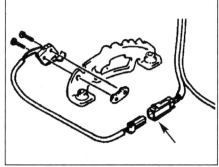

8.19 Disconnect the P-position switch connector (arrowed), then check for continuity in Park

Connector	Terminal	⊖ probe connected to	Condition	Measurement value
A	a	B—b	P range, selector lever release button not depressed	0Ω
A	b	B—b	Constant	0Ω
B	a	B—b	Brake pedal released → depressed	0V → B+
B	b (harness side)	Body	Constant	0Ω
B	c	B—b	Ignition switch ON	B+
B	d	B—b	Ignition switch OFF	B+

B+: Battery positive voltage

8.29 Shift-lock terminal guide and voltage/continuity table

20 Using an ohmmeter check the switch for continuity between the connector terminals with the shift lever in the Park (P) position and the shift lever release button in the released/locked position.

21 Repeat the continuity test with the shift lever release button depressed; depressing the release button should open the switch, breaking continuity.

22 If the switch fails any of these tests, renew it.

23 Reconnect the P-range switch connector.

24 Fit the indicator panel.

25 Fit the front and rear console.

26 Connect the negative battery cable.

Shift-lock actuator

27 Remove the front and rear console (see Chapter 11).

28 Shift the shift lever to the Park (P) position.

29 Turn the ignition switch ON (engine OFF), and using a volt-ohmmeter, check the terminal voltages and continuity **(see illustration)**.

Caution: When checking continuity between terminal B (harness side) and earth, disconnect connector B.

30 If the actuator fails any of these tests, renew it.

31 Turn the ignition switch OFF and fit the front and rear console.

9 Transmission mount - check and renewal

1 Insert a large screwdriver between the transmission mount and its bracket and lever the two apart **(see illustration)**.

2 The transmission mount should not move excessively. If it does, renew the mount.

3 To renew a mount, support the transmission with a jack, remove the nuts and bolts and remove the mount. It may be necessary to raise the transmission slightly to provide enough clearance to remove the mount.

4 Refitting is the reverse of removal.

10 Automatic transmission - removal and refitting

Removal

1 Disconnect the cables from the battery.

> ⚠️ *Warning: When removing the battery cables always detach the negative cable first and hook it up last.*

2 Remove the battery and battery tray.

3 Remove the intake air hose and air cleaner assembly (see Chapter 4).

4 Set the handbrake.

5 Loosen the front wheel nuts no more than 1/4 turn, then raise the vehicle and support it securely on axle stands. Remove the wheels

and the splash shield(s). **Note:** *All models have a splash shield on the left side of the engine compartment, inside the wheel well; 1995 and later models have a shield on the right side which must also be removed.*

6 Remove the starter (see Chapter 5).

7 Drain the transmission lubricant into a suitable container (see Chapter 1).

8 Separate the driveshaft(s) from the transmission and remove the intermediate shaft if so equipped (see Chapter 8). Support the end of the driveshaft with a wire or rope. **Note:** *It is not necessary to completely remove the driveshafts; you can detach the inner CV joints and suspend them out of the way. However, you'll have more room to work if you remove the driveshafts. And this is a good time to inspect the CV joint boots for tears and deterioration and, if necessary, repack them with new CV joint grease (see Chapter 8).*

9 Remove the anti-roll bar (see Chapter 10).

10 Disconnect the speedometer cable **(see illustration)** (on 1995 and later models disconnect the speed sensor electrical connector and the range switch connector) and shift selector cables (see Section 5).

9.1 Try to lever the mount from side-to-side or up-and-down with a screwdriver

10.10 Disconnect the speedometer cable (arrowed) from the transmission

10.11 Unplug the inhibitor switch (left arrow) and the solenoid valve connectors (right arrow)

10.12 Mark the throttle cable casing at the mounting bracket (arrowed) so it can be reinstalled

10.17 Remove the engine sump-to-transmission bolts (arrowed)

10.19 Remove the bolts securing the No. 2 engine mount to the transmission

11 Unplug the inhibitor switch and the solenoid valve at the connectors on top of the transmission **(see illustration)**.

12 Clearly mark the throttle cable casing at the bracket on the throttle body **(see illustration)** so that it can be reinstalled in the same position and remove the throttle cable. **Note:** *It is very important that the casing be reinstalled in the same position on the bracket; otherwise, the transmission will not shift correctly.*

13 Detach any cable or wire harness clamps from the engine and/or transmission and set the cables and harnesses aside.

14 Support the engine. This can be done from above by using an engine hoist, or by placing a jack (with a wood block as an insulator) under the engine sump. The engine must be supported at all times while the transmission is out of the vehicle.

15 Remove the engine support subframe **(see illustration 4.24)** and on 1995 and later models with the 1.8 litre engine remove the transverse subframe.

16 Remove the front exhaust pipe assembly (see Chapter 4).

17 Remove the 5 engine sump-to-transmission bolts **(see illustration)**.

18 Remove the No. 1 engine mount located at the rear side of the transmission, toward the bulkhead.

19 Remove the No. 2 engine mount located on the front side of the transmission **(see illustration)**.

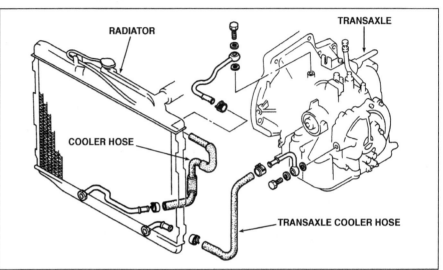

10.21 Locate the cooler hoses on the side and top of the transmission and disconnect them

20 Remove the No. 4 engine mount located above the transmission near the battery/battery tray area.

21 Disconnect the transmission oil cooler inlet and outlet hoses **(see illustration)**.

22 Support the transmission with a jack (preferably a special jack made for this purpose). If you're using a trolley jack, be sure to place a wood block between the lifting pad and the transmission to protect the cast aluminium housing. Safety chains

will help steady the transmission on the jack.

23 Remove the torque converter inspection cover. Mark the relationship of the torque converter to the driveplate so they can be installed in the same position **(see illustration)**. Remove the six torque converter mounting bolts. Turn the crankshaft for access to each one in turn.

24 Remove the four engine-to-transmission bolts **(see illustration)**.

10.23 Mark the relationship of the torque converter to the driveplate

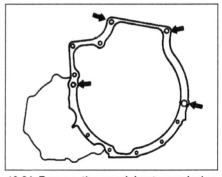

10.24 Remove the remaining transmission nut and bolts

25 Make a final check that all wires and hoses have been disconnected from the transmission.

26 Lower the left end of the engine, then roll the transmission and jack toward the side of the vehicle. Once the input shaft is clear of the splines in the torque converter, lower the transmission and remove it from under the vehicle. Try to keep the transmission as level as possible.

27 Move the transmission to the side to disengage it from the engine block dowel pins and make sure the torque converter is detached from the driveplate. Secure the torque converter to the transmission so that it will not fall out during removal. Lower the transmission from the vehicle.

Refitting

28 Make sure that the torque converter is securely engaged in the transmission prior to refitting.

29 With the transmission secured to the jack as on removal, raise it into position and then carefully move it forward. Be sure to keep it level so the torque converter does not slide forward.

30 Move the transmission carefully into place until the dowel pins are engaged and the torque converter is engaged.

31 Rotate the torque converter to align the bolt holes with the holes in the driveplate. The match marks on the torque converter and driveplate, made during paragraph 23, must align.

32 Fit the four bolts securing the transmission to the engine. Tighten the bolts to the torque listed in this Chapter's Specifications.

33 Fit the torque converter-to-driveplate bolts. Tighten them to the torque listed in this Chapter's Specifications. Fit the torque converter inspection cover.

34 Fit the five engine sump-to-transmission bolts. Tighten them to the torque listed in this Chapter's Specifications.

35 Remove the transmission support jack.

36 Reconnect the transmission oil cooler inlet and outlet hoses.

Caution: The hose ends and tubing they mate with have alignment marks. Be sure to align these marks when sliding the hoses on and ensure that the hoses are fully seated before refitting the clamp. Ensure that the hose clamps are positioned so that they do not interfere with any other parts.

37 Fit the engine mounts and tighten the bolts securely.

38 Fit the front exhaust pipe assembly (see Chapter 4).

39 Fit the engine support subframe and the transverse subframe if so equipped. Tighten the bolts to the torque listed in this Chapter's Specifications.

40 Remove the engine support jack or hoist.

41 Attach any cable or wire harness clamps previously removed from the engine and/or transmission.

42 Refit the throttle cable aligning the mark made during paragraph 12 with the bracket to ensure the cable is installed in the original position.

43 Fit and adjust the inhibitor switch and the solenoid valve electrical connectors (see Section 7).

44 Connect and adjust the shift cable (see Section 5) and the speedometer cable/sensor.

45 Fit the anti-roll bar (see Chapter 10).

46 Fit and/or connect the driveshaft(s) to the transmission and the intermediate shaft is so equipped (see Chapter 8).

47 Fit the starter (see Chapter 5).

48 Fit the wheels. Lower the vehicle and tighten the wheel nuts to the torque listed in Chapter 1 Specifications.

49 Fill the transmission with the proper type and amount of fluid (see Chapter 1).

50 Fit the intake air hose and resonance chamber.

51 Fit the battery and battery tray.

52 Connect the battery cables.

 Warning: When connecting the battery cables always attach the positive cable first.

53 Road test the vehicle to check for proper transmission operation and check for leakage.

Notes

Chapter 8
Clutch and driveshafts

Contents

Degrees of difficulty

Easy, suitable for novice with little experience	Fairly easy, suitable for beginner with some experience	Fairly difficult, suitable for competent DIY mechanic 	Difficult, suitable for experienced DIY mechanic	Very difficult, suitable for expert DIY or professional

Specifications

Clutch
Fluid type . . . . See *Lubricants and fluids*
Pedal freeplay . . . . See Chapter 1

Driveshaft
Driveshaft standard length (1990 to 1994 models)
  1.3 litre models
    Right . . . . 918.9 mm
    Left . . . . 640.4 mm
  1.6 litre models
    Right . . . . 919.3 mm
    Left . . . . 637.8 mm
  1.8 litre models
    Right . . . . 630.7 mm
    Left . . . . 621.2 mm
Driveshaft standard length (1995 and later models)
  1.3 litre models
    Right . . . . 595.5 to 605.5 mm
    Left . . . . 653.5 to 663.5 mm
  1.5 litre models
    Manual gearbox
      Right . . . . 595.5 to 605.5 mm
      Left . . . . 653.5 to 663.5 mm
    Automatic gearbox
      Right . . . . 595.5 to 605.5 mm
      Left . . . . 649.5 to 659.5 mm
  1.8 litre models
    Right . . . . 640.9 to 650.9 mm
    Left . . . . 647.3 to 657.3 mm

Torque specifications

	lbf ft	Nm
Clutch master cylinder mounting nuts	14 to 18	19 to 24
Clutch pressure plate-to-flywheel bolts	14 to 19	19 to 26
Clutch release cylinder mounting bolts	14 to 17	19 to 23
Driveshaft/hub locknut	174 to 235	236 to 319
Intermediate shaft support bracket bolts	32 to 45	43 to 61
Wheel nuts	65 to 87	89 to 118

1 General information

The information in this Chapter deals with the components from the engine to the front wheels, except for the transmission, which is dealt with in Chapters 7A and 7B. For the purposes of this Chapter, these components are grouped into two categories: clutch and driveshafts. Separate Sections within this Chapter offer general descriptions and checking procedures for both groups.

Since nearly all the procedures covered in this Chapter involve working under the vehicle, make sure it's securely supported on sturdy axle stands or a hoist where the vehicle can be easily raised and lowered.

2 Clutch - description and check

1 All vehicles with a manual transmission use a single dry plate, diaphragm spring type clutch (see illustration). The clutch disc has a splined hub which allows it to slide along the splines of the transmission input shaft. The clutch and pressure plate are held in contact by spring pressure exerted by the diaphragm in the pressure plate.
2 The clutch release system is operated by hydraulic pressure. The hydraulic release system consists of the clutch pedal, a master cylinder, a fluid reservoir, the hydraulic line, a slave cylinder which actuates the clutch release lever, and the clutch release bearing.
3 When pressure is applied to the clutch pedal to release the clutch, hydraulic pressure is exerted against the outer end of the clutch release lever. As the lever pivots, the shaft fingers push against the release bearing. The bearing pushes against the fingers of the diaphragm spring of the pressure plate assembly, which in turn releases the clutch plate.
4 Terminology can be a problem regarding the clutch components because common names have in some cases changed from that used by the manufacturer. For example, the driven plate is also called the clutch plate or disc, the pressure plate assembly is sometimes referred to as the clutch cover, the clutch release bearing is sometimes called a throw-out bearing, and the release cylinder is sometimes called the operating or slave cylinder.
5 Other than replacing components that have obvious damage, some preliminary checks should be performed to diagnose a clutch system failure.

a) The first check should be of the fluid level in the clutch/brake reservoir (see "Weekly checks!"). If the fluid level is low, add fluid as necessary and inspect the hydraulic clutch system for leaks. If the reservoir has run dry, bleed the system (see Section 8) and retest the clutch operation.
b) To check 'clutch-spin down time,' run the engine at normal idle speed with the transmission in Neutral (clutch pedal up - engaged). Disengage the clutch (pedal down), wait several seconds and shift the transmission into Reverse. No grinding noise should be heard. A grinding noise would most likely indicate a problem in the pressure plate or the clutch disc.
c) To check for complete clutch release, run the engine (with the handbrake applied to prevent movement) and hold the clutch pedal approximately 1/2-inch from the floor. Shift the transmission between 1st gear and Reverse several times. If the shift is not smooth, component failure is indicated. Check the release cylinder pushrod travel. With the clutch pedal depressed completely the release cylinder pushrod should extend substantially. If it doesn't, check the fluid level in the reservoir.
d) Visually inspect the clutch pedal bushing at the top of the clutch pedal to make sure there is no sticking or excessive wear.
e) Under the vehicle, check that the clutch release lever is solidly mounted on the ball stud.

3 Clutch components - removal, inspection and refitting

Warning: Dust produced by clutch wear and deposited on clutch components may contain asbestos, which is hazardous to your health. DO NOT blow it out with compressed air and DO NOT inhale it. DO NOT use petrol or petroleum based solvents to remove the dust. Brake system cleaner should be used to flush the dust into a drain pan. After the clutch components are wiped clean with a rag, dispose of the contaminated rags and cleaner in a labelled, covered container.

Removal

1 Access to the clutch components is normally accomplished by removing the transmission, leaving the engine in the vehicle. If, of course, the engine is being removed for major overhaul, then the opportunity should always be taken to check the clutch for wear and renew worn components as necessary. The relatively low cost of the clutch components compared to the time and labour involved in gaining access to them warrants their renewal any time the engine or transmission is removed, unless they are new or in near-perfect condition. The following procedures assume that the engine will stay in place.

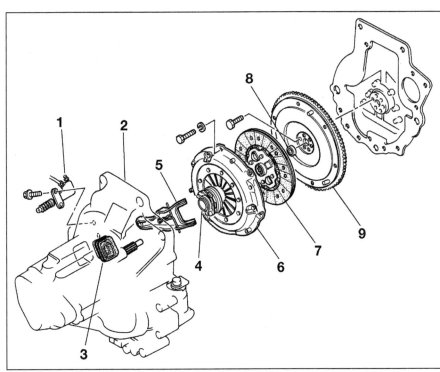

2.1 Typical clutch components

1 Clutch release cylinder	4 Release bearing	7 Clutch disc
2 Transmission	5 Clutch release fork	8 Pilot bearing
3 Boot	6 Clutch cover	9 Flywheel

3.6 Mark the relationship of the pressure plate to the flywheel

3.10 Examine the clutch disc for evidence of excessive wear

3.12a Examine the pressure plate friction surface for score marks, cracks or overheating (blue spots)

2 Remove the release cylinder (see Section 7). Hang it out of the way with a piece of wire - it isn't necessary to disconnect the pipe or hose.

3 Remove the transmission from the vehicle (see Chapter 7, Part A). Support the engine while the transmission is out. Preferably, an engine hoist should be used to support it from above. However, if a jack is used underneath the engine, make sure a piece of wood is used between the jack and sump to spread the load.

Caution: The pick-up for the oil pump is very close to the bottom of the sump. If the pan is bent or distorted in any way, engine oil starvation could occur.

4 The release fork and release bearing can remain attached to the transmission for the time being.

5 To support the clutch disc during removal, fit a clutch alignment tool through the clutch disc hub.

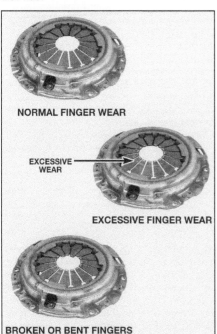

NORMAL FINGER WEAR

EXCESSIVE WEAR

EXCESSIVE FINGER WEAR

BROKEN OR BENT FINGERS

3.12b Replace the pressure plate if any of these conditions are noted

6 Carefully inspect the flywheel and pressure plate for indexing marks. The marks are usually an X an O or a white letter. If they cannot be found, scribe marks yourself so the pressure plate and the flywheel will be in the same alignment during refitting **(see illustration)**.

7 Slowly loosen the pressure plate-to-flywheel bolts. Work in a diagonal pattern and loosen each bolt a little at a time until all spring pressure is relieved. Then hold the pressure plate securely and completely remove the bolts, followed by the pressure plate and clutch disc.

Inspection

8 Ordinarily, when a problem occurs in the clutch, it can be attributed to wear of the clutch driven plate assembly (clutch disc). However, all components should be inspected at this time.

9 Inspect the flywheel for cracks, heat checking, score marks and other damage. If the imperfections are slight, a machine workshop can resurface it to make it flat and smooth.

10 Inspect the lining on the clutch disc. There should be at least 1.6 mm (0.06 in) of lining above the rivet heads. Check for loose rivets, distortion, cracks, broken springs and other obvious damage **(see illustration)**. As mentioned above, ordinarily the clutch disc is replaced as a matter of course, so if in doubt about the condition, renew it.

3.14 Centre the clutch disc in the pressure plate with a clutch alignment tool

11 The release bearing should be replaced along with the clutch disc (see Section 4).

12 Check the machined surface and the diaphragm spring fingers of the pressure plate **(see illustrations)**. If the surface is grooved or otherwise damaged, renew the pressure plate assembly. Also check for obvious damage, distortion, cracking, etc. Light glazing can be removed with emery cloth or sandpaper. If a new pressure plate is indicated, new or factory rebuilt units are available.

Refitting

13 Before refitting, carefully wipe the flywheel and pressure plate machined surfaces clean. It's important that no oil or grease is on these surfaces or the lining of the clutch disc. Handle these parts only with clean hands.

14 Position the clutch disc and pressure plate with the clutch held in place with an alignment tool **(see illustration)**. Make sure it's installed properly (most renewal clutch plates will be marked 'flywheel side' or something similar - if not marked, fit the clutch disc with the damper springs or cushion toward the transmission).

15 Tighten the pressure plate-to-flywheel bolts only finger tight, working around the pressure plate.

16 Centre the clutch disc by ensuring the alignment tool is through the splined hub and into the recess in the crankshaft. Wiggle the tool up, down or side-to-side as needed to centre the disc. Tighten the pressure plate-to-flywheel bolts a little at a time, working in a criss-cross pattern to prevent distortion of the cover. After all of the bolts are finger-tight, tighten them to the torque listed in this Chapter's Specifications. Remove the alignment tool.

17 Using high-temperature grease, lubricate the inner groove of the release bearing (see Section 4). Also place grease on the release lever contact areas and the transmission input shaft bearing retainer.

18 Fit the clutch release bearing (see Section 4).

19 Fit the transmission, release cylinder and all components removed previously, tightening all fasteners to the proper torque specifications.

4 Clutch release bearing and lever - removal, inspection and refitting

⚠️ **Warning: Dust produced by clutch wear and deposited on clutch components may contain asbestos, which is hazardous to your health. DO NOT blow it out with compressed air and DO NOT inhale it. DO NOT use petrol or petroleum-based solvents to remove the dust. Brake system cleaner should be used to flush it into a drain pan. After the clutch components are wiped clean with a rag, dispose of the contaminated rags and cleaner in a labelled, covered container.**

Removal

1 Disconnect the negative cable from the battery.
2 Remove the transmission (see Chapter 7).
3 Remove the clutch release lever from the ball stud, then remove the bearing from the lever **(see illustration)**.

Inspection

4 Hold the bearing by the outer race and rotate the inner race while applying pressure **(see illustration)**. If the bearing doesn't turn smoothly, or if it's noisy, renew the bearing/hub assembly with a new one. Wipe the bearing with a clean rag and inspect it for damage, wear and cracks. Don't immerse the bearing in solvent - it is sealed for life and soaking or dipping in solvent would ruin it. Also check the release lever for cracks and bends.

Refitting

5 Fill the inner groove of the release bearing with high-temperature grease. Also apply a light coat of the same grease to the transmission input shaft splines and the front bearing retainer **(see illustration)**.
6 Lubricate the release lever ball socket, lever ends and release cylinder pushrod socket with high-temperature grease **(see illustration)**.
7 Attach the release bearing to the release lever.

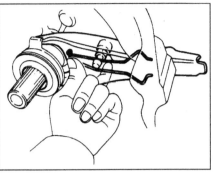

4.3 Reach behind the release lever and disengage the lever from the ball stud

8 Slide the release bearing onto the transmission input shaft front bearing retainer while passing the end of the release lever through the opening in the clutch housing. Push the clutch release lever onto the ball stud until it's firmly seated.
9 Apply a light coat of high-temperature grease to the face of the release bearing where it contacts the pressure plate diaphragm fingers.
10 The remainder of refitting is the reverse of the removal procedure.

5 Pilot bearing - inspection and renewal

1 A pilot bearing, pressed into the rear of the crankshaft, supports the front of the transmission input shaft. The needle roller bearing is greased at the factory and does not require additional lubrication. The pilot bearing should be inspected whenever the clutch components are removed. Due to its inaccessibility, if you are in doubt as to its condition, renew it.
2 Remove the transmission (see Chapter 7, Part A).
3 Remove the clutch components (see Section 3).
4 Inspect the bearing for excessive wear, scoring, lack of grease, dryness or obvious damage **(see illustration 2.1 for location)**. If any of these conditions are noted, the bearing

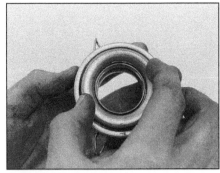

4.4 Check the operation of the bearing

should be replaced. An electric torch will be helpful to direct light into the recess.
5 The bearing must be pulled from its hole in the crankshaft, gripping the bearing at the rear. Special tools are available, but you may be able to get by with an alternative tool or fabricated tool. One method that works well is to use a slide-hammer with a small tip that has two adjustable hooks, 180° apart. Such tips are commonly available for slide-hammers, and are often included with better-quality slide-hammer kits. A slide-hammer is a tool with many uses, such as pulling dents from body parts and removing seals; you'll use it for more things than just removing bushings. If a slide-hammer with the correct hooked tip is not available, try to find a hooked tool that will fit into the bearing hole and hook behind the bearing, then clamp a large pair of locking pliers to the tool and strike the pliers, near the jaws, to pull the bearing out.
6 To fit the new bearing, lightly lubricate the outside surface with multi-purpose grease, then drive it into the recess with a hammer and a bearing driver or a clutch alignment tool. Make sure that the bearing seal faces toward the transmission. Don't allow the pilot bearing to become cocked in the bore. Tap into place until it's flush with the edge of the bearing bore.
7 Lubricate the pilot bearing with high-temperature grease.
8 Fit the clutch components (see Section 3).
9 Fit the transmission (see Chapter 7, Part A).

6 Clutch master cylinder - removal, overhaul and refitting

Note: *Before beginning this procedure, contact local parts stores and dealer service departments concerning the purchase of a rebuild kit or a new master cylinder. Availability and cost of the necessary parts may dictate whether the cylinder is rebuilt or replaced with a new one. If you decide to rebuild the cylinder, inspect the bore as described in paragraph 10 before purchasing parts.*

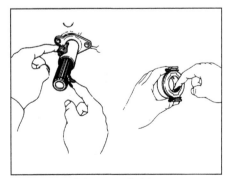

4.5 Apply a light coat of high-temperature grease to the transmission bearing retainer

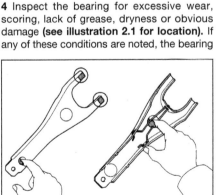

4.6 Apply high temperature grease to the release lever in the areas indicated

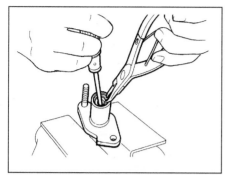

6.7 While holding the piston down remove the circlip

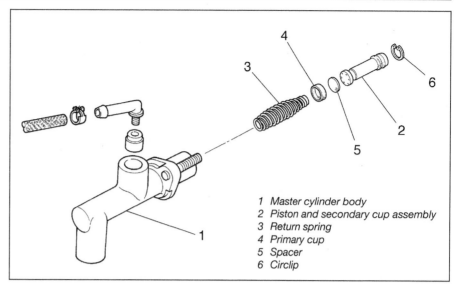

1 Master cylinder body
2 Piston and secondary cup assembly
3 Return spring
4 Primary cup
5 Spacer
6 Circlip

6.8 Clutch master cylinder components

Removal

1 Disconnect the negative cable and then the positive cable from the battery. Remove the battery hold-down clamp and the battery cover. Remove the battery.
Caution: If the stereo in your vehicle is equipped with an anti-theft system, make sure you have the correct code before disconnecting the battery.
2 Remove the bolt securing the diagnosis connector and move the connector aside.
3 At the clutch master cylinder, remove the clamp and the reservoir fluid hose; plug the hose to keep from draining the reservoir and lay it aside. Have rags handy as some fluid will be lost when the hose and hydraulic line are removed.
Caution: Don't allow brake fluid to come into contact with paint, as it will damage the finish.
4 Disconnect the hydraulic line at the clutch master cylinder. If available, use a flare-nut spanner on the fitting, to protect the fitting from being rounded off.
5 From under the dash, remove the nuts which attach the master cylinder to the bulkhead. Remove the master cylinder, again being careful not to spill fluid from the master cylinder.

Overhaul

6 Turn the master cylinder over and allow the trapped fluid to drain from the hose/pipe connection into a pan.
7 Place the cylinder in a vice with the piston end up. Push the piston down with a Phillips screwdriver and remove the circlip with pliers **(see illustration)**.
Caution: Do not damage the push rod contact surface of the piston.
8 Tap the master cylinder on a block of wood to eject the piston, spacer, primary cup and spring from inside the bore **(see illustration)**.
Note: *If the rebuild kit supplies a complete piston assembly, ignore the paragraphs which don't apply.*
9 Carefully remove the seal from the piston.
10 Inspect the bore of the master cylinder for deep scratches, score marks and ridges. The surface must be smooth to the touch. If the bore isn't perfectly smooth, the master

cylinder must be replaced with a new or factory rebuilt unit.
11 If the cylinder will be rebuilt, use the new parts contained in the rebuild kit and follow any specific instructions which may have accompanied the rebuild kit. Wash all parts to be re-used with brake cleaner, denatured alcohol or clean brake fluid. DO NOT use petroleum-based solvents.
12 Attach a new seal to the piston. The seal lips must face away from the pushrod end of the piston.
13 Lubricate the bore of the cylinder, the spring, primary cup, spacer and piston with plenty of fresh brake fluid.
14 Carefully guide the spring, primary cup, spacer and piston into the cylinder bore.
15 Again place the cylinder in a vice with the piston end up. Push the piston down with a Phillips screwdriver and fit a new circlip **(see illustration 6.7)**.

Refitting

16 Dab a small amount of grease on the end of the pushrod. Position the master cylinder on the pushrod and against the bulkhead, refitting the mounting nuts finger-tight.
17 Connect the hydraulic line to the master cylinder, moving the cylinder slightly as necessary to thread the fitting properly into the bore. Don't cross-thread the fitting as it's installed.
18 Tighten the mounting nuts and the hydraulic line fitting securely.
19 Reconnect the reservoir hose to the master cylinder.
20 Refit the diagnosis connector and the battery.
21 Fill the clutch/brake fluid reservoir with brake fluid conforming to DOT 3 specifications and bleed the clutch system (see Section 8).
22 Check the clutch pedal height and freeplay (see Chapter 1).

7 Clutch release cylinder - removal, overhaul and refitting

Note: *Before beginning this procedure, contact local parts stores and dealer service departments concerning the purchase of a rebuild kit or a new release cylinder. Availability and cost of the necessary parts may dictate whether the cylinder is rebuilt or replaced with a new one. If it's decided to rebuild the cylinder, inspect the bore as described in paragraph 8 before purchasing parts.*

Removal

1 Disconnect the negative cable from the battery.
Caution: If the stereo in your vehicle is equipped with an anti-theft system, make sure you have the correct code before disconnecting the battery.
2 Raise the vehicle and support it securely on axle stands.
3 Disconnect the hydraulic line at the release cylinder. If available, use a flare-nut spanner on the fitting, which will prevent the fitting from being rounded off. Have a small can and rags handy, as some fluid will be spilled as the line is removed. Cap the fluid line.
4 Remove the release cylinder mounting bolts.
5 Remove the release cylinder.

Overhaul

6 Remove the pushrod and the boot **(see illustration overleaf)**.
7 Tap the cylinder on a block of wood to eject the piston and seal. Remove the spring from inside the cylinder.
8 Carefully inspect the bore of the cylinder. Check for deep scratches, score marks and ridges. The bore must be smooth to the touch. If any imperfections are found, the

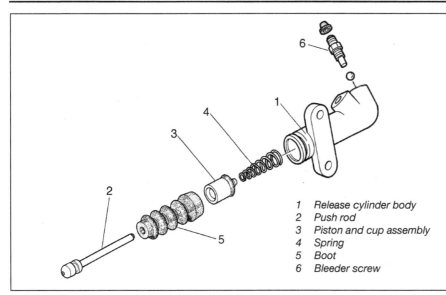

1 Release cylinder body
2 Push rod
3 Piston and cup assembly
4 Spring
5 Boot
6 Bleeder screw

7.6 Clutch release cylinder components

release cylinder must be replaced with a new one.

9 Using the new parts in the rebuild kit, assemble the components using plenty of fresh brake fluid for lubrication. Note the installed direction of the spring and the seal.

Refitting

10 Fit the release cylinder on the clutch housing. Make sure the pushrod is seated in the release fork pocket.
11 Connect the hydraulic line to the release cylinder. Tighten the connection.
12 Fill the clutch master cylinder with brake fluid (conforming to DOT 3 specifications).
13 Bleed the system (see Section 8).
14 Lower the vehicle and connect the negative battery cable.

8 Clutch hydraulic system - bleeding

1 The hydraulic system should be bled of all air whenever any part of the system has been removed or if the fluid level has been allowed to fall so low that air has been drawn into the master cylinder. The procedure is similar to bleeding a brake system.
2 Fill the clutch/brake reservoir with new brake fluid.
Caution: Do not re-use any of the fluid coming from the system during the bleeding operation or use fluid which has been inside an open container for an extended period of time.
3 Raise the vehicle and place it securely on axle stands to gain access to the release cylinder, which is located on the left side of the clutch housing.
4 Locate the bleed screw on the clutch release cylinder (next to the fitting for the hydraulic fluid line). Remove the dust cap

which fits over the bleed screw and push a length of plastic hose over the valve. Place the other end of the hose into a clear container with about two inches of brake fluid in it. The hose end must be submerged in the fluid.
5 Have an assistant depress the clutch pedal and hold it. Open the bleed screw on the release cylinder, allowing fluid to flow through the hose. Close the bleed screw when fluid stops flowing from the hose. Once closed, have your assistant release the pedal.
6 Continue this process until all air is evacuated from the system, indicated by a full, solid stream of fluid being ejected from the bleed screw each time and no air bubbles in the hose or container. Keep a close watch on the fluid level in the reservoir; if the level drops too low, air will be sucked back into the system and the process will have to be started all over again.
7 Fit the dust cap and lower the vehicle. Check carefully for proper operation before placing the vehicle in normal service.

9 Clutch start switch - check and renewal

Check

1 Check the clutch pedal height and freeplay (see Chapter 1).
2 Verify that the engine will not start when the clutch pedal is released. Verify that the engine will start when the clutch pedal is depressed all the way.
3 If the clutch start switch doesn't perform as described, adjust and, if necessary, renew it.
4 Locate the switch on the clutch pedal assembly and unplug the electrical connector.
5 Verify that there is continuity between the clutch start switch terminals when the switch is ON (pedal depressed) **(see illustration)**.

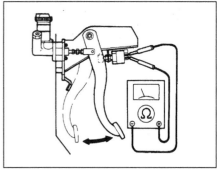

9.5 Check the continuity of the clutch start switch

6 Verify that no continuity exists between the switch terminals when the switch is OFF (pedal released).
7 If the switch fails either of the tests, renew it.

Renewal

8 Unplug the electrical connector. Loosen the locknuts and remove the switch.
9 Refitting is the reverse of removal.
10 Adjust the pedal height (see Chapter 1)
11 Verify again that the engine doesn't start when the clutch pedal is released, and does start when the pedal is depressed.

10 Driveshafts - general information and inspection

1 Power is transmitted from the transmission to the wheels through a pair of driveshafts. The inner end of each driveshaft is splined into the differential side gears. The outer ends of the driveshafts are splined to the axle hubs and locked in place by a large locknut.
2 The inner ends of the driveshafts are equipped with sliding constant velocity joints, which are capable of both angular and axial motion. Each inner joint assembly consists of a tripod bearing and a joint housing (outer race) in which the joint is free to slide in and out as the driveshaft moves up and down with the wheel. The joints can be dismantled and cleaned in the event of a boot failure (see Section 13), but if any parts are damaged, the joints must be replaced as a unit.
3 The outer CV joints are the 'balljoint' type which have ball bearings running between an inner race and an outer cage, allowing angular but not axial movement. The outer joints should be cleaned, inspected and repacked, but they cannot be dismantled. If an outer joint is damaged, it must be replaced along with the driveshaft (the outer joint and driveshaft are sold as a single component). On vehicles equipped with the 1.8 litre engine there is an intermediate/joint shaft between the transmission and the driveshaft to the right wheel. This shaft is supported by a bracket at the outer end where it mates with the driveshaft.

4 The boots should be inspected periodically for damage and leaking lubricant. Torn CV joint boots must be replaced immediately or the joints can be damaged. Boot renewal involves removal of the driveshaft (see Section 11). **Note:** *Some car accessory outlets carry 'split' type renewal boots, which can be installed without removing the driveshaft from the vehicle. This is a convenient alternative; however, the driveshaft should be removed and the CV joint dismantled and cleaned to ensure the joint is free from contaminants such as moisture and dirt which will accelerate CV joint wear.* The most common symptom of worn or damaged CV joints, besides lubricant leaks, is a clicking noise in turns, a clunk when accelerating after coasting and vibration at motorway speeds. To check for wear in the CV joints and driveshaft shafts, grasp each axle (one at a time) and rotate it in both directions while holding the CV joint housings, feeling for play indicating worn splines or sloppy CV joints. Also check the driveshaft shafts for cracks, dents and distortion.

11 Driveshaft -
removal and refitting

Removal

1 Disconnect the cable from the negative terminal of the battery.
Caution: If the stereo in your vehicle is equipped with an anti-theft system, make sure you have the correct code before disconnecting the battery.
2 Set the handbrake.
3 Loosen the front wheel nuts 1/4 turn. Using a hammer and punch, unstake the driveshaft hub locknut and loosen it 1/4 turn. Raise the vehicle and support it securely on axle stands. Remove the wheels.
4 Remove the driveshaft hub locknut. To prevent the hub from turning, wedge a lever between two of the wheel studs and allow the lever to rest against the ground **(see illustration)**.
5 To loosen the driveshaft from the hub splines, tap the end of the driveshaft with a

11.4 Use a large lever to immobilise the hub while loosening the driveshaft hub nut

soft-faced hammer **(see illustration)** or a hammer and a brass punch. **Note:** *Don't attempt to push the end of the driveshaft through the hub yet. Applying force to the end of the driveshaft, beyond just breaking it loose from the hub, can damage the driveshaft or transmission. If the driveshaft is stuck in the hub splines and won't move, it may be necessary to remove the brake disc (see Chapter 9) and push it from the hub with a two-jaw puller after paragraph 9 is performed.*
6 Remove the engine splash shield(s). **Note:** *All models have a splash shield on the left side of the engine compartment, inside the wheel well; 1995 and later models also have a shield on the right side which must be removed.*
7 Remove the nut and bolt securing the anti-roll bar to the control arm (see Chapter 10).
8 Disconnect the tie-rod from the steering knuckle (see Chapter 10).
9 Separate the lower ball joint from the control arm (see Chapter 10).
10 Pull out on the steering knuckle and detach the driveshaft from the hub **(see illustration)**. Don't let the driveshaft hang by the inner CV joint after the outer end has been detached from the steering knuckle, as the inner joint could become damaged. Support the outer end of the driveshaft with a piece of wire, if necessary.
11 Place a drain pan underneath the transmission to catch the lubricant that will spill out when the driveshafts are removed. Gently lever the inner CV joint out of the transmission being careful not to damage the

11.5 Using a brass punch, strike the end of the driveshaft sharply with a hammer

dust cover or oil seal **(see illustration)**. On vehicles with an intermediate shaft slide the driveshaft off the shaft.
12 Refer to Chapter 7 for the driveshaft oil seal renewal procedure.

Refitting

13 Refitting is the reverse of the removal procedure, but with the following additional points:
a) *Fit a new clip on the end of the driveshaft inner CV joint, apply molybdenum based grease to the splines and wipe the transmission oil seal with transmission oil.*
b) *With the end gap of the clip facing up, push the driveshaft sharply in to seat the clip on the inner CV joint in the groove of the differential side gear.*
Caution: The sharp edges of the driveshaft circlip can slice or puncture the oil seal.
c) *Fit a new driveshaft hub locknut, and tighten securely (do not attempt to tighten it fully until the vehicle is resting on its wheels)*
d) *Fit the wheel and wheel nuts, lower the vehicle and tighten the wheel nuts to the torque listed in the Chapter 1 Specifications.*
e) *Tighten the driveshaft hub locknut to the torque listed in this Chapter's Specifications and stake the locknut with a punch (see illustration).*
f) *Check the transmission lubricant and add, if necessary, to bring it to the proper level (see Chapter 1).*

11.10 Pull the steering knuckle out and slide the end of the driveshaft out of the hub

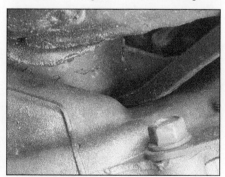

11.11 Separate the inner end of the driveshaft from the transmission

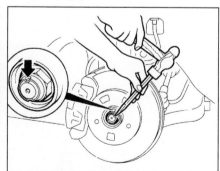

11.13 Tighten the locknut to the specified torque and use a punch to stake the nut so it cannot loosen

13.3 Lift the tabs on all the boot clamps with a screwdriver, then open the clamps

13.4 Remove the boot from the inner CV joint and slide the joint housing from the tripod

12 Intermediate shaft - removal and refitting (1.8 litre models only)

Note: *If the shaft does not rotate smoothly and freely by hand, the support bracket bearing will probably need to be replaced. The bearing is pressed into the bracket and should be taken to an automotive engineering workshop if it needs renewal.*

Removal

1 If you do not plan to service the driveshaft CV joints, it is not necessary to remove the right driveshaft in order to remove the intermediate shaft. In this case follow the procedure in Section 11 with the following changes:

a) *Do not loosen and remove the driveshaft hub locknut and separate the driveshaft from the hub as described in paragraphs 3, 4, 5 and 10.*

b) *After separating the driveshaft from the intermediate shaft (paragraph 11), move the driveshaft clear and support it with a*

block or wire. Don't let the driveshaft hang by the outer CV joint as the joint could be damaged.

2 Remove the three bolts securing the intermediate shaft bracket to the vehicle and gently lever/pull the shaft from the transmission being careful not to damage the oil seal.

Refitting

3 Refitting is the reverse of the removal procedure:

13 Driveshaft boot renewal and CV joint inspection

Note: *If the CV joints must be overhauled (usually due to torn boots), explore all options before beginning the job. Complete rebuilt driveshafts are available on an exchange basis, which eliminates much time and work. Whichever route you choose to take, check on the cost and availability of parts before dismantling the vehicle.*

1 Remove the driveshaft (see Section 11).

Dismantling

2 Mount the driveshaft in a vice with wood-lined jaws (to prevent damage to the driveshaft). Check the CV joint for excessive play in the radial direction, which indicates worn parts. Check for smooth operation throughout the full range of motion for each CV joint. If a boot is torn, dismantle the joint, clean the components and inspect for damage due to loss of lubrication and possible contamination by foreign matter.

3 Using a small screwdriver, lever the retaining tabs on the clamps up to loosen them and slide them off **(see illustration)**.

4 Using a screwdriver, carefully lever up on the edge of the outer boot and push it away from the CV joint. Old and worn boots can be cut off. Pull the inner CV joint boot back from the housing and slide the housing from the tripod **(see illustration)**.

5 Mark the tripod and driveshaft to ensure that they are reassembled properly.

6 Remove the tripod joint circlip with a pair of pliers **(see illustration)**.

7 Use a hammer and a brass punch to drive the tripod joint from the driveshaft **(see illustration)**.

13.6 Remove the circlip with a pair pliers

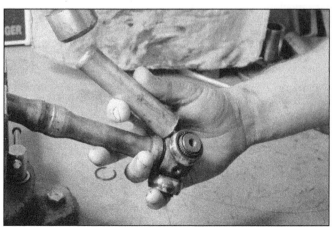

13.7 Drive the tripod joint from the driveshaft with a brass punch and hammer

13.10a Wrap the splined area of the driveshaft with tape to prevent damage to the boots

13.10b Install the tripod with the recessed portion of the splines facing the driveshaft

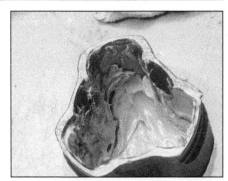

13.10c Place grease at the bottom of the CV joint housing

13.10d Insert the tripod into the housing, followed by the rest of the grease

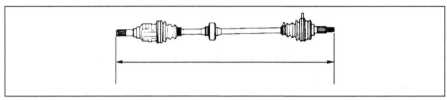

13.11 The driveshaft length should be set before the boot clamps are tightened

8 If you have not already cut them off, remove both boots. If you're working on a right-side driveshaft, you'll also have to cut off the clamp for the dynamic damper and slide the damper off.

Check

9 Thoroughly clean all components, including the outer CV joint assembly, with solvent until the old CV joint grease is completely removed. Inspect the bearing surfaces of the inner tripods and housings for cracks, pitting, scoring and other signs of wear. It's very difficult to inspect the bearing surfaces of the inner and outer races of the outer CV joint, but you can at least check the surfaces of the ball bearings themselves. If they are in good shape, the races probably are too; if they are not, neither are the races. If the inner CV joint is worn, you can buy a new inner CV joint and fit it on the old driveshaft; if the outer CV joint is worn, you must purchase a new outer CV joint *and* driveshaft (they are sold preassembled).

Reassembly

10 Wrap the splines on the end of the driveshaft with electrical tape to protect the boots from the sharp edges of the splines **(see illustration)**. Slide the clamps and boot(s) onto the driveshaft, then place the tripod on the shaft. **Note:** *If you are working on a right side driveshaft, be sure to fit the dynamic damper and a new clamp before refitting the inner boot.* Apply grease to the tripod assembly and inside the housing. Insert the tripod into the housing and pack the remainder of the grease around the tripod **(see illustrations)**.

11 Slide the boot into place, making sure both ends seat in their grooves. Adjust the length of the driveshaft to the dimension listed in this Chapter's Specifications **(see illustration)**.

12 Equalise the pressure in the boot, then tighten and secure the boot clamps **(see illustrations)**.

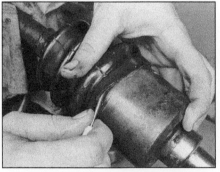

13.12a Equalise the pressure inside the boot with a screwdriver between the boot and the outer race

13.12b To install the new clamps, bend the tang down . . .

13.12c . . . then tap the tabs over to hold it in place

Notes

Chapter 9
Brakes

Contents

Degrees of difficulty

| Easy, suitable for novice with little experience | | Fairly easy, suitable for beginner with some experience | | Fairly difficult, suitable for competent DIY mechanic | | Difficult, suitable for experienced DIY mechanic | | Very difficult, suitable for expert DIY or professional | 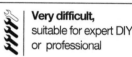 |

Specifications

General

Brake fluid type	See *Lubricants and fluids*
Brake pedal height	
1990 to 1994	193 to 196 mm
1995 and later	17.9 to 21.9 mm
Brake pedal freeplay	
1990 to 1994	3.0 to 8.0 mm
1995 and later	4.0 to 12.0 mm
Brake light switch-to-pedal clearance	See procedure
Servo pushrod-to-master cylinder piston clearance	0.1 to 0.4 mm
ABS sensor-to-toothed wheel clearance	0.3 to 1.1 mm
Pedal reserve	70 mm

Disc brakes

Minimum brake pad thickness	See Chapter 1
Front disc thickness	
1.3 litre models	18.0 mm
All except 1.3 litre models	22.0 mm
Rear disc thickness	9.0 mm
Disc runout limit (front and rear)	0.1 mm

Drum brakes

Drum inside diameter	200.0 mm

Handbrake

Handbrake lever travel	5 to 7 clicks

Torque specifications

	lbf ft	Nm
Brake hose-to-caliper banjo bolts	16 to 21	22 to 28
Front caliper bolts	29 to 36	39 to 49
Rear caliper bolts	34 to 44	46 to 60
Master cylinder-to-brake servo nuts	7 to 12	9 to 16
Vacuum servo mounting nuts	14 to 18	19 to 24
Wheel cylinder mounting bolts	7 to 9	9 to 12
Wheel nuts	See Chapter 1	

1 General information

The vehicles covered by this manual are equipped with hydraulically-operated front and rear brake systems. The front brakes are disc type and the rear brakes are drum or disc type. Both the front and rear brakes are self-adjusting. The disc brakes automatically compensate for pad wear, while the drum brakes incorporate an adjustment mechanism which is activated as the handbrake is applied.

Hydraulic system

The hydraulic system consists of two separate circuits. The master cylinder has separate reservoirs for the two circuits, and, in the event of a leak or failure in one hydraulic circuit, the other circuit will remain operative. A dual proportioning valve on the bulkhead provides brake balance between the front and rear brakes.

Vacuum servo

The vacuum servo, utilising engine manifold vacuum and atmospheric pressure to provide assistance to the hydraulically operated brakes, is mounted on the bulkhead in the engine compartment.

Handbrake

The handbrake operates on the rear brakes only, through cable actuation. It's activated by a lever mounted in the centre console.

Service

After completing any operation involving dismantling of any part of the brake system, always test drive the vehicle to check for proper braking performance before resuming normal driving. When testing the brakes, perform the tests on a clean, dry, flat surface.

Conditions other than these can lead to inaccurate test results.

Test the brakes at various speeds with both light and heavy pedal pressure. The vehicle should stop evenly without pulling to one side or the other.

Avoid locking the brakes, because this slides the tyres and diminishes braking efficiency and control of the vehicle.

Tyres, vehicle load and wheel alignment are factors which also affect braking performance.

2 Anti-lock Brake System (ABS) - general information

1 The Anti-lock Brake System (ABS) is designed to maintain vehicle steerability, directional stability and optimum deceleration under severe braking conditions and on most road surfaces. It does this by monitoring the rotational speed of each wheel and controlling the brake line pressure to each wheel during braking. This prevents the wheel from locking up.

Components

Actuator assembly

2 The ABS hydraulic unit consists of an electric hydraulic pump, solenoid valves, flow control valves, buffer and damper chamber, and is located in the engine compartment. The electric pump provides hydraulic pressure to the brakes, modulating brake line pressure during ABS operation, by turning on/off the solenoid valves and opening/closing the flow control valves in the ABS hydraulic unit. The buffer chamber stores hydraulic fluid from the brakes for smooth decrease of pressure. The damper chamber decreases pump noise and vibration. The hydraulic unit is controlled by the ABS control module, located under the dash at the driver's side. A fail-safe mode, operated by the fail-safe relay, mounted in the engine compartment near the left side

headlight, returns the brake system to conventional operation if there is a malfunction in the ABS, and the ABS warning light comes on.

Speed sensors

3 The speed sensors, which are located at each wheel, generate small electrical pulsations when the toothed sensor rotors are turning, sending a variable voltage signal to the ABS control module indicating wheel rotational speed.

4 The front speed sensors (see illustration) are mounted at the front wheel hubs in close relationship to the toothed sensor rotors, which are integral with the outer constant velocity (CV) joints.

5 The rear wheel sensors are bolted to the brake backing plates or axle carriers (see illustration). The sensor rotors are integral with the rear brake hub.

ABS computer

6 The ABS control module, mounted under the dashboard, is the 'brain' of the ABS system, in conjunction with the vehicle CPU. The function of the ABS Control Module is to accept and process information received from the wheel speed sensors to control the hydraulic line pressure, avoiding wheel lock up. The ABS Control Module also constantly monitors the system, even under normal driving conditions, to find faults within the system.

7 If a problem develops within the system, an 'ABS' light will glow on the dashboard. A diagnostic code will also be stored in the ECU, which, when retrieved by a service technician, will indicate the problem area or component.

Diagnosis and repair

8 If a dashboard warning light comes on and stays on while the vehicle is in operation, the ABS system requires attention. Although a special electronic ABS diagnostic tester is

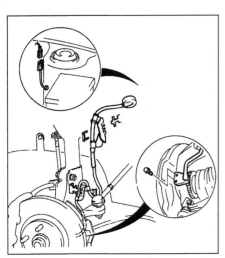

2.4 ABS front wheel speed sensor and sensor rotor

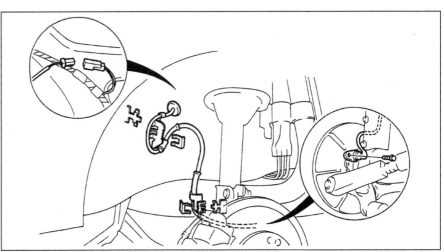

2.5 ABS rear wheel speed sensor and sensor rotor

necessary to properly diagnose the system, the home mechanic can perform a few preliminary checks before taking the vehicle to a dealer service department or other repair workshop which is equipped with a tester.

a) Check the brake fluid level in the reservoir.
b) Check that all electrical connectors are securely connected.
c) Check the fuses.

Caution: Do not attempt to use the vehicle until repairs are accomplished.

9 Additional checks that can be performed to assist you before dealer diagnosis and/or repair, that may help you discuss the problem with the dealer service representatives, are as follows:

With a fully charged vehicle battery, turn the ignition switch ON, and check that the ABS warning light goes out after 2 to 4 seconds.

If the light stays on after 2 to 4 seconds, the ABS control module is detecting a failure and will not activate the ABS hydraulic unit. See the dealer for servicing. Turn the ignition switch OFF.

Carefully jack up the vehicle on a level surface and securely support using axle stands. Shift the transmission to neutral or N range.

Release the handbrake. Rotate each wheel by hand, making sure that excessive brake drag does not exist.

Locate the Data Link Connector under the bonnet at the bulkhead, near the battery, and place a jumper wire between terminals TBS and GND.

Starting with the right front wheel, have an assistant depress the brake pedal while you check that the right front wheel will not rotate by hand.

With the brake pedal still depressed, turn the ignition switch ON and verify that the brake is released momentarily (approximately 1/2 second) and the wheel turns when pressure reduction from the ABS automatically cycles on and off. Perform the same check on the other wheels in order, left front, right rear, and left rear.

If the system tests are satisfactory for momentary brake release (the previous two steps above), then the piping to the ABS hydraulic unit is OK, the braking system

3.1 Always wash the brakes with brake cleaner before caliper removal

including the hydraulic unit is OK, the electrical system (solenoid, ABS motor) in the ABS hydraulic unit is OK, and the ABS control module and its output system including relay, solenoid, wiring harness are OK. Not checked by the above tests are the ABS input system/harness, intermittent failures, and fluid leakage.

Caution: Do not drive the vehicle until repairs are completed.

10 The vehicle should be diagnosed and repaired by a dealer service department or other repair workshop.

3 Disc brake pads (front) - renewal

Warning: Dust created by the brake system may contain asbestos, which is harmful to your health. Never blow it out with compressed air and don't inhale any of it. Clean the brake assembly with brake cleaner before any brake work. An approved filtering mask should be worn when working on the brakes. Do not, under any circumstances, use petroleum-based solvents to clean brake parts.

Note: If an overhaul is indicated (usually because of fluid leakage), explore all options before beginning the job. New and factory rebuilt calipers are available on an exchange basis, which makes this job quite easy. If you decide to rebuild the calipers, make sure a

3.4 Depress the piston inward fully to make room for the new pads

rebuild kit is available before proceeding. Always rebuild the calipers in pairs (front pair and/or rear pair) - never rebuild just one of them. Be careful when handling the new brake pads - do not touch the lining surface with your fingers to eliminate any oil contamination, which will affect braking efficiency.

1 Loosen the front wheel nuts, raise the front of the vehicle and place it securely on axle stands. Remove the wheel. **Note:** Work on one brake assembly at a time, using the opposite side brake assembly for reference if necessary. Wash the brake assembly with brake system cleaner before beginning work **(see illustration)**.

2 If you are checking the brake pads for wear, see Chapter 1. Inspect the brake disc carefully as described in Section 5. If machining is necessary, follow the brake disc removal procedure in Section 5.

3 Open the bonnet and remove the cap from the brake fluid reservoir.

4 With the old pads in place, press against the pad on the piston side of the caliper, displacing the caliper piston inward fully **(see illustration)**. As the piston is pressed inward, watch the fluid level in the brake fluid reservoir rise, being careful to remove any excess so that fluid will not spill over.

5 Remove the W-shaped clip from the caliper **(see illustration)**.

6 Remove the pad pins and M-shaped spring from the caliper **(see illustration)**.

7 Remove the pads, the anti-squeal shim, the outer shim, and the inner shim **(see illustration)**.

8 Apply a coating of high-temperature brake

3.5 Remove the W-shaped clip from the caliper

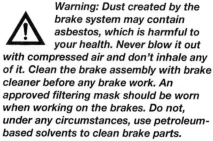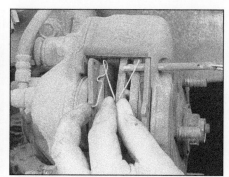

3.6 Remove the pad pins and M-shaped spring from the caliper

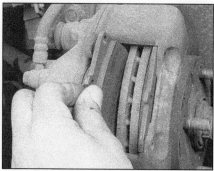

3.7 Remove the pads, the anti-squeal shim, the outer shim, and the inner shim

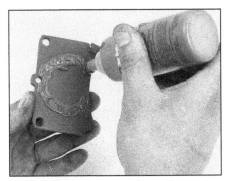

3.8 Apply brake grease or anti-squeal compound to the brake pad backing plates

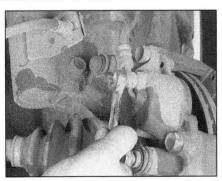

4.2a Remove the brake hose banjo bolt

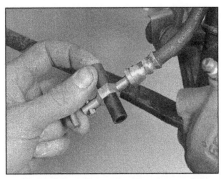

4.2b Using a piece of rubber hose of the appropriate size, plug the brake line

grease or anti-squeal compound to the brake pad backing plates **(see illustration)**. Be careful to not get any on or near the brake pad friction surfaces.

9 With the caliper piston pushed inward fully, fit the new pads with the anti-squeal shim, the outer shim, and the inner shim.

10 Refit the pad pins, M-shaped spring, and the W-shaped clip.

11 Repeat paragraphs 4 to 11 for the opposite wheel brake pad renewal.

12 Check the brake fluid level and remove or add brake fluid as necessary. Refit the reservoir cap.

 Warning: Press the brake pedal several times and recheck the brake fluid level in the reservoir before driving the vehicle.

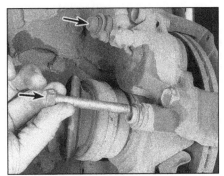

4.7 Remove the caliper mounting bolts (arrowed)

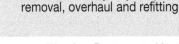

4 Disc brake caliper (front) - removal, overhaul and refitting

 Warning: Dust created by the brake system may contain asbestos, which is harmful to your health. Never blow it out with compressed air and don't inhale any of it. An approved filtering mask should be worn when working on the brakes. Do not, under any circumstances, use petroleum-based solvents to clean brake parts. Use brake system cleaner.

Note: *If an overhaul is indicated (usually because of fluid leakage), explore all options before beginning the job. New and factory rebuilt calipers are available on an exchange basis, which makes this job quite easy. If you decide to rebuild the calipers, make sure a rebuild kit is available before proceeding. Always rebuild the calipers in pairs - never rebuild just one of them.*

Removal

1 Loosen the front wheel nuts, raise the front of the vehicle and place it securely on axle stands. Remove the wheel and prepare for dismantling.

2 Remove the brake hose bolt (banjo bolt) and disconnect the brake hose from the caliper. Plug the brake hose to keep

contaminants out of the brake system and to prevent losing any more brake fluid than is necessary **(see illustrations)**. **Note:** *Don't disconnect the hose if you are only removing the caliper for access to other components.*

3 Remove the W-shaped clip from the caliper **(see illustration 3.5)**.

4 Remove the M-shaped spring from the caliper **(see illustration 3.6)**.

5 Remove the pad pins from the caliper **(see illustration 3.6)**.

6 Push the caliper piston inward if necessary **(see illustration 3.4)** to remove the pads, the anti-squeal shim, the outer shim, and the inner shim **(see illustration 3.7)**.

7 Remove the caliper mounting bolts **(see illustration)**.

8 Remove the caliper **(see illustration)** and the two guide plates at the caliper mounting points.

Overhaul

9 To overhaul the caliper, remove the bolt sleeves and the boots **(see illustration)**.

10 Remove the caliper piston retaining ring and dust boot **(see illustration)**.

11 Before you remove the piston, place a wood block or some rags between the piston and caliper to prevent damage as it is removed.

12 To remove the piston from the caliper, apply compressed air from a foot pump to the brake fluid hose connection on the caliper

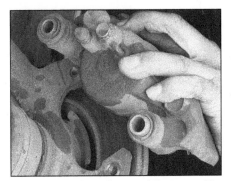

4.8 Remove the caliper and the two guide plates (not shown)

4.9 Remove the caliper bolt sleeves and boots

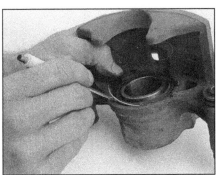

4.10 Using a small screwdriver, remove the cylinder boot set ring

4.12 Use compressed air to force the piston out of its bore

4.15 Remove the seal from the piston using a plastic or wooden tool, such as a pencil

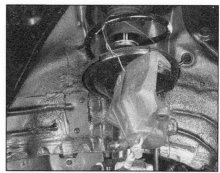

5.2 Hang the caliper with a piece of wire - do not allow the caliper to hang by the brake hose

body **(see illustration)**. Use only enough pressure to ease the piston out of its bore.

 Warning: Be careful not to place your fingers between the piston and the caliper, as the piston may come out with some force.

13 Remove the rubber cap and bleed screw.

14 Inspect the mating surfaces of the piston and caliper bore wall. If there is any scoring, rust, pitting or bright areas, renew the complete caliper unit with a new one. Emery cloth can be used to remove light corrosion and stains.

15 If these components are in good condition, remove the piston seal from the caliper bore **(see illustration)**.

16 Wash all the components with brake system cleaner and allow them to dry.

17 To reassemble the caliper, you should already have the correct rebuild kit for your vehicle.

18 Lubricate the new piston seal and the piston with brake fluid and fit the piston seal in its groove in the caliper bore.

19 Fit the piston into the caliper bore. Do not force the piston into the bore, but make sure it is squarely in place, then apply firm (but not excessive) force by hand to fit it.

20 Fit the new piston dust boot and retaining ring.

21 Refit the bleed screw and rubber cap.

22 Clean the bolt sleeves and lightly coat

them with high-temperature grease. Refit the sleeves and boots.

23 At this time, inspect the brake disc to be sure that it is reusable (see Section 5).

Refitting

24 Fit the caliper by reversing the removal procedure. Remember to renew the copper sealing washers (gaskets) at the brake hose-to-caliper connection (new washers normally come with the rebuild kit).

25 Bleed the brake circuit according to the procedure in Section 12. Make sure there are no leaks from the hose connections. Test the brakes carefully before returning the vehicle to normal service.

5 Brake disc - inspection, removal and refitting

Inspection

1 Loosen the wheel nuts, raise the vehicle and support it securely on axle stands. Remove the wheel and fit the wheel nuts to hold the disc in place. It may be necessary to place washers under the nuts so the disc is held tightly to the hub.

2 Remove the brake caliper as outlined (front brakes see Section 4, rear brakes see Section 9) but it is not necessary to disconnect the

brake hose. After removing the caliper bolts, suspend the caliper out of the way with a piece of wire **(see illustration)**.

3 Visually inspect the disc surface for score marks and other damage. Light scratches and shallow grooves are normal after use and may not always be detrimental to brake operation, but deep scoring - over 1.0 mm (0.04 in) - requires refinishing by an automotive engineering workshop. Be sure to check both sides of the disc **(see illustration)**. If pulsating has been noticed during normal application of the brakes, suspect disc runout - the ABS system may cause pulsating of the pedal during emergency stops.

4 To check disc runout, place a dial indicator at a point about 13 mm (0.5 in) from the outer edge of the disc **(see illustration)**. Set the indicator to zero and rotate the disc slowly by hand. The indicator reading should not exceed the specified allowable runout limit. If it does, the disc must be refinished by an automotive engineering workshop. **Note:** *The discs could be resurfaced regardless of the dial indicator reading, as this will impart a smooth finish and ensure a perfectly flat surface, eliminating any brake pedal pulsation or other undesirable symptoms related to questionable discs. At the very least, if you elect not to have the discs resurfaced, remove the glaze from the surface with emery cloth or sandpaper, using a swirling motion* **(see illustration)**.

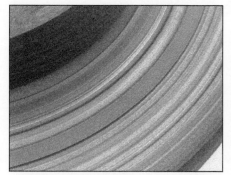

5.3 The pads were obviously neglected; wear this severe means the disc must be replaced

5.4a To check disc runout, mount a dial indicator as shown and rotate the disc

5.4b Using a swirling motion, remove the glaze from the disc surface with sandpaper or emery cloth

5.5a The minimum wear dimension is cast into the back side of the disc

5.5b Use a micrometer to measure disc thickness

5 It is critical that the disc is not machined to a thickness less than the specified minimum thickness. The minimum wear (or discard) thickness is cast into the inside of the disc **(see illustration)**. The disc thickness can be checked with a micrometer **(see illustration)**.

Removal

6 Remove the wheel nuts which were installed to hold the disc in place and remove the disc from the hub. On models equipped with ABS, unplug the electrical connector for the speed sensor, remove the clips fastening the hydraulic brake line to the strut, remove the bolts holding the sensor at the toothed wheel, and remove the sensor.

Refitting

7 Place the disc in position over the wheel studs.
8 Fit the caliper. Tighten the caliper bolts to the torque listed in this Chapter's Specifications.
9 Refit the ABS wheel sensor if removed, refitting in the reverse order of removal. Make sure the speed sensor-to-toothed rotor clearance is within the range listed in this Chapter's Specifications.
10 Fit the wheel, then lower the vehicle to the earth. Tighten the wheel nuts to the torque listed in the Chapter 1 Specifications.
11 Check the fluid level in the brake reservoir. Remove or add fluid as needed. Depress the brake pedal a few times to bring the brake pads into contact with the disc. Bleeding won't be necessary unless the brake

6.4a Mark the relationship of the drum to the hub

hose was disconnected from the caliper. Check the operation of the brakes carefully before driving the vehicle.

6 Drum brake shoes - renewal

 Warning: Drum brake shoes must be replaced on both wheels at the same time - never renew the shoes on only one wheel. Also, the dust created by the brake system may contain asbestos, which is harmful to your health. Never blow it out with compressed air and don't inhale any of brake dust. An approved filtering mask should be worn when working on the brakes. Do not, under any circumstances, use petroleum-based solvents to clean brake parts. Use brake system cleaner only. **Caution: Whenever the brake shoes are renewed, the return and hold-down springs should also be renewed. Due to the continuous heating/cooling cycle to which the springs are subjected, spring tension decreases over a period of time and may allow the shoes to drag on the drum and wear at a much faster rate than normal.**

1 Loosen the wheel nuts, raise the rear of the vehicle and support it securely on axle stands. Chock the front wheels to keep the vehicle from rolling.
2 Release the handbrake.
3 Remove the wheel. If checking brake shoe linings for wear, see Chapter 1. Also, check the brake wheel cylinder for any signs of fluid leakage. If fluid leakage is found, repair the wheel cylinder (see Section 7). **Note:** *All four rear brake shoes at both rear wheels must be replaced at the same time, but to avoid mixing up parts, work on only one brake assembly, and when complete, repair the opposite wheel before driving the vehicle.*
4 Follow the accompanying illustrations for the brake shoe renewal procedure **(see illustrations 6.4a to 6.4v)**. Be sure to stay in

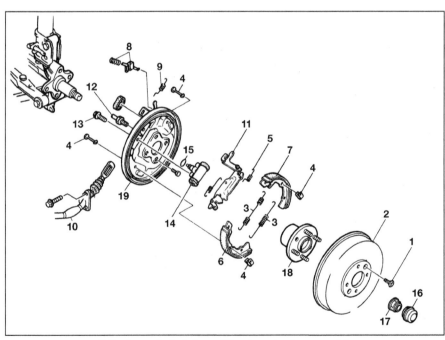

6.4b An exploded view of the drum brake assembly

1 Drum retention screw	7 Brake shoe - trailing side	13 Wheel cylinder mounting bolt(s)
2 Brake drum	8 Stopper spring and clip	14 Wheel cylinder
3 Return springs	9 Return spring	15 Wheel cylinder gasket
4 Hold-down pin and spring	10 Handbrake cable	16 Hub cap
5 Anti-rattle spring	11 Handbrake operating lever assembly	17 Spindle locknut
6 Brake shoe - leading side	12 Brake line and fitting	18 Wheel hub
		19 Brake backing plate

6.4c Remove the drum retaining screws

6.4d Thread bolts into the holes to unseat the drum if it's stuck - check the handbrake is fully released . . .

6.4e . . . and pull the brake drum off

6.4f Clean the brake assembly with brake cleaner and allow it to dry;
DO NOT USE COMPRESSED AIR

6.4g Unhook the upper return spring from the shoes . . .

6.4h . . . then unhook the lower return spring from the shoes

6.4i Remove the leading shoe hold-down pin and spring by pushing in and turning the pin 1/4 turn . . .

6.4j . . . remove the trailing shoe hold-down pin and spring and remove the leading shoe

6.4k Remove the anti-rattle spring from the adjuster and trailing shoe . . .

6.4l . . . and remove the trailing shoe

6.4m Apply high-temperature grease to the shoe contact points on the backing plate

6.4n Push the handbrake operating lever assembly over and hold until . . .

6.4o . . . the trailing brake shoe is installed and then . . .

6.4p . . . fit the trailing shoe hold-down pin and spring by pushing in and turning the pin 1/4 turn

6.4q Depress the wheel cylinder piston on the front side and . . .

6.4r . . . fit the leading shoe and its hold-down pin and spring

6.4s Fit the lower return spring . . .

6.4t . . . and the upper return spring . . .

6.4u . . . and the anti-rattle spring

6.4v The completed assembly looks like this

6.5 The maximum drum diameter is cast into the drum

order and read the caption under each illustration. **Note:** *If the brake drum cannot be easily pulled off the axle and shoe backing plate assembly, make sure the handbrake is completely released. If the drum still cannot be pulled off, the brake shoes will have to be retracted. This is done by loosening the handbrake cable nut until the handbrake lever at the brake backing plate returns to its stop. The drum should now come off.*

Refitting

5 Before refitting the brake drum, check it for cracks, score marks, deep scratches and hard spots, which will appear as small discoloured areas. If the hard spots cannot be removed with fine emery cloth or if any of the other conditions listed above exist, the drum must be taken to an automotive engineering workshop to have it resurfaced. **Note:** *Professionals recommend resurfacing the drums each time a brake job is done. Resurfacing will eliminate the possibility of out-of-round drums. If the drums are worn so much that they cannot be resurfaced without exceeding the maximum allowable diameter (stamped into the drum), then new ones will be required* **(see illustration)**. *At the very least, if you elect not to have the drums resurfaced, remove the glaze from the surface with emery cloth or sandpaper, using a swirling motion.*

6 Before refitting the brake drum, have an assistant depress the brake pedal while you check for operation of the automatic adjuster. Fit the brake drum on the axle flange.
7 Mount the wheel and fit the wheel nuts. Make sure the new brake shoes are adjusted so there is no brake drag with the brake pedal released (see Section 14).
8 Lower the vehicle and tighten the wheel nuts to the torque listed in the Chapter 1 Specifications.
9 Make a number of forward and reverse stops and operate the handbrake and check for satisfactory pedal action. Check the operation of the brakes carefully before driving the vehicle.

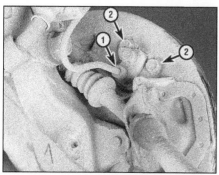

7.4 Disconnect the brake line fitting (1), then remove the two wheel cylinder bolts (2)

7 Wheel cylinder - removal, overhaul and refitting

Note: *If an overhaul is indicated (usually because of fluid leaks or sticky operation), explore all options before beginning the job. New wheel cylinders are available, which makes this job quite easy. If you decide to rebuild the wheel cylinder, make sure a rebuild kit is available before proceeding. Never overhaul only one wheel cylinder - always rebuild both of them. If the wheel cylinder shows evidence of brake fluid leakage, all brake components must be cleaned and the brake shoes must be renewed if contaminated with brake fluid (see Section 6).*

Removal

1 Raise the rear of the vehicle and support it securely on axle stands. Chock the front wheels to keep the vehicle from rolling.
2 Remove the brake shoe assembly (see Section 6).

3 Remove all dirt and foreign material from around the wheel cylinder.
4 Disconnect the brake line **(see illustration)** with a flare-nut spanner, if available. Don't pull the brake line away from the wheel cylinder.
5 Remove the wheel cylinder mounting bolts.
6 Detach the wheel cylinder from the brake backing plate and place it on a clean workbench. Immediately plug the brake line to prevent fluid loss and contamination.

Overhaul

7 Remove the bleed screw, dust boots, piston cups, pistons, spring, and spring caps from the wheel cylinder body **(see illustration)**.
8 Clean the wheel cylinder with brake fluid, denatured alcohol or brake system cleaner.

⚠️ *Warning: Do not, under any circumstances, use petroleum-based solvents to clean brake parts.*

9 Use filtered, unlubricated compressed air to dry the wheel cylinder and blow out the passages.
10 Check the bore for corrosion and score marks. Emery cloth (see your local automotive parts supplier) can be used to remove light corrosion and stains, but the cylinder must be replaced with a new one if the defects cannot be removed easily, or if the bore is scored.
11 Lubricate the wheel cylinder bore, new piston cups and pistons with brake fluid.

⚠️ *Warning: Always use fresh brake fluid from a new, previously unopened container.*

12 Assemble the wheel cylinder components. Make sure the piston cup lips face inward.

Refitting

13 Place the wheel cylinder in position and fit the mounting bolts finger tight. Connect the

brake line to the cylinder, being careful not to cross-thread the fitting, but do not tighten the brake line at this time.
14 Tighten the wheel cylinder mounting bolts to the torque listed in this Chapter's Specifications.
15 Tighten the brake line securely and fit the brake shoe assembly (see Section 6).
16 Bleed the brakes (see Section 12).
17 Check the operation of the brakes carefully before driving the vehicle.

8 Disc brake pads (rear) - renewal

⚠️ *Warning: Disc brake pads must be replaced on both rear wheels at the same time - never renew the pads on only one wheel. The dust created by the brake system may contain asbestos, which is harmful to your health. Never blow brake dust out with compressed air and don't inhale any of it. An approved filtering mask should be worn when working on the brakes. Do not, under any circumstances, use petroleum-based solvents to clean brake parts. Use brake system cleaner only*

1 Remove the cap from the brake fluid reservoir.
2 Loosen the wheel nuts, raise the rear of the vehicle and support it securely on axle stands. Chock the wheels at the front.
3 Remove the wheels. Work on one brake assembly at a time, using the assembled brake for reference if necessary.
4 If checking brake pads for wear, see Chapter 1. Inspect the brake disc carefully as outlined in Section 5. If machining is necessary, follow the information in that Section to remove the disc, at which time the pads can be removed as well.

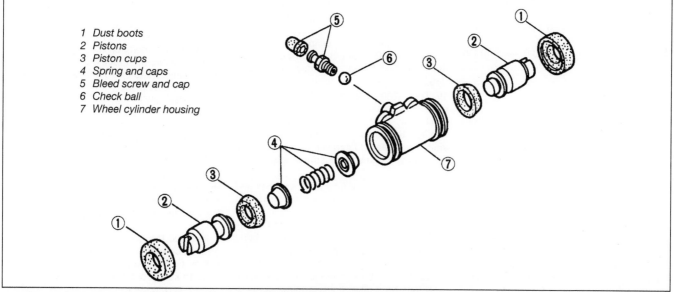

1 Dust boots
2 Pistons
3 Piston cups
4 Spring and caps
5 Bleed screw and cap
6 Check ball
7 Wheel cylinder housing

7.7 Typical wheel cylinder assembly

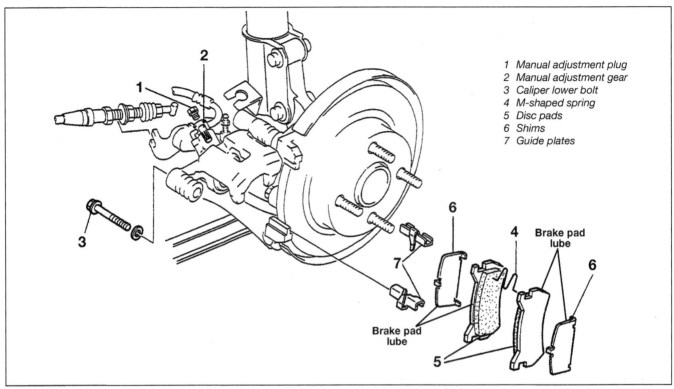

1 Manual adjustment plug
2 Manual adjustment gear
3 Caliper lower bolt
4 M-shaped spring
5 Disc pads
6 Shims
7 Guide plates

Brake pad lube

Brake pad lube

8.6 Rear disc brake pad details

5 Open the bonnet, and carefully remove the cap from the brake fluid reservoir.

6 Remove the plug from the manual adjustment gear screw **(see illustration)**.

7 Pull the brake caliper piston inward by rotating the manual adjustment gear anti-clockwise with an Allen spanner **(see illustration)**. As the piston is pulled inward, watch the fluid level in the brake fluid reservoir rise, being careful to remove any excess so the fluid will not spill over.

8 Remove the lower caliper bolt **(see illustration 8.6)**.

9 Remove the M-shaped spring from the caliper **(see illustration 8.6)**.

10 Rotate and swing the caliper up, with the upper bolt remaining in place.

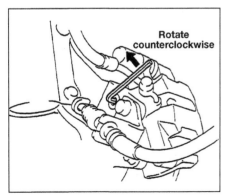

Rotate counterclockwise

8.7 Using an Allen spanner, rotate the manual adjustment gear anti-clockwise to retract the brake pads

11 Remove the brake pads, shim plates and the caliper guide plates **(see illustration 8.6)**.

12 With the new brake pads ready, apply a light coating of high-temperature brake grease or anti-squeal compound to the brake pad backing plates **(see illustration 3.8)**. Be careful to not get any on or near the brake pad friction surfaces.

13 With the caliper piston pushed inward fully, refit the caliper guides

14 Fit new pads with the outer shim and the inner shim, and the M-shaped spring **(see illustration 8.6)**.

15 Refit the lower caliper bolt **(see illustration 8.6)**. Tighten the caliper bolts to the torque listed in this Chapter's Specifications.

16 Turn the manual adjustment gear clockwise (opposite the direction shown in illustration 8.7) until the caliper piston contacts the brake disc. Then turn the manual adjustment gear 1/3 turn anti-clockwise.

17 Refit the manual adjustment gear screw plug.

18 Check the brake fluid reservoir level and remove or add brake fluid as necessary. Refit the brake fluid reservoir cap.

19 After the job has been completed, firmly depress the brake pedal a few times to bring the pads into contact with the disc.

20 Repeat paragraphs 6 to 19 for the opposite wheel brake pad renewal. Check the level of the brake fluid, adding some if necessary. Check the operation of the brakes

carefully before placing the vehicle into normal service.

21 Check the handbrake cable adjustment.

9 Disc brake caliper (rear) -
removal, overhaul and refitting

⚠️ *Warning: Dust created by the brake system may contain asbestos, which is harmful to your health. Never blow it out with compressed air and do not inhale any of it. An approved filtering mask should be worn when working on the brakes. Do not, under any circumstances, use petroleum-based solvents to clean brake parts. Use brake system cleaner.*

Note: *The caliper can be removed without disturbing the pads. If the caliper mounting bracket or brake disc are to be removed, the pads must also be taken from the mounting.*

Removal

1 Loosen the rear wheel nuts, raise the rear of the vehicle and place it securely on axle stands. Remove the wheel.

2 Remove the handbrake cable from the caliper.

3 Remove the brake hose bolt (banjo bolt) and disconnect the brake hose from the caliper **(see illustration 4.2a)**. Plug the brake hose to keep contaminants out of the brake system and to prevent losing any more brake fluid than is necessary **(see illustration 4.2b)**.

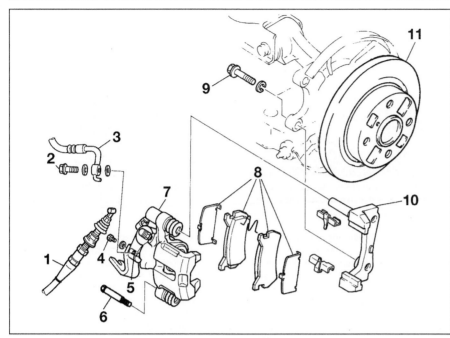

9.4 Rear brake caliper refitting details

1 Handbrake cable
2 Banjo fitting bolt
3 Brake line
4 Manual adjustment plug
5 Manual adjustment gear
6 Caliper lower bolt
7 Caliper
8 Disc pads, springs, shims
9 Caliper bracket bolt
10 Caliper mounting bracket
11 Disc

4 Remove the rear disc manual adjustment plug **(see illustration 8.6).**

5 Move the brake caliper piston inward by rotating the manual adjustment gear anti-clockwise **(see illustration 8.7).**

6 Remove the lower caliper bolt **(see illustration 8.6).**

7 Remove the M-shaped spring from the caliper **(see illustration 8.6).**

8 Remove the upper caliper bolt, and lift the caliper away.

9 Remove the brake pads, shim plates from the side of each pad, and the caliper guide plates **(see illustration 9.4).**

10 Remove the mounting bracket from the wheel hub **(see illustration 9.4).**

11 Remove the brake disc. If the vehicle is equipped with ABS, unplug the speed sensor electrical connector, remove the clips fastening the hydraulic brake line to the strut,

remove the bolts holding the sensor at the toothed wheel, and remove the sensor.

Overhaul

12 Due to the complexity of the rear calipers on these models, we do not recommend overhauling them. Replacing them as a pair with rebuilt units will provide better service for less cost.

Refitting

13 Fit the caliper by reversing the removal procedure. Remember to renew the copper sealing washers (gaskets) at the brake hose-to-caliper connection.

14 If the vehicle is equipped with ABS, refit the ABS wheel sensor. Make sure the clearance between the sensor and the toothed rotor is as listed in this Chapter's Specifications.

15 Bleed the brake circuit according to the

procedure in Section 12. Make sure there are no leaks from the hose connections. Test the brakes carefully before returning the vehicle to normal service.

16 Check the handbrake adjustment.

---

10 Master cylinder - removal, overhaul and refitting

Note: *Before deciding to overhaul the master cylinder, check on the availability and cost of a new or factory rebuilt unit and also the availability of a rebuild kit. If you decide to rebuild the cylinder, inspect the bore as described in paragraph 12 before purchasing parts.*

Removal

1 Unplug the electrical connector for the fluid level warning switch **(see illustration).** Check continuity at the level sensor terminals; no continuity should be measured when the fluid level is above MIN.

2 Carefully remove the brake fluid reservoir cap and remove as much fluid as possible from the reservoir with a syringe. Check continuity of the level sensor; continuity should be measured when fluid level is below the MIN level.

3 Remove the nuts and washers attaching the master cylinder to the vacuum servo **(see illustration).**

4 Place rags under the fittings and prepare caps or plastic bags to cover the ends of the lines once they are disconnected. Loosen the fittings at the ends of the brake lines where they enter the master cylinder **(see illustration).** To prevent rounding off the flats, use a flare-nut spanner, which wraps around the fitting hex.

Caution: Brake fluid will damage paint. Cover all body parts and be careful not to spill fluid during this procedure.

5 Pull the brake lines away from the master cylinder and plug the ends to prevent contamination.

6 Pull the master cylinder off the studs to remove it. Again, be careful not to spill the fluid as this is done.

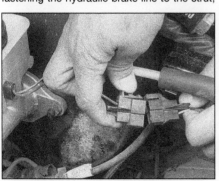

10.1 Unplug the electrical connector for the fluid level warning switch

10.3 Remove the master cylinder mounting bolts

10.4 Loosen the brake line fittings with a flare-nut spanner

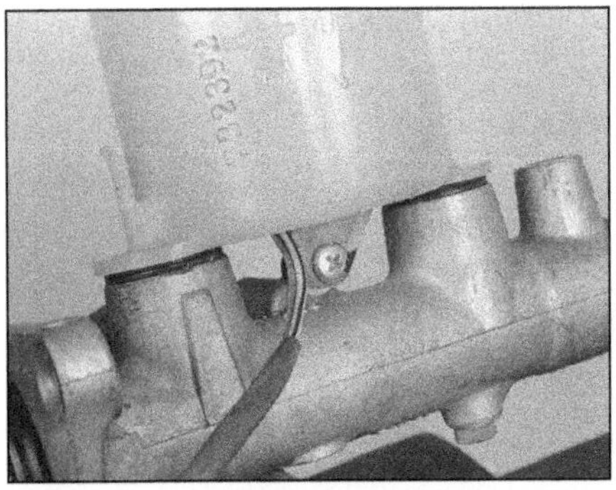

10.8a The brake fluid reservoir is retained by a screw

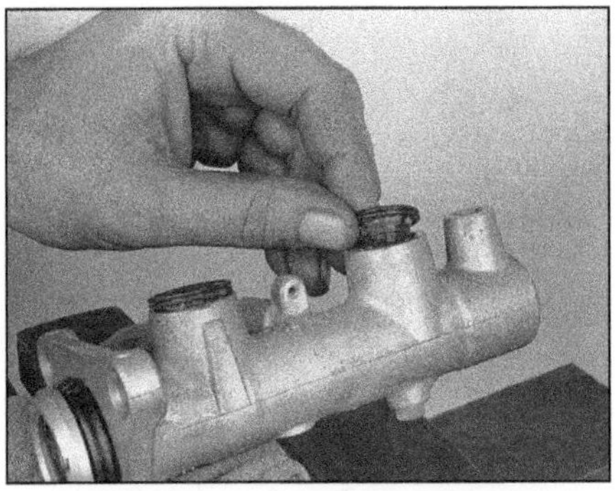

10.8b After the reservoir has been removed, pull the grommets from the master cylinder body

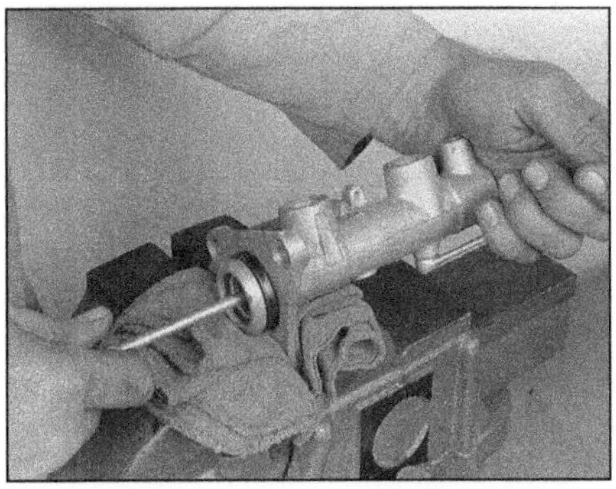

10.9 Using a Phillips screwdriver, depress the pistons, then remove the stopper bolt

Overhaul

7 Before attempting the overhaul of the master cylinder, obtain the proper rebuild kit, which will contain the necessary renewal parts and also any instructions which are specific to your model.

8 Remove the reservoir retaining screw, pull off the reservoir and remove the grommets **(see illustrations)**.

9 Place the cylinder in a vice and use a punch or Phillips screwdriver to depress the pistons until they bottom against the other end of the master cylinder. Hold the pistons in this position and remove the stopper bolt from the master cylinder **(see illustration)**.

10 Carefully remove the circlip at the end of the master cylinder **(see illustration)**.

11 The internal components can now be removed from the bore **(see illustrations)**. Make a note of the proper order of the components so they can be returned to their original locations. **Note:** *The two springs are different, so pay particular attention to their installed order.*

12 Carefully inspect the bore of the master cylinder. Any deep score marks or other damage mean that a new master cylinder is required. DO NOT attempt to hone the bore.

13 Renew all parts included in the rebuild kit, following any instructions in the kit. Clean all re-used parts with brake system cleaner.

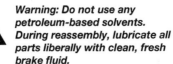

Warning: Do not use any petroleum-based solvents. During reassembly, lubricate all parts liberally with clean, fresh brake fluid.

14 Push the assembled components into the bore, bottoming them against the end of the master cylinder, then fit the stopper bolt.

15 Fit the new circlip, making sure it's seated properly in the groove.

16 Fit the reservoir grommets, reservoir and reservoir mounting screw.

17 Before refitting the master cylinder, it should be bench bled. Since you'll have to apply pressure to the master cylinder piston and, at the same time, control flow from the brake line outlets, the master cylinder should be mounted in a vice, with the jaws of the vice clamping on the mounting flange.

18 Insert threaded plugs into the brake line outlet holes and tighten them so no air will leak past them, but not so tight that they cannot be easily loosened.

19 Fill the reservoir with brake fluid of the recommended type (see *Lubricants and fluids*).

20 Remove one plug and push the piston assembly into the bore to expel the air from the master cylinder. A large Phillips screwdriver can be used to push on the piston assembly.

21 To prevent air from being drawn back into the master cylinder, the plug must be replaced and tightened before releasing the pressure on the piston.

22 Repeat the procedure until only brake fluid is expelled from the brake line outlet hole. When only brake fluid is expelled, repeat the procedure at the other outlet hole and plug. Be sure to keep the master cylinder reservoir filled with brake fluid to prevent the introduction of any additional air into the master cylinder system while bleeding it.

23 Since high pressure is not involved in the bench bleeding procedure, an alternative to the removal and renewal of the plugs with each stroke of the piston assembly is available. Before pushing in on the piston assembly, remove the plug as described in paragraph 20. Before releasing the piston, however, instead of replacing the plug, simply put your finger tightly over the hole to keep air from being drawn back into the master cylinder. Wait several seconds for brake fluid to be drawn from the reservoir into the bore, then depress the piston again, removing your finger as brake fluid is expelled. Be sure to put your finger back over the hole each time before releasing the piston, and when the bleeding procedure is complete for that outlet, renew the plug and tighten it before going on to the other port.

Refitting

24 Fit the master cylinder over the studs on the vacuum servo, fit the washers, and tighten the nuts only finger-tight at this time. Don't forget to use a new gasket.

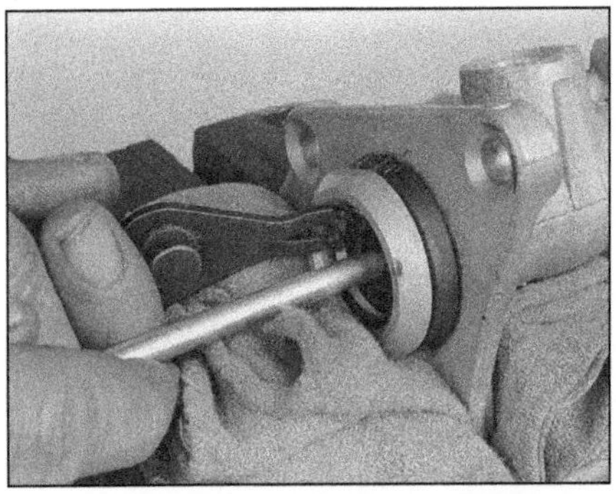

10.10 Depress the pistons again and remove the snap-ring with a pair of circlip pliers

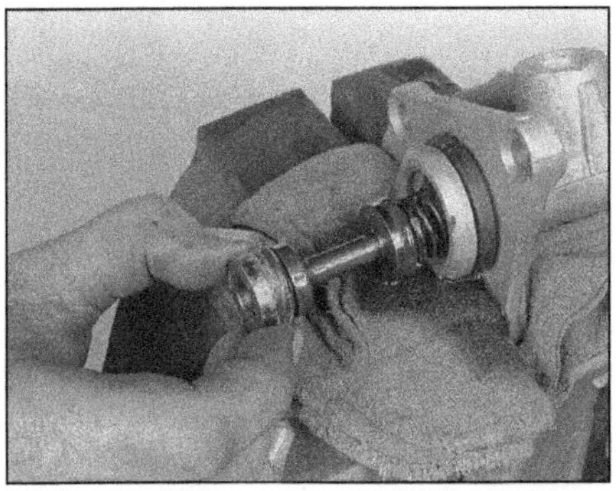

10.11a After the circlip has been removed, the primary (No. 1) piston assembly can be removed

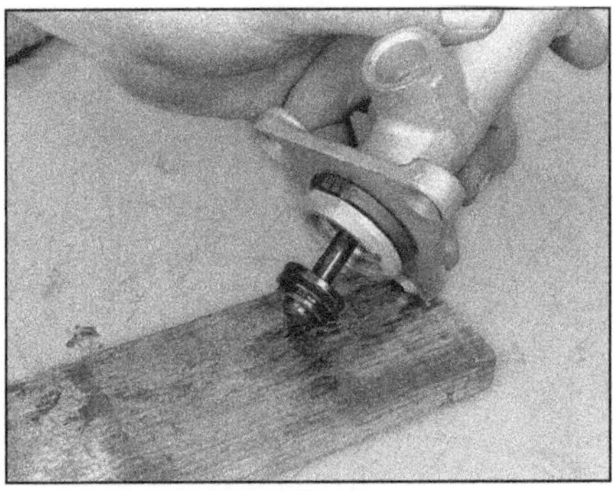

10.11b If necessary, tap the master cylinder against a block of wood to eject the secondary piston

10.27 Depress the pedal and hold it down, and loosen the fitting nut, allowing the air and fluid to escape

11.3 Unscrew the brake line threaded fitting with a flare-nut spanner

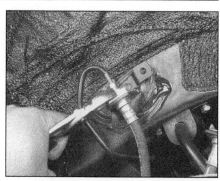

11.4 Pull off the U-clip with a pair of pliers

25 Thread the brake line fittings into the master cylinder. Since the master cylinder is still loose, it can be moved slightly so the fittings thread in easily by hand. Be careful not to strip the threads as the fittings are tightened.

26 Tighten the master cylinder mounting nuts to the torque listed in this Chapter's Specifications. Tighten the brake line fittings securely using a flare-nut spanner.

27 Fill the master cylinder reservoir with fluid, then bleed the master cylinder and the brake system (see Section 12). To bleed the master cylinder on the vehicle, have an assistant depress the brake pedal and hold it down while you loosen the fitting to allow air and fluid to escape (see illustration). Tighten the fitting, then allow your assistant to return the pedal to its rest position. Repeat this procedure on all fittings until the fluid is free of air bubbles. Check the operation of the brake system carefully before driving the vehicle.

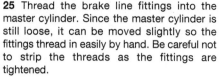

11 Brake hoses and lines - inspection and renewal

Inspection

1 About every six months, with the vehicle raised and supported securely on axle stands, the rubber hoses which connect the steel brake lines with the front and rear brake assemblies should be inspected for cracks, chafing of the outer cover, leaks, blisters and other damage. These are important and vulnerable parts of the brake system and inspection should be complete. A light and mirror will be helpful for a thorough check. If a hose exhibits any of the above conditions, renew it.

Renewal

Front brake hose

2 Loosen the wheel nuts, raise the vehicle and support it securely on axle stands. Remove the wheel.

3 At the frame bracket, unscrew the brake line fitting from the hose (see illustration).

Use a flare-nut spanner to prevent rounding off the corners and hold the hose fitting with an open-end spanner.

4 Remove the U-clip from the female fitting at the bracket with a pair of pliers (see illustration), then pass the hose through the bracket.

5 At the caliper end of the hose, remove the banjo fitting bolt, then separate the hose from the caliper. Note that there are two copper sealing washers on either side of the fitting - these sealing washers should be replaced with new ones during refitting.

6 To fit the hose, pass the caliper fitting end through any bracket, as necessary, then connect the fitting to the caliper with the banjo bolt and new copper sealing washers. Make sure the locating lug on the fitting is engaged with the hole in the caliper, then tighten the bolt to the torque listed in this Chapter's Specifications.

7 Push the hose support into the strut bracket and fit the U-clip, as necessary. Make sure the hose is not twisted between the caliper and any brackets.

8 Route the hose into the frame bracket, again making sure it is not twisted, then connect the brake line fitting, starting the threads by hand. Fit the U-clip, then tighten the fitting securely.

9 Bleed the caliper (see Section 12).

10 Fit the wheel and wheel nuts, lower the vehicle and tighten the wheel nuts to the torque listed in the Chapter 1 Specifications.

Rear brake hose

11 The rear brake hose serves as the flexible connection between two rigid metal lines, one on the body and the other on the suspension. Both ends of the hose are attached to these metal lines with threaded fittings and U-clips. Refer to paragraphs 2, 3 and 4 above. Be sure to bleed the wheel cylinder when you're done (see Section 12).

Metal brake lines

12 When replacing brake lines, be sure to use the correct parts. Don't use copper tubing for any brake system components. Purchase steel brake lines from a dealer or car accessory outlet.

13 Pre-fabricated brake line, with the tube ends already flared and fittings installed, is available at car accessory outlets and dealer parts departments. These lines are also bent to the proper shapes.

14 When refitting the new line, make sure it is securely supported in the bracket(s) and has plenty of clearance between moving or hot components.

15 After refitting, check the master cylinder fluid level and add fluid as necessary. Bleed the brake system (see Section 12) and test the brakes carefully before driving the vehicle in traffic.

12 Brake hydraulic system - bleeding

Warning: Wear eye protection when bleeding the brake system. If the fluid comes in contact with your eyes, immediately rinse them with water and seek medical attention. Do not get any brake fluid on the brake pads.

Note: *Bleeding the hydraulic system is necessary to remove any air that manages to find its way into the system when it has been opened during removal and refitting of a hose, line, caliper or master cylinder.*

1 If a brake line is disconnected at the brake master cylinder, or if air has entered it due to low fluid level in the brake master cylinder reservoir, all four wheels must be bled.

2 If a brake line was disconnected only at one wheel, then only that caliper or wheel cylinder must be bled.

3 If a brake line is disconnected at a fitting located between the master cylinder and any of the brakes, that part of the system served by the disconnected brake line must be bled.

4 Remove any residual vacuum from the servo by applying the brake several times with the engine off.

5 Remove the master cylinder reservoir cover and fill the reservoir with brake fluid. Refit the cover. **Note:** *Check the fluid level often during the bleeding operation and add fluid as*

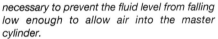

12.8 When bleeding the brakes, a hose is connected to the bleed screw and submerged in brake fluid

13.6 Detach the hose from the servo

13.10a Remove the clip and pin (centre arrow); to detach the servo, remove the four mounting nuts

necessary to prevent the fluid level from falling low enough to allow air into the master cylinder.

6 Have an assistant on hand, as well as a supply of new brake fluid, a clear plastic container partially filled with clean brake fluid, a length of plastic, rubber or vinyl tubing to fit over the bleed valve and a spanner to open and close the bleed valve.

7 For a brake system bleeding of all four wheels, begin at the left rear wheel; remove the bleed cap and attach the vinyl hose to the bleed valve. Loosen the bleed valve slightly, then tighten it to a point where it is snug but can still be loosened quickly and easily. If bleeding only specific wheels or portions of the brake system, follow the appropriate paragraphs below.

8 Place one end of the tubing over the bleed valve and submerge the other end in brake fluid in the container **(see illustration)**.

9 Have the assistant pump the brakes slowly a few times to get pressure in the system, then hold the pedal down firmly.

10 While the pedal is held down, open the bleed valve just enough to allow a flow of fluid to leave the valve. Watch for air bubbles to exit the submerged end of the tubing. When the fluid flow slows after a couple of seconds, close the valve and have your assistant release the pedal.

11 Repeat paragraphs 9 and 10 until no more air is seen leaving the tubing, then tighten the bleed valve securely and proceed to the right front wheel, the right rear wheel and the left front wheel, in that order, and perform the same procedure. Be sure to check the fluid in the master cylinder reservoir frequently, keeping it about 3/4 full during bleeding. **Note:** *Always use new, fresh brake fluid. Old fluid or fluid from an opened container contains moisture which will deteriorate the brake system components.*

12 At the end of the operation, refill the master cylinder with fluid to the MAX mark on the reservoir.

13 Check the operation of the brakes. The pedal should feel solid when depressed, with no sponginess. If necessary, repeat the entire brake system bleeding.

⚠️ **Warning: Do not operate the vehicle if you are in doubt about the effectiveness of the brake system.**

13 Vacuum servo - check, removal and refitting

Operating check

1 Depress the brake pedal several times with the engine off and make sure there's no change in the pedal reserve distance (distance from the pedal to the floor).

2 Depress the pedal and start the engine. If the pedal goes down slightly, operation is normal.

Airtightness check

3 Start the engine and turn it off after one or two minutes. Depress the brake pedal slowly several times. If the pedal depresses less each time, the servo is airtight.

4 Depress the brake pedal while the engine is running, then stop the engine with the pedal held depressed. If there is no change in the pedal reserve travel after holding the pedal for 30 seconds, the servo is airtight. **Note:** *If the*

airtightness check fails in either paragraph above, first try checking and/or replacing the servo vacuum hose/check valve and repeat the airtightness check.

Removal

5 Vacuum servo units shouldn't be dismantled. They require special tools not normally found in most automotive repair stations or workshops. Because of its critical relationship to brake performance, the servo should be replaced with a new or rebuilt one.

6 Disconnect the vacuum hose/check valve leading from the engine to the servo **(see illustration)**. Be careful not to damage the hose when removing it from the fitting.

7 Remove the brake master cylinder (see Section 10).

8 Remove the steering column lower finish panel (see Chapter 11).

9 Remove the pedal return spring.

10 Locate the pushrod clevis pin connecting the servo to the brake pedal **(see illustrations)**. Remove the spring clip from the clevis pin with pliers and pull out the clevis pin.

11 Remove the four nuts holding the brake servo to the bulkhead **(see illustration 13.10a)**.

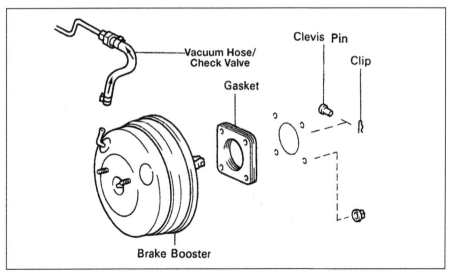

13.10b Vacuum servo refitting details

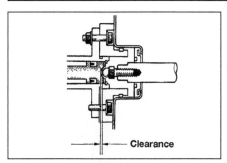

13.15a There should be a little clearance between the servo pushrod and the master cylinder pushrod

13.15b Hold the serrated portion of the rod with a pair of pliers and turn the adjusting screw in or out

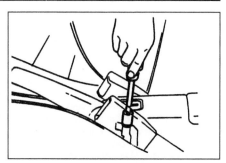

14.3 Remove the cover and turn the adjusting nut until the desired lever travel is obtained

You may need a light to see the mounting nuts.

12 Slide the servo straight out from the bulkhead until the studs clear the holes. Be careful not to tear or damage the brake servo gasket between the bulkhead and the servo.

Refitting

13 Refitting is basically the reverse of removal. Tighten the servo mounting nuts to the torque listed in this Chapter's Specifications. Be sure to use a new clevis retaining clip if the old clip is loose.

14 When refitting the servo vacuum hose/check valve, be sure to fit the vacuum hose/check valve with the arrows on the vacuum hose toward the engine.

15 If the vacuum servo unit is being replaced, the clearance between the master cylinder piston and the pushrod in the vacuum servo must be measured and, if necessary, adjusted. Using a depth micrometer or vernier caliper, measure the distance from the pocket of the primary piston to the master cylinder mounting flange. Next, with the engine running for vacuum applied to the servo (or vacuum applied by a vacuum pump, if desired), measure the distance from the end of the vacuum servo pushrod to the mounting face of the servo where the master cylinder mounting flange seats **(see illustration)**. Subtract the depth of the piston pocket from the protrusion of the pushrod to calculate the clearance and compare your findings with the

values listed in this Chapter's Specifications. If necessary, turn the adjusting screw on the end of the servo pushrod until the clearance is within the specified limit **(see illustration)**.

16 After the final refitting of the master cylinder and brake hoses and lines, the brake pedal height and freeplay must be adjusted and the brake system must be bled. See the appropriate Sections of this Chapter for the procedures.

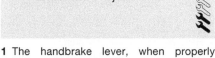

14 Handbrake - adjustment

1 The handbrake lever, when properly adjusted, should travel five to seven clicks, when a moderate pulling force is applied. If it travels less than the specified minimum number of clicks, the handbrake may not be releasing completely and could cause the rear brakes to drag. If the lever can be pulled up more than the specified maximum number of clicks, the handbrake may not hold adequately on an incline, allowing the car to roll.

2 To gain access to the handbrake cable adjuster, remove the rear console (see Chapter 11).

3 Remove the adjusting nut clip and adjust nut **(see illustration)**. Turn the adjusting nut until the desired travel is attained. Tighten the locknut.

4 Fit the rear console.

15 Handbrake cables - renewal

Equaliser-to-brake lever cable

1 Loosen the rear wheel nuts, raise the rear of the vehicle and support it securely on axle stands. Chock the front wheels. Remove the wheel.

2 Make sure the handbrake is completely released. Remove the console at the handbrake lever (see Chapter 11).

3 Remove the handbrake lever adjusting nut.

4 Under the vehicle, it is best to remove the exhaust and heat shield components in the area of the handbrake cable connection to the handbrake lever. Remove the return spring and front handbrake cable **(see illustration)**.

5 Pry out the rubber grommet from the floorpan and pull the front cable out.

6 Refitting is the reverse of removal. Apply a light coat of grease to the portion of the cable end that engages with the equaliser. And coat the sealing edge of the rubber grommet with silicone to ensure that it remains watertight.

Equaliser-to-brake cable

7 Remove the handbrake cable mounting bolts (on vehicles with drum brakes) located along the vehicle chassis, or the nuts (on vehicles with rear disc brakes) from the handbrake cable floorpan mounts **(see illustrations)**.

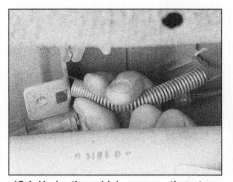

15.4 Under the vehicle, remove the return spring and front handbrake cable

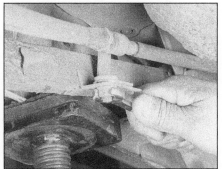

15.7a Remove the cable bolts (drum brakes) or cable bracket nuts (disc brakes) and detach the cable

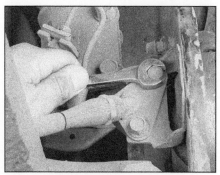

15.7b Remove the cable bolts or nuts at the rear brake assembly

Detach the handbrake cable from the rear wheel.

8 Remove the parking cable retaining clip at the bracket end **(see illustration)**.

9 Detach the handbrake cable from the equaliser **(see illustration)**. Pull the cable out from under the vehicle.

10 Refitting is the reverse of removal. Apply a light coat of grease to the portion of the cable end that engages with the equaliser.

11 Adjust the handbrake when the handbrake cable is reinstalled (see Section 14).

16 Brake pedal -
check and adjustment

Pedal height

1990 to 1994 models

1 Measure the pedal height **(see illustration)** and compare your measurement with the pedal height listed in this Chapter's Specifications.

2 If the pedal height is incorrect, adjust it as follows:

3 Unplug the electrical connector from the brake light switch.

4 Loosen the brake light switch locknut and turn the brake switch until it does not contact the pedal.

5 Loosen the pushrod locknut.

6 Adjust the pedal height by turning the pedal pushrod.

7 Tighten the pushrod locknut.

8 Turn the brake light switch until it lightly contacts the pedal stop.

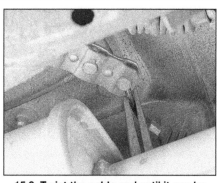

15.8 Remove the retaining clip at the equaliser and detach the forward end of the handbrake cable

9 Turn the brake light switch an additional 1/2 turn.

10 Tighten the brake light switch locknut.

11 Plug in the brake light switch electrical connector.

12 Check that brake lights come on when the brake pedal is depressed, and go off when the brake pedal is released.

13 Check the pedal freeplay (see below).

1995 and later models

Note: *It may be necessary to use a new brake light switch assembly each time brake pedal adjustment is made.*

14 Remove the brake light switch.

15 Measure the pedal height **(see illustration)** and compare your measurement with the pedal height listed in this Chapter's Specifications.

16 If the pedal height is incorrect, adjust it as follows:

15.9 Twist the cable end until it can be removed from the equaliser

17 Loosen the locknut B and turn nut A until it does not contact the pedal **(see illustration 16.15)**.

18 Loosen the pushrod locknut D. Adjust the pedal height by turning the pedal pushrod C.

19 Tighten locknut D.

20 Turn the nut A so there is a clearance between nut A and the pedal of 0.1 to 1.0 mm (0.004 to 0.04 in).

21 Tighten locknut B.

22 Fit the brake switch.

23 Check that brake lights come on when the brake pedal is depressed, and go off when the brake pedal is released.

24 Check the pedal freeplay (see below).

Pedal freeplay

25 Stop the engine if it's running, and depress the brake pedal several times until there's no more vacuum left in the servo.

26 Gently press the pedal by hand until you feel some resistance, then measure the distance between the fully released pedal and the point at which you feel resistance **(see illustration)**. Compare your measurement with the pedal freeplay listed in this Chapter's

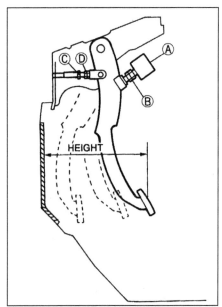

16.1 Pedal height is the distance between the pedal and the bulkhead when the pedal is released

A *Switch*	C *Pushrod*
B *Locknuts*	D *Locknuts*

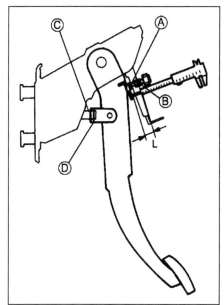

16.15 Pedal height is the distance between the pedal and the switch bracket when the pedal is released

A *Locknut*	C *Pushrod*	L *Pedal*
B *Nut*	D *Locknuts*	*height*

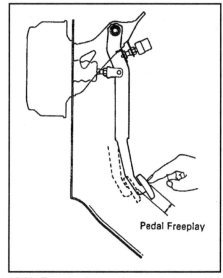

16.26 Freeplay is the distance between the pedal when released and the point when resistance is felt

Specifications. If the pedal freeplay is incorrect, adjust it as follows:

27 Adjust the brake pedal pushrod to obtain the specified pedal freeplay, then adjust the brake light switch as described. If the pedal freeplay cannot be adjusted properly, troubleshoot the brake system.

Pedal reserve

28 Start the engine, depress the brake pedal a few times, then press down hard and hold it.

29 Pedal reserve travel is measured from the floor to the top of the pedal while it is held depressed. Compare your measurement to the pedal reserve listed in this Chapter's Specifications.

30 If the pedal reserve is less than specified, check the adjustment of the rear brake shoes, malfunction of the automatic adjuster in rear drum brakes, and/or the vacuum servo pushrod-to-master cylinder piston clearance. If the brake pedal feels spongy, bleed the brake system (see Section 12).

17 Brake light switch - check and renewal

Check

1 The brake light switch is located on a bracket at the top of the brake pedal. The switch activates the brake lights at the rear of the vehicle when the pedal is depressed.

2 To check the brake light switch, simply note whether the brake lights come on when the pedal is depressed and go off when the pedal is released. If they do not function correctly, adjust the switch as described in Section 16 (adjusting the switch is part of brake pedal adjustment).

3 If the lights still do not come on, either the switch is not getting voltage, the switch itself is defective, or the circuit between the switch and the lights is defective. There is always the remote possibility that all of the brake light bulbs are burned out, but this is not very likely.

4 Use a voltmeter or test light to verify that there's voltage present at one side of the switch connector. If no voltage is present, troubleshoot the circuit from the switch to the fuse box. If there is voltage present, check for voltage on the other terminal when the brake pedal is depressed. If no voltage is present, renew the switch. If there is voltage present, troubleshoot the circuit from the switch to the brake lights (see the wiring diagrams at the end of Chapter 12).

Renewal

5 Disconnect the negative battery cable from the battery.

6 Unplug the electrical connector for the brake light switch.

7 Loosen the brake switch locknut and unscrew the switch from the pedal bracket.

8 Refitting is the reverse of removal.

9 Adjust the brake pedal and brake light switch (see Section 16).

Notes

Chapter 10
Suspension and steering systems

Contents

Degrees of difficulty

Easy, suitable for novice with little experience	Fairly easy, suitable for beginner with some experience	Fairly difficult, suitable for competent DIY mechanic 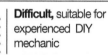	Difficult, suitable for experienced DIY mechanic 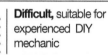	Very difficult, suitable for expert DIY or professional

Specifications

Torque specifications	lbf ft	Nm
Wheel nuts	65 to 87	89 to 118
Front suspension		
Anti-roll bar		
Bracket bolts		
1990 to 1994	32 to 43	43 to 58
1995 and later	50 to 65	68 to 88
Link nuts		
1990 to 1994	Tighten to 19.1 mm (0.75 in) of exposed thread	
1995 and later	32 to 44	43 to 60
Balljoints		
Balljoint-to-control arm bolt/nuts	69 to 86	94 to 117
Balljoint-to-steering knuckle nut	32 to 41	43 to 56
Control arm		
Front pivot bolt	69 to 93	94 to 126
Rear pivot **bolt**	69 to 93	49 to 126
Rear pivot **nut**	69 to 86	49 to 117
Strut-to-steering knuckle bolts/nuts		
1990 to 1994	69 to 93	94 to 126
1995 and later	76 to 93	103 to 126
Strut upper mounting nuts		
1990 to 1992	22 to 30	30 to 41
1993 to 1994, 1995 and later	34 to 46	46 to 62
Suspension support-to-piston rod nut	58 to 81	79 to 110

Torque specifications (continued)

	lbf ft	Nm
Rear suspension		
Anti-roll bar		
Link nuts		
1990 to 1994	Tighten to 17.5 mm (0.69 in) of exposed thread	
1995 and later	32 to 44	43 to 60
Bushing retainer bolts/nuts	32 to 43	43 to 58
Drum brake backing plate-to-rear spindle bolts		
1990 to 1994	33 to 43	45 to 58
1995 and later	34 to 49	46 to 66
Hub and bearing assembly to rear spindle locknut	130 to 173	176 to 235
Lateral link suspension arm No. 1 & No. 2 **outboard** nut/bolt		
1990 to 1994	63 to 86	85 to 117
1995 and later	64 to 86	87 to 117
Lateral link suspension arm No. 1 & No. 2 **inboard** nut/bolt		
1990 to 1994	50 to 70	68 to 95
1995 and later - front arm bolt/nut	64 to 86	87 to 117
1995 and later - rear arm cam plate bolt/nut	26 to 39	35 to 53
Strut-to-spindle nuts/bolts	69 to 93	94 to 126
Strut upper mounting nuts	34 to 46	46 to 62
Suspension support-to-piston rod nut	41 to 49	56 to 66
Trailing link strut rod **front** nuts/bolts		
1990 to 1994	47 to 68	64 to 92
1995 and later **bolt**	55 to 73	75 to 99
1995 and later - brake cable bracket **nut** on strut rod	14 to 18	19 to 24
Trailing link strut rod **rear** nuts/bolts		
1990 to 1994	69 to 93	94 to 126
1995 and later (bolt)	69 to 93	94 to 126
Steering		
Airbag module-to-steering wheel screws (1995 and later only)	6 to 9	8 to 12
Power steering pressure hose banjo nut		
1990 to 1994	12 to 17	16 to 23
1995 and later	18 to 26	24 to 35
Steering gear bracket nuts (*see procedure for torque sequence*)	28 to 38	38 to 52
Steering wheel nut	29 to 36	39 to 49
Tie-rod ends		
Tie-rod end-to-steering knuckle nut	32 to 41	43 to 56
Tie-rod end locknut	26 to 36	35 to 49
U-joint-to-pinion shaft pinch-bolt	14 to 19	19 to 26

1 General information

The front suspension (**see illustration**) is a MacPherson strut design. The upper end of each strut/coil spring assembly is attached to the vehicle's body strut support. The lower end of the strut assembly is connected to the upper end of the steering knuckle. The steering knuckle is attached to a balljoint mounted on the outer end of the suspension control arm. An anti-roll bar reduces body roll.

The rear suspension (**see illustration**) also utilises strut/coil spring assemblies. The upper end of each strut is attached to the vehicle body. The lower end of each strut is attached to an axle carrier (spindle). The carrier is located by a pair of suspension arms on each side, and a longitudinally mounted strut rod between the body and each carrier.

The rack-and-pinion steering gear is located behind the engine/transmission assembly and actuates the tie-rods, which are attached to the steering knuckles. The inner ends of the tie-rods are protected by rubber boots which should be inspected periodically for secure attachment, tears and leaking lubricant.

The manual steering system consists of the steering wheel and column, connected by universal joints to the rack and pinion steering gear. The power steering system consists of a belt-driven pump and associated lines and hoses which assists in actuating the rack and pinion steering gear. The power steering pump reservoir should be checked periodically (see Chapter 1). Looseness in the steering can be caused by wear in the steering shaft universal joints, the steering gear, the tie-rod ends, and loose retaining bolts.

Precautions

Frequently, when working on the suspension or steering system components, you may come across fasteners which seem impossible to loosen. These fasteners on the underside of the vehicle are continually subjected to water, road grime, mud, etc., and can become rusted or 'seized,' making them extremely difficult to remove. In order to unscrew these stubborn fasteners without damaging them (or other components), be sure to use a generous amount of penetrating oil and allow it to soak in for a while. Using a wire brush to clean exposed threads will also ease removal of the nut or bolt and prevent damage to the threads. Sometimes a sharp blow with a hammer and flat-faced punch (do not use a sharp-pointed or sharp-edged punch) will break the bond between nut and bolt threads, but care must be taken to prevent the punch from slipping off the fastener and ruining the threads. Heating the stuck fastener and surrounding area with a torch sometimes helps too, but this is not recommended because of the obvious dangers associated with heat and flame sources. Long breaker bars and extension pipes will increase leverage, but never use an extension pipe on a ratchet - the ratcheting mechanism could be damaged. Sometimes tightening the nut or bolt first will help to break it loose. Fasteners that require drastic measures to remove should always be renewed.

1.1 Front suspension and related components

1 Front anti-roll bar link bolt*
2 Support crossmember
3 Control arm
4 Balljoint
5 Strut/coil spring assembly
6 Right driveshaft assembly
7 Left driveshaft assembly
8 Rack-and-pinion steering gear
*Anti-roll bar and clamps not shown

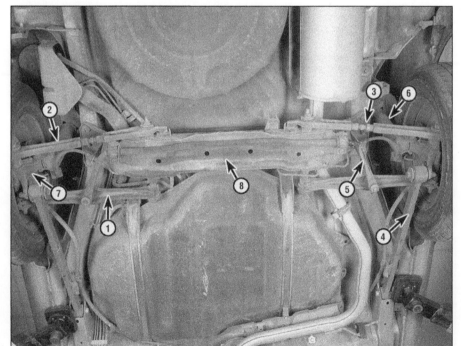

1.2 Rear suspension components

1 Rear lateral suspension arm - No. 1
2 Rear lateral suspension arm - No. 2
3 Rear arm toe adjuster (1990 to 1994; 1995 and later use cam plate adjusters)
4 Strut rod (trailing link)
5 Rear anti-roll bar
6 Strut/coil spring assembly
7 Rear spindle
8 Rear suspension crossmember

Since most of the procedures dealt with in this Chapter involve jacking up the vehicle and working underneath it, a good pair of axle stands will be needed. A hydraulic trolley jack is the preferred type of jack to lift the vehicle, and it can also be used to support certain components during various operations.

⚠ *Warning: Never, under any circumstances, rely on a jack to support the vehicle while working on it. Whenever any of the suspension or steering fasteners are loosened or removed they must be inspected and, if necessary, replaced with new ones of the same part number or of original equipment grade, material strength, size, quality and design. Torque specifications must be followed for proper reassembly and component retention. Never attempt to heat or straighten any suspension or steering components. Instead, renew any bent or otherwise damaged part with a new one.*

2 Strut assembly (front) - removal, inspection and refitting

Note: *When disposing of a used strut assembly, return them to your automotive parts store or dealer - some struts are gas-charged and require special disposal procedures.*

Removal

1 Loosen the wheel nuts, raise the vehicle and support it securely on axle stands. Remove the wheel.
2 Unbolt the brake hose bracket from the strut. If the vehicle is equipped with ABS, detach the speed sensor wiring harness from the strut by removing the clamp bracket bolt.
3 Remove the strut-to-knuckle nuts **(see illustration)** and knock the bolts out with a hammer and punch.
4 Separate the strut from the steering knuckle. Be careful not to overextend the inner CV joint. Also, do not let the steering knuckle fall outward and strain the brake hose.

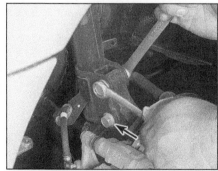

2.3 Remove the two nuts, then knock out the bolts (arrowed) with a hammer and flat-nosed punch

2.5 Remove the upper mounting nuts (arrowed)

3.3 Fit the spring compressor until all pressure is relieved from the upper spring seat

3.4 Remove the piston shaft nut

5 Support the strut and spring assembly with one hand and remove the strut-to-body nuts **(see illustration)**. Remove the assembly out from the wheelarch.

Inspection

6 Check the strut body for leaking fluid, dents, cracks and other obvious damage which would warrant repair or renewal.
7 Check the coil spring for chips or cracks in the spring coating (this will cause premature spring failure due to corrosion). Inspect the spring seat for cuts and general deterioration.
8 If any undesirable conditions exist, proceed to the strut dismantling procedure (see Section 3).

Refitting

9 Guide the strut assembly up into the wheelarch and insert the upper mounting studs through the holes in the body. Once the studs protrude, fit the nuts to prevent the strut from falling back downward. The help of an assistant is recommended, as the strut is heavy and awkward.
10 Slide the steering knuckle into the strut flange and insert the two bolts. Fit the nuts and tighten them to the torque listed in this Chapter's Specifications.
11 Connect the brake hose bracket to the strut and tighten the bolt securely. If the vehicle is equipped with ABS, fit the speed sensor wiring harness bracket.
12 Fit the wheel and wheel nuts, then lower the vehicle and tighten the wheel nuts to the torque listed in this Chapters specifications.

13 Tighten the upper mounting nuts to the torque listed in this Chapter's Specifications.
14 Have the front end alignment checked, and if necessary, adjusted.

3 Strut/spring assembly - renewal

1 If the struts or coil springs exhibit the telltale signs of wear (leaking fluid, loss of damping capability, chipped, sagging or cracked coil springs) explore all options before beginning any work. The strut/shock absorber assemblies are not serviceable and must be replaced if a problem develops. However, strut assemblies complete with springs may be available on an exchange basis, which eliminates much time and work. Whichever repair/renewal method you choose, check on the cost and availability of parts before dismantling your vehicle.

 Warning: Dismantling a strut is potentially dangerous and utmost attention must be directed to the job, or serious injury may result. Use only a high-quality spring compressor and carefully follow the manufacturer's instructions furnished with the tool. After removing the coil spring from the strut assembly, set it aside in a safe, isolated area.

Dismantling

2 Remove the strut assembly following the procedure described in the previous Section.

Mount the strut assembly in a vice. Line the vice jaws with wood or rags to prevent damage to the unit and do not tighten the vice excessively.
3 Following the tool manufacturer's instructions, fit the spring compressor (which can be obtained at most car accessory outlets or equipment yards on a daily rental basis) on the spring and compress it sufficiently to relieve all pressure from the upper spring seat **(see illustration)**.
4 Loosen the piston shaft nut **(see illustration)**. It may be necessary to hold the shaft from turning while loosening the nut.
5 Remove the nut and suspension support **(see illustration)**. Mark the suspension support so that it will be reinstalled with the same side inboard (there is a factory 'direction indicator' marking that faces inboard, away from (opposite) the side of the strut with the lower bracket mounting holes; you should mark the orientation when dismantling). Inspect the bearing in the suspension support for smooth operation. If it does not turn smoothly, renew the suspension support. Check the rubber portion of the suspension support for cracking and general deterioration. If there is any separation of the rubber, renew it.
6 Lift the spring seat and upper insulator from the piston shaft **(see illustration)**. Check the rubber spring seat for cracking and hardness, replacing it if necessary.
7 Carefully lift the compressed spring from the assembly **(see illustration)** and set it in a safe place.

3.5 Lift the suspension support off the piston shaft

3.6 Remove the spring seat from the piston shaft

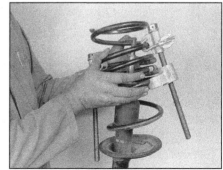

3.7 Remove the compressed spring assembly

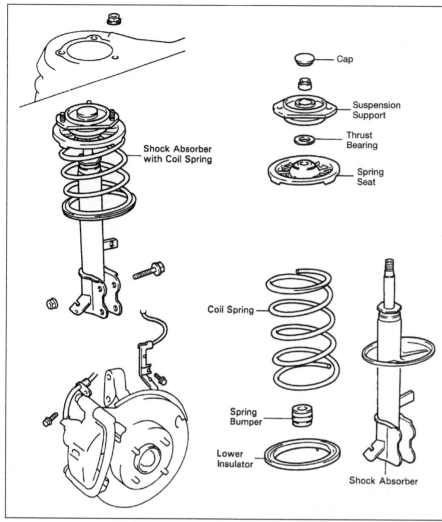

3.10 Typical strut and coil spring assembly details

Labels in illustration:
- Cap
- Suspension Support
- Thrust Bearing
- Spring Seat
- Shock Absorber with Coil Spring
- Coil Spring
- Spring Bumper
- Lower Insulator
- Shock Absorber

⚠ **Warning: Keep the ends of the spring pointed away from your body.**

8 Slide the rubber bumper off the piston shaft.

9 Check the lower insulator (if equipped) for wear, cracking and hardness and renew it if necessary.

Reassembly

10 If the lower insulator is being replaced, set it into position with the step (dropped portion) seated in the lowest part of the seat. Extend the damper rod to its full length and fit the rubber bumper **(see illustration)**. Apply rubber lubricant to the rubber bumper contact surfaces.

11 Place the coil spring onto the lower insulator, with the end of the spring resting in the step (lowest part of the insulator) **(see illustration)**.

12 Fit the upper insulator and upper spring seat. Apply rubber lubricant to the upper insulator contact surfaces.

13 Fit the bearing and suspension support to the piston shaft. Locate the suspension support with the direction indicator mark in line with the lower bracket, away from (opposite) the lower bracket mounting holes (as removed in the steps above).

14 Fit the nut and partially tighten it.

15 Remove the spring compressor tool.

16 Tighten the suspension support to the torque listed in this Chapter's Specifications.

17 Fit the strut assembly following the procedure outlined previously (see Section 2).

4 Anti-roll bar and bushings (front) - removal and refitting

Removal

1 Loosen the front wheel nuts. Raise the front of the vehicle and support it securely on axle stands. Apply the handbrake and chock the rear wheels to keep the vehicle from rolling off the stands. Remove the front wheels. Remove the engine undercover.

2 If you're working on a 1990 to 1994 model, remove the anti-roll bar link nut, bolt, bushings and washers **(see illustration)**. Store the parts in order as they were

3.11 When refitting the spring, place the end into the recessed portion of the lower seat (arrowed)

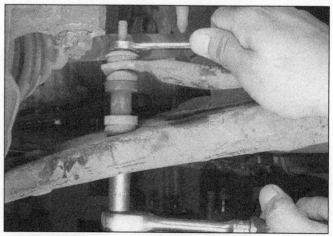

4.2a Remove the link nut, bushings, spacer, washers and link bolt

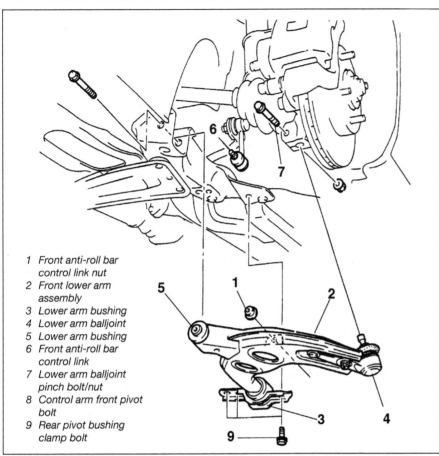

1 Front anti-roll bar control link nut
2 Front lower arm assembly
3 Lower arm bushing
4 Lower arm balljoint
5 Lower arm bushing
6 Front anti-roll bar control link
7 Lower arm balljoint pinch bolt/nut
8 Control arm front pivot bolt
9 Rear pivot bushing clamp bolt

4.2b Front suspension details - 1995 and later models

mounted, for correct reassembly later. If you're working on a 1995 or later model, remove the anti-roll bar control link nut at the lower arm assembly (see illustration).

3 Store the parts as they were mounted, for correct reassembly later.

4 Remove the nuts from the steering gear and pull the steering gear forward.

5 Support the engine (the preferred method is using a hoist above the engine).

6 Remove the front crossmember mounting bolts (see illustration 1.1), and lower the crossmember slowly.

7 Unbolt the anti-roll bar brackets from the crossmember (see illustration).

8 With the anti-roll bar off the vehicle, inspect the bracket bushings. If they are cracked, worn or deteriorated, renew them.

9 Clean the bushing area of the anti-roll bar with a stiff wire brush to remove any rust or dirt.

Refitting

10 Apply rubber lubricant to the bushings at the anti-roll bar clamp brackets and at the anti-roll bar ends (attachments to the suspension A-arm).

4.7 To detach the front anti-roll bar from the crossmember, remove the bolt from the bushing brackets

5.5 Remove the pinch bolt (arrowed) and nut, then lever the balljoint stud from the steering knuckle

Caution: Do not use petroleum or mineral-based lubricants or brake fluid - they will lead to deterioration of the bushings.

11 Refitting is the reverse of removal. Fit the bushings on the anti-roll bar with the bushing flat bottom/split facing the crossmember, and with the bushing located on the anti-roll bar at the refitting position line painted on the anti-roll bar. **Note:** *On 1995 and later models, fit the anti-roll bar bracket in the direction shown by the arrow marked on the bracket.* Fit and tighten the anti-roll bar bracket nuts to the torque listed in this Chapter's Specifications.

12 Raise the crossmember into position. Fit and tighten the crossmember bolts to the torque listed in this Chapter's Specifications.

13 Move the steering gear back into position and fit the steering gear mounting bracket nuts (see Section 19). Tighten the steering gear mounting nuts to the torque listed in this Chapter's Specifications.

14 Fit the anti-roll bar link bolt, bushings, washers, and nut in the order as removed in the paragraphs above and tighten to the specified length of exposed thread, or torque, as listed in this Chapter's Specifications.

5 Control arm - removal, inspection and refitting

Removal

1 Loosen the wheel nuts on the side to be dismantled, raise the front of the vehicle, support it securely on axle stands and remove the wheel.

2 Remove the anti-roll bar link nut (see illustrations 4.2a and 4.2b), bushings, washers and bolt.

3 Remove the control arm front pivot bolt and washer (see illustration 4.2b).

4 Remove the control arm rear pivot bushing clamp bolts (see illustration 4.2b). **Note:** *It is not necessary to remove the pivot bushing nut that retains the control arm bushing unless you are replacing the bushing.*

5 Remove the pinch bolt and nut holding the steering knuckle to the lower balljoint (see illustration), then pry the control arm balljoint from the steering knuckle.

6 Remove the control arm.

7 If replacing the lower balljoint, detach the lower balljoint from the control arm.

Inspection

8 Check the control arm for damage or distortion and the bushings for wear, replacing parts as necessary. **Do not** attempt to straighten a bent control arm.

Refitting

9 Refitting is the reverse of removal. Tighten all of the fasteners to the torque values listed in this Chapter's Specifications. **Note:** *Before tightening the pivot bolts, raise the outer end*

of the control arm with a trolley jack to simulate normal ride height.

10 Fit the wheel and wheel nuts, lower the vehicle and tighten the wheel nuts to the torque listed in this Chapters specifications.

11 It is a good idea to have the front wheel alignment checked and, if necessary, adjusted after this job has been performed.

6 Balljoints - renewal

1 Loosen the wheel nuts, raise the vehicle and support it securely on axle stands. Remove the wheel.

2 Remove the pinch bolt and nut holding the steering knuckle to the lower balljoint. Pry the control arm balljoint from the steering knuckle **(see illustration 5.5)**.

3 Remove the bolt and nuts securing the balljoint to the control arm **(see illustration)**. Separate the balljoint from the control arm with a lever.

4 To fit the balljoint, insert the balljoint threaded stud through the hole in the lower A-arm and fit the nut, but do not tighten the nut yet.

5 Fit the balljoint mounting bolt and nut. Tighten the balljoint bolt and nuts to the torque listed in this Chapter's Specifications.

6 Insert the balljoint into the steering knuckle fully, and fit the pinch bolt and nut. Tighten to the torque listed in this Chapter's Specifications.

7 Fit the wheel and wheel nuts. Lower the vehicle and tighten the wheel nuts to the torque listed in this Chapters specifications.

7 Steering knuckle and hub - removal and refitting

 Warning: Dust created by the brake system may contain asbestos, which is harmful to your health. Never blow it out with compressed air and do not inhale any of it. Do not, under any circumstances, use petroleum-based solvents to clean brake parts. Use brake system cleaner only.

Removal

1 Loosen the wheel nuts, raise the vehicle and support it securely on axle stands. Remove the wheel.

2 Remove the brake caliper and the brake disc (see Chapter 9); it is not necessary to disconnect the brake hose. Suspend the brake assembly from the coil spring with a piece of wire. Disconnect the brake hose from the strut.

3 If the vehicle is equipped with ABS, remove the wheel speed sensor.

4 Loosen, but don't remove the strut-to-steering knuckle nuts and bolts (see Section 2).

5 Separate the tie-rod end from the steering knuckle arm (see Section 17).

6 Remove the pinch bolt and nut holding the steering knuckle to the lower balljoint **(see illustration 5.5)**. Pry the control arm balljoint from the steering knuckle.

7 Push the driveshaft from the hub as described in Chapter 8. Support the end of the driveshaft with a piece of wire.

8 The strut-to-knuckle bolts can now be removed.

9 Carefully separate the steering knuckle from the strut and lift out the steering knuckle.

Refitting

10 Guide the steering knuckle and hub assembly into position, inserting the driveshaft into the hub.

11 Push the steering knuckle into the strut flange and fit the bolts and nuts, but do not tighten them yet.

12 Insert the balljoint into the steering knuckle and fit the pinch bolt and nut. Tighten the balljoint pinch bolt and nut to the torque listed in this Chapter's Specifications.

13 If you are refitting a new balljoint, fit it on the control arm (see Section 5), but do not tighten the bolt and nuts yet.

14 Attach the tie-rod to the steering knuckle arm (see Section 17). Tighten the strut bolt nuts, the balljoint-to-control arm bolt and nuts and the tie-rod nut to the torque listed in this Chapter's Specifications. Fit a new tie rod nut split pin.

15 Place the brake disc on the hub and fit the caliper as outlined in Chapter 9.

16 Fit the driveshaft/hub nut and tighten it to the torque listed in the Chapter 8 Specifications.

17 Fit the wheel and wheel nuts.

18 Lower the vehicle and tighten the wheel nuts to the torque listed in this Chapters specifications.

8 Hub and bearing assembly (front) - removal and refitting

1 Due to the special tools and expertise required to press the hub and bearing from the steering knuckle, this job should be left to a professional mechanic. However, the steering knuckle and hub may be removed and the assembly taken to a dealer service department or other repair workshop. See Section 7 for the steering knuckle and hub removal procedure.

9 Anti-roll bar and bushings (rear) - removal and refitting

1 Loosen the rear wheel nuts. Raise the rear of the vehicle and place it securely on axle stands. Remove the rear wheels.

2 If you're working on a 1990 to 1994 model, remove the anti-roll bar link nut **(see illustration)**, bolt, bushings and washers. Store the parts in order, for correct reassembly later. If you're working on a 1995 or later model, remove the anti-roll bar control link nut at the strut assembly **(see**

6.3 Remove the balljoint bolt and nuts from the control arm and remove the balljoint

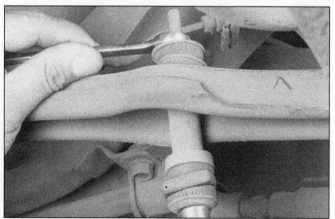

9.2a Remove the bushing nut, bushings, spacer, washers and bushing bolt (arrowed)

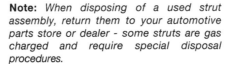

9.2b Rear anti-roll bar details - 1995 and later models

| 1 | Rear anti-roll bar control link | 2 | Rear anti-roll bar clamp | 4 | Lower control link nut |
| | | 3 | Rear anti-roll bar | 5 | Upper control link nut |

illustration). Store the parts as they were mounted, for correct reassembly later.

3 Unbolt the anti-roll bar bushing clamps from the body **(see illustration)**.

4 The anti-roll bar can now be removed from the vehicle. Pull the bushings off the anti-roll bar using a rocking motion.

5 Check the bushings for wear, hardness, distortion, cracking and other signs of deterioration, replacing them if necessary. Also check the anti-roll bar link bushings for the same conditions, and renew if necessary.

6 Using a wire brush, clean the areas of the bar where the bushings ride. Refitting is the reverse of the removal procedure. Apply rubber lubricant to the bushings prior to refitting.

Caution: Do not use petroleum-based products or brake fluid, as these will damage the rubber.

7 Fit the bushings at the anti-roll bar brackets with the bushing flat bottom/split facing the crossmember, and with the bushing located on the anti-roll bar at the refitting position line painted on the anti-roll bar.

8 Fit and tighten the anti-roll bar bracket nuts to the torque listed in this Chapter's Specifications.

9 Fit the anti-roll bar end bushings, washers, and nut in the order as removed in the Steps above and tighten to the specified length of exposed thread as listed in this Chapter's Specifications.

10 Strut assembly (rear) - removal, inspection and refitting

Note: When disposing of a used strut assembly, return them to your automotive parts store or dealer - some struts are gas charged and require special disposal procedures.

Removal

1 Loosen the rear wheel nuts, raise the rear of the vehicle and support it securely on axle stands. Remove the wheel.

2 Remove the clip and detach the brake hose

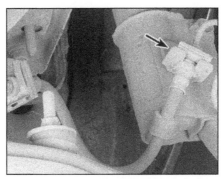

10.2 Remove the clip (arrowed) and pass the hose fitting through the slot (1990 to 1994 model shown)

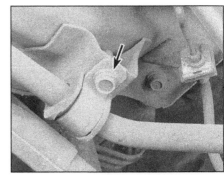

9.3 Remove the bolts (arrowed) from the bushing brackets (1990 to 1994 model shown)

from the bracket on the strut **(see illustration)**. If the vehicle is equipped with ABS, detach the wheel speed sensor wire from the strut.

3 Support the spindle with a trolley jack.

4 Remove the strut-to-spindle bolt nuts. Don't let the spindle fall outward, as this could strain the brake hose.

5 Access the upper strut mounting bolts through the boot on four-door models, and through the passenger compartment/hatch door on two-door models, removing trim as necessary (see Chapter 11). Have an assistant support the strut, then remove the upper strut-to-body mounting nuts **(see illustration)**. Remove the strut assembly.

Inspection

6 Follow the inspection procedures described in Section 2. If you determine that the strut assembly must be dismantled for renewal of the strut or the coil spring, refer to Section 3.

7 When reassembling the strut, make sure the suspension support is aligned as removed, according to the procedure to note the location of the suspension support during dismantling, which is with the two mounting studs lined up with the centre of the piston rod.

Refitting

8 Manoeuvre the assembly up into the wheelarch and insert the mounting studs through the holes in the body. Fit the nuts, but don't tighten them yet.

10.5 To detach the upper end of the rear strut from the vehicle, remove these nuts (arrowed)

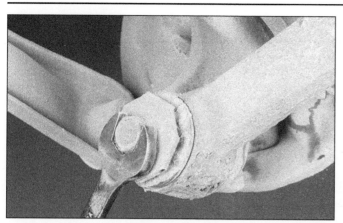

11.3 To detach the rear strut rod from the spindle, remove this bolt - 1990 to 1994 shown

11.4 To disconnect the strut rod from the body, remove this bolt - 1990 to 1994 shown

9 Push the spindle into the strut lower bracket and fit the bolts and nuts, tightening them to the torque listed in this Chapter's Specifications.
10 Attach the brake hose to the strut bracket and fit the clip. If the vehicle is equipped with ABS, attach the wheel speed sensor wire to the strut.
11 Fit the wheel and wheel nuts, lower the vehicle and tighten the wheel nuts to the torque listed in this Chapters specifications.
12 Tighten the strut upper mounting nuts to the torque listed in this Chapter's Specifications.
13 Repeat Steps 1 through 7 for the other strut.
14 Refit any trim removed (see Chapter 11).

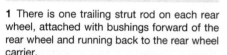

11 Strut rod - removal and refitting

1 There is one trailing strut rod on each rear wheel, attached with bushings forward of the rear wheel and running back to the rear wheel carrier.
2 Loosen the wheel nuts, raise the vehicle and support it securely on axle stands. Remove the wheel.
3 Remove the strut rod-to-spindle bolt (see illustration). On 1995 and later models remove the handbrake cable bracket (see illustration 12.1b).
4 Remove the strut rod-to-body bracket bolt (see illustration) and detach the rod from the vehicle.
5 Refitting is the reverse of the removal procedure, but don't tighten the bolts until the suspension is raised by a jack to simulate normal ride height. Be sure to tighten the bolts to the torque listed in this Chapter's Specifications.
6 Fit the wheel and wheel nuts, then lower the vehicle. Tighten the wheel nuts to the torque listed in this Chapters specifications.

12 Suspension arms - removal and refitting

Removal

1 The lateral suspension arms are the two parallel suspension arms mounted on the rear crossmember (two arms for each rear wheel) (see illustrations). Loosen the rear wheel nuts, raise the rear of the vehicle and support it securely on axle stands.
2 Chock the front wheels and remove the rear wheel.
3 Support the rear wheel carrier with a trolley jack. If you're working on a 1995 or later model, mark the suspension arm cam plate

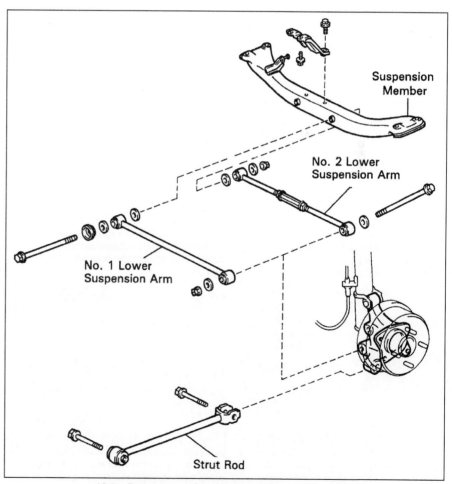

12.1a Rear suspension details - 1990 to 1994 models

Suspension Member

No. 2 Lower Suspension Arm

No. 1 Lower Suspension Arm

Strut Rod

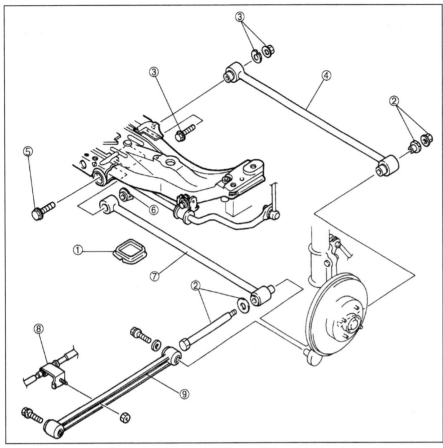

12.1b Rear suspension details - 1995 and later models

1 Crossmember bolt access caps
2 Suspension arm bolts, washers, nuts
3 Suspension arm adjusting cam plate, cam bolt, nut
4 No. 2 suspension arm (lateral link)
5 Suspension arm-to-crossmember bolt, nut
6 Suspension arm-to-crossmember bolt, nut
7 No. 1 Suspension arm (lateral link)
8 Brake cable bracket (on strut rod) and nut
9 Strut rod (trailing link)

settings for proper refitting later and remove the crossmember access covers **(see illustration 12.1b)**.

4 Remove the nut, washer, and bolt from the inboard end of the suspension arm at the suspension crossmember **(see illustration)** and remove the bolt.

5 Remove the nut, washer, and bolt from the outboard end of the suspension arm (at the rear spindle) **(see illustration)**.

6 Remove the lateral suspension arms.
Caution: On 1990 to 1994 models, DO NOT loosen the locknuts or turn the adjuster on the rear lateral suspension arms; moving this affects the rear wheel toe alignment.

Refitting

7 Refitting is the reverse of removal.

8 If you're working on a 1995 or later model, fit the cam plate so the notch faces the same direction as the adjusting cam bolt and align with the marks made prior to removal for proper refitting.

9 Using a trolley jack, raise the spindle to simulate normal ride height, then tighten all suspension fasteners to the torque listed in this Chapter's Specifications. If you replaced a rear lateral suspension arm (the adjustable lateral suspension arm), have the rear wheel toe adjusted by an alignment workshop as soon as you are done.

10 Fit the wheel and wheel nuts, then lower the vehicle to the earth. Tighten the wheel nuts to the torque listed in this Chapters specifications.

11 Have the rear wheel alignment checked.

13 Hub and bearing assembly and rear brake assembly - removal and refitting

⚠ *Warning: Dust created by the brake system may contain asbestos, which is harmful to your health. Never blow it out with compressed air and don't inhale any of it. Do not, under any circumstances, use petroleum-based solvents to clean brake parts. Use brake system cleaner only.*
Note: *Due to the special tools required to renew the bearing, the hub and bearing assembly should not be dismantled by the home mechanic. The assembly can be removed, however, and taken to a dealer service department or other repair workshop to have the bearing replaced.*

Removal

Drum brake models

1 Loosen the wheel nuts, raise the vehicle and support it securely on axle stands. Remove the wheel.

2 Remove the centre hub cap.

3 Remove the drum retaining screws and pull the brake drum from the hub (see Chapter 9).

4 Using a hammer and punch, unstake the hub locknut. Remove the hub locknut at the rear hub spindle **(see illustration)**.

12.4 Remove the nut and washer - 1990 to 1994 shown

12.5 To detach the rear lateral suspension arms from the spindle, remove the nut and bolt

13.4 To remove the hub and bearing assembly, remove the centre hub locknut

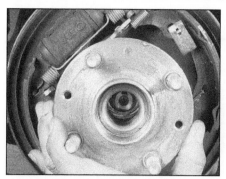

13.5 Remove the hub and bearing assembly from the spindle

13.18 Stake (punch) the locknut lip down into the spindle groove, to prevent the locknut from loosening

5 Remove the hub and bearing assembly from its seat and from the brake assembly **(see illustration)**.

6 On 1990 to 1994 models, the rear axle hub can be removed from the bearing to allow renewal of the bearing. Due to the special tools required to do this, you'll have to take the hub and bearing assembly to an automotive engineering workshop and have the old bearing pulled off the hub and a new bearing pressed on (you can re-use the hub itself, as long as it is in good condition).

7 On 1995 and later models the hub and bearing must be replaced as an assembly.

8 For brake backing plate assembly removal, see Section 14.

Disc brake models

9 Loosen the wheel nuts, raise the vehicle and support it securely on axle stands. Remove the wheel.

10 Remove the centre hub cap.

11 Using a hammer and punch, unstake the hub locknut. Remove the hub locknut at the rear hub spindle.

12 Remove the brake caliper and brake disc (see Chapter 9). It is not necessary to disconnect the brake hose or detach the handbrake cable. Suspend the brake assembly from the coil spring with a piece of wire.

13 Remove the hub and bearing assembly from the spindle.

14 Refer to Steps 6 and 7 above.

15 Remove the dust cover if necessary.

Refitting

Rear drum brake models

16 Check that the brake assembly mounting bolts are tightened onto the rear spindle assembly to the torque listed in this Chapter's Specifications.

17 Fit the hub and bearing assembly on the spindle and fit a new locknut. Tighten the locknut to the torque listed in this Chapter's Specifications.

18 Using a punch and hammer, stake the locknut lip down into the spindle groove, to prevent the locknut from loosening **(see illustration)**.

19 Refit the brake tubing to the brake assembly.

20 Fit the handbrake cable.

21 Fit the hub cap over the locknut, the brake drum and drum retaining screws, and the wheel. Lower the vehicle and tighten the wheel nuts to the torque listed in this Chapters specifications.

Disc brake models

22 Fit the dust cover, if removed, and tighten the mounting bolts to the torque listed in this Chapter's Specifications.

23 Fit the hub and bearing assembly on the spindle.

24 Fit the brake disc.

25 Fit a new locknut on the spindle. Tighten the locknut to the torque listed in this Chapter's Specifications.

26 Using a punch and hammer, stake the locknut lip down into the spindle groove, to prevent the locknut from loosening **(see illustration 13.18)**.

27 Fit the centre hub cap.

28 Fit the brake caliper (see Chapter 9).

29 Fit the wheel. Lower the vehicle and tighten the wheel nuts to the torque listed in this Chapters specifications.

---

14 Rear spindle - removal and refitting

⚠️ **Warning: Dust created by the brake system may contain asbestos, which is harmful to your health. Never blow it out with compressed air and don't inhale any of it. Do not, under any circumstances, use petroleum-based solvents to clean brake parts. Use brake system cleaner only.**

Removal

Drum brake models

1 Loosen the wheel nuts, raise the vehicle and support it securely on axle stands. Remove the wheel.

2 Remove the centre hub cap.

3 Unstake the locknut and remove the hub locknut at the rear hub spindle **(see illustration 13.4)**.

4 Remove the drum retaining screws and

pull the brake drum from the hub (see Chapter 9).

5 Remove the hub and bearing assembly from its seat, manoeuvring it out through the brake assembly.

6 Remove the brake line and the brake backing plate bolts, then remove the brake assembly from the rear spindle. It is not necessary to dismantle the brake shoe assembly or disconnect the handbrake cable from the backing plate. Suspend the backing plate and brake assembly from the coil spring with a piece of wire. **Note:** *If removing the rear brake backing plate assembly completely, detach the handbrake cable (see Chapter 9).*

7 If you're working on a 1995 or later model, remove the wheel speed sensor from its spindle mount.

8 Support the spindle with a jack. Remove the suspension strut-to-spindle bolts.

9 Remove the trailing arm-to-spindle nut and washer and remove the lateral strut-to-spindle bolt.

10 Remove the spindle.

Disc brake models

11 Loosen the wheel nuts, raise the vehicle and support it securely on axle stands. Remove the wheel.

12 Remove the centre hub cap.

13 Unstake the locknut and remove the hub locknut at the rear hub spindle.

14 Remove the brake caliper and brake disc (see Chapter 9). It is not necessary to disconnect the brake hose or detach the handbrake cable. Suspend the backing plate and brake assembly from the coil spring with a piece of wire.

15 Remove the hub and bearing assembly from its seat.

16 Remove the dust cover if necessary.

17 If you're working on a 1995 or later model, remove the wheel speed sensor from the spindle.

18 Support the spindle with a jack. Remove the suspension strut-to-spindle bolts (see Section 10).

19 Remove the trailing arm-to-spindle nut and washer and remove the lateral strut-to-spindle bolt (see Section 12).

20 Remove the spindle.

Refitting

Drum brake models

21 Inspect the spindle for cracks, deformation and signs of wear. If it is worn out, renew it with a new spindle.

22 Refitting is the reverse of removal.

23 Fit the suspension arm bolt/nut and the strut rod bolts and nuts. Raise the spindle to simulate normal ride height, then tighten the fasteners to the torque values listed in this Chapter's Specifications.

24 If you're working on a 1995 or later model, reattach the wheel speed sensor to the spindle.

25 Remove the trolley jack from under the spindle. Attach the brake assembly to the spindle, and tighten the brake assembly mounting bolts to the torque listed in this Chapter's Specifications. Fit a new locknut. Tighten the locknut to the torque listed in this Chapter's Specifications and stake the locknut into the spindle groove **(see illustration 13.18)**.

26 Fit the hub/bearing.

27 Connect the brake line.

28 Fit the rear brake drum (see Chapter 9).

29 Fit the wheel and wheel nuts.

30 Lower the vehicle and tighten the wheel nuts to the torque listed in this Chapters specifications.

Disc brake models

31 Inspect the spindle for cracks, deformation and signs of wear. If it is worn out, renew it with a new spindle.

32 Refitting is the reverse of removal.

33 Fit the suspension arm bolt/nut and the strut rod bolts and nuts. Raise the spindle to simulate normal ride height, then tighten the fasteners to the torque values listed in this Chapter's Specifications.

34 Remove the trolley jack from under the spindle.

35 If you're working on a 1995 or later model, reattach the wheel speed sensor to the spindle.

36 Fit the dust cover and tighten the mounting bolts to the torque listed in this Chapter's Specifications.

37 Fit the hub and bearing assembly on the spindle. Fit a new locknut on the spindle. Tighten the locknut to the torque listed in this Chapter's Specifications.

38 Using a punch and ball peen hammer, stake the locknut lip down into the spindle groove, to prevent the locknut from loosening **(see illustration 13.18)**.

39 Fit the centre hub cap. Remove the jack from under the spindle.

40 Fit the brake disc. Fit the brake disc retaining screws and tighten them to the torque listed in this Chapter's Specifications.

41 Fit the brake caliper (see Chapter 9).

42 Fit the wheel. Lower the vehicle and tighten the wheel nuts to the torque listed in this Chapters specifications.

15 Steering system - general information

1 All models are equipped with rack-and-pinion steering. The steering gear is bolted to the engine cradle and operates the steering knuckles via tie-rods. The inner ends of the tie-rods are protected by rubber boots which should be inspected periodically for secure attachment, tears and leaking lubricant.

2 On models with power steering, the power assist system consists of a belt-driven pump and associated lines and hoses. The fluid level in the power steering pump reservoir should be checked periodically (see Chapter 1).

16.1 Remove the under-dash panel and unplug the electrical connector in the airbag wiring harness

3 The steering wheel operates the steering shaft, which actuates the steering gear through universal joints. Looseness in the steering can be caused by wear in the steering shaft universal joints, the steering gear, the tie-rod ends or loose retaining bolts.

16 Steering wheel - removal and refitting

 Warning: 1995 and later models are equipped with airbags. The airbag is armed and can inflate whenever the battery is connected. To prevent accidental deployment (and possible injury), turn the ignition key to LOCK and disconnect the negative battery cable whenever working near airbag components. After the battery is disconnected, wait at least two minutes before beginning work (the system has a back-up capacitor that must fully discharge). For more information see Chapter 12.

Removal

1 Turn the ignition key to LOCK , then disconnect the cable from the negative terminal of the battery. If the vehicle is equipped with an airbag system, wait at least two minutes before proceeding. Also, if the vehicle is equipped with an airbag, disconnect

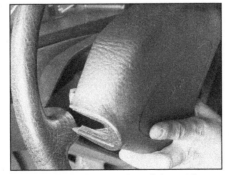

16.3a Lift the horn pad straight out from the steering wheel and . . .

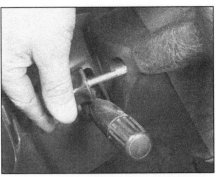

16.2 On 1990 to 1994 models, remove the horn pad retaining screws behind the steering wheel

the electrical connector for the airbag wiring harness below the dash **(see illustration)**.

2 Turn the ignition key to off and turn the steering wheel so the wheels are pointing straight ahead, then remove the screws on the backside of the horn pad to the steering wheel **(see illustration)**.

 Warning: On 1995 and later models, follow the airbag servicing instructions prior to proceeding with any steps that may involve the airbag system:

DO NOT dismantle any airbag component.

DO NOT attempt repair of the airbag system wiring harness.

DO NOT inspect or check the airbag system using an ohmmeter, because this can cause inadvertent deployment of the airbag.

DO NOT disconnect the airbag module (SAS) with the ignition switch ON - this could cause inadvertent airbag deployment.

DO NOT handle or carry the airbag with the trim cover facing you.

When handling the airbag, DO NOT set the airbag module down with the trim cover facing down.

DO NOT touch a deployed airbag for at least 15 minutes - it can be extremely hot.

Contact a dealer for proper disposal of a used airbag.

3 On 1994 and earlier models, lift the horn pad from the steering wheel and remove the electrical connector behind the steering wheel cover **(see illustrations)**. On 1995 and later

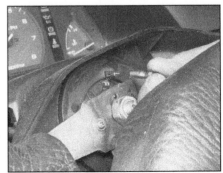

16.3b . . . remove the electrical connector behind the horn pad

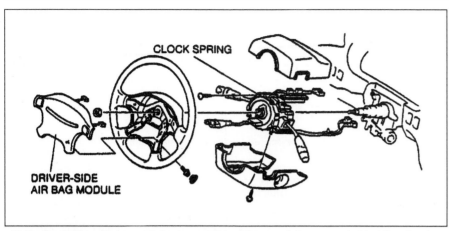

16.3c On 1995 and later models, remove the airbag module screws behind the steering wheel

16.4 Remove the steering wheel nut

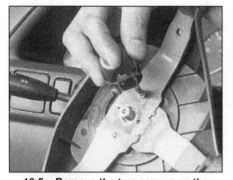

16.5a Remove the two screws on the steering wheel spokes and attach a steering wheel puller

16.5b Use a steering wheel puller to remove the steering wheel

models, remove the airbag attaching screws and detach the airbag module from the steering wheel. Disconnect the module electrical connectors (see illustration).

 Warning: Set the airbag module down with the trim side facing up.

4 Remove the steering wheel locknut (see illustration), then mark the relationship of the steering shaft to the hub (if marks do not already exist or do not line up) to simplify refitting and ensure steering wheel alignment.
5 Remove the two steering wheel spoke

screws to expose the threaded puller holes (see illustration) and attach a steering wheel puller. Use the puller to disconnect the steering wheel from the shaft (see illustration).

Refitting

6 Make sure that the front wheels are facing straight ahead.
7 To fit the wheel, align the mark on the steering wheel hub with the mark on the shaft and slip the wheel onto the shaft. Fit the nut and tighten it to the torque listed in this Chapter's Specifications.

8 On 1995 and later models, plug in the electrical connector for the airbag module and flip down the locking tab.
9 On 1995 and later models, make sure the airbag module electrical connector is positioned correctly and that the wires do not interfere with anything, then fit the airbag module and tighten the retaining screws to the torque listed in this Chapter's Specifications.
10 On 1990 to 1994 models, fit the horn pad and retaining screws.
11 Connect the negative battery cable. On models with an airbag, reconnect the electrical connector for the airbag wiring harness under the dash.

17 Tie-rod ends - removal and refitting

Removal

1 Loosen the wheel nuts. Raise the front of the vehicle, support it securely on axle stands, chock the rear wheels and set the handbrake. Remove the front wheel.
2 Remove the split pin (see illustration) and loosen the nut on the tie-rod end stud.
3 Hold the tie rod with a pair of locking pliers or spanner and loosen the locknut enough to mark the position of the tie-rod end in relation to the threads (see illustrations).

17.2 Remove the split pin from the castle nut and loosen - but don't remove - the nut

17.3a Loosen the locknut . . .

17.3b . . . then mark the position of the tie-rod end in relation to the threads

17.4 Disconnect the tie-rod end from the steering knuckle arm with a puller

4 Disconnect the tie rod from the steering knuckle arm with a puller **(see illustration)**.
5 Unscrew the tie-rod end from the tie-rod.

Refitting

6 Thread the tie-rod end to the marked position on the tie-rod and insert the tie-rod stud into the steering knuckle arm. Tighten the locknut securely.
7 Fit the castle nut on the stud and tighten it to the torque listed in this Chapter's Specifications. Fit a new split pin. If the hole for the cotter pin does not line up with one of the slots in the nut, turn the nut an additional amount until it slides through easily.
8 Fit the wheel and wheel nuts. Lower the vehicle and tighten the wheel nuts to the torque listed in this Chapters specifications.
9 Have the wheel alignment checked.

18 Steering gear boots - renewal

1 Loosen the wheel nuts, raise the vehicle and support it securely on axle stands. Remove the wheel.
2 Remove the tie-rod end and locknut (see Section 17).
3 Remove the steering gear boot clamps. Slide the boot off.
4 Before refitting the new boot, wrap the threads and serrations on the end of the steering rod with a layer of tape so the small end of the new boot is not damaged during refitting.
5 Place a new inner clamp over the steering gear.
6 Slide the new boot into position on the steering gear until it seats in the groove in the steering rod and fit clamps. Tighten the clamps securely.
7 Remove the tape and fit the tie-rod end locknut and tie-rod end (see Section 17).
8 Fit the wheel and wheel nuts. Lower the vehicle and tighten the wheel nuts to the torque listed in this Chapters specifications.

19 Steering gear - removal and refitting

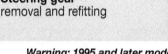

Warning: 1995 and later models are equipped with airbags. Make sure the steering shaft is not turned while the steering gear is removed or you could damage the airbag system. To prevent the shaft from turning, turn the ignition key to the lock position before beginning work or run the seat belt through the steering wheel and clip the seat belt into place. Make sure the ignition switch is OFF.

Removal

1 Disconnect the cable from the negative terminal of the battery. If the vehicle is equipped with an airbag, wait at least two minutes before proceeding. Loosen the front wheel nuts, raise the front of the vehicle and support it securely on axle stands. Apply the handbrake and remove the wheels. Remove the engine undercover splash shield.
2 If equipped with power steering, place a drain pan under the steering gear. Detach the power steering pressure and return lines **(see illustration)** and cap or cover the ends to prevent excessive fluid loss and contamination.

3 Mark the relationship of the steering column universal joint at the steering gear input shaft. Remove the steering column universal joint pinch bolt **(see illustration)**.
4 Remove the steering column cover plates on the bulkhead in the engine compartment. To remove, mounting nuts are located under the dashboard in side the vehicle.
5 Separate the tie-rod ends from the steering knuckle arms (see Section 17).
6 On manual transmission vehicles with power steering, remove the extension bar/control rod, located under the steering gear.
7 Support the steering gear and remove the steering gear bracket mounting nuts **(see illustration)**. Separate the steering column shaft from the steering gear input shaft and remove the steering gear assembly.

Warning: Do NOT turn the steering wheel while the steering gear is removed. If the steering wheel is inadvertently turned, recentre the steering wheel.

8 Check the steering gear mounting grommets for excessive wear or deterioration, replacing them if necessary.

Refitting

9 Raise the steering gear into position and connect the steering gear input shaft and the steering shaft universal joint, aligning the marks.
10 Fit the steering gear mounting brackets and nuts and tighten them to the torque listed in this Chapter's Specifications. **Note:** *Torque the upper bracket nuts first, then the lower nuts.*
11 Connect the tie-rod ends to the steering knuckle arms (see Section 17).
12 Fit the universal joint pinch bolt and tighten it to the torque listed in this Chapter's Specifications.
13 If equipped with power steering, connect the power steering pressure and return hoses to the steering gear and fill the power steering pump reservoir with the recommended fluid (see Chapter 1).
14 Lower the vehicle and bleed the steering system (see Section 21).

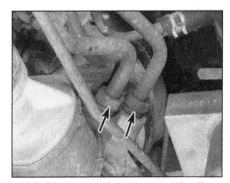

19.2 Disconnect the power steering line fittings (arrowed)

19.3 Mark the relationship of the joint to the input shaft and remove the U-joint pinch-bolt (arrowed)

19.7 Remove the steering gear bracket nuts (arrowed), two on this bracket and two on the other side bracket

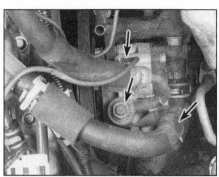

20.3a Detach the hose (right arrow), the pressure line (centre arrow) and the switch (top arrow)

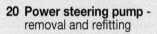

20 Power steering pump -
removal and refitting

Removal

1 Disconnect the cable from the negative battery terminal.
2 Using a large syringe, suck as much fluid out of the power steering fluid reservoir as possible. Place a drain pan under the vehicle to catch any fluid that spills out when the hoses are disconnected. Cap or cover the hoses to prevent entry of dirt or other contaminants.
3 Loosen the clamp and disconnect the fluid return hose from the pump **(see illustrations)**. Detach the electrical connector from the pressure sensor on the pump, if applicable.
4 Remove the pressure line-to-pump banjo nut **(see illustrations 20.3a and 20.3b)**, then detach the line from the pump.
5 Check the banjo bolt seals and renew if necessary.
6 Raise the front of the vehicle and place it securely on axle stands.
7 Loosen the pivot bolt/nut and adjuster bolt **(see illustration)**, and remove the drivebelt (see Chapter 1).
8 Remove the pivot, adjuster and mounting bolts/nuts, then remove the pump from the vehicle.

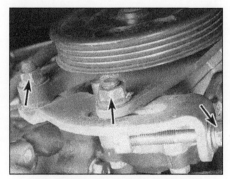

20.7 Besides the pivot bolt and nut, remove the adjuster bolts and nut (arrowed) - 1990 to 1994 shown

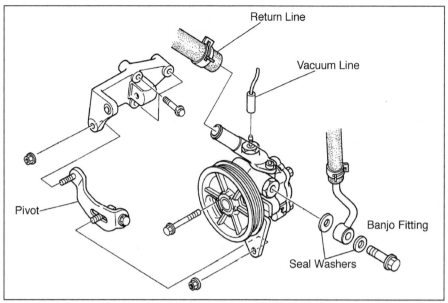

Return Line

Vacuum Line

Banjo Fitting

Seal Washers

Pivot

20.3b Detach the return line, remove the pressure line banjo fitting, and remove the vacuum line

9 If access to engine components is required, remove the pump mounting bracket mounting bolts and remove the mounting bracket.

Refitting

10 Refitting is the reverse of removal. Be sure to tighten the pressure line fitting or banjo bolt to the torque listed in this Chapter's Specifications. Adjust the drivebelt tension following the procedure described in Chapter 1.
11 Top off the fluid level in the reservoir (see Chapter 1) and bleed the system (see Section 21).

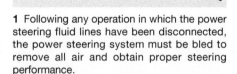

21 Power steering system -
bleeding

1 Following any operation in which the power steering fluid lines have been disconnected, the power steering system must be bled to remove all air and obtain proper steering performance.
2 Before starting the engine and with the front wheels in the straight ahead position, check the power steering fluid level and, if low, add fluid until it reaches the L (Low) mark on the dipstick.
3 Start the engine and allow it to run at fast idle. Recheck the fluid level and add more new, fresh power steering fluid if necessary to reach the L mark on the dipstick.
4 Bleed the system by turning the wheels from side to side, without hitting the stops. This will work the air out of the system. Continuously check the reservoir and keep the reservoir full of fluid as this is done.
5 When the air is worked out of the system, return the wheels to the straight ahead position and keep the vehicle running for

several more minutes before shutting it off, or road test as follows before shutting the engine off.
6 Road test the vehicle to be sure the steering system is functioning normally and is noise-free.
7 Recheck and top off the power steering fluid level to the F (Full) mark on the dipstick while the engine is at normal operating temperature. Add fluid if necessary (see Chapter 1).

22 Wheels and tyres -
general information

All vehicles covered by this manual are equipped with radial tyres. Use of other sizes or types of tyres may affect the ride and handling of the vehicle. Don't mix different types of tyres, such as radials and bias belted, on the same vehicle as handling may be seriously affected. It is recommended that tyres be replaced in pairs on the same axle, but if only one tyre is being replaced, be sure it's the same size, type, structure and tread design as the other, with the same or better tread wear rating, traction rating, and temperature rating.

Because tyre pressure has a substantial effect on handling and wear, the pressure on all tyres should be checked at least once a week or before any extended trips (see *Weekly checks*). Make sure that tyres are not worn below the tread depth wear indicators moulded into the tread or depth measured is at least the recommended depth in your owner's handbook or as recommended by the tyre manufacturer.

These models are factory-equipped with either steel or aluminium wheels. If alkaline compounds (road salt or saltwater) get on aluminium wheels, flush both the outside and inside the wheels with water soon. Wheels must be renewed if they are bent, dented, leak air, have elongated bolt holes, are heavily rusted or corroded, have wobble that is noticeable visually (the radial runout is excessive) or if the wheel nuts will not stay tight. Wheel repairs that use welding or peening are not recommended. Never use a temporary spare for more than the prescribed driving distance and speed, and do not use the temporary spare wheel with a standard tyre.

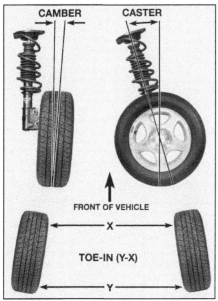

23.1 Camber, caster and toe-in angles

Tyre and wheel balance is important in the overall handling, braking, and performance of the vehicle. Unbalanced wheels can adversely affect handling and ride characteristics as well as tyre life. Whenever a tyre is installed on a wheel, the tyre and wheel should be balanced by a workshop with the proper equipment. Make sure the tyre workshop uses an off-vehicle tyre balancer whenever balancing the wheels/tyres, or damage to the front transmission could result.

23 Wheel alignment - general information

A wheel alignment refers to the adjustments made to the wheels so they are in proper angular relationship to the suspension and the ground. Wheels that are out of proper alignment not only affect vehicle control, but also increase tyre wear. The front end angles normally measured are camber, caster and toe-in **(see illustration)**. On the front end, toe-in and camber are adjustable. The only adjustment possible on the rear is toe-in. The other angles should be measured to check for bent or worn suspension parts.

Getting the proper wheel alignment is a very exacting process, requiring complicated alignment machines to perform the job properly. Because of this, you should have a workshop with a four-wheel alignment machine and technician with the proper training to properly perform these tasks. However, we give the following information describing the basic idea of what is involved with wheel alignment so you can better understand the process and deal intelligently with the workshop that does the work.

Toe-in is the turning in of the wheels. The purpose of a toe specification is to ensure stability with controlled parallel rolling of the wheels. In a vehicle with zero toe-in, the distance between the front edges of the wheels will be the same as the distance between the rear edges of the wheels. The actual amount of toe-in is normally only a fraction of an inch. On the front end, toe-in is adjusted by the tie-rod end position on the tie-rod. On the rear end, it is adjusted by an adjuster on the rear suspension lateral link arm. Incorrect toe-in will cause the tyres to wear by making them scrub excessively on the road surface, and will cause the vehicle to be less stable, especially during straight line driving.

Camber is the tilt of the wheels from vertical when viewed from the end of the vehicle. When the wheels tilt out at the top, camber is positive (+). When the wheels tilt in at the top, camber is negative (–). The amount of tilt is measured in degrees from vertical; this measurement is the camber angle. This angle affects the amount of tyre tread which contacts the road and compensates for changes in the suspension geometry when the vehicle is cornering or travelling over varying surfaces. It is adjusted on the front end by replacing the lower strut-to-steering knuckle bolt with a special adjusting bolt.

Caster is the tilting of the front steering axis from the vertical. A tilt toward the rear is positive caster and a tilt toward the front is negative caster. Caster is for directional stability by causing the steering to tend to return to centre.

Chapter 11
Body

Contents

Degrees of difficulty

Easy, suitable for novice with little experience	Fairly easy, suitable for beginner with some experience	Fairly difficult, suitable for competent DIY mechanic	Difficult, suitable for experienced DIY mechanic	Very difficult, suitable for expert DIY or professional

1 General information

The models covered by this manual feature a 'unibody' construction, using a floor pan with front and rear frame side rails which support the body components, front and rear suspension systems and other mechanical components. Certain components are particularly vulnerable to accident damage and can be unbolted and repaired or replaced. Among these parts are the body mouldings, bumpers, bonnet and boot lids and all glass.

Only general body maintenance practices and body panel repair procedures within the scope of the do-it-yourselfer are included in this Chapter.

2 Body - maintenance

The general condition of a vehicle's bodywork is the one thing that significantly affects its value. Maintenance is easy, but needs to be regular. Neglect, particularly after minor damage can lead quickly to further deterioration and costly repair bills. It is important also to keep watch on those parts of the vehicle not immediately visible, for instance the underside, inside all the wheel arches, and the lower part of the engine compartment.

The basic maintenance routine for the bodywork is washing - preferably with a lot of water, from a hose. This will remove all the loose solids which may have stuck to the vehicle. It is important to flush these off in such a way as to prevent grit from scratching the finish. The wheel arches and underframe need washing in the same way, to remove any accumulated mud, which will retain moisture and tend to encourage rust. Paradoxically enough, the best time to clean the underframe and wheel arches is in wet weather, when the mud is thoroughly wet and soft. In very wet weather, the underframe is usually cleaned of large accumulations automatically, and this is a good time for inspection.

Periodically, except on vehicles with a wax-based underbody protective coating, it is a good idea to have the whole of the underframe of the vehicle steam-cleaned, engine compartment included, so that a thorough inspection can be carried out to see what minor repairs and renovations are necessary. Steam-cleaning is available at many garages, and is necessary for the removal of the accumulation of oily grime, which sometimes is allowed to become thick in certain areas. If steam-cleaning facilities are not available, there are some excellent grease solvents available which can be brush-applied; the dirt can then be simply hosed off. Note that these methods should not be used on vehicles with wax-based underbody protective coating, or the coating will be removed. Such vehicles should be inspected annually, preferably just prior to Winter, when the underbody should be washed down, and any damage to the wax coating repaired. Ideally, a completely fresh coat should be applied. It would also be worth considering the use of such wax-based protection for injection into door panels, sills, box sections, etc, as an additional safeguard against rust damage, where such protection is not provided by the vehicle manufacturer.

After washing paintwork, wipe off with a chamois leather to give an unspotted clear finish. A coat of clear protective wax polish will give added protection against chemical pollutants in the air. If the paintwork sheen has dulled or oxidised, use a cleaner/polisher combination to restore the brilliance of the shine. This requires a little effort, but such dulling is usually caused because regular washing has been neglected. Care needs to be taken with metallic paintwork, as special non-abrasive cleaner/polisher is required to avoid damage to the finish. Always check that the door and ventilator opening drain holes and pipes are completely clear, so that water can be drained out. Brightwork should be treated in the same way as paintwork. Windscreens and windows can be kept clear of the smeary film which often appears, by the use of proprietary glass cleaner. Never use any form of wax or other body or chromium polish on glass.

3 Vinyl trim - maintenance

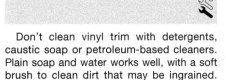

Don't clean vinyl trim with detergents, caustic soap or petroleum-based cleaners. Plain soap and water works well, with a soft brush to clean dirt that may be ingrained. Wash the vinyl as frequently as the rest of the vehicle.

After cleaning, application of a high quality rubber and vinyl protectant will help prevent oxidation and cracks. The protectant can also be applied to weatherstripping, vacuum lines and rubber hoses, which often fail as a result of chemical degradation, and to the tyres.

4 Upholstery and carpets - maintenance

Mats and carpets should be brushed or vacuum-cleaned regularly, to keep them free of grit. If they are badly stained, remove them from the vehicle for scrubbing or sponging, and make quite sure they are dry before refitting. Seats and interior trim panels can be kept clean by wiping with a damp cloth. If they do become stained (which can be more apparent on light-coloured upholstery), use a little liquid detergent and a soft nail brush to scour the grime out of the grain of the material. Do not forget to keep the headlining clean in the same way as the upholstery. When using liquid cleaners inside the vehicle, do not over-wet the surfaces being cleaned. Excessive damp could get into the seams and padded interior, causing stains, offensive odours or even rot.

 HAYNES HiNT *If the inside of the vehicle gets wet accidentally, it is worthwhile taking some trouble to dry it out properly, particularly where carpets are involved. Do not leave oil or electric heaters inside the vehicle for this purpose.*

5 Body repair - minor damage

Repairs of minor scratches in bodywork

If the scratch is very superficial, and does not penetrate to the metal of the bodywork, repair is very simple. Lightly rub the area of the scratch with a paintwork renovator, or a very fine cutting paste, to remove loose paint from the scratch, and to clear the surrounding bodywork of wax polish. Rinse the area with clean water.

Apply touch-up paint to the scratch using a fine paint brush; continue to apply fine layers of paint until the surface of the paint in the scratch is level with the surrounding paintwork. Allow the new paint at least two weeks to harden, then blend it into the surrounding paintwork by rubbing the scratch area with a paintwork renovator or a very fine cutting paste. Finally, apply wax polish.

Where the scratch has penetrated right through to the metal of the bodywork, causing the metal to rust, a different repair technique is required. Remove any loose rust from the bottom of the scratch with a penknife, then apply rust-inhibiting paint to prevent the formation of rust in the future. Using a rubber or nylon applicator, fill the scratch with bodystopper paste. If required, this paste can be mixed with cellulose thinners to provide a very thin paste which is ideal for filling narrow scratches. Before the stopper-paste in the scratch hardens, wrap a piece of smooth cotton rag around the top of a finger. Dip the finger in cellulose thinners, and quickly sweep it across the surface of the stopper-paste in the scratch; this will ensure that the surface of the stopper-paste is slightly hollowed. The scratch can now be painted over as described earlier in this Section.

Repairs of dents in bodywork

When deep denting of the vehicle's bodywork has taken place, the first task is to pull the dent out, until the affected bodywork almost attains its original shape. There is little point in trying to restore the original shape completely, as the metal in the damaged area will have stretched on impact, and cannot be reshaped fully to its original contour. It is better to bring the level of the dent up to a point which is about 3 mm below the level of the surrounding bodywork. In cases where the dent is very shallow anyway, it is not worth trying to pull it out at all. If the underside of the dent is accessible, it can be hammered out gently from behind, using a mallet with a wooden or plastic head. Whilst doing this, hold a suitable block of wood firmly against the outside of the panel, to absorb the impact from the hammer blows and thus prevent a large area of the bodywork from being 'belled-out'.

Should the dent be in a section of the bodywork which has a double skin, or some other factor making it inaccessible from behind, a different technique is called for. Drill several small holes through the metal inside the area - particularly in the deeper section. Then screw long self-tapping screws into the holes, just sufficiently for them to gain a good purchase in the metal. Now the dent can be pulled out by pulling on the protruding heads of the screws with a pair of pliers.

The next stage of the repair is the removal of the paint from the damaged area, and from an inch or so of the surrounding 'sound' bodywork. This is accomplished most easily by using a wire brush or abrasive pad on an electric drill, although it can be done just as effectively by hand, using sheets of abrasive paper. To complete the preparation for filling, score the surface of the bare metal with a screwdriver or the tang of a file, or alternatively, drill small holes in the affected area. This will provide a really good 'key' for the filler paste.

To complete the repair, see the Section on filling and respraying.

Repairs of rust holes or gashes in bodywork

Remove all paint from the affected area, and from an inch or so of the surrounding 'sound' bodywork, using an abrasive pad or a wire brush on an electric drill. If these are not available, a few sheets of abrasive paper will do the job most effectively. With the paint removed, you will be able to judge the severity of the corrosion, and therefore decide whether to renew the whole panel (if this is possible) or to repair the affected area. New body panels are not as expensive as most people think, and it is often quicker and more satisfactory to fit a new panel than to attempt to repair large areas of corrosion.

Remove all fittings from the affected area, except those which will act as a guide to the original shape of the damaged bodywork (eg headlight shells etc). Then, using tin snips or a hacksaw blade, remove all loose metal and any other metal badly affected by corrosion. Hammer the edges of the hole inwards, in order to create a slight depression for the filler paste.

Wire-brush the affected area to remove the powdery rust from the surface of the remaining metal. Paint the affected area with rust-inhibiting paint, if the back of the rusted area is accessible, treat this also.

Before filling can take place, it will be necessary to block the hole in some way. This can be achieved by the use of aluminium or plastic mesh, or aluminium tape.

Aluminium or plastic mesh, or glass-fibre matting, is probably the best material to use for a large hole. Cut a piece to the approximate size and shape of the hole to be filled, then position it in the hole so that its edges are below the level of the surrounding bodywork. It can be retained in position by several blobs of filler paste around its periphery.

Aluminium tape should be used for small or very narrow holes. Pull a piece off the roll, trim it to the approximate size and shape required, then pull off the backing paper (if used) and stick the tape over the hole; it can be overlapped if the thickness of one piece is insufficient. Burnish down the edges of the tape with the handle of a screwdriver or similar, to ensure that the tape is securely attached to the metal underneath.

Bodywork repairs - filling and respraying

Before using this Section, see the Sections on dent, deep scratch, rust holes and gash repairs.

Many types of bodyfiller are available, but generally speaking, those proprietary kits which contain a tin of filler paste and a tube of resin hardener are best for this type of repair. A wide, flexible plastic or nylon applicator will be found invaluable for imparting a smooth and well-contoured finish to the surface of the filler.

Mix up a little filler on a clean piece of card or board - measure the hardener carefully (follow the maker's instructions on the pack), otherwise the filler will set too rapidly or too slowly. Using the applicator, apply the filler paste to the prepared area; draw the applicator across the surface of the filler to achieve the correct contour and to level the surface. As soon as a contour that approximates to the correct one is achieved, stop working the paste - if you carry on too long, the paste will become sticky and begin to 'pick-up' on the applicator. Continue to add thin layers of filler paste at 20-minute intervals, until the level of the filler is just proud of the surrounding bodywork.

Once the filler has hardened, the excess can be removed using a metal plane or file. From then on, progressively-finer grades of abrasive paper should be used, starting with a 40-grade production paper, and finishing with a 400-grade wet-and-dry paper. Always wrap the abrasive paper around a flat rubber, cork, or wooden block - otherwise the surface of the filler will not be completely flat. During the smoothing of the filler surface, the wet-and-dry paper should be periodically rinsed in water. This will ensure that a very smooth finish is imparted to the filler at the final stage.

At this stage, the 'dent' should be surrounded by a ring of bare metal, which in turn should be encircled by the finely 'feathered' edge of the good paintwork. Rinse the repair area with clean water, until all of the dust produced by the rubbing-down operation has gone.

Spray the whole area with a light coat of primer - this will show up any imperfections in the surface of the filler. Repair these imperfections with fresh filler paste or bodystopper, and once more smooth the surface with abrasive paper. Repeat this

spray-and-repair procedure until you are satisfied that the surface of the filler, and the feathered edge of the paintwork, are perfect. Clean the repair area with clean water, and allow to dry fully.

 If bodystopper is used, it can be mixed with cellulose thinners to form a really thin paste which is ideal for filling small holes.

The repair area is now ready for final spraying. Paint spraying must be carried out in a warm, dry, windless and dust-free atmosphere. This condition can be created artificially if you have access to a large indoor working area, but if you are forced to work in the open, you will have to pick your day very carefully. If you are working indoors, dousing the floor in the work area with water will help to settle the dust which would otherwise be in the atmosphere. If the repair area is confined to one body panel, mask off the surrounding panels; this will help to minimise the effects of a slight mis-match in paint colours. Bodywork fittings (eg chrome strips, door handles etc) will also need to be masked off. Use genuine masking tape, and several thicknesses of newspaper, for the masking operations.

Before commencing to spray, agitate the aerosol can thoroughly, then spray a test area (an old tin, or similar) until the technique is mastered. Cover the repair area with a thick coat of primer; the thickness should be built up using several thin layers of paint, rather than one thick one. Using 400-grade wet-and-dry paper, rub down the surface of the primer until it is really smooth. While doing this, the work area should be thoroughly doused with water, and the wet-and-dry paper periodically rinsed in water. Allow to dry before spraying on more paint.

Spray on the top coat, again building up the thickness by using several thin layers of paint. Start spraying at one edge of the repair area, and then, using a side-to-side motion, work until the whole repair area and about 2 inches of the surrounding original paintwork is covered. Remove all masking material 10 to 15 minutes after spraying on the final coat of paint.

Allow the new paint at least two weeks to harden, then, using a paintwork renovator, or a very fine cutting paste, blend the edges of the paint into the existing paintwork. Finally, apply wax polish.

Plastic components

With the use of more and more plastic body components by the vehicle manufacturers (eg bumpers. spoilers, and in some cases major body panels), rectification of more serious damage to such items has become a matter of either entrusting repair work to a specialist in this field, or renewing complete components. Repair of such damage by the DIY owner is not really feasible, owing to the cost of the equipment and materials required

for effecting such repairs. The basic technique involves making a groove along the line of the crack in the plastic, using a rotary burr in an electric drill. The damaged part is then welded back together, using a hot-air gun to heat up and fuse a plastic filler rod into the groove. Any excess plastic is then removed, and the area rubbed down to a smooth finish. It is important that a filler rod of the correct plastic is used, as body components can be made of a variety of different types (eg polycarbonate, ABS, polypropylene).

Damage of a less serious nature (abrasions, minor cracks etc) can be repaired by the DIY owner using a two-part epoxy filler repair material. Once mixed in equal proportions, this is used in similar fashion to the bodywork filler used on metal panels. The filler is usually cured in twenty to thirty minutes, ready for sanding and painting.

If the owner is renewing a complete component himself, or if he has repaired it with epoxy filler, he will be left with the problem of finding a suitable paint for finishing which is compatible with the type of plastic used. At one time, the use of a universal paint was not possible, owing to the complex range of plastics encountered in body component applications. Standard paints, generally speaking, will not bond to plastic or rubber satisfactorily. However, it is now possible to obtain a plastic body parts finishing kit which consists of a pre-primer treatment, a primer and coloured top coat. Full instructions are normally supplied with a kit, but basically, the method of use is to first apply the pre-primer to the component concerned, and allow it to dry for up to 30 minutes. Then the primer is applied, and left to dry for about an hour before finally applying the special-coloured top coat. The result is a correctly-coloured component, where the paint will flex with the plastic or rubber, a property that standard paint does not normally possess.

6 Body repair - major damage

Major damage must be repaired by an auto body workshop specifically equipped to perform unibody repairs. These workshops have the specialised equipment required to do the job properly.

If the damage is extensive, the body must be checked for proper alignment or the vehicle's handling characteristics may be adversely affected and other components may wear at an accelerated rate.

Due to the fact that all of the major body components (bonnet, wings, etc.) are separate and replaceable units, any seriously damaged components should be replaced rather than repaired. Sometimes the components can be found in a breakers yard that specialises in used vehicle components, often at considerable savings over the cost of new parts.

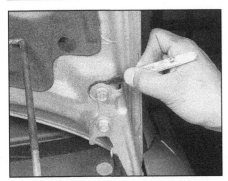

9.1 Before removing the bonnet, mark around the hinge plate

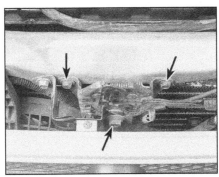

9.10 The bonnet latch mounting bolts (arrows and additional bolts below)

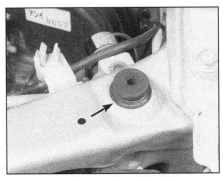

9.11 Adjust the bonnet bumpers (arrowed) so that the bonnet is flush with the wings and grille

7 Hinges and locks - maintenance

Once every 5000 miles, or every four months, the hinges and latch assemblies on the doors, bonnet and boot should be given a few drops of light oil or lock lubricant. The door latch strikers should also be lubricated with a thin coat of grease to reduce wear and ensure free movement. Lubricate the door and boot locks with spray-on graphite lubricant.

8 Windscreen and fixed glass - renewal

Renewal of the windscreen and fixed glass requires the use of special fast-setting adhesive/caulk materials and some specialised tools. It is recommended that these operations be left to a dealer or a workshop specialising in glass work.

9 Bonnet - removal, refitting and adjustment

Note: *The bonnet is heavy and somewhat awkward to remove and fit - at least two people should perform this procedure.*

Removal and refitting

1 Scribe or felt tip marks around the hinges to ensure proper alignment during refitting (see illustration).
2 Use blankets or pads to cover the cowl area of the body and wings. This will protect the body and paint as the bonnet is removed.
3 Disconnect the windscreen washer tube at the bonnet.
4 Have an assistant support the bonnet. Remove the hinge-to-bonnet bolts.
5 Lift off the bonnet.
6 Refitting is the reverse of removal.

Adjustment

7 Fore-and-aft and side-to-side adjustment of the bonnet is done by moving the hinge plate slot after loosening the bolts.
8 Scribe or felt tip mark a line around the entire hinge plate so you can judge the amount of movement (see illustration 9.1).
9 Loosen the bolts or nuts and move the bonnet into correct alignment. Move it only a little at a time. Tighten the hinge bolts and carefully lower the bonnet to check the position.
10 If necessary after refitting, the entire bonnet latch assembly can be adjusted up-and-down as well as from side-to-side on the radiator support so the bonnet closes securely, and is flush with the wings. To make the adjustment, scribe or felt tip mark a line around the bonnet latch mounting bolts to aid alignment when refitting, then loosen the bolts and reposition the latch assembly to align with the striker on the bonnet, as necessary (see illustration). Following adjustment, retighten the mounting bolts.
11 The bonnet bumpers on the body and on the bonnet should support the bonnet so that the bonnet is flush with the wings (see illustration) when closed. Note: *Adjust the latch so the bonnet engages securely when closed and the bonnet bumpers are slightly compressed for proper alignment with the wings and grille.*
12 The bonnet latch assembly, as well as the hinges, should be periodically lubricated with white lithium-base grease to prevent binding and wear.

10 Bonnet release latch and cable - removal and refitting

Latch

1 Scribe or felt tip mark a line around the latch to aid alignment when refitting, then remove the bonnet latch mounting bolts (see illustration 9.10). Remove the latch.
2 Disconnect the bonnet release cable by removing the cable retaining clip near the bonnet latch and disengaging the cable from the latch assembly (see illustration).

3 Refitting is the reverse of removal. Note: *Adjust the latch so the bonnet engages securely when closed and the bonnet bumpers are slightly compressed (see Section 9).*

Cable

4 Disconnect the bonnet release cable from the latch.
5 Attach a piece of thin wire or string to the end of the cable and unfasten all remaining cable retaining clips.
6 Working in the passenger compartment, remove the passenger's side kick panel. Then remove the release lever mounting bolts and detach the bonnet release lever.
7 Pull the cable and grommet rearward into the passenger compartment until you can see the wire or string. Ensure that the new cable has a grommet attached, then remove the old cable from the wire or string and renew it with the new cable.
8 Working in the engine compartment, pull the wire or string back through the bulkhead.
9 Refitting is the reverse of removal. Note: *Push on the cable grommet with your fingers from inside the passenger compartment to seat the grommet into the bulkhead correctly.*

11 Radiator grille - removal and refitting

1 On 1990 to 1994 models, remove radiator grille by removing the grille screw shown and

10.2 Lever off the retaining clip and remove the cable from the latch assembly

pulling the grille away from the body **(see illustrations)**, using a small screwdriver if necessary at the grille attachment clips to release the clips. Check the condition of the clips and renew as necessary. On 1995 and later models, remove the upper seal filler, remove the grille screws shown and lift the grille away from the body **(see illustration)**.

2 On 1990 to 1994 models, remove the screw from both front direction indicator/running light (combination light), and remove both combination lights.

3 On 1990 to 1994 models, remove the screws from the lower grille mouldings and remove both lower grille mouldings.

4 Refitting is the reverse of removal. **Note:** *When refitting the radiator grille, make sure to fit grille retaining clips, as applicable, into the grille, align them with the refitting holes in the body, and press the grille securely in place.*

12 Bumpers - removal and refitting

Note: *The bumper assembly is heavy and somewhat awkward to remove and fit - support the bumper when the bolts are removed - have an assistant help you when performing this procedure.*

Front bumper

1 Apply the handbrake, raise the vehicle and support it securely on axle stands. Remove the under cover splash shield. Open the bonnet.

2 Disconnect the cable from the negative battery terminal and disconnect any wiring that would interfere with bumper removal.

3 Remove the screws from both front direction indicators and remove both direction indicator lights.

4 Remove the radiator grille (see Section 11).

5 Remove the headlights (see Chapter 12).

6 Remove the screws from the lower grille mouldings and remove both lower grille mouldings.

7 Remove the screw(s) attaching the bumper fascia (bumper cover) to the wing at the area of the wheel cutout, and on 1990 to 1994

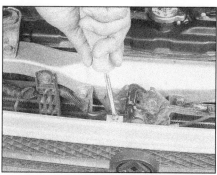

11.1a For 1990 to 1994 models, remove the grille clip retaining screw . . .

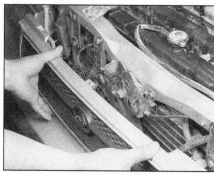

11.1b . . . and pull off the radiator grille. Check the condition of the clips

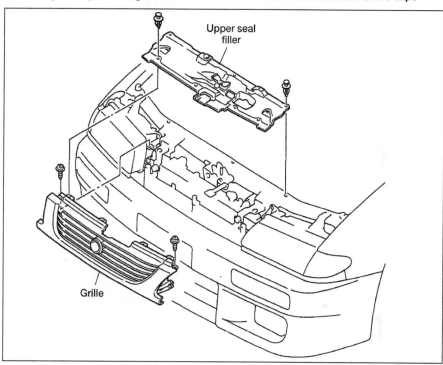

Upper seal filler

Grille

11.1c For 1995 and later models, remove the upper seal filler, remove the screws, and lift off the grille

models, remove the screws retaining the bumper cover at the grille area **(see illustrations)**.

8 On 1990 to 1994 models, working under the bumper, remove the attaching screws at both angle brackets **(see illustration)** and then remove the front bumper reinforcement (main steel beam attached to the body) by removing

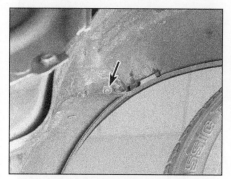

12.7a Unscrew the bumper cover screw (arrowed) under the wing lip - 1990 to 1994 model shown

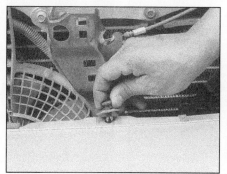

12.7b Unscrew and pull out the bumper cover fasteners at the grille area - 1990 to 1994 model shown

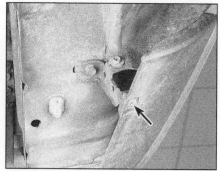

12.8a Remove the bumper angle bracket screws (arrowed), located near the wheel opening - 1990 to 1994 shown

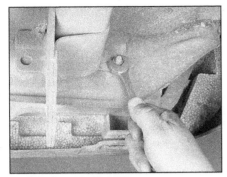

12.8b Remove the reinforcement bolts, and remove the bumper cover - 1990 to 1994 shown

the bumper reinforcement retention bolts **(see illustration)**. On 1995 and later models, working under the bumper, remove the attaching screws along the bottom of the bumper cover. Then remove the front bumper reinforcement nuts from the body attachment points in the grille area **(see illustration)**. Carefully remove the bumper while disconnecting the front direction indicator light connectors, and lower the bumper to the floor or to padded wooden blocks for additional dismantling. Front wing removal can be done at this time by removal of the wing bolts.

9 Remove the bumper cover bolts attaching the cover to the bumper reinforcement. On 1990 to 1994 models, push out the upper bumper cover tabs that are inserted into the slots at the top of the bumper reinforcement.

10 Remove the bumper cover from the bumper reinforcement and remove the energy-absorbing foam, located between the cover and reinforcement.

11 Refitting is the reverse of the removal procedure.

Rear bumper

12 Apply the handbrake, raise the vehicle and support it securely on axle stands.

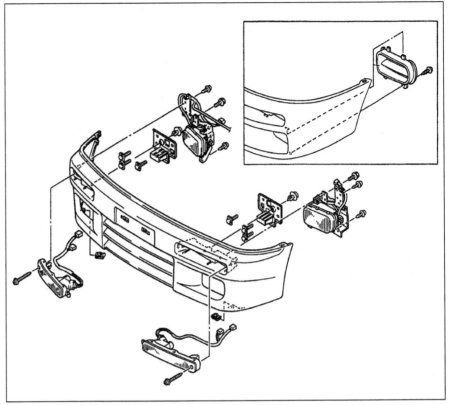

12.8c 1995 and later front bumper details

13 Disconnect the cable from the negative battery terminal and disconnect any wiring that would interfere with bumper removal.

14 Remove the rear stop/direction indicator light (combination lights) (see Chapter 12).

15 On 1990 to 1994 models, inside the boot, remove the boot end trim. On 1995 and later models, remove the boot side trim panels.

16 Where fitted, remove the two bumper bracket covers at the boot end, located inside the boot **(see illustration)** and remove the

bumper reinforcement attachment nuts **(see illustration)**.

17 Remove the rear side marker lights from the bumper.

18 On 1990 to 1994 hatchback models, remove the rear number plate light.

19 On 1990 to 1994 models, remove the rear bumper retainer bar, along the top of the bumper assembly. On 1995 and later models, remove the rear wheel cutout extensions (flaps and splash shields), remove the bolts under the bumper cover, on the top of the

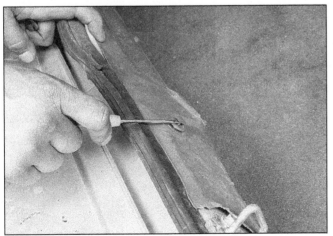

12.16a Remove the inside boot end trim . . .

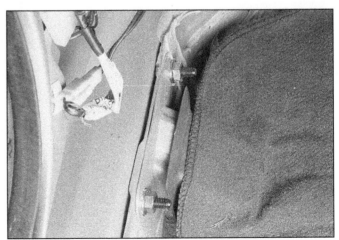

12.16b . . . exposing the bumper reinforcement bar attaching studs and nuts - 1990 to 1994 shown

bumper cover, and the nuts inside the boot **(see illustration)**.

20 Where fitted, remove the screws attaching the bumper cover to the wing at the area of the wheel cutout **(see illustration)**.

21 On 1990 to 1994 models, working under the bumper, remove the rear bumper reinforcement (main steel beam attached to the body) by removing the bumper reinforcement retention bolts. Carefully lower the bumper part way, supporting the hatchback model bumper while its number plate wiring harness and number plate holder are removed. Carefully lower the bumper fully onto padded wooden blocks for additional dismantling.

22 On 1990 to 1994 models, remove the bumper cover bolts attaching the cover to the bumper reinforcement **(see illustrations)**. Remove the bumper cover from the bumper reinforcement and the energy-absorbing foam, located between the cover and reinforcement.

23 On 1995 and later models, remove the bumper cover bolts attaching the cover to the bumper reinforcement, and remove the bumper cover from the bumper reinforcement and the energy-absorbing foam. Remove the side marker lights and other attached parts as required.

24 On 1990 to 1994 models, remove both rear mud flaps as necessary.

25 Refitting is the reverse of the removal procedure.

13 Door trim panel - removal and refitting

Removal

1 On manual window models, remove the window crank by working a cloth back-and-forth behind the handle to dislodge the retainer **(see illustration)**. A special tool is available for this purpose, but it is not essential. With the retainer removed, pull off the handle. On electric window models, disconnect the battery, pry out the switch assembly, unplug the electrical connector and remove the switch assembly.

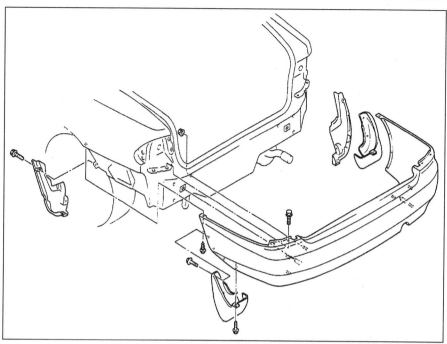

12.19 1995 and later rear bumper details

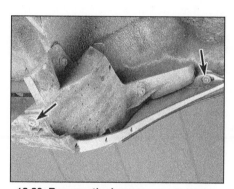

12.20 Remove the bumper cover screws (arrowed) at the wheel openings - 1990 to 1994 shown

2 For front doors, remove the trim cover inside the door which covers the outside mirror (see Section 26). For rear doors, remove the trim cover inside the door which fills the window corner area. For rear doors

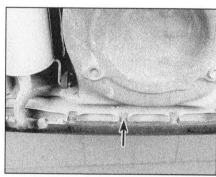

12.22a Remove the rear bumper cover bolts (arrowed) and wing bolts (not shown) from the rear bumper and . . .

with electric windows, remove the pull handle bracket screw, located in the finger pocket on the door trim panel.

3 Remove the screw from the inside door latch handle **(see illustration)**, pull out the

12.22b . . . remove the bumper reinforcement bolts (arrowed), then remove the bumper - 1990 to 1994 shown

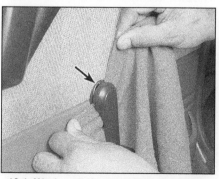

13.1 Work a cloth up behind the window handle until the retainer (arrowed) is pushed up

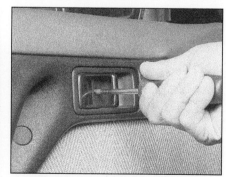

13.3a Remove the door latch handle screw . . .

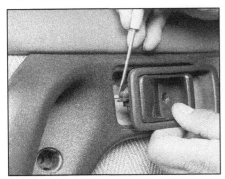

13.3b ... pull out the latch handle, detach the rod, and remove the handle - 1990 to 1994 shown

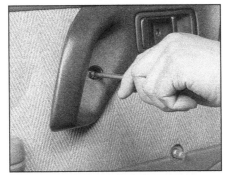

13.4 Remove the screw cap and screw from the door latch cover - 1990 to 1994 shown

13.5 Remove the inside door arm rest/handle - 1990 to 1994 shown

latch handle, detach the door pull rod **(see illustration)**, and remove the door latch handle.

4 Remove the screw trim cap and screw from the door latch handle trim panel **(see illustration)**. On 1995 and later front doors, remove the door panel reflector.

5 On 1990 to 1994 models, remove the inside door arm rest/handle **(see illustration)**.

6 Remove the door trim panel screw cover (1990 to 1994) **(see illustration)** and remove the screw. Insert a special trim panel removal tool, a wide putty knife, or a thin screwdriver between the door trim panel and door to disengage the door trim retaining clips. Work

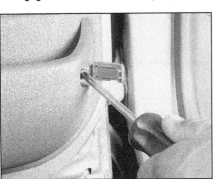

13.6a Remove the door trim panel screw cover and remove the screw - 1990 to 1994 shown

around the outer edge until the panel is loose **(see illustration)**.

7 Make sure all of the door trim retaining clips are disengaged. Remove the door trim panel from the vehicle by gently pulling it upwards and out, while disconnecting any electrical connectors.

8 On 1995 and later models, remove the square seal pads between the door trim panel and watershield plastic sheet, or leave it in place if re-using the watershield. For access to inside the door, remove the plastic watershield. Peel back the plastic cover, taking care not to tear it **(see illustration)**.

Refitting

9 To fit the door trim panel, first press the watershield back into place. If necessary, add more sealant to hold it in place.

10 Prior to refitting of the door trim panel, be sure to refit any clips which may have come out of the door trim panel during removal.

11 Place the door trim panel in position, making sure that any door panel electrical connectors are connected or routed through the panel as necessary. Press the door trim panel into place until the clips are seated.

12 On 1990 to 1994 models, refit and securely tighten the arm rest/handle screws. On 1995 and later front doors, refit the reflector on the door trim panel.

13 For front doors, refit the outside mirror trim cover, located on the inside of the door.

For rear doors with an electric window, fit the pull handle bracket screw, located in the finger pocket on the door trim panel.

14 Refit the inside door handle.

15 Fit the manual window crank or electric window switch assembly.

14 Door latch, lock cylinder and handles - removal and refitting

1 Remove the door trim panel and the plastic watershield (see Section 13).

Door latch

2 Reach inside the door and disconnect the control links from the latch.

3 Mark the location of the door latch prior to removal. Remove the latch retaining screws from the end of the door **(see illustration)**.

4 Detach the door latch. If equipped with electric door locks, remove the door lock solenoid.

5 Refitting is the reverse of removal. Align the door latch and tighten the door latch screws securely.

Lock cylinder and outside handle

6 Through the door inside access hole, remove the outside handle retention

13.6b Use a trim panel removal tool to detach the trim panel retaining clips

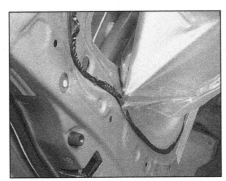

13.8 If the plastic watershield is peeled off carefully, it can be re-used

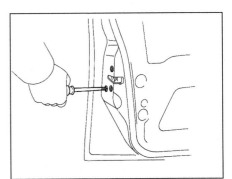

14.3 Remove the latch screws from the end of the door

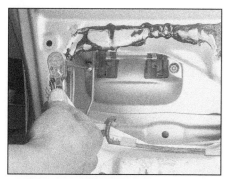

14.6 Remove the outside handle retention bolts/nuts

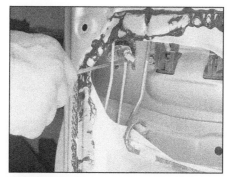

14.7 Remove the control rod from the lock cylinder

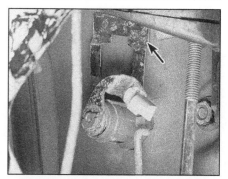

14.8 Lever the retaining clip (arrowed) upwards and off the lock cylinder

bolts/nuts **(see illustration)**. On 1995 and later models, remove the lock cylinder electrical switch retainer and remove the switch.

7 Remove the control rod from the lock cylinder **(see illustration)**.

8 Use pliers or a screwdriver to lever the retaining clip upwards and off the lock cylinder **(see illustration)**.

9 Pull the outside handle and lock cylinder **(see illustration)** from the door.

10 Refitting is the reverse of removal.

11 The door key cylinder electrical switch may be tested if necessary without removal. Disconnect the electrical connector. Check that the electrical continuity between the terminals is 0 ohms (no resistance) when in the unlocked position, and is 1 k-ohms when in the locked position.

Inside handle

12 Refer to Section 13 for removal and refitting.

15 Door window glass - removal, refitting and adjustment

1 Remove the door trim panel and the plastic watershield (see Section 13).

2 On 1990 to 1994 front windows, open the window to approximately 4 inches from the fully open position. On 1990 to 1994 rear windows, fully open the window. On 1995 and later front windows, fully open the window. On 1995 and later rear windows, raise the glass approximately two inches from fully closed.

3 Disconnect the negative battery cable.

4 On 1990 to 1994 rear door windows, remove the centre channel strip by carefully lifting the door weatherstrip on the top of the door, and removing the centre channel screw and clip **(see illustration)**. On 1995 and later rear door windows, remove the glass guide channel at the rear of the window.

5 On 1990 to 1994 rear door windows, remove the window regulator from the large opening.

6 Place a rag inside the door panel to help prevent scratching the glass. Remove the glass mounting bolts.

7 Remove the glass by pulling it up and out of the door.

8 On 1990 to 1994 models, remove rear door quarter window glass and carefully pull the weatherstrip free, removing any clips or attachment points - do not pull too hard as this may damage the weatherstrip.

9 Refitting is the reverse of removal.

10 Window glass adjustment is by means of slotted adjustment screws. Loosen the adjustment screws, position and hold the glass fully closed in the door frame, and lightly tighten the adjustment screws. Wind the window slowly, checking for smooth travel. Adjust vertically and horizontally to obtain full closure with smooth travel as the window is wound up and down.

16 Window regulator - removal and refitting

1 Remove the door trim panel and watershield (see Section 13).

2 Remove the door glass. For rear doors, remove both the roll-up window and the quarter window (see Section 15). **Note:** *To remove the door glass run channel only, paragraph 6 below, the glass does not need to be removed.*

3 Mark or measure the location of the manual or electric window regulator assembly for refitting alignment.

4 For electric windows, disconnect the electrical connector.

5 Unbolt the window regulator assembly and remove the regulator through the door frame access hole **(see illustration)**.

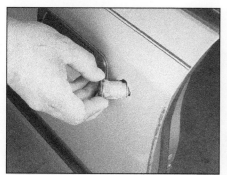

14.9 Pull the lock cylinder and outside handle (not shown) from the door

15.4 Remove the centre channel by lifting the weatherstrip and removing the screw/clip

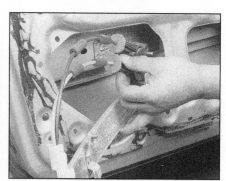

16.5 Unbolt the window regulator assembly and remove from the door - 1990 to 1994 shown

16.6 Remove the door glass run channel as necessary

6 Remove the door glass run channel as necessary **(see illustration)**.
7 Refitting is the reverse of removal. During refitting, apply multi-purpose grease to the regulator rollers.

17 Door - removal, refitting and adjustment

Removal and refitting

1 Disconnect the negative cable from the battery.
2 On 1990 to 1994 models, pull back the wiring connector boot at the door hinge area,

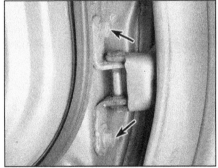

17.5 Mark the door hinge bolt locations (arrowed)

and disconnect the electrical connector. On 1995 and later models, pull the small pin on the top of the door jamb electrical connector, then unplug the electrical connector.
3 Position a jack or axle stands under the door or have an assistant available to support the door when the hinge bolts are removed **(see illustration)**. **Note:** *If a jack or stand is used, place a rag between it and the door to protect the door paint.*
4 Remove the door stop strut bolt **(see illustration)**.
5 Mark around the door hinges and hinge bolts to aid alignment when refitting **(see illustration)**.
6 Remove the hinge-to-door bolts and carefully detach the door.
7 Refitting is the reverse of removal. Adjust and securely tighten the door hinge bolts and striker bolts, if removed, as described below.

Adjustment

8 Following refitting, locate the alignment marks made during door removal. Make sure the door is aligned properly and adjust it if necessary as follows:
a) *Up-and-down and forward-and-backward adjustments are made by loosening the hinge-to-body bolts and moving the door, as necessary. A special offset tool may be required to reach some of the bolts* **(see illustration)**.
b) *In-and-out and up-and-down adjustments are made by loosening the door side*

17.3 Use axle stands padded with rags to support the door during the removal and refitting procedures

17.4 Remove the bolt and detach the stop strut

hinge bolts and moving the door, as necessary. A special offset tool may be required to reach some of the bolts **(see illustration)**.
c) *The door lock striker can also be adjusted both up-and-down and sideways to provide a positive engagement with the locking mechanism. This is done by loosening the screws and moving the striker by hand or by lightly tapping with a soft-faced hammer, as necessary* **(see illustration)**.

18 Rear quarter glass - renewal

Saloon models (1990 to 1994 only)

1 Remove the rear door trim panel and the plastic watershield (see Section 13).
2 Disconnect the negative battery cable.
3 Fully open the roll-up door glass.
4 Remove the centre channel strip by carefully lifting the door weatherstrip on the top of the door, and removing the centre channel screw and clip **(see illustration 15.4)**.
5 Remove rear quarter window glass and carefully pull the weatherstrip free, removing any clips or attachment points - do not pull too hard as this may damage the weatherstrip.

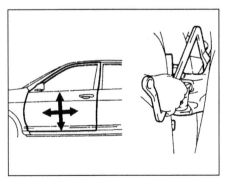

17.8a When adjusting the door, a special spanner such as this one will make the job easier

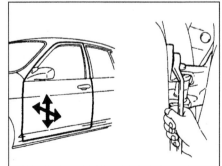

17.8b Adjust the door up-and-down or in-and-out after loosening the hinge-to-door bolts

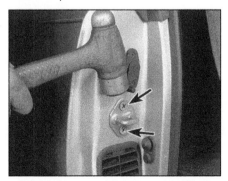

17.8c Adjust the striker by loosening the screws (arrowed) and gently tapping the striker

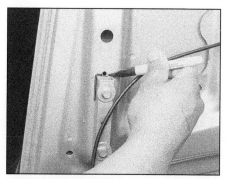

19.6 Mark around the boot lid hinges prior to removal of the lid

6 Refitting is the reverse of the removal procedure.

Hatchback models

7 Remove the upper seatbelt anchor.
8 Remove the inside pillar trim.
9 Remove the quarter window latch.
10 Pull out the quarter window glass.
11 Remove the quarter window hinges and outside moulding from the quarter window, as necessary.
12 Refitting is the reverse of the removal procedure.

19 Boot lid - removal, refitting and adjustment

Note: *The boot lid is heavy and somewhat awkward to remove and fit - have an assistant available to perform this procedure.*
1 Disconnect the negative battery cable.
2 Remove the lid lock cover inside the boot lid.
3 Disconnect and remove the boot opener release cable from the boot lid.
4 Disconnect the electrical wiring harness from the boot lid.
5 With the boot lid open, cover the edges of the boot compartment with pads or cloths to protect the painted surfaces when the boot lid is removed.
6 Make alignment marks around the hinge mounting bolts to aid alignment when refitting **(see illustration)**.
7 While supporting the boot lid, remove the boot lid-to-hinge bolts on both hinges and lift off the boot lid.
8 If the boot lid springs are to be removed, note the location of the hooked end of each spring at the notches in both the right hand and left hand brackets. Remove the springs from the right hand and left hand brackets using pliers to grip near the hooked end of each spring. **Note:** *The boot lid springs can be removed with the boot lid still installed, by opening the boot lid fully and securely supporting the boot lid open while removing the springs.*
9 If necessary, remove the boot lid latch by marking the latch position and removing the bolts, the latch and the lock cylinder.

10 Refitting is the reverse of removal. **Note:** *When refitting the boot lid, align the hinge with the marks made during removal. If the springs were removed, securely support the boot lid fully open and refit the springs in the brackets as removed above. Proper spring adjustment ensures that the boot lid is held open fully by the springs. If necessary, adjust the springs by resetting the hooked ends of the springs into alternate notches in the brackets.*
11 After refitting, carefully close the boot lid and check for proper alignment with the wings and bumper panel.
12 Forward-and-backward and side-to-side adjustments are made by loosening the hinge-to-lid bolts and gently moving the boot lid into correct alignment.
13 To adjust the lid so it is flush with the body when closed, open the lid and slightly loosen the lid mounting bolts and loosen the latch striker, tap the striker lightly, close the lid to check alignment, open the lid and securely tighten all bolts. Recheck closing and opening again.

20 Rear hatch - removal, refitting and adjustment

Note: *The rear hatch is heavy and somewhat awkward to remove and fit - at least two people should perform this procedure.*
1 Disconnect the negative battery cable.
2 On 1990 to 1994 models, remove the hatch wiring harness near the hatch hinge by removing the lower, side and manifold interior trim panels, the rear seat belt upper anchor, and the rear pillar trim panels.
3 On 1990 to 1994 models, remove the rear portion of the headliner.
4 On 1990 to 1994 models, disconnect the window washer tubing.
5 With the hatch open, cover the edges of the compartment with pads or cloths to protect the painted surfaces when the hatch is removed.
6 Scribe or felt tip mark alignment marks around the hinges to use for alignment when refitting.
7 Scribe or felt tip mark around the striker to aid alignment when refitting, remove the hatch striker, disconnect the opener cable.
8 Have an assistant support the hatch while detaching the hatch support strut (see Section 21).
9 While an assistant supports the hatch, remove the hatch-to-hinge bolts on both sides and lift the hatch off.
10 To remove the opener cable, if necessary, remove the driver's door scuff plate (1990 to 1994) or hatch lever cover (1995 and later), boot side cover and quarter trim on the driver's side, the opener lever near the front seat, and the rear seat cushion.
11 If necessary, remove the hatch lock by removing the hatch inner trim panel, removing the lock retainer clip, lock cylinder, and lock assembly.

12 Refitting is the reverse of removal. **Note:** *When refitting the hatch, align the hinges with the scribe marks made during removal.*
13 After refitting, carefully close the hatch and check for proper alignment with the hatch opening and the hatch seats tightly against the weatherstrip.
14 Adjustments to the hatch position are made by loosening the hinge to hatch bolts or nuts and gently moving the hatch into correct alignment with the top and bottom sides of the hatch opening.
15 The hatch lock is adjusted by partially loosening the lid hinge bolts and striker bolts, then slowly closing the hatch. Carefully reopen the hatch, tighten the striker and recheck the lock by opening and closing the hatch. Adjust so that the hatch closes fully align with the hatch opening, and seats tightly against weatherstrip.

21 Rear hatch support strut(s) - renewal

⚠ **Warning: The support strut is filled with pressurised gas - do not dismantle this component. If faulty, renew it with a new one.**

Note: *The rear hatch is heavy and somewhat awkward to hold securely while replacing the struts - at least two people should perform this procedure.*
1 Open the hatch fully and support it in the open position.
2 Remove the strut bolts and detach the strut from the hatch and the body.
3 Refitting is the reverse of the removal procedure.

22 Centre console - removal and refitting

1 Disconnect the negative battery cable.

Rear console

2 Remove the rear console screws, and remove the rear console **(see illustration)**.

22.2 Remove the screws and remove the rear console - 1990 to 1994 shown

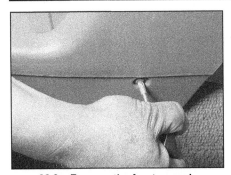

22.3a Remove the front console screws . . .

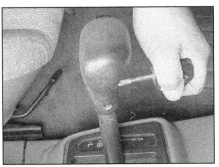

22.3b . . . the gear knob, and . . .

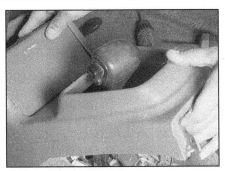

22.3c . . . detach the front console - 1990 to 1994 shown

Front console - at the shift lever

3 Remove the ashtray, remove the gear knob, remove the front console screws, and remove the console (see illustrations). Disconnect any electrical connectors. **Note:** *On 1990 to 1994 models there are two types of front consoles - a one-piece full front console with integral drawer, and a two-piece small console with a tray slot.*

4 Refitting is the reverse of the removal procedure.

23.2 Remove the steering column lower cover screws and remove the cover

23.4 Remove the steering column upper cover screws and remove the cover - 1990 to 1994 shown

23 Steering column covers - removal and refitting

1 Remove the steering column lower cover screws.
2 Remove the steering column lower cover (see illustration), detaching the electrical connector (1990 to 1994 models).
3 Remove the steering column upper cover screws.
4 Remove the steering column upper cover (see illustration).
5 Refitting is the reverse of the removal procedure.

24 Instrument cluster bezel - removal and refitting

1 Disconnect the cable from the negative battery terminal.
2 On 1990 to 1994 models, remove the side panel and screw retaining the instrument bezel (see illustration).
3 Remove the instrument cluster bezel screws (see illustrations).
4 To remove front-mounted switches, pop out any switches on this panel and disconnect the electrical connectors (see illustrations).

24.2 Remove the side panel and the screw (arrowed) retaining the instrument bezel

24.3a Remove the screw retaining the instrument cluster bezel

24.3b Remove the instrument cluster bezel screws here and along the bottom of the panel

24.4a Pop out any switches on the instrument bezel panel . . .

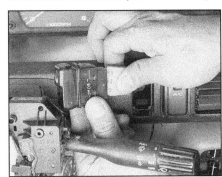

24.4b . . . and disconnect the electrical connectors from this panel

24.5 Carefully lift out the instrument cluster bezel - 1990 to 1994 shown

5 Grasp the instrument bezel securely and carefully remove it **(see illustration)**, to detach any pull-out clips, and disconnect any remaining electrical connectors. On 1995 and later models, pull the instrument bezel away to detach the clips from the instrument panel.
6 Refitting is the reverse of the removal procedure.

25 Dashboard - removal and refitting

 Warning: 1995 and later models are equipped with airbags. The airbag is armed and can inflate whenever the battery is connected. To prevent accidental deployment (and possible injury), turn the ignition key to LOCK and disconnect the negative battery cable whenever working near airbag components. After the battery is disconnected, wait at least two minutes before beginning work (the system has a back-up capacitor that must fully discharge). For more information see Chapter 12.
Note: *The project car was left-hand drive; bear this in mind when following these procedures.*
1 Turn the ignition key OFF, then disconnect the cable from the negative terminal of the battery. If the vehicle is equipped with an airbag system, wait at least two minutes before proceeding.
Caution: For models equipped with airbags, follow the airbag servicing instructions prior to proceeding with any steps that may involve working around the airbags.
DO NOT dismantle any airbag component.
DO NOT attempt repair of airbag system wiring harness.
DO NOT inspect or check the airbag system using an ohmmeter, because this can cause inadvertent deployment of the airbag.
DO NOT disconnect the airbag module (SAS) with the ignition switch ON - this could cause inadvertent airbag deployment.

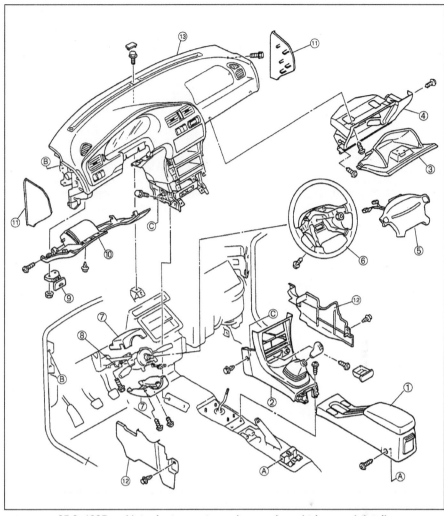

25.2 1995 and later instrument panel, console and trim panel details

1 Rear console	5 Driver's side airbag module
2 Front console	6 Steering wheel
3 Glove compartment door	7 Steering column covers
4 Glove compartment interior (cover)	8 Steering shaft
9 Bonnet release lever	
10 Lower panel	
11 Side panels	
12 Side wall	
13 Dashboard	

DO NOT handle or carry the airbag with the trim cover facing you when it has been removed and is live (has not been deployed).
When handling the airbag, DO NOT set the airbag module down with the trim cover facing down.
DO NOT touch a deployed airbag for at least 15 minutes - it can be extremely hot.
Contact a dealer for proper disposal of a used airbag.
2 If you're working on a 1995 or later model, refer to the accompanying illustration **(see illustration)** and use the following illustrations in this Section (showing a 1990 to 1994 model) for reference.
3 Remove the rear and front consoles (see Section 22). Remove the two console side walls, visible with the front console removed **(see illustrations)**.
4 On 1990 to 1994 models, remove the

ventilation outlet panel on the right side of the dash over the glove box.
5 Remove steering column lower and upper covers (see Section 23).

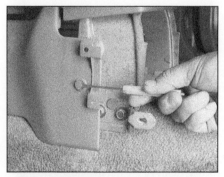

25.3a With the front console removed, remove the console side wall fasteners . . .

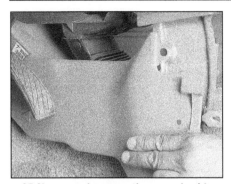

25.3b . . . and remove the console side wall on both sides

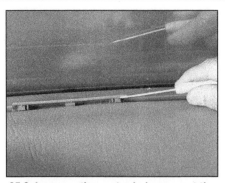

25.6 Lever up the centre hole cover at the windscreen vent panel and remove the centre screw . . .

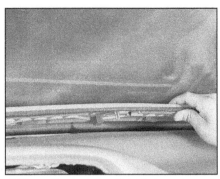

25.7 . . . then unsnap the windscreen vent panel

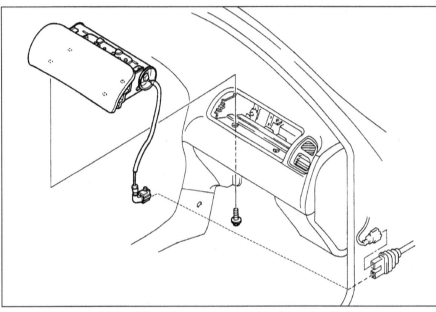

25.8 1995 and later passenger-side airbag details

pulling it up on the right side, slide it to the right and remove the door. Then remove the dashboard right side panel at the end of the dashboard, and remove the glove compartment.

c) Remove the passenger side airbag module as follows:

d) Disconnect the airbag electrical connector.

e) Remove the airbag retaining screws from inside the glove compartment area (glove compartment removed).

f) Lift out the passenger side airbag assembly **(see illustration)**.

g) Remove the driver's side airbag module and the steering wheel (see Chapter 10).

h) Detach the steering shaft from the dashboard.

9 Unsnap the dashboard right and left side panels at the ends of the dashboard **(see illustration 24.2)**.

10 Detach the bonnet release knob from under the dashboard. Remove the lower panel retaining screws from the underdash panel at the driver's side, remove the nut behind the bonnet release knob and lower the knob, then pull out the underdash panel while disconnecting any electrical connectors **(see illustrations)**.

11 Remove the instrument cluster bezel (see Section 24).

12 On 1990 to 1994 models, remove the glove compartment and remove the

6 Unsnap the centre hole cover on the top of the dashboard at the windscreen vent panel **(see illustration)**. Remove the screw at the centre of the windscreen vent panel.

7 Carefully unsnap the windscreen vent panel and remove it from the top of the dashboard **(see illustration)**.

8 On 1995 and later models:

a) Remove the windscreen pillar (A-pillar) trim panels by pulling the pillar trim back to disengage the clips and pin, then pull upward to disengage the hook from the body.

b) Remove the glove compartment door by

25.10a Remove the nut behind the bonnet release knob to detach the knob . . .

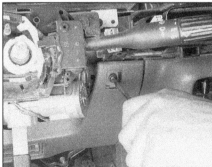

25.10b . . . and remove the screws attaching the driver's side underdash panel . . .

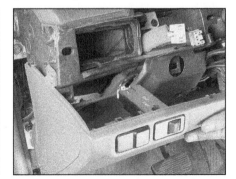

25.10c . . . and remove the underdash panel

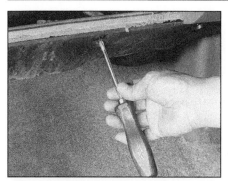

25.12 Remove the underdash panel at the right side of the dash

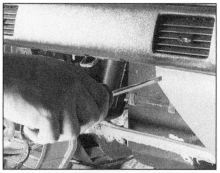

25.13a Remove the right side dash panel screws . . .

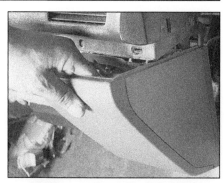

25.13b . . . pull out the dash panel, removing the electrical connector

underdash panel under the glove box **(see illustration)**.

13 On 1990 to 1994 models, remove the dash panel **(see illustrations)** and electrical connector at the right side of the glove compartment.

14 To remove the centre dash panel housing the radio and heater controls, remove the radio trim panel, remove the radio mounting screws, the radio aerial, power and earth cables, remove the heater controls, remove the centre dash panel screws and lift off the housing **(see illustration)**.

15 Remove the upper glove compartment cover inside the dashboard.

16 On 1990 to 1994 models, remove the control wires from the heater unit and the blower unit **(see illustration)**. On 1995 and later models with wire-type heater controls,

remove the air MIX wire, air INTAKE wire, and MODE wire, the dashboard main electrical connector at the bottom left side of the dashboard, the CPU and PCM connectors, and the orange and blue steering wheel airbag module connectors. On 1995 and later models with the Logic-type heater control unit, remove the PCM connectors, the blower unit connector, the air MIX actuator connector, dashboard main connector, the CPU connector, the orange and blue steering wheel airbag module connectors, and the cabin temperature sensor from the air duct.

17 As necessary, remove the centre vertical dashboard frame mount near the floor.

18 Carefully remove the dashboard **(see illustration)**, while disconnecting the electrical connectors at the left side of the dash, the blower unit, and at the underdash

fuse/electrical circuit breaker at the driver's side.

19 Refitting is the reverse of removal. When refitting the dashboard and reconnecting the heater controls, see Chapter 3 for control adjustment.

26 Outside mirror - removal and refitting

Manual mirror

1 Pry off the mirror control handle screw cover, remove the handle shaft screw, remove the handle **(see illustrations)**.

2 Detach the mirror cover inside the door by using a small screwdriver to pry the cover free from the door **(see illustration)**.

25.14 Remove the centre dash panel housing - 1990 to 1994 shown

25.16 Detach the heater unit and blower unit control wires - 1990 to 1994 shown

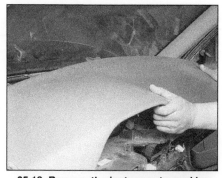

25.18 Remove the instrument panel by tilting and lifting away from the bulkhead

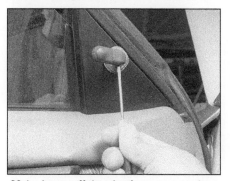

26.1a Lever off the plastic cover panel . . .

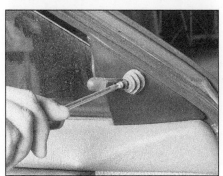

26.1b . . . and remove the handle shaft screw and handle

26.2 Lever off the mirror panel inside the door

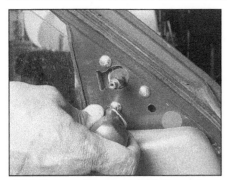

26.3 Remove the mirror retaining screws to remove the mirror

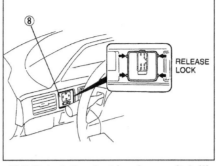

26.7 Detach the electric mirror switch (8) from the instrument panel

27.3a Detach the seat rail bolt covers, unbolt the front seat rail bolts from the floor . . .

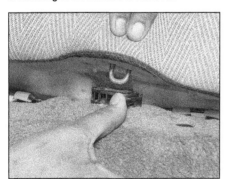

27.3b . . . then detach the electrical connector and remove the seat from the vehicle

3 Remove the mirror retaining screws from inside the door and detach the mirror **(see illustration)**.

Electric mirror

4 Detach the mirror cover inside the door by using a small screwdriver to pry the cover free from the door **(see illustration 26.2)**.
5 Remove the mirror retaining screws from inside the door and detach the mirror.
6 Unplug the electric mirror electrical connector.
7 If necessary to check or repair the electric mirror switch, detach the electric mirror switch from the instrument panel **(see illustration)**.
8 Refitting is the reverse of removal.

Mirror glass renewal

1990 to 1994 manual and electric type, 1995 and later manual type

9 Using a hot air blower, heat the mirror.
10 Adjust the mirror so that one edge of the mirror is accessible.
11 While keeping the mirror hot, insert a thin scraper between the mirror glass and the mirror frame, and carefully pry the mirror loose.
12 Remove all remaining adhesive from the back of the mirror glass.
13 Warm the frame with a hot air blower, and gently press the mirror glass in place. Allow to cool before driving.

1995 and later electric mirror

14 Push at the top of the mirror glass.
15 Pull the bottom of the mirror glass and remove the mirror from the housing.
16 Fit the mirror by hooking the top of the mirror glass onto the frame, then pressing the sides and bottom of the mirror.

27 Seats - removal and refitting

Front seats

1 Disconnect the seat belt buckle electrical connector near the floor.

2 Remove the seat forward/back travel release handle cover at the side of the seat.
3 Remove the seat rail retaining bolts at the floor, disconnect the electrical connector, and lift the seats from the vehicle **(see illustrations)**.
4 Refitting is the reverse of removal.

Rear seats

5 On saloon models, detach the retaining clips at the base of the rear seat near the floor **(see illustration)**, lift the front of the cushion up, then pull it out toward the front of the vehicle.
6 On hatchback models, depress the retaining clips at the base of the rear seat cushion **(see illustration 27.5)**, pull the rear seat cushion up and remove it from the vehicle.
7 On saloon models with rear split-folding seatback, remove the side cushion lower nut, unsnap the side cushion from the body, and lift out the side cushions. On saloon models with a standard one-piece seatback and with split-folding seatbacks, remove the seat back retaining bolts, lift up on the seat back to remove the seat back from the body **(see illustrations)**. On split-folding seatback models, the rear seat back latches are removable, as necessary.
8 On hatchback models with the rear split-folding seatback, remove the seat back retaining bolts, lift up on the seat back to

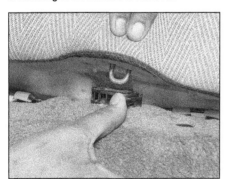

27.5 Press the rear seat cushion retaining clip and lift the rear seat bottom cushion

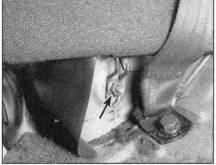

27.7a Remove the rear seatback retaining bolts (arrowed) . . .

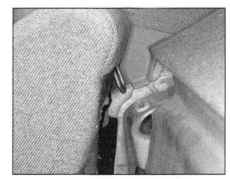

27.7b . . . and pull up the seatback to remove the upper retaining clips from the slots

remove the seat back from the body. On split-folding seatback models, the rear seat back latches are removable, as necessary. On hatchback models with a standard one-piece seatback, remove the seat back retaining bolts, lift up on the seat back to remove the seat back from the body. On 1995 and later models with the rear seat centre folding armrest, remove the screws from the armrest mount at the seatback to remove the armrest.

9 The saloon rear package trim panel is removed by removing the rear seatback, removing the high-mounted stoplight, removing the push-pull fasteners and pulling the trim panel forward to disengage the clips on the trim panel from the body.

10 Refitting is the reverse of removal. During refitting, route the seat belts between the seat bottom and the seatback for accessibility after seat refitting.

28 Seat belts - check

1 Check the seat belts, buckles, latch plates and guide loops for any obvious damage or signs of wear.

2 Make sure the seat belt reminder light (if fitted) comes on when the key is turned on.

3 Check that the passive front seat belt drive mechanisms (as applicable) actuate properly during use to travel and latch in place when driver or passenger is seated.

4 The seat belts are designed to lock up during a sudden stop or impact, yet allow free movement during normal driving. The retractors should hold the belt against your chest while driving and rewind the belt when the buckle is unlatched. Check the retractor on each seat belt locks when the belt is quickly pulled. **Note:** *Do not remove the belt retractor covers or dismantle the retractors, as the ELR (Emergency Locking Retractor) has a spring that will unwind and cannot be rewound.*

5 If any of the above checks reveal problems with the seat belt system, disconnect the negative battery cable, and renew the seat belt components and retractor assemblies as necessary.

Notes

Chapter 12
Chassis electrical system

Contents

Degrees of difficulty

Easy, suitable for novice with little experience	**Fairly easy,** suitable for beginner with some experience	**Fairly difficult,** suitable for competent DIY mechanic	**Difficult,** suitable for experienced DIY mechanic	**Very difficult,** suitable for expert DIY or professional

1 General information

The electrical system is a 12-volt, negative earth type. Power for the lights and all electrical accessories is supplied by a lead/acid-type battery which is charged by the alternator.

This Chapter covers repair and service procedures for the various electrical components not associated with the engine. Information on the battery, alternator, distributor and starter motor can be found in Chapter 5.

It should be noted that, when portions of the electrical system are serviced, the cable should be disconnected from the negative battery terminal to prevent electrical shorts and/or fires.

Caution: If the stereo in your vehicle is equipped with an anti-theft system, make sure you have the correct code before disconnecting the battery in any of the following procedures.

2 Electrical fault finding - general information

A typical electrical circuit consists of an electrical component, any switches, relays, motors, fuses, fusible links or circuit breakers related to that component and the wiring and electrical connectors that link the component to both the battery and the chassis. To help you pinpoint an electrical circuit problem, wiring diagrams are included at the end of this Chapter.

Before tackling any troublesome electrical circuit, first study the appropriate wiring diagrams to get a complete understanding of what makes up that individual circuit. Trouble spots, for instance, can often be narrowed down by noting if other components related to the circuit are operating properly. If several components or circuits fail at one time, chances are the problem is in a fuse or earth connection, because several circuits are often routed through the same fuse and earth connections.

Electrical problems usually stem from simple causes, such as loose or corroded connections, a blown fuse, a melted fusible link or a bad relay. Visually inspect the condition of all fuses, wires and connections in a problem circuit before troubleshooting it.

If testing instruments are going to be utilised, use the diagrams to plan ahead of time where you will make the necessary connections in order to accurately pinpoint the trouble spot.

The basic tools needed for electrical troubleshooting include a circuit tester or voltmeter (a 12-volt bulb with a set of test leads can also be used), a continuity tester, which includes a bulb, battery and set of test leads, and a jumper wire, preferably with a circuit breaker incorporated, which can be used to bypass electrical components. Before attempting to locate a problem with test instruments, use the wiring diagram(s) to decide where to make the connections.

Electrical troubleshooting is simple if you keep in mind that all electrical circuits are basically electrical current running from the battery, through the wires, switches, relays, fuses and fusible links to each electrical component (light bulb, motor, etc.) and to earth, from which it is passed back to the battery. Any electrical problem is an interruption in the flow of electricity to the electrical component and back to the battery.

Voltage checks

Voltage checks should be performed if a circuit is not functioning properly. Connect one lead of a circuit tester to either the battery negative terminal or a known good earth. Connect the other lead to an electrical connector in the circuit being tested, preferably nearest to the battery or fuse. If the bulb of the tester lights, voltage is present, which means that the part of the circuit between the electrical connector and the battery is problem free. Continue checking the rest of the circuit in the same fashion. When you reach a point at which no voltage is present, the problem lies between that point and the last test point with voltage. Most of the time the problem can be traced to a loose connection. **Note:** *Keep in mind that some circuits receive voltage only when the ignition key is in the Accessory or Run position.*

Finding a short

One method of finding shorts in a circuit is to remove the fuse and connect a test light or voltmeter to the fuse terminals in its place with all the relevant components switched off. There should be no voltage present in the circuit. Move the wiring harness from side to side while watching the test light. If the bulb goes on, there is a short to earth somewhere in that area, probably where the insulation has rubbed through. The same test can be performed on each component in the circuit, even a switch.

Earth check

Perform a earth test to check whether a component is properly earthed. Disconnect the battery and connect one lead of a self-powered test light, known as a continuity

tester, to a known good earth. Connect the other lead to the wire or earth connection being tested. If the bulb goes on, the earth is good. If the bulb does not go on, the earth is not good.

Continuity check

A continuity check is done to determine if there are any breaks in a circuit - if it is passing electricity properly. With the circuit off (no power in the circuit), a self-powered continuity tester can be used to check the circuit. Connect the test leads to both ends of the circuit (or to the 'power' end and a good earth), and if the test light comes on the circuit is passing current properly. If the light doesn't come on, there is a break somewhere in the circuit. The same procedure can be used to test a switch, by connecting the continuity tester to the power in and power out sides of the switch. With the switch turned on, the test light should come on.

Finding an open circuit

When diagnosing for possible open circuits, it is often difficult to locate them by sight because corrosion or terminal misalignment are hidden by the electrical connectors. Merely wiggling an electrical connector on a sensor or in the wiring harness may correct the open circuit condition. Remember this when an open circuit is indicated when troubleshooting a circuit. Intermittent problems may also be caused by corroded or loose connections.

3 Fuses - general information

Note: *The project car was left-hand drive; component locations may vary.*

1 The electrical circuits of the vehicle are protected by a combination of fuses, circuit breakers and fusible links. The main fuse block is located in the engine compartment on the driver's side, and the interior fuse box is located under the instrument panel on the driver's side of the dashboard **(see illustrations)**.

2 Each of the fuses is designed to protect a specific circuit, and the various circuits are identified on the fuse panel itself. the main fuse block in the engine compartment supplies circuit with high current draws, such as the fuel injection, headlights, cooling fan, air conditioner, etc. The interior fuse box supplies current to the remainder of the circuits; interior lights, radio, door locks, electric windows, instrument panel, wipers, exterior lights, etc.

3 Blade type fuses are employed in the main fuse block and the fuse box **(see illustration)**. **Note:** *When replacing a fuse, do not attempt to use pliers - always use the fuse puller tool supplied in the fuse box cover for safe removal and renewal, without damaging the fuse itself or neighbouring fuses.* If an electrical component fails, always check the fuse first. A blown fuse is easily identified through the

3.1a The main fuse block is located in the engine compartment, near the battery

3.1b The interior fuse box is located near the driver's side kick panel

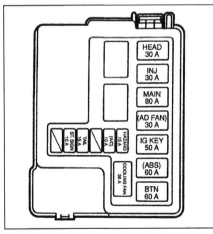

3.1c 1995 and later model main fuse block details

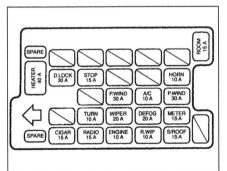

3.1d 1995 and later model interior fuse box details

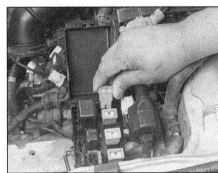

3.3a The main fuses supply circuits with a high current draw

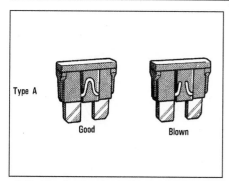

3.3b The fuses are blade type fuses that can be visually checked

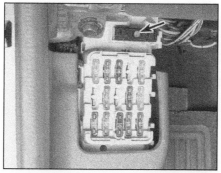

4.2 Press the reset button (arrowed) to reset the circuit breaker - 1994 and earlier models

clear plastic body. Visually inspect the element for evidence of damage **(see illustration)**, or where possible, perform a continuity check across the fuse terminals with the fuse removed from the fuse block or box. If a continuity check is necessary the blade terminal tips are exposed in the fuse body.

4 Be sure to renew blown fuses with the correct type. Fuses of different ratings are physically interchangeable, but only fuses of the proper rating should be used. Replacing a fuse with one of a higher or lower value than specified is not recommended. Each electrical circuit needs a specific amount of protection. The amperage value of each fuse is moulded into the fuse body.

5 If the renewal fuse immediately fails, this indicates a more serious problem than just a failed or defective fuse. Don't renew it again until the cause of the problem is isolated and corrected. In most cases, this will be a short circuit in the wiring caused by a broken or deteriorated wire, or a failed electrical component.

6 The fuse box under the instrument panel is mounted on the joint box which connects major wiring harnesses and houses the Central Processing Unit (CPU). The CPU controls electrical systems. For access, the kick panel trim must be removed. The CPU is removable for inspection or renewal. A Powertrain Control Module (PCM) is located at the floor behind the centre console. The PCM controls engine operation. **Note:** *If the fuse box ROOM fuse is burned out, the dashboard malfunction light will be ON; to renew, turn the ignition switch to LOCK and fit the new fuse.*

4 Circuit breakers - general information

Note: *The project car was left-hand drive; component locations may vary.*

1 On some models the circuit breaker resets itself automatically, an electrical overload in a circuit breaker protected system will cause the circuit to fail momentarily, then come back on. If the circuit does not come back on,

check it immediately. Note, however, that some circuit breakers must be reset manually. Once the electrical problem is corrected, and the circuit breaker resets, the circuit breaker will resume its normal function.

2 On 1994 and earlier models, to reset the heater manual circuit breaker, press in the circuit breaker reset button, located above the fuse box at the driver's kick panel enclosure **(see illustration)**.

5 Relays - general information

Note: *The project car was left-hand drive; component locations may vary.*

1 Many electrical accessories in the vehicle use relays to transmit the electrical signal to the component. If the relay is defective, that component will not operate properly.

2 The flasher relay, door lock timer relay, horn relay, side marker/tail/number plate/tail Illumination (TNS) relay, wiper relay (1994 and earlier), and the headlight relay are located in one relay assembly under the dashboard on the driver's side. The DRL (Daytime Running Light) control unit and relay are located under the dashboard on the passenger's side. On 1995 and later models, the horn relay is located on the passenger side panel forward of the door opening.

3 If a faulty relay is suspected, it can be removed and tested by a dealer or other qualified workshop. Defective relays must be replaced as a unit.

6 Direction indicator/hazard flashers - check and renewal

 Warning: 1995 and later models are equipped with airbags. The airbag is armed and can inflate anytime the battery is connected. To prevent accidental deployment (and possible injury), turn the ignition key to LOCK and disconnect the negative battery cable whenever working near airbag components. After the battery is disconnected, wait at least two minutes before beginning work (the system has a back-up capacitor that must fully discharge). For more information see Section 26.

Note: *The project car was left-hand drive; component locations may vary.*

1 The direction indicator/hazard flasher, a small canister-shaped unit located near the fuse box under the dashboard at the driver's side, flashes the direction indicators and the hazard flashers. On 1994 and earlier models, it is mounted on a bracket with the horn relay, TNS relay, headlight relay, and wiper relay. On 1995 and later models, it is located behind the dashboard lower panel under the steering wheel **(see illustration)** and is removed by

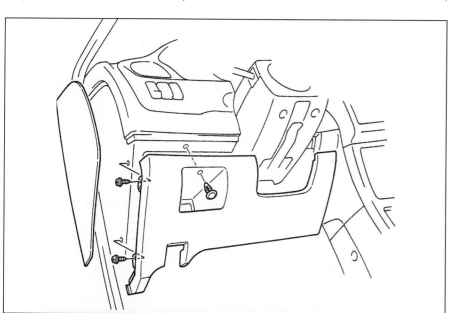

6.1 1995 and later model driver's side lower dash panel removal details

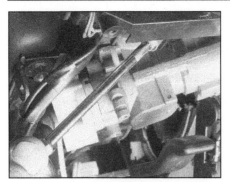

7.5 Remove the combination switch mounting screws - 1994 and earlier model shown

7.6 Slip the combination switch off the steering column and unplug electrical connector(s)

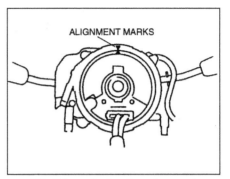

7.7 Airbag clockspring alignment marks

detaching the dashboard left side panel, the lower panel screws, and the push fastener.

2 When the flasher unit is functioning properly, an audible click can be heard during its operation. If the direction indicators fail on one side or the other and the flasher unit does not make its characteristic clicking sound, a faulty direction indicator bulb is indicated.

3 Flasher relay check: With ignition switch on, operate direction indicator switch right and left, checking front and rear direction indicators are flashing; actuate the hazard warning switch and check both front and rear signals flash.

4 If both direction indicators fail to flash, the problem may be a blown fuse, a faulty flasher unit, a failed bulb, a broken switch or a loose or open electrical connection. If a quick check of the fuse box indicates that the direction indicator fuse has blown, check the wiring for a short before refitting a new fuse.

5 To renew the flasher, remove the flasher from its mounting bracket, and pull the flasher out of the electrical connector.

6 Also, if a faulty flasher is suspected, it can be removed and tested by a dealer or other qualified workshop. Defective flashers must be replaced as a unit. Make sure that the renewal unit is identical to the original. Compare the old one to the new one before refitting it.

7 If one side only fails to flash properly, check for burnt out bulbs.

8 Refitting is the reverse of removal.

7 Combination switch - removal and refitting

Warning: 1995 and later models are equipped with airbags. The airbag is armed and can inflate anytime the battery is connected. To prevent accidental deployment (and possible injury), turn the ignition key to LOCK and disconnect the negative battery cable whenever working near airbag components. After the battery is disconnected, wait at least two minutes before beginning work (the system has a

back-up capacitor that must fully discharge). For more information see Section 26.

Note: *The project car was left-hand drive; component locations may vary.*

1 Disconnect the negative battery cable.

2 On 1995 and later models, disable the driver's airbag and remove the airbag assembly (see Chapter 10).

3 Remove the steering wheel (see Chapter 10).

4 Remove the steering column upper and lower covers (see Chapter 11).

5 Remove the combination switch retaining screws **(see illustration)**, clips and latch behind the combination switch.

6 Disconnect the electrical connectors and slide the combination switch off the column **(see illustration)**.

Warning: On models equipped with airbags, handle the combination switch/clockspring assembly very carefully.
Damage to the clockspring could cause an airbag system failure resulting in serious personal injury.

7 Refitting is the reverse of removal. On models equipped with airbags, ensure the clockspring is centred properly before refitting

the combination switch/clockspring assembly onto the steering shaft as follows:

a) *Position the front wheels pointing straight ahead.*

b) *Gently rotate the clockspring inner hub clockwise to the end of its stop. Do not force it against the stop.*

c) *Rotate the clockspring 2 and 3/4 turns anti-clockwise.*

d) *Align the mark on the inner hub with the mark on the housing* **(see illustration)**.

8 Combination switch - check

Warning: 1995 and later models are equipped with airbags. The airbag is armed and can inflate anytime the battery is connected. To prevent accidental deployment (and possible injury), turn the ignition key to LOCK and disconnect the negative battery cable whenever working near airbag components. After the battery is disconnected, wait at least two minutes before beginning work (the system has a back-up capacitor that must fully

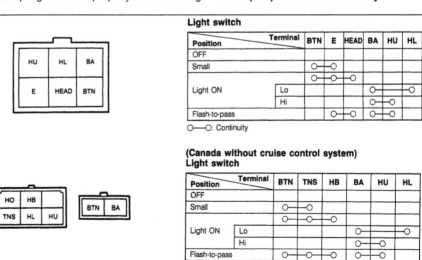

Light switch

Position	Terminal	BTN	E	HEAD	BA	HU	HL
OFF							
Small			O—O				
				O—O			
Light ON	Lo					O—O	
	Hi					O—O	
Flash-to-pass			O—O			O—O	

O—O: Continuity

(Canada without cruise control system)
Light switch

Position	Terminal	BTN	TNS	HB	BA	HU	HL
OFF							
Small		O—O					
			O—O				
Light ON	Lo					O—O	
	Hi					O—O	
Flash-to-pass		O—O	O—O			O—O	

8.5a Light control switch terminal guide and continuity table - 1994 and earlier models

*discharge). For more information see
Section 26.*

1 Disconnect the negative cable at the battery.

2 On 1995 and later models, disable the driver's airbag and remove the airbag assembly (see Chapter 10).

3 Remove the steering wheel (see Chapter 10).

4 Remove the steering column upper and lower covers (see Chapter 11).

5 On the combination switch assembly, check for continuity between the indicated terminals using an ohmmeter with the light switch, direction indicator switch, and wiper/washer switch in each of the indicated positions **(see illustrations)**.

6 If the continuity between terminals is not as specified in the illustrations, renew the combination switch. Refer to Section 7 for combination switch refitting and centring the clockspring, if equipped. See Chapter 10 for steering wheel and airbag refitting.

9 Ignition switch - check and renewal

**Warning: 1995 and later models
are equipped with airbags. The
airbag is armed and can inflate
anytime the battery is
connected. To prevent accidental
deployment (and possible injury), turn the
ignition key to LOCK and disconnect the
negative battery cable whenever working
near airbag components. After the battery
is disconnected, wait at least two minutes
before beginning work (the system has a
back-up capacitor that must fully
discharge). For more information see
Section 26.**

Note: *The project car was left-hand drive;
component locations may vary.*

1 Disconnect the negative battery cable.

2 On 1995 and later models, disable the driver's airbag.

3 Remove the steering column upper and lower covers (see Chapter 11).

4 Remove the lower dash panel **(see illustration 6.1)**.

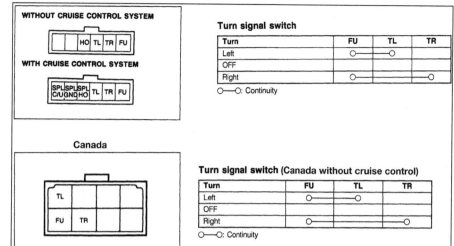

Turn signal switch			
Turn	FU	TL	TR
Left	O——————O		
OFF			
Right	O——————	——————O	

O——O: Continuity

Turn signal switch (Canada without cruise control)			
Turn	FU	TL	TR
Left	O——————O		
OFF			
Right	O——————	——————O	

O——O: Continuity

**8.5b Direction indicator switch terminal guide continuity table -
1994 and earlier models**

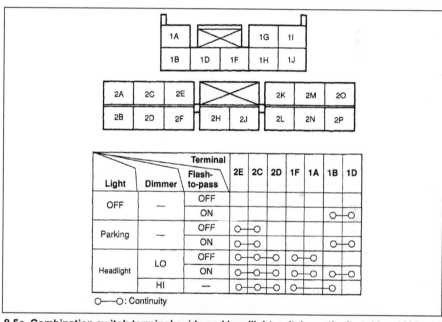

Light	Dimmer	Flash-to-pass	2E	2C	2D	1F	1A	1B	1D
OFF	—	OFF							
		ON						O—O	
Parking	—	OFF	O—O						
		ON	O—O					O—O	
Headlight	LO	OFF	O—O—O		O—O				
		ON	O—O—O		O—O			O—O	
	HI	—	O—O—O		O—O				

O——O: Continuity

**8.5c Combination switch terminal guide and headlight switch continuity table - 1995 and
later models**

Switch position	Terminal	1I	1H	1G
Left		O——————O		
OFF				
Right		O——————	——————O	

O——O: Continuity

**8.5d Direction indicator switch continuity table - 1995 and later
models**

Switch position		One-touch	2K	2L	2N	2J	2M
Wiper switch	OFF	OFF	O——————	——————O			
		ON		O——————	——————O		
	LO				O——————O		
	HI			O——————O		
Washer switch	ON				O——————O	

O——O: Continuity

**8.5e Windscreen wiper and washer switch continuity table - 1995
and later models**

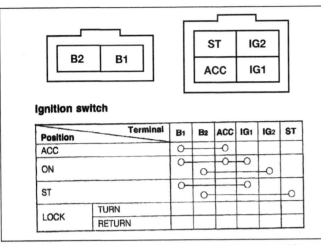

Ignition switch

Position		Terminal B₁	B₂	ACC	IG₁	IG₂	ST
ACC		O—		—O			
ON		O—		—O—	—O		
			O—		—O		
ST		O—			—O		
			O—				—O
LOCK	TURN						
	RETURN						

9.6a Ignition switch terminal guide and continuity table - 1994 and earlier models

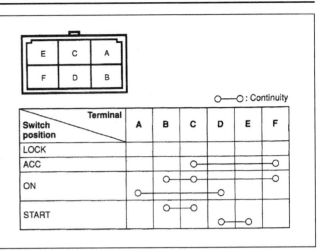

O——O : Continuity

Switch position	Terminal A	B	C	D	E	F
LOCK						
ACC			O—		—O	—O
ON	O—		—O—	—O		—O
START	O—		—O—	—O		
					O—	—O

9.6b Ignition switch terminal guide and continuity table - 1995 and later models

Check

5 Trace the wire from the ignition switch to the electrical connector and unplug the connector.
6 Check for continuity with switch in each indicated position (see illustrations).

Renewal

7 Disconnect the electrical connector from the switch.
8 Remove the screw and separate the switch from the steering lock assembly (see illustration).
9 Refitting is the reverse of removal.

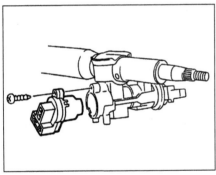

9.8 Ignition switch refitting details

10 Headlight bulb - renewal

Warning: Halogen gas-filled bulbs are under pressure and may shatter if the surface is scratched or the bulb is dropped. Wear eye protection and handle the bulbs carefully, grasping only the base. Keep bulbs away from children. Allow the bulb to cool before removal. Do not touch the surface of the bulb with your fingers because the oil from your skin could cause it to overheat and fail prematurely. If you do touch the bulb surface, wipe the bulb clean with methylated spirits.

Note: *The headlight bulb renewal procedure steps in this Section do not affect headlight aim.*

1 Make sure the headlight switch is OFF.
2 Open the bonnet.
3 Locate the headlight bulb at the rear of the headlight assembly.
4 On 1994 and earlier models, disconnect the electrical connector from the bulb by squeezing the tabs and pulling the electrical connector away from the headlight, then rotate the retainer ring anti-clockwise (when viewed from the engine compartment) about one-eighth of a turn (see illustrations). On 1995 and later models, disconnect the electrical connector from the bulb and remove the retaining ring.
5 Remove the bulb base (see illustration).
6 Make sure the bulb is cool to touch. Grasp the headlight bulb base and carefully pull the bulb out (don't rotate the bulb while removing it). Note: *Use the protective cover and carton from the new bulb to promptly dispose of the old bulb.*
7 Fit the new headlight bulb with the flat side of the plastic base facing upward, by gently inserting the glass portion of the bulb into the socket. The base of the bulb may need to be rotated slightly clockwise or anti-clockwise when inserting it to align the grooves on the bulb base with the tabs in the socket. When the grooves are aligned, push the bulb firmly into the socket.
8 Slide the bulb retaining ring over the plastic base of the bulb. On 1994 and earlier models, lock the retaining ring by rotating it clockwise (when viewed from the engine compartment). The retaining ring will lock fully when rotated sufficiently and solid resistance is felt.
9 Push the electrical connector into the rear

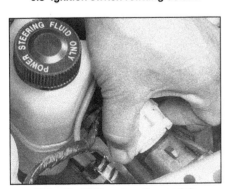

10.4a On 1994 and earlier models, squeeze the tabs and then pull the connector from the headlight bulb

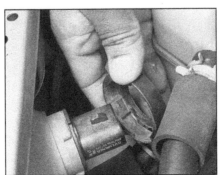

10.4b Rotate the bulb retaining ring anti-clockwise about one-eighth of a turn and remove it

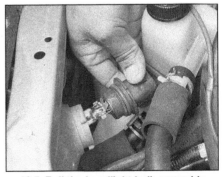

10.5 Pull the headlight bulb assembly straight out of the housing

11.2 Remove the combination light screws and remove the light assembly - 1994 and earlier shown

11.4a Remove the headlight-mounting screws from the front support . . .

11.4b . . . and the wing

of the bulb base until it snaps and locks into position.

10 Switch on the headlights and check for proper operation.

11 Headlight housing - removal and refitting

1 Disconnect the negative battery cable.

2 Remove the front combination light (direction indicator/side marker light) retaining screw(s), remove the combination light bulb electrical connector, and pull the combination light assembly off the vehicle **(see illustrations 11.2 and 13.3)**.

3 Remove the headlight bulb electrical connector and remove the headlight bulb (see Section 10).

 Warning: Halogen gas-filled bulbs are under pressure and may shatter if the surface is scratched or the bulb is dropped. Wear eye protection and handle the bulbs carefully, grasping only the base. Keep bulbs away from children. Allow the bulb to cool before removal. Do not touch the surface of the bulb with your fingers because the oil from your skin could cause it to overheat and fail prematurely. If you do touch the bulb surface, wipe the bulb clean with methylated spirits.

4 Remove the headlight assembly side mounting bolt, accessible with the combination light (direction indicator/side marker light) off the vehicle and remove the headlight assembly front mounting bolt, accessible near the grille **(see illustrations)**.

5 On 1994 and earlier models, remove the fastener behind the headlight assembly **(see illustration)**. On 1995 and later models, remove the nut at the top of the headlight assembly **(see illustration)**.

6 On 1994 and earlier models, remove the lower grille moulding fasteners and the lower grille moulding **(see illustration)**.

7 Remove the headlight housing (lens) assembly.

8 Refitting is the reverse of removal. Refer to Section 10 for headlight bulb refitting.

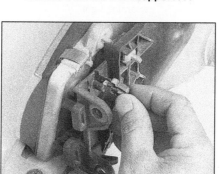

11.5a Remove the headlight clip behind the assembly (unit removed from vehicle for clarity) . . .

12 Headlights - adjustment
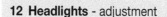

Note: *It is important that the headlights are aimed correctly. If adjusted incorrectly they could blind the driver of an oncoming vehicle and cause a serious accident or seriously reduce your ability to see the road. The headlights should be checked for proper aim every 12 months and any time a new headlight is installed or front end body work is performed. It should be emphasised that the following information is only an interim step which will provide temporary adjustment until the headlights can be adjusted by a properly equipped workshop.*

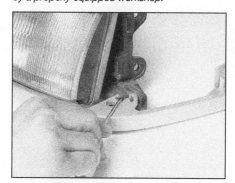

11.6 Remove the lower grille moulding screws and remove the moulding

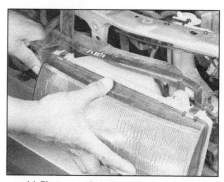

11.5b . . . and remove the headlight assembly

1 1994 and earlier models have two adjustment screws, one to the side controlling left-and-right movement and one above the light for up-and-down movement that are accessible from the front of the headlight housing **(see illustration)**, with the combination light (direction indicator/side marker light assembly) removed, and the bonnet open. 1995 and later models have two adjustment screws, one toward the centre of the vehicle controlling left-and-right movement and one closest to the wing for up-and-down movement. They are accessible from the back of the headlight housing with the bonnet open.

2 Have the headlight adjustment checked by a dealer service department at the earliest opportunity.

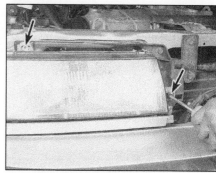

12.1 1994 and earlier headlight adjustment screws (arrowed)

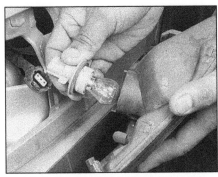

13.3 Rotate the bulb holders to remove the combination light (direction indicator) bulb from the housing

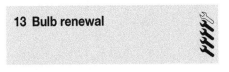

13 Bulb renewal

Front direction indicator, parking and side marker

1 Remove the front light (direction indicator/side marker light) retaining screw(s) (see Section 11).

2 Remove the light assembly (see Section 11).

3 On 1994 and earlier models, twist the light bulb holder (socket) anti-clockwise and pull it out of the light assembly **(see illustration)**. On 1995 and later models, pull the bulb/socket assembly from its light assembly socket.

4 On 1994 and earlier models, while holding the combination light bulb holder, rotate the bulb to remove it. Renew the bulb.

5 On 1995 and later models, pull the bulb from its socket and renew the bulb.

6 Refitting is the reverse of removal.

Rear brake, direction indicator, tail, reversing lights, and side marker

Saloon

7 Open the boot lid.

8 Inside the boot, remove the light housing/bulb socket holder **(see illustration)**.

9 Twist the combination light bulb being

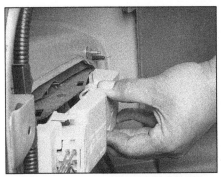

13.8 Remove fasteners to pull out the rear brake light, taillight, direction indicator, or reversing light

replaced to remove it from its holder (socket) **(see illustration)**.

10 To remove the combination light assembly entirely, open the boot lid and remove the combination light assembly retaining nut. On 1994 and earlier models, the retaining nut is inside the boot. On 1995 and later models, the wing-mounted lights are retained by screws exposed when the boot lid is open. On 1995 and later models, the boot lid mounted (inboard) combination light is retained by through bolts from inside the boot lid. Remove the combination light assembly and gasket, while disconnecting the wiring electrical connector **(see illustration)**.

11 On 1994 and earlier models, to remove the saloon rear side marker light, remove the two screws, twist the bulb holder (socket), and pull the bulb to remove it. Press in the new bulb.

12 Refitting is the reverse of removal.

Hatchback

13 Open the rear hatch.

14 Inside the boot area, open either the brake/taillight/side marker light access panel, the direction indicator access panel, or the reversing light access panel depending on the bulb to be replaced.

15 Twist the combination light bulb holder (socket) anti-clockwise for the bulb(s) being replaced and pull them out of the light assembly.

16 Holding the combination light bulb holder

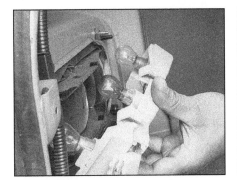

13.9 Remove the taillight bulb holder (socket) to renew the bulbs

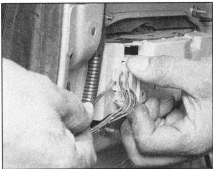

13.10 From inside the boot, disconnect the combination light assembly wiring harness (saloon models)

(socket), rotate the bulb being replaced to remove it. Renew the bulb.

17 To remove the combination light assembly, open the rear hatch and remove the combination light assembly retaining nut (inside the boot). Remove the combination light assembly and gasket, while disconnecting the wiring electrical connector.

18 Refitting is the reverse of removal.

Number plate light

Saloon

19 Remove the rear number plate for access.

20 On 1994 and earlier models, twist and pull the number plate light holder (socket) out of the slot in the car body. Twist the bulb to remove it. Renew the bulb.

21 On 1995 and later models, remove the lens screws and pull the bulbs out. Renew the bulbs.

22 Refitting is the reverse of removal

Hatchback

23 Above the rear number plate, remove the number plate light screws and remove the lens. **Note:** *There are two identical rear number plate lights.*

24 Pull the bulb to remove it. Press in the new bulb.

High-mounted brake light

Saloon

25 On 1994 and earlier models, remove the two high-mounted brake light housing push-pull retaining pins or retaining screws **(see illustration)**. Remove the high-mounted brake

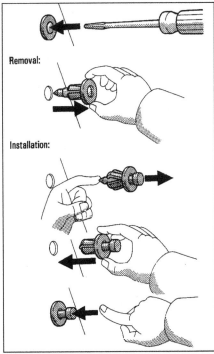

13.25 Push-pull retainer removal and refitting details (saloon high-mounted brake light)

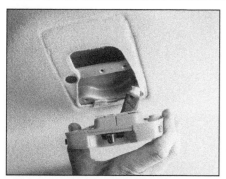

13.34a Remove the screws retaining the overhead light assembly

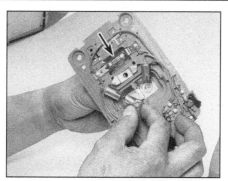

13.34b Remove the overhead map light bulbs

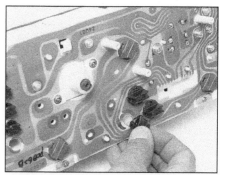

13.36 The instrument cluster light bulbs are removed from the backside of the cluster

light housing. Twist and pull the high-mounted brake light holder (socket) and pull it out of the light housing. Twist the bulb to remove it. Renew the bulb.

26 On 1995 and later models, remove the push fasteners to remove the light housing cover.

27 On 1995 and later models, remove the bulb holder from the housing. Renew the bulb.

28 Refitting is the reverse of removal.

Hatchback

29 On the exterior of the hatch, remove the high-mounted stop-light retaining screws.

30 Rotate the bulb holder (socket) anti-clockwise to remove it from the high-mounted brake light assembly.

31 Pull the bulb to remove it. Press in the new bulb.

32 Refitting is the reverse of removal.

Interior lights

33 For the interior light mounted at the centre of the roof, pull the light lens off, and pull the bulb from its holder (socket). Renew the bulb and press the light lens in place.

34 For models with a sunroof, remove the map lights (spot lights) in the overhead panel by removing the rearview mirror, slide back the panel cover, remove the panel, and pull out the map light bulb(s) **(see illustrations)**.

Press in the new bulb(s). Refitting is the reverse of removal.

35 For models without a sunroof, remove the map lights (spot lights) mounted at the centre of the roof by pulling the light lens off, remove the light housing, and twisting the bulb(s) to remove them. Renew the bulb(s). Refitting is the reverse of removal.

Instrument cluster illumination

36 To gain access to the instrument cluster illumination light(s), the instrument cluster will have to be removed (see Section 17). The bulb(s) can then be removed and replaced from the rear of the cluster **(see illustration)**.

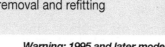

14 Radio and speakers - removal and refitting

Warning: 1995 and later models are equipped with airbags. The airbag is armed and can inflate anytime the battery is connected. To prevent accidental deployment (and possible injury), turn the ignition key to LOCK and disconnect the negative battery

cable whenever working near airbag components. After the battery is disconnected, wait at least two minutes before beginning work (the system has a back-up capacitor that must fully discharge). For more information see Section 26. Caution: If the stereo in your vehicle is equipped with an anti-theft system, make sure you have the correct code before disconnecting the battery.

Radio

1 Disconnect the negative cable at the battery.

2 Remove the radio trim bezel **(see illustration)**.

3 Remove the radio retaining screws, pull the radio out far enough to unplug the electrical connector and the aerial lead and remove the radio **(see illustrations)**.

4 Refitting is the reverse of removal.

Speakers

5 Remove the front door trim panel (see Chapter 11).

6 Remove the speaker retaining screws/nuts. Unplug the electrical connector and remove the speaker **(see illustration)**.

7 Refitting is the reverse of removal.

14.2 Carefully lever the trim bezel from around the radio

14.3a Remove the radio retaining screws

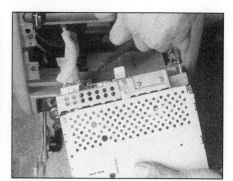

14.3b Pull the radio out of the instrument panel and disconnect the connectors and aerial lead

15 Aerial -
removal and refitting

1 Unplug the cable from the radio. On 1995 and later models, Remove the lower dash panel at the driver's side (see Chapter 11) and disconnect the aerial jack. **Note:** *The aerial may be tested if desired, by checking continuity at the aerial cable plug end. The aerial should have full continuity (no resistance).*
2 On 1994 and earlier models, loosen any aerial cable clamps found. For electric aerials, disconnect the electrical power connector.
3 On 1994 and earlier models, remove the aerial mount screws or threaded mounting clamp, as necessary. On 1995 and later models, pull the aerial out of the vehicle windscreen post A-pillar.
4 Remove the aerial, while pulling out the cable.
5 Refitting is the reverse of removal. On 1995 and later models, tape the aerial jack to the aerial drain tubing, pass the aerial into the A-pillar aerial hole. Connect the aerial base and fit.

16 Instrument cluster -
removal and refitting

 Warning: 1995 and later models are equipped with airbags. The airbag is armed and can inflate anytime the battery is connected. To prevent accidental deployment (and possible injury), turn the ignition key to LOCK and disconnect the negative battery cable whenever working near airbag components. After the battery is disconnected, wait at least two minutes before beginning work (the system has a back-up capacitor that must fully discharge). For more information see Section 26.

1 Disconnect the cable from the negative battery terminal.
2 Remove the steering wheel (see Chapter 10). Remove the steering column upper and lower covers (see Chapter 11).
3 Remove the instrument cluster bezel (see Chapter 11).
4 Remove the instrument cluster retaining screws and pull the cluster away from the dashboard.
5 Disconnect the speedometer cable from the instrument cluster. **Note:** *Lubrication of a noisy speedometer cable may be done by injecting lithium grease or other suitable lubricant into the speedometer cable housing when disconnected from the instrument cluster.*

14.6 Remove the electrical connector and the speaker attaching screws to remove the speaker

6 Unplug the electrical connectors and remove the cluster.
7 Refitting is the reverse of removal.

17 Horn -
check and renewal

Check

1 Disconnect the electrical connector from the horn under the car.
2 Test the horn by carefully connecting battery voltage to the two horn terminals with jumper wires from the battery.
3 If the horn doesn't sound, renew it. If it does sound, the problem lies in the steering wheel horn switch, horn relay (see Section 5) or the wiring between components.

Renewal

4 Disconnect the electrical connector and remove the bracket bolt **(see illustration)**.
5 Refitting is the reverse of removal.

18 Wiper motor -
check and renewal

Note: *The project car was left-hand drive; component locations may vary.*

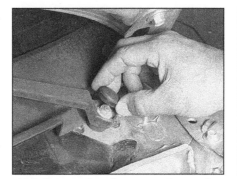

18.6 Remove the wiper arm nut cover for access to the retaining nut

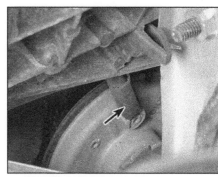

17.4 Disconnect the horn electrical connector (arrowed) and remove the horn mounting bolts

1 The windscreen wiper motor is located in the engine compartment. The rear wiper motor (Hatchback model only) is mounted in the rear hatchback door.

Check

Windscreen wiper/washer switch
2 Refer to Section 8 for the wiper and washer switch check procedure.

Wiper motor
3 If a motor doesn't work or doesn't park properly and the wiper switch checks okay, the relay or the motor must be replaced.

Renewal

Windscreen wiper motor
4 Disconnect the cable from the negative battery terminal.
5 Unplug the electrical connector from the wiper motor.
6 Remove the wiper arm plug for access to the wiper arm retaining nut **(see illustration)**. Remove the nut and lift the arm off the shaft.
7 Remove the cowl grille by removing the cowl grille fastener cover buttons and screws and remove the cowl grille **(see illustrations)**.

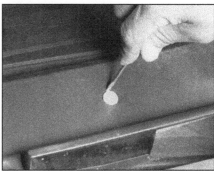

18.7a Remove the cowl grille buttons and screws

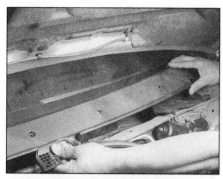
18.7b Lift the cowl grille

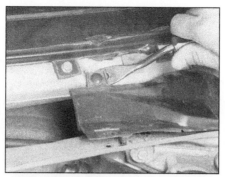
18.8 Remove the wiper linkage baffle

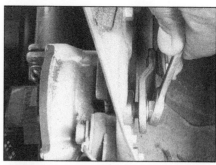
18.9 Remove the wiper motor to linkage nut and detach the linkage arm

18.11a Unbolt the wiper motor mounting bolts

18.11b Remove the wiper motor assembly

8 Remove the baffle (cover) over the wiper at the left (driver's) side **(see illustration)**.
9 Remove the wiper motor linkage nut from the wiper motor driveshaft **(see illustration)** and detach the linkage arm.
10 Mark the wiper motor bracket position before removing the motor from the bracket.
11 Remove the wiper motor bracket retaining bolts, then lower the wiper motor and bracket assembly and remove it from the vehicle **(see illustrations)**.
12 Refitting is the reverse of removal.

Rear wiper motor

13 Remove the wiper arm, then remove the shaft spindle nuts and washers. **Note:** *Clean the wiper arm spindle splines before refitting of the wiper arms.*
14 Unplug the electrical connector, detach the wiper linkage, remove the retaining bolts and lower the motor through the rear hatch access hole as an assembly.
15 Refitting is the reverse of removal.

19 Rear window demister switch - check and renewal

> *Warning: 1995 and later models are equipped with airbags. The airbag is armed and can inflate anytime the battery is connected. To prevent accidental deployment (and possible injury), turn the ignition key to LOCK and disconnect the negative battery cable whenever working near airbag components. After the battery is disconnected, wait at least two minutes before beginning work (the system has a back-up capacitor that must fully discharge). For more information see Section 25.*

1 Detach the cable from the negative battery terminal.
2 Remove the instrument cluster bezel (see

Section 17) and access the rear demister switch.
3 Use an ohmmeter to check for continuity at the indicated terminals with the switch in the indicated positions **(see illustration)**.
4 Renew the switch if the continuity is not as specified.

20 Rear window demister - check and repair

1 The rear window demister consists of a grid of horizontal heater filament elements baked onto the glass surface.
2 Small breaks in the element can be repaired without removing the rear window.

Check

3 Turn the ignition switch and demister system switches to ON.
4 Determine which side of the window demister heat grid is negative (connected to earth), and which side is positive (connected to 12 volts).
5 When measuring voltage during the next two tests, wrap a piece of aluminium foil around the tip of each voltmeter probe.
6 Press the foil-covered positive voltmeter probe against the positive side of the demister grid with your finger **(see illustration)**.
7 Using the voltmeter negative probe, check the voltage at the centre of each heater filament element **(see illustration)**. If the voltage is 5 volts, the wire is okay (there is no break). If the voltage is high (10 to 12 volts), the wire is broken between the centre of the

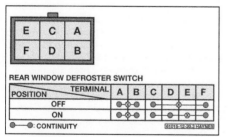
19.3 Rear window defogger switch terminal guide and continuity table

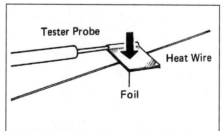
20.6 Wrap a piece of foil around the negative probe of the voltmeter and press it against the wire

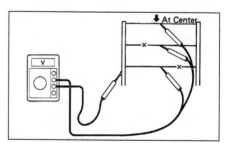
20.7 Check the voltage with the negative lead at the *centre* of each wire

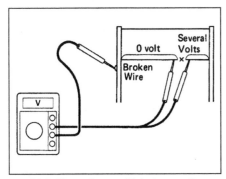

20.9 The point at which the needle deflects from zero to several volts is where the wire is broken

element and the positive end. If the voltage is 0-volts the wire is broken between the centre of the element and earth.

8 To find the break, place the voltmeter positive lead against the demister positive terminal.

9 Place the voltmeter negative lead with the foil strip against the heater wire at the positive terminal end and slide it toward the negative terminal end. The point at which the voltmeter deflects from zero to several volts is the point at which the heater filament element is broken **(see illustration)**. Make note of the location of the area of the heater filament break **Note:** *If the heat element is not broken, the voltmeter will indicate no voltage at the positive end of the heat element but gradually increase to about 12-volts.*

Repair

10 Repair the break in the element using a repair kit specifically recommended for this purpose.

11 Follow the instructions on the packet.

---

21 Cruise control system - description and check

Note: *The project car was left-hand drive; component locations may vary.*

1 The cruise control system maintains vehicle speed with a cruise control unit (computer), located in the passenger compartment under the dashboard behind the heater blower unit, a speed sensor to signal the cruise control unit, and an actuator located in the engine compartment. The actuator is connected to the throttle linkage by a cable. The cruise control system also consists of the steering wheel cruise control switches, speed sensor in the instrument cluster, brake light switch, clutch switch for vehicles with manual transmissions, and associated wiring **(see illustration)**. Some features of the system requires special testers and diagnostic procedures which are beyond the scope of the home mechanic. Listed below are some general procedures that may be used to locate common problems.

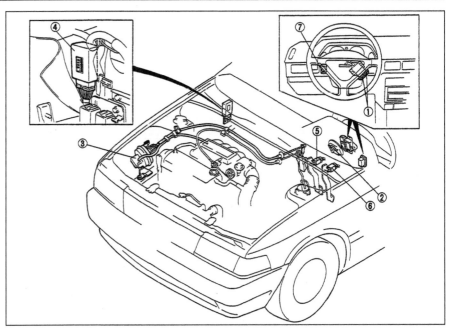

21.1 Typical cruise control system components

1	Cruise control switch	4	Cruise control unit	6	Clutch switch
2	Speed sensor	5	Brake light switch	7	Main switch
3	Actuator				

2 Check the cruise control fuse labelled METER (1994 and earlier models) which fuses the instrument panel and STOP fuse (1995 and later models), at the fuse box (see Section 3).

3 Have an assistant operate the brake pedal while you check the operation of the brake lights (voltage from the brake light and clutch switch on vehicles with manual transmission deactivates the cruise control).

4 If the brake lights don't come on or don't shut off, correct the problem and retest the cruise control. Check the clutch switch (Chapter 8).

5 Visually inspect the vacuum hose connected to the actuator, check the control cable between the cruise control actuator and the throttle linkage, and renew as necessary.

6 Check the control cable freeplay as follows: Remove the cable clip and adjust the nut so that the actuator control cable freeplay is approximately 0.8 mm (0.13 in) to

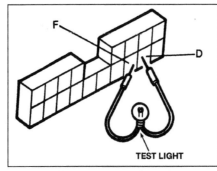

21.7 Cruise control unit electrical connector and test light hook up - 1994 and earlier shown

4.75 mm (0.19 in) when the cable is pressed lightly by your finger.

7 On 1994 and earlier models, a quick test of the remainder of the cruise control system is performed as follows, using a 1.4 watt test light with probes connected between terminals D and F of the cruise control connector **(see illustration)**, located under the dash on the cruise control unit behind the heater blower unit (see Chapter 3 for access). Connect the test light with the cruise control connector still connected to the cruise control unit, and with the Terminal D probe pushed through open Terminal D hole to the electrical connector pin on the control unit.

8 Turn the ignition switch ON, and shift the gear selector lever to D or R on automatic transmission vehicles, or to any gear except neutral on manual transmission vehicles. Check the cruise control Main switch is OFF (Main indicator light is OFF).

9 Press the Resume/Accel switch and the Main switch simultaneously to activate the system test. The Main indicator light will come on. Then operate each switch described below and obtain the two-digit problem code numbers (light flashes is the first digit of the problem code and then the second set of flashes is the second digit of the problem code). Example: Three flashes, a slight delay, then five flashes, indicates problem Code 35.

10 Pressing Set/Coast switch, problem Code 21 indicates trouble with the cruise control switch.

11 Pressing Resume/Accel switch, problem Code 22 indicates trouble with the cruise control switch.

12 Depressing brake pedal, problem Code 31 indicates trouble with the brake light switch.

13 Turning Ignition switch ON, shift the gear selector lever to P or N on automatic transmission vehicles, or depressing the clutch on manual transmission vehicles, problem Code 35 indicates trouble with the inhibitor switch (see Chapter 6) or clutch switch (see Chapter 8).

14 Test drive the vehicle above 25 mph, problem Code 37 indicates trouble with the speed sensor or trouble (electrical short or open) in the cruise control system wiring harness.

15 Finally, test drive the vehicle to determine if the cruise control is now operating properly. If the problem is not found with the above procedures, immediately take the vehicle to a dealer service department or an automotive electrical specialist for further diagnosis and repair.

22 Electric rear view mirrors - description and check

Note: *The project car was left-hand drive; component locations may vary.*

1 The electric rear view mirrors use two motors to move the glass; one for up-and-down adjustments and one for left-right adjustments.

2 The control switch has a selector portion which sends voltage to the left or right side mirror. With the ignition key in the ACC position, roll down the windows and operate the mirror control switch through all functions (left-right and up-down) for both the left and right side mirrors.

3 Listen carefully for the sound of the electric motors running in the mirrors.

4 If the motors can be heard but the mirror glass doesn't move, the drive mechanism inside the mirror is most likely defective. Remove and dismantle the mirror to locate the problem (see Chapter 11).

5 If the mirrors do not operate and no sound comes from the electric motors in the mirrors, check the radio fuse in the fuse box located under the left side of the dash (see Section 3).

6 If the radio fuse is okay, remove the mirror control switch on the dashboard and access the back of the mirror control switch without disconnecting the electrical connector. Turn the ignition ON and check for voltage at the switch. There should be voltage at one terminal.

7 If no voltage is measured at the mirror control switch, check for a short circuit or open in the wiring harness between the fuse panel and the mirror control switch.

8 If voltage is measured at the mirror control switch, disconnect the mirror control switch electrical connector and check wiring harness electrical connector side to check the electric outside mirrors for continuity between terminals A and C, C and D, A and L, and A and B **(see illustration)**. If continuity is not measured at any of these terminals, check the wiring harness and connectors in the doors to the electric outside mirrors. If the wiring is okay, renew the electric outside mirror(s).

9 Check the mirror control switch for continuity in all its operating positions **(see illustration)**. If the switch does not have continuity, it should be replaced.

23 Electric door lock system - description and check

Note: *The project car was left-hand drive; component locations may vary.*

1 The electric door lock system operates the door lock actuators mounted in each door. The system consists of the switches, actuators and associated wiring located in the doors and the relay located under the dash at the driver's side of the vehicle. Diagnosis can usually be limited to simple checks of the

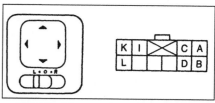

22.8 Electric rear view mirror driver's control switch and switch terminal guide

wiring connections and actuators for minor faults which can be easily repaired.

2 Electric door lock systems are operated by bi-directional actuator motors located in the doors. The lock switches have two operating positions: Lock and Unlock. These switches activate a timer unit which in turn connects voltage to the door lock actuator motors. Depending on which way the timer unit is activated, polarity is reversed, allowing the two sides of the circuit to be used alternately for Lock (down) and Unlock (up).

3 Always check the circuit protection first. The Room fuse provides circuit protection to the electric door lock switches. The door lock fuse protects the timer unit and actuator motors.

4 Operate the door lock switches in both directions (Lock and Unlock) with the engine off. Listen for the faint sound of the timer unit 'click' or the sound of the actuator motor in the door.

5 If no sound is heard, check for voltage at the door lock switches. If no voltage is present, check the wiring between the fuse box and the door lock switches for shorts and opens.

6 If voltage is present but no click or sound is heard, remove the door lock switch and test the switch for continuity. On 1995 and later models, insert a 1 k-ohm resistor between terminals A and B when testing for continuity in the switch Lock position. Renew the switch if there's no continuity in both switch positions **(see illustrations)**.

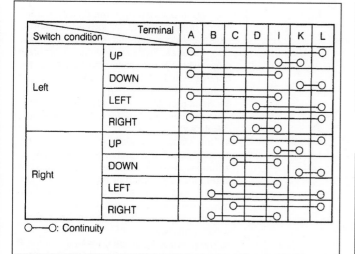

Switch condition	Terminal	A	B	C	D	I	K	L
Left	UP	O				O—O		O
	DOWN	O					O—O	O
	LEFT	O			O			O
	RIGHT	O			O			O
Right	UP			O		O—O		O
	DOWN			O			O—O	O
	LEFT	O		O				O
	RIGHT	O		O				O

O——O: Continuity

22.9 Electric rear view mirror driver's control switch continuity table

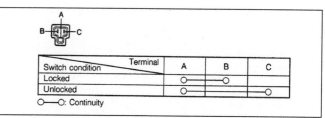

Switch condition	Terminal	A	B	C
Locked		O—O		
Unlocked			O—O	

O——O: Continuity

24.6a Electric door lock switch terminal guide and continuity table - 1994 and earlier

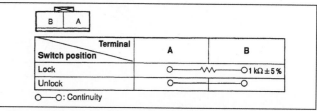

Switch position	Terminal	A	B
Lock		O—WW—O	1kΩ±5%
Unlock		O——O	

O——O: Continuity

23.6b Electric door lock switch terminal guide and continuity table - 1995 and later

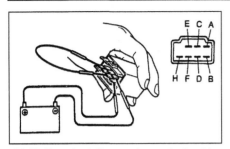

23.10 Door lock timer unit terminal guide and test connections - 1994 and earlier

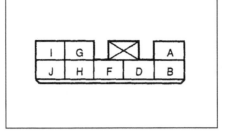

23.11 Door lock timer unit terminal guide - 1995 and later

7 If the switch has continuity but no sound is heard from the actuator motors in the doors, check the wiring between the switch and the timing unit for continuity. Also check the wiring between the timing unit and the actuator motors for continuity. Repair the wiring if no continuity is measured.

8 If all but one door lock actuator motor operates, remove the trim panel from the affected door (see Chapter 11) and check for voltage at the actuator motor while the door lock switch is operated. One of the connector terminals should have voltage in the Lock position; the other should have voltage in the Unlock position.

9 If the inoperative actuator motor is receiving voltage, but fails to operate, renew the actuator motor.

10 If none of the door lock actuator motors operate, or if they only operate electrically one direction (either up or down only), check the timer unit by using jumpers from the battery **(see illustration)**. The timer unit is located under the driver's left side trim panel in front of the door opening. On 1994 and earlier models, disconnect the timer unit and connect a test wire from the positive battery terminal to the timer unit terminal B, and the timer unit terminal A to earth (negative battery terminal, then connect a jumper wire between timer unit terminals H and D or H and C. The door timer unit should click. If the timer unit does not click, renew the timer unit.

11 On 1995 and later models, do not disconnect the timer unit. Use a voltmeter with the negative test lead to vehicle earth. Backprobe the timer unit terminals and check the following terminals under the indicated conditions **(see illustration)**:

a) *Terminal A - when actuator is moved to locked position, applied voltage should go from 0-volts to 12-volts then back to 0-volts.*

b) *Terminal B - when driver's door lock actuator is moved to unlocked position, applied voltage should go from 0-volts to 12-volts then back to 0-volts.*

c) *Terminal F - when actuator door lock is moved to unlocked position, applied voltage should go from 0-volts to 12-volts then back to 0-volts.*

d) *Terminal G - when actuator door lock is moved to unlocked position, applied voltage should go from 12-volts to 0-volts then back to 12-volts.*

e) *Terminal H - when actuator door lock is moved to locked position, applied voltage should go from 12-volts to 0-volts then back to 12-volts.*

f) *Terminal I - should measure 12-volts.*

g) *Terminal J - when connected to earth should have continuity at all times.*

Note: *It is common for door lock harness wires to break in the portion of the harness between the body and door (opening and closing the door fatigues and may eventually break the wires).*

24 Electric window system - description and check

1 The electric window system operates the electric motors mounted in the doors which lower and raise the windows. The system consists of the control switches, the motors (regulators), glass mechanisms and associated wiring **(see illustration)**.

2 Electric windows are wired so they can be lowered and raised from the driver's control switch or by sub-switches located at the front passenger door, and both rear doors on four-door vehicles. Each window has a separate motor which is reversible. The position of the control switch determines the polarity and therefore the direction of motor operation.

3 Circuit protection is provided by the electric window fuse in the fuse box under the dashboard.

4 The electric window system will only operate when the ignition switch is ON. In addition, when OFF, the electric window safety lockout switch at the driver's control switch disables the switches at the passenger's window also. Always check this switch before troubleshooting an electric window problem.

5 These procedures are general in nature. If you cannot locate the problem, take the vehicle to a dealer service department or other qualified repair facility.

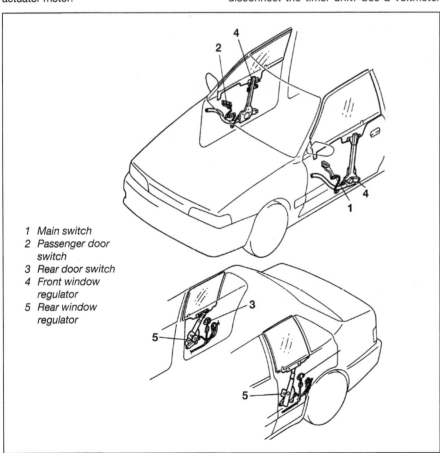

1 *Main switch*
2 *Passenger door switch*
3 *Rear door switch*
4 *Front window regulator*
5 *Rear window regulator*

24.1 Typical electric window system components

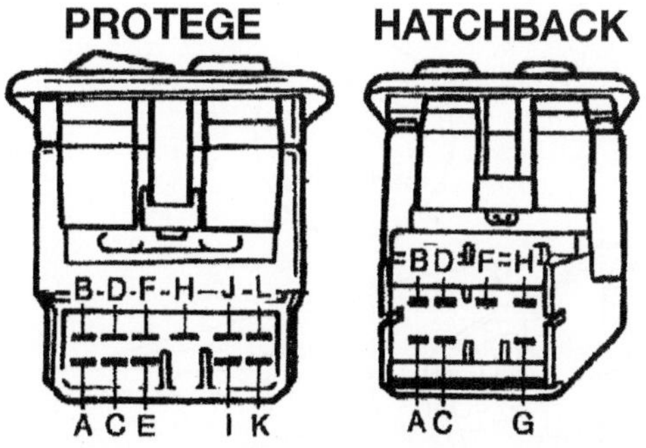

Switch condition \ Terminal	PROTEGE A	PROTEGE F	Hatchback H	Hatchback G
ON	O—	—O	O—	—O
OFF				

O—O: Continuity

24.7 Electric window safety lockout switch terminal guide and continuity table

6 If the electric windows don't work at all, check the electric window fuse in the fuse box.

7 If only the rear windows are inoperative, or if the windows only operate from the driver's control switch, check the electric window safety lockout switch for continuity in the unlocked position **(see illustration)**. Renew the switch if no continuity is measured.

8 Check the wiring between the switches and fuse box for continuity. Repair the wiring, if necessary.

9 If only one window is inoperative from the driver's control switch, try the other control switch at the window. **Note:** *This does not apply to the driver's door window.*

10 If the same window works from one switch, but not the other, check the non-operative switch for continuity **(see illustrations)**.

11 If the switch tests OK, check for a short or open in the wiring between the affected switch and the window motor.

12 If one window is inoperative from both switches, remove the trim panel from the non-operative door and check for voltage at the motor while the switch is operated.

13 If voltage is reaching the motor, disconnect the glass from the regulator (see Chapter 11). Move the window up and down by hand while checking for binding and damage. Also check for binding and damage to the regulator. If the regulator is not damaged and the window moves up and down smoothly, renew the motor. If binding or damage is found, lubricate and repair or renew parts, as necessary.

14 If voltage is not measured at window motor, check the wiring in the circuit for continuity between the switches and motors. Consult the wiring diagram for the vehicle. Check that each switch applies voltage to the motor when the switch is turned on. If voltage is not applied, renew the window motor.

15 Test all electric windows after repair to confirm proper operation.

Switch	Front·LH				Front·RH				Rear·LH				Rear·RH			
Terminal PROTEGE	A	B	D	H	A	H	J	L	A	C	E	H	A	H	I	K
Switch condition / Terminal Hatchback	H	F	C	D	H	D	A	B								
UP	O		O		O		O		O	O			O			O
		O		O		O		O			O	O		O	O	
OFF		O	O	O		O	O	O		O	O	O		O	O	O
DOWN	O	O				O	O		O		O		O		O	
			O	O	O			O		O		O		O		O

O—O: Continuity

24.10a Electric window driver's control switch continuity table - 1994 and earlier

M	K	I	☒		C	A
N	L	J	H	F	D	B

Switch position \ Terminal	Driver L	Driver N	Driver H	Driver F	Passenger D	Passenger B	Passenger H	Passenger F	Left rear M	Left rear K	Left rear J	Left rear F	Right rear A	Right rear C	Right rear J	Right rear F
UP	O		O		O		O		O		O		O		O	
		O		O		O		O		O		O		O		O
OFF (with power-cut switch at ON)	O	O		O	O	O		O	O	O		O	O	O		O
DOWN		O	O			O	O			O	O			O	O	
	O			O	O			O	O			O	O			O
AUTO DOWN		O	O													
	O			O												

O—O: Continuity

24.10b Electric window driver's control switch terminal guide and continuity table - 1995 and later

E	☒	A
F	D	B

Switch position \ Terminal	A	B	D	E	F
UP		O	O		
	O			O	
OFF	O			O	
			O		O
DOWN		O		O	
			O		O

O—O: Continuity

24.10c Electric window passenger control switch terminal guide and continuity table - 1995 and later

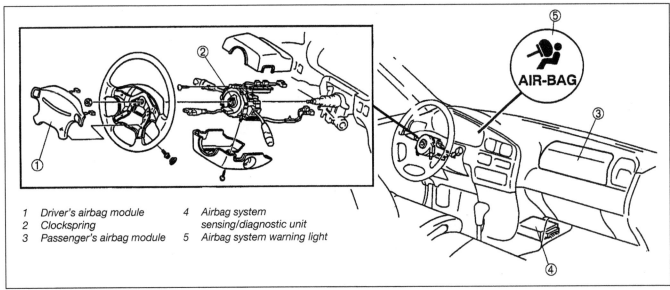

1 Driver's airbag module
2 Clockspring
3 Passenger's airbag module
4 Airbag system sensing/diagnostic unit
5 Airbag system warning light

25.1 Typical airbag system components

25 Airbag system - general information

The 1995 and later models are equipped with a Supplemental Restraint System (SRS), more commonly known as 'airbags.' This system is designed to protect the driver and front seat passenger from serious injury in the event of a head-on or frontal collision. It consists of airbag modules in the centre of the steering wheel and the passenger side of the instrument panel, and a sensing/diagnostic unit located inside the passenger compartment **(see illustration)**.

Airbag modules

The airbag modules contain a housing incorporating the cushion (airbag) and inflator unit. The inflator assembly is mounted on the back of the housing over a hole through which gas is expelled, inflating the bag almost instantaneously when an electrical signal is sent from the system. The specially wound wire that carries this signal to the driver's module is called a clockspring. The clockspring is a flat, ribbon-like electrically conductive tape which is wound many times so that It can transmit an electrical signal regardless of steering wheel position.

Central airbag sensing/diagnostic unit

The airbag sensing/diagnostic unit contains the safing sensor and an on-board microprocessor which monitors the operation of the system. It checks this system every time the vehicle is started, causing the AIRBAG warning light to go on, then off, if the system is operating properly. If there is a fault in the system, the light will go on and stay on and the airbag sensing/diagnostic unit will store fault codes indicating the nature of the fault. If the AIRBAG light goes on and stays on, the vehicle should be taken to your dealer immediately for service.

Servicing components near the airbag system

Nevertheless, there are times when you need to remove the steering wheel, radio or service other components on or near the instrument panel. At these times, you'll be working around components and wiring harnesses for the airbag system. Airbag system wiring is easy to identify; they're all covered by a bright yellow conduit. Do not unplug the connectors for the airbag system wiring, except to disable the system. And do not use electrical test equipment on the airbag system wiring. **ALWAYS DISABLE THE AIRBAG SYSTEM BEFORE WORKING NEAR THE AIRBAG SYSTEM COMPONENTS OR RELATED WIRING.**

Disabling the airbag system

1 Turn the steering wheel to the straight ahead position, place the ignition switch in Lock and remove the key.

2 Disconnect the cable from the negative battery terminal.

3 Wait two minutes for the back-up capacitor to discharge.

Enabling the airbag system

4 Connect the cable to the negative battery terminal.

5 Turn the ignition key to ON and verify that the AIRBAG warning light comes on for approximately six seconds, then goes off.

26 Wiring diagrams

Since it is not possible to include all wiring diagrams for every year covered by this manual, the following diagrams are those that are typical and most commonly needed.

Prior to troubleshooting any circuits, check the fuse and circuit breakers to make sure they are in good condition. Make sure the battery is properly charged and has clean, tight cable connections (see Chapter 1).

When checking the wiring system, make sure that all electrical connectors are clean, with no broken or loose pins. When unplugging an electrical connector, do not pull on the wires, only on the connector housings themselves.

Key to symbols

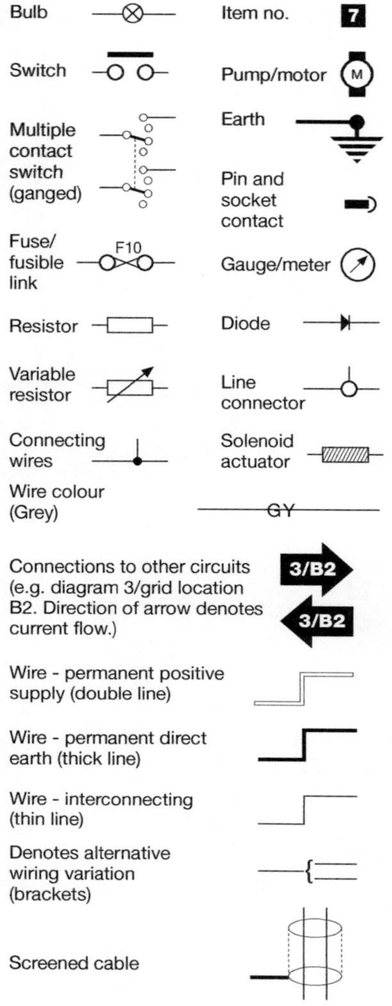
Bulb
Item no.
7
Switch
Pump/motor
M
Multiple contact switch (ganged)
Earth
Pin and socket contact
Fuse/ fusible link
F10
Gauge/meter
Resistor
Diode
Variable resistor
Line connector
Connecting wires
Solenoid actuator
Wire colour (Grey)
GY
Connections to other circuits (e.g. diagram 3/grid location B2. Direction of arrow denotes current flow.)
3/B2
3/B2
Wire - permanent positive supply (double line)
Wire - permanent direct earth (thick line)
Wire - interconnecting (thin line)
Denotes alternative wiring variation (brackets)
Screened cable

Typical engine fusebox (in engine compartment)

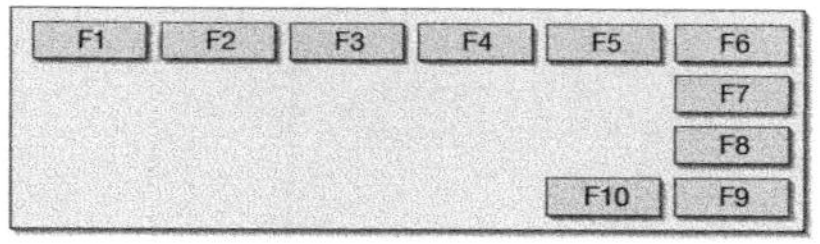
F1
F2
F3
F4
F5
F6
F7
F8
F10
F9

Typical engine fusebox (carburetor models)

Fuse	*Rating*	*Colour*	*Circuit protected*
F1	30A	Pink	PTC heater
F2	30A	Pink	Headlights
F3	80A	Black	Main fuse - protection of all circuits
F4	60A	Yellow	Hazard, interior, door lock, brake and tail lights, Alternator
F5	-		Not used
F6	30A	Pink	Cooling fan
F7	20A	Yellow	Additional cooling fan for air conditioning
F8	-		Not used
F9	-		Not used
F10	-		Not used

Typical engine fusebox (fuel injection models)

Fuse	*Rating*	*Colour*	*Circuit protected*
F1	30A	Pink	Fuel injection system
F2	30A	Pink	Headlights
F3	80A	Black	Main fuse - protection of all circuits
F4	60A	Yellow	Hazard, interior, door lock, brake and tail lights, Alternator
F5	60A	Yellow	Anti-lock brake system
F6	30A	Pink	Cooling fan
F7	20A	Yellow	Additional cooling fan for air conditioning
F8	-		Not used
F9	10A	Red	Engine control unit
F10	30A	Green	ABS valve

Typical passenger fusebox (in passenger compartment)

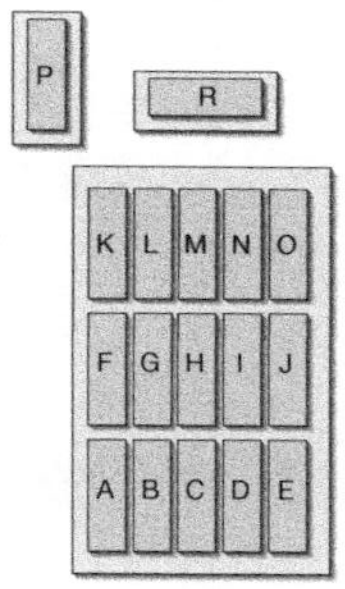
P
R
K
L
M
N
O
F
G
H
I
J
A
B
C
D
E

Typical passenger fusebox

Fuse	*Rating*	*Colour*	*Circuit protected*
A	10A	Red	Rear wiper and washer
B	10A	Red	Hazard warning
C	10A	Red	Clock, interior light, luggage compartment light
D	15A	Blue	Engine control system
E	15A	Blue	Radio (cassette), electric mirror, cigarette lighter
F	30A	Green	Central locking
G	7.5A	Brown	Dim-dip lights
H	30A	Green	Electric windows
i	10A	Red	Gauges, reversing lights indicators
J	20A	Yellow	Windscreen wipers and washers
K	15A	Blue	Brake lights, horn
L	10A	Red	Rear lights, parking lights, instrument cluster illumination, number plate light
M	15A	Blue	Sunroof
N	-		Not used
O	20A	Yellow	Rear window demister
P	10A	Red	Rear fog lights
Q	-	-	Not used
Circuit breaker			
R	30A		Heater fan motor

H29676
C. J. TURK

Diagram 1 : Information for wiring diagrams - up to 1995

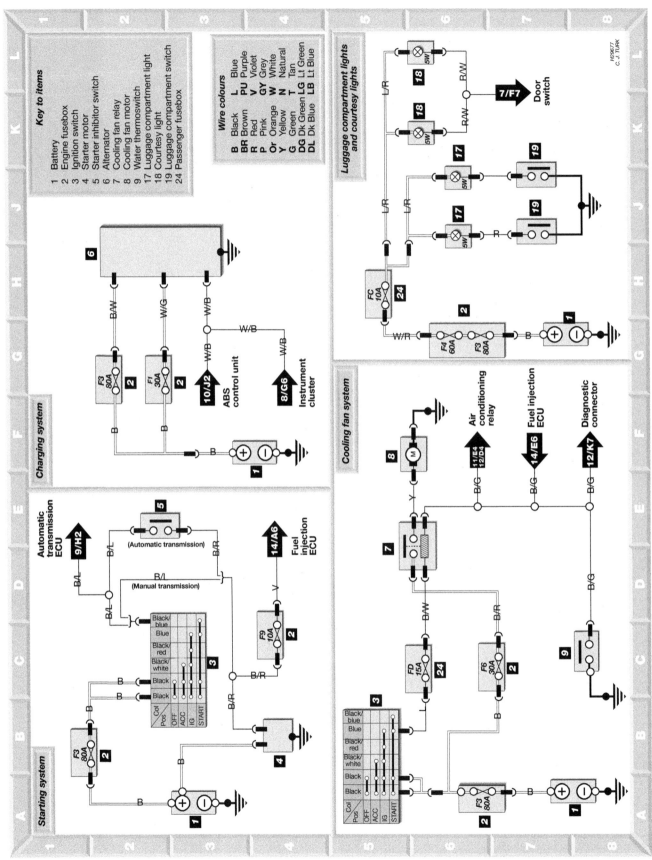

Diagram 2 : Typical starting, charging, cooling fan, luggage compartment and courtesy lights - up to 1995

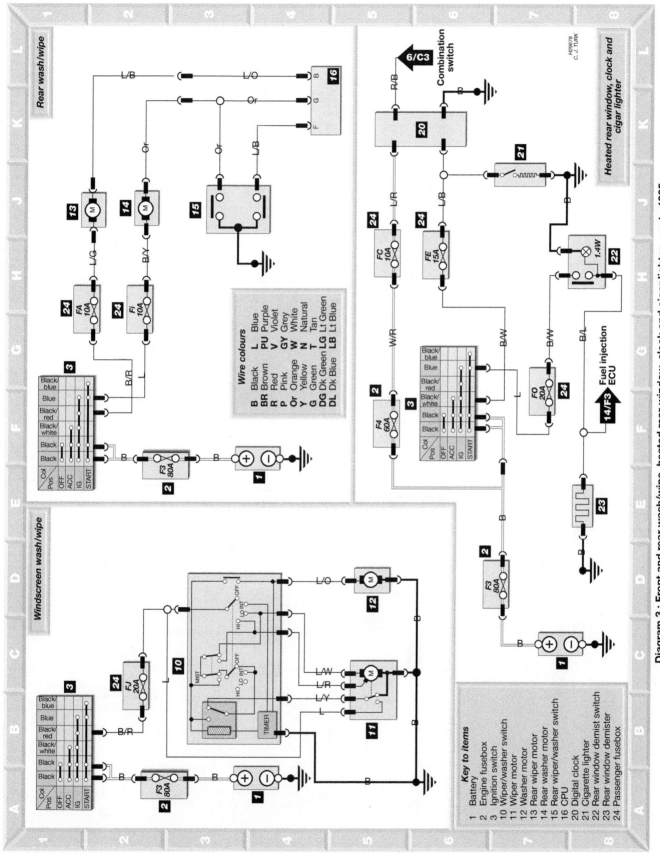

Rear wash/wipe

Windscreen wash/wipe

Heated rear window, clock and cigar lighter

6/C3 Combination switch

Fuel injection ECU 14/F3

Wire colours

B	Black	L	Blue
BR	Brown	PU	Purple
R	Red	V	Violet
P	Pink	GY	Grey
Or	Orange	W	White
Y	Yellow	N	Natural
G	Green	T	Tan
DG	Dk Green	LG	Lt Green
DL	Dk Blue	LB	Lt Blue

Key to items

1 Battery
2 Engine fusebox
3 Ignition switch
10 Wiper/washer switch
11 Wiper motor
12 Washer motor
13 Rear wiper motor
14 Rear washer motor
15 Rear wiper/washer switch
16 CPU
20 Digital clock
21 Cigarette lighter
22 Rear window demist switch
23 Rear window demister
24 Passenger fusebox

H29678
C. J. TURK

Diagram 3 : Front and rear wash/wipe, heated rear window, clock and cigar lighter – up to 1995

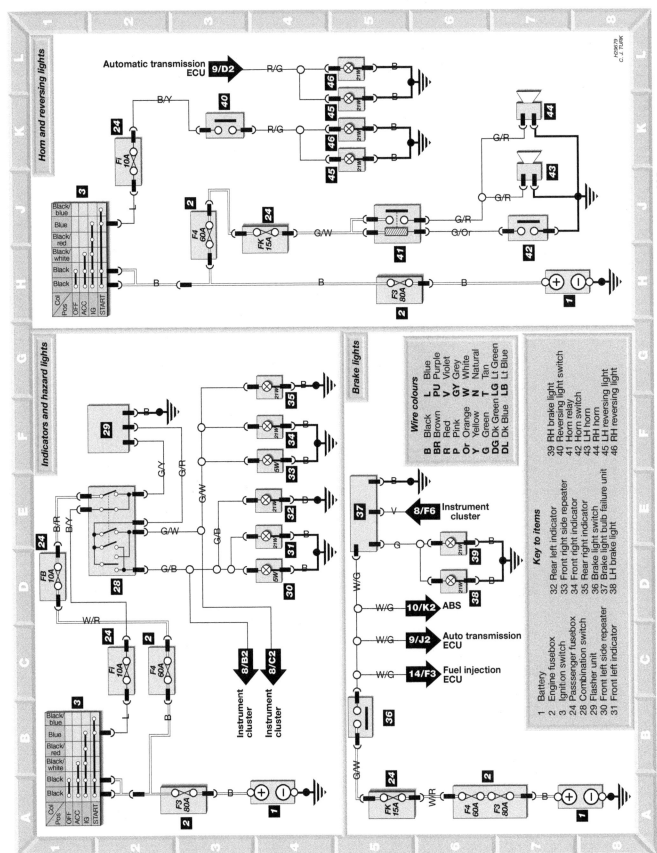

H29679
C. J. TURK

Diagram 4 : Indicators and hazard warning lights, brake lights, horn and reversing lights - up to 1995

Wire colours

B	Black	L	Blue
BR	Brown	PU	Purple
R	Red	V	Violet
P	Pink	GY	Grey
Or	Orange	W	White
Y	Yellow	N	Natural
G	Green	T	Tan
DG	Dk Green	LG	Lt Green
DL	Dk Blue	LB	Lt Blue

Key to items

1 Battery
2 Engine fusebox
3 Ignition switch
24 Passsenger fusebox
28 Combination switch
29 Flasher unit
30 Front left side repeater
31 Front left indicator
32 Rear left indicator
33 Front right side repeater
34 Front right indicator
35 Rear right indicator
36 Brake light switch
37 Brake light bulb failure unit
38 LH brake light
39 RH brake light
40 Reversing light switch
41 Horn relay
42 Horn switch
43 LH horn
44 RH horn
45 LH reversing light
46 RH reversing light

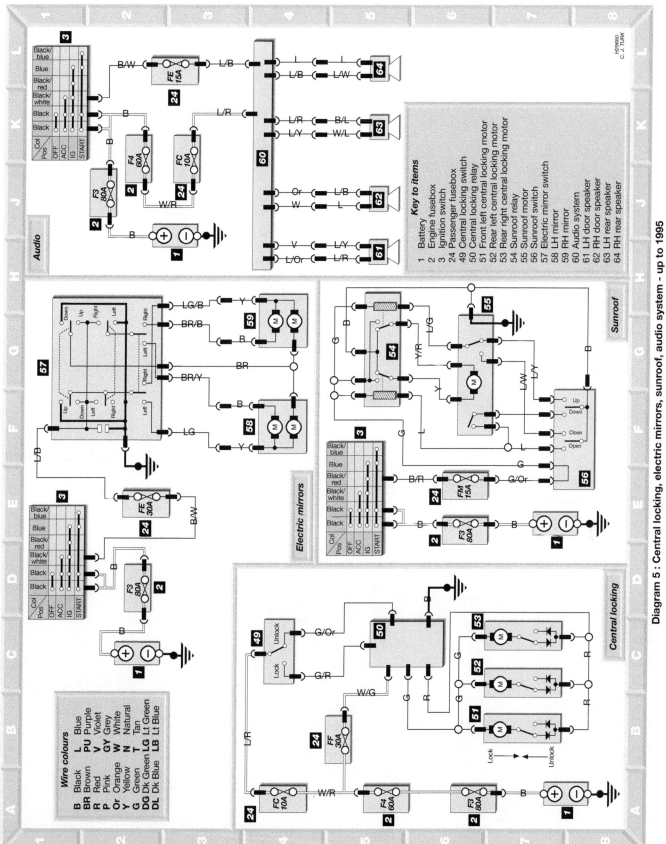

Diagram 5 : Central locking, electric mirrors, sunroof, audio system - up to 1995

H29680
C. J. TURK

Key to items

1 Battery
2 Engine fusebox
3 Ignition switch
24 Passenger fusebox
49 Central locking switch
50 Central locking relay
51 Front left central locking motor
52 Rear left central locking motor
53 Rear right central locking motor
54 Sunroof relay
55 Sunroof motor
56 Sunroof switch
57 Electric mirror switch
58 LH mirror
59 RH mirror
60 Audio system
61 LH door speaker
62 RH door speaker
63 LH rear speaker
64 RH rear speaker

Wire colours

B Black
BR Brown
R Red
P Pink
Or Orange
Y Yellow
G Green
DG Dk Green
DL Dk Blue
L Blue
PU Purple
V Violet
GY Grey
W White
N Natural
T Tan
LG Lt Green
LB Lt Blue

Audio

Electric mirrors

Sunroof

Central locking

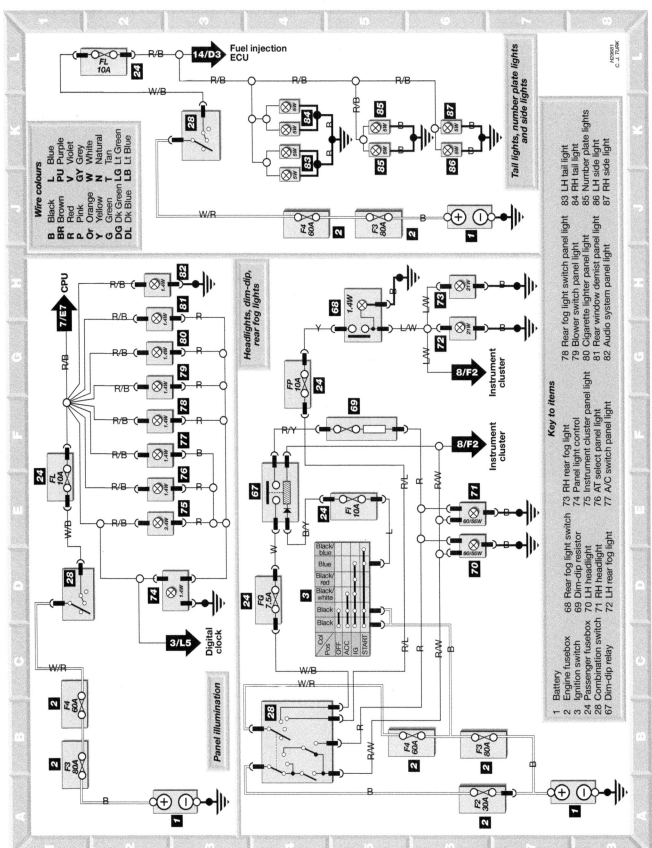

Diagram 6 : Exterior and interior lighting – up to 1995

Wire colours

B	Black	L	Blue
BR	Brown	PU	Purple
R	Red	V	Violet
P	Pink	GY	Grey
Or	Orange	W	White
Y	Yellow	N	Natural
G	Green	T	Tan
DG	Dk Green	LG	Lt Green
DL	Dk Blue	LB	Lt Blue

Key to items

1 Battery
2 Engine fusebox
3 Passenger fusebox
24 Combination switch
28 Dim-dip relay
67 Dim-dip relay
68 Rear fog light switch
69 Dim-dip resistor
70 LH headlight
71 RH headlight
72 LH rear fog light
73 RH rear fog light
74 Panel light control
75 Instrument cluster panel light
76 AT select panel light
77 A/C switch panel light
78 Rear fog light switch panel light
79 Blower switch panel light
80 Cigarette lighter panel light
81 Rear window demist panel light
82 Audio system panel light
83 LH tail light
84 RH tail light
85 Number plate lights
86 LH side light
87 RH side light

Fuel injection ECU

Tail lights, number plate lights and side lights

Headlights, dim-dip, rear fog lights

Instrument cluster

Instrument cluster

Panel illumination

Digital clock

H29881
C. J. TURK

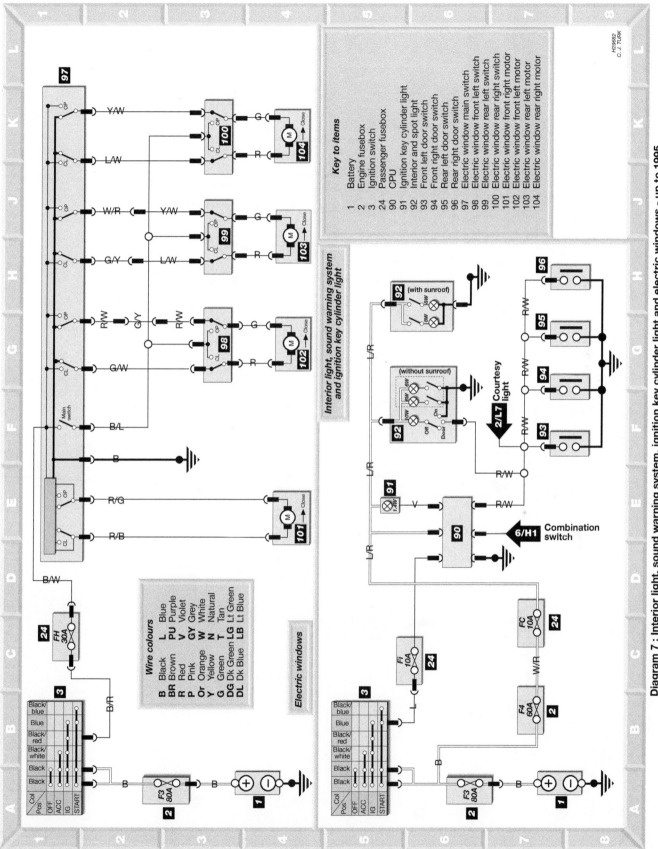

Key to items

1 Battery
2 Engine fusebox
3 Ignition switch
24 Passenger fusebox
90 CPU
91 Ignition key cylinder light
92 Interior and spot light
93 Front left door switch
94 Front right door switch
95 Rear left door switch
96 Rear right door switch
97 Electric window main switch
98 Electric window front left switch
99 Electric window rear left switch
100 Electric window front right switch
101 Electric window front left motor
102 Electric window front right motor
103 Electric window rear left motor
104 Electric window rear right motor

Interior light, sound warning system and ignition key cylinder light

Electric windows

Wire colours

B	Black	L	Blue
BR	Brown	PU	Purple
R	Red	V	Violet
P	Pink	GY	Grey
Or	Orange	W	White
Y	Yellow	N	Natural
G	Green	T	Tan
DG	Dk Green	LG	Lt Green
DL	Dk Blue	LB	Lt Blue

Diagram 7 : Interior light, sound warning system, ignition key cylinder light and electric windows – up to 1995

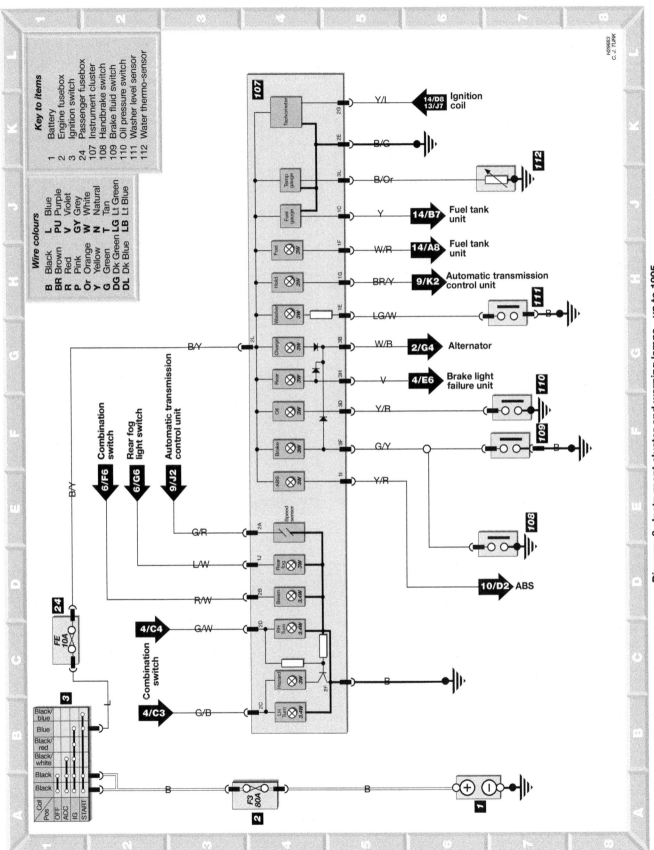

Diagram 8 : Instrument cluster and warning lamps - up to 1995

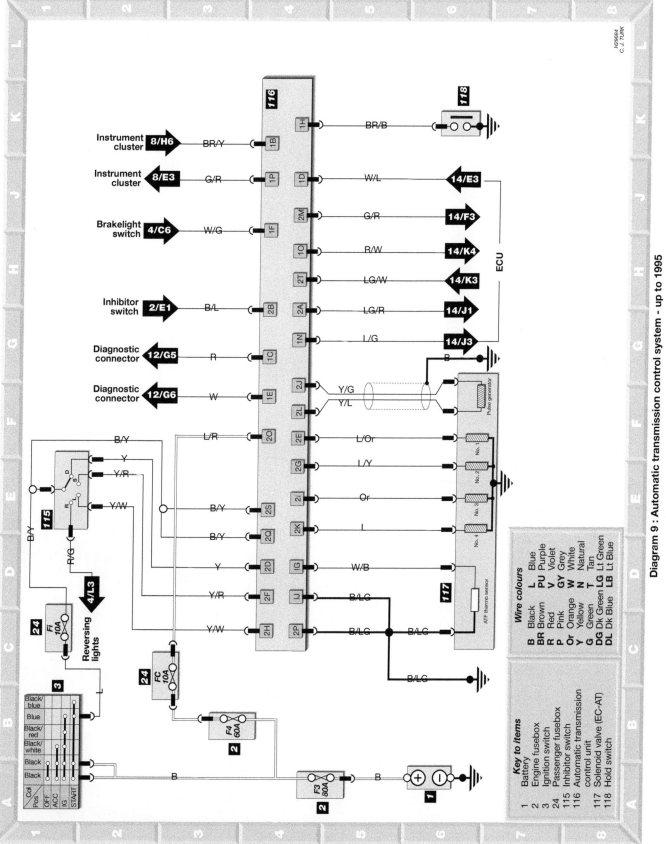

Diagram 9 : Automatic transmission control system - up to 1995

Wire colours

B	Black	L	Blue
BR	Brown	PU	Purple
R	Red	V	Violet
P	Pink	GY	Grey
Or	Orange	W	White
Y	Yellow	N	Natural
G	Green	T	Tan
DG	Dk Green	LG	Lt Green
DL	Dk Blue	LB	Lt Blue

Key to items

1 Battery
2 Engine fusebox
3 Ignition switch
24 Passenger fusebox
115 Inhibitor switch
116 Automatic transmission control unit
117 Solenoid valve (EC-AT)
118 Hold switch

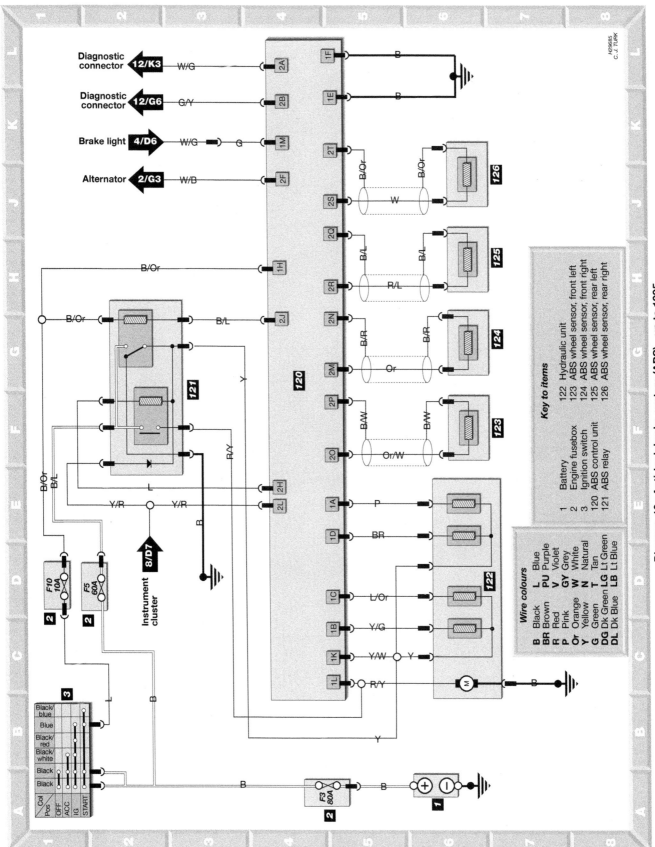

Diagram 10 : Anti-lock brake system (ABS) - up to 1995

Key to items

122 Hydraulic unit
123 ABS wheel sensor, front left
124 ABS wheel sensor, front right
125 ABS wheel sensor, rear left
126 ABS wheel sensor, rear right

1 Battery
2 Engine fusebox
3 Ignition switch
120 ABS control unit
121 ABS relay

Wire colours

B Black	**L** Blue		
BR Brown	**PU** Purple		
R Red	**V** Violet		
P Pink	**GY** Grey		
Or Orange	**W** White		
Y Yellow	**N** Natural		
G Green	**T** Tan		
DG Dk Green	**LG** Lt Green		
DL Dk Blue	**LB** Lt Blue		

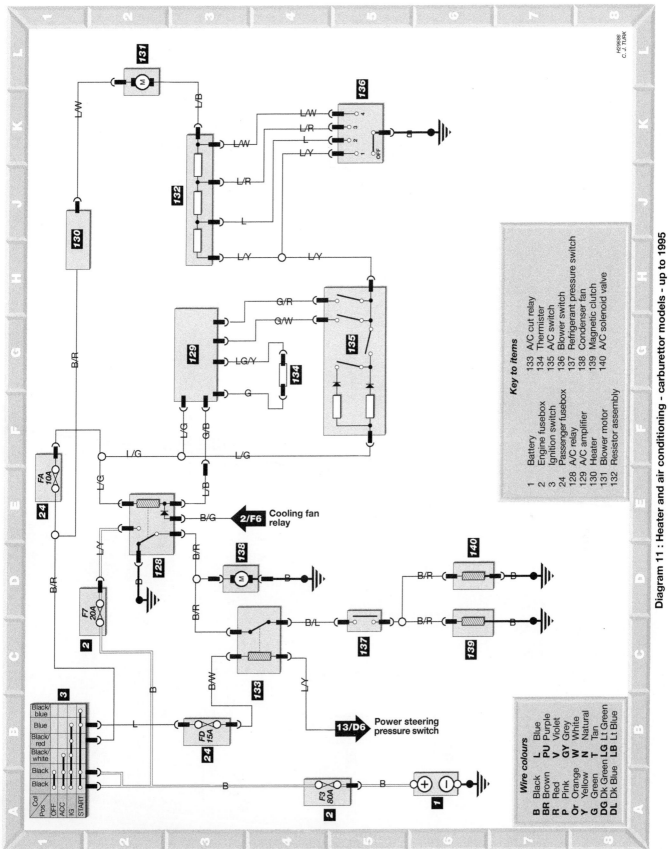

Diagram 11 : Heater and air conditioning - carburettor models - up to 1995

Key to items

1	Battery
2	Engine fusebox
3	Ignition switch
24	Passenger fusebox
128	A/C relay
129	A/C amplifier
130	Heater
131	Blower motor
132	Resistor assembly
133	A/C cut relay
134	Thermister
135	A/C switch
136	Blower switch
137	Refrigerant pressure switch
138	Condenser fan
139	Magnetic clutch
140	A/C solenoid valve

Wire colours

B	Black	**L**	Blue
BR	Brown	**PU**	Purple
R	Red	**V**	Violet
P	Pink	**GY**	Grey
Or	Orange	**W**	White
Y	Yellow	**N**	Natural
G	Green	**T**	Tan
DG	Dk Green	**LG**	Lt Green
DL	Dk Blue	**LB**	Lt Blue

Cooling fan relay 2/F6

Power steering pressure switch 13/D6

H20686
C.J. TURK

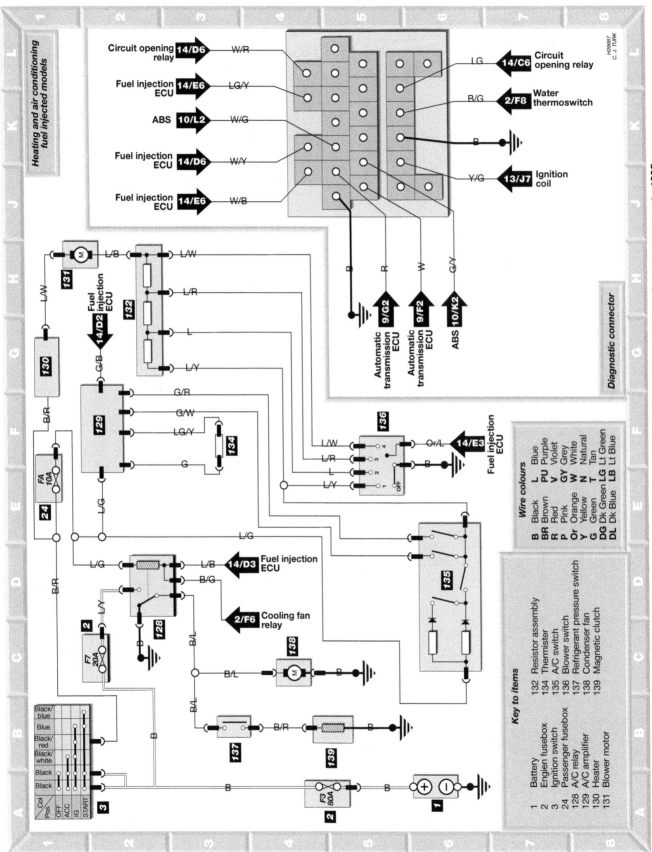

Diagram 12 : Heater and air conditioning - fuel injection models and diagnostic connector - up to 1995

Heating and air conditioning fuel injected models

Circuit opening relay **14/D6** W/R
Fuel injection ECU **14/E6** LG/Y
ABS **10/L2** W/G
Fuel injection ECU **14/D6** W/Y
Fuel injection ECU **14/E6** W/B

LG **14/C6** Circuit opening relay
B/G **2/F8** Water thermoswitch
Y/G **13/J7** Ignition coil

Automatic transmission ECU **9/G2**
Automatic transmission ECU **9/F2**
ABS **10/K2**

Diagnostic connector

Fuel injection ECU **14/D2**

Fuel injection ECU **14/E3**

Fuel injection ECU **14/D3**

Cooling fan relay **2/F6**

Wire colours

B	Black	**L**	Blue	**PU** Purple
BR	Brown	**V**	Violet	
R	Red	**GY**	Grey	
P	Pink	**W**	White	
Or	Orange	**N**	Natural	
Y	Yellow	**T**	Tan	
G	Green	**DG** Dk Green **LG** Lt Green		
		DL Dk Blue **LB** Lt Blue		

Key to items

1	Battery
2	Engien fusebox
3	Ignition switch
24	Passenger fusebox
128	A/C relay
129	A/C amplifier
130	Heater
131	Blower motor
132	Resistor assembly
134	Thermister
135	A/C switch
136	Blower switch
137	Refrigerant pressure switch
138	Condenser fan
139	Magnetic clutch

Col Pos OFF ACC IG START

Black/ blue
Blue
Black/ red
Black/ white
Black
Black

H29687
C.J.TURK

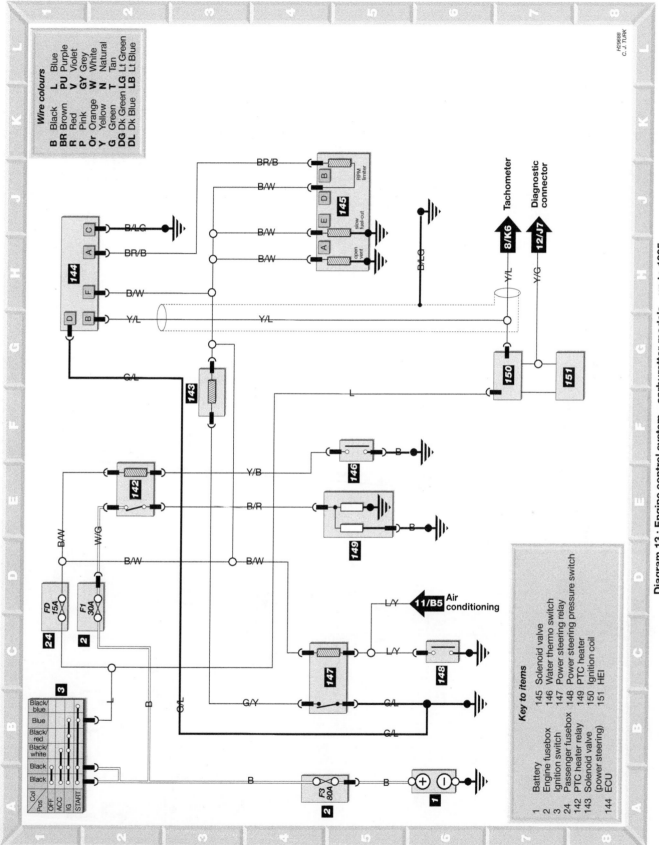

Diagram 13 : Engine control system – carburettor models – up to 1995

Wire colours

B	Black	L	Blue
BR	Brown	PU	Purple
R	Red	V	Violet
P	Pink	GY	Grey
Or	Orange	W	White
Y	Yellow	N	Natural
G	Green	T	Tan
DG	Dk Green	LG	Lt Green
DL	Dk Blue	LB	Lt Blue

Key to items

1	Battery	145	Solenoid valve
2	Engine fusebox	146	Water thermo switch
3	Ignition switch	147	Power steering relay
24	Passenger fusebox	148	Power steering pressure switch
142	PTC heater relay	149	PTC heater
143	Solenoid valve	150	Ignition coil
	(power steering)	151	HEI
144	ECU		

Tachometer **8/K6**

Diagnostic connector **12/J7**

Air conditioning **11/B5**

H29688
C. J. TURK

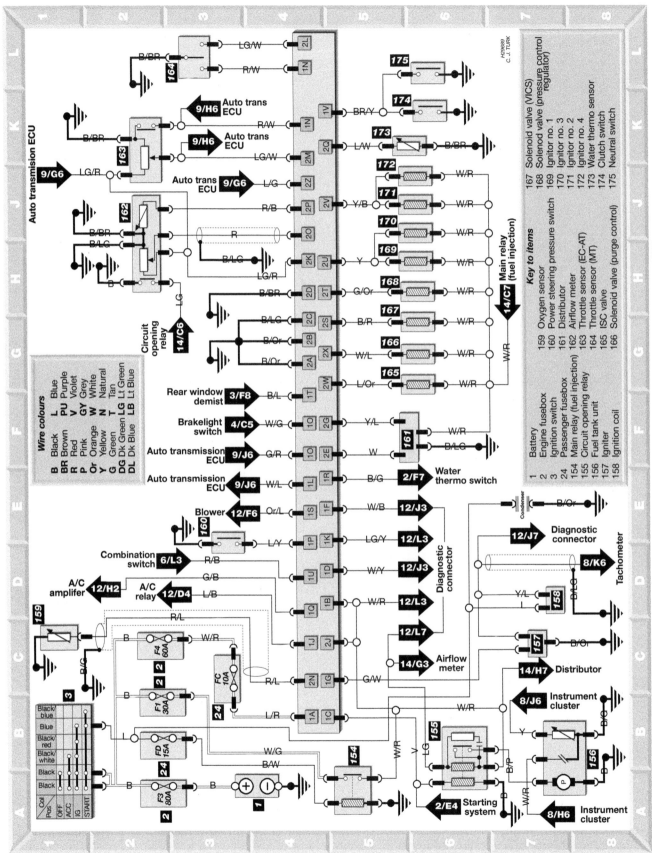

Diagram 14 : Engine control system - fuel injection models - up to 1995

Key to items

1	Battery
2	Engine fusebox
3	Ignition switch
24	Passenger fusebox
154	Main relay (fuel injection)
155	Circuit opening relay
156	Fuel tank unit
157	Igniter
158	Ignition coil
159	Oxygen sensor
160	Power steering pressure switch
161	Distributor
162	Airflow meter
163	Throttle sensor (EC-AT)
164	Throttle sensor (MT)
165	ISC valve
166	Solenoid valve (purge control)
167	Solenoid valve (VICS)
168	Solenoid valve (pressure control regulator)
169	Ignitor no. 1
170	Ignitor no. 3
171	Ignitor no. 2
172	Ignitor no. 4
173	Water thermo sensor
174	Clutch switch
175	Neutral switch

Wire colours

B	Black	L	Blue
BR	Brown	PU	Purple
R	Red	V	Violet
P	Pink	GY	Grey
Or	Orange	W	White
Y	Yellow	N	Natural
G	Green	T	Tan
DG	Dk Green	LG	Lt Green
DL	Dk Blue	LB	Lt Blue

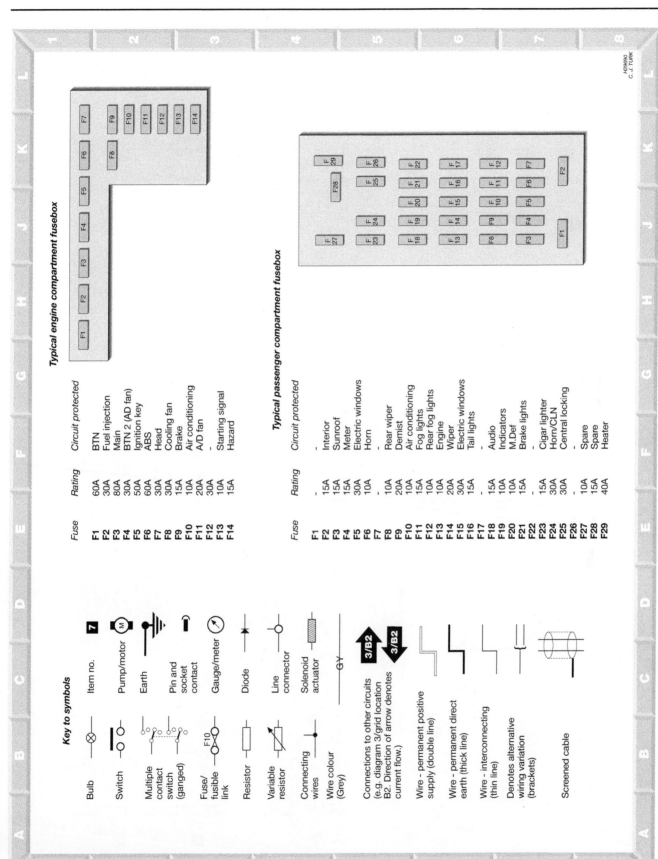

Typical engine compartment fusebox

Fuse	Rating	Circuit protected
F1	60A	BTN
F2	30A	Fuel injection
F3	80A	Main
F4	30A	BTN 2 (AD fan)
F5	50A	Ignition key
F6	60A	ABS
F7	30A	Head
F8	30A	Cooling fan
F9	15A	Brake
F10	10A	Air conditioning
F11	20A	A/D fan
F12	30A	-
F13	10A	Starting signal
F14	15A	Hazard

Typical passenger compartment fusebox

Fuse	Rating	Circuit protected
F1	-	-
F2	15A	Interior
F3	15A	Sunroof
F4	15A	Meter
F5	30A	Electric windows
F6	10A	Horn
F7	-	-
F8	10A	Rear wiper
F9	20A	Demist
F10	10A	Air conditioning
F11	15A	Fog lights
F12	10A	Rear fog lights
F13	10A	Engine
F14	20A	Wiper
F15	30A	Electric windows
F16	15A	Tail lights
F17	-	-
F18	15A	Audio
F19	10A	Indicators
F20	10A	M.Def
F21	15A	Brake lights
F22	-	-
F23	15A	Cigar lighter
F24	30A	Horn/CLN
F25	30A	Central locking
F26	-	-
F27	10A	Spare
F28	15A	Spare
F29	40A	Heater

Key to symbols

Bulb
Switch
Multiple contact switch (ganged)
Fuse/ fusible link
Resistor
Variable resistor
Connecting wires
Wire colour (Grey)
Connections to other circuits (e.g. diagram 3/grid location B2. Direction of arrow denotes current flow.)
Wire – permanent positive supply (double line)
Wire – permanent direct earth (thick line)
Wire – interconnecting (thin line)
Denotes alternative wiring variation (brackets)
Screened cable

Item no.
Pump/motor
Earth
Pin and socket contact
Gauge/meter
Diode
Line connector
Solenoid actuator

Diagram 15 : Information for wiring diagrams - 1995 onwards

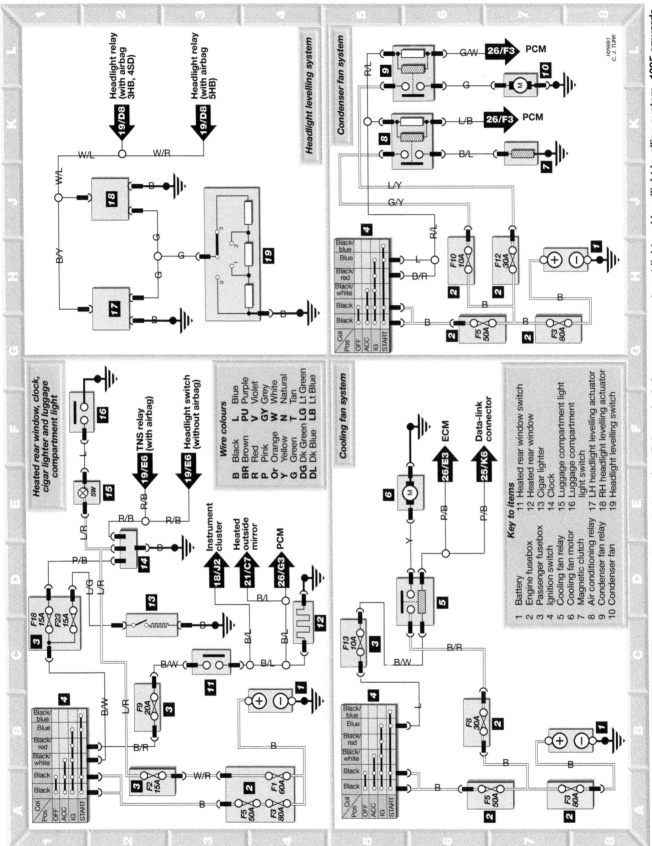

Diagram 16 : Typical cooling fan, condenser fan, heated rear window, cigar lighter, clock, luggage compartment light and headlight levelling system -1995 onwards

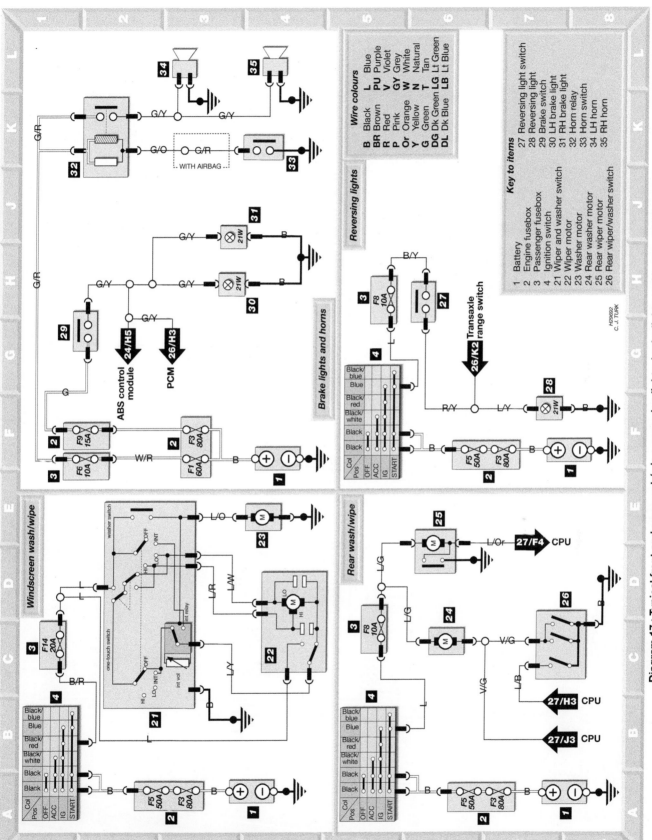

Wire colours

B Black	**L** Blue
BR Brown	**PU** Purple
R Red	**V** Violet
P Pink	**GY** Grey
Or Orange	**W** White
Y Yellow	**N** Natural
G Green	**T** Tan
DG Dk Green	**LG** Lt Green
DL Dk Blue	**LB** Lt Blue

Key to items

1 Battery
2 Engine fusebox
3 Passenger fusebox
4 Ignition switch
21 Wiper and washer switch
22 Wiper motor
23 Washer motor
24 Rear washer motor
25 Rear wiper motor
26 Rear wiper/washer switch
27 Reversing light switch
28 Reversing light
29 Brake switch
30 LH brake light
31 RH brake light
32 Horn relay
33 Horn switch
34 LH horn
35 RH horn

H29692
C. J. TURK

Diagram 17 : Typical front and rear wash/wipe, reversing lights, brake lights and horns - 1995 onwards

Brake lights and horns

Reversing lights

Windscreen wash/wipe

Rear wash/wipe

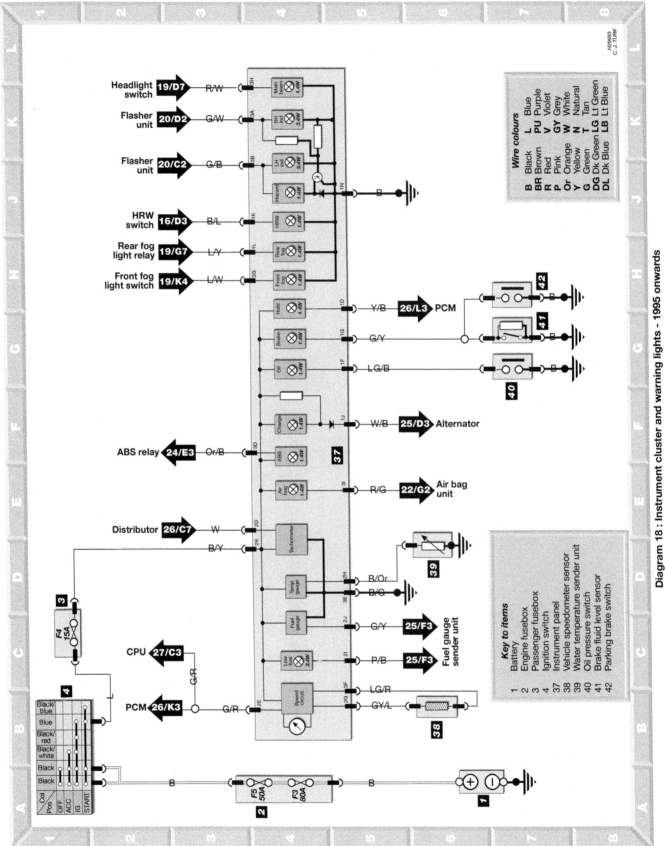

Diagram 18 : Instrument cluster and warning lights - 1995 onwards

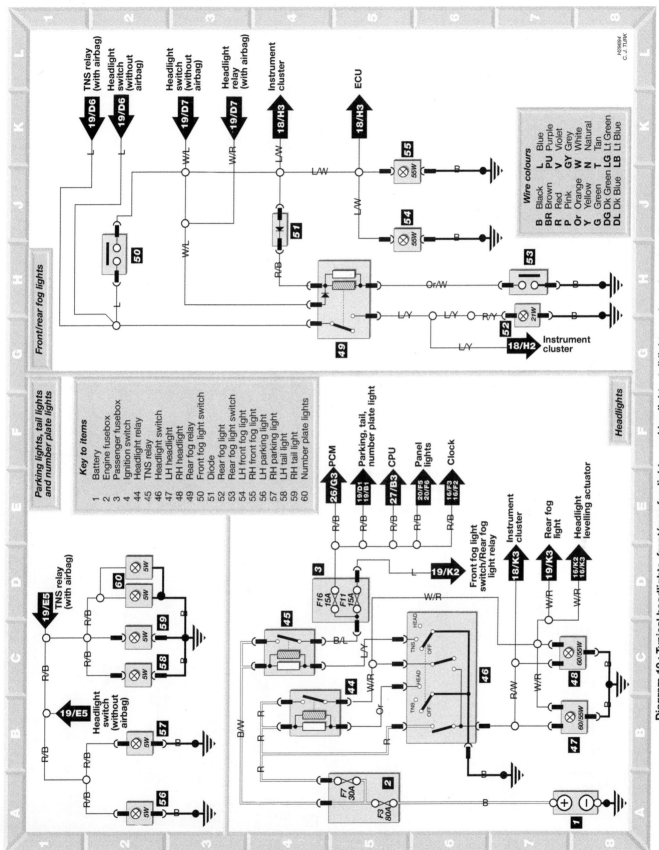

Diagram 19 : Typical headlights, front/rear fog lights, parking lights, tail lights and number plate lights – 1995 onwards

Key to items

1 Battery
2 Engine fusebox
3 Passenger fusebox
4 Ignition switch
44 Headlight relay
45 TNS relay
46 Headlight switch
47 LH headlight
48 RH headlight
49 Rear fog relay
50 Front fog light switch
51 Diode
52 Rear fog light
53 Rear fog light switch
54 LH front fog light
55 RH front fog light
56 LH parking light
57 RH parking light
58 LH tail light
59 RH tail light
60 Number plate lights

Wire colours

B	Black	L	Blue
BR	Brown	PU	Purple
R	Red	V	Violet
P	Pink	GY	Grey
Or	Orange	W	White
Y	Yellow	N	Natural
G	Green	T	Tan
DG	Dk Green	LG	Lt Green
DL	Dk Blue	LB	Lt Blue

H29694
C. J. TURK

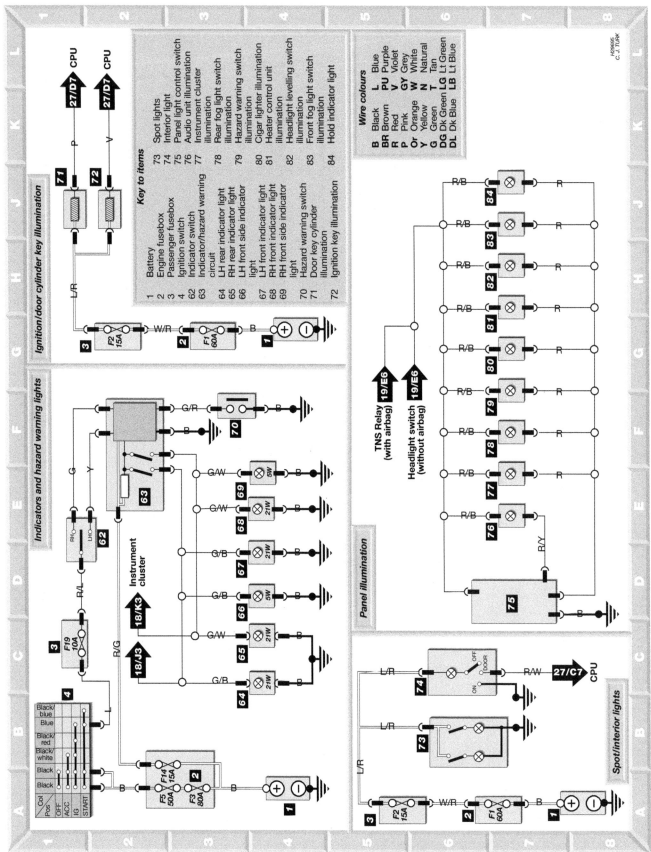

Ignition/door cylinder key illumination

Indicators and hazard warning lights

Panel illumination

Spot/interior lights

Key to items

1	Battery	
2	Engine fusebox	
3	Passenger fusebox	
4	Ignition switch	
62	Indicator switch	
63	Indicator/hazard warning circuit	
64	LH rear indicator light	
65	RH rear indicator light	
66	LH front side indicator light	
67	LH front indicator light	
68	RH front indicator light	
69	RH front side indicator light	
70	Hazard warning switch	
71	Door key cylinder illumination	
72	Ignition key illumination	
73	Spot lights	
74	Interior light	
75	Panel light control switch	
76	Audio unit illumination	
77	Instrument cluster illumination	
78	Rear fog light switch illumination	
79	Hazard warning switch illumination	
80	Cigar lighter illumination	
81	Heater control unit illumination	
82	Headlight levelling switch illumination	
83	Front fog light switch illumination	
84	Hold indicator light	

Wire colours

B	Black	L	Blue
BR	Brown	PU	Purple
R	Red	V	Violet
P	Pink	GY	Grey
Or	Orange	W	White
Y	Yellow	N	Natural
G	Green	T	Tan
DG	Dk Green	LG	Lt Green
DL	Dk Blue	LB	Lt Blue

TNS Relay (with airbag)

Headlight switch (without airbag)

Instrument cluster

Diagram 20 : Indicators and hazard warning lights, key illumination, spot/interior lights and panel illumination – 1995 onwards

H29695
C. J. TURK

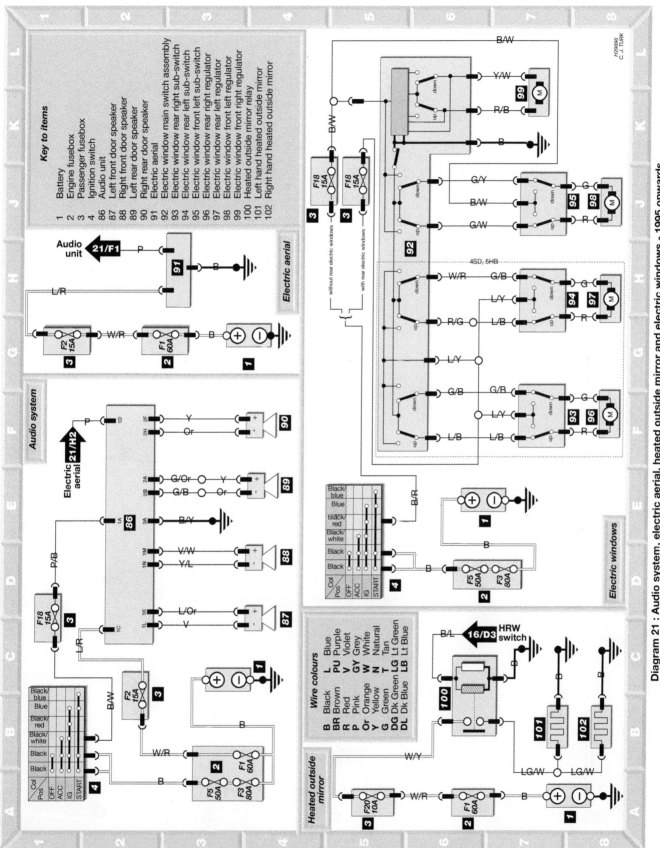

Key to items

1	Battery
2	Engine fusebox
3	Passenger fusebox
4	Ignition switch
86	Audio unit
87	Left front door speaker
88	Right front door speaker
89	Left rear door speaker
90	Right rear door speaker
91	Electric aerial
92	Electric window main switch assembly
93	Electric window rear right sub-switch
94	Electric window rear left sub-switch
95	Electric window front left sub-switch
96	Electric window rear right regulator
97	Electric window rear left regulator
98	Electric window front left regulator
99	Electric window front right regulator
100	Heated outside mirror relay
101	Left hand heated outside mirror
102	Right hand heated outside mirror

Wire colours

B	Black	L	Blue
BR	Brown	PU	Purple
R	Red	V	Violet
P	Pink	GY	Grey
Or	Orange	W	White
Y	Yellow	N	Natural
G	Green	T	Tan
Dg	Dk Green	LG	Lt Green
DL	Dk Blue	LB	Lt Blue

Audio unit 21/F1

Electric aerial

Audio system

Electric aerial 21/H2

Electric windows

Heated outside mirror

HRW switch 16/D3

Diagram 21 : Audio system, electric aerial, heated outside mirror and electric windows - 1995 onwards

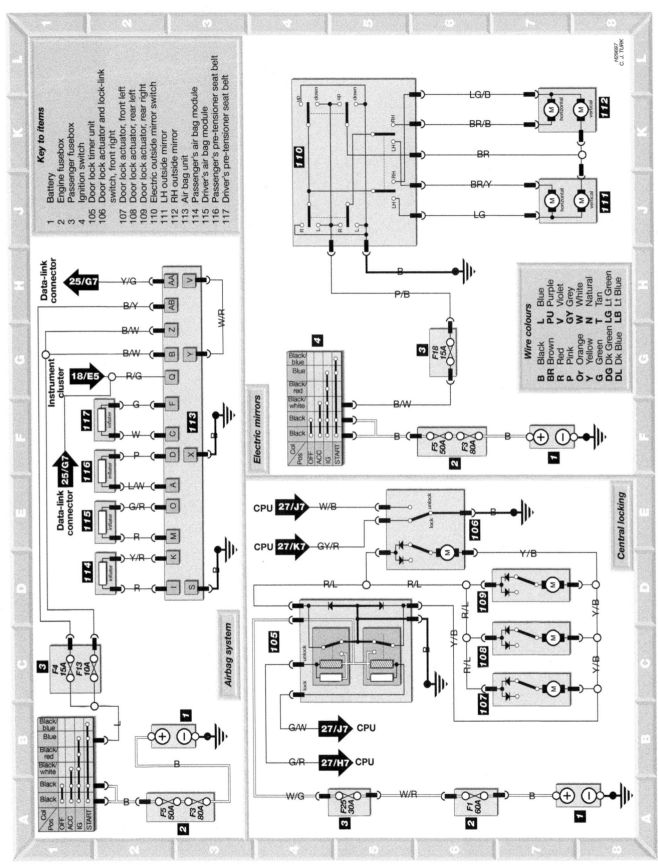

H29697
C. J. TURK

Key to items

1 Battery
2 Engine fusebox
3 Passenger fusebox
4 Ignition switch
105 Door lock timer unit
106 Door lock actuator and lock-link switch, front right
107 Door lock actuator, front left
108 Door lock actuator, rear left
109 Door lock actuator, rear right
110 Electric outside mirror
111 LH outside mirror
112 RH outside mirror
113 Air bag unit
114 Passenger's air bag module
115 Driver's air bag module
116 Passenger's pre-tensioner seat belt
117 Driver's pre-tensioner seat belt

Wire colours

B	Black	L	Blue	PU	Purple
BR	Brown	V	Violet		
R	Red	GY	Grey		
P	Pink	W	White		
Or	Orange	N	Natural		
Y	Yellow	T	Tan		
G	Green	LG	Lt Green		
DG	Dk Green	LB	Lt Blue		
DL	Dk Blue				

Electric mirrors

Airbag system

Central locking

Diagram 22 : Central locking, electric mirrors and airbag system - 1995 onwards

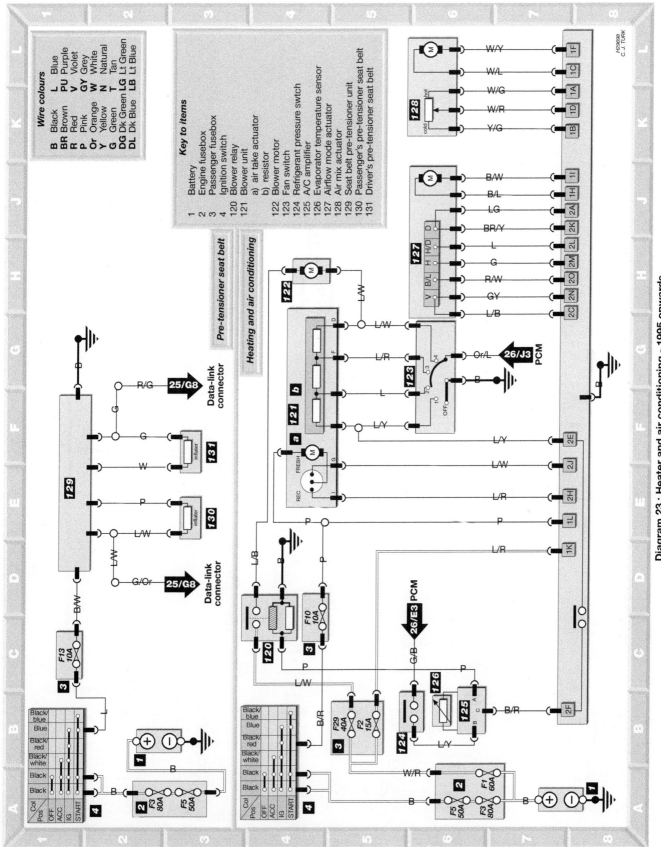

Wire colours

B	Black	**L**	Blue
BR	Brown	**PU**	Purple
R	Red	**V**	Violet
P	Pink	**GY**	Grey
Or	Orange	**W**	White
Y	Yellow	**N**	Natural
G	Green	**T**	Tan
DG	Dk Green	**LG**	Lt Green
DL	Dk Blue	**LB**	Lt Blue

Key to items

1 Battery
2 Engine fusebox
3 Passenger fusebox
4 Ignition switch
120 Blower relay
121 Blower unit
  a) air take actuator
  b) resistor
122 Blower motor
123 Fan switch
124 Refrigerant pressure switch
125 A/C amplifier
126 Evaporator temperature sensor
127 Airflow mode actuator
128 Air mix actuator
129 Seat belt pre-tensioner unit
130 Passenger's pre-tensioner seat belt
131 Driver's pre-tensioner seat belt

Pre-tensioner seat belt

Heating and air conditioning

Data-link connector

Data-link connector

Diagram 23 : Heater and air conditioning - 1995 onwards

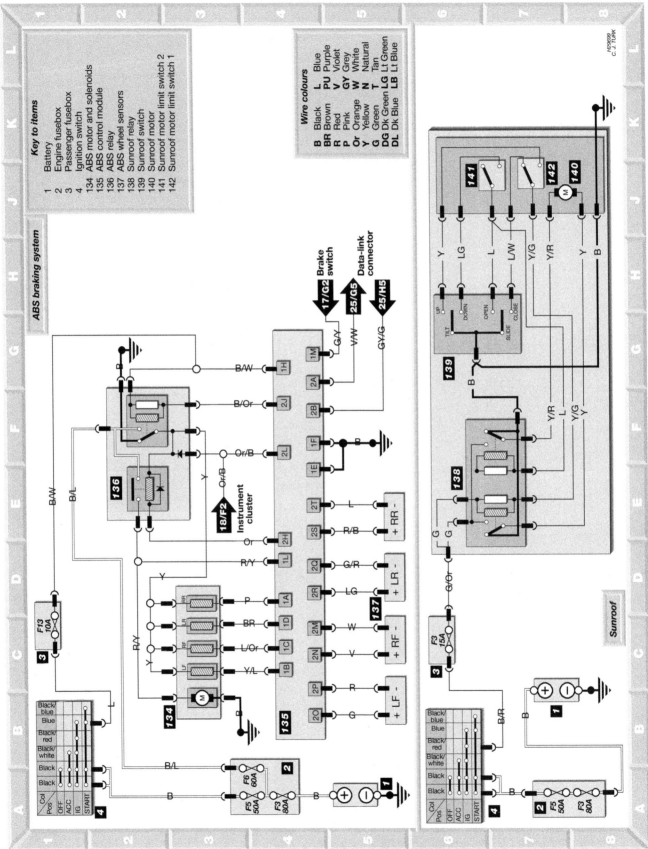

Key to items

1 Battery
2 Engine fusebox
3 Passenger fusebox
4 Ignition switch
134 ABS motor and solenoids
135 ABS control module
136 ABS relay
137 ABS wheel sensors
138 Sunroof relay
139 Sunroof switch
140 Sunroof motor
141 Sunroof motor limit switch 2
142 Sunroof motor limit switch 1

Wire colours

B	Black	L	Blue
BR	Brown	PU	Purple
R	Red	V	Violet
P	Pink	GY	Grey
Or	Orange	W	White
Y	Yellow	N	Natural
G	Green	T	Tan
DG	Dk Green	LG	Lt Green
DL	Dk Blue	LB	Lt Blue

ABS braking system

Sunroof

Diagram 24 : ABS braking system, sunroof – 1995 onwards

H29699
C. J. TURK

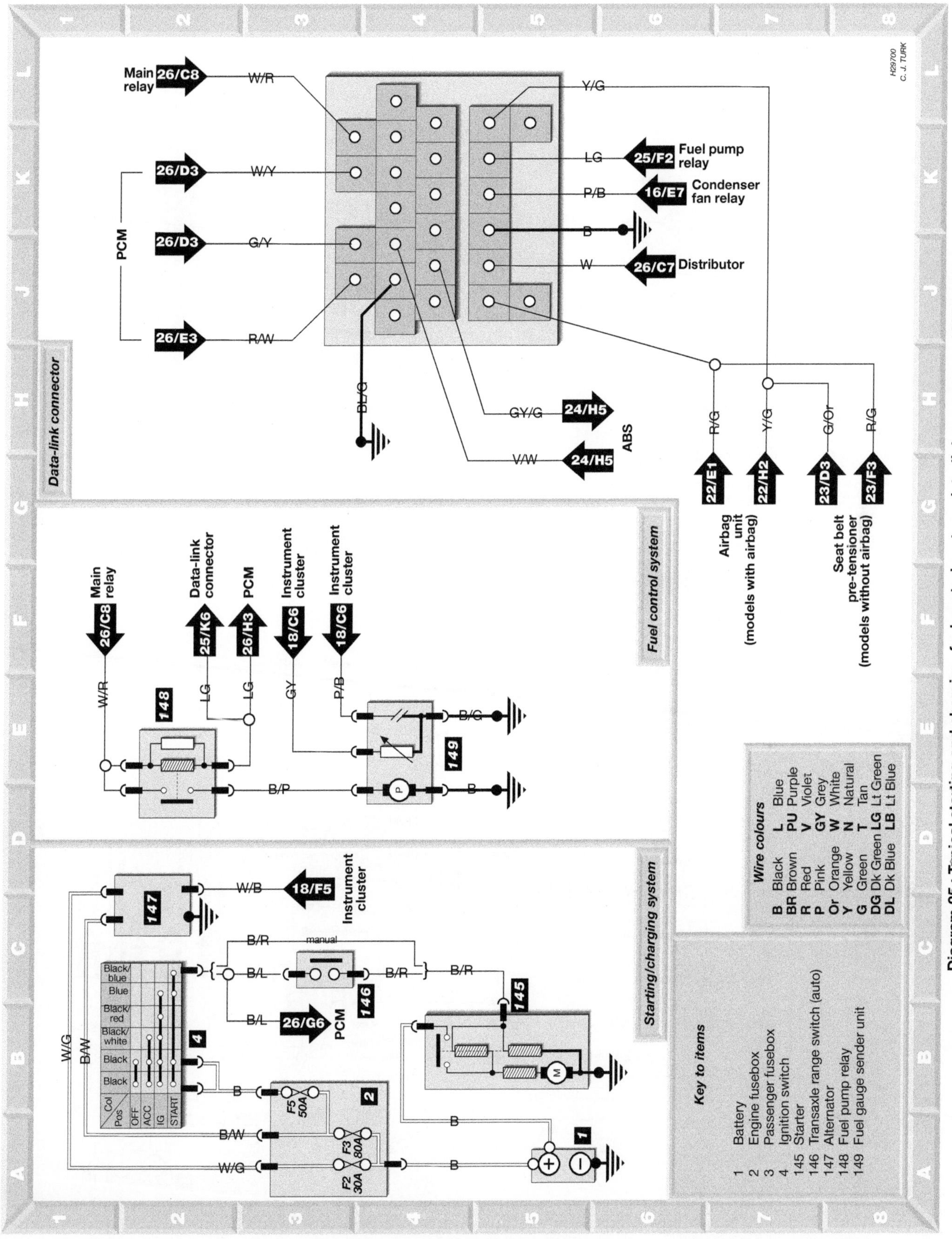

H29700
C. J. TURK

Data-link connector

Main relay 26/C8 —W/R—

26/D3 —W/Y—
PCM
26/D3 —G/Y—

26/E3 —R/W—

BL/O

Y/G

LG 25/F2 Fuel pump relay

P/B 16/E7 Condenser fan relay

B

W 26/C7 Distributor

GY/G 24/H5

V/W 24/H5 ABS

R/G 22/E1 Airbag unit (models with airbag)

Y/G 22/H2

G/Or 23/D3

R/G 23/F3 Seat belt pre-tensioner (models without airbag)

Fuel control system

26/C8 Main relay
25/K6 Data-link connector
26/H3 PCM
18/C6 Instrument cluster
18/C6 Instrument cluster

W/R
148
LG
LG
GY
P/B

B/G

149

B/P B

Starting/charging system

W/B 18/F5 Instrument cluster

147

B/R manual
B/L 146 B/R B/R 145
B/L 26/G6 PCM

Black/blue
Blue
Black/red
Black/white
Black
Black

| Col Pos | OFF | ACC | IG | START |

4

W/G
B/W

F5 50A

F3 80A
F2 30A

2

B

B

M

B

1

Wire colours

B Black	**L** Blue		
BR Brown	**PU** Purple		
R Red	**V** Violet		
P Pink	**GY** Grey		
Or Orange	**W** White		
Y Yellow	**N** Natural		
G Green	**T** Tan		
DG Dk Green	**LG** Lt Green		
DL Dk Blue	**LB** Lt Blue		

Diagram 25 : Typical starting and charging, fuel control system, data-link connector – 1995 onwards

Key to items

1 Battery
2 Engine fusebox
3 Passenger fusebox
145 Starter
146 Transaxle range switch (auto)
147 Alternator
148 Fuel pump relay
149 Fuel gauge sender unit

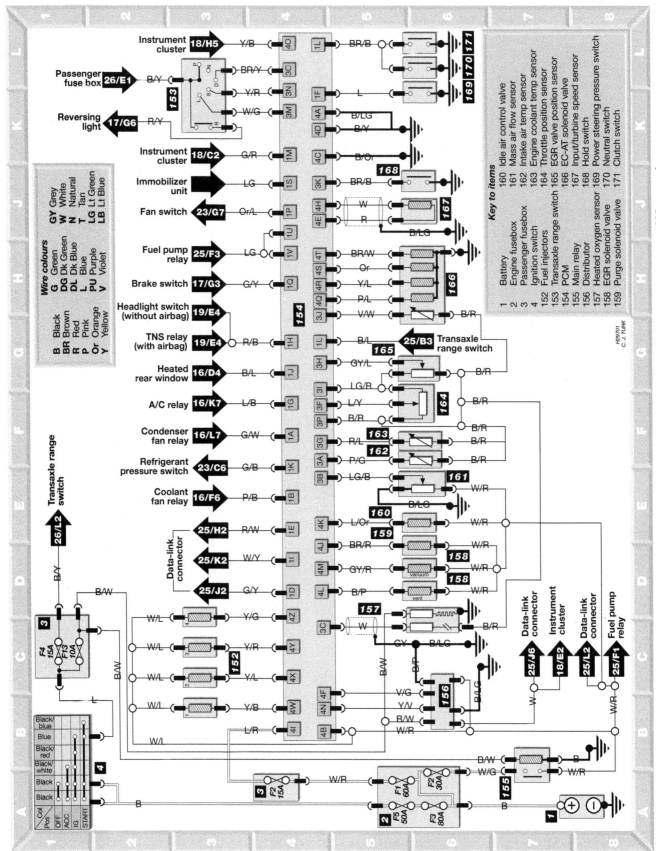

Diagram 26 : Typical engine control system, ignition system and EC-AT control system – 1995 onwards

Wire colours

GY	Grey	W	White
G	Green	N	Natural
DG	Dk Green	T	Tan
DL	Dk Blue	LG	Lt Green
L	Blue	LB	Lt Blue
PU	Purple		

B	Black		
BR	Brown		
R	Red	P	Pink
Or	Orange		
Y	Yellow	V	Violet

Key to items

1 Battery
2 Engine fusebox
3 Passenger fusebox
4 Ignition switch
152 Fuel injectors
153 Transaxle range switch
154 PCM
155 Main relay
156 Distributor
157 Heated oxygen sensor
158 EGR solenoid valve
159 Purge solenoid valve
160 Idle air control valve
161 Mass air flow sensor
162 Intake air temp sensor
163 Engine coolant temp sensor
164 Throttle position sensor
165 EGR valve position sensor
166 EC-AT solenoid valve
167 Input/turbine speed sensor
168 Hold switch
169 Power steering pressure switch
170 Neutral switch
171 Clutch switch

H29701
C. J. TURK

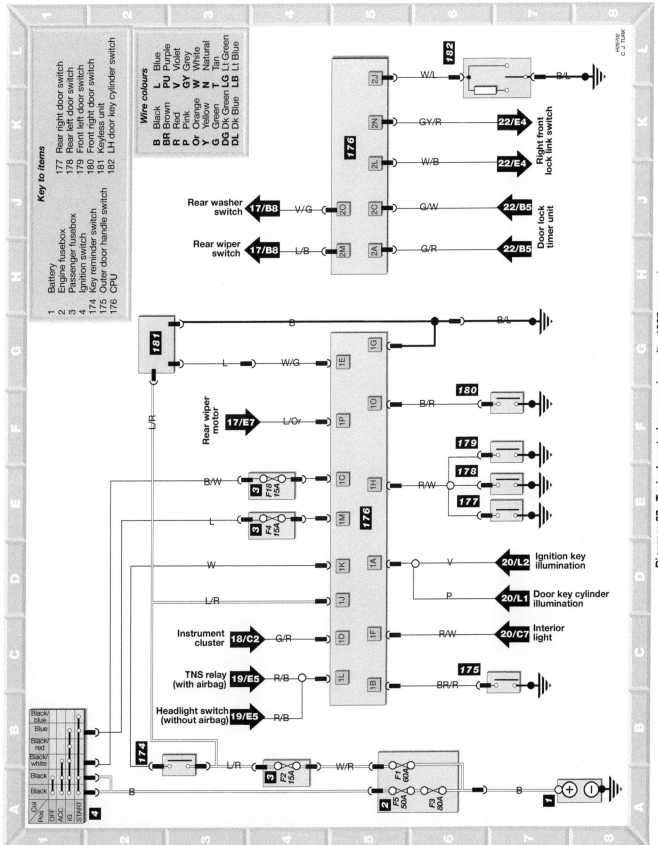

Key to items

1 Battery
2 Engine fusebox
3 Passenger fusebox
4 Ignition switch
174 Key reminder switch
175 Outer door handle switch
176 CPU
177 Rear right door switch
178 Rear left door switch
179 Front left door switch
180 Front right door switch
181 Keyless unit
182 LH door key cylinder switch

Wire colours

B	Black	L	Blue
BR	Brown	PU	Purple
R	Red	V	Violet
P	Pink	GY	Grey
Or	Orange	W	White
Y	Yellow	N	Natural
G	Green	T	Tan
DG	Dk Green	LG	Lt Green
DL	Dk Blue	LB	Lt Blue

Diagram 27 : Typical central processing unit – 1995 onwards

Notes

Dimensions

Overall length	
1991 to 1994	4225 mm (166.5 in)
1995 and later	4335 mm (170.8 in)
Overall width	
1991 to 1994	1645 mm (64.8 in)
1995 and later	1695 mm (66.8 in)
Overall height	
1991 to 1994	1430 mm (56.3 in)
1995 and later	1420 mm (59.9 in)
Wheelbase	
1991 to 1994	2400 mm (94.6 in)
1995 and later	2605 mm (102.6 in)

Conversion factors

Length (distance)

Inches (in)	x 25.4	=	Millimetres (mm)	x 0.0394	=	Inches (in)
Feet (ft)	x 0.305	=	Metres (m)	x 3.281	=	Feet (ft)
Miles	x 1.609	=	Kilometres (km)	x 0.621	=	Miles

Volume (capacity)

Cubic inches (cu in; in³)	x 16.387	=	Cubic centimetres (cc; cm³)	x 0.061	=	Cubic inches (cu in; in³)
Imperial pints (Imp pt)	x 0.568	=	Litres (l)	x 1.76	=	Imperial pints (Imp pt)
Imperial quarts (Imp qt)	x 1.137	=	Litres (l)	x 0.88	=	Imperial quarts (Imp qt)
Imperial quarts (Imp qt)	x 1.201	=	US quarts (US qt)	x 0.833	=	Imperial quarts (Imp qt)
US quarts (US qt)	x 0.946	=	Litres (l)	x 1.057	=	US quarts (US qt)
Imperial gallons (Imp gal)	x 4.546	=	Litres (l)	x 0.22	=	Imperial gallons (Imp gal)
Imperial gallons (Imp gal)	x 1.201	=	US gallons (US gal)	x 0.833	=	Imperial gallons (Imp gal)
US gallons (US gal)	x 3.785	=	Litres (l)	x 0.264	=	US gallons (US gal)

Mass (weight)

Ounces (oz)	x 28.35	=	Grams (g)	x 0.035	=	Ounces (oz)
Pounds (lb)	x 0.454	=	Kilograms (kg)	x 2.205	=	Pounds (lb)

Force

Ounces-force (ozf; oz)	x 0.278	=	Newtons (N)	x 3.6	=	Ounces-force (ozf; oz)
Pounds-force (lbf; lb)	x 4.448	=	Newtons (N)	x 0.225	=	Pounds-force (lbf; lb)
Newtons (N)	x 0.1	=	Kilograms-force (kgf; kg)	x 9.81	=	Newtons (N)

Pressure

Pounds-force per square inch (psi; lbf/in²; lb/in²)	x 0.070	=	Kilograms-force per square centimetre (kgf/cm²; kg/cm²)	x 14.223	=	Pounds-force per square inch (psi; lbf/in²; lb/in²)
Pounds-force per square inch (psi; lbf/in²; lb/in²)	x 0.068	=	Atmospheres (atm)	x 14.696	=	Pounds-force per square inch (psi; lbf/in²; lb/in²)
Pounds-force per square inch (psi; lbf/in²; lb/in²)	x 0.069	=	Bars	x 14.5	=	Pounds-force per square inch (psi; lbf/in²; lb/in²)
Pounds-force per square inch (psi; lbf/in²; lb/in²)	x 6.895	=	Kilopascals (kPa)	x 0.145	=	Pounds-force per square inch (psi; lbf/in²; lb/in²)
Kilopascals (kPa)	x 0.01	=	Kilograms-force per square centimetre (kgf/cm²; kg/cm²)	x 98.1	=	Kilopascals (kPa)
Millibar (mbar)	x 100	=	Pascals (Pa)	x 0.01	=	Millibar (mbar)
Millibar (mbar)	x 0.0145	=	Pounds-force per square inch (psi; lbf/in²; lb/in²)	x 68.947	=	Millibar (mbar)
Millibar (mbar)	x 0.75	=	Millimetres of mercury (mmHg)	x 1.333	=	Millibar (mbar)
Millibar (mbar)	x 0.401	=	Inches of water (inH₂O)	x 2.491	=	Millibar (mbar)
Millimetres of mercury (mmHg)	x 0.535	=	Inches of water (inH₂O)	x 1.868	=	Millimetres of mercury (mmHg)
Inches of water (inH₂O)	x 0.036	=	Pounds-force per square inch (psi; lbf/in²; lb/in²)	x 27.68	=	Inches of water (inH₂O)

Torque (moment of force)

Pounds-force inches (lbf in; lb in)	x 1.152	=	Kilograms-force centimetre (kgf cm; kg cm)	x 0.868	=	Pounds-force inches (lbf in; lb in)
Pounds-force inches (lbf in; lb in)	x 0.113	=	Newton metres (Nm)	x 8.85	=	Pounds-force inches (lbf in; lb in)
Pounds-force inches (lbf in; lb in)	x 0.083	=	Pounds-force feet (lbf ft; lb ft)	x 12	=	Pounds-force inches (lbf in; lb in)
Pounds-force feet (lbf ft; lb ft)	x 0.138	=	Kilograms-force metres (kgf m; kg m)	x 7.233	=	Pounds-force feet (lbf ft; lb ft)
Pounds-force feet (lbf ft; lb ft)	x 1.356	=	Newton metres (Nm)	x 0.738	=	Pounds-force feet (lbf ft; lb ft)
Newton metres (Nm)	x 0.102	=	Kilograms-force metres (kgf m; kg m)	x 9.804	=	Newton metres (Nm)

Power

Horsepower (hp)	x 745.7	=	Watts (W)	x 0.0013	=	Horsepower (hp)

Velocity (speed)

Miles per hour (miles/hr; mph)	x 1.609	=	Kilometres per hour (km/hr; kph)	x 0.621	=	Miles per hour (miles/hr; mph)

Fuel consumption*

Miles per gallon (mpg)	x 0.354	=	Kilometres per litre (km/l)	x 2.825	=	Miles per gallon (mpg)

Temperature

Degrees Fahrenheit = (°C x 1.8) + 32   Degrees Celsius (Degrees Centigrade; °C) = (°F - 32) x 0.56

It is common practice to convert from miles per gallon (mpg) to litres/100 kilometres (l/100km), where mpg x l/100 km = 282

Spare parts are available from many sources, including maker's appointed garages, accessory shops, and motor factors. To be sure of obtaining the correct parts, it will sometimes be necessary to quote the vehicle identification number. If possible, it can also be useful to take the old parts along for positive identification. Items such as starter motors and alternators may be available under a service exchange scheme - any parts returned should be clean.

Our advice regarding spare parts is as follows.

Officially appointed garages

This is the best source of parts which are peculiar to your car, and which are not otherwise generally available (eg, badges, interior trim, certain body panels, etc). It is also the only place at which you should buy parts if the vehicle is still under warranty.

Accessory shops

These are very good places to buy materials and components needed for the maintenance of your car (oil, air and fuel filters, light bulbs, drivebelts, greases, brake pads, touch-up paint, etc). Components of this nature sold by a reputable shop are usually of the same standard as those used by the car manufacturer.

Besides components, these shops also sell tools and general accessories, usually have convenient opening hours, charge lower prices, and can often be found close to home. Some accessory shops have parts counters where components needed for almost any repair job can be purchased or ordered.

Motor factors

Good factors will stock all the more important components which wear out comparatively quickly, and can sometimes supply individual components needed for the overhaul of a larger assembly (eg, brake seals and hydraulic parts, bearing shells, pistons, valves). They may also handle work such as cylinder block reboring, crankshaft regrinding, etc.

Tyre and exhaust specialists

These outlets may be independent, or members of a local or national chain. They frequently offer competitive prices when compared with a main dealer or local garage, but it will pay to obtain several quotes before making a decision. When researching prices, also ask what "extras" may be added - for instance fitting a new valve and balancing the wheel are both commonly charged on top of the price of a new tyre.

Other sources

Beware of parts or materials obtained from market stalls, car boot sales or similar outlets. Such items are not invariably sub-standard, but there is little chance of compensation if they do prove unsatisfactory. in the case of safety-critical components such as brake pads, there is the risk not only of financial loss, but also of an accident causing injury or death.

Second-hand components or assemblies obtained from a car breaker can be a good buy in some circumstances, but this sort of purchase is best made by the experienced DIY mechanic.

Vehicle identification numbers

Modifications are a continuing and unpublicised process in vehicle manufacturing. Since spare parts manuals and lists are compiled on a numerical basis, the individual vehicle numbers are essential to correctly identify the component required.

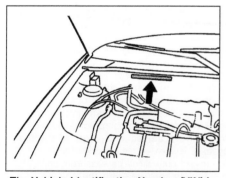

The Vehicle Identification Number (VIN) is stamped into the bulkhead

The engine identification number is stamped on a pad at the rear of the engine block

Vehicle Identification Number (VIN)

This very important identification number is located on the bulkhead inside the engine compartment (see illustration). It contains information such as where and when the vehicle was manufactured, the model year and the body style.

Engine identification number

The engine identification number can be found stamped on a pad on either the right rear or left rear of the cylinder block (see illustration).

Transmission identification number

The transmission identification information can be found on a bar code label located on the transmission bellhousing.

Radio/cassette unit anti-theft system - precaution

The radio/cassette/CD player/autochanger unit fitted to your Mazda may be equipped with a built-in security code to deter thieves. If the power source to the unit is cut, the anti-theft system will activate. Even if the power source is immediately reconnected, the radio/cassette unit will not function until the correct security code has been entered. Therefore, if you do not know the correct security code for the unit, I **do not** disconnect the battery negative lead, or remove the radio/cassette unit from the vehicle.

The procedure for reprogramming a unit that has been disconnected from its power supply varies from model to model - consult the handbook supplied with the unit for specific details or refer to your Mazda dealer.

Whenever servicing, repair or overhaul work is carried out on the car or its components, observe the following procedures and instructions. This will assist in carrying out the operation efficiently and to a professional standard of workmanship.

Joint mating faces and gaskets

When separating components at their mating faces, never insert screwdrivers or similar implements into the joint between the faces in order to prise them apart. This can cause severe damage which results in oil leaks, coolant leaks, etc upon reassembly. Separation is usually achieved by tapping along the joint with a soft-faced hammer in order to break the seal. However, note that this method may not be suitable where dowels are used for component location.

Where a gasket is used between the mating faces of two components, a new one must be fitted on reassembly; fit it dry unless otherwise stated in the repair procedure. Make sure that the mating faces are clean and dry, with all traces of old gasket removed. When cleaning a joint face, use a tool which is unlikely to score or damage the face, and remove any burrs or nicks with an oilstone or fine file.

Make sure that tapped holes are cleaned with a pipe cleaner, and keep them free of jointing compound, if this is being used, unless specifically instructed otherwise.

Ensure that all orifices, channels or pipes are clear, and blow through them, preferably using compressed air.

Oil seals

Oil seals can be removed by levering them out with a wide flat-bladed screwdriver or similar implement. Alternatively, a number of self-tapping screws may be screwed into the seal, and these used as a purchase for pliers or some similar device in order to pull the seal free.

Whenever an oil seal is removed from its working location, either individually or as part of an assembly, it should be renewed.

The very fine sealing lip of the seal is easily damaged, and will not seal if the surface it contacts is not completely clean and free from scratches, nicks or grooves. If the original sealing surface of the component cannot be restored, and the manufacturer has not made provision for slight relocation of the seal relative to the sealing surface, the component should be renewed.

Protect the lips of the seal from any surface which may damage them in the course of fitting. Use tape or a conical sleeve where possible. Lubricate the seal lips with oil before fitting and, on dual-lipped seals, fill the space between the lips with grease.

Unless otherwise stated, oil seals must be fitted with their sealing lips toward the lubricant to be sealed.

Use a tubular drift or block of wood of the appropriate size to install the seal and, if the seal housing is shouldered, drive the seal down to the shoulder. If the seal housing is unshouldered, the seal should be fitted with its face flush with the housing top face (unless otherwise instructed).

Screw threads and fastenings

Seized nuts, bolts and screws are quite a common occurrence where corrosion has set in, and the use of penetrating oil or releasing fluid will often overcome this problem if the offending item is soaked for a while before attempting to release it. The use of an impact driver may also provide a means of releasing such stubborn fastening devices, when used in conjunction with the appropriate screwdriver bit or socket. If none of these methods works, it may be necessary to resort to the careful application of heat, or the use of a hacksaw or nut splitter device.

Studs are usually removed by locking two nuts together on the threaded part, and then using a spanner on the lower nut to unscrew the stud. Studs or bolts which have broken off below the surface of the component in which they are mounted can sometimes be removed using a stud extractor. Always ensure that a blind tapped hole is completely free from oil, grease, water or other fluid before installing the bolt or stud. Failure to do this could cause the housing to crack due to the hydraulic action of the bolt or stud as it is screwed in.

When tightening a castellated nut to accept a split pin, tighten the nut to the specified torque, where applicable, and then tighten further to the next split pin hole. Never slacken the nut to align the split pin hole, unless stated in the repair procedure.

When checking or retightening a nut or bolt to a specified torque setting, slacken the nut or bolt by a quarter of a turn, and then retighten to the specified setting. However, this should not be attempted where angular tightening has been used.

For some screw fastenings, notably cylinder head bolts or nuts, torque wrench settings are no longer specified for the latter stages of tightening, "angle-tightening" being called up instead. Typically, a fairly low torque wrench setting will be applied to the bolts/nuts in the correct sequence, followed by one or more stages of tightening through specified angles.

Locknuts, locktabs and washers

Any fastening which will rotate against a component or housing during tightening should always have a washer between it and the relevant component or housing.

Spring or split washers should always be renewed when they are used to lock a critical component such as a big-end bearing retaining bolt or nut. Locktabs which are folded over to retain a nut or bolt should always be renewed.

Self-locking nuts can be re-used in non-critical areas, providing resistance can be felt when the locking portion passes over the bolt or stud thread. However, it should be noted that self-locking stiffnuts tend to lose their effectiveness after long periods of use, and should then be renewed as a matter of course.

Split pins must always be replaced with new ones of the correct size for the hole.

When thread-locking compound is found on the threads of a fastener which is to be re-used, it should be cleaned off with a wire brush and solvent, and fresh compound applied on reassembly.

Special tools

Some repair procedures in this manual entail the use of special tools such as a press, two or three-legged pullers, spring compressors, etc. Wherever possible, suitable readily-available alternatives to the manufacturer's special tools are described, and are shown in use. In some instances, where no alternative is possible, it has been necessary to resort to the use of a manufacturer's tool, and this has been done for reasons of safety as well as the efficient completion of the repair operation. Unless you are highly-skilled and have a thorough understanding of the procedures described, never attempt to bypass the use of any special tool when the procedure described specifies its use. Not only is there a very great risk of personal injury, but expensive damage could be caused to the components involved.

Environmental considerations

When disposing of used engine oil, brake fluid, antifreeze, etc, give due consideration to any detrimental environmental effects. Do not, for instance, pour any of the above liquids down drains into the general sewage system, or onto the ground to soak away. Many local council refuse tips provide a facility for waste oil disposal, as do some garages. If none of these facilities are available, consult your local Environmental Health Department, or the National Rivers Authority, for further advice.

With the universal tightening-up of legislation regarding the emission of environmentally-harmful substances from motor vehicles, most vehicles have tamperproof devices fitted to the main adjustment points of the fuel system. These devices are primarily designed to prevent unqualified persons from adjusting the fuel/air mixture, with the chance of a consequent increase in toxic emissions. If such devices are found during servicing or overhaul, they should, wherever possible, be renewed or refitted in accordance with the manufacturer's requirements or current legislation.

OIL CARE

FOLLOW THE CODE

OIL BANK LINE
0800 66 33 66
www.oilbankline.org.uk

Note: It is antisocial and illegal to dump oil down the drain. To find the location of your local oil recycling bank, call this number free.

Introduction

A selection of good tools is a fundamental requirement for anyone contemplating the maintenance and repair of a motor vehicle. For the owner who does not possess any, their purchase will prove a considerable expense, offsetting some of the savings made by doing-it-yourself. However, provided that the tools purchased meet the relevant national safety standards and are of good quality, they will last for many years and prove an extremely worthwhile investment.

To help the average owner to decide which tools are needed to carry out the various tasks detailed in this manual, we have compiled three lists of tools under the following headings: *Maintenance and minor repair, Repair and overhaul*, and *Special*. Newcomers to practical mechanics should start off with the *Maintenance and minor repair* tool kit, and confine themselves to the simpler jobs around the vehicle. Then, as confidence and experience grow, more difficult tasks can be undertaken, with extra tools being purchased as, and when, they are needed. In this way, a *Maintenance and minor repair* tool kit can be built up into a *Repair and overhaul* tool kit over a considerable period of time, without any major cash outlays. The experienced do-it-yourselfer will have a tool kit good enough for most repair and overhaul procedures, and will add tools from the *Special* category when it is felt that the expense is justified by the amount of use to which these tools will be put.

Maintenance and minor repair tool kit

The tools given in this list should be considered as a minimum requirement if routine maintenance, servicing and minor repair operations are to be undertaken. We recommend the purchase of combination spanners (ring one end, open-ended the other); although more expensive than open-ended ones, they do give the advantages of both types of spanner.

- ☐ *Combination spanners:*
  Metric - 8 to 19 mm inclusive
- ☐ *Adjustable spanner - 35 mm jaw (approx.)*
- ☐ *Spark plug spanner (with rubber insert) - petrol models*
- ☐ *Spark plug gap adjustment tool - petrol models*
- ☐ *Set of feeler gauges*
- ☐ *Brake bleed nipple spanner*
- ☐ *Screwdrivers:*
  Flat blade - 100 mm long x 6 mm dia
  Cross blade - 100 mm long x 6 mm dia
  Torx - various sizes (not all vehicles)
- ☐ *Combination pliers*
- ☐ *Hacksaw (junior)*
- ☐ *Tyre pump*
- ☐ *Tyre pressure gauge*
- ☐ *Oil can*
- ☐ *Oil filter removal tool*
- ☐ *Fine emery cloth*
- ☐ *Wire brush (small)*
- ☐ *Funnel (medium size)*
- ☐ *Sump drain plug key (not all vehicles)*

Repair and overhaul tool kit

These tools are virtually essential for anyone undertaking any major repairs to a motor vehicle, and are additional to those given in the *Maintenance and minor repair* list. Included in this list is a comprehensive set of sockets. Although these are expensive, they will be found invaluable as they are so versatile - particularly if various drives are included in the set. We recommend the half-inch square-drive type, as this can be used with most proprietary torque wrenches.

The tools in this list will sometimes need to be supplemented by tools from the *Special* list:

- ☐ *Sockets (or box spanners) to cover range in previous list (including Torx sockets)*
- ☐ *Reversible ratchet drive (for use with sockets)*
- ☐ *Extension piece, 250 mm (for use with sockets)*
- ☐ *Universal joint (for use with sockets)*
- ☐ *Flexible handle or sliding T "breaker bar" (for use with sockets)*
- ☐ *Torque wrench (for use with sockets)*
- ☐ *Self-locking grips*
- ☐ *Ball pein hammer*
- ☐ *Soft-faced mallet (plastic or rubber)*
- ☐ *Screwdrivers:*
  Flat blade - long & sturdy, short (chubby), and narrow (electrician's) types
  Cross blade – long & sturdy, and short (chubby) types
- ☐ *Pliers:*
  Long-nosed
  Side cutters (electrician's)
  Circlip (internal and external)
- ☐ *Cold chisel - 25 mm*
- ☐ *Scriber*
- ☐ *Scraper*
- ☐ *Centre-punch*
- ☐ *Pin punch*
- ☐ *Hacksaw*
- ☐ *Brake hose clamp*
- ☐ *Brake/clutch bleeding kit*
- ☐ *Selection of twist drills*
- ☐ *Steel rule/straight-edge*
- ☐ *Allen keys (inc. splined/Torx type)*
- ☐ *Selection of files*
- ☐ *Wire brush*
- ☐ *Axle stands*
- ☐ *Jack (strong trolley or hydraulic type)*
- ☐ *Light with extension lead*
- ☐ *Universal electrical multi-meter*

Sockets and reversible ratchet drive

Brake bleeding kit

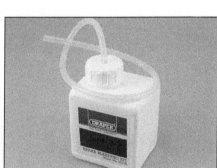

Torx key, socket and bit

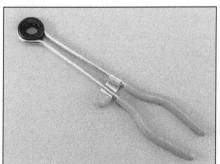

Hose clamp

Angular-tightening gauge

Special tools

The tools in this list are those which are not used regularly, are expensive to buy, or which need to be used in accordance with their manufacturers' instructions. Unless relatively difficult mechanical jobs are undertaken frequently, it will not be economic to buy many of these tools. Where this is the case, you could consider clubbing together with friends (or joining a motorists' club) to make a joint purchase, or borrowing the tools against a deposit from a local garage or tool hire specialist. It is worth noting that many of the larger DIY superstores now carry a large range of special tools for hire at modest rates.

The following list contains only those tools and instruments freely available to the public, and not those special tools produced by the vehicle manufacturer specifically for its dealer network. You will find occasional references to these manufacturers' special tools in the text of this manual. Generally, an alternative method of doing the job without the vehicle manufacturers' special tool is given. However, sometimes there is no alternative to using them. Where this is the case and the relevant tool cannot be bought or borrowed, you will have to entrust the work to a dealer.

- ☐ Angular-tightening gauge
- ☐ Valve spring compressor
- ☐ Valve grinding tool
- ☐ Piston ring compressor
- ☐ Piston ring removal/installation tool
- ☐ Cylinder bore hone
- ☐ Balljoint separator
- ☐ Coil spring compressors (where applicable)
- ☐ Two/three-legged hub and bearing puller
- ☐ Impact screwdriver
- ☐ Micrometer and/or vernier calipers
- ☐ Dial gauge
- ☐ Stroboscopic timing light
- ☐ Dwell angle meter/tachometer
- ☐ Fault code reader
- ☐ Cylinder compression gauge
- ☐ Hand-operated vacuum pump and gauge
- ☐ Clutch plate alignment set
- ☐ Brake shoe steady spring cup removal tool
- ☐ Bush and bearing removal/installation set
- ☐ Stud extractors
- ☐ Tap and die set
- ☐ Lifting tackle
- ☐ Trolley jack

Buying tools

Reputable motor accessory shops and superstores often offer excellent quality tools at discount prices, so it pays to shop around.

Remember, you don't have to buy the most expensive items on the shelf, but it is always advisable to steer clear of the very cheap tools. Beware of 'bargains' offered on market stalls or at car boot sales. There are plenty of good tools around at reasonable prices, but always aim to purchase items which meet the relevant national safety standards. If in doubt, ask the proprietor or manager of the shop for advice before making a purchase.

Care and maintenance of tools

Having purchased a reasonable tool kit, it is necessary to keep the tools in a clean and serviceable condition. After use, always wipe off any dirt, grease and metal particles using a clean, dry cloth, before putting the tools away. Never leave them lying around after they have been used. A simple tool rack on the garage or workshop wall for items such as screwdrivers and pliers is a good idea. Store all normal spanners and sockets in a metal box. Any measuring instruments, gauges, meters, etc, must be carefully stored where they cannot be damaged or become rusty.

Take a little care when tools are used. Hammer heads inevitably become marked, and screwdrivers lose the keen edge on their blades from time to time. A little timely attention with emery cloth or a file will soon restore items like this to a good finish.

Working facilities

Not to be forgotten when discussing tools is the workshop itself. If anything more than routine maintenance is to be carried out, a suitable working area becomes essential.

It is appreciated that many an owner-mechanic is forced by circumstances to remove an engine or similar item without the benefit of a garage or workshop. Having done this, any repairs should always be done under the cover of a roof.

Wherever possible, any dismantling should be done on a clean, flat workbench or table at a suitable working height.

Any workbench needs a vice; one with a jaw opening of 100 mm is suitable for most jobs. As mentioned previously, some clean dry storage space is also required for tools, as well as for any lubricants, cleaning fluids, touch-up paints etc, which become necessary.

Another item which may be required, and which has a much more general usage, is an electric drill with a chuck capacity of at least 8 mm. This, together with a good range of twist drills, is virtually essential for fitting accessories.

Last, but not least, always keep a supply of old newspapers and clean, lint-free rags available, and try to keep any working area as clean as possible.

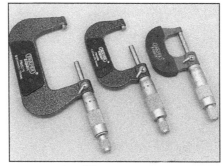

Micrometers

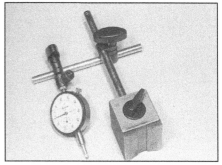

Dial test indicator ("dial gauge")

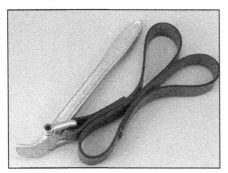

Strap wrench

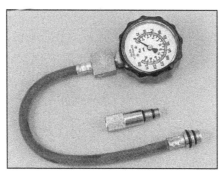

Compression tester

Fault code reader

This is a guide to getting your vehicle through the MOT test. Obviously it will not be possible to examine the vehicle to the same standard as the professional MOT tester. However, working through the following checks will enable you to identify any problem areas before submitting the vehicle for the test.

Where a testable component is in borderline condition, the tester has discretion in deciding whether to pass or fail it. The basis of such discretion is whether the tester would be happy for a close relative or friend to use the vehicle with the component in that condition. If the vehicle presented is clean and evidently well cared for, the tester may be more inclined to pass a borderline component than if the vehicle is scruffy and apparently neglected.

It has only been possible to summarise the test requirements here, based on the regulations in force at the time of printing. Test standards are becoming increasingly stringent, although there are some exemptions for older vehicles.

An assistant will be needed to help carry out some of these checks.

The checks have been sub-divided into four categories, as follows:

1 Checks carried out **FROM THE DRIVER'S SEAT**

2 Checks carried out **WITH THE VEHICLE ON THE GROUND**

3 Checks carried out **WITH THE VEHICLE RAISED AND THE WHEELS FREE TO TURN**

4 Checks carried out on **YOUR VEHICLE'S EXHAUST EMISSION SYSTEM**

---

1 Checks carried out **FROM THE DRIVER'S SEAT**

Handbrake

☐ Test the operation of the handbrake. Excessive travel (too many clicks) indicates incorrect brake or cable adjustment.

☐ Check that the handbrake cannot be released by tapping the lever sideways. Check the security of the lever mountings.

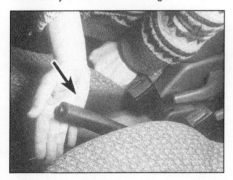

Footbrake

☐ Depress the brake pedal and check that it does not creep down to the floor, indicating a master cylinder fault. Release the pedal, wait a few seconds, then depress it again. If the pedal travels nearly to the floor before firm resistance is felt, brake adjustment or repair is necessary. If the pedal feels spongy, there is air in the hydraulic system which must be removed by bleeding.

☐ Check that the brake pedal is secure and in good condition. Check also for signs of fluid leaks on the pedal, floor or carpets, which would indicate failed seals in the brake master cylinder.

☐ Check the servo unit (when applicable) by operating the brake pedal several times, then keeping the pedal depressed and starting the engine. As the engine starts, the pedal will move down slightly. If not, the vacuum hose or the servo itself may be faulty.

Steering wheel and column

☐ Examine the steering wheel for fractures or looseness of the hub, spokes or rim.

☐ Move the steering wheel from side to side and then up and down. Check that the steering wheel is not loose on the column, indicating wear or a loose retaining nut. Continue moving the steering wheel as before, but also turn it slightly from left to right.

☐ Check that the steering wheel is not loose on the column, and that there is no abnormal

movement of the steering wheel, indicating wear in the column support bearings or couplings.

Windscreen, mirrors and sunvisor

☐ The windscreen must be free of cracks or other significant damage within the driver's field of view. (Small stone chips are acceptable.) Rear view mirrors must be secure, intact, and capable of being adjusted.

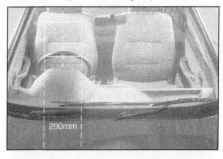

☐ The driver's sunvisor must be capable of being stored in the "up" position.

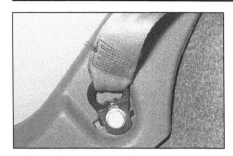

Seat belts and seats

Note: *The following checks are applicable to all seat belts, front and rear.*

☐ Examine the webbing of all the belts (including rear belts if fitted) for cuts, serious fraying or deterioration. Fasten and unfasten each belt to check the buckles. If applicable, check the retracting mechanism. Check the security of all seat belt mountings accessible from inside the vehicle.

☐ Seat belts with pre-tensioners, once activated, have a "flag" or similar showing on the seat belt stalk. This, in itself, is not a reason for test failure.

☐ The front seats themselves must be securely attached and the backrests must lock in the upright position.

Doors

☐ Both front doors must be able to be opened and closed from outside and inside, and must latch securely when closed.

2 Checks carried out WITH THE VEHICLE ON THE GROUND

Vehicle identification

☐ Number plates must be in good condition, secure and legible, with letters and numbers correctly spaced – spacing at (A) should be at least twice that at (B).

☐ The VIN plate and/or homologation plate must be legible.

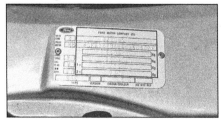

Electrical equipment

☐ Switch on the ignition and check the operation of the horn.

☐ Check the windscreen washers and wipers, examining the wiper blades; renew damaged or perished blades. Also check the operation of the stop-lights.

☐ Check the operation of the sidelights and number plate lights. The lenses and reflectors must be secure, clean and undamaged.

☐ Check the operation and alignment of the headlights. The headlight reflectors must not be tarnished and the lenses must be undamaged.

☐ Switch on the ignition and check the operation of the direction indicators (including the instrument panel tell-tale) and the hazard warning lights. Operation of the sidelights and stop-lights must not affect the indicators - if it does, the cause is usually a bad earth at the rear light cluster.

☐ Check the operation of the rear foglight(s), including the warning light on the instrument panel or in the switch.

☐ The ABS warning light must illuminate in accordance with the manufacturers' design. For most vehicles, the ABS warning light should illuminate when the ignition is switched on, and (if the system is operating properly) extinguish after a few seconds. Refer to the owner's handbook.

Footbrake

☐ Examine the master cylinder, brake pipes and servo unit for leaks, loose mountings, corrosion or other damage.

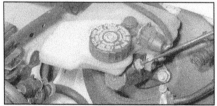

☐ The fluid reservoir must be secure and the fluid level must be between the upper (**A**) and lower (**B**) markings.

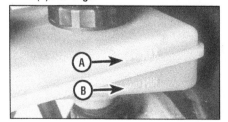

☐ Inspect both front brake flexible hoses for cracks or deterioration of the rubber. Turn the steering from lock to lock, and ensure that the hoses do not contact the wheel, tyre, or any part of the steering or suspension mechanism. With the brake pedal firmly depressed, check the hoses for bulges or leaks under pressure.

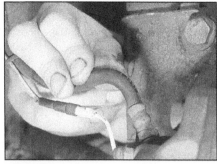

Steering and suspension

☐ Have your assistant turn the steering wheel from side to side slightly, up to the point where the steering gear just begins to transmit this movement to the roadwheels. Check for excessive free play between the steering wheel and the steering gear, indicating wear or insecurity of the steering column joints, the column-to-steering gear coupling, or the steering gear itself.

☐ Have your assistant turn the steering wheel more vigorously in each direction, so that the roadwheels just begin to turn. As this is done, examine all the steering joints, linkages, fittings and attachments. Renew any component that shows signs of wear or damage. On vehicles with power steering, check the security and condition of the steering pump, drivebelt and hoses.

☐ Check that the vehicle is standing level, and at approximately the correct ride height.

Shock absorbers

☐ Depress each corner of the vehicle in turn, then release it. The vehicle should rise and then settle in its normal position. If the vehicle continues to rise and fall, the shock absorber is defective. A shock absorber which has seized will also cause the vehicle to fail.

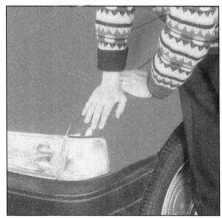

Exhaust system

☐ Start the engine. With your assistant holding a rag over the tailpipe, check the entire system for leaks. Repair or renew leaking sections.

3 Checks carried out
WITH THE VEHICLE RAISED AND THE WHEELS FREE TO TURN

Jack up the front and rear of the vehicle, and securely support it on axle stands. Position the stands clear of the suspension assemblies. Ensure that the wheels are clear of the ground and that the steering can be turned from lock to lock.

Steering mechanism

☐ Have your assistant turn the steering from lock to lock. Check that the steering turns smoothly, and that no part of the steering mechanism, including a wheel or tyre, fouls any brake hose or pipe or any part of the body structure.
☐ Examine the steering rack rubber gaiters for damage or insecurity of the retaining clips. If power steering is fitted, check for signs of damage or leakage of the fluid hoses, pipes or connections. Also check for excessive stiffness or binding of the steering, a missing split pin or locking device, or severe corrosion of the body structure within 30 cm of any steering component attachment point.

Front and rear suspension and wheel bearings

☐ Starting at the front right-hand side, grasp the roadwheel at the 3 o'clock and 9 o'clock positions and rock gently but firmly. Check for free play or insecurity at the wheel bearings, suspension balljoints, or suspension mountings, pivots and attachments.
☐ Now grasp the wheel at the 12 o'clock and 6 o'clock positions and repeat the previous inspection. Spin the wheel, and check for roughness or tightness of the front wheel bearing.

☐ If excess free play is suspected at a component pivot point, this can be confirmed by using a large screwdriver or similar tool and levering between the mounting and the component attachment. This will confirm whether the wear is in the pivot bush, its retaining bolt, or in the mounting itself (the bolt holes can often become elongated).

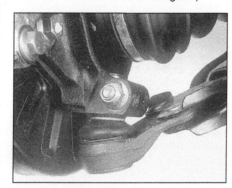

☐ Carry out all the above checks at the other front wheel, and then at both rear wheels.

Springs and shock absorbers

☐ Examine the suspension struts (when applicable) for serious fluid leakage, corrosion, or damage to the casing. Also check the security of the mounting points.
☐ If coil springs are fitted, check that the spring ends locate in their seats, and that the spring is not corroded, cracked or broken.
☐ If leaf springs are fitted, check that all leaves are intact, that the axle is securely attached to each spring, and that there is no deterioration of the spring eye mountings, bushes, and shackles.

☐ The same general checks apply to vehicles fitted with other suspension types, such as torsion bars, hydraulic displacer units, etc. Ensure that all mountings and attachments are secure, that there are no signs of excessive wear, corrosion or damage, and (on hydraulic types) that there are no fluid leaks or damaged pipes.
☐ Inspect the shock absorbers for signs of serious fluid leakage. Check for wear of the mounting bushes or attachments, or damage to the body of the unit.

Driveshafts
(fwd vehicles only)

☐ Rotate each front wheel in turn and inspect the constant velocity joint gaiters for splits or damage. Also check that each driveshaft is straight and undamaged.

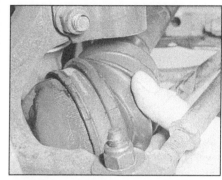

Braking system

☐ If possible without dismantling, check brake pad wear and disc condition. Ensure that the friction lining material has not worn excessively, (A) and that the discs are not fractured, pitted, scored or badly worn (B).

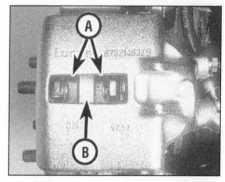

☐ Examine all the rigid brake pipes underneath the vehicle, and the flexible hose(s) at the rear. Look for corrosion, chafing or insecurity of the pipes, and for signs of bulging under pressure, chafing, splits or deterioration of the flexible hoses.
☐ Look for signs of fluid leaks at the brake calipers or on the brake backplates. Repair or renew leaking components.
☐ Slowly spin each wheel, while your assistant depresses and releases the footbrake. Ensure that each brake is operating and does not bind when the pedal is released.

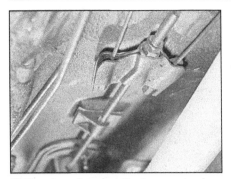

☐ Examine the handbrake mechanism, checking for frayed or broken cables, excessive corrosion, or wear or insecurity of the linkage. Check that the mechanism works on each relevant wheel, and releases fully, without binding.

☐ It is not possible to test brake efficiency without special equipment, but a road test can be carried out later to check that the vehicle pulls up in a straight line.

Fuel and exhaust systems

☐ Inspect the fuel tank (including the filler cap), fuel pipes, hoses and unions. All components must be secure and free from leaks.

☐ Examine the exhaust system over its entire length, checking for any damaged, broken or missing mountings, security of the retaining clamps and rust or corrosion.

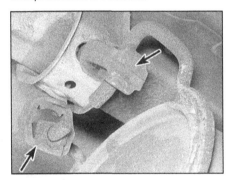

Wheels and tyres

☐ Examine the sidewalls and tread area of each tyre in turn. Check for cuts, tears, lumps, bulges, separation of the tread, and exposure of the ply or cord due to wear or damage. Check that the tyre bead is correctly seated on the wheel rim, that the valve is sound and properly seated, and that the wheel is not distorted or damaged.

☐ Check that the tyres are of the correct size for the vehicle, that they are of the same size and type on each axle, and that the pressures are correct.

☐ Check the tyre tread depth. The legal minimum at the time of writing is 1.6 mm over at least three-quarters of the tread width. Abnormal tread wear may indicate incorrect front wheel alignment.

Body corrosion

☐ Check the condition of the entire vehicle structure for signs of corrosion in load-bearing areas. (These include chassis box sections, side sills, cross-members, pillars, and all suspension, steering, braking system and seat belt mountings and anchorages.) Any corrosion which has seriously reduced the thickness of a load-bearing area is likely to cause the vehicle to fail. In this case professional repairs are likely to be needed.

☐ Damage or corrosion which causes sharp or otherwise dangerous edges to be exposed will also cause the vehicle to fail.

4 Checks carried out on YOUR VEHICLE'S EXHAUST EMISSION SYSTEM

Petrol models

☐ Have the engine at normal operating temperature, and make sure that it is in good tune (ignition system in good order, air filter element clean, etc).

☐ Before any measurements are carried out, raise the engine speed to around 2500 rpm, and hold it at this speed for 20 seconds. Allow the engine speed to return to idle, and watch for smoke emissions from the exhaust tailpipe. If the idle speed is obviously much too high, or if dense blue or clearly-visible black smoke comes from the tailpipe for more than 5 seconds, the vehicle will fail. As a rule of thumb, blue smoke signifies oil being burnt (engine wear) while black smoke signifies unburnt fuel (dirty air cleaner element, or other carburettor or fuel system fault).

☐ An exhaust gas analyser capable of measuring carbon monoxide (CO) and hydrocarbons (HC) is now needed. If such an instrument cannot be hired or borrowed, a local garage may agree to perform the check for a small fee.

CO emissions (mixture)

☐ At the time of writing, for vehicles first used between 1st August 1975 and 31st July 1986 (P to C registration), the CO level must not exceed 4.5% by volume. For vehicles first used between 1st August 1986 and 31st July 1992 (D to J registration), the CO level must not exceed 3.5% by volume. Vehicles first

used after 1st August 1992 (K registration) must conform to the manufacturer's specification. The MOT tester has access to a DOT database or emissions handbook, which lists the CO and HC limits for each make and model of vehicle. The CO level is measured with the engine at idle speed, and at "fast idle". The following limits are given as a general guide:

At idle speed -
CO level no more than 0.5%
At "fast idle" (2500 to 3000 rpm) -
CO level no more than 0.3%
(Minimum oil temperature 60°C)

☐ If the CO level cannot be reduced far enough to pass the test (and the fuel and ignition systems are otherwise in good condition) then the carburettor is badly worn, or there is some problem in the fuel injection system or catalytic converter (as applicable).

HC emissions

☐ With the CO within limits, HC emissions for vehicles first used between 1st August 1975 and 31st July 1992 (P to J registration) must not exceed 1200 ppm. Vehicles first used after 1st August 1992 (K registration) must conform to the manufacturer's specification. The MOT tester has access to a DOT database or emissions handbook, which lists the CO and HC limits for each make and model of vehicle. The HC level is measured with the engine at "fast idle". The following is given as a general guide:

At "fast idle" (2500 to 3000 rpm) -
HC level no more than 200 ppm
(Minimum oil temperature 60°C)

☐ Excessive HC emissions are caused by incomplete combustion, the causes of which can include oil being burnt, mechanical wear and ignition/fuel system malfunction.

Diesel models

☐ The only emission test applicable to Diesel engines is the measuring of exhaust smoke density. The test involves accelerating the engine several times to its maximum unloaded speed.

Note: It is of the utmost importance that the engine timing belt is in good condition before the test is carried out.

☐ The limits for Diesel engine exhaust smoke, introduced in September 1995 are:

Vehicles first used before 1st August 1979:
Exempt from metered smoke testing, but must not emit "dense blue or clearly visible black smoke for a period of more than 5 seconds at idle" or "dense blue or clearly visible black smoke during acceleration which would obscure the view of other road users".

Non-turbocharged vehicles first used after 1st August 1979: 2.5m-1

Turbocharged vehicles first used after 1st August 1979: 3.0m-1

☐ Excessive smoke can be caused by a dirty air cleaner element. Otherwise, professional advice may be needed to find the cause.

Engine

- [ ] Engine backfires
- [ ] Engine diesels (continues to run) after switching off
- [ ] Engine hard to start when cold
- [ ] Engine hard to start when hot
- [ ] Engine lacks power
- [ ] Engine lopes while idling or idles erratically
- [ ] Engine misses at idle speed
- [ ] Engine misses throughout driving speed range
- [ ] Engine rotates but will not start
- [ ] Engine runs with oil pressure light on
- [ ] Engine stalls
- [ ] Engine starts but stops immediately
- [ ] Engine stumbles on acceleration
- [ ] Engine surges while holding accelerator steady
- [ ] Engine will not rotate when attempting to start
- [ ] Oil puddle under engine
- [ ] Pinking or knocking engine sounds during acceleration or uphill
- [ ] Starter motor noisy or excessively rough in engagement

Engine electrical system

- [ ] Alternator light fails to come on when key is turned on
- [ ] Alternator light fails to go out
- [ ] Battery will not hold a charge

Fuel system

- [ ] Excessive fuel consumption
- [ ] Fuel leakage and/or fuel odour

Cooling system

- [ ] Coolant loss
- [ ] External coolant leakage
- [ ] Internal coolant leakage
- [ ] Overcooling
- [ ] Overheating
- [ ] Poor coolant circulation

Clutch

- [ ] Clutch pedal stays on floor
- [ ] Clutch slips (engine speed increases with no increase in vehicle speed
- [ ] Grabbing (chattering) as clutch is engaged
- [ ] High pedal effort
- [ ] Noise in clutch area
- [ ] Pedal travels to floor - no pressure or very little resistance
- [ ] Transmission rattling (clicking)
- [ ] Unable to select gears

Manual transmission

- [ ] Clicking noise in turns
- [ ] Clunk on acceleration or deceleration
- [ ] Knocking noise at low speeds
- [ ] Leaks lubricant
- [ ] Hard to shift
- [ ] Noise most pronounced when turning
- [ ] Noisy in all gears
- [ ] Noisy in neutral with engine running
- [ ] Noisy in one particular gear
- [ ] Slips out of gear
- [ ] Vibration

Automatic transmission

- [ ] Engine will start in gears other than Park or Neutral
- [ ] Fluid leakage
- [ ] General shift mechanism problems
- [ ] Transmission fluid brown or has burned smell
- [ ] Transmission slips, shifts roughly, is noisy or has no drive in forward or reverse gears
- [ ] Transmission will not downshift with accelerator pedal pressed to the floor

Driveshafts

- [ ] Clicking noise in turns
- [ ] Shudder or vibration during acceleration
- [ ] Vibration at highway speeds

Brakes

- [ ] Brake pedal feels spongy when depressed
- [ ] Brake pedal travels to the floor with little resistance
- [ ] Brake roughness or chatter (pedal pulsates)
- [ ] Dragging brakes
- [ ] Excessive brake pedal travel
- [ ] Excessive pedal effort required to stop vehicle
- [ ] Grabbing or uneven braking action
- [ ] Noise (high-pitched squeal when the brakes are applied)
- [ ] Handbrake does not hold
- [ ] Vehicle pulls to one side during braking

Suspension and steering systems

- [ ] Abnormal noise at the front end
- [ ] Abnormal or excessive tyre wear
- [ ] Cupped tyres
- [ ] Erratic steering when braking
- [ ] Excessive pitching and/or rolling around corners or during braking
- [ ] Excessive play or looseness in steering system
- [ ] Excessive tyre wear on inside edge
- [ ] Excessive tyre wear on outside edge
- [ ] Hard steering
- [ ] Poor returnability of steering to centre
- [ ] Rattling or clicking noise in steering gear
- [ ] Shimmy, shake or vibration
- [ ] Suspension bottoms
- [ ] Tyre tread worn in one place
- [ ] Vehicle pulls to one side
- [ ] Wander or poor steering stability
- [ ] Wheel makes a thumping noise

Introduction

This section provides an easy reference guide to the more common problems which may occur during the operation of your vehicle. These problems and their possible causes are grouped under headings denoting various components or systems, such as Engine, Cooling system, etc. They also refer you to the chapter and/or section which deals with the problem.

Remember that successful troubleshooting is not a mysterious black art practised only by professional mechanics. It is simply the result of the right knowledge combined with an intelligent, systematic approach to the problem. Always work by a process of elimination, starting with the simplest solution and working through to the most complex - and

never overlook the obvious. Anyone can run the gas tank dry or leave the lights on overnight, so don't assume that you are exempt from such oversights.

Finally, always establish a clear idea of why a problem has occurred and take steps to ensure that it doesn't happen again. If the electrical system fails because of a poor connection, check the other connections in the system to make sure that they don't fail as well. If a particular fuse continues to blow, find out why - don't just renew one fuse after another. Remember, failure of a small component can often be indicative of potential failure or incorrect functioning of a more important component or system.

Engine

Engine will not rotate when attempting to start

☐ Battery terminal connections loose or corroded (Chapter 1).
☐ Battery discharged or faulty (Chapter 1).
☐ Automatic transmission not completely engaged in Park (Chapter 7) or clutch pedal not completely depressed (Chapter 8).
☐ Broken, loose or disconnected wiring in the starting circuit (Chapters 5 and 12).
☐ Starter motor pinion jammed in flywheel ring gear (Chapter 5).
☐ Starter solenoid faulty (Chapter 5).
☐ Starter motor faulty (Chapter 5).
☐ Ignition switch faulty (Chapter 12).
☐ Starter pinion or flywheel teeth worn or broken (Chapter 5).
☐ Defective fusible link (see Chapter 12).

Engine rotates but will not start

☐ Fuel tank empty.
☐ Battery discharged (engine rotates slowly) (Chapter 5).
☐ Battery terminal connections loose or corroded (Chapter 1).
☐ Leaking fuel injector(s), faulty fuel pump, pressure regulator, etc. (Chapter 4).
☐ Broken or stripped timing belt Chapter 2).
☐ Ignition components damp or damaged (Chapter 5).
☐ Worn, faulty or incorrectly gapped spark plugs (Chapter 1).
☐ Broken, loose or disconnected wiring in the starting circuit (Chapter 5).
☐ Broken, loose or disconnected wires at the ignition coils or faulty coils (Chapter 5).
☐ Defective crankshaft sensor or PCM (see Chapter 6).

Engine hard to start when cold

☐ Battery discharged or low (Chapter 1).
☐ Malfunctioning fuel system (Chapter 4).
☐ Faulty coolant temperature sensor or intake air temperature sensor (Chapter 6).
☐ Fuel injector(s) leaking (Chapter 4).
☐ Faulty ignition system (Chapter 5).

Engine hard to start when hot

☐ Air filter clogged (Chapter 1).
☐ Fuel not reaching the fuel injection system (Chapter 4).
☐ Corroded battery connections, especially earth (Chapter 1).
☐ Faulty coolant temperature sensor or intake air temperature sensor (Chapter 6).

Starter motor noisy or excessively rough in engagement

☐ Pinion or flywheel gear teeth worn or broken (Chapter 5).
☐ Starter motor mounting bolts loose or missing (Chapter 5).

Engine starts but stops immediately

☐ Loose or faulty electrical connections at ignition coil (Chapter 5).
☐ Insufficient fuel reaching the fuel injector(s) (Chapters 4).
☐ Vacuum leak at the gasket between the intake manifold/plenum and throttle body (Chapter 4).
☐ Fault in the engine control system (Chapter 6).
☐ Intake air leaks, broken vacuum lines (see Chapter 4)

Oil puddle under engine

☐ Sump gasket and/or sump drain bolt washer leaking (Chapter 2).
☐ Oil pressure sending unit leaking (Chapter 2).
☐ Valve covers leaking (Chapter 2).
☐ Engine oil seals leaking (Chapter 2).

Engine lopes while idling or idles erratically

☐ Vacuum leakage (Chapters 2 and 4).
☐ Leaking EGR valve (Chapter 6).
☐ Air filter clogged (Chapter 1).
☐ Fuel pump not delivering sufficient fuel to the fuel injection system (Chapter 4).
☐ Leaking head gasket (Chapter 2).
☐ Timing belt and/or pulleys worn (Chapter 2).
☐ Camshaft lobes worn (Chapter 2).

Engine misses at idle speed

☐ Spark plugs worn or not gapped properly (Chapter 1).
☐ Faulty spark plug leads (Chapter 1).
☐ Vacuum leaks (Chapters 2 and 4).
☐ Faulty ignition coil(s) (Chapter 5).
☐ Uneven or low compression (Chapter 2).
☐ Faulty fuel injector(s) (Chapter 4).

Engine misses throughout driving speed range

☐ Fuel filter clogged and/or impurities in the fuel system (Chapter 1).
☐ Low fuel output at the fuel injector(s) (Chapter 4).
☐ Faulty or incorrectly gapped spark plugs (Chapter 1).
☐ Leaking spark plug leads (Chapters 1 or 5).
☐ Faulty emission system components (Chapter 6).
☐ Low or uneven cylinder compression pressures (Chapter 2).
☐ Burned valves (Chapter 2).
☐ Weak or faulty ignition system (Chapter 5).
☐ Vacuum leak in fuel injection system, throttle body, intake manifold or vacuum hoses (Chapter 4).

Engine (continued)

Engine stumbles on acceleration
- ☐ Spark plugs fouled (Chapter 1).
- ☐ Problem with fuel injection system (Chapter 4).
- ☐ Fuel filter clogged (Chapters 1 and 4).
- ☐ Fault in the engine control system (Chapter 6).
- ☐ Intake manifold air leak (Chapters 2 and 4).
- ☐ EGR system malfunction (Chapter 6).

Engine surges while holding accelerator steady
- ☐ Intake air leak (Chapter 4).
- ☐ Fuel pump or fuel pressure regulator faulty (Chapter 4).
- ☐ Problem with fuel injection system (Chapter 4).
- ☐ Problem with the emissions control system (Chapter 6).

Engine stalls
- ☐ Idle speed incorrect (Chapter 1).
- ☐ Fuel filter clogged and/or water and impurities in the fuel system (Chapters 1 and 4).
- ☐ Ignition components damp or damaged (Chapter 5).
- ☐ Faulty emissions system components (Chapter 6).
- ☐ Faulty or incorrectly gapped spark plugs (Chapter 1).
- ☐ Faulty spark plug leads (Chapter 1).
- ☐ Vacuum leak in the fuel injection system, intake manifold or vacuum hoses (Chapters 2 and 4).

Engine backfires
- ☐ Emission control system not functioning properly (Chapter 6).
- ☐ Faulty spark plug leads or coil(s) (Chapter 5).
- ☐ Problem with the fuel injection system (Chapter 4).
- ☐ Vacuum leak at fuel injector(s), intake manifold or vacuum hoses (Chapters 2 and 4).
- ☐ Burned valves or incorrect valve timing (Chapter 2).

Engine lacks power
- ☐ Worn camshaft lobes (Chapter 2).
- ☐ Burned valves or incorrect valve timing (Chapter 2).
- ☐ Faulty spark plug leads or faulty coil (Chapters 1 and 5).
- ☐ Faulty or incorrectly gapped spark plugs (Chapter 1).
- ☐ Problem with the fuel injection system (Chapter 4).
- ☐ Plugged air filter (Chapter 1).
- ☐ Brakes binding (Chapter 9).
- ☐ Automatic transmission fluid level incorrect (Chapter 1).
- ☐ Clutch slipping (Chapter 8).
- ☐ Fuel filter clogged and/or impurities in the fuel system (Chapters 1 and 4).
- ☐ Emission control system not functioning properly (Chapter 6).
- ☐ Low or uneven cylinder compression pressures (Chapter 2).
- ☐ Restricted exhaust system (Chapters 4).

Pinking or knocking engine sounds during acceleration or uphill
- ☐ Incorrect grade of fuel.
- ☐ Problem with the engine control system (Chapter 6).
- ☐ Fuel injection system faulty (Chapter 4).
- ☐ Improper or damaged spark plugs or wires (Chapter 1).
- ☐ EGR valve not functioning (Chapter 6).
- ☐ Vacuum leak (Chapters 2 and 4).

Engine runs with oil pressure light on
- ☐ Low oil level (*Weekly checks*).
- ☐ Idle rpm below specification (Chapter 1).
- ☐ Short in wiring circuit (Chapter 12).
- ☐ Faulty oil pressure sender (Chapter 2).
- ☐ Worn engine bearings and/or oil pump (Chapter 2).

Engine diesels (continues to run) after switching off
- ☐ Idle speed too high (Chapter 1).
- ☐ Excessive engine operating temperature (Chapter 3).
- ☐ Excessive carbon deposits on valves and pistons (see Chapter 2).

Engine electrical system

Battery will not hold a charge
- ☐ Alternator drivebelt defective or not adjusted properly (Chapter 1).
- ☐ Battery electrolyte level low (Chapter 1).
- ☐ Battery terminals loose or corroded (Chapter 1).
- ☐ Alternator not charging properly (Chapter 5).
- ☐ Loose, broken or faulty wiring in the charging circuit (Chapter 5).
- ☐ Short in vehicle wiring (Chapter 12).
- ☐ Internally defective battery (Chapters 1 and 5).

Alternator light fails to go out
- ☐ Faulty alternator or charging circuit (Chapter 5).
- ☐ Alternator drivebelt defective or out of adjustment (Chapter 1).
- ☐ Alternator voltage regulator inoperative (Chapter 5).

Alternator light fails to come on when key is turned on
- ☐ Warning light bulb defective (Chapter 12).
- ☐ Fault in the printed circuit, dash wiring or bulb holder (Chapter 12).

Fuel system

Excessive fuel consumption
- ☐ Dirty or clogged air filter element (Chapter 1).
- ☐ Emissions system not functioning properly (Chapter 6).
- ☐ Fuel injection system not functioning properly (Chapter 4).
- ☐ Low tyre pressure or incorrect tyre size (*Weekly checks*).

Fuel leakage and/or fuel odour
- ☐ Leaking fuel feed or return line (Chapters 1 and 4).
- ☐ Tank overfilled.
- ☐ Evaporative canister filter clogged (Chapters 1 and 6).
- ☐ Problem with fuel injection system (Chapter 4).

Cooling system

Overheating
- [ ] Insufficient coolant in system (*Weekly checks*).
- [ ] Water pump defective (Chapter 3).
- [ ] Radiator core blocked or grille restricted (Chapter 3).
- [ ] Thermostat faulty (Chapter 3).
- [ ] Electric coolant fan inoperative or blades broken (Chapter 3).
- [ ] Radiator cap not maintaining proper pressure (Chapter 3).

Overcooling
- [ ] Faulty thermostat (Chapter 3).
- [ ] Inaccurate temperature gauge sending unit (Chapter 3).

External coolant leakage
- [ ] Deteriorated/damaged hoses; loose clamps (Chapters 1 and 3).
- [ ] Water pump defective (Chapter 3).
- [ ] Leakage from radiator core or coolant reservoir bottle (Chapter 3).
- [ ] Engine drain or water jacket core plugs leaking (Chapter 2).

Internal coolant leakage
- [ ] Leaking cylinder head gasket (Chapter 2).
- [ ] Cracked cylinder bore or cylinder head (Chapter 2).

Coolant loss
- [ ] Too much coolant in system (Chapter 1).
- [ ] Coolant boiling away because of overheating (Chapter 3).
- [ ] Internal or external leakage (Chapter 3).
- [ ] Faulty pressure cap (Chapter 3).

Poor coolant circulation
- [ ] Inoperative water pump (Chapter 3).
- [ ] Restriction in cooling system (Chapters 1 and 3).
- [ ] Thermostat sticking (Chapter 3).

Clutch

Pedal travels to floor - no pressure or very little resistance
- [ ] Master cylinder or release cylinder faulty (Chapter 8).
- [ ] Fluid line, hose or connection leaking (Chapter 8).
- [ ] No fluid in reservoir (Chapter 8).
- [ ] Broken release bearing or fork (Chapter 8).

Unable to select gears
- [ ] Faulty transmission (Chapter 7).
- [ ] Faulty clutch disc or pressure plate (Chapter 8).
- [ ] Faulty release lever or release bearing (Chapter 8).
- [ ] Faulty shift lever assembly or rods (Chapter 8).

Clutch slips (engine speed increases with no increase in vehicle speed)
- [ ] Clutch plate worn (Chapter 8).
- [ ] Clutch plate is oil soaked by leaking rear main seal (Chapter 8).
- [ ] Clutch plate not seated (Chapter 8).
- [ ] Warped pressure plate or flywheel (Chapter 8).
- [ ] Weak diaphragm springs (Chapter 8).
- [ ] Clutch plate overheated. Allow to cool.

Grabbing (chattering) as clutch is engaged
- [ ] Oil on clutch plate lining, burned or glazed facings (Chapter 8).
- [ ] Worn or loose engine or transmission mounts (Chapters 2 and 7).
- [ ] Worn splines on clutch plate hub (Chapter 8).
- [ ] Warped pressure plate or flywheel (Chapter 8).
- [ ] Burned or smeared resin on flywheel or pressure plate (Chapter 8).

Transmission rattling (clicking)
- [ ] Release fork loose (Chapter 8).
- [ ] Low engine idle speed (Chapter 1).

Noise in clutch area
- [ ] Faulty bearing (Chapter 8).

Clutch pedal stays on floor
- [ ] Broken release bearing or fork (Chapter 8).
- [ ] Clutch master cylinder piston binding in bore (Chapter 8).

High pedal effort
- [ ] Master cylinder piston binding in bore (Chapter 8).
- [ ] Pressure plate faulty (Chapter 8).

Manual transmission

Knocking noise at low speeds
- [ ] Worn driveshaft constant velocity (CV) joints (Chapter 8).
- [ ] Worn side gear shaft counterbore in differential case (Chapter 7A).*

Noise most pronounced when turning
- [ ] Differential gear noise (Chapter 7A).*

Clunk on acceleration or deceleration
- [ ] Loose engine or transmission mounts (Chapters 2 and 7A).
- [ ] Worn differential pinion shaft in case.*
- [ ] Worn side gear shaft counterbore in differential case (Chapter 7A).*
- [ ] Worn or damaged driveshaft inboard CV joints (Chapter 8).

Clicking noise in turns
- [ ] Worn or damaged outboard CV joint (Chapter 8).

Vibration
- [ ] Rough wheel bearing (Chapters 1 and 10).
- [ ] Damaged driveshaft (Chapter 8).
- [ ] Out of round tyres (*Weekly checks*).
- [ ] Tyre out of balance (Chapters 1 and 10).
- [ ] Worn CV joint (Chapter 8).

Noisy in neutral with engine running
- [ ] Damaged input gear bearing (Chapter 7A).*
- [ ] Damaged clutch release bearing (Chapter 8).

Manual transmission (continued)

Noisy in one particular gear

☐ Damaged or worn constant mesh gears (Chapter 7A).*
☐ Damaged or worn synchronisers (Chapter 7A).*
☐ Bent reverse fork (Chapter 7A).*
☐ Damaged fourth speed gear or output gear (Chapter 7A).*
☐ Worn or damaged reverse idler gear or idler bushing (Chapter 7A).*

Noisy in all gears

☐ Insufficient lubricant (Chapter 7A).
☐ Damaged or worn bearings (Chapter 7A).*
☐ Worn or damaged input gear shaft and/or output gear shaft (Chapter 7A).*

Leaks lubricant

☐ Driveshaft seals worn (Chapter 7A).
☐ Excessive amount of lubricant in transmission (Chapters 1 and 7A).
☐ Loose or broken input gear shaft bearing retainer (Chapter 7A).*
☐ Input gear bearing retainer O-ring and/or lip seal damaged (Chapter 7A).*
☐ Vehicle speed sensor O-ring leaking (Chapter 7A).

Slips out of gear

☐ Worn or improperly adjusted linkage (Chapter 7A).
☐ Transmission loose on engine (Chapter 7A).
☐ Shift linkage does not work freely, binds (Chapter 7A).
☐ Input gear bearing retainer broken or loose (Chapter 7A).*
☐ Foreign material between clutch cover and engine housing (Chapter 7A).
☐ Worn shift fork (Chapter 7A).*

Hard to shift

☐ Shift linkage loose or worn (Chapter 7A).
☐ *Although the corrective action necessary to remedy the symptoms described is beyond the scope of this manual, the above information should be helpful in isolating the cause of the condition so that the owner can communicate clearly with a professional mechanic.*

Automatic transmission

Note: *Due to the complexity of the automatic transmission, it is difficult for the home mechanic to properly diagnose and service this component. For problems other than the following, the vehicle should be taken to a dealer or transmission workshop.*

Fluid leakage

☐ Automatic transmission fluid is a deep red colour. Fluid leaks should not be confused with engine oil, which can easily be blown onto the transmission by air flow.
☐ To pinpoint a leak, first remove all built-up dirt and grime from the transmission housing with degreasing agents and/or steam cleaning. Then drive the vehicle at low speeds so air flow will not blow the leak far from its source. Raise the vehicle and determine where the leak is coming from. Common areas of leakage are:
Pan (Chapters 1 and 7)
Dipstick tube (Chapters 1 and 7)
Transmission oil lines (Chapter 7)
Speed sensor (Chapter 7)
Driveshaft oil seals (Chapter 7).

Transmission fluid brown or has a burned smell

☐ Transmission fluid overheated (Chapter 1).

Engine will start in gears other than Park or Neutral

☐ Neutral start switch out of adjustment or malfunctioning (Chapter 7B).

General shift mechanism problems

☐ Chapter 7, Part B, deals with checking and adjusting the shift linkage on automatic transmissions. Common problems which may be attributed to poorly adjusted linkage are:
Engine starting in gears other than Park or Neutral.
Indicator on shifter pointing to a gear other than the one actually being used.
Vehicle moves when in Park.
☐ Refer to Chapter 7B for the shift linkage adjustment procedure.

Transmission will not downshift with accelerator pedal pressed to the floor

☐ The transmission is electronically controlled. This type of problem - which is caused by a malfunction in the control unit, a sensor or solenoid, or the circuit itself - is beyond the scope of this book. Take the vehicle to a dealer service department or a competent automatic transmission workshop.

Transmission slips, shifts roughly, is noisy or has no drive in forward or reverse gears

☐ There are many probable causes for the above problems, but the home mechanic should be concerned with only one possibility - fluid level. Before taking the vehicle to a repair workshop, check the level and condition of the fluid as described in Chapter 1. Correct the fluid level as necessary or change the fluid and filter if needed. If the problem persists, have a professional diagnose the cause.

Driveshafts

Clicking noise in turns

☐ Worn or damaged outboard CV joint (Chapter 8).

Shudder or vibration during acceleration

☐ Excessive toe-in (Chapter 10).
☐ Incorrect spring heights (Chapter 10).
☐ Worn or damaged inboard or outboard CV joints (Chapter 8).
☐ Sticking inboard CV joint assembly (Chapter 8).

Vibration at highway speeds

☐ Out of balance front wheels and/or tyres (Chapters 1 and 10).
☐ Out of round front tyres (Chapters 1 and 10).
☐ Worn CV joint(s) (Chapter 8).

Brakes

Note: *Before assuming that a brake problem exists, make sure that:*
The tyres are in good condition and properly inflated (Weekly checks).
The front end alignment is correct (Chapter 10).
The vehicle is not loaded with weight in an unequal manner.

Vehicle pulls to one side during braking

☐ Incorrect tyre pressures (*Weekly checks*).
☐ Front end out of alignment (have the front end aligned).
☐ Front, or rear, tyre sizes not matched to one another.
☐ Restricted brake lines or hoses (Chapter 9).
☐ Malfunctioning drum brake or caliper assembly (Chapter 9).
☐ Loose suspension parts (Chapter 10).
☐ Loose calipers (Chapter 9).
☐ Excessive wear of brake shoe or pad material or disc/drum on one side.

Noise (high-pitched squeal when the brakes are applied)

☐ Front and/or rear disc brake pads worn out. The noise comes from the wear sensor rubbing against the disc (does not apply to all vehicles). Renew pads with new ones immediately (Chapter 9).

Excessive brake pedal effort required to stop vehicle

☐ Malfunctioning power brake servo (Chapter 9).
☐ Partial system failure (Chapter 9).
☐ Excessively worn pads or shoes (Chapter 9).
☐ Piston in caliper or wheel cylinder stuck or sluggish (Chapter 9).
☐ Brake pads or shoes contaminated with oil or grease (Chapter 9).
☐ Brake disc grooved and/or glazed (Chapter 1).
☐ New pads or shoes installed and not yet seated. It will take a while for the new material to seat against the disc or drum.

Brake roughness or chatter (pedal pulsates)

☐ Excessive lateral runout (Chapter 9).
☐ Uneven pad wear (Chapter 9).
☐ Defective disc (Chapter 9).

Excessive brake pedal travel

☐ Partial brake system failure (Chapter 9).
☐ Insufficient fluid in master cylinder (Chapters 1 and 9).
☐ Air trapped in system (Chapters 1 and 9).

Dragging brakes

☐ Incorrect adjustment of brake light switch (Chapter 9).
☐ Master cylinder pistons not returning correctly (Chapter 9).
☐ Restricted brakes lines or hoses (Chapters 1 and 9).
☐ Incorrect handbrake adjustment (Chapter 9).

Grabbing or uneven braking action

☐ Malfunction of proportioning valve (Chapter 9).
☐ Malfunction of power brake servo unit (Chapter 9).
☐ Binding brake pedal mechanism (Chapter 9).

Brake pedal feels spongy when depressed

☐ Air in hydraulic lines (Chapter 9).
☐ Master cylinder mounting bolts loose (Chapter 9).
☐ Master cylinder defective (Chapter 9).

Brake pedal travels to the floor with little resistance

☐ Little or no fluid in the master cylinder reservoir caused by leaking caliper piston(s) (Chapter 9).
☐ Loose, damaged or disconnected brake lines (Chapter 9).

Handbrake does not hold

☐ Handbrake linkage improperly adjusted (Chapters 1 and 9).

Suspension and steering systems

Note: *Before attempting to diagnose the suspension and steering systems, perform the following preliminary checks:*
Tyres for wrong pressure and uneven wear.
Steering universal joints from the column to the rack and pinion for loose connectors or wear.
Front and rear suspension and the rack and pinion assembly for loose or damaged parts.
Out-of-round or out-of-balance tyres, bent rims and loose and/or rough wheel bearings.

Vehicle pulls to one side

☐ Mismatched or uneven tyres (Chapter 10).
☐ Broken or sagging springs (Chapter 10).
☐ Wheel alignment out-of-specifications (Chapter 10).
☐ Front brake dragging (Chapter 9).

Abnormal or excessive tyre wear

☐ Wheel alignment out-of-specifications (Chapter 10).
☐ Sagging or broken springs (Chapter 10).
☐ Tyre out-of-balance (Chapter 10).
☐ Worn strut damper (Chapter 10).
☐ Overloaded vehicle.
☐ Tyres not rotated regularly.

Wheel makes a thumping noise

☐ Blister or bump on tyre (Chapter 10).
☐ Improper strut damper action (Chapter 10).

Shimmy, shake or vibration

☐ Tyre or wheel out-of-balance or out-of-round (Chapter 10).
☐ Loose or worn wheel bearings (Chapters 1, 8 and 10).
☐ Worn tie-rod ends (Chapter 10).
☐ Worn lower balljoints (Chapters 1 and 10).
☐ Excessive wheel runout (Chapter 10).
☐ Blister or bump on tyre (Chapter 10).

Hard steering

☐ Lack of lubrication at balljoints, tie-rod ends and rack and pinion assembly (Chapter 10).
☐ Front wheel alignment out-of-specifications (Chapter 10).
☐ Low tyre pressure(s) (Chapters 1 and 10).

Poor returnability of steering to centre

☐ Lack of lubrication at balljoints and tie-rod ends (Chapter 10).
☐ Binding in balljoints (Chapter 10).
☐ Binding in steering column (Chapter 10).
☐ Lack of lubricant in steering gear assembly (Chapter 10).
☐ Front wheel alignment out-of-specifications (Chapter 10).

Suspension and steering systems (continued)

Abnormal noise at the front end

☐ Lack of lubrication at balljoints and tie-rod ends (Chapters 1 and 10).
☐ Damaged strut mounting (Chapter 10).
☐ Worn control arm bushings or tie-rod ends (Chapter 10).
☐ Loose anti-roll bar (Chapter 10).
☐ Loose wheel nuts (Chapters 1 and 10).
☐ Loose suspension bolts (Chapter 10)

Wander or poor steering stability

☐ Mismatched or uneven tyres (Chapter 10).
☐ Lack of lubrication at balljoints and tie-rod ends (Chapters 1 and 10).
☐ Worn strut assemblies (Chapter 10).
☐ Loose anti-roll bar (Chapter 10).
☐ Broken or sagging springs (Chapter 10).
☐ Wheels out of alignment (Chapter 10).

Erratic steering when braking

☐ Wheel bearings worn (Chapter 10).
☐ Broken or sagging springs (Chapter 10).
☐ Leaking wheel cylinder or caliper (Chapter 10).
☐ Warped rotors or drums (Chapter 10).

Excessive pitching and/or rolling around corners or during braking

☐ Loose anti-roll bar (Chapter 10).
☐ Worn strut dampers or mountings (Chapter 10).
☐ Broken or sagging springs (Chapter 10).
☐ Overloaded vehicle.

Suspension bottoms

☐ Overloaded vehicle.
☐ Worn strut dampers (Chapter 10).
☐ Incorrect, broken or sagging springs (Chapter 10).

Cupped tyres

☐ Front wheel or rear wheel alignment out-of-specifications (Chapter 10).
☐ Worn strut dampers (Chapter 10).
☐ Wheel bearings worn (Chapter 10).
☐ Excessive tyre or wheel runout (Chapter 10).
☐ Worn balljoints (Chapter 10).

Excessive tyre wear on outside edge

☐ Inflation pressures incorrect (*Weekly checks*).
☐ Excessive speed in turns.
☐ Front end alignment incorrect (excessive toe-in). Have professionally aligned.
☐ Suspension arm bent or twisted (Chapter 10).

Excessive tyre wear on inside edge

☐ Inflation pressures incorrect (*Weekly checks*).
☐ Front end alignment incorrect (toe-out). Have professionally aligned.
☐ Loose or damaged steering components (Chapter 10).

Tyre tread worn in one place

☐ Tyres out-of-balance.
☐ Damaged or buckled wheel. Inspect and renew if necessary.
☐ Defective tyre (*Weekly checks*).

Excessive play or looseness in steering system

☐ Wheel bearing(s) worn (Chapter 10).
☐ Tie-rod end loose (Chapter 10).
☐ Steering gear loose (Chapter 10).
☐ Worn or loose steering intermediate shaft (Chapter 10).

Rattling or clicking noise in steering gear

☐ Steering gear loose (Chapter 10).
☐ Steering gear defective.

A

ABS (Anti-lock brake system) A system, usually electronically controlled, that senses incipient wheel lockup during braking and relieves hydraulic pressure at wheels that are about to skid.

Air bag An inflatable bag hidden in the steering wheel (driver's side) or the dash or glovebox (passenger side). In a head-on collision, the bags inflate, preventing the driver and front passenger from being thrown forward into the steering wheel or windscreen.

Air cleaner A metal or plastic housing, containing a filter element, which removes dust and dirt from the air being drawn into the engine.

Air filter element The actual filter in an air cleaner system, usually manufactured from pleated paper and requiring renewal at regular intervals.

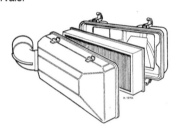

Air filter

Allen key A hexagonal wrench which fits into a recessed hexagonal hole.

Alligator clip A long-nosed spring-loaded metal clip with meshing teeth. Used to make temporary electrical connections.

Alternator A component in the electrical system which converts mechanical energy from a drivebelt into electrical energy to charge the battery and to operate the starting system, ignition system and electrical accessories.

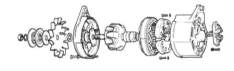

Alternator (exploded view)

Ampere (amp) A unit of measurement for the flow of electric current. One amp is the amount of current produced by one volt acting through a resistance of one ohm.

Anaerobic sealer A substance used to prevent bolts and screws from loosening. Anaerobic means that it does not require oxygen for activation. The Loctite brand is widely used.

Antifreeze A substance (usually ethylene glycol) mixed with water, and added to a vehicle's cooling system, to prevent freezing of the coolant in winter. Antifreeze also contains chemicals to inhibit corrosion and the formation of rust and other deposits that would tend to clog the radiator and coolant passages and reduce cooling efficiency.

Anti-seize compound A coating that reduces the risk of seizing on fasteners that are subjected to high temperatures, such as exhaust manifold bolts and nuts.

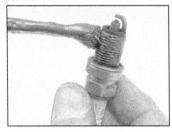

Anti-seize compound

Asbestos A natural fibrous mineral with great heat resistance, commonly used in the composition of brake friction materials. Asbestos is a health hazard and the dust created by brake systems should never be inhaled or ingested.

Axle A shaft on which a wheel revolves, or which revolves with a wheel. Also, a solid beam that connects the two wheels at one end of the vehicle. An axle which also transmits power to the wheels is known as a live axle.

Axle assembly

Axleshaft A single rotating shaft, on either side of the differential, which delivers power from the final drive assembly to the drive wheels. Also called a driveshaft or a halfshaft.

B

Ball bearing An anti-friction bearing consisting of a hardened inner and outer race with hardened steel balls between two races.

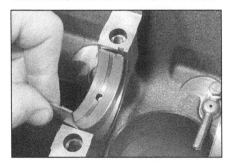

Bearing

Bearing The curved surface on a shaft or in a bore, or the part assembled into either, that permits relative motion between them with minimum wear and friction.

Big-end bearing The bearing in the end of the connecting rod that's attached to the crankshaft.

Bleed nipple A valve on a brake wheel cylinder, caliper or other hydraulic component that is opened to purge the hydraulic system of air. Also called a bleed screw.

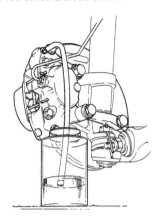

Brake bleeding

Brake bleeding Procedure for removing air from lines of a hydraulic brake system.

Brake disc The component of a disc brake that rotates with the wheels.

Brake drum The component of a drum brake that rotates with the wheels.

Brake linings The friction material which contacts the brake disc or drum to retard the vehicle's speed. The linings are bonded or riveted to the brake pads or shoes.

Brake pads The replaceable friction pads that pinch the brake disc when the brakes are applied. Brake pads consist of a friction material bonded or riveted to a rigid backing plate.

Brake shoe The crescent-shaped carrier to which the brake linings are mounted and which forces the lining against the rotating drum during braking.

Braking systems For more information on braking systems, consult the *Haynes Automotive Brake Manual*.

Breaker bar A long socket wrench handle providing greater leverage.

Bulkhead The insulated partition between the engine and the passenger compartment.

C

Caliper The non-rotating part of a disc-brake assembly that straddles the disc and carries the brake pads. The caliper also contains the hydraulic components that cause the pads to pinch the disc when the brakes are applied. A caliper is also a measuring tool that can be set to measure inside or outside dimensions of an object.

Camshaft A rotating shaft on which a series of cam lobes operate the valve mechanisms. The camshaft may be driven by gears, by sprockets and chain or by sprockets and a belt.

Canister A container in an evaporative emission control system; contains activated charcoal granules to trap vapours from the fuel system.

Canister

Carburettor A device which mixes fuel with air in the proper proportions to provide a desired power output from a spark ignition internal combustion engine.

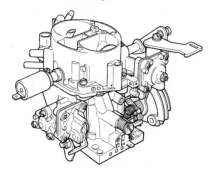

Carburettor

Castellated Resembling the parapets along the top of a castle wall. For example, a castellated balljoint stud nut.

Castellated nut

Castor In wheel alignment, the backward or forward tilt of the steering axis. Castor is positive when the steering axis is inclined rearward at the top.

Catalytic converter A silencer-like device in the exhaust system which converts certain pollutants in the exhaust gases into less harmful substances.

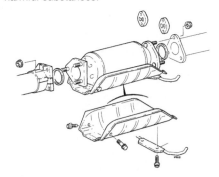

Catalytic converter

Circlip A ring-shaped clip used to prevent endwise movement of cylindrical parts and shafts. An internal circlip is installed in a groove in a housing; an external circlip fits into a groove on the outside of a cylindrical piece such as a shaft.

Clearance The amount of space between two parts. For example, between a piston and a cylinder, between a bearing and a journal, etc.

Coil spring A spiral of elastic steel found in various sizes throughout a vehicle, for example as a springing medium in the suspension and in the valve train.

Compression Reduction in volume, and increase in pressure and temperature, of a gas, caused by squeezing it into a smaller space.

Compression ratio The relationship between cylinder volume when the piston is at top dead centre and cylinder volume when the piston is at bottom dead centre.

Constant velocity (CV) joint A type of universal joint that cancels out vibrations caused by driving power being transmitted through an angle.

Core plug A disc or cup-shaped metal device inserted in a hole in a casting through which core was removed when the casting was formed. Also known as a freeze plug or expansion plug.

Crankcase The lower part of the engine block in which the crankshaft rotates.

Crankshaft The main rotating member, or shaft, running the length of the crankcase, with offset "throws" to which the connecting rods are attached.

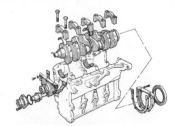

Crankshaft assembly

Crocodile clip See Alligator clip

D

Diagnostic code Code numbers obtained by accessing the diagnostic mode of an engine management computer. This code can be used to determine the area in the system where a malfunction may be located.

Disc brake A brake design incorporating a rotating disc onto which brake pads are squeezed. The resulting friction converts the energy of a moving vehicle into heat.

Double-overhead cam (DOHC) An engine that uses two overhead camshafts, usually one for the intake valves and one for the exhaust valves.

Drivebelt(s) The belt(s) used to drive accessories such as the alternator, water pump, power steering pump, air conditioning compressor, etc. off the crankshaft pulley.

Accessory drivebelts

Driveshaft Any shaft used to transmit motion. Commonly used when referring to the axleshafts on a front wheel drive vehicle.

Driveshaft

Drum brake A type of brake using a drum-shaped metal cylinder attached to the inner surface of the wheel. When the brake pedal is pressed, curved brake shoes with friction linings press against the inside of the drum to slow or stop the vehicle.

Drum brake assembly

E

EGR valve A valve used to introduce exhaust gases into the intake air stream.

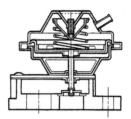

EGR valve

Electronic control unit (ECU) A computer which controls (for instance) ignition and fuel injection systems, or an anti-lock braking system. For more information refer to the *Haynes Automotive Electrical and Electronic Systems Manual.*

Electronic Fuel Injection (EFI) A computer controlled fuel system that distributes fuel through an injector located in each intake port of the engine.

Emergency brake A braking system, independent of the main hydraulic system, that can be used to slow or stop the vehicle if the primary brakes fail, or to hold the vehicle stationary even though the brake pedal isn't depressed. It usually consists of a hand lever that actuates either front or rear brakes mechanically through a series of cables and linkages. Also known as a handbrake or parking brake.

Endfloat The amount of lengthwise movement between two parts. As applied to a crankshaft, the distance that the crankshaft can move forward and back in the cylinder block.

Engine management system (EMS) A computer controlled system which manages the fuel injection and the ignition systems in an integrated fashion.

Exhaust manifold A part with several passages through which exhaust gases leave the engine combustion chambers and enter the exhaust pipe.

Exhaust manifold

F

Fan clutch A viscous (fluid) drive coupling device which permits variable engine fan speeds in relation to engine speeds.

Feeler blade A thin strip or blade of hardened steel, ground to an exact thickness, used to check or measure clearances between parts.

Feeler blade

Firing order The order in which the engine cylinders fire, or deliver their power strokes, beginning with the number one cylinder.

Flywheel A heavy spinning wheel in which energy is absorbed and stored by means of momentum. On cars, the flywheel is attached to the crankshaft to smooth out firing impulses.

Free play The amount of travel before any action takes place. The "looseness" in a linkage, or an assembly of parts, between the initial application of force and actual movement. For example, the distance the brake pedal moves before the pistons in the master cylinder are actuated.

Fuse An electrical device which protects a circuit against accidental overload. The typical fuse contains a soft piece of metal which is calibrated to melt at a predetermined current flow (expressed as amps) and break the circuit.

Fusible link A circuit protection device consisting of a conductor surrounded by heat-resistant insulation. The conductor is smaller than the wire it protects, so it acts as the weakest link in the circuit. Unlike a blown fuse, a failed fusible link must frequently be cut from the wire for replacement.

G

Gap The distance the spark must travel in jumping from the centre electrode to the side

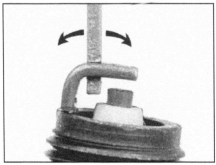

Adjusting spark plug gap

electrode in a spark plug. Also refers to the spacing between the points in a contact breaker assembly in a conventional points-type ignition, or to the distance between the reluctor or rotor and the pickup coil in an electronic ignition.

Gasket Any thin, soft material - usually cork, cardboard, asbestos or soft metal - installed between two metal surfaces to ensure a good seal. For instance, the cylinder head gasket seals the joint between the block and the cylinder head.

Gasket

Gauge An instrument panel display used to monitor engine conditions. A gauge with a movable pointer on a dial or a fixed scale is an analogue gauge. A gauge with a numerical readout is called a digital gauge.

H

Halfshaft A rotating shaft that transmits power from the final drive unit to a drive wheel, usually when referring to a live rear axle.

Harmonic balancer A device designed to reduce torsion or twisting vibration in the crankshaft. May be incorporated in the crankshaft pulley. Also known as a vibration damper.

Hone An abrasive tool for correcting small irregularities or differences in diameter in an engine cylinder, brake cylinder, etc.

Hydraulic tappet A tappet that utilises hydraulic pressure from the engine's lubrication system to maintain zero clearance (constant contact with both camshaft and valve stem). Automatically adjusts to variation in valve stem length. Hydraulic tappets also reduce valve noise.

I

Ignition timing The moment at which the spark plug fires, usually expressed in the number of crankshaft degrees before the piston reaches the top of its stroke.

Inlet manifold A tube or housing with passages through which flows the air-fuel mixture (carburettor vehicles and vehicles with throttle body injection) or air only (port fuel-injected vehicles) to the port openings in the cylinder head.

J

Jump start Starting the engine of a vehicle with a discharged or weak battery by attaching jump leads from the weak battery to a charged or helper battery.

L

Load Sensing Proportioning Valve (LSPV) A brake hydraulic system control valve that works like a proportioning valve, but also takes into consideration the amount of weight carried by the rear axle.

Locknut A nut used to lock an adjustment nut, or other threaded component, in place. For example, a locknut is employed to keep the adjusting nut on the rocker arm in position.

Lockwasher A form of washer designed to prevent an attaching nut from working loose.

M

MacPherson strut A type of front suspension system devised by Earle MacPherson at Ford of England. In its original form, a simple lateral link with the anti-roll bar creates the lower control arm. A long strut - an integral coil spring and shock absorber - is mounted between the body and the steering knuckle. Many modern so-called MacPherson strut systems use a conventional lower A-arm and don't rely on the anti-roll bar for location.

Multimeter An electrical test instrument with the capability to measure voltage, current and resistance.

N

NOx Oxides of Nitrogen. A common toxic pollutant emitted by petrol and diesel engines at higher temperatures.

O

Ohm The unit of electrical resistance. One volt applied to a resistance of one ohm will produce a current of one amp.

Ohmmeter An instrument for measuring electrical resistance.

O-ring A type of sealing ring made of a special rubber-like material; in use, the O-ring is compressed into a groove to provide the sealing action.

O-ring

Overhead cam (ohc) engine An engine with the camshaft(s) located on top of the cylinder head(s).

Overhead valve (ohv) engine An engine with the valves located in the cylinder head, but with the camshaft located in the engine block.

Oxygen sensor A device installed in the engine exhaust manifold, which senses the oxygen content in the exhaust and converts this information into an electric current. Also called a Lambda sensor.

P

Phillips screw A type of screw head having a cross instead of a slot for a corresponding type of screwdriver.

Plastigage A thin strip of plastic thread, available in different sizes, used for measuring clearances. For example, a strip of Plastigage is laid across a bearing journal. The parts are assembled and dismantled; the width of the crushed strip indicates the clearance between journal and bearing.

Plastigage

Propeller shaft The long hollow tube with universal joints at both ends that carries power from the transmission to the differential on front-engined rear wheel drive vehicles.

Proportioning valve A hydraulic control valve which limits the amount of pressure to the rear brakes during panic stops to prevent wheel lock-up.

R

Rack-and-pinion steering A steering system with a pinion gear on the end of the steering shaft that mates with a rack (think of a geared wheel opened up and laid flat). When the steering wheel is turned, the pinion turns, moving the rack to the left or right. This movement is transmitted through the track rods to the steering arms at the wheels.

Radiator A liquid-to-air heat transfer device designed to reduce the temperature of the coolant in an internal combustion engine cooling system.

Refrigerant Any substance used as a heat transfer agent in an air-conditioning system. R-12 has been the principle refrigerant for many years; recently, however, manufacturers have begun using R-134a, a non-CFC substance that is considered less harmful to

the ozone in the upper atmosphere.

Rocker arm A lever arm that rocks on a shaft or pivots on a stud. In an overhead valve engine, the rocker arm converts the upward movement of the pushrod into a downward movement to open a valve.

Rotor In a distributor, the rotating device inside the cap that connects the centre electrode and the outer terminals as it turns, distributing the high voltage from the coil secondary winding to the proper spark plug. Also, that part of an alternator which rotates inside the stator. Also, the rotating assembly of a turbocharger, including the compressor wheel, shaft and turbine wheel.

Runout The amount of wobble (in-and-out movement) of a gear or wheel as it's rotated. The amount a shaft rotates "out-of-true." The out-of-round condition of a rotating part.

S

Sealant A liquid or paste used to prevent leakage at a joint. Sometimes used in conjunction with a gasket.

Sealed beam lamp An older headlight design which integrates the reflector, lens and filaments into a hermetically-sealed one-piece unit. When a filament burns out or the lens cracks, the entire unit is simply replaced.

Serpentine drivebelt A single, long, wide accessory drivebelt that's used on some newer vehicles to drive all the accessories, instead of a series of smaller, shorter belts. Serpentine drivebelts are usually tensioned by an automatic tensioner.

Serpentine drivebelt

Shim Thin spacer, commonly used to adjust the clearance or relative positions between two parts. For example, shims inserted into or under bucket tappets control valve clearances. Clearance is adjusted by changing the thickness of the shim.

Slide hammer A special puller that screws into or hooks onto a component such as a shaft or bearing; a heavy sliding handle on the shaft bottoms against the end of the shaft to knock the component free.

Sprocket A tooth or projection on the periphery of a wheel, shaped to engage with a chain or drivebelt. Commonly used to refer to the sprocket wheel itself.

Starter inhibitor switch On vehicles with an

automatic transmission, a switch that prevents starting if the vehicle is not in Neutral or Park.

Strut See MacPherson strut.

T

Tappet A cylindrical component which transmits motion from the cam to the valve stem, either directly or via a pushrod and rocker arm. Also called a cam follower.

Thermostat A heat-controlled valve that regulates the flow of coolant between the cylinder block and the radiator, so maintaining optimum engine operating temperature. A thermostat is also used in some air cleaners in which the temperature is regulated.

Thrust bearing The bearing in the clutch assembly that is moved in to the release levers by clutch pedal action to disengage the clutch. Also referred to as a release bearing.

Timing belt A toothed belt which drives the camshaft. Serious engine damage may result if it breaks in service.

Timing chain A chain which drives the camshaft.

Toe-in The amount the front wheels are closer together at the front than at the rear. On rear wheel drive vehicles, a slight amount of toe-in is usually specified to keep the front wheels running parallel on the road by offsetting other forces that tend to spread the wheels apart.

Toe-out The amount the front wheels are closer together at the rear than at the front. On front wheel drive vehicles, a slight amount of toe-out is usually specified.

Tools For full information on choosing and using tools, refer to the *Haynes Automotive Tools Manual*.

Tracer A stripe of a second colour applied to a wire insulator to distinguish that wire from another one with the same colour insulator.

Tune-up A process of accurate and careful adjustments and parts replacement to obtain the best possible engine performance.

Turbocharger A centrifugal device, driven by exhaust gases, that pressurises the intake air. Normally used to increase the power output from a given engine displacement, but can also be used primarily to reduce exhaust emissions (as on VW's "Umwelt" Diesel engine).

U

Universal joint or U-joint A double-pivoted connection for transmitting power from a driving to a driven shaft through an angle. A U-joint consists of two Y-shaped yokes and a cross-shaped member called the spider.

V

Valve A device through which the flow of liquid, gas, vacuum, or loose material in bulk may be started, stopped, or regulated by a movable part that opens, shuts, or partially obstructs one or more ports or passageways. A valve is also the movable part of such a device.

Valve clearance The clearance between the valve tip (the end of the valve stem) and the rocker arm or tappet. The valve clearance is measured when the valve is closed.

Vernier caliper A precision measuring instrument that measures inside and outside dimensions. Not quite as accurate as a micrometer, but more convenient.

Viscosity The thickness of a liquid or its resistance to flow.

Volt A unit for expressing electrical "pressure" in a circuit. One volt that will produce a current of one ampere through a resistance of one ohm.

W

Welding Various processes used to join metal items by heating the areas to be joined to a molten state and fusing them together. For more information refer to the *Haynes Automotive Welding Manual*.

Wiring diagram A drawing portraying the components and wires in a vehicle's electrical system, using standardised symbols. For more information refer to the *Haynes Automotive Electrical and Electronic Systems Manual*.

Note: *References throughout this index are in the form - Chapter number • page number*

Preserving Our Motoring Heritage

< The Model J Duesenberg Derham Tourster. Only eight of these magnificent cars were ever built – this is the only example to be found outside the United States of America

Almost every car you've ever loved, loathed or desired is gathered under one roof at the Haynes Motor Museum. Over 300 immaculately presented cars and motorbikes represent every aspect of our motoring heritage, from elegant reminders of bygone days, such as the superb Model J Duesenberg to curiosities like the bug-eyed BMW Isetta. There are also many old friends and flames. Perhaps you remember the 1959 Ford Popular that you did your courting in? The magnificent 'Red Collection' is a spectacle of classic sports cars including AC, Alfa Romeo, Austin Healey, Ferrari, Lamborghini, Maserati, MG, Riley, Porsche and Triumph.

A Perfect Day Out

Each and every vehicle at the Haynes Motor Museum has played its part in the history and culture of Motoring. Today, they make a wonderful spectacle and a great day out for all the family. Bring the kids, bring Mum and Dad, but above all bring your camera to capture those golden memories for ever. You will also find an impressive array of motoring memorabilia, a comfortable 70 seat video cinema and one of the most extensive transport book shops in Britain. The Pit Stop Cafe serves everything from a cup of tea to wholesome, home-made meals or, if you prefer, you can enjoy the large picnic area nestled in the beautiful rural surroundings of Somerset.

> John Haynes O.B.E., Founder and Chairman of the museum at the wheel of a Haynes Light 12.

< Graham Hill's Lola Cosworth Formula 1 car next to a 1934 Riley Sports.

The Museum is situated on the A359 Yeovil to Frome road at Sparkford, just off the A303 in Somerset. It is about 40 miles south of Bristol, and 25 minutes drive from the M5 intersection at Taunton.
Open 9.30am - 5.30pm (10.00am - 4.00pm Winter) 7 days a week, *except Christmas Day, Boxing Day and New Years Day*
Special rates available for schools, coach parties and outings Charitable Trust No. 292048